# Warman's®
# Advertising

## DON & ELIZABETH JOHNSON

Published by

krause
publications

700 East State St., Iola, WI 54990-0001
715-445-2214
www.krause.com

Please, call or write us for our free catalog of antiques and collectibles publications.
To place an order or receive our free catalog, call 800-258-0929. For editorial comment and further information,
use our regular business telephone at (715) 445-2214

Library of Congress Catalog Number: 00-102687
ISBN: 0-87341-850-6

Printed in the United States of America

**On the cover, clockwise from top right, are:** Sign, paper, 2-sided, "Rocky Ford Cigars," 9-1/2" h, 11-3/4" w,
$425; box, cardboard, litho paper, "Ko-We-Ba Rolled Oats, Kothe, Wells & Bauer Co., Indianapolis," 1 lb., $185; pitcher, yellowware,
Red Wing Saffron, rust and white stripes, ink stamp advertising "N. Frudden & Son, Lumbermen Since 1889, Nora Springs, Iowa,"
base ink-stamped "Red Wing Saffron Ware," spout chips, 6-1/2" high. $100; tin, vertical pocket, litho tin, "Bull Dog Cut Plug DeLuxe,"
1910 tax stamp, unopened, 4-5/8" h, $725; sign, tin, die-cut, bottle-shape, "Pepsi-Cola 5¢ Sparkling, Satisfying, Pepsi-Cola, Made Only By
Pepsi-Cola Company, Long Island City, N.Y., Bottled Locally by Authorized Bottlers From Coast to Coast, 12 Ounces,"
29-1/2" h, 8-1/4" w, $560; and box, wooden, machine dovetails, slide lid, paper labels, "Williams' Root Beer Extract,
The Williams & Carleton Co., Hartford, Ct.," 7-1/2" h, 9-3/4" w, 5-1/4' d, $400.

# ACKNOWLEDGMENTS

To Kris Manty, our editor, thanks for a smooth project from beginning to end. It really was fun. (Even if we did inadvertently send you a blank disk.)

To Ellen Schroy, author of numerous Warman's titles and the backbone of Krause Publication's antiques and collectibles line, you're the best. Thanks for all the help along the way.

The authors would also like to thank the following auctioneers, who were instrumental in providing catalogs and illustrations for this book. We cannot adequately express our appreciation. Without your assistance, this project would not have been possible. Thank you!

**Mark Anderton**
**Collectors Auction Services**
**RR 2, Box 431 Oakwood Rd.**
**Oil City, PA 16301**
**814-677-6070**
**www.caswel.com**

**Chris Fricker**
**Fricker Auctions**
**P.O. Box 852**
**Bloomington, IL 61702**

**Gary Metz**
**Gary Metz's Muddy River Trading Company**
**P.O. Box 1430**
**Salem, VA 24153**
**540-387-5070**

**Wm. Morford**
**Rd. #2**
**Cazenovia, NY 13035**
**315-662-7625**

**Sandy Rosnick**
**15 Front St.**
**Salem, MA 01970**
**978-741-1130**

**Buffalo Bay Auction Co.**
**5244 Quam Circle**
**Rogers, MN 55374**
**612-428-8480**
**www.buffalobayauction.com**

To the following friends and colleagues who assisted in obtaining photographs and additional pricing information for this book, we are also deeply indebted.

**Terry C. Abernathy**
**Abernathy Auction & Real Estate Co.**
**Liberty, IN**

**W.B. Addison**
**Addison Auction**
**Greenfield, IN**

**Barry and Barbara Carter**
**Knightstown Antique Mall**
**Knightstown, IN**

**Jim Dragoo**
**Dragoo Auction Co.**
**Chesterfield, IN**

**Kim and Mary Kokles**
**Indianapolis Antique Advertising Show**
**Garland, TX**

**Mike Koons**
**Roger Koons**
**Koons Auction & Realty Co.**
**Connersville, IN**

**Doug Moore**
**'Tiques & Toys**
**Cicero, IN**

**Andrew Walther**
**Shane Hawkins**
**Walther & Hawkins Auctioneers**
**Centerville, IN**

And lastly, but certainly of no less importance, we are sincerely grateful to our baby-sitters extraordinaire—those individuals who gave freely of both their time and energy to corral and entertain two rambunctious preschoolers: Curt, Cheryl, Kaitlyn, and Emily Ferrell; Paige Fischer; Phyllis Johnson; and Joann Smith.

# DEDICATION

**In memory of Glenda Hughes**

An example for us all, she withstood the ravages of disease with determination, unwavering courage, and quiet dignity—ever-confident that the situation was in God's hands. The scent of lilacs and the sound of her laughter shall forever be entwined in my heart.

**Elizabeth Johnson**

**In memory of Jon Brecka**

Collecting is a great thing. But, it should never be the only thing that drives a person's life. The late Clark Garrett used to tell fellow antique dealers, "Remember, it's just merch."

That's merch, as in merchandise. His point was simply this: Don't get attached to material things. To realize the strength of his message, understand that Garrett dealt in the best. Even today, years after his death, items selling with the provenance of "ex Clark Garrett" are placed on a higher plateau. If Garrett once owned something, it was good.

Your 1903 Coca-Cola calendar might be spectacular. Your Shell gas globe might be mint. Your Burley Boy vertical pocket tin might be flawless. But it's still just merch. It's just stuff.

What does your collection do? Does it bring you joy? Hopefully. By its very nature, antique advertising attracts attention. It wouldn't rank as one of the top-rated collectibles if it wasn't so appealing. But never forget that advertising is inanimate. It has no life, no soul. It can't talk to you, can't crack a joke that brightens a gloomy day, can't offer a tender word on a lonely evening. Only people can do that.

My world got a little smaller last year with the death of a friend, Jon Brecka. His passing emphasized the fact that the things around me, things I greatly enjoy, are just that—things. Reduced to their essentials, they are nothing. They don't hold the breath of God within them. They are of no consequence. Take away one or all of those objects, and my life can go on without despair. Yours, too.

I hold in my heart a deep sense of loss for my friend, who helped shape the antiques and collectibles hobby through his positions at the Antique Trader and Krause Publications. Jon's age was one of his greatest assets. At 35, he had decades of work and untold years of influence ahead of him. When his life was cut short, the loss reverberated beyond his family and friends. It touched an entire industry.

His death speaks of the uncertainty of life. It nudges our subconscious, whispering that the things we collect will never be of true importance. They are just merch—simply things we hang on our walls, set on our shelves or place in our homes. Enjoy them, but don't misplace your passions. Love was never intended for inanimate objects. Instead, it's a gift we freely give to family and friends, and, most importantly, to the God who created us.

Collecting is a great thing, but there's no greater joy that can fill one's life than knowing God, which comes through a personal relationship with Jesus Christ. It is to the Creator of all things that we give thanks for this project and for the hope and joy that we have discovered in our lives.

**Don Johnson**

*"Do not store up for yourselves treasures on earth, where moth and rust destroy, and where thieves break in and steal. But store up for yourselves treasures in heaven, where moth and rust do not destroy, and where thieves do not break in and steal. For where your treasure is, there your heart will be also. -*
*-Matthew 6:19-21 (NIV)*

# GENERAL INTRODUCTION

## Some lessons we learn too late.

As if straight from the hand of Norman Rockwell, that autumn day in 1986 was painted with the vivid colors of maple trees and punctuated by the staccato cry of an auctioneer. Following the deaths of the owners of a rural Indiana estate, an auction crew had been hired to sell literally everything the family owned, from stacks of stained doilies to acreage and outbuildings. Tables loaded with a mix of household goods and antiques made the trip worthwhile, but one treasure went practically unnoticed in the barn that day.

The crowd had thinned considerably by the time the auctioneer began selling the items in the outbuildings, starting with the main barn. Since the central bay had already been cleaned out, he sold the contents of the three remaining sections: a granary on the left, a granary on the right, and a haymow. With no one bidding against me, I effortlessly purchased the contents of the haylofts for five dollars, making what seemed like the buy of the day. Few people had climbed the wooden ladder to peek inside, where the owners of the property had stored an old wooden barber's chair.

Competing for the contents of the building's ground floor required only a little more effort. The granaries had been used as the family's trash dump, holding what seemed to be a century's worth of cans, bottles, and other garbage. Fending off just one other bidder, I bought the granary on the left for three dollars. However, a frowning woman with an intense look on her face appeared determined to pay whatever it took for the privilege of rooting through the trash in the right granary, and I eventually gave in. I scoffed at her fifteen-dollar acquisition, wondering to myself how anyone could justify paying so much for what amounted to nothing more than a heap of rubbish.

Unidentified restaurant, circa 1924. The tobacco counter displays cigar signs and boxes for El Producto, Van Dam, Cuban Rose, Bankable, and White Owl. The countertop showcase includes Camel cigarettes. On the wall is a sign, "We Serve Nun Better Coffee, The Best In All America," near a Kellogg's Corn Flakes box under an inverted U-shaped display.

## Or had she seen something I missed?

After a while, I ventured to her side of the structure. "I'm just curious," I said. "What's in there that made you bid on the contents?" Her frown deepened. "What's in yours?" she asked, answering my question with a question.

"Nothing in particular," I said. "Mostly, I just wanted to see what I could find."

"Me too," she said, returning to her work excavating a mound of tin cans.

Despite having lost the battle over the right granary, I was pleased with my acquisitions as I drove out of the barnyard that day. My barber's chair was proudly ensconced in the bed of my Ford truck, a cardboard box filled with an assortment of tins, cans, and bottles chattering beside it. What a great day!

Nearly fifteen years later, I can't name a single advertising item I pulled out of that barn. But I can tell you this—as a young collector, I wasn't nearly as smart as I thought I was. Although I unearthed some collectible advertising in that granary, I hadn't a clue about what I was leaving behind. Lining the wall at the far end of building were stacks of oil cans. Quarts. Gallons. It's impossible to remember what other sizes were there or which makers were represented. All I know is that they were dirty and, to my untrained eye, didn't look like they were worth the trouble of hauling away. So I didn't. As far as I know, those oil cans are still in that old barn in west-central Indiana.

In my ignorance, what oil cans did I leave behind? A quart Husky with its lively dog motif? A Phillips Trop-Artic with images of igloos and palm trees? A Deep Rock gallon showing an early race car? Probably not. More than likely, the cans were common and of minimal value. But, they did have some value, which I wasn't smart enough to realize at the time. Additionally, there's always the possibility I left behind a gem, something good enough it might even have brightened the countenance of my dour-faced competitor that day. I hope she kicked around on my side of the barn after I left. I hope she recognized the value of those cans on which I didn't want to dirty my hands.

What was the treasure in the barn that day? Was it the barber's chair, which I sold at auction a few years later, the profit barely enough to justify having hauled the thing off the property? Was it the assortment of advertising I dug from beneath the rubble of someone's life? Or, was the treasure still in that granary when I went to sleep at the end of the day?

## One man's junk...

The mistake I made at that long-ago auction has been repeated by many people over the years. You can't know everything. If you collect popcorn tins, chances are good you don't know much about tobacco pouches. If your main interest is Texaco, you probably aren't well-versed in Mr. Peanut. Or, maybe you don't know much about antique advertising, other than the fact that you like certain pieces. That's great! Welcome to the hobby. And, what a hobby it is.

This book is designed to provide an overview of the antique advertising market. The number of companies and the diversity of products represented herein serve as a reminder that, in the field of antique advertising, one man's junk truly is another man's treasure.

Our goal in writing *Warman's Advertising* has been to cover the broad middle market of antique advertising. We've included only a few pieces of newer advertising, and we've avoided many of the top-of-the-line items. Instead, the focus is on vintage advertising that, for the most part, collectors will find both available and affordable.

What's here? A bit of anything and everything. Only in a price guide about antique advertising will you find back-to-back listings for a display showing pig guts (Moorman) and a tin depicting a semi-nude woman peddling wafers (Morman Elders Damtana Wafers). Check the headings for "Shamrock" and you'll discover four different products: gasoline, coffee, milk, and rolled oats.

During the late-19th and early-20th centuries, when advertising images were enjoying their heyday, no one was concerned about being politically correct. Manufacturers often used the race card to their advantage, creating images wild enough to start riots by today's standards. Yet, advertising from that era also serves as reminder for us in the 21st century. We see society's attitudes frozen in those images.

Despite some unsavory designs, the antique advertising market is driven primarily by fun, carefree graphics adorning thousands of objects, from gas globes to street signs, from talcum tins to coffee cans. One of our favorites is a Baby Bunting Rolled Oats container showing a cherub playing a panpipe while rabbits dance nearby. The graphics are simply delightful. Nothing in contemporary advertising compares.

It's there that modern advertising has failed the public. Today's products and signs are largely unimaginative. Cereal boxes showcase high-paid athletes; motor oil is sold in text-only plastic containers. Where is the creativity? Even Campbell's let us down when it discontinued the long-standing red-and-white soup cans that had become an icon to millions of Americans. Is nothing sacred?

## Hey, bidder, bidder, bidder!

Today's collectors face the daunting task of sifting through what is now three centuries' worth of advertising. How did we distill all of those products and promotions into *Warman's Advertising*? We did so with the help of five auctioneers who specialize in antique advertising. The majority of the items included in this price guide were sold at their cataloged auc-

Fishburn's Corner, Junction Highways 10 and 35, South End, Bass Lake, Knox, Ind. The Sinclair station on the left has a round sign for "Sinclair H-C Gasoline," a rectangular sign for "Sinclair Credit Cards," and 2 pumps with Sinclair gas globes. The Texaco station on the right has Coca-Cola signs on two sides and a Coke cooler near one entrance.

Fred Norton, Groceries, Provisions, Cigars & Tobacco. Soft Drinks. Location unknown. Above the shop owner's name are hands holding Nabisco boxes. The window is filled with boxes of Chipso. In front of the window is an Eisenlohr's Cinco Cigars sign, and a Mail Pouch strip sign is on the steps.

tions during a 15-month period immediately preceding publication. We've also listed prices from several smaller advertising and general-line auctions.

With only a few exceptions, the price listed is what someone actually paid for the item, and that figure includes buyer's premiums, when in effect. Might an item be worth more than its value here? Might it be worth less? On both counts, the answer is a resounding yes. But, we're convinced that auctions continue to serve as the best yardstick for measuring such a broad marketplace. It's at public auction that the concept of supply and demand is transformed from mere theory into reality.

We don't by any means intend to discount the traditional market, however. The full-time antiques dealers who specialize in advertising are true professionals, and their prices are generally accurate. But, when dealing with sellers who aren't as knowledgeable in the field, one can see great disparity in the prices of antique advertising. At one antique mall, we saw a 50-pound lard can tagged $15. Just a few weeks later, we spotted an identical can in lesser condition, but the asking price was nearly four times as much. Auctions remove the guesswork of determining price and pit eager buyers against each other to see what the market will bear.

## More than just values

This book is a new addition to the Warman's line. As part of the "Encyclopedia of Antiques and Collectibles," it goes beyond merely providing values for the items listed. Additional information sure to be of value to readers is presented throughout the book. Company histories, as well as lists of collectors' clubs, reference materials, and museums are included for most categories. Because so many books and clubs dealing with antique advertising are of a more general nature, more inclusive lists are available in the book's appendices.

We've tried to provide listings that contain more details than those in most other price guides. Vague listings have always been a problem in the industry. If a price guide simple states "Union Leader tobacco tin" without any further description, the value given is useless. Not only was Union Leader packaged in several different vertical pocket tins, but other forms also exist, including a cylindrical container and a horizontal box. The same holds true for many other types of advertising, whether it's a Swansdown Coffee can, a Dr. Pepper thermometer or a Sinclair sign.

We've included detailed descriptions whenever possibly. Our intent is to provide readers with a visual image of the object, noting variations, colors, size, etc. When comparing an actual item with a listing in this book, we hope it will be readily apparent whether you're looking at the same thing described here.

The biggest names in advertising can be found in these pages. Our category for Coca-Cola is the longest of any in the book. Yet, we believe other companies deserve equal attention as well. All of the Coke listings in the world won't do you any good if you're holding a Monarch typewriter ribbon tin and want to know what it's worth. Much of this price guide consists of categories having only one or two listings. Although those sections may be scant, their importance lies in their contribution to understanding the much larger realm of antique advertising.

We've limited the number of abbreviations in the descriptions to decrease the need to constantly flip to a key explaining those truncated words. Since price guides generally sound as if Tonto wrote them, we've also tried to make our descriptions less stilted.

We hope you like what you see and that you find this book useful. Readers who would like to contribute to the next edition are welcome to provide us with historical information on companies, as well as information regarding reference material, clubs, or museums which don't appear in this work. Auctioneers with cataloged sales specializing in advertising are also welcome to submit catalogs and prices realized for inclusion in future editions.

Finally, we're always glad to hear what you think.

**Don and Elizabeth Johnson**
**5110 S. Greensboro Pike**
**Knightstown, IN 46148**
**djohnson@spitfire.net**

Unidentified location, 1931. "Vernor's Ginger Ale" painted-wood roadside sign.

Unidentified store, Indiana. The window has two similar Owl Cigar signs and a Gen. Arthur sign, with a Sandow sign below. Displayed in the store window is a pyramid of cigar boxes, including Sandow, Famo and Little Joe. The two vertical signs flanking the door read "Cigars and Tobacco" and "Confectionery." To the right is an "Indianapolis News Sold Here" sign.

# STATE OF THE MARKET

HOT! That one word best sums up the market for antique advertising. Collectors are spending more money and showing increased enthusiasm for the field, and antique advertising has become one of America's favorite collecting categories. Don't look for that fever pitch to subside anytime soon.

Top-of-the-line items continue to generate the most interest. Dealers and auctioneers have no problems finding buyers for their best merchandise, even though collectors are having to pay premium prices. Buyers are willing to dig deep into their pockets to acquire that special piece to hang on their wall or display on a shelf.

But it's not just the rare and the unusual that are changing hands quickly. While activity is more subdued in the area of middle-market advertising, there's still great interest in any piece that is in pristine condition. As always, condition is king.

## Pop Goes The Market

One recent trend has been the increased interest in soda collectibles. Coca-Cola has long ruled the soda market, and no company will ever knock Coke off its mountaintop. But as prices for Coke memorabilia escalated, collectors began finding themselves priced out of the market. Not wanting to give up collecting, they turned their attention to other soda companies. Almost overnight, 7Up, Dr. Pepper, Orange-Crush and Moxie found new life in a hoard of buyers with money to spend. And, the transformation of the soda market hasn't been limited to the bigger names in soft drinks. Off brands such as Clicquot Club have also been targeted by collectors.

Does that mean the market for Coca-Cola has reached its peak? Not in your lifetime! Coke continues to climb in stature, with plenty of collectors fueling the ever-increasing prices. Oddly enough, new collectibles (think QVC) have greatly boosted the vintage Coke market. The scenario goes something like this: A person buys a Coca-Cola music box from one of the home-shopping channels, but has no interest in other Coke collectibles. Before long, that person begins seeing more Coke memorabilia and realizes the scope of the Coke market. Suddenly he picks up another piece or two and, just like that, his passive interest turns into an active desire to buy more. A collector is born, and the Coke market gets new life.

## Long May They Stand

Don't think soda's getting all the glory these days. Instead, it's really only the new kid on the block. The long-standing veterans of the advertising marketplace remain in place. Gas and oil collectibles are as hot as ever and are becoming increasingly difficult to find. Sales of breweriana are going strong, with no signs of abating, and tobacco-related collectibles remain in demand.

Advertising that falls under the various food and drink categories, from chewing gum displays to coffee tins, are eagerly sought, with Planters Peanuts items especially desired. Other top-selling niches in the market are as varied as match holders, paper clips, celluloid, and veterinary items. In addition, buyers are showing an increased interest in items from the first half of the 20th century.

## The Pendulum Swings

Of course, not everything is a Super Collectible, with a red "S" on its chest and flowing cape on its back. The dealers and auctioneers we talked to identified several areas where interest has waned. That's to be expected since advertising, like any field of antiques and collectibles, goes through cycles.

Among the items that aren't as strong today as they were in the recent past are razor tins and condom tins. Victorian images have also fallen off the pace lately, largely because the graphics don't appeal to younger buyers. And, because of the increasing numbers of reproductions, collectors have grown particularly leery of clocks.

## Condition Is King

Regardless of the category, whether it's Coke or Kodak, condition remains the most important factor in determining the value of an item. Auctioneer Gary Metz explained it this way, "Condition rules the roost."

Buyers are putting faith in the sage advice offered by countless dealers and collectors over the years: Buy the best you can afford. Most collectors purchase out of passion rather than simply for investment potential. Yet, wise buyers know that an item in excellent condition is much more likely to increase in value than the same piece in lesser condition. The marketplace is full of rusty 1-pound, keywind coffee cans without a home. But, find an unopened example of any brand in mint condition, and collectors will be competing for adoption rights. It's there that the hunt really begins.

A Prince Albert sign showing Chief Joseph is a good example of the importance of condition in determining value. Consider these auction prices: a sign in cond. 7 sold for $1,650 compared to one in cond. 9.25+ that realized $3,822.50. The same sign has also sold for more than $6,000. Why the difference? The phase of the moon? A healthy stock market? Nope. It's condition.

## Image is everything

While condition is king, other factors are also crucial in determining the desirability and value of an item. Graphics are at the top of that list.

Consider a Newsboy Tobacco litho-paper sign in its original frame, which was tagged $14,500 at The Original Indianapolis Antique Advertising Show. Several factors accounted for the piece's five-figure price. Condition played a key role, since the sign was in great shape and in its original frame marked "National Tobacco Works." But what made the sign a true knock-out was its fantastic graphics, showing children scrapping in a street for a plug of tobacco, while a man was walking past a cigar store Indian in the background.

The greater the image, the better the colors, the more desirable the item will be. Consider Polarine, which made several styles of half-gallon oil cans. The plain version showing the company's triangular logo garners only a fraction of the price of the example with color graphics of an open-top touring sedan driving through the countryside.

Rarity also comes into play when determining value, although it is typically a few rungs down the ladder on the scale of importance. A previously unknown Coca-Cola sign is certainly rare, but if it has been used for target practice and is covered with rust, its value in unrestored condition will be minimal when compared to other desirable Coke signs of the same vintage in pristine original condition.

Some advertising can be classified as rare (with few, if any, additional examples existing) yet still have little value. A tip tray with only plain text for a merchant and without graphics, will appeal only minimally to collectors. It might be the only known example, but its rarity is trumped by its anonymity and the absence of interesting graphics.

## Other factors

Local markets still play a role in determining the value of an item. Specialty advertising items generally generate maximum interest in the area in which they originated. An advertising plate from a bank in Dubuque, Iowa, will be of minimal interest in Florida.

However, the antiques and collectibles field continues to evolve into a community where the effects of geography have been greatly diminished by advancing technology. Catalog auctions initially went a long way toward leveling the playing field of buyers in different parts of the country. The Internet has even further removed those obstacles.

## Other factors: The sequel

Keep in mind that prices can also be affected by a number of other factors. It's not uncommon for two individuals at an auction to decide they absolutely must own an item, and they'll empty their bank accounts rather than let the other person walk away with the piece in hand.

The same thing happens when family members bid on pieces that are of sentimental value. A run-of-the-mill keywind Maxwell House coffee can might bring ten times its true value if two cousins get into a bidding war over the can in which their grandmother kept her egg money.

We recently witnessed another good example of the role outside factors can play in determining the value of a piece of advertising. The item was a Schlitz postcard mailed on April 19, 1912, and the early graphics were appealing. But when the piece was offered at auction, the Schlitz collectors were outbid by a Titanic memorabilia collector, who was attracted by the card's message, "Wasn't the shipwreck awful, so many people gone who enjoyed life with all their wealth & good health…"

## A little off the top?

Most collectors remain purists when it comes to vintage advertising—they understand the necessity of restoration, but they would rather own pieces in great original condition. Given the choice between buying a Phillips 66 sign restored to cond. 9.5 and the same sign in original shape at cond. 8, they're more likely to prefer the latter. In today's marketplace, serious collectors need to be knowledgeable enough about restoration techniques to be able to identify those items that have been touched up. The best way to learn the nuances of restored advertising is to handle as many original pieces as possible. Most professional auctioneers and dealers are willing to spend time educating collectors.

The following are general tips for spotting restoration:

*Paper will show slight variations in color.

*Tin will show textural differences.

*Porcelain signs will show a gloss difference, having a duller (satin) look.

*Reverse-painted glass will show differences in registration.

## Four troublemakers

Just as Mary couldn't seem to shake that pesky little lamb of hers, the antiques and collectibles industry has four tagalongs of its own: reproductions, fakes, forgeries, and fantasy items.

Of the four, the reproductions category is the only one that isn't always considered something akin to the Black Death. When properly marked and dated, reproductions serve as a valuable tool for helping to fill holes in collections. Reproduction gas globes and lenses have allowed many collectors to top off their gas pump when an original globe was either unavailable or unaffordable. Examples clearly marked "Reproduction" remove the question of whether a collector is getting the real thing or being stuck with an imposter. Likewise, newer Roly Poly tobacco canisters have allowed many collectors to fill gaps in their collection by obtaining a contemporary example until they could acquire an original.

Fakes, forgeries, and fantasy items have always had a negative connotation on the antiques market. Whether handled by unwitting dealers or unscrupulous sellers, such items have caused much wailing and gnashing of teeth by collectors who later learned they had spent good money on bad merchandise.

What's a collector to do? Study. Subscribe to newsletters. Talk to other dealers and collectors. As much as possible, handle legitimate merchandise as well as reproductions, fakes, forgeries, and fantasy items. Hands-on experience is still the best teacher.

## Where'd you get that?

When it comes to finding merchandise, dealers carrying middle-line advertising often say they can't find or can't afford inventory. That's typically not true of dealers selling higher-end goods. Sometimes it takes a little more patience, but they continue to turn up great pieces.

Where's a collector to look? Specialty advertising auctions remain the lifeblood of the advertising market. In addition to selling a general line of advertising, most specialty auctioneers have at least one field in which they excel: soda, tobacco, gas and oil, coffee, etc.

Specialized advertising shows are another great source for items. When it comes to shows, the mecca is The Original Indianapolis Antique Advertising Show, held three times a year in Indianapolis, Ind. Promoted by Kim and Mary Kokles, this show remains the best anywhere, with more than 125 hand-picked dealers who carry just about every type of advertising imaginable. Other great shows also exist and shouldn't be overlooked.

General-line antique shows remain another arena where advertising can often be ferreted out. One dealer we talked to has better luck at higher-quality shows, noting, "If someone's paying a lot for booth rent, you can figure they'll have something good to sell." At the opposite end of the spectrum, don't discount flea markets. It might take a lot more looking to turn up a jewel, but great pieces are still being discovered.

Likewise, antique shops and antique malls are another source of antique advertising.

And then there's the Internet...

## The 'I' word

Love it. Hate it. The Internet is here, and it's not going away. The auctioneers we interviewed all agreed that the Internet has increased their business, becoming an additional tool for them to use to better serve their clients.

Several dealers, however, expressed concern over the WWF-style sales methods used by many non-professional sellers on the Internet. As with pro wrestling, what those online sellers are offering isn't always what it appears to be.

Internet auctions can be especially brutal when it comes to unknowledgeable or unscrupulous sellers misrepresenting merchandise, especially when dealing with an item's condition. The biggest disadvantage to buying online, whether from an auction or through an electronic storefront, is that the buyer can't inspect the merchandise, putting him at the mercy of the seller to accurately described the item and disclose any flaws. Even if the seller offers a return policy (and we firmly believe all online sellers should), it's still disappointing to receive a piece that wasn't what it was said to be and then have to hassle with shipping it back.

That's not to say the Internet is bad thing or that every seller is a con artist. Cyberspace is a great tool that many dealers and auctioneers have used to expand their business, and it's been the number-one factor in closing the gap between regional pricing differences. A buyer stuck on the plains of North Dakota is no longer isolated from the rest of the world as long as he has a computer and Internet access. Suddenly, he becomes a viable buyer in the world marketplace.

## Buying 101

Following are two simple guidelines for safer and more productive purchases.

*Know your seller. When you find a dealer or auctioneer who handles the type of merchandise you collect, build a relationship with that person. Give the seller a "want" list, and chances are good he'll contact you when he acquires something of interest to you. Full-time, professional dealers and auctioneers know their livelihood depends on treating their customers honestly and fairly.

*Buy from sellers who will stand behind their merchandise. As much as possible, patronize dealers and auctioneers who offer a guarantee of authenticity for all the merchandise they sell. When buying on the Internet, look for sellers who offer a return policy, preferably one that allows you to send back the item for a full refund within a reasonable amount of time. Many professional dealers who sell on the Internet or by mail-order have a no-questions-asked refund policy, allowing an item to be returned for any reason.

## Parting words

Everything we've written to this point is worthless if you don't remember two simple words: Have fun. Collecting should be a hobby. Enjoy it. Share it with your family members and friends. Revel in the opportunity to hunt for great merchandise. Rejoice in a wonderful find. And, if the passion for collecting antique advertising ever becomes an aggravating, obsessive search that leaves you kicking the cat and mad at the world, it's time to sell your signs and tins and take up gardening or synchronized swimming.

Collecting should be fun. We hope it always remains so. Best of luck in your search.

# APPENDIX A

## References

### Advertising

Steve Batson, *Country Store Counter Jars and Tins*, Schiffer Publishing, 1997

Michael Bruner, *Encyclopedia of Porcelain Enamel Advertising*, 2nd ed., Schiffer Publishing

Michael Bruner, *More Porcelain Enamel Advertising*, Schiffer Publishing, 1997

Irene Davis, *Collecting Paint Advertising and Memorabilia*, Schiffer Publishing, 2000

Douglas Congdon-Martin, *America for Sale: A Collector's Guide to Antique Advertising*, Schiffer Publishing, 1991

Douglas Congdon-Martin and Robert Biondi, *Country Store Antiques: From Cradles to Caskets*, Schiffer Publishing, 1991

Douglas Congdon-Martin and Robert Biondi, *Country Store Collectibles*, Schiffer Publishing, 1990

Len Davidson, *Vintage Neon*, Schiffer Publishing, 1999

Fred Dodge, *Antique Tins*, Book I, 1995 (1997 value update); Book II, 1998, Collector Books

Ted Hake, *Hake's Guide to Advertising Collectibles*, Wallace-Homestead, 1992

Jim Harmon, *Radio & TV Premiums*, Krause Publications, 1997

Bill and Pauline Hogan, *Charlton Standard Catalogue of Canadian Country Store Collectables*, Charlton Press, 1996

Ray Klug, *Antique Advertising Encyclopedia*, 3rd ed., Schiffer Publishing

Ralph and Terry Kovel, *The Label Made Me Buy It*, Crown Publishers, 1998

Hal Morgan, *Symbols of America*, Viking, 1986

Alice L. Muncaster and Ellen Sawyer, *The Dog Made Me Buy It!*, Crown Publishers, 1990

Richard A. Penn, *Mom and Pop Stores*, R.S. Pennyfield's, 1998

Robert Reed, *Bears and Dolls in Advertising*, Antique Trader Books, 1998

Robert Reed, *Paper Advertising Collectibles: Treasures from Almanacs to Window Signs*, Antique Trader Books, 1998

Loretta Metzger Rieger and Lagretta Metzger Bajorek, *Children's Paper Premiums in American Advertising 1890-1990s*, Schiffer Publishing, 2000

B.J. Summers, *Advertising Memorabilia*, 2nd ed., Collector Books, 1999

David L. Wilson, *General Store Collectibles*, vol. 1; 1994, vol. 2, 1998, Collector Books

David Zimmerman, *Encyclopedia of Advertising Tins: Smalls and Samples*, vol. I, 1994; vol. II, 1999, Collector Books

### Advertising Characters

Mark Chase and Michael Kelly, *Collectible Drinking Glasses*, Collector Books, 1996

Albert and Shelly Coito, *Elsie the Cow and Borden's Collectibles*, Schiffer Publishing, 2000

Warren Dotz, *Advertising Character Collectibles*, Collector Books, 1993 (1997 value update)

Warren Dotz, *What a Character! 20th Century American Advertising Icons*, Chronicle Books, 1996

Joan Stryker Grubaugh, *A Collector's Guide to the Gerber Baby*, self-published, 1997

Ted Hake, *Hake's Price Guide to Character Toy Premiums*, Collector Books, 1996

Ted Hake, *Hake's Price Guide to Character Toys*, 2nd ed., Avon Books, 1998

Jim Harmon, *Radio & TV Premiums*, Krause Publications, 1997

John Hervey, *Collector's Guide to Cartoon & Promotional Drinking Glasses*, L-W Book Sales, 1990 (1995 value update)

Mary Jane Lamphier, *Zany Characters of the Ad World*, Collector Books, 1995

David Longest, *Character Toys and Collectibles*, 1st series, 1984 (1992 value update); 2nd series, 1987 (1990 value update), Collector Books

Carol and Gene Markowski, *Tomart's Price Guide to Character & Promotional Glasses*, 2nd ed., Tomart Publications, 1993

Rex Miller, *The Investor's Guide to Vintage Character Collectibles*, Krause Publications, 1999

Alice L. Muncaster and Ellen Sawyer, *The Dog Made Me Buy It!*, Crown Publishers, 1990

Myra Yellin Outwater, *Advertising Dolls*, Schiffer Publishing, 1997

Robert M. Overstreet, *Overstreet Premium Ring Price Guide*, 2nd ed., Collector Books, 1996

Robert Reed, *Bears and Dolls in Advertising*, Antique Trader Books, 1998

Jon D. Swartz and Robert C. Reinehr, *Handbook of Old-Time Radio*, Scarecrow Press, 1993

Tom Tumbusch, *Tomart's Price Guide to Radio Premium and Cereal Box Collectibles*, Wallace-Homestead, 1991

David and Micki Young, *Campbell's Soup Collectibles from A to Z*, Krause Publications, 1998

## Ashtrays

Art Anderson, *Casinos and Their Ashtrays*, self-published, 1994

Nancy Wanvig, *Collector's Guide to Ashtrays*, 2nd ed., Collector Books, 1999

## Aunt Jemima

Jean Williams Turner, *Collectible Aunt Jemima*, Schiffer Publishing, 1994

## Automobilia

David K. Bausch, *The Official Price Guide to Automobilia*, House of Collectibles, 1996

Jim and Nancy Schaut, *American Automobilia*, Wallace-Homestead, 1994

Leila Dunbar, *Automobilia*, Schiffer Publishing, 1998

Ron Kowalke and Ken Buttolph, *Car Memorabilia Price Guide*, 2nd ed., Krause Publications, 1997

## Black Memorabilia

Patiki Gibbs, *Black Collectibles Sold in America*, Collector Books, 1987 (1996 value update)

Kenneth Goings, *Mammy and Uncle Mose*, Indiana University Press, 1994

Kyle Husfloen, ed., *Black Americana Price Guide*, Antique Trader Books, 1997

Jan Lindenberger, *More Black Memorabilia*, Schiffer Publishing, 1995

J.L. Mashburn, *Black Americana: A Century of History Preserved on Postcards*, Colonial House, 1996

Dawn Reno, *Encyclopedia of Black Collectibles*, Wallace-Homestead, 1996

J.P. Thompson, *Collecting Black Memorabilia*, L-W Book Sales, 1996

Jean Williams Turner, *Collectible Aunt Jemima*, Schiffer Publishing, 1994

## Borden's

Albert and Shelly Coito, *Elsie the Cow and Borden's Collectibles*, Schiffer Publishing, 2000

## Bottles (also see Milk Bottles)

Philip Hopper, *Anchor Hocking Commemorative Bottles and Other Collectibles*, Schiffer Publishing, 2000

Rich Sweeney, *Collecting Applied Color Label Soda Bottles*, 2nd ed., self-published, 1995

Jeff Wichman, *The Best of the West: Antique Western Bitters Bottles*, Pacific Glass Books (1700 37th St., Suite 203, Sacramento, CA 95814), 1999

## Breweriana

Donna S. Baker, *Vintage Anheuser-Busch: An Unofficial Collector's Guide*, Schiffer Publishing, 1999

George J. Baley, *Back Bar Breweriana*, L-W Book Sales, 1992

Donald Bull, *Price Guide to Beer Advertising, Openers and Corkscrews*, self-published, 1981

Gary Straub, *Collectible Beer Trays*, Schiffer Publishing, 1995

Herb and Helen Haydock, *World of Beer Memorabilia*, Collector Books, 1997

Thomas Toepfer, *Beer Cans*, L-W Book Sales, 1976 (1995 value update)

## Campbell's

Doug Collins, *America's Favorite Food: The Story of Campbell Soup Company*, Harry N. Abrams, 1994

David and Micki Young, *Campbell's Soup Collectibles from A to Z*, Krause Publications, 1998

## Cereal Boxes and Premiums

Scott Bruce, *Cereal Box Bonanza: The 1950s*, Collector Books, 1996

Scott Bruce, *Cereal Boxes & Prizes: 1960s*, Flake World Publishing, 1998

Scott Bruce and Bill Crawford, *Cerealizing America*, Faber and Faber, 1995

Jim Harmon, *Radio & TV Premiums*, Krause Publications, 1997

Tom Tumbusch, *Tomart's Price Guide to Radio Premium and Cereal Box Collectibles*, Wallace-Homestead, 1991

## Character & Promotional Glasses

Mark Chase and Michael Kelly, *Collectible Drinking Glasses*, Collector Books, 1996

John Hervey, *Collector's Guide to Cartoon & Promotional Drinking Glasses*, L-W Book Sales, 1990 (1995 value update)

Carol and Gene Markowski, *Tomart's Price Guide to Character & Promotional Glasses*, 2nd ed., Tomart Publications, 1993

## Clocks

Michael Bruner, *Advertising Clocks: America's Timeless Heritage*, Schiffer Publishing, 1995

Jerry Maltz, *Baird Advertising Clocks*, self-published (31 Turner Dr., New Rochelle, NY 10804), 1998

Coca-Cola

Gael de Courtivron, *Collectible Coca-Cola Toy Trucks*, Collector Books, 1995

Shelly Goldstein, *Goldstein's Coca-Cola Collectibles*, Collector Books, 1991 (1996 value update)

Deborah Goldstein-Hill, *Price Guide to Vintage Coca-Cola Collectibles 1896-1965*, Krause Publications, 1999

Bob and Debra Henrich, *Coca-Cola Commemorative Bottles*, Collector Books, 1998

William McClintock, *Coca-Cola Trays*, rev. 2nd ed., Schiffer Publishing, 2000

Allan Petretti, *Petretti's Coca-Cola Collectibles Price Guide*, 10th ed., Antique Trader Books, 1997

Allan Petretti and Chris Beyer, *Classic Coca-Cola Serving Trays*, Antique Trader Books, 1998

Randy Schaeffer and Bill Bateman, *Coca-Cola: A Collector's Guide to New and Vintage Coca-Cola Memorabilia*, Running Press, 1995

Joyce Spontak, *Commemorative Coca-Cola Bottles: An Unauthorized Guide*, Schiffer Publishing, 1998

B.J. Summers, *B.J. Summers' Guide to Coca-Cola*, 2nd ed., Collector Books, 1999

B.J. Summers, *B.J. Summers' Pocket Guide to Coca-Cola*, 2nd ed., Collector Books, 2000

Al and Helen Wilson, *Wilson's Coca-Cola Guide*, Schiffer Publishing, 1997

## Coffee Tins

James H. Stahl, *Collectors Guide to Key-Wind Coffee Tins*, L-W Book Sales, 1991

## Cookbooks

Bob Allen, *Guide to Collecting Cookbooks and Advertising Cookbooks*, Collector Books, 1990 (1995 value update)

Linda J. Dickinson, *Price Guide to Cookbooks and Recipe Leaflets*, Collector Books, 1990 (1995 value update)

## Cracker Jack

Alex Jaramillo, *Cracker Jack Prizes*, Abbeville Press, 1989

Ravi Pina, *Cracker Jack Collectibles*, Schiffer Publishing, 1995

Larry White, *Cracker Jack Toys: The Complete, Unofficial Guide for Collectors*, Schiffer Publishing, 1997

## Dolls

Myra Yellin Outwater, *Advertising Dolls*, Schiffer Publishing, 1997

Joleen Ashman Robison and Kay Sellers, *Advertising Dolls*, Collector Books, 1980 (1994 value update)

Robert Reed, *Bears and Dolls in Advertising*, Antique Trader Books, 1998

## Drugstore Collectibles

Al Bergevin, *Drugstore Tins & Their Prices*, Wallace-Homestead, 1990

A. Walker Bingham, *Snake-Oil Syndrome: Patent Medicine Advertising*, Christopher Publishing House, 1994

Douglas Congdon-Martin, *Drugstore & Soda Fountain Antiques*, Schiffer Publishing, 1991

Patricia McDaniel, *Drugstore Collectibles*, Wallace-Homestead, 1994

## Elsie the Cow (see Borden's)

## Ephemera

Lagretta Metzger Bajorek, *America's Early Advertising Paper Dolls*, Schiffer Publishing, 1999

Robert Reed, *Paper Advertising Collectibles: Treasures from Almanacs to Window Signs*, Antique Trader Books, 1998

Loretta Metzger Rieger and Lagretta Metzger Bajorek, *Children's Paper Premiums in American Advertising 1890-1990s*, Schiffer Publishing, 2000

Mary Young, *Collector's Guide to Magazine Paper Dolls*, Collector Books, 1990

## Gerber

Joan Stryker Grubaugh, *A Collector's Guide to the Gerber Baby*, self-published, 1997

## Jewel Tea

C.L. Miller, *Jewel Tea Grocery Products*, Schiffer Publishing, 1996

## Knives

Richard D. White, *Advertising Cutlery*, Schiffer Publishing, 1999

## Labels

Joe Davidson, *Fruit Crate Art*, Wellfleet Press, 1990

Lynn Johnson and Michael O'Leary, *En Route: Label Art from the Golden Age of Air Travel*, Chronicle Books, 1993

Ralph and Terry Kovel, *The Label Made Me Buy It*, Crown Publishers, 1998

Gordon T. McClelland and Jay T. Last, *Fruit Box Labels: An Illustrated Guide to Citrus Labels*, Hillcrest Press, 1995

Gerard S. Petrone, *Cigar Box Labels: Portraits of Life, Mirrors of History*, Schiffer Publishing, 1998

## Letter Openers

Everett Grist, *Collector's Guide to Letter Openers*, Collector Books, 1998

*Collector's Digest Letter Openers: Advertising & Figural*, L-W Book Sales, 1996

## Matchcovers & Match Holders

Jean and Franklin Hunting, *Collectible Match Holders for Tabletops and Walls*, Schiffer Publishing, 1998

Bill Retskin, *The Matchcover Collector's Price Guide*, 2nd ed., Antique Trader Books, 1997

## Milk Bottles

John Tutton, *Udderly Beautiful*, self-published (1967 Ridgeway Rd., Front Royal, VA 22630), no date

## Motorcycle Collectibles

Leila Dunbar, *Motorcycle Collectibles*, Schiffer Publishing, 1996

Leila Dunbar, *More Motorcycle Collectibles*, Schiffer Publishing, 1997

## Neon Signs

Len Davidson, *Vintage Neon*, Schiffer Publishing, 1999

## Oyster Cans

Jim and Vivian Karsnitz, *Oyster Cans*, Schiffer Publishing, 1993

## Paint

Irene Davis, *Collecting Paint Advertising and Memorabilia*, Schiffer Publishing, 2000

## Paper Dolls

Lagretta Metzger Bajorek, *America's Early Advertising Paper Dolls*, Schiffer Publishing, 1999

Mary Young, *Collector's Guide to Magazine Paper Dolls*, Collector Books, 1990

## Pepsi-Cola

James C. Ayers, *Pepsi-Cola Bottles Collectors Guide*, self-published, 1995

Everette and Mary Lloyd, *Pepsi-Cola Collectibles*, Schiffer Publishing, 1993

Bill Vehling and Michael Hunt, *Pepsi-Cola Collectibles*, vol. 1, 1990 (1993 value update), vol. 2, 1990 (1992 value update), vol. 3, 1993 (1995 value update), L-W Book Sales

## Petroliana

Mark Anderton, *Encyclopedia of Petroliana*, Krause Publications, 1999

Mark Anderton and Sherry Mullen, *Gas Station Collectibles*, Wallace-Homestead/Krause, 1994

Robert W. D. Ball, *Texaco Collectibles*, Schiffer Publishing, 1994

Scott Benjamin and Wayne Henderson, *Gas Globes: Pennzoil to Union and Affiliates*, Schiffer Publishing, 1999

Scott Benjamin and Wayne Henderson, *Gas Pump Globes*, Motorbooks International, 1993

Scott Benjamin and Wayne Henderson, *Oil Company Signs*, Motorbooks International, 1995

Scott Benjamin and Wayne Henderson, *Sinclair Collectibles*, Schiffer Publishing, 1997

Mike Bruner, *Gasoline Treasures*, Schiffer Publishing, 1996

Todd P. Helms, *The Conoco Collector's Bible*, Schiffer Publishing, 1995

Todd P. Helms and Chip Flohe, *A Collection of Vintage Gas Station Photographs*, Schiffer Publishing, 1997

J. Sam McIntyre, *The Esso Collectibles Handbook: Memorabilia from Standard Oil of New Jersey*, Schiffer Publishing, 1998

Rick Pease, *Filling Station Collectibles*, Schiffer Publishing, 1994

Rick Pease, *Petroleum Collectibles*, Schiffer Publishing, 1997

Rick Pease, *Service Station Collectibles*, Schiffer Publishing, 1996

Rick Pease, *A Tour with Texaco: Antique Advertising and Memorabilia*, Schiffer Publishing, 1997

Sonya Stenzler and Rick Pease, *Gas Station Collectibles*, Schiffer Publishing, 1993

Charles Whitworth, *Gulf Oil Collectibles*, Schiffer Publishing, 1998

## Planters Peanuts

Jan Lindenberger, *Planters Peanut Collectibles Since 1961*, Schiffer Publishing, 1995

## Playing Cards

Everett Grist, *Advertising Playing Cards*, Collector Books, 1992

## Radio Premiums

Ted Hake, *Hake's Price Guide to Character Toy Premiums*, Collector Books, 1996

Jim Harmon, *Radio & TV Premiums*, Krause Publications, 1997

Robert M. Overstreet, *Overstreet Premium Ring Price Guide*, 2nd ed., Collector Books, 1996

Tom Tumbusch, *Tomart's Price Guide to Radio Premium and Cereal Box Collectibles*, Wallace-Homestead, 1991

## Railroad Collectibles

Stanley L. Baker, *Railroad Collectibles*, 4th ed., Collector Books, 1990 (1996 value update)

Barbara J. Conroy, *Restaurant China: Restaurant, Airline, Ship & Railroad Dinnerware*, vol. 1, 1998; vol. 2, 1999, Collector Books

Richard Luckin, *Dining on Rails: An Encyclopedia of Railroad China*, RK Publishing, 1998

## Restaurant China

Barbara J. Conroy, *Restaurant China: Restaurant, Airline, Ship & Railroad Dinnerware*, vol. 1, 1998; vol. 2, 1999, Collector Books

## Soda Fountain Collectibles

Douglas Congdon-Martin, *Drugstore and Soda Fountain Antiques*, Schiffer Publishing, 1991

## Soft Drink Collectibles

Tom Morrison, *Root Beer: Advertising and Collectibles*, Schiffer Publishing, 1992

Tom Morrison, *More Root Beer: Advertising and Collectibles*, Schiffer Publishing, 1997

Allan Petretti, *Petretti's Soda Pop Collectibles Price Guide*, 2nd ed., Antique Trader Books, 1999

Rich Sweeney, *Collecting Applied Color Label Soda Bottles*, 2nd ed., 1995

## Souvenir and Commemorative Items

Wayne Bednersch, *Collectible Souvenir Spoons*, Collector Books, 1998

Arene Burgess, *Collector's Guide to Souvenir Plates*, Schiffer Publishing, 1996

Monica Lynn Clements and Patricia Rosser Clements, *Popular Souvenir Plates*, Schiffer Publishing, 1998

Laurence W. Williams, *Collector's Guide to Souvenir China: Keepsakes of a Golden Era*, Collector Books, 1998

## Tape Measures

*Collector's Digest Advertising & Figural Tape Measures*, L-W Book Sales, 1995

## Tobacciana

Edwin Barnes and Wayne Dunn, *Cigar-Label Art Visual Encyclopedia with Index and Price Guide*, self-published, 1995

Douglas Congdon-Martin, *Camel Cigarette Collectibles, The Early Years 1913-1963*, Schiffer Publishing, 1996

Douglas Congdon-Martin, *Camel Cigarette Collectibles 1964-1995*, Schiffer Publishing, 1997

Douglas Congdon-Martin, *Tobacco Tins*, Schiffer Publishing, 1992

Jero L. Gardner, *The Art of the Smoke*, Schiffer Publishing, 1998

Joe Giesenhagen, *The Collector's Guide to Vintage Cigarette Packs*, Schiffer Publishing, 1999

Gerard S. Petrone, *Cigar Box Labels: Portraits of Life, Mirrors of History*, Schiffer Publishing, 1998

Gerard S. Petrone, *Tobacco Advertising: The Great Seduction*, Schiffer Publishing, 1996

Dr. Fernando Righini and Marco Papazonni, *The International Collectors' Book of Cigarette Packs*, Schiffer Publishing, 1998

Jerry Terranova and Douglas Congdon-Martin, *Antique Cigar Cutters & Lighters*, Schiffer Publishing, 1996

Jerry Terranova and Douglas Congdon-Martin, *Great Cigar Stuff for Collectors*, Schiffer Publishing, 1997

A.M.W. van Weert, *Legend of the Lighter*, Electra, 1995

Neil Wood, *Collecting Cigarette Lighters*, vol. 1, 1994, vol. 2, 1995, L-W Book Sales

Neil Wood, *Smoking Collectibles*, L-W Book Sales, 1994

## Trade Cards

Dave Cheadle, *Victorian Trade Cards*, Collector Books, 1996

## Uncle Sam

Gerald Czulewicz, *Foremost Guide to Uncle Sam Collectibles*, Collector Books, 1995

Nicholas Steward, *James Montgomery Flagg: Uncle Sam and Beyond*, Collector's Press, 1997

## W.T. Rawleigh

C.L. Miller, *Door to Door Collectibles: Salves, Lotions, Pills and Potions from W.T. Rawleigh*, Schiffer Publishing, 1998

# APPENDIX B

## Periodicals

### Advertising

*Advertising Collectors Express*, P.O. Box 221, Mayview, MO 64071

*Let's Talk Tin*, 1 S. Beaver Lane, Greenville, SC 29605

*Paper & Advertising Collector*, P.O. Box 500, Mount Joy, PA 17552

*Paper Collectors' Marketplace*, P.O. Box 128, Scandinavia, WI 54977

*Tin Fax Newsletter*, 205 Brolley Woods Dr., Woodstock, GA 30188

*Tin Type Newsletter*, P.O. Box 440101, Aurora, CO 80044

*Trade Card Journal*, 143 Main St., Brattleboro, VT 05301

### Automobilia

*Mobilia Magazine*, P.O. Box 575, Middlebury, VT 05753

### Black Memorabilia

*Blackin'*, 559 22nd Ave., Rock Island, IL 61201

*Lookin Back at Black*, 6087 Glen Harbor Dr., San Jose, CA 95123

### Breweriana

*All About Beer*, 1627 Marion Ave., Durham, NC 27705

*Barley Corn News*, P.O. Box 2328, Falls Church, VA 22042

*Suds 'n Stuff*, 4765 Galacia Way, Oceanside, CA 92056

### Campbell

*Soup Collector*, 414 Country Lane Ct., Wauconda, IL 60084

### Cereal Boxes

*Flake*, P.O. Box 481, Cambridge, MA 02140

### Character & Promotional Glasses

*Collector Glass News*, P.O. Box 308, Slippery Rock, PA 16057

### Circus Items

*Circus Report*, 525 Oak St., El Cerrito, CA 94530

### Drugstore Collectibles

*Drugstore Memories*, Hook's American Drugstore Museum, 1180 E. 38th St., Indianapolis, IN 46205

*Siren Soundings*, 1439 Main St., Brewster, MA 02631

### Ice Cream Collectibles

*The Ice Screamers*, P.O. Box 465, Warrington, PA 18976

### Labels

*Banana Label Times*, P.O. Box 159, Old Town, FL 32860

### Matchcovers

*Match Hunter*, 740 Poplar, Boulder, CO 80304

*Matchcover Classified*, 16425 Dam Rd. #3, Clearlake, CA 95422

### McDonald's

*Collecting Tips Newsletter*, P.O. Box 633, Joplin, MO 64802

### Petroliana

*Check the Oil!*, 30 W. Olentangy St., Powell, OH 43065 <www.oldgas.com/info/cto.htm>

*Petroleum Collectibles Monthly*, P.O. Box 556, LaGrange, OH 44050 <www.pcmpublishing.com>

### Premiums

*Box Top Bonanza*, 3403 46th Ave., Moline, IL 61265

*Premium Collectors Magazine*, 1125 Redman Ave., St. Louis, MO 63138

*The Premium Watch Watch*, 24 San Rafael Dr., Rochester, NY 14618

*The Toy Ring Journal*, P.O. Box 544, Birmingham, MI 48012

### Soda Fountain Collectibles

*The Ice Screamers*, P.O. Box 465, Warrington, PA 18976

### Soft Drink Collectibles

*Club Soda*, P.O. Box 489, Troy, ID 83871 <www.club-soda.net>

*Painted-Label Soda Bottles*, 1055 Ridgecrest Dr., Goodlettsville, TN 37072 <www.gono.com/vir-mus/museum.htm>

*Root Beer Float*, 609 Devils Ln., Walworth, WI 53184

### Souvenir and Commemorative Items

*Antique Souvenir Collectors News*, P.O. Box 562, Great Barrington, MA 01230

### Tobacciana

*The Cigar Label Gazette*, P.O. Box 3, Lake Forest, CA 92630

### Trade Cards

*Trade Card Journal*, 109 Main St., Brattleboro, VT 05301

### Typewriter Ribbon Tins

*Ribbon Tin News*, 28 The Green, Watertown, CT 06795

### Watches, Advertising

*The Premium Watch Watch*, 24 San Rafael Dr., Rochester, NY 14618

# APPENDIX C

## Collectors' Clubs; Associations

### Advertising

Advertising Cup and Mug Collectors of America, P.O. Box 680, Solon, IA 52333

Antique Advertising Assoc. of America, P.O. Box 1121, Morton Grove, IL 60053 <www.pastimes.org>

The Ephemera Society of America, Inc., P.O. Box 95, Cazenovia, NY 13035 <www.ephemerasociety.org>

National Assoc. of Paper & Advertising Collectors, P.O. Box 500, Mount Joy, PA 17552

Porcelain Advertising Collectors Club, P.O. Box 381, Marshfield Hills, MA 02051

Tin Container Collectors Assoc., P.O. Box 440101, Aurora, CO 80044

Trade Card Collector's Assoc., 3706 S. Acoma St., Englewood, CO 80110

## Advertising Characters

Campbell Kids Collectors, 649 Bayview Dr., Akron, OH 44319

Campbell Soup Collector Club, 414 Country Lane Ct., Wauconda, IL 60084

Charlie Tuna Collectors Club, 7812 N.W. Hampton Rd., Kansas City, MO 64152

Peanut Pals, 804 Hickory Grade Rd., Bridgeville, PA 15017

R.F. Outcault Society, 103 Doubloon Dr., Slidell, LA 70461 (Buster Brown and the Yellow Kid)

## Ashtrays

Ashtray Collectors Club. P.O. Box 11652, Houston, TX 77283

## Black Memorabilia

Black Memorabilia Collector's Assoc., 2482 Devoe Terrace, Bronx, NY 10468

## Bottle Openers

Figural Bottle Opener Collectors Club, 9697 Gwynn Park Dr., Ellicott City, MD 21042 <www.dol.net/~c-llesser>

Just for Openers, P.O. Box 64, Chapel Hill, NC 27514 <www.mindspring.com/~jfo>

## Bottles

National Assoc. of Milk Bottle Collectors, Inc., 4 Ox Bow Rd., Westport, CT 06880 <www.collectoroline.com~NAMBC ~wp.html>

Painted Soda Bottles Collectors Assoc., 9418 Hilmer Dr., La Mesa, CA 91942 <www.collectoronline.com/PSBCA/PSBCA.html>

## Breweriana

American Breweriana Assoc. Inc., P.O. Box 11157, Pueblo, CO 81001 <www.a-b-a.com>

Beer Can Collectors of America, 747 Merus Ct., Fenton, MO 63026 <www.bcca.com/index.html>

Capitol City Chapter of the Beer Can Collectors of America, P.O. Box 287, Brandywine, MD 20613

East Coast Breweriana Assoc., P.O. Box 64, Chapel Hill, NC 27514 <www.mindspring.com/~jfo>

Gambrinus Chapter of the Beer Can Collectors of America, 985 Maebelle Way, Westerville, OH 43081

National Assoc. of Breweriana Advertising, 1380 W. Wisconsin Ave., Apt. 232, Oconomowoc, WI 53066

## Buster Brown / The Yellow Kid

R.F. Outcault Society, 103 Doubloon Dr., Slidell, LA 70461

## Calendars

Calendar Collector Society, 18222 Flower Hill Way #299, Gaithersburg, MD 20879 <www.collectors.org/ccs>

Calendar Plate Collectors Club, 710 N. Lake Shore Dr., Tower Lakes, IL 60010

## Campbell

Campbell Kids Collectors, 649 Bayview Dr., Akron, OH 44319

Campbell Soup Collector Club, 414 Country Lane Ct., Wauconda, IL 60084 <www.soupcollector.com>

## Casino Memorabilia

Casino Chip & Gaming Token Collectors Club, P.O. Box 340345, Columbus, OH 43234 <www.chequers.com>

## Cereal Boxes and Premiums

Sugar-Charged Cereal Collectors, 5400 Cheshire Meadows Way, Fairfax, VA 22032

## Character & Promotional Glasses

Promotional Glass Collectors Assoc., 2654 S.E. 23rd St., Albany, OR 97321

## Cigars and Cigarettes (see Tobacciana)

## Circus Items

Circus Historical Society, 4102 Idaho Ave., Nashville, TN 37209

Society for the Preservation of Circus Art, P.O. Box 311192, Enterprise, AL 36331

## Coca-Cola

Cavanagh's Coca-Cola Christmas Collector's Society, 1000 Holcomb Woods Pkwy., Suite 440B, Roswell, GA 30076

Coca-Cola Collectors Club International, P.O. Box 49166, Atlanta, GA 30359 <www.cocacolaclub.org>

The Cola Club, P.O. Box 158715, Nashville, TN 37215 <www.nostalgiapubs.com/ppals/colaclub.html>

Florida West Coast Chapter of the Coca-Cola Collectors Club International, 1007 Emerald Dr., Brandon, FL 33511

## Cracker Jack

Cracker Jack Collectors Assoc., P.O. Box 16033, Philadelphia, PA 19114 <www.collectoronline.com/CJCA>

## Credit Cards

American Credit Card Collectors Society, P.O. Box 2465, Midland, MI 48641

## Dr. Pepper

Dr. Pepper 10-2-4 Collector's Club, 3100 Monticello, Suite 890, Dallas, TX 75205 <www.drpep.com/clubpage.htm>

## Drugstore Collectibles

The Drug Store Collector, 3851 Gable Lane Dr., #513, Indianapolis, IN 46208

## Ephemera

Aeronautica & Air Label Collectors Club, P.O. Box 1239, Elgin, IL 60121

American Business Card Club, P.O. Box 460297-K, Aurora, CO 80046

Assoc. of Map Memorabilia Collectors, 8 Amherst Rd., Pelham, MA 01002

Calendar Collectors Society, 18222 Flower Hill Way, #299, Gaithersburg, MD 20879 <www.collectors.org/CCS>

Ephemera Society of America, Inc., 105 Hawthorne Dr., Camillus, NY 13031 <www.ephemerasociety.org>

National Assoc. of Paper & Advertising Collectors, P.O. Box 500, Mount Joy, PA 17552

Paper Collectors' Marketplace, P.O. Box 128, Scandinavia, WI 54977

## Grapette

Grapette Collectors Club, 2240 Highway 27N, Nashville, AR 71852

## Kodak

International Kodak Historical Society, P.O. Box 21, Paoli, PA 19301

## Labels

Aeronautica & Air Label Collectors Club, P.O. Box 1239, Elgin, IL 60121

American Antique Graphics Society, 5185 Windfall Rd., Medina, OH 44256

The Citrus Label Society, 131 Miramonte Dr., Fullerton, CA 92365

Florida Citrus Label Collectors Assoc., P.O. Box 547636, Orlando, FL 32854 <www.members.aol.com/burnassoc.>

Fruit Crate Label Society, Rt. 2, Box 695, Chelan, WA 98816

International Seal, Label and Cigar Band Society, 8915 E. Bellevue St., Tucson, AZ 85715

Produce Seal Society, 4113 Paint Rock Dr., Austin, TX 78731

Society of Antique Label Collectors, P.O. Box 24811, Tampa, FL 33623

## Matchcovers

The American Matchcover Collecting Club, P.O. Box 18481, Asheville, NC 28814 <www.matchcovers.com>

Casino Matchcover Club, 5001 Albridge Way, Mt. Laurel, NJ 08054

Liberty Bell Matchcover Club, 5001 Albridge Way, Mount Laurel, NJ 08054

The Long Beach Matchcover Club, 2501 W. Sunflower H-5, Santa Ana, CA 92704

New Moon Matchbox & Label Club, P.O. Box 192, Cascade, MD 21719

Pacific Northwest Matchcover Collector's Club, 9424 Odin Way, Bothell, WA 98011 <www.halcyon.com/rlauck/pnmcc.html>

Rathkamp Matchcover Society, 432 N. Main St., Urbana, OH 43078 <www.psyber.com/~rmsed>

Trans-Canada Matchcover Club, P.O. Box 219, Caledonia, Ontario, Canada NOA-1A0

Windy City Matchcover Club of Illinois, 3104 Fargo Ave., Chicago, IL 60645

## Match Safes

International Match Safe Assoc., P.O. Box 791, Malaga, NJ 08328

## McDonald's

McD International Pin Club, 3587 Oak Ridge, Slatington, PA 18080 <www.mipc.com>

McDonald's Collectors Club, 255 New Lenox Rd., Lenox, MA 01240

## Moxie

Moxie Enthusiasts Collectors Club of America, Route 375, Box 164, Woodstock, NY 12498

New England Moxie Congress, 445 Wyoming Ave., Millburn, NJ 07041 <www.xensei.com/users/iraseski>

## Nabisco

Inner Seal Collectors Club, 6609 Billtown Rd., Louisville, KY 40299

POW-WOW, P.O. Box 24751, Minneapolis, MN 55424 <www.shazam.imginc.com/fca> (Nabisco Straight Arrow Promotion 1948-1954)

## Pepsi-Cola

Ozark Mountain Pepsi Collectors Club, 9101 Columbus Ave. S, Bloomington, MN 55420

Pepsi-Cola Collectors Club, P.O. Box 817, Claremont, CA 91711 <www.pepsigifts.com/pccinfo.html>

## Petroliana

American Petroleum Collectors/Iowa Gas, 6555 Colby Ave., Des Moines, IA 50311

International Petroliana Collectors Assoc., P.O. Box 937, Powell, OH 43065

Iowa Gas Swap Meet, 2417 Linda Dr., Des Moines, IA 50322 <www.home.stlnet.com/~jimpotts/iowagas>

Oil Can Collectors Club, 4213 Derby Ln., Evansville, IN 47715 <www.oilcancollectors.com>

World Oil Can Collector's Organization, 20 Worley Rd., Marshall, NC 28753

## Planters Peanuts

Peanut Pals, P.O. Box 652, St. Clairsville, OH 43950 <www.commserve.com/mrpeanut/ppals.html>

## Railroad Collectibles

Railroadiana Collectors Association, P.O. Box 4894, Diamond Bar, CA 91765

## Saloon & Bar Collectibles

International Swizzle Stick Collectors Assoc., P.O. Box 1117, Bellingham, WA 98227

## Soda Fountain Collectibles

The Ice Screamers, P.O. Box 465, Warrington, PA 18976

National Assoc. of Soda Jerks, P.O. Box 115, Omaha, NE 68101

## Soda Machines

Club Soda, P.O. Box 489, Troy, ID 83871 <www.club-soda.net>

## Soft Drink Collectibles

The Cola Club, P.O. Box 158715, Nashville, TN 37215 <www.nostalgiapubs.com/ppals/colaclub.html>

Dr. Pepper 10-2-4 Collector's Club, 3100 Monticello, Suite 890, Dallas, TX 75205

Grapette Collectors Club, 2240 Highway 27N, Nashville, AR 71852

Moxie Enthusiasts Collectors Club of America, Route 375, Box 164, Woodstock, NY 12498

National Pop Can Collectors, 19201 Sherwood Green Way, Gaithersburg, MD 20879

New England Moxie Congress, 445 Wyoming Ave., Millburn, NJ 07041

Painted Soda Bottle Collectors Assoc., 9418 Hilmer Dr., La Mesa, CA 91942 <www.collectoronline.com/psbca/psbca.html>

Ozark Mountain Pepsi Collectors Club, 9101 Columbus Ave. S, Bloomington, MN 55420

Pepsi-Cola Collectors Club, P.O. Box 817, Claremont, CA 91711

The Society of Root Beer Cans & Bottles, P.O. Box 571, Lake Geneva, WI 53147

## Souvenir and Commemorative Items

American Spoon Collectors, 7408 Englewood Ln., Raytown, MO 64133

Antique Souvenir Collectors News, P.O. Box 562, Great Barrington, MA 01230

Northeastern Spoon Collectors Guild, 8200 Boulevard East, North Bergen, NJ 07047

The Scoop Club, 84 Oak Ave., Shelton, CT 06484

## Star-Kist

Charlie Tuna Collectors Club, 7812 N.W. Hampton Rd., Kansas City, MO 64152

## Thermometers

Thermometer Collectors Club of America, 6130 Rampart Dr., Carmichael, CA 95608

## Tobacciana

Camel Joe & Friends, 2205 Hess Dr., Cresthill, IL 60435

Cigar Label Collectors International, P.O. Box 66, Sharon Center, OH 44274

Cigarette Pack Collectors Assoc., 61 Searle St., Georgetown MA 01833 <www.hometown.aol.com/cigpack/index.html>

International Lighter Collectors, P.O. Box 536, Quitman, TX 75783

International Seal, Label and Cigar Band Society, 8915 E. Bellevue St., Tucson, AZ 85715

Piedmont Tobacco Memorabilia & Collector's Club, Rt. 1, Box 324, King, NC 27021

Pocket Lighter Preservation Guild, P.O. Box 1054, Addison, IL 60101

Tin Tag Collectors Club, Route 2, Box 55, Pittsburgh, TX

75686 <www.collectoronline.com/club~TTCC.html>

### Tokens

Casino Chip & Gaming Token Collectors Club, P.O. Box 340345, Columbus, OH 43234 <www.ccgtcc.com>

### Trade Cards

Trade Card Collectors Assoc., P.O. Box 284, Marlton, NJ 08053 <www.members.aol.com/tccahomepg>

United States Cartophilic Society, P.O. Box 4020, Saint Augistine, FL 32085

# APPENDIX D

## Museums

### Advertising

American Advertising Museum, 5035 SE 24th Ave., Portland, OR 97202

Creatability Toys Museum of Advertising Icons, 1550 Maruga Ave., Suite 504, Miami, FL 33146, phone 305-663-7374 <www.toymuseum.com/main.html>

National Signs of the Times Museum, 407 Gilbert Ave., Cincinnati, OH, phone 513-421-2050 or 800-925-1110 <www.sign-museum.org>

### Bottles and Beverage Containers

The Museum of Beverage Containers & Advertising, 1055 Ridgecrest Dr., Goodlettsville, TN 37072, phone 615-859-5236 <www.gono.com/vir-mus/museum.htm>

National Bottle Museum, 76 Milton Ave., Ballston Spa, NY 12020, phone 518-885-7589 <www.crisny.org/not~for~profit/nbm>

### Breweriana

American Museum of Brewing History & Arts, Oldenberg Brewing Company, 400 Buttermilk Pike Exit, Ft. Mitchell, KY 41017, phone 606-341-7223 <www.realbeer.com/oldenberg/museum.html>

### Coca-Cola

Biedenharn Candy Company & Museum of Coca-Cola Memorabilia, 1107 Washington St., Vicksburg, MS 39180, phone 601-638-6514 <www.cdiguide.com>

Schmidt's Coca-Cola Museum, P.O. Box 848, 1201 N. Dixie, Elizabethtown, KY 42701, phone 502-769-3320 x 237

The World of Coca-Cola Pavilion, 55 Martin Luther Dr., Atlanta, GA 30303, phone 404-676-5151 <www.cocacola.com/museum>

### Coffee

Arbuckles' Coffee Museum, 97 16th Ave. SW, Cedar Rapids, IA 52404, phone 319-363-1242

### Cracker Jack

COSI Columbus, 280 E. Broad St., Columbus, OH 43215, phone 614-228-2674 <www.cosi.org>

### Dr Pepper

Dr Pepper Museum, 300 S. 5th St., Waco, TX 76701, phone 254-757-1025 or 800-527-7096 <www.drpeppermuseum.com>

### Drugstore and Pharmaceutical

Hook's American Drugstore Museum, 1180 E. 38th St., Indianapolis, IN 46205

New England Fire & History Museum, The Schmidt Apothecary Shop, 1439 Main St., Brewster, MA 02631, phone 508-1896-5711

### Neon Signs

Neon Museum of Philadelphia, 2140 Mount Vernon St., Philadelphia, PA 19130

Rocket City Neon Advertising Museum, 1554 NE 3rd Ave., Camas. WA 98607

### Thermometers

Porter Thermometer Museum, 49 Zarahelma Rd., P.O, Box 944, Onset, MA 02558, phone 508-295-5504

### Tobacciana

National Cigar Museum, P.O. Box 3000, Pismo Beach, CA 93448, phone 805-773-6777 <www.cigarnews.com/national-cigarmuseum.

### Trademarks

U.S. Patent & Trademark Museum, 2121 Crystal Dr., Arlington, VA 22202, phone 703-305-8341

# APPENDIX E

## Shows

The Original Indianapolis Antique Advertising Show, Kim and Mary Kokles, P.O. Box 495092, Garland, TX 75049, phone 972-240-1987

## Auction Services

Aiglatson Auctions, P.O. Box 3173, Framington, MA 01705, phone 508-877-0538 (trade cards and tobacco cards only)

Antique Bottle Connection, 147 Reserve Rd., Libby, MT 59923, phone 406-293-8442 (Western antique bottles, patent medicine bottles and related items)

Autopia Advertising Auctions, 15209 NE 90th St., Redmond, WA 98052, phone 425-883-7653 (advertising)

Buffalo Bay Auction Co., 5244 Quam Circle, Rogers, MN 55374, phone 612-428-8480 <www.buffalobayauction.com> (advertising)

Cerebro, P.O. Box 327, East Prospect, PA 17317, phone 717-252-3685 or 800-695-2235 (tobacco ephemera and advertising labels)

Chris Fricker, P.O. Box 852, Bloomington, IL 61702, phone 309-663-5828 <www.frickerauctions.com> (advertising)

Cigar-Label Art, P.O. Box 3902, Mission Viejo, CA 92691, phone 949-582-7686 <www.cigarlabelart.com> (cigar labels)

Collectors Auction Services, RR 2, Box 431 Oakwood Rd., Oil City, PA 16301, phone 814-677-6070 <http://www.caswel.com/> (oil, gas, country store, and advertising)

Daniel Auction Company, P.O. Box 594, Sylvester, GA 31791, phone 912-776-3998 (semi-annual antique advertising auction)

Dave Beck Auctions, P.O. Box 435, Mediapolis, IA 52637, phone 319-394-3943 (advertising mirrors, fobs, pinbacks, radio premiums, and signs)

Fink's Off the Wall Auctions, 108 E. 7th St., Lansdale, PA 19446, phone 215-855-9732 <www.finksauctions.com> (breweriana)

Frank's Antiques & Auctions, P.O. Box 516, Hilliard, FL 32046, phone 904-845-2870 (advertising)

Gary Metz's Muddy River Trading Company, P.O. Box 1430, Salem, VA 24153, phone 540-387-5070 (advertising and soda collectibles)

Gene Harris Antique Auction Center, Inc., P.O. Box 476, Marshalltown, IA 50158, phone 800-862-6674 <www.harrisantiqueauction.com> (advertising)

Gold Coast Trading, P.O. Box 600, Smithtown, NY 11787, phone 516-979-6607 (cigar box labels)

Hake's Americana & Collectibles, P.O. Box 1444, York, PA 17405, phone 717-848-1333 (Americana, character, and personality collectibles)

Harry Schenck, RR #1, Box 268A, Beech Creek, PA 16822, phone 570-726-4161 (advertising)

Howard B. Parzow, P.O. Box 3464, Gaithersburg, MD 20885, phone 301-977-6741 (drug store, apothecary, Americana, country store, and advertising)

James D. Julia Auctioneers, Inc., P.O. Box 830, Rte. 201, Fairfield, ME 04937, phone 207-453-7125 <www.juliaauctions.com> (advertising)

Jerry Madsen, 4624 W. Woodland Rd., Edina, MN 55424, phone 612-926-7775 (Nipper, needle tins, and advertising)

Leslie's Main Street Antiques, 934 Main St., Newberry, SC 29108, phone 803-276-8600 or 888-321-8600<www.leslieantiques.com> (American pharmacy collectibles)

Lynn Geyer's Advertising Auctions, 300 Trail Ridge, Silver City, NM 88061, phone 505-538-2341 (advertising and breweriana)

Manochio Enterprises, P.O. Box 2010, Saratofa, CA 95070, phone 408-996-1963 (firecracker labels)

McMurray Antiques & Auctions, P.O. Box 393, Kirkwood, NY 13795, phone 607-775-2321 (apothecary, drugstore, patent medicines, pills, tins, and advertising items)

Meisner's Auction Service, P.O. Box 115, Rt. 20 & 22, New Lebanon, NY 12125, phone 518-766-5002 (automobilia and petroliana)

Mike Smith's Patent Medicine Auction, 7431 Covington Hwy., Lithonia, GA 30058, phone 770-482-5100 <www.buffalo~road.com> (veterinary patent medicines and advertising)

New Orleans Auction Galleries, Inc., 801 Magazine St., New Orleans, LA 70130, phone 504-566-1849 <www.neworleansauction.com> (labels)

Noel Barrett Antiques, Carversville Rd., Box 300, Carversville, PA 18923 phone, 215-297-5109 (labels)

Nostalgia Publications, Inc., 21 S. Lake Dr., Hackensack, NJ 07601, phone 201-488-4536 <www.nostalgiapubs.com> (Coca-Cola and other soft drink collectibles)

Ohio Cola Traders, 4411 Bazetta Rd., Cortland, OH 44410, phone 330-637-0357 (Coca-Cola memorabilia)

Past Tyme Pleasures, 2491 San Ramon Valley Blvd., Suite 1-204, San Ramon, CA 94583, phone 925-484-4488 (advertising)

Patriotic Americana, 2671 Youngstown Rd. SE, Warren, OH 44484, phone 330-369-1192 (firecracker labels)

Pop Shoppe Auctions, 10556 Combie Rd. #106521, Auburn, CA 95602, phone 530-268-6333 (6pm-9pm) (ACL soda bottles)

Poster Auctions International, Inc., 601 W. 26th St., New York, NY 10001, phone 212-787-4000 <www.posterauction.com> (antique advertising posters)

Randy Inman Auctions, Inc., P.O. Box 726, Waterville, ME 04903, phone 207-872-6900 <www.inmanauctions.com> (advertising)

Richard Opfer Auctioneering, Inc., 1919 Greenspring Dr., Timonium, MD 21093, phone 410-252-5035 <www.opferauction.com> (advertising)

Sandy Rosnick, 15 Front St., Salem, MA 01970, phone 978-741-1130 (advertising)

Stanton's Auctioneers & Realtors, P.O. Box 146, 144 S. Main St., Vermontville, MI 49096, phone 517-726-0181 (advertising)

Victorian Casino Antiques, 1421 S. Main St., Las Vegas, NV 89104, phone 702-382-2466 (advertising)

Victorian Images, P.O. Box 284, Marlton, NJ 08053, phone 609-953-7711 <www. tradecards.com/vi> (trade cards, advertising, and tobacco)

Wm. Morford, Rd. #2, Cazenovia, NY 13035, phone 315-662-7625 (advertising)

# TIPS FOR USING THIS BOOK

## Category headings

*Listings are presented alphabetically. Depending on the item, some products using a person's name may be listed under the first name or initial, while others may be listed under a last name.

*Category heads sometimes carry descriptors to help identify the product (such as Three Cadets Condoms).

## Colors

Colors are described to the best of our ability, but, because photographs do not always reproduce well, we don't guarantee the colors listed will always be accurate. The biggest problem we encountered when working from catalogs was distinguishing similar tones, such as cobalt and black or ivory and yellow. In some case we've simply listed questionable colors as "dark" or "light."

## Condition

Condition quoted with each listing is taken from descriptions used by the auctioneers. Some auction houses use a letter system: G for Good, VG for Very Good, and EXC for Excellent. Other firms rely on a number system, grading on a scale of 6 to 10, where 10 is mint condition.

The use of two numbers separated by a hyphen (cond. 8.5-9) indicates the range in which that particular item falls. The use of numbers separated by a slash (cond. 9/8) indicates the condition of two sides of the same object, generally a sign.

Keep in mind that determining condition is not an exact science, and the applied grades are subjective.

The following grading system, used by Sandy Rosnick, is consistent with that used by most auction companies specializing in antique advertising:

| | | |
|---|---|---|
| 10 | = | mint |
| 9.5 | = | near-mint |
| 8.5 | = | outstanding |
| 8 | = | excellent |
| 7.5 | = | fine-plus |
| 7 | = | fine |
| 6.5 | = | fine-minus (good) |
| 6 | = | poor |

By comparison, the following grading system used by Buffalo Bay includes additional details:

10 = Mint, unused or unopened—no wear or fading.

9 = Very minor imperfections, primarily to areas subject to wear (lids and rims on tins, light roll creases on mail-order calendars and paper items, soiling on print edges, light paper loss on containers opened by string pull, etc.), but all image areas are near-mint.

8 = Light scratches, minor dents, very light edge rusting or litho loss at edges, minute edge tears that may go into the image area, color is very good to excellent and overall the item views nicely at 3 feet.

7 = Heavier scratching or flaking, light dents, pitting or rust spots, or light fading, stains or soiling. Tears in excess of 3 inches but not into the primary image, edge damage, etc., very presentable at 6 feet.

6 = Very noticeable damage or deterioration.

## Descriptions

To be consistent, we have used the following terms throughout the book:

*Change trays are listed as tip trays.

*Coffee containers are listed as cans.

*Posters are listed as paper signs.

*Rolled oats containers are listed as boxes, even when cylindrical.

*Signs are 1-sided unless noted. Flange signs are always 2-sided.

*Tin and litho tin are, in most cases, synonymous.

## Measurements

Measurements quoted are taken from descriptions used by the auctioneers. The measurements are typically accurate to within one-quarter of an inch, but they are not guaranteed. Some listings for the same item may show differences in size, depending on the source of the listing. We have not made adjustments to compensate in these cases.

When known, measurements are listed in the following order: height, width, and depth. Abbreviations are used to designate those dimensions. When a catalog description provided measurements without a clear sense of order, we used the descriptions as quoted by the auctioneer, typically in the following format: 6" x 6-1/2" x 5-1/2". In a few cases, only one measurement was included in the auction catalog.

## Values

Values for most items are actual prices paid at auction, including buyer's premiums. For clarity, some prices have been rounded to the nearest 50 cents or $1.3-D= three-dimensional

## Abbreviations

| | | | | | | | | | | | |
|---|---|---|---|---|---|---|---|---|---|---|---|
| approx | = | approximately | gal | = | gallon | mkd | = | marked | pr | = | pair |
| coin-op | = | coin-operated | ground | = | background | NM | = | near mint | pt | = | pint |
| cond. | = | condition | h | = | height | NOS | = | new old stock | qt | = | quart |
| d | = | depth | illust | = | illustration | NRFB | = | never removed | sq | = | square |
| dec | = | decorated | kt | = | karat | from | | box | oz | = | ounce(s) |
| dia | = | diameter | l | = | length | orig | = | original | VG | = | very good |
| EXC | = | excellent | lb | = | pound(s) | pg | = | page(s) | w | = | width |
| G | = | Good | litho | = | lithographed | pc | = | piece(s) | | | |

# A

## AA-1 Motor Oil

Can, tin, "AA-1 Motor Oil, Pure Paraffin Base, Reliable and Economical," white text, black ground, shows sky-scrapers/plane/tractor/race car/train, Phoenix Oil Co., Augusta, GA, cond. 7, qt, 5-1/2" h, 4" dia ......... 126.50

## AAA

Sign, porcelain, 2-sided
    Oval, with hanger, "Approved AAA," cobalt/white, red border, cond. 7, 24" h, 38" w......................... 258.50
    Oval, "Auto Club of Missouri, AAA, Emergency Service," white text, cobalt ground, red border, cond. 8, 22-1/2" h, 30" w ............................................ 143.00

## A&P

**History:** What began in 1859 as a one-man operation in New York City harbor resulted in the first chain of general food stores in the United States. George Huntington Hartford purchased tea by the shipload and sold it at dockside for one third of what the other vendors were charging. He named his enterprise the Great American Tea Company. To expand the geographical

Tin, "A&P Mustard, Sultana Spice Mills, Take Grandmother's Advice, Use A.&.P. Spices," yellow ground, wear, scratches, 3-1/4" h, $35.

scope of his business, he started selling tea, coffee, and other grocery items from Wells Fargo wagons.

Following completion of the first transcontinental railroad in 1869, Hartford began referring to his stores as The Great Atlantic & Pacific Tea Company. Unfortunately, the chain was not established on the West Coast until after Hartford's death in 1917.

Sign
    Glass, reverse-painted, beveled edge, "A&P Established 1859," white text with black trim, red ground, small surface loss on background, 15" dia ... 121.00
    Porcelain, "Welcome to A&P! Free Parking, Please! One Hour Only! The Next Hour Is For Your Neighbor," cartoon image of 5 cars/drivers, white/black text, red-white-red ground, cond. G, 24" h, 36" w...........330.00

## A&W Root Beer

**History:** From a mixture of roots and berries, barks and herbs, a frosty mug was born.

Roy Allen and Frank Wright began peddling their concoction in 1919 in Lodi, Calif. The success of their 5¢ beverage resulted in the creation of three additional stores in California.

The initials of the founders' names were first used in conjunction with the product in Houston, Texas, in 1922. The company was sold in 1950, and, during the subsequent expansion, was referred to as the A&W Root Beer Company. Many acquisitions and sales have occurred over the years, but the A&W trademark remains one that is readily recognized.

The company first produced beverages in cans and bottles for the grocery store trade in 1971, with the addition of sugar-free products in 1974.

Animation cel, hand painted, A&W Root Beer Bear surrounded by 4 children, color print background, with matching animation drawing, from 1970s commercials, cel 12" h, 10" w ........................................... 66.00
Banner
    Nylon, oval A&W logo, white ground, cond. EXC, 2' 11" h, 4' 11-1/2" w ...................................... 50.00
    Plastic, "New, Try My Huge Dagwood Burger," Dagwood at left, A&W logo upper-right, blue ground, contemporary .................................................. 12.50
Jug, syrup, glass, paper label, "A&W Root Beer, Take Some Home," white text in upper/lower panels, prices for gal, 1/2-gal, qt beside image of full syrup jug, label fading/foxing, 1 gal .............................. 31.00
Lunch box, plastic, "Kids…Remember what the Great Root Bear says:…" cartoon bear at left, white panel, orange box, 6" h, 8" w ..................................... 85.00
Mug, glass, clear, "Ice Cold," white/red/black bull's-eye logo, cond. EXC, 4-1/2" h, 2-3/4" dia ................. 115.00
Poster, paper, "The Unbelievable Float" over A&W Root Beer Bear on beach with mug, "A&W Root Beer & Ice Cream" on white courtesy panel at bottom, bottle/ice cream container lower-right, cond. EXC, 18" h, 24" w ................................................................. 37.00
Wristwatch, ladies', "75 Years" under A&W logo, gold text, black ground/band, orig case ...................... 95.00

## Abbey Garden Coffee
Can, litho tin
    "Abbey Garden Coffee, A Blend of Genuine Ankola Mocha and Java," trees/abbey in medallion, red ground, cond. 8-, 1 lb, 6-1/4" h, 4-1/8" dia . 1,815.00
    "Genuine Ankola Mocha and Java," trees/abbey in medallion, red ground, rust, 1 lb, 6-1/4" h, 4" dia ................................................................. 275.00

## Abington Hotel
Sign, tin, self-framing, name in red in upper-left, hotel/ street scene with horse-buggies/trolley, cond. G, 28-1/4" h, 22" w ............................................... 231.00

## Acme Coffee
Can, litho tin, pry lid, "Acme Brand Vacuum Packed Steel Cut Coffee, Distributed by American Stores Co., Phila.," mountain/river scenes over brown ground with white

dots, lid bent, rust/fading/scratches, 1 lb, 4-1/4" h, 5-1/4" dia ................................................................ 66.00

## Acme Hair Vigor
Bottle, glass, mold blown, label under glass, "Acme Hair Vigor, Phil. Eisemann," red text, white ground, cond. EXC, 8-1/4" h, 2-7/8" dia ...................................... 550.00

## Acme Louse Killer
Can, paper label on cardboard, "Acme Louse Killer, Teur de Poux," red/black text in yellow circle surrounded by 8 round vignettes of farm animals, blue ground, unopened, cond. NM, 5-1/2" h, 3-1/8" dia ........... 70.50

## Acorn Stoves and Ranges
Sign, litho tin, embossed, couple under acorn-shaped trade sign of Ye Stove Store, poem in old English, cond. 8.5, 7" h, 4-3/4" w ...................................... 440.00

## Acropolis Coffee
Can, keywind, litho tin, shows Parthenon, red ground, cond. 7.5+, 1 lb, 3-1/2" h, 5" dia ......................... 176.00

## Adams' Barley Wheat Taffy Chewing Gum
Box, cardboard, "Adams' Barley Wheat Taffy Chewing Gum," 2 flaps opening at center, text in red repeated on each flap, 2 canted images of different women, with paper liner, cond. 8-, 1" h, 7-1/2" w, 9" d ................. 99.00

## Adams Chewing Gum
Box
    Cardboard, "Adams Pepsin Tutti Frutti Gum, Peppermint Flavor," red/white text, green ground, "The Original Chicle Gum" in red diamond, cond. EXC, 4-1/4" h, 6-3/8" w, 5-1/4" d ......................................... 1,072.50

**Sign, paper, wooden frame, "Adams Pure Chewing Gum," 9-1/4" h, 8-3/4" w, $80.**

Tin, ribbon, litho tin, Addressograph, 2" h, $12.

Cardboard, "Adams Sappota Chewing Gum," flap covers show 2 Victorian woman, plaid trim, cond. 8-8.5, 7-1/2" h, 8-1/2" w ............................................ 88.00

Litho tin, "Adams Pepsin Tutti Frutti Gum," cond. 5, 6" h ................................................................ 132.00

Labels, paper, lot of 6, "Adams Tutti Frutti Chewing Gum, 144 Pieces," Victorian actresses, unused, 8-1/4 to 9-1/2" h, 4" w ................................................... 357.50

Sign, paper, "Adams' Red Rose Chewing Gum," white text around red border, canted rectangular image of 6 women with strand of roses, "If you follow We will shed fairest Roses where you tread...," cond. G, 6-1/4" h, 12-3/4" w ............................................................ 66.00

## Addison Typewriter Ribbon

Tin, litho tin, "Addison" in red on black/white Deco image of New York City skyscrapers, cond. 8.5, 3/4" h, 2-1/2" dia ........................................................ 198.00

## Addressograph (See Photo)

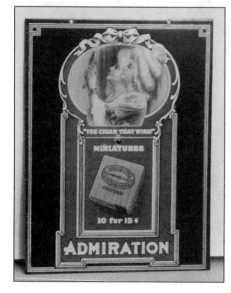

Sign, tin, easel-back, "The Cigar That Wins, Miniatures, 10 for 15¢, Admiration," Colonial woman looking in mirror, 1910s-1920s, cond. 9-9.25, 7-1/2" h, 5-1/2" w, $143. (Photo courtesy of Gary Metz, Muddy River Trading Co.)

## Admiral Radios/Refrigerators

Clock, neon, round, "Radios, Admiral, Refrigerators" white/red on black circle, black numbers except 12/3/6/9 are stars, dim orig neon, not running properly, circa 1940s, cond. 7, 20" dia ..................................... 187.00

## Admiral Rough Cut

Can, litho tin, knob top, round portrait of admiral, ship background, gold on dark ground, cond. 8, 6" h, 5" dia ................................................................. 67.00

## Admiration Cigars (See Photo)

## Admiration Coffee (See Photo)

## Aero Brand Coffee

Can, litho tin, round medallion with biplane, brown over yellow ground, Thompson, Elliott Limited, Vancouver BC, cond. 7+, 1 lb, 5-5/8" h, 4-1/8" dia .......................... 385.00

## Aero Motor Oil

Can, litho tin, "Super Refined Aero Motor Oil, 100% Pennsylvania Pure, 2500 Mile Guarantee," black/red/white text, white plane at top of black oval, red over black ground, Christenson Oil Co., Portland OR, cond. 8, qt, 5-1/2" h, 4" dia ......................................... 132.00

## Aeroshell

Can, tin

"Aeroshell Lubricating Oil, A mineral base oil for aero engines and high precision motor car and motor cycle engines," yellow shell flanked by wings, yellow text, red ground, London, cond. 7, gal, 10-1/2" h, 8-1/4" w, 3-1/2" d ...................................... 605.00

"Aeroshell Oil," red text over yellow shell logo with wings, white-yellow-red ground, replaced cap, scratches/fading, 9-1/2" h, 6-1/4" w, 2-1/2" d ........................... 55.00

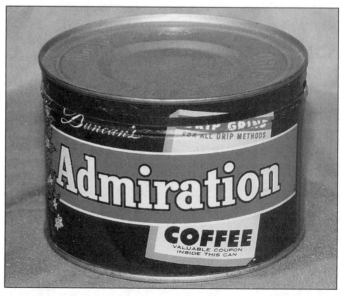

Can, keywind, litho tin, "Duncan's Admiration Coffee, Duncan Coffee Co., Houston, Tx.," 1 lb, $68.

Trade card, paper, "Agate Iron Ware, It is a perfect article, Just as the makers say, and as I can't destroy it, My Advice is, buy to day," advertises Massachusetts merchant on back, $15.

## Aetna A Plus

Gas globe lens, glass, "Aetna Plus" in white on large red "A" on white ground, red border, cond. 7.5, 13-1/2" dia............................................................. 55.00

## After Dinner Salted Peanuts

Can, litho tin, "After Dinner Wholesome Crisp Salted Peanuts, Bosman & Lohman Co., Norfolk, Va., U.S.A.," red text on yellow area, blue ground, lid cond. 5, can cond. 6.5-7, 5 lb ............................................................. 143.00
Pail, litho tin, 2" h.......................................................... 16.50

## Aircraft Rolled Oats

Can, cardboard, round, "Aircraft Brand Rolled Oats," sheaf of oats on white ground, landscape above lower black border, red text, The Donald Company, Grand Island NE, cond. 9-, 1 lb 4 oz .................................................... 302.50

## Agalion Motor Oil

Can, tin, "Agalion Motor Oil" in white under lion's face, red ground, Northern Oil & Fuel Corp., Watertown NY, no bottom, cond. 7, gal, 11" h, 8" w, 3" d .......... 385.00

## Agate Iron Ware (See Photo)

## Air-Float

Tin, litho tin, small top
"Air-Float Borated Baby Powder," round portrait of infant, Talcum Puff Co., Toronto & Jacksonville FL, cond. 8-, 6" h .................................................... 55.00
"Air-Float Talcum Powder," oval portrait of woman, flowers, green/purple on white ground, Talcum Puff Co., New York, cond. 8.5, 4-1/2" h, 2-1/2" w, 1-1/4" d ......................................................... 181.50

## Airport Coffee

Can, keywind, litho tin, yellow/black text and design, shows plane taking flight, Albrecht Grocer Co., Akron OH, cond. 7.5, 1 lb, 4" h, 5" dia........................ 158.50

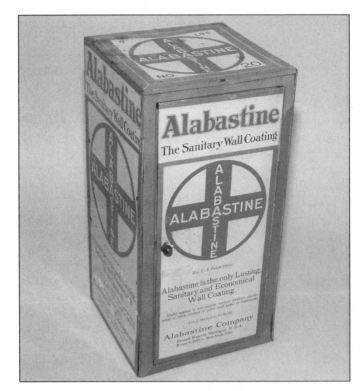

Cabinet, tin, "Alabastine, The Sanitary Wall Coating...Alabastine Company, Grand Rapids, Mich.," lettered "5 LBS, NO. 20" on top, wear, 16-1/4" h, 8-1/8" sq, $85.

## Alabastine (See Photo)

## Alka Seltzer

**History:** Dr. Franklin L. Miles began practicing medicine in Elkhart, Ind., in 1875, and, shortly thereafter, he began practicing his pharmacological skills. The Miles Medical Company was formed in 1884 to sell his home remedies. Along with several partners, he was responsible for creating an impressive array of restoratives and tonics, some of which were still being sold in the 1970s.

Alka-Seltzer was first marketed in October 1931 and was widely advertised. In 1935, the company became Miles Laboratories, Inc. The Speedy Alka-Seltzer character debuted in 1954 and pitched the fizzy product until 1964.

Thermometer, aluminum/glass, "For Headache, Upset Stomach," Speedy, minor scratches/pitting, 12" d................................................................ 412.50

## Allen & Ginter

Insert cards, cardboard, Indian Chiefs, complete set of 50, remnants of glue from scrapbook, most cond. EXC, 3-1/4" h, 1-1/2" w...................................... 577.50

## Allis-Chalmers

Sign, porcelain, diamond, "A-C, Allis-Chalmers," blue text in white seal, orange ground, cond. EXC, 6" h, 6" w..................................................................88.00

## Altex

Tin, litho tin, "Altex Air Tested Prophylactics, 3 for 50¢, Western Rubber Co., Canada," brown/cream, cond. 7-, 1/4" h, 2-1/8" w, 1-5/8" d ..........................330.00

## Alumni Burley Cut

Tin, vertical pocket, litho tin, black text, red oval shows man in mortar board, books flank medallion, white ground, United States Tobacco Co., front cond. 8+, back cond. 6, 4" h, 3" w ................................... 827.00

## Amalie Motor Oil

Clock, lightup, metal body, glass face, "Amalie Pennsylvania Motor Oil" in white on red oval, white ground, cond. 7, 15" dia ............................................................. 242.00

## American Agriculture Chemical Co.

Sign, flange, porcelain, round, "Authorized Agent, The American Agricultural Chemical Company, AA Quality, Fertilizers," bull's-eye design in red/white/blue, cond. 8+, 20" dia........................................................ 330.00

## American Bank Protection Co.

Sign, glass, reverse-painted, shield shape, "Danger, This Value Is Protected by Electrical Steel Lining and Alarms, American Bank Protection Co., Minneapolis, Minn., P. Pause & Co. Chicago," minor flaking, some paint spots lifting, 14" h, 18" w ................................................... 258.50

## American Beauty Bread

Thermometer, painted wood, "American Beauty Bread, Welcome Baking Company, Oakland, Calif.," 15" h, 6" w, $110.

Tin, litho tin, vertical box, concave, "American Eagle Chewing Tobacco," text in banners on dark ground, crossed leaves behind "American Eagle," top shows woman on eagle, cond. 7.5, 5" h, 6" w, 4-1/2" d, $220.

## American Can Company

Pail, litho tin, "Compliments of Tin-Ware Dept., American Can Company, Manufacturers of Tin Ware & Cans," black/gold text, red ground, 1905 premium Southern Hardware Jobbers Association convention, cond. 7, 1-3/4" h, 1-5/8" dia .............................................357.50

## American Club Ginger Ale

Sign, cardboard, classic nude, cond. 9.5, 11" sq ........ 176.00

## American Coffee

Can, cardboard, tin top/bottom, "American Mocha & Java, Golden Eagle Brand, Packed by Cobb, Bates & Yerxa Co., Importers, Boston, Mass.," gold eagle, red ground, 3 lb, cond. 8+, 8" h, 5-1/2" sq ................................... 154.00

## American Duplex Co.

Trade sign, tin/metal, coffeepot, "American Duplex Co., Louisville, Kentucky," silver over black body, stains/dents, 29" h, 22" w ........................................... 495.00

## American Eagle Tobacco

Tin, flat pocket, litho tin, "American Eagle Chewing Tobacco, American Eagle Tobacco Co., Detroit, Mich.," woman with banner riding on back of flying eagle, wreath at edges, cond. 8-, 5/8" h, 3-5/8" w, 2-3/8" d .......................................................... 935.00

## American Express

Sign

Cardboard, "To Send Money anywhere, at any time, for any purpose, use - American Express Money Orders," red/white text, money order on black ground, "For Sale At Express Offices, Drug and Stationery Stores" on white panel at bottom, dated Sept 1921, framed, tears/stains/fading/creases, 17" h, 13" w.................................................. 55.00

Painted metal, flange, die-cut, shield shape, "American Express Credit Cards," oval warrior in center, black/yellow text, yellow over black ground, bubbling/scratches, 23-3/4" h, 18-3/4" w .............. 55.00

Porcelain, "American Express Travelers Cheques Accepted Here," chips at grommet holes/edges, 4-1/2" h, 10" w.................................................. 99.00

Porcelain, flange, "American Express Co., Money Orders, Foreign Drafts, Travelers Checques, Letters of Credit, Telegraphic Transfers," white on cobalt ground, circa 1914, cond. 7-8........................... 302.50

## American Gasoline

Gas globe

2 lenses, high-profile metal body, "American Certified Quality Gasoline," clear text on white ground, red circle in center under horizontal white bar, paint loss to lenses, body repainted, lens cond. 7, body cond. 9, 15" dia.................................................. 170.50

2 lenses, wide glass body, "American" in blue on white panel, red ground above, blue ground below, all cond. 9, 12-1/2" dia.................................... 253.00

Gas globe lens, 2 lenses, "American Gas" in white on blue border of red bull's-eye logo, cond. 8.5, 15" dia.................................................. 231.00

Insert, gas pump, glass, "American" in black, oval torch logo at left, white ground with lower red border, cond. 8.5, 3-1/2" h, 24-1/2" w ........................ 66.00

Sign, porcelain, 2-sided, oval, "American" torch logo in red/white/blue, missing flame, cond. 8+, 44-1/2" h, 73-1/2" w.................................................. 357.50

## American Lady Coffee

Can, tin, slip lid, "American Lady Coffee," portrait of woman in round blue wreath, red text, white ground, Haas-Lieber Grocery Co., St. Louis, soiling/fading/rusted top-bottom, 3 lb, 9-1/2" h, 5-1/2" w ........................................ 154.00

## American Locomotive Co.

Photograph, framed, "American Locomotive Company, New York City" on orig mat, "New York Central" on coal car, "Jan 1929" near track, cond. EXC, 15 5/8" h, 29-1/2" w ........................................... 154.00

## American Mills Coffee

Can, litho tin, small top, "American Mills Blend Coffee, J.S. Silvers & Bro., Cranbury, N.J.," round image of man opening lion's mouth, red/black, cond. 8+, 5-1/2" h, 4-3/4" dia............................................. 687.50

## American Snuff

Fan, cardboard, wooden handle, railroad image, reverse shows factory/1934-1935 calendars, cond. 8+, 14-3/4"h, 7-5/8" w ................................... 44.00

## American Typewriter Ribbon

Tin, litho tin, "American Brand Typewriter Ribbon, N.N. Storms Co.," image of old Indian, red ground, cond. 8+, 2" h, 1-3/4" sq ............................................. 231.00

## American Union

Tin, vertical pocket

Cardboard, tin top/bottom, slide opener, "Smoke and Chew American Union Cut Plug," name in round seal with red ribbon, red/white/blue ground, cond. 7, 3-3/4" h, 3" w ................................................. 276.00

Litho tin, slide opener, "Smoke and Chew American Union Cut Plug, Flake Cut, The Pinkerton Tobacco Co., Toledo, Ohio," reverse reads "Feiner Rauchen und Kauen Tabak," name in round seal with red ribbon, red/white/blue ground, cond. 8, 3-3/4" h, 3" w................................................. 554.00

## American Wood Powder

Can, tin, "The American Wood Powder, Every Can Of This Powder Is Tested As To Penetration And Force, Gives Greater Penetration Than Black Powder," 1890s, cond. 8, 7" h, 6" dia.............................. 165.00

## America's Best Coffee

Can, paper label over cardboard, "America's Best Blended Coffee," Indian chief on 2 sides/lid, MJB Kellam Co., Binghamton NY, cond. 8.5, 1 lb, 5-3/8" h, 4-1/8" dia .......................................... 962.50

## Ammo Washing Powder

Sign, trolley, cardboard, "How do you do without Ammo," black/red text in yellow diamond, ground with 4 scenes of woman cleaning, 1920s, cond. 8, 11" h, 21" w................................................. 33.00

## Amoco

Can, tin, "Amoco French Dry Cleaner," oval orange/black logo, white text, white over purple ground, purple band

Can, litho tin, "Amoco Motor Grease, American Oil Company," scratches/dents, 1 lb, $15.

at top, cond. 7+, gal, 10-3/4" h, 5-3/4" w,
4-3/4" d............................................ 49.50
Display, tire rack
Painted metal, 2-sided, oval "Amoco" logo, "Tires,
Tubes" in gray above/below, arched red/white/blue
ground, cond. 7, 7" h, 12-1/2" w ..................... 88.00
Painted metal, 2-sided, oval "Amoco" logo above
"Tires" in black on white arch, green ground, cond.
8/7.5, 7" h, 12-1/2" w ...................................... 93.50
Tin/wire, "Amoco 120, Super Tire," blue/red/white text,
white over blue ground, cond. 8, 8-1/2" h, 13" w,
10" d ............................................................. 22.00
Gas globe
2 lenses, high-profile metal body, "Amoco" in white on
black horizontal band with white top/bottom border,
red ground, lens cond. 8, body cond. 7,
15-1/2" dia ................................................. 330.00
1 lens, high-profile metal body, "Amoco-Gas" in white on
black band, white stripe above/below name, red
ground, both cond. 8, 15" dia ......................... 385.00
Pen/pencil set, Cross, metal die-cut oval logo on upper
pocket clasp, pen does not close, cond. 8,
5-3/8" l............................................................ 27.50
Punch board, "Amoco Motor Oil Bonus Board, 64 Cash
Winners," "Standard" oval logo upper-left, shows 4 oil
cans upper-right, playing area in red/blue/green/black
quarters, unused, cond. EXC, 10-1/8" h, 9-3/4" w, lot
of 2 ............................................................. 60.50
Sign
Cardboard, "...step ahead, Mighty Amoco," close-up of
bass drummer, red/black oval logo lower-right,
cond. 8, 28" h, 61" w......................................110.00

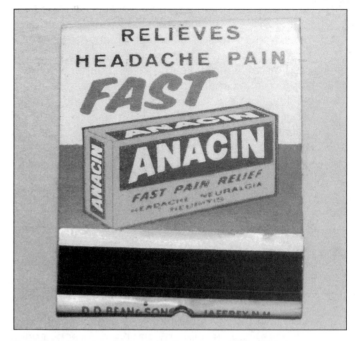

**Matchbook, advertises Anacin on one side, Dristan on other, $1.**

Porcelain, 2-sided, "American Amoco Gas Courtesy
Cards Honored Here," red/black oval logo, white/
black text, 2 red stars, white ground, cond. 7, 15" h,
24" w........................................................... 104.50
Tin, embossed, "Amoco Battery Cable Service," red/black
oval, white band with stars over black band, 1950s-
1960s, cond. 7.5-8, 10" h, 17" w....................... 121.00

# Amolin (See Photo)

# Anacin (See Photo)

# Anchor Buggy Co.

Sign, cloth, "It's too good for the money, It's an Anchor, Ask
any Anchor Agent, Made by Anchor Buggy Co., Cincinnati, Ohio," woman in white dress with laurel wreath, No.
02 buggy in white oval, green ground, cond. VG, 64" h,
38" w.........................................................742.50

# Andes Stoves & Ranges

Match holder, cardboard, die-cut, tin holder/striker, shield
shape, "Use Andes Stoves and Ranges, Best In The
World, Always Give Satisfaction," lists New York merchant, shows girl in floral bonnet, cond. VG, 6-1/4" h,
4-5/8" w .......................................................... 170.50

# Angelus Marshmallows

Pocket mirror, oval, cherub with horn/box, blue ribbon,
cond. 8 ......................................................... 143.00
Tape measure, pocket type, celluloid, "Try" over box of
"Angelus Marshmallows," "The Cracker Jack Co., Chi-
cago" at bottom, yellow ground, shows marshmallow tin
on back, cond. 9+, 1-1/2" dia................................82.50
Tin, sample, litho tin, round, paper label on top, "Angelus
Marshmallows, A Message of Purity" in oval design on

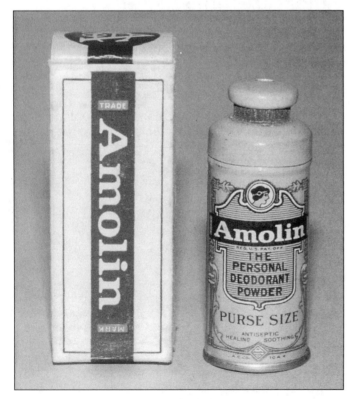

**Tin, litho tin, "Amolin, The Personal Deodorant Powder,
Purse Size," orig paper box, 2-5/8" h, $10.**

side, Cracker Jack Co., 1930s-1940s,
cond. 8.5 ......................................................... 220.00
Sign, cardboard, "One Taste Invites Another," shows 2
boxes, one open with marshmallows spilling out,
green ground with black border, reverse pictures large
black/white Cracker Jack sign, cond. 8.5+, 8-3/4" h,
11-1/2" w ......................................................... 154.00

## Anglo-Saxon Tobacco

Tin, litho tin, embossed, "Anglo-Saxon Smoking Tobacco,
W.B. Reid & Co., Toronto," crossed American/British
flags, wreath, cond. 7.5, 4" h, 6" w.................... 353.00

## Anheuser-Busch

**History:** Eberhard Anheuser was devoted to suds. In
1857, the soap manufacturer purchased a failing
brewery and hired Adolphus Busch, his son-in-law, as
a salesman. Incorporating the most modern production methods of the period, Anheuser was the first to
pasteurize beer, and the first to refrigerate the finished
product during summer shipping.

The company's most famous advertising featured a
bloody battle scene, "Custer's Last Fight" by F. Otto
Becker, and more than 9 million copies were repro-
duced on cardboard, paper, and tin for distribution to
bars and patrons.

Among its many brands, Budweiser was introduced
in 1876, Malt-Nutrine in 1895, Michelob in 1896, and
Busch in 1955.

One of the company's most popular promotional items,
a pocketknife with a peephole in one end and a picture of
Adolphus inside, was produced in 47 variations.

**Reference:** Donna S. Baker, *Vintage Anheuser-Busch:
An Unofficial Collector's Guide*, Schiffer Publishing, 1999

Pocket mirror, celluloid, oval, "Anheuser-Busch Ginger Ale,
St. Louis, Mo., U.S.A.," red A/eagle logo, white text, black
ground, gold border, 2-3/4"...................................... 88.00
Sign, paper, "The Father of Waters," Indians on raft with
keg/crate, new frame, 13-1/4" h, 19" w.................... 88.00

## Anker-Holth Cream Separator

Sign, porcelain, "We Use The Anker-Holth Cream Separator," white text, blue ground, cond. 8+, 10" h,
14" w ................................................................. 231.00

## Ant. Bernier, Ltee.

Can, tin, "Ant. Bernier, Ltee., Quebec" in white on blue
oval border, shows early car, "American Packed, High
Grade" in red/white, red ground, cond. 7, gal, 12" h,
8" w, 3" d .......................................................... 660.00

## Antonella

Tin, vertical pocket, litho tin, "Antonella [wood-like text]
Mild Pipe Blend" scroll shows peace pipe, brown
ground, cond. 8.5............................................... 477.00

## Arcadia Smoking Mixture

Tin, horizontal box, litho tin, lions flank "sub hoc signo

Can, oil, "Archer
Lubricants, Archer
Petroleum Corp.,"
unopened, 1 quart,
$30.

vinces," Callum's Cigar Stores, Toronto, cond. 8, 2" h,
5" w, 3-5/8" d ..................................................... 103.00

## Archer Lubricants

Box, oversized countertop display, cardboard, Indian with
ear-of-corn body, circa 1920s, 5-5/8" h, 9-5/8" w,
18" d ................................................................. 385.00
Tin, "Archer Lubricants," Indian with bow/arrow, cond. 8,
2 gal .................................................................... 85.00

## Ardath Cigarettes

Tin, vertical pocket, litho tin, hinged lid, "Ardath Cigarettes Splendo, Mild Natural Egyptian Blend, Ardath
Tobacco Co., London," held 25 cigarettes, cond. 7.5,
3-1/4" h, 4" w, 1" d ............................................... 37.50

## Arm-Chair Club

Can, litho tin, screw top, "Arm-Chair Club, English Mixture, Pipe Tobacco," silhouette of man reading paper
in armchair, red ground, Royal Canadian Tobacco Co.,
Toronto, cond. 7.5 ................................................ 27.50

## Arm & Hammer

**History:** This company had its roots in a relatively
small endeavor named the Vulcan Spice Mills. As his
trademark, founder James Austin Church used the
arm of Vulcan, the Roman god of war, striking an anvil
with a hammer.

Originally, Church used the logo only to identify his
spices and mustard. After joining his father at Church &
Company in 1867, the label was used for baking soda.

A competing product, Cow Brand baking soda,
was being sold by another relative, and the two companies eventually merged in 1896 to form Church &
Dwight Company.

Display, cardboard, "Arm & Hammer Soda, This Is An
Enlarged Copy, Small Card In Each Package," shows

Box, paper, "Arm & Hammer Bicarbonate of Soda," unopened, 2 oz, $15.

Indigo Bunting trade card, trade card on back and company history, edge wear, 14-3/4" h, 11-3/4" w ............................................. 104.50

Shipping box, wood, paper labels on 4 sides, "Arm & Hammer Soda, Church & Co., New York," round arm/hammer logo in white/red/blue, top-corner edge break, no lid, cond. 8-, 8-1/2" h, 20" w, 16" d ........................ 27.50

Sign, paper, identifies 14 birds, "Arm & Hammer Soda" sign on tree over oval text box and box of product, framed, cond. G, 26" h, 18" w ........................... 121.00

## Armour

**History:** Philip Danforth Armour and John Plankinton moved their provision business from Milwaukee, Wis., to Chicago in 1867 and chose the name Armour and Company.

Their meat-processing operation expanded quickly, necessitating several moves, until they settled in at the Union Stock Yards. Before 1872, all of the pork and lamb they processed was salt-cured. After that time, natural ice and newly developed coolers were used to preserve the meat.

Canned meat was first produced in 1879, and the company's Veribest trademark for its expanding line of canned products was introduced around the turn of the century. Fruits and vegetables, peanut butter and jelly, and even soda fountain supplies were included.

The company's packaging has been revamped several times over the years, with the modified star and rectangle trademark being introduced in 1963. Now a part of the Armour-Dial family, products range from soap, plant food, and floor cleaner to a plethora of food items.

Box, cardboard, "Armour's Oats, Breakfast, Luncheon and Dinner," elf holding stalk of oats, Armour Grain Co., Chicago, yellow ground, cond. 7.5+, 7-1/4" h, 4-1/4" dia .................................................... 50.50

Pail, litho tin, "Armour's Veribest Peanut Butter," text in oval with blue border/horizontal panel, nursery rhyme characters/animals on yellow ground, cond. 8.25, 1 lb, 4" h, 3-1/2" dia ............................................. 302.50

Sign
Heavy paper, "For Breakfast, Luncheon and Dinner Use Armour's Oats, Worthwhile Recipes on Every Package," shows elf with stalk of oats beside product, newer frame, Armour Grain Co., cond. VG, 26-3/4" h, 21" w ............................................. 93.50

Tin, "Armour's Star" in yellow, shows wrapped packages at top, 3 plates of ham served various ways, black chef slicing ham at bottom, white text under images, edge wear/dents/back rusted, 37-1/2" h, 13" w .............................................................. 550.00

Tin, embossed, "Armour Franks, Plump, Juicy, Tender!, Sold Exclusively," boy eating hotdog, name in black panel with red star, white ground, dark band at bottom, cond. 8.5+, 11-1/2" h, 15-1/4" w ............. 198.00

Tin over cardboard, beveled, "Armour's 3X Oleomargarine," shows biscuits, margarine and box of product, cond. 8-, 13" h, 19" w ............................ 220.00

## Armstrong Tires

Sign, tin, embossed, round corners, "Armstrong Rhino-Flex Tires," rhino lower-left, red/black text, white ground, black border, cond. 8, 18" h, 60" w ................................... 170.50

## Asa Candler & Co.

Billhead, 1888, druggists, framed/matted, cond. 9-9.5 ................................................................. 522.50

## Ashland

Gas globe
2 lenses, wide glass body, "Ashland Flying Octanes," diagonal "Ashland," red/black text, black triangular Ethyl logo lower-right, white ground, lens cond. 9/8.5, body cond. 9, 13-1/2" dia ...................... 423.50

New plastic body with 2 glass lenses, "Ashland Flying Octanes," diagonal "Ashland," red/green text, black triangular Ethyl logo lower-right, white ground, lens cond. 8, body cond. 9, 13-1/2" dia ............... 605.00

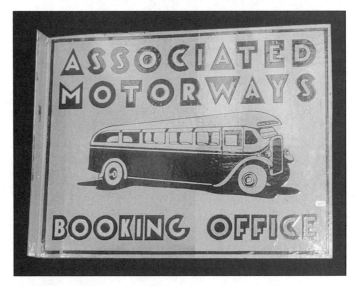

**Sign, flange, porcelain, green and orange, "Associated Motorways Booking Office," $5,850.**

Gas globe lens, glass, "Ashland Flying Octanes," diagonal "Ashland," red/green text, white ground, cond. 8, 13-1/2" dia.............................................. 132.00
Sign, porcelain, 2-sided, octagonal, "Ashland Oil Products," red/green text, white ground, cond. 7, 60" h, 90" w .......................................................... 209.00

## Associated Motor Oil

Can, tin, "Associated Motor Oil" in white over image of early tanker truck, red ground, Associated Oil Co., San Francisco, cond. 7, gal, 10-1/2" h, 8" w, 3" d................ 715.00

## Associated Motorways (See Photo)

## Astrostar Tires

Sign, tin, self-framing, black text, airplane lower-right, green ground, cond. 8, 15-1/2" h, 60" w.......................... 126.50

## Athlete Smoking Mixture

Tin, litho tin, athlete in outdoor scene, D. Ritchie & Co., Montreal, cond. 7+, 4" h, 6" w ..........................115.50

## Atkinson Hasserick & Co.

Oil can, cut metal, soldered, sliding lid, "K" embossed at top, "Machine Oil" stamped on reverse, "1/2 pint 16" stamped on bottom, minor dents/scratches, 2-3/4" h, 2-1/2" w, 8-1/2" d.................................... 49.50

## Atlantic

Gas globe
  1 lens, wide glass body, "Atlantic" in white on red panel with thin line above/below name, white ground, lens glued to body, lens cond. 8, body cond. 9, 13-1/2" dia ................................................. 121.00
  2 lenses, narrow Gill glass body, "Atlantic Hi-Arc," blue "Atlantic," white "Hi-Arc" on blue panel with short red stripes above/below, white ground, lens cond. 8.5, body cond. 8, 13-1/2" dia.................................. 368.50
Letter opener, brass, shows early Atlantic Refining Co. asphalt truck, cond. 8, 8-3/4" l............................. 33.00

**Pump sign, porcelain, "Atlantic," white text, red ground, cond. 8, 9" h, 13" w, $88. (Photo courtesy of Collectors Auction Services)**

Sign
  Metal, 2-sided, "Atlantic Paraffine Base Motor Oil, Aviation, A Pennsylvania Oil," vertical airplane, red/black text, white ground, black border, cond. 7...........528.00
  Painted metal, flange, "Atlantic Motor Oils, Light-Medium-Heavy and Polarine," red/white text, black ground, cond. 7, 13-1/2" h, 18" w ................. 275.00
  Porcelain, individual red text, spells out "ATLANTIC," cond. 7, 15" h, all............................................. 148.50
  Porcelain, pump sign, curved to fit visible pump, "The Atlantic Refining Company," crossed arrows under "Atlantic," black text, white logo on red panel, white ground, restored, cond. 8+, 13" sq .............. 330.00

## Atlas

Tin, paper label on cardboard, "Atlas Cayenne Pepper," blue Atlas holding globe on shoulders, white/black text, orange panel on cobalt ground, Woolson Spice Co., Toledo, 2 oz, cond. 8.5+ ......................................... 44.00

## Atlas Assurance Co.

Sign, porcelain, "Atlas Assurance Co. Limited of London, Established 1808," man holding world on his shoulders, scratches, chips at edges, 11-3/4" h, 17-3/4" w........................................................... 198.00

## Atlas Bantam (See Photo)

## Atlas Tires

Display, tire rack, tin/wire
  "Atlas" in white on red ground, blue band at bottom, white border, cond. 8, 8-1/2" h, 13" w, 10" d .................................................... 55.00
  "Atlas Plycon, The Round Tire" in white, red ground, blue band at bottom, white border, cond. 8, 8-1/2" h, 13" w, 10" d.................................................... 27.50
Sign, porcelain
  "Atlas Tires," white text, red ground, "Guaranteed By The Standard Oil Co. Of Ohio" in white seal, 2 corners with diagonal bands, cond. 7, 24" h, 71" w........................................................... 825.00

**Peanut machine, "Atlas Bantam 5¢, The Atlas Mfg & Sales Co., Cleveland, Ohio" decal, nickel-plated metal with glass dome, embossed top, 11-1/2" h, $175.**

"Tires, Atlas, Batteries," white text, "Atlas" is vertical, "Guaranteed by Standard Oil Company" round logo bottom-right, orange ground, 2 corners with diagonal bands, cond. 8, 60" h, 15-7/8" w ............. 357.50

## Aunt Hannah's Bread

Pot scraper, litho tin, "Baur's Pot and Pan Scraper Fits Any Corner of Pot or Pan, Always Look for this Label, It Guarantees Pure, Sweet, Wholesome Bread, Baur Bros. Co., The Cleanest Bakery in America, Pittsburgh, Pa.," cond. 8-, 3" h, 3-3/8" w ............... 1,155.00

## Aunt Jemima

**History:** The Pearl Milling Company first used the image of Aunt Jemima in 1889. The company's owner, Charles G. Underwood, had been searching for a symbol his company could use for a new self-rising pancake mix. Reportedly, a team of blackface comedians performing a cake walk to a song called "Aunt Jemima" served as his inspiration.

After the business was sold to R.T. Davis Mill & Manufacturing Company, the new owners launched Aunt Jemima to fame with a display at the 1893 Columbian Exposition in Chicago. A thin woman named Nancy Green (who certainly didn't resemble the robust trademark) was hired to portray Aunt Jemima. Reportedly, she flipped more than a million pancakes during the fair's run. Anna Robinson was the model for the more modern version of the trademark that was introduced in 1936.

According to company legend, Aunt Jemima was originally a cook on a plantation in Louisiana. Uncle Mose, Diana, and Wade were also part of the family. The first Aunt Jemima cloth dolls were introduced in 1896, and composition dolls were sold in 1931.

**Doll, cloth, stuffed, "Aunt Jemima's Pancake Flour Pickaninny Doll, Wade Davis, The Davis Milling Co., St. Joseph, Mo.," 11" h, $225.**

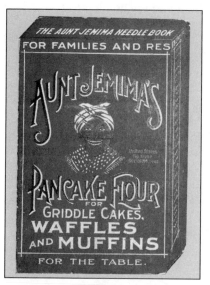

Needle case, paper, opens, "The Aunt Jemima Needle Book for Families and Res, Aunt Jemima's Pancake Flour for Griddle Cakes, Waffles and Muffins for the Table," 5-1/4" h, 3-1/2" w, $250.

**Reference:** Jean Williams Turner, *Collectible Aunt Jemima*, Schiffer Publishing, 1994

Sack, cloth, "Aunt Jemima Degerminated Yellow Corn Meal," shows Aunt Jemima, yellow fabric, unopened, sewn repair to tear, 25 lb, 10" h, 11" w ............. 121.00

Sign, cardboard, 2-sided, string-hung, "Aunt Jemima's Pancake Flour," Aunt Jemima in red blouse with white dots, white scarf with red dots, cond. 8.5+, 6" h, 4" w ............................................................... 1,650.00

Toy, string climber, cardboard, die-cut, 2-pc, top shows red box of Aunt Jemima Pancake Flour, "I'se In Town Honey," 4" h, 2-1/4" w, bottom has climbing Aunt Jemima, "Le' Me To It, It's Worth Climbing For Aunt Jemima's Pancake Flour," 13-1/4" h, 6" w, cond. 8+ ...................................................... 7,590.00

## Aunt Lydia's Thread

Display, countertop, wood dovetailed box, "Aunt Lydia, Aunt Lydia's Button & Carpet Thread, Extra Strong" in stencil/paint, with 4 boxes, 11-1/4" w ................................ 253.00

## Autoline Oil

Sign, porcelain, 2-sided, oval, "Autoline Oil, for your motor's sake," white/black text, red ground, cond. 8, 20" h, 30" w ........................................................ 220.00

## Autumn Leaf Rolled Oats

Box, cardboard, round, "Autumn Leaf Brand Rolled Oats" under leaves, red/dark text, The Burt-Zaiser Co., Burlington IA, side paper loss, cond. 7, 1 lb 4 oz ................ 27.50

## Avon Polish

Sign, tin, "Avon Brilliant Polish For Boots And Leggings," pictures round green tin mkd "Avon Polish, High Class Boot Polish, Preserves The Leather," yellow ground, black border, cond. G, 8" h, 3" w ......................... 71.50

Cabinet, wood, 2 dovetailed drawers with round metal handles, beveled top, drawers mkd "A.W. Co." and "Roll Braid" in faded gold lettering, minor scratches, 8" h, 16-1/2" w, 15 3/4" d ................................. 231.00

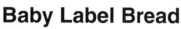

# B

## B-1 Lemon-Lime Soda

Sign

Celluloid, round, "We Serve B-1 Lemon-Lime Soda Plus Vitamin B," black/white text, red center, white border, 1940s, cond. 9.5, 6" dia ...................... 27.50

Tin, die-cut, embossed, bottle shape, red "B-1 Lemon-Lime Soda" round logo on green bottle, ©1940, nail hole/scratches/yellowing, 28" h, 8" w .............. 88.00

## B-A

Gas globe, 2 different lenses, wide glass body, "B-A Peerless Ethyl," centered "B-A Service Products" logo, red text at rim, white ground; "B-A Ethyl," logo at top, red text, white ground, lens cond. 8/7, body cond. 8.5, 13-1/2" dia ......................................................... 495.00

## B&B Baby Talc

Tin, litho tin, sample, various animal pull toys, elephant with orange "B&B" balloon, white ground, orange top/bottom borders, Bauer & Black, Chicago, cond. 8+, 2-1/4" h, 1-1/2" w, 7/8" d .................................. 137.50

## B&L Oysters (See Photo)

## Baby Bunting Rolled Oats

Box, paper on cardboard, cherub playing instrument with dancing rabbits, Rowe-Fawcett Co., New Albany IN, cond. 8+, 1-1/4 lb, 7-5/8" h, 4-1/2" dia ........... 1,430.00

**Tin, litho tin, "Delicious B&L Brand Oysters," Bivalve Oyster Packing Co., Bivalve, Md., green ground, 7-1/2" h, 6-5/8" dia, $40.**

## Baby Label Bread

Sign, litho tin, "Baby Label Brand, Matthaei Bread Co. Registered Honey Bread," child dressed in white sitting in red high chair, blue/red ground, oak frame, cond. 8.5, 19-1/2" h, 15-1/4" w .......................... 302.50

## Baby Stuart Coffee

Can, pry lid, paper label on tin, "Baby Stuart Brand Steel Cut Roasted Coffee," oval image of baby Stuart, red/black text, white ground, cond. 8.5, 1 lb ............. 357.50

## Bagdad Coffee

Pail, slip lid, litho tin, "Bagdad Brand Coffee," 3 Arabs in arched panel, cobalt/light-blue text, red ground, no lid, cond. 8.5, 5 lb ..................................................... 66.00

## Bagdad Tobacco

Tin, vertical pocket, litho tin

Short version, "Bagdad Short Cut Perfection of Blends For Pipe or Cigarette Smoking," circular medallion with man in turban, flanked by leaves, blue ground, cond. 8.5..................................................... 132.00

Short version, plain lid, "Bagdad Short Cut For Pipe Smoking," circular medallion with man in turban,

**Humidor, porcelain, "Bagdad," 6-1/2" h, $150.**

flanked by flags, blue ground, litho top,
cond. 9 ............................................................ 285.00
Tall version, "Bagdad Short Cut For Pipe Smoking," cir-
cular medallion with man in turban, flanked by flags,
blue ground, litho top, cond. 8, 4-1/4" h ........... 440.00

# Bagley's Wild Fruit Tobacco

Lunch box, litho tin, "Bagley's Wild Fruit Flake Cut
Tobacco, Smoking, Chewing," red/gold on blue
ground, cond. 8+ ................................................. 167.00

# Baker's

**History:** In 1765, an immigrant chocolate maker from
Ireland, John Hannon, persuaded Dr. James Baker to
finance a chocolate mill in Dorchester, Mass. While
on a trip to the West Indies to purchase cocoa beans,
Hannon was presumably lost at sea in 1779.

Dr. Baker began running the company and introduced his own blend of chocolate, Baker's, in 1780.
His grandson, Walter, joined the company in 1818,
and the name was subsequently changed to Walter
Baker Company in 1824.

The company's trademark of a woman in a long
dress and apron and holding a serving tray was
adopted in 1883. Based on a 1745 painting of wait-
ress Anna Baltauf in a Viennese chocolate shop, the
symbol was one of the first United States trademarks.

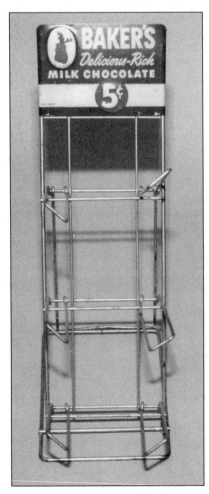

**Rack, wire, tin sign at
top, "Baker's Delicious
Rich Milk Chocolate
5¢," 12-1/2" h, $55.**

The company became part of General Foods in
1927, and both were acquired by the Philip Morris conglomerate in 1985.

In the things-aren't-always-as-they-seem category:
Baker's German Sweet Chocolate, which is still sold
today, has absolutely no connection to Germany.
Instead, the product is named for an Englishman
whose name was German.

Dish, covered, porcelain, "Baker's Cocoa," woman-with-
tray logo, red/white, 2-1/2" h, 5" dia ................. 385.00
Tin, litho tin, 2-pc, "Baker's Cocoa," woman with tray,
cond. 7.5, 1-1/8" h, 3-3/8" dia .......................... 132.00

# Bald Eagle Whiskey

Tray, litho tin, oval, "Petts Bald Eagle Whiskey," woman
and cherub, circa 1890s, cond. 8.5, 16-5/8" h,
13-5/8" w ........................................................ 742.50

# Balko Trailers (See Photo)

# Ballantine

Sign, tin, "Drink Ballantine XXX Ale," three white inter-
locking rings, "Purity, Body, Flavor," blue ground,
dents/scratches, 22" h, 70" w .......................... 137.50
Thermometer, round, "Ask the man for...Ballantine beer,"
3 blue rings with "Purity, Body, Flavor," cond. 8.25,
12" dia ............................................................... 99.00

# Baltimore Enamel and Novelty Co.

Sign, porcelain, Indian chief over blue/red lettering, red
border, scattered chips, 10" h, 6" w ................. 330.00

# Bambino Smoking Tobacco

Tin, vertical pocket, litho tin, silhouette of Babe Ruth,
orange ground, cond. 8 ................................. 2,928.00

**Clip, "Balko Trailers, Ladysmith, Wis., Large or Small We
Haul Them All," button is 1-5/8" by 2-3/8", $10.**

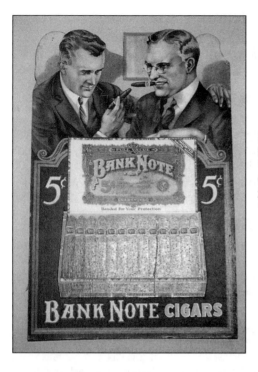

Display, card-board standup, "Bank Note Cigars, 5¢," 21-1/2" h, 14" w, $50.

## Bank Note Cigars (See Photo)

## Banner Boy

Tin, litho tin, boy holding "Banner Boy" banner, "Allspice" stamped on tin, cond. 7.5-8, 3-3/4" h, 2-1/4" w, 1-1/4" d.............................................................. 231.00

## Banner Milk

Sign, porcelain, "Banner Milk, It Tastes Better," red text on white ground, white "Milk" in red oval, scratches/fading, 14" h, 24" w ............................................ 77.00

## Bardahl Motor Oil (See Photo)

## Barking Dog Smoking Mixture

Pack, paper, foil-lined, "Barking Dog Smoking Mixture, Never Bites, London Depot 22 New Bond Street," central image of dog ................................................. 44.00

## Barney Oldfield Tires

Blotter, "If Barney Trusts Them, You Can, Barney Oldfield Tires, The Most Trustworthy Tires Built," merchant info to left of early "14" racer, green ground, cond. 8+, 3-1/4" h, 6" w .......................................................................110.00

## Barnsdall Gasoline

Gas globe, milk glass, 3-pc, "Barnsdall Gasoline, Be Square," B-in-square logo, red/blue text, white ground, cond. EXC, 15-1/2" dia..................................... 605.00

## Barnum's Animals Crackers

Box, cardboard, "Barnum's Animals Crackers," caged circus animals, white text, red ground, pre-1954, cond. 9, 2-3/4" h, 5" w, 2" d................................................ 33.00

Can, tin, "Bardahl racing oil, 4-Cycle Motor Oil," unopened, qt, $20.

## Barq's

**History:** Edward Charles Edmond Barq and one of his brothers formed their own bottling company in New Orleans in 1890. Even though they were awarded a medal for their soft drink, Orangine, the business didn't prosper.

Edward moved to Biloxi, Miss., in 1897, still experimenting and still hoping to find the perfect soft drink formula. Then, in 188, Edward arrived at just the right mix of ingredients to make Barq's Root Beer. Since then, the company has relied primarily on word of mouth to advertise its product.

Barq's is currently the second most popular root beer (behind A&W) in America.

Calendar holder, tin over cardboard, beveled edge, string-hung, "Drink Barq's, It's Good," bottle at right, red/white on black ground, some mid 1950s pages, cond. 8, 19" h, 8" w .......................................... 253.00

Sign, tin, embossed letters, "Drink Barq's, It's Good," NOS, 12" h, 30" w, $100.

Sign, tin over cardboard, beveled edge, string-hung, "Drink Barq's, It's Good," sandwich/plate of pickles by glass/bottle, 1950s, cond. 7.75, 14" h, 11" w........................ 209.00

## Barrus Mustard

Tin, store size, "Barrus Mustard, Boston," round image of spread-wing eagle on world, yellow ground, circa 1880s, cond. 8, 10 lb, 11-1/4" h, 7" sq.............. 1,045.00

## Bartels Beer

Cigar/cigarette/match holder, tin, cone shape, "Bartels Malt Extract," bearded man with stein, red ground, 3 holes for cigars/cigarettes, removable match holder on top, cond. G, 4" h, base 4-5/8" dia ................... 660.00

Sign, litho tin, "Bartels Beer" in white on dark border, "BBCo" on white center, minor scratches/dents, 18-1/2" dia................................................. 82.50

## Bartels Root Beer

Tray, metal, "Bartels Brilliant Old Devonshire, Crown & Root Beer, Syracuse, N.Y.," woman holding glass in round medallion, green ground, cond. 8+, 12" d.............. 412.50

## Barthold Mixture

Tin, square corner, litho tin, "Barthold Mixture, Peter Hauptmann & Co., St. Louis," Statue of Liberty at left, red/black design, cond. 7.5, 2-1/4" h, 4-1/2" w, 3-1/4" d................................................ 258.50

## Bartholomay Brewing Co.

Sign, cardboard, "Compliments of Bartholomay Brew. Co., Rochester, N.Y." at bottom, woman with grain on winged wheel in sky, slightly faded/stains/wear, 40" h, 29" w ................................................ 687.50

Tip tray, litho tin, "Beers, Ales & Porter, In Kegs & Bottles," woman with grains on winged wheel in sky, text around edge, cond. 8.25, 4-1/4" dia.................. 143.00

## Bartlett Springs Mineral Water

Tray, litho tin, deer and fawn drinking in woods, oversized bottle behind them, Bartlett Springs Co., San Francisco, cond. 8+, 13" dia.................................... 550.00

## Base Ball Tobacco

Pack, paper, "Base Ball Tobacco For Cigarette And Pipe," white text, red ground, baseball at top lettered "More and Better," cigarettes/pipe at bottom, Larus & Bro., empty, cond. 8, 4-1/2" h, 3" w................... 277.00

## Bathasweet Rice Powder

Tin, litho tin, sample, "Trial Size, Bathasweet Rice Powder, Exquisitely Perfumed, Antiseptically Pure, The Only Safe Toilet Powder For the Nursery and Home," cond. 8, 2-5/8" h, 1-1/4" dia ................................ 50.50

## Battle Axe Shoes

Shoe horn, litho tin, "Buy Battle Axe Shoes, The Sign of Quality, Stephen Putney Shoe Co., Richmond, Va.," hand with axe, cond. 8.5+, 4-1/2" h, 1-3/4" w .................. 253.00

## Battle Ax Plug

Label, paper on wood, "Battle Axe Plug, That's All," yellow text, black ground, shows arm with weapon, cond. 7.5, 10-1/2" sq.................................................... 27.50

## Battleship Coffee

Tin, keywind, litho tin
"Battleship Coffee, It's The Flavor!," blue/red text, shows ship, red vertical band, lid possibly replaced, cond. 7, 1 lb, 3-1/2" h, 5" dia ......................... 67.00
Drip grind, warship on both sides in blues, white ground, cond. 8, 1 lb...................................... 88.00

## Baxter-Schenkelberger & Co.

Sign, paper, "Two Soles with but a single thought, Baxter-Schenkelberger & Co., Boston, London," left/right soles at top, seated bum in suit/soleless shoes, art by Hy Mayer, fading/creases/tears, 27-5/8" h, 19-3/4" w........................................................ 286.00

## Baxter's Cigars

Sign, tin, embossed, "Baxter's" at top, "Drum 5¢ Cigar, Beat All, How Good They Are" on drumhead, red text, white ground, dented corners, cond. G, 13-3/4" h 9-1/2" w.............................................................. 88.00

## Bayer Aspirin

**History:** Ease his pain. That's what a German chemist was hoping to do for his father when he experimented with acetylsalicylic acid. The result: aspirin. First made available to physicians by Friedrich Bayer and Company in 1899, aspirin quickly became the number-one drug in the world.

Doll, cloth, "Bear Brand Hosiery," wear, 9-1/4" h, $165.

Children's Chewable Aspirin was introduced in 1952, and Bayer Aspirin even went to the moon with the Apollo astronauts in 1969.

Display, cardboard, die-cut, fold-out sides, "Genuine Aspirin, Does not depress the heart," shows woman in orange hat with box of product, "Look for the Bayer Cross" under oversized "Bayer" aspirin on left/ring wing, The Bayer Co., New York, NY, stitched seams, paper loss/crease/bent corners/warped, 33-3/4" h, 42-5/8" w .......................................................... 176.00

## Bear Brand Hosiery (See Photo)

## Beechcraft

Sign, porcelain, 2-sided, oval, "Certified Beechcraft Service," red text, white ground, cond. 8, 17" h, 24" w ................................................................ 390.50

## Beechnut

Tin, litho tin, polychrome scene of Beechnut plant/ Mohawk Valley, circa 1930s, 12-1/2" l ................. 25.00

## Beech-Nut Gum

Box, display, cardboard, "Beech-Nut Nut Flavored Chewing Gum, 5¢," girl at left, pack at right, front with red oval logo, cond. 8, 5-1/4" h, 6" w, 4-1/4" d ................. 154.00

Sign, porcelain, "Beech-Nut Chewing Tobacco, Quality made it famous," red/white pack, blue ground, 1920s-1930s, cond. 7.5, 46" h, 30" w, $330. (Photo courtesy of Gary Metz, Muddy River Trading Co.)

Display, countertop

Cardboard, 3-D stick of "Beech-Nut Spearmint Gum," oval "Beech-Nut Brand" logo at left, black/red text, green/white ground, unused, cond. 9.25, 15" l, 4-1/4" sq ....................................................... 60.50

Tin, 4 tiers, "Beech-Nut Peppermint Flavored Chewing Gum, 5¢," marquee shows girl, side shows/lists 5 flavors, cond. 7.5, 15" h, 6-1/2" w ................. 141.00

Sign, cardboard

Die-cut, easel back, woman in red dress/top hat with "Beech-Nut Gum" drum, unused, cond. NM, 38" h, 14-1/4" w .................................................... 302.50

Trolley, "Beech-Nut Gum presents radio's most interesting program, Chandu The Magician," magician's face/packs of gum, circa 1932, cond. NM, 11" h, 21" w ................................................................ 187.00

"Finest Peppermint Flavor, Beech-Nut Gum," 2 female golfers, circa 1930s, cond. 8+, 9" h, 16" w ................................................................ 176.00

"It costs you no more to enjoy Beech-Nut...the Quality Gum," pack of peppermint gum in center, white/yellow text, blue ground, framed, fold/crease, 22-1/2" h, 46-1/2" w ............................................................ 104.50

"Refreshingly yours: Beech-Nut Gum," woman's face/ 2 packs, yellow ground, cond. 8+, 16" h, 44" w ................................................................ 110.00

## Beech-Nut Tobacco

Bin, litho tin, slant lid, "We keep it Fresh, Beech-Nut Chewing Tobacco, Quality Made it Famous," shows red/white package, blue ground, cond. 7, 8-5/8" x 9-7/8" x 8-1/8" ................................................. 467.50

## Beeline Antifreeze

Can, tin, "Beeline Permanent Type Antifreeze And Coolant," gold oval at top with bee on red circle, red over white ground, Frontier Refining Co., Denver, cond. 8/ 7.5, 1 gal, 9-1/2" h, 7" w, 4" d .......................... 115.50

## Beeman's Pepsin Gum

Pocket mirror, "Beeman's Pepsin Gum, good for digestion, for sale everywhere," bald man, white text, blue ground, cond. 9.5 ................................................ 176.00

## Bee Starch

Sign, litho paper, "Use Only Bee Starch in the Laundry, Requires No Cooking," nude child with 2 boxes of product flying on back of bee, framed, trimmed/ repairs, cond. 7, 22-1/2" h, 15" w ................... 1,155.00

## Belar Cigars

Sign, tin, self-framing, easel/hung, "Flor De Belar Cigars, Perfection of Quality," flanked by 2 styles of cigars, gold ground, wood-motif tin frame, cond. VG, 7-3/8" h, 9-7/8" w ............................................................. 49.50

## Belfast Cut Plug

Tin, litho tin, "Belfast Cut Plug, Smoke or Chew," shield with "Cigars" in white text on green circle, green text, dark ground, cond. 9, 4" x 6" .............................. 27.50

Sign, porcelain, 2-sided, "Public Telephone" with "Bell System" in bell logo, white on blue ground, manufacturer's defects of white speckling under finish, 5-1/2" h, 12-1/2" w, $198. (Photo courtesy of Collectors Auction Services)

# Bell System

**History:** A superintendent at AT&T designed the now-famous trademark of a blue bell as a way to pay homage to Alexander Graham Bell, who invented the telephone.

Originally, the words "Long Distance Telephone" appeared inside the bell's outline, which was approved as a service symbol in early 1889. After local telephone equipment was connected with long-distance stations in 1895, the wording in the symbol was changed to "Local and Long Distance Telephone." In 1939, the words "American Telephone & Telegraph Co. and Associated Companies" appeared between a pair of circles that surrounded the bell, and "Bell System" was printed on the bell. Several changes to the design were made over the years, and numerous variations exist, but by 1969 all wording had been removed from the symbol.

Paperweight, cobalt glass, bell-shaped, "Local & Long Distance Telephone," fired-on white text, 3" h, 3-1/4" dia .......................................................... 209.00
Sign, porcelain
   "Bell System, American Telephone & Telegraph Co. And Associated Companies," cobalt bell logo/text on white circle, cobalt ground, 1930s-1940s, cond. 7.5-8, 11" sq .................................................. 38.50
   Flange, "Bell System, Public Telephone," bell logo in center, cobalt/white, cond. G, 18" sq ............ 275.00

Sign, tin, raised letters, "Belmont Orange Bud, A Fruit Drink," 8-3/4" h, 19-1/2" w, $65.

Cigar box, paper, "Ben Bey Cadets, It's a pleasure," full, wrappers with 1926 revenue stamps, $30.

# Belmont

Tin, vertical pocket, litho tin, concave, Canadian, 2 pipes over shield with "B," blue ground, cond. 8-8.5 ................................................................ 578.00

# Belmont Orange Bud (See Photo)

# Ben Bey Tobacco

Tin, litho tin, running horse/rider with gun, circa 1922, cond. 8.5+, 3" h, 9" w, 6-1/2" d ........................... 82.50

# Bendheim Bros. & Co. Perique Mixture

Tin, litho tin, "Bendheim Bros. & Co. Original Perique Mixture, New York, U.S.A.," banner/leaf design in yellow/black, floral border, 1890s, cond. 8-, 1-1/8" h, 5" w, 3" d ................................................................ 429.00

# Bendix Radio

Clock, glass face/cover, cardboard body, "Bendix Radio, Product of Bendix Aviation Corporation," white text in red circle, black numbers in white border, arrow backwards on second hand, 15" dia ......................... 220.00
Sign, flange, metal, round, "Bendix Vacuum Power" in white/black panels in center, "Sales And Service, BK--Hydrovac" around border, red/white text, red/white/black design, chips/scratches, 18" h, 18" w .................... 253.00

# Benford's Golden Giant Spark Plug

Tin, litho tin, plug on one side, horse on other, yellow ground, cond. 7.5-8, 4-1/2" h, 1-3/8" sq ............ 220.00

Tin, litho tin, "Ben-Hur Marjoram," 2 oz, $15.

# Ben Franklin

Gas globe, 2 lenses, glass Gill ripple body, "Ben Franklin Premium Regular," central portrait, red/white text, red border with some white at bottom, all cond. 9, 13-1/2" dia .................................................... 4,675.00

# Bengal Peanut Butter

Pail, litho tin, "Bengal Brand Quality Peanut Butter," cartoon images of tiger, child on rocking horse, girl with doll, cond. 7.5+, 14 oz, 3-3/4" h, 3-1/2" dia ................... 687.50

# Ben-Hur

Can, keywind, litho tin, "Ben-Hur Coffee, Vacuum Packed To Protect Freshness," yellow horses, white text, red ground, top cond. 7, body cond. 8.5, 1 lb ................ 42.00

# Ben Hur Motor Oil

Can, litho tin, "Ben Hur Premium Quality Motor Oil," red/ black/white text under racing horses, red ground, black trim, Ben Hur Oil Co., Los Angeles, New Orleans, cond. 8.5, qt, 5-1/2" h, 4" dia .............. 165.00

# Bennett Sloan Tea

Tin, litho tin, "Bennett Sloan & Co. Teas and Coffees, Choice Family Tea," detailed scenes of forest, tea set, green ground, cond. 8-, 8-1/2" h, 3-1/2" sq ........... 154.00

# Bentley & Settle

Bin, counter-style, stenciled tin, "Bentley & Settle Wholesale Grocers, Syracuse, N.Y." and "Ginger," medallion shows woman, floral design, black ground, door at bottom, hinged lid at top, cond. 8+, 12" h, 8" w, 8-1/2" d ........................................................ 1,045.00

# Benzol

Gas globe, 2 lenses, narrow glass body, "Benzol Premium Blend," white text under red/white/blue star logo, blue ground, lens cond. 8.5, body cond. 9, 13-1/2" dia........................................................ 770.00

# Berger Beer

Sign, tin, die-cut
    Woman holding "Berger" bottle, yellow majorette uniform/"Berger" hat/red boots, cond. VG, 19-1/8" h, 4-1/4" w ........................................................110.00
    Woman holding "Berger 45" bottle, yellow 1-pc swimsuit, red "Miss Berger" drape, "Any" in yellow circle by head, cond. VG, 18-1/2" h, 6-1/2" w.................. 110.00

# Berghoff Beer

Sign, tin over cardboard, "Right on every Point, Berghoff Beer," 2 hunting dogs in weeds/snow, cond. 9+, 13" h, 21" w ................................................................ 132.00

# Berry Brothers

Pocket mirror, celluloid, round
    "Berry Brothers Celebrated Varnishes and Architectural Finishes," child in straw hat holding handle to wooden crate (with lettering) turned into cart, dog inside, cond. EXC, 1-3/4" h, 2-3/4" w ......................................275.00
    "The Berry Brothers Toy Wagon," 2 children/dog in front of wagon, 2 children in wagon made of wooden crate, cond. 8.5 ............................... 440.00

Can, litho tin, pry top, "Best Value Brand Coffee, The Weideman Co. Cleveland, Ohio," 1 lb, $180. (Front side of can, back side is on the next page).

Can, litho tin, pry top, "Best Value Brand Coffee, The Weideman Co. Cleveland, Ohio," 1 lb, $180. (Back)

# Berwind Briquets

Sign, tin, "Why Go South? Burn Berwind Briquets," 2 robins/ birdhouse at left, black/red text, white ground, creases/ bubbling/dented corners, 14" h, 20" w ...................... 82.50

# BesTaste Coffee

Can, keywind, litho tin, "Drip Grind BesTaste Fine Quality Coffee, Distributed by BesTaste Products Co., Buffalo, N.Y.," bust of chef, red/dark ground, cond. 9, 1 lb ................................................................. 293.00

# Best Value Coffee (See Photos)

# Bettendorf Wagon

Ashtray, litho tin, "The Bettendorf Steel Gear Wagon, Bettendorf Axle Company, Davenport, Iowa," green wagon with red wheels, ornamented scalloped border, circa 1902, 3-1/4" h, 5" l .................................... 121.00

# Betz Beer

Sign, glass, reverse-painted, lighted, metal housing, "Betz Beer, Ale-Porter" under "B" keystone logo, flaking on glass, rust, 17" dia ................................. 165.00

# Beverly Farms Milk

Clock, lightup, Pam style, glass face/cover, metal case, "Beverly Farms Milk," red text/farm scene/dots for hours, yellow ground, cond. VG, 15" dia ............. 55.00

# Beverwyck

Can, conetop, litho tin, "Beverwyck Irish Brand Cream Ale," white text on green 3-leaf clover in white oval, shield BBBB logo, 2-tone green ground, has contents, Beverwyck Breweries, Albany NY, rust, 7-3/4" h, 4" dia ................................................................. 88.00

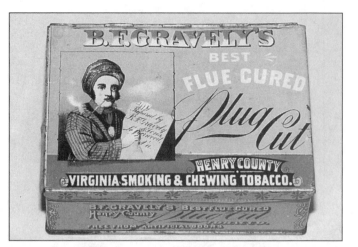

Tin, square corner, "B.F. Gravely's Best Flue Cured Plug Cut, Henry County, Virginia Smoking & Chewing Tobacco," light-blue ground, red strip at bottom, cond. 7.5, rectangular, $79.

# B.F. Gravely

Tin, vertical pocket, litho tin, "B.F. Gravely & Sons Special Pipe Tobacco, Crimp Cut," person in red turban, light-blue ground, cond. 8-9 .................................. 1,577.00

# Bickmore Gall Salve

Sign, cardboard, "Bickmore Gall Salve for all wounds and sores on animals, Be sure and work the horse," line of white horses crossing mountain pass, yellow/white text, framed, cond. 9, 20" h, 32" w ...................... 66.00

Display, countertop, cardboard with easel back, "Bickmore Easy-Shave Cream, 35¢," 31" h, 21" w, $65.

## Bickmore Easy-Shave Cream
(See Photo)

## Bicycle Gum

Tin, litho tin, sliding lid, "Zeno Bicycle Wild Cherry," tandem bike, cond. 7-, 3/4" h, 3-1/4" w, 1" dia ................... 440.00

## Big Ben Tobacco

Tin, vertical pocket, litho tin
"Big Ben Smoking Tobacco For Pipe & Cigarettes," horse/landscape, red ground, cond. 9 ...........119.00
"Specimen" version, "Big Ben Smoking Tobacco For Pipe & Cigarettes," horse/landscape, red ground, cond. 7.5 ...................................... 33.00

## Big Boy Cola

Sign, cardboard, "Ice Cold Big Boy, A Real Cola, 12-Fl Oz., 5¢," round red "Big Boy" logo by tilted bottle, ice motif on blue ground, scratches, 22" h, 14" w ...................... 44.00

## Big Boy Spark Plug

Tin, litho tin, 3-sided, boy holding "Big Boy" sign on front, 1898 spark plug on other 2 sides, red/white checkered corners, cond. 7+, 4-1/4" h, 1-3/4" w ................. 220.00

## Bigger Hair Tobacco

Pack, "Bigger Hair Tobacco, Chew or Smoke," bust of Fiji Islander with rings in her nose/ears, yellow ground, unopened, cond. 7.5 .........................................110.00

## Big Giant Cola

Sign, tin, embossed, rolled lip, "More For Your Money, 16 ounces, Big Giant Cola," tilted bottle at right, white/black/red text, white panel on red ground, cond. G, 11-1/2" h, 23-1/2" w.................................................. 49.50

Sign, hanging, button-type, "Ice Cold Birch-O Served Here," mint, 8-7/8" dia, $60.

Sign, hanging, tin, convex, "Red Star, Birds Eye," 11-1/2" h, $60.

## Big Sister Peanut Butter

Pail, litho tin, "Big Sister Brand Peanut Butter," white text at top, orange band at bottom, dark ground with witch on broomstick, boy/girl on peanut, owl on moon, cond. 7-7.5, 1 lb ........................................................ 354.00

## Billups

Bank, tin, gas pump motif, "Billups Premium" in white on red ring around Ethyl triangular logo, "New Highest Octane" at bottom, white panel on red ground, cond. 8/7, 4" h, 2-1/4" w, 1-5/8" d ................................. 187.00

## Binghamton Mirror Works

Pocket mirror, celluloid, oval, portrait of woman with flowers in hair, cond. 9+, 2-3/4" h, 1-3/4" w............. 176.00

## Birch-O (See Photo)

## Birds Eye (See Photo)

## Bireley's

Door push, litho tin, embossed
"Drink (shows bottle of Bireley's), Non-Carbonated Beverage," black text, orange ground, cond. 8.75, 12" h .............................................................. 66.00
"Drink Bireley's, for Real Fruit Taste," shows large-mouth bottle/cut orange, black text, yellow ground, cond. 7.75-8, 10" h ......................................... 77.00
Sign, litho tin, embossed
"Drink Bireley's, For Real Fruit Taste," 4 bottles with oranges/grapes/lemons/tomatoes, 1941, cond. 8.25-8.5, 4" h, 20" w ..................................... 302.50

"Got a minute? Enjoy Bire-ley's Real Fruit Taste, Not A Bubble In A Bottle, It's Not Carbonated, Bireley's" 4 bottles, leaves/red banner, black on white ground, yellow/blue borders, late 1940s-early 1950s, cond. 9.25............... 715.00

Thermometer, tin

"Bireley's Orange Drink, Not A Bubble In The Bottle," slanted bottle, yellow ground, 1949, cond. 9.5, 16" h, 4-1/2" w ...................... 467.50

Rounded corners, "Drink Bire-ley's" at top, "Non-Carbonated Beverages" at bottom, tilted orange bottle at left, tube at right on white panel, yellow ground, circa 1950, cond. 8.25+, 15-3/4" h, 4-1/2" w.............. 170.50

## Bit-O-Honey

Sign, litho tin, embossed, "Schutter's Bit-O-Honey Candy with toasted almonds 5¢," product on table with almonds, yellow text, black ground, cond. 6.5, 9" h, 20" w ................................................. 220.00

## Black and White

Tin, vertical pocket

Short version, "National Cigar Stand Black and White Crushed Plug," capitol building icon, cond. 8+........................................... 484.00

Tall version, "Black and White Roll Cut Smoking Tobacco," cond. 7.5-8 .................................. 250.00

## Black Cat Shoe Polish

Clock, windup, tin sign, "Black Cat Shoe Dressing & Superba Polish, Challenge the World," black cat at left, products across bottom, large round clock face at top, yellow ground, wood frame, soiling/paint loss, 23-1/2" h, 17-1/2" w.............................................. 990.00

## Black-Draught

Sign, flange, metal, "Black-Draught, a good laxative," black text, white ground, scratches/fading, 6-1/2" h, 12" w ...................................................110.00

## Black Kow

Sign, tin, embossed, "Drink Black Kow In Bottles, 5¢," lady cow with bottle at left, white/black text, central white oval on red ground, Welch Fruit Products, fading/stains/ creases/chips, 11-3/4" h, 23-3/4" w.......................... 88.00

## Blackman's

Dispenser, black glass, "Blackman's" in oval, cond. 8-8.5 ....................................................... 22.00

## Blackstone Cigars

Sign, porcelain, embossed, "Waitt & Bond, Blackstone, Smoked From Coast To Coast," white/yellow text, blue ground, cond. 8.5, 12" h, 35-3/4" w................... 495.00

## Blanchard Ice Cream

Sign, mechanized, battery-operated, "Blanchard Brand Delicious Ice Cream, Good for Babies," baby lying on back reaching up to dish of ice cream, orig box, cond. 8.5, 24" h, 19" w............................................... 495.00

## Blanke's Coffee

Bin, wood, "C.F. Blanke & Co. Roasted Coffee, Drink Blanke's Exposition Brand Roasted Coffee," black stencil, paint loss/cracks to wood, 33" h, 22" w, 16" d................................................................. 770.00

Can

Small top, litho tin, square, "Blanke's Mojav Coffee," woman on horse, green ground, cond. 7.5, 2 lb.......................................................................... 88.00

Same design as above, red ground, light fading, cond. 8-, 2 lb............................................................. 82.50

Milk pail, litho tin, "Blanke's Portonilla Coffee," woman on horseback, cond. 7+, 10" h, 5-1/2" dia.............. 275.00

## Blatz Beer

**History:** Born in Bavaria in 1826, Valentine Blatz first worked as an apprentice in his father's brewery and was then employed by a larger brewery with facilities in a number of German cities. In 1851, shortly after emigrating to America, Blatz started his own brewery, which was destroyed by fire in 1872. After rebuilding, the Blatz brand became one of the first beers to be sold in cities other than the one in which it was produced, thereby gaining national recognition.

Sign, porcelain, steeply curved, orig iron corner mounting bracket, "Blatz Beer" oval logo in red 6-point star, white text, cobalt ground, 1920s-1930s, cond. 7.5-8, 18" h, 15" w....................................................... 522.50

## Bloodhound

Sign, tin

Embossed, "Authorized Dealer for 'A Dog-gone Good Chew,' Bloodhound," red dog, yellow ground, 1940s-1950s, cond. 8.5+, 12" h, 18" w......... 357.50

"A Dog-gone Good Chew, Bloodhound," red dog/picture of product, yellow ground, circa 1940s, cond. 7.5, 18" h, 28" w .......................................... 132.00

## Bludwine

**Sign, flange, litho tin, "Ice Cold Bludwine For Your Health's Sake, 5¢," bottle and grapes on white, diagonal red band on dark ground, cond. 8.5-9, 10" h, 13" w, $660. (Photo courtesy Gary Metz, Muddy River Trading Co.)**

## Blue and Scarlet Plug Cut

Lunch box, litho tin, "Blue and Scarlet Plug Cut, Manufactured Solely by the Booker Tobacco Co. Incorporated, Richmond, Va.," red/blue/gold ground, missing clasp, cond. 7 ............................................................. 94.00

## Blue Bird

Sign, tin over cardboard, string hanger, "Let's drink Blue Bird, More delicious than Grape Juice!," red text, yellow ground, cond. 9, 6"h, 9" w ............................ 82.50

## Blue Bird Handkerchiefs

Display, store display box, litho metal, "Blue Bird, A Mans Handkerchief," hinged top with glass insert displaying 4 early product boxes, white text, woodgrain ground, circa 1920s, cond. 8+, 6-3/4" x 11-1/2" x 8".................... 550.00

## Bluebird Smoking Mixture

Tin, horizontal box, litho tin, "Bluebird Smoking Mixture, Bluebird For Happiness," shows bird on blue cloud-like design, diagonal band, The Rock City Tobacco Co., cond. 7.5-8, 2-3/8" h, 4-1/4" w, 3" d .................... 66.00

## Blue Boar

Tin, litho tin
Pry lid, "Blue Boar Rough Cut," blue boar in yellow oval, dark ground, cond. 8.5, 3-3/4" x 4-1/4" .. 28.00
Slip lid, "Blue Boar Rough Cut," square scene of dogs with hunter killing boar, dark ground, cond. 7.5, 5" h, 5" dia................................................................. 28.00

## Blue Bonnet Coffee

Can, keywind, litho tin, woman in blue hat flanked by blue flowers, white over blue ground, Springfield Grocer Co., Springfield, Mo., 1 lb, 4" h, 5" dia .............. 302.50

## Blue Buckle Work Garments

Sign, porcelain, "Blue Buckle Work Garments, Strong for Work, Overalls, Pants, Shirts," white with blue text, cracking of porcelain, chips to mounting holes, fading and water stain, warped, 4-1/2" h, 13" w .......... 126.50

## Blue Coral

Banner, canvas, "Protect Your Car Now, Salute to Quality, Blue Coral Treatment, Preserves, Restores, Beautifies Fine Car Finishes," woman with doorman under awning, 2 product containers at right, cond. 8+ .................. 104.50

## Blue Daisy

Tin, paper label, "Blue Daisy Brand Mace, Packed Expressly for Rasse Wholesale Grocer Co., Fairbury, Neb.," round medallion with flowers, 1 oz, 3-1/4" h, 1-3/4" w, 1-3/8" d.............................................. 440.00

## Blue Flame

Sign, Plexiglas, chain hanger, "Closed for Holiday, for emergencies please call:," Reddy Kilowatt/Blue Flame logo, 1960s, cond. 9-9.5, 9" h, 10" w ................. 60.50

Tin, paper label, "Blue Jewel Ground Red Pepper, Jewel Food Stores, Chicago," 1-1/2 oz, $95.

## Blue Flame Coffee

Pail, tin, "The Blue Flame New Process Coffee," white text in blue panel, red boxes/cups at lower left/right, white ground, Griggs Copper & Co. Coffee Roasters, St. Paul, rust/scratches/dents, 14" h .................. 60.50

## Blue-Jay

Display box, "Blue-Jay Corn and Bunion Plasters make hard roads easy, They stop the pain instantly and Remove the corn in 48 hours," yellow sign with blue jay by railroad track with 2 hoboes, 3-3/4" h, 18-1/4" w, 8-3/4" d .......................................................... 187.00

## Blue Jewel (See Photo)

## Blue Ribbon Coffee

Can, litho tin, "Blue Ribbon Brand Steel Cut Coffee," UTCO symbol in center, white/black text, black triangle on white over blue ground, blue lid, Ulry Talbert Co., Grand Island NE, cond. EXC, 1 lb, 6" h, 4-1/4" dia.......................................................... 89.00

## Blu-Flame

Gas globe, 1 lens, wide glass body, "Blu-Flame" in black text over blue/white flames on yellow ground, lens epoxied to body, lens cond. 8.5, body cond. 9, 13-1/2" dia......................................................... 198.00

## Blu-J Brooms

Display, metal, 2 embossed tin signs on sides, "Merkle's Blu-J, Merkle Broom Co.," faded/rust/bends, 35" h, 22-3/4" w, 10" d.................................................................. 110.00
Hanger, cardboard, die-cut, 2-sided, blue jay clinging to broom, cond. 8, 10-1/2" h, 4" w........................ 467.50

Tin, litho tin, "Blue Spot 5¢ Mild,"5-1/2" h, 4-3/4" sq, $300.

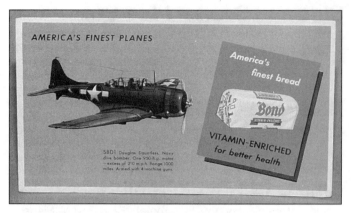

Blotter, paper, "America's Finest Planes" series, SBD1 Douglas Dauntless, Navy dive bomber, $17.50.

## Blue Spot (See Photo)

## Boardman's Putnam Coffee

Can, keywind, litho tin, rider in white circle, "Boardman's" in red, "Putnam Coffee" on white band, blue ground, cond. 7.5+, 1 lb, 4" h, 5-1/8" dia...................... 276.00

## Bob White Baking Powder

Can, paper label over tin, round, "Bob White Baking Powder," quail in oval, white text, red ground, "Save this label front..." on white band at bottom, cond. 8-, 4 oz .................................................................. 60.50

## Bo-Ka Coffee

Can, keywind, litho tin, "Bo-Ka Coffee," green coffee-picking panel, white text, red ground, Reid-Murdoch & Co., Chicago, cond. 8.5 ..................................... 60.50

## Bollard's Own Smoking Mixture

Tin, litho tin, slip lid, round portrait of man, yellow ground, cond. 8.5, 1-3/4" h, 3-1/4" dia ............................. 75.00

## Bon-Air

Tin, vertical pocket, litho tin, "Bon-Air Smoking Mixture, A Tobacco Both You And Your Pipe Will Enjoy, Cannot Bite The Tongue," black text, white ground with red stripes, cond. 9+ ............................................... 491.00

## Bon Ami (See Photo)

## Bond Bread

Display, broom holder, wood with porcelain sign, "Fresh Bond Bread," white text, red seal, cream ground, red border, holds 6 brooms, wear to framework, edge chips to sign, 40-1/2" h, 19" w......................... 220.00
Poster, textured, "Easter Greetings, Bond, General Baking Company," girl watering potted lilies, product shown, cond. 9.5, 38" h, 13" w........................... 49.50

## Bond Street

Tin, vertical pocket, litho tin
Sample, "Bond Street Aromatic Pipe Tobacco, 90 Years," street scene, cond. 8.5.................... 143.00

Box, sample, paper with paper label, "Bon Ami Powder, The Bon Ami Co., New York," 2-1/2" h, $5.

Can, tin with paper label, "Bonny Lass Brand, Michigan Fruit Canners Inc., General Office: Benton Harbor, Mich.," unopened, torn label, $10.

Tin, litho tin, "Bonnie Lee White Hulless Pop Corn, 'It Pops,' Bonnie Lee Pop Corn Co., Van Buren, Ind.," unopened, 10 oz, $225.

Can, paper label, "Borden's Sweetened Chocolate Flavored Malted Milk, Made by the Borden Company, New York, N.Y.," 1 lb, $58.

"Bond Street Pipe Tobacco, Established Over 100 Years," street scene, sealed, cond. 9 ............. 27.50

## Bonny Lass (See Photo)

## Bonnie Lee (See Photo)

## Booth's Oysters

Sign, tin, embossed, "Booth's Oval Brand Oysters," white text, red oval over sunburst on black ground, "A. Booth & Co. Oysters Fish and Canned Goods" on blue ground at bottom, new frame, touch-ups to chips/scratches, 30" h, 22" w ...................................... 357.50

## Booth's Talcum

Tin, "A Healing Soothing Deodorant, Booth's Compound Derma-Talcum," 5 cherubs with roses, paper chips on cap, 4-1/8" h, 2-1/8" w...................................... 330.00

## Boot Jack Plug Tobacco

Boot jack, cast iron, embossed, "Use Musselman's Boot Jack Plug Tobacco," floral design, 10" l, 3-1/4" w .............................................................. 60.50

## Borax Extract of Soap

Sign, tin, "Borax Extract of Soap" in white, "For Washing Everything" on white panel, red ground, white border, cond. VG, 7" h, 24" w......................................... 104.50

## Borden's

**History:** Gail Borden was working in Texas in 1849 when a frontier trader introduced him to Pinole, an Indian food made of dried, pulverized buffalo meat, dried and crushed hominy, and beans. Borden experimented with the idea, and his dried biscuit of wheat flour and beef was ultimately awarded a medal at the Great Council Exhibition in London in 1851. Because the biscuits would keep indefinitely and could be reconstituted with water, they were an answer to the problems of long-term food storage before the days of refrigeration and inexpensive canning.

During his return trip from England, Borden was prodded to action once again. Realizing that the children onboard the ship had no fresh milk, Borden vowed to find a way to can milk. He theorized that it would be possible to condense milk by boiling off much of its

Sign, porcelain, 2-sided, "Borden's Ice Cream, You Know it's Pure," 1920s-1930s, 19" h, 21" w, $1,705. (Photo courtesy of Gary Metz, Muddy River Trading Co.)

water, and by 1856 he had patented a process to do so. Jeremiah Milbank became a partner in Gail Borden, Jr., and Company in 1857, and the business changed its name to New York Condensed Milk Company in 1858. The company grew slowly until it began receiving orders for condensed milk to feed the Union Army during the Civil War. After the war, business improved, and the company operated several plants, eventually becoming Borden Condensed Milk Company in 1899 and then The Borden Company in 1919.

The company's first trademark consisted of an American bald eagle, and its condensed milk was named Eagle Brand. Its most recognized trademark, Elsie the cow, first appeared in print ads in 1936, and a live Elsie was on show at the New York World's Fair in 1939. Elsie's popularity necessitated the creation of a family for her—a husband named Elmer, a son named Beauregard, a daughter named Beulah, and, in 1957, twin calves named Lobelia and Larabee.

**Reference:** Albert and Shelly Coito, *Elsie the Cow and Borden's Collectibles*, Schiffer Publishing, 2000

Can, metal, metal lid, "Borden's Richer Malted Milk" repeated three times around can, denting to lid, minor scratches, 8-1/2" h, 6" dia .................................. 121.00

Clock, glass face/cover, metal case, electric, "Borden's Milk & Cream Sold Here," red on white ground with floral center, black 3/6/9/12, partial decal of Elsie on cover, yellowing, 20-1/2" dia ............................ 170.50

Jar, heavy glass soda fountain jar, "Borden's The Improved Malted Milk" label, domed metal lid embossed "Borden's," dents to lid, 9-3/8" h, 6-5/8" dia .................. 522.50

Salt/pepper shakers, ceramic, waist-up figural of "Elsie" and "Elmer," cond. VG, 4" h, pr .......................... 99.00

Sign
    Neon over porcelain, die-cut, Elsie with front hooves over arched section, lights yellow/white, cond. VG ...................................................... 1,870.00
    Tin, "Bordens" in white on red oval, Elsie/yellow petal image to left, red "Trucks" with pointing hand at bottom, white ground, yellow border, minor scratches, 12" h, 24" w ................................................... 176.00
    Tin, embossed, Elsie/yellow daisy, white ground, cond. 9, 17-1/2" sq .............................................. 154.00
    Tin, embossed, die-cut, 2-sided, circular top with "Borden's Ice Cream" under Elsie/yellow daisy, red/white text, white over black ground, rectangular bottom with curved ends, "Tony's Mkt," black on white panel, cond. VG, 56" h, 51" w, 9" d .............. 742.50

## Bossy Brand Cigars

Lamp, white glass globe on metal stem above clear glass base with handle, "Buy The Incomparable Bossy Brand 5¢ Cigar, Look For The Star On Every Cigar," black cow, scratches/soiling, 7-1/2" h, 4" w ............................ 880.00

## Boston Belting Co.

Sign, stone-litho paper, "Boston Belting Co., Original Manufacturer of Vulcanized Rubber Goods," elaborate scenes of factory/lighthouse/natives working on tropical

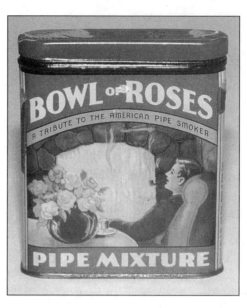

Tin, vertical pocket, litho tin, short version, "Bowl of Roses Pipe Mixture," man smoking in chair by bowl of roses, cond. 8, 3-5/8" h, $242.

plantation, framed, light staining, cond. 8.5, 17-1/2" h, 13-1/4" w .............................................................. 440.00

## Boston Garter

Display box, wood with 4 glass sides, "Boston Garter Velvet Grip," edge wear/scratches, some wood splitting, 5-3/4" h, 9-3/4" w, 14" d ..................................... 176.00

Display cabinet, wood with front glass window, rear door exposes 3 shelves, decals on 3 sides, minor wear, 12-1/2" h, 11" w ................................................... 440.00

## Boston Herald

Tip tray, litho tin, round, "The Boston Herald, The Sunday Herald" on red rim, "On Sale Everywhere, A Paper Made For All" flanks running paperboy on yellow ground, cond. 8.5 .............................................. 66.00

## Boston Trade

Cigar cutter, countertop, oak base, paper label, shows Boston landmark, cond. 8+, 6" h, 8" w, 4-3/4" d ............ 302.50

## Bowe's Seal Fast

Sign, tin, embossed, "Safe tire repairs - Bowe's Seal Fast, Patent Process, We fix flats," "Seal Fast" in red seal, red/black/white text, white over black ground, cond. 8, 20" h, 15" w ............................................. 99.00

## Bowey's Root Beer

Sign, porcelain, curved barrel sign, "Bowey's Root Beer, Creamy or Solid," white text, mug lettered "Old Style," 1930s-1940s, cond. 6.5-7, 11" h, 13" w ............ 176.00

## Bowl of Roses

Tin, vertical pocket, litho tin, tall version, "Bowl of Roses Pipe Mixture," man smoking in chair by bowl of roses, cond. 7.5 ......................................................... 341.00

## Boyce Moto Meter

Sign, metal, die-cut, 2-sided, "Boyce Moto Meter, Authorized Service Station," white/red text, woman in red jacket/hat pointing to product on car, cond. 8/7 ...................................................... 3,135.00

## Boyd's

Dispenser, metal, porcelain interior, electric, "Boyd's Hot Fudge," paint chips to base, scratches, crazing to interior, spoon missing, 10" h, 7" dia...................... 220.00

## Boye Needle Co.

Display, wood, glass panel in front, oval decal logo, for crochet hooks, 1920s, The Boye Needle Co., cond. 8.5, 8" x 7-1/2" x 5-1/2" .................................... 187.00

## BP

Sign, porcelain, "Appointed Oil Fired Heating Installer" in black on white ground, Shell logo at left, "BP" logo at right, white ground, red/yellow/orange flames on black ground at top, chips/scratches/stain, 13-1/4" h, 18-1/4" w .......................................................... 231.00

## Brandywine Coffee

Can, keywind, litho tin, "Brandywine Coffee," semi-circular panel shows camper cooking over open fire, "It's Dandy Fine" above image, "Down on the Brandywine" below, white text, red ground, Page Coffee Co., St. Joseph/Kansas City, repainted lid, body cond. 8.25, 1 lb ..................................................................... 214.50

## Brandy Wine Soda

Sign, cardboard, "Let's Drink Brandy Wine," pinup with bottle on flying eagle, circa 1939, cond. 8+, 22" dia................................................................. 231.00

**Tin, sample, litho tin, "F.W. McNess' Breakfast Cocoa, Furst-McNess Company, Freeport, Illinois," 2-1/4" h, $77.**

## Breakfast Cocoa (See Photo)

## Br'er Fox Pop Corn

Tin, litho tin, cartoon image of fox in blue jacket/red-striped pants holding box beside "Always Fine" in white rectangle, red/blue checkered ground, no lid, cond. 8+, 10 lb, 9-1/2" h, 6-1/2" dia .................... 71.50

## Breyer's Ice Cream

Sign, porcelain, die-cut, 2-sided
"Eat Breyer's Ice Cream, Quality all-ways," green leaf/red text on white, green ground, NOS, 28" h, 20" w.......................................................... 555.50
"Sodas" in white at rectangular top, "Eat Breyer's Ice Cream, Quality all-ways," leaf/red text on white oval, restored, 27" h, 36" w.......................... 660.00

## Bride Rose Tobacco

Pouch, cloth, "Bride Rose Cut Plug Mixture," single rose, Harry Weissinger, full, cond. 8+ ......................... 55.00

## Briggs

Tin, vertical pocket, litho tin, "Briggs Pipe Mixture, When a Feller Needs a Friend," seal-shaped area lettered "Complimentary Tin, Not For Sale," hand holding pipe, brown ground, full, cond. 8.5 ........................... 165.00

## Briggs & Stratton

Thermometer, glass front, plastic frame, metal band, round, "Briggs & Stratton 4 Cycle Gasoline Engines, Authorized Parts-Service," dial shows in window at top, circa 1940s-1950s, cond. 8-8.5, 14" dia................................253.00

## Briscoe Motor Sales

Letter opener, metal, 2 slug plates on end, "Briscoe Motor Sales Co., Briscoe & Liberty Cars, Frank Bishop, Pres.," cond. 8, 10" l ...............................11.00

## Broadway Brewing Co.

Tip tray, litho tin, round, "Broadway Brewing Co., Buffalo, N.Y., Pure Beers," hand holding battle ax, cond. 9.25 ......................................................... 71.50

## Bromo Seltzer

**History:** Captain Isaac Emerson first concocted Bromo-Seltzer in a Baltimore drugstore in 1888, building a plant to process the product in 1891.

Hazel Atlas made the first of the now-famous blue bottles, but Maryland Glass Corporation took over in 1907 with a completely automated system. Their bottles are marked with an "M."

Metal seals were developed for the large bottles in 1920 and for the small bottles in 1928. Until that time, corks were inserted to contain the product. In 1954, the switch was made to the metal screw cap.

Dispenser, cobalt glass bottle, metal arm, cobalt metal base, "Bromo Seltzer Emerson Drug Co." on bottle, "The

Container, wooden, paper label, "Brooklyn Mills Pepper, 10 Lbs, Wm. Waring & Son, Brooklyn," 14-1/2" h, 12" dia, $225.

Bin, store display, litho tin, "Brother Jonathan Chewing Tobacco, F.F. Adams Tobacco Co., Milwaukee, Wis.," cond. 8-, 12" h, 8-1/4" dia, $6,050. (Photo courtesy of Wm. Morford)

Emerson Drug Co. of Baltimore City Maryland" on base, cond. EXC, 16-1/4" h, 4-1/2" w, 6" d ...................... 363.00

# Brookfield Rye

Sign, litho tin, self-framed, "Made famous by public favor, Rare, Old Perfect, Brookfield Rye," semi-nude woman holding bottle, cond. 8+, 33" h, 23" w ............. 3,850.00

# Brooklyn Mills Pepper (See Photo)

# Brotherhood Tobacco

Lunch box, litho tin, black shield, red ground, canted top, cond. 8.5 ....................................................... 229.00

# Brother Jonathan

# Browder Gasoline

Gas globe lens, glass, "Browder Special Gasoline," red/white text, blue center with wide white border, cond. 8.5 ................................................................... 181.50

# Brown Bear Blend

Pack, paper, foil-lined, "Brown Bear Blend, Made Exclusively for Liggett's," white text, brown bear in white circle under 3 Bs forming a triangle, cond. 9 .......... 27.50

# Browniekar

Pinback button, celluloid, "Browniekar, Mfg by Omar Motor Co.," cartoon scene of man in early open auto, cond. EXC, 1-1/4" dia........................................ 440.00

# Brownie Salted Peanuts

Can, litho tin, "Brownie Brand Salted Peanuts, The More I Eat, The More I Want," yellow oval shows brownie, white text, blue ground, United Fig & Date Co., Chicago-New York, dents/scratches/stains/rusted top-bottom, 10 lb, 8-3/4" h 8-1/2" dia ............................ 72.50

# Brown Seed Co.

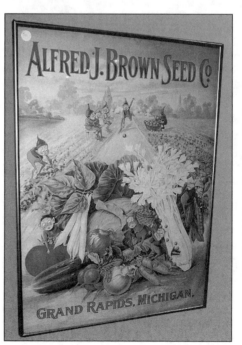

Sign, litho paper, "Alfred J. Brown Seed Company, Grand Rapids, Mich., Stecher Litho Co.," shows Palmer Cox's Brownies, near-mint, 33" h, 24" w, $2,500.

**Match holder, litho tin, "The Brown Shoe Co's Star-Five-Star $2.50 Shoes," wear, rust, 9" h, 4-7/8" w, $250.**

# Brown Shoe Co. (See Photo)

## Brown's-Oyl

Sign, tin, embossed, "Brown's-Oyl for Fords," can-shaped character with "Brownie" on red hat, black ground, cond. 8, 20" h, 13-1/4" w ....................... 357.50

## Brucks Jubilee

Sign, tin, embossed, die-cut, "Drink Brucks Jubilee Beers-Ale, Over 85 Years Continuous Brewing," black/red text inside horseshoe, cond. 8.25, 11-1/4" h, 11-1/2" w .......................................... 126.50

## Brundage Peanut Butter

Bin, countertop store bin, litho tin, "Brundage Star Maid Peanut Butter," maid with tray in front of star, blue/gold text, white ground, Brundage Bros., Toledo, Ohio, cond. 7.5, 25 lb, 9-1/4" h, 10" dia ...................... 127.50

## Bubble Up

Screen door brace, embossed metal, "Be Alive!, Drink Bubble Up, 5¢," yellow ground, cond. 7.5-8, 12" x 6" ............................................................. 132.00

## Buck Cigar

Sign, metal, die-cut, shape of a buck's head, "Buck Cigar, King of the Range," rust spotting, scratches/soiling, 12-1/4" h, 10-1/4" w .......................................... 825.00

## Buckeye Beer

Sign, litho tin, embossed
  Strip sign, "Buckeye Beer, Months In Brew - Then Served To You," black/red text flanked by waiters with tray/banner, white ground, circa 1950s, cond. 9.75, 13" w ...................................................... 93.50

"Buckeye Beer On Draught Here," man with red/white/blue top hat at left, same man with banner at right, black/red text, white ground, black/red border, scratches/soiling, 2-3/4" h, 13-1/2" w ............. 77.00

## Buckeye Root Beer

Dispenser, ceramic, "Buckeye Root Beer, Cleveland Fruit Juice Co.," oval medallion with mug over leaves, early replacement pump, cond. 8.5+, 15" h, 9" dia . 3,520.00
Dispenser, ceramic, orig marked pump, tree trunk motif, "Buckeye Root Beer" in white circle, 1920s-1930s, cond. 8.75 ............................................... 1,155.00
Mug, ceramic, "Buckeye Root Beer" on black ring, figural handle, cracks/chips, 6-1/4" h, 3-5/8" dia........... 22.00

## Buckhorn

Cigarette case, litho tin, shows elk head, red ground, cond. 9 .............................................................. 38.50

## Buckingham Cigarettes

Box, cardboard, flat 50, cardboard case shows 3 guards holding cards saying "Season's Greetings," crest logo, cond. 8 ............................................................. 92.50

## Buckingham Tobacco

Door push, litho tin, "Smoke Bagley's Buckingham Cut Plug, Your Next Tobacco," red/white text, 2 red panels, white ground, cond. 9, 5" h, 3" w ..................... 335.50
Tin, vertical pocket, litho tin
  Sample, "Buckingham Bright Cut Plug Smoking Tobacco, Trial Package," colorful text on black ground, cond. 8+ .......................................... 157.00
  "Buckingham Bright Cut Plug Smoking Tobacco," side says "Cut Plug," colorful text on black ground, cond. 8-9 .................................................................. 84.00
  "Buckingham Bright Cut Plug Smoking Tobacco," side

**Tin, litho tin, "Buckingham Bright Cut Plug Smoking Tobacco, John J. Bagley & Co., The American Tobacco Co., Successor Mfr.," wear, scratches, 3-3/4" h, 4-1/2" d, $75.**

has "American Tob." verbiage, colorful text on black
ground, cond. 9................................................ 77.00

## Budweiser Barley Malt Syrup

Sign, cardboard, cutout, easel-back
    Couple holding can of product, larger can in fore-
ground, cond. 8.25-8.5, 21" h, 13" w ............ 275.00
    Couple holding can of product, larger can in fore-
ground, orig envelope, circa 1930s, cond. 8.25, 3' h,
2' w ................................................................ 302.50

## Budweiser Beer

**History:** Anheuser-Busch introduced Budweiser beer in
1876, and it quickly became their best-selling brand.

Although Anheuser-Busch brewed the drink, Carl Con-
rad registered the trademark in 1878, and it wasn't until
1891 that the company gained the rights to the name.

In a 1950 bid for corporate sponsorship, Budweiser
became the first beer to sponsor a television show,
"The Ken Murray Variety Show."

The trademark "A" with an eagle was first used in
1872. A variety of advertising slogans have been used
over the years, including "Old Time Flavor" (1935),
"Pick a Pair" (1957), and "Where There's Life, There's
Bud" (1957).

Other breweries have used the name Budweiser,
including the DuBois Brewing Company of Dubois,
Pennsylvania, which used the name from 1905 until
they were restrained from doing so in 1970. Also hoping to capitalize on the brand's popularity, the Budweiser Brewing Company of Brooklyn, New York,
began selling Bud as early as 1885.

**Sign, litho tin, 1-sided, cardboard easel back with chain
hanger, "Budweiser Served here..., 12 oz. Bottle," 15" h,
12" w, $40.**

**Tray, tin, pictures paddlewheeler at busy dock, "Budweiser,
King of Bottled Beer," scene titled, "St. Louis Levee In
Early Seventies," 1914 copyright, $140.**

Calendar, tin over cardboard, chain-hung, slots for calendar inserts, "Budweiser, Preferred Everywhere," bottle
and pilsner glass on silver tray, red ground, minor
scratches/dents/rust, 22-1/2" h, 12" w .............. 247.50
Clock
    Plastic case with 8 Clydesdales pulling wagon, electric
clock/lights, "World's Champion Clydesdale Team,"
"Budweiser" red bowtie logo, clock face missing,
20" h, 36" w ................................................... 176.00
    Plastic, pocket watch form, electric, "Budweiser 1876,
King of Beers," A-B logo in center, red text, white
Roman numerals, 15-1/2" dia ......................... 55.00
Sign, cardboard
    "Attack On The Overland Stage 1860, Budweiser" on
lower cardboard frame, shows stagecoach attack,
©1952, tears/dented edges, 28-1/2" h,
41" w............................................................. 121.00
    "Budweiser Girl," outdoor scene of woman in red dress
holding bottle, A-B logo lower-right, newer wood
frame, water stains/scratches/tears/top corners
missing, 35" h, 20-1/2" w .............................. 660.00
    "Budweiser, King Of Beers" in red panel, shows 8 Cly-
desdales pulling beer wagon, stain/fading/
scratches, 20" h, 47-1/4" w............................. 55.00
    "Custer's Last Stand Presented By Budweiser" on
lower cardboard frame, shows Battle of Little Big
Horn, cond. G, 24" h, 41" w.......................... 121.00
Sign, glass, reverse-painted, die-cast metal holder with
eagle logo, footed wood base, "We Feature Budweiser
Draught Beer, Preferred Everywhere," white on red
ground, holder mkd "Anheuser-Busch, St. Louis, Mo."
with eagle logo, cond. 9-, 9-1/2" h, 18-1/2" w,
3" d.................................................................. 424.60
Sign, litho tin over wood, embossed, "Anheuser-Busch
Budweiser, King Of Bottled Beer," A-B logo at left,
white text, all on red except "Budweiser" on black
ground, 1930s-1940s, cond. 8.25-8.5, 20" h,
72" w ............................................................... 715.00
Tumbler, Christmas theme, 1940s-1950s, orig
box ..................................................................... 8.50

## Budweiser Smoking Tobacco

Tin, vertical pocket, cardboard, "Budweiser Highest Grade Granulated Cut Plug Smoking Tobacco," red ground, cond. 8.5 ............................................... 515.00

## Buell's Brighton Blend Coffee

Can, litho tin, twist lid, "Buell's Brighton Blend Coffee, Merit—that's all!," woman with cup, red/black text, white ground, cond. G, 6" h, 4-1/2" dia ............. 176.00

## Buffalo Brand Peanuts

Tin, litho tin, "Buffalo Brand Fancy Salted Peanuts, F.M. Hoyt & Co., Amesbury, Mass.," red text in yellow oval ring, buffalo in center, red ground, cond. 7.5, 10 lb, 9-1/2" h, 8-1/4" dia .................................................. 50.50

## Buffalo Brand Peanut Butter

Pail, litho tin, "Buffalo Brand Peanut Butter, F.M. Hoyt & Co., Amesbury, Mass," red text in gold ring, buffalo in center, red ground, cond. 8, 1 lb ...................... 231.00

## Buffalo Club Rye Whiskey

Sign, litho tin, "Buffalo Club Rye Whiskey," white text in red ring around buffalo head, "C.E. Person's Sons, Importers and Distillers, Buffalo, N.Y.," in black at top/ bottom, white ground, cond. VG, 34" h, 23-1/2" w ...................................................... 522.50

## Buick

Pocket mirror, celluloid, round, "J.F. McCreary & Son, 6 Cylinder Buick, Beaver Falls, Pa.," happy/sad face in center with "The Man That Buys From Us, The Man That Don't Buy From Us," 4 digit phone number, cond. EXC, 2-1/4" dia ................................................. 33.00

Sign

Metal, 2-sided, "Authorized Buick Service, Valve In Head," white text, "Buick" in diagonal over red center, black border, cond. 7, 18" dia ................. 242.00

Porcelain, "Authorized Buick Service," white text, "Buick" on cobalt logo with "Valve-In-Head Motor Cars" in border, white inner circle, cobalt border, cond. 7+ ...................................................... 852.50

Thermometer, porcelain, rounded top/bottom, diagonal "Buick" in white on sq white border at top, "Motor Cars" in white at bottom, "Bishop Buick Company" in white courtesy block, cobalt ground, white border, cond. 6, 27" h, 7" w ...................................................... 495.00

## Buick Oil

Can, litho tin, early car on road with "Best Oil For All Buick Models" on billboard, green design, gold text, white ground, Monarch Mfg. Co., Council Bluffs IA, Toledo OH, Los Angeles CA, cond. 7, gal, 7-1/2" h, 5-1/2" w ...................................................... 176.00

## Builder's Rolled Oats

Box, cardboard, round, "Builder's Brand Quick Cooking Rolled Oats," red cup on front, "Builder Bill" in blue/

Sign, cardboard, die-cut, 2-sided, "Bull Dog Cut Plug," rough edges, 8-1/2" h, $180.

white-striped bib overalls on back, yellow ground, cond. 9-, 3 lb ...................................................... 165.00

## Bulldog Seats

Sign, embossed tin, oval, "Use Bulldog Seats, Joints Won't Let Go," shows black/white bulldog standing on wooden toilet seat, cond. 7.5-8, 6-1/2" h, 9-3/4" w .............................................................. 880.00

## Bull Dog Tobacco

Match holder, litho tin, die-cut, "Won't Bite, Bull Dog Cut Plug Deluxe Straight Leaf, Finest Bright Burley Tobacco," red bulldog at top, considerable wear/hanger torn, cond. 7-, 6-1/2" h, 3-1/4" w .......................... 148.50

Tin, vertical pocket, paper label on cardboard, tin top and bottom, "Bull Dog Smoking DeLuxe," red bulldog and "Won't Bite" in oval medallion flanked by pipes, blue ground, cond. 9- ................................................ 770.00

Tin, vertical pocket, litho tin

Oval, "Bull Dog Smoking DeLuxe," red bulldog and "Won't Bite" in oval medallion flanked by pipes, 2-tone blue ground, cond. 8+, short version ................. 575.00

"Bull Dog Cut Plug DeLuxe," red bulldog and "Won't Bite" in oval medallion flanked by pipes, 2-tone ground, large dog, full, cond. 8, 4.5" h .......... 605.00

## Bull Durham

Box, display, cardboard, "Genuine Bull Durham Tobacco, Roll Your Own," bull at broken wooden fence, sealed, contains 2 dozen sealed bags with stamps and hang tags, box cond. 8.5, mint bags ......................... 212.00

Sign

Cardboard, "Genuine Bull Durham," shows bull at fence, packet of product, cond. 8.5+, 7-3/4" h, 10-7/8" w ...................................................... 577.50

Litho tin, embossed, "Bull Durham, 1 oz. bag 5¢," shows bull at fence/packet of product, framed, cond. NM, 16" h, 12-1/2" w .......................... 907.50

## Bull Frog Shoe Polish

Tin, "Bull Frog Shoe Polish," frog in center, gold/black

text, red ground, S.M. Bixby & Co., New York, cond. 7.5+, 2-3/4" dia................................................ 107.80

## Bull's Eye Beer

Sign, porcelain, "Bull's Eye Beer, Golden West Brewing Co's, Oakland, California," red/blue text, white ground, central image of red/white/blue bull's eye, cond. NM, 18" sq................................................... 522.50

## Bundy Typewriter Ribbon

Tin, litho tin, "Bundy Typewriter Co.," giant standing over building, blue on gold ground, cond. 8+, 3/4" h, 2-5/8" dia ........................................................ 44.00

## Bunnies Salted Peanuts

Tin, "Bunnies Salted Peanuts, G.E. Barbour Co. Limited, Saint John, N.B.," dancing rabbit in top hat/blue coat/ red pants, red ground, cond. 8+, 11" h, 7-3/4" dia ....................................................... 412.50

## Bunny Bread

Door bar, metal, "Everybody Loves Bunny Enriched Bread," smiling rabbit face, red "Bunny" in white oval, black text, yellow ground, cond. G, 3" h, 28" w ............................................................. 242.00

Sign, tin, embossed, "Everybody Loves Bunny Enriched Bread," red "Bunny" beside cartoon face of rabbit on white oval, black text, yellow ground, red border, cond. G, 12" h, 27-3/4" w........................................... 357.50

## Bunte

Tin, litho tin, slip top, "Bunte Marshmallows, Made By Bunte Brothers, Chicago U.S.A.," child in sailor-type outfit beside large tin of marshmallows, another view shows factory, cond. 8, 5 lb, 5" h, 12-3/4" dia .................. 226.00

**Tin, litho tin, "Bunte Fine Hard Candies," screw top, wear/ scratches/rust, 5 lb, $25.**

## Burger Beer

Clock, tin face, "Burger Bohemian Beer," white text on red/black oval, black numbers, white ground, cond. 8-, 14-1/2" h, 18-1/2" w ........................................ 71.50

## Burgess Batteries

Display, countertop, painted metal, "New Burgess Batteries" on front, "Burgess Flashlight Batteries" on side, hinged top shows zebra holding battery/advertising, blue ground, chips/scratches/some paint loss, 14-3/4" h, 10-3/4" w, 11-3/4" d ...................................... 33.00

## Burham Safety Razor

Tin, litho metal, shows razor, black text, red ground, with orig razor, cond. 8, 7/8" h, 3-1/4" w, 1-7/8" d ................. 165.00

## Burley Boy

Tin, vertical pocket, litho tin, "The White Man's Hope" in white oval with red trim, "Bagley's Burley Boy," boy with fists up, cond. 8+ ..................................... 999.00

## Burnishine

Sign, cardboard
Die-cut standup, "A Quick Shine for A Long Time, Burnishine Polishes All Metal," man shining bank sign, chauffeur shining car, cond. 9-9.25, 13" h, 6-1/2" w ......................................................... 38.50
Easel-back, "A Quick Shine for A Long Time, Burnishine Polishes All Metal," chauffeur shining car, man shining bank sign, cond. 9.75, 15" h, 10" w ................... 77.00
Sign, tin, embossed, "Bright Up! Burnishine Will Polish All Metals, Try It," red/white/blue, 1910s-1920s, cond. NM, 7-1/2" h, 5-1/2" w....................................... 49.50

## Bursley's Coffee

Can, keywind, litho tin, taller version, cup of coffee over

**Sign, tin, embossed, "Branch of Golden Sheaf Bakery, Manufacturers of Buster Brown Bread," Buster Brown at left, Tige at right, sheaf of wheat top center, white/red/yellow text, green ground, cond. 8.75+, 20" h, 28" w, $1,155. (Photo courtesy of Gary Metz, Muddy River Trading Co.)**

"Bursley's" in script, "Coffee" in white on black band, orange ground, Bursley & Co., Fort Wayne, Ind., cond. 9, 1 lb .............................................. 60.50

## Busch Beer

Sign, paper, metal strips at top/bottom, "Busch Beer, John B. Busch Brewing Co.," Victorian table scene, gold foil border, framed, cond. 9, 19-1/2" h, 15-1/2" w .......................................... 242.00

## Buster Brown Bread (See Photo)

## Buster Brown Shoes

**History:** Richard Felton Outcault first introduced the mischievous Buster Brown and his dog Tige in a New York Herald comic strip in 1902. During the St. Louis World's Fair Exposition of 1904, the characters were sold to merchants for use as trademarks. Outcault's idea to license rights to his comic figures was particularly innovative for the early 1900s. Subsequently, more than 50 different products incorporated the Buster Brown names and likenesses. Outcault's comic strip was discontinued in 1920. The Buster Brown Gang debuted on radio in 1943, and they appeared on television from 1951 until 1954.

Clock, lightup, glass face/cover, metal body, "Buster Brown, America's Favorite Children's Shoe," red/black text under Buster Brown/Tige, black numbers, Pam Clock Co., cond. EXC, 15" dia .......................... 550.00

Figural head, Fiberglas, sits on tank to inflate balloons, 21" h, 20" w, 24" dia .......................................... 137.50

**Bill hook, "Buster Brown Vacation Days Carnival," 2-1/4" dia, 6-1/2" l, $20.**

Game, skill game, celluloid, "Buster Brown Shoes" over Buster Brown/Tige, 5 bb's to put in their eyes/teeth, back shows foot/bones, "Room For Every Toe, Buster Brown Shaping Last Shoes," 1920s, cond. EXC, 2-1/8" dia.................................................. 127.50

Pocket mirror, celluloid, round, "Buster Brown Shoes, First Because of the Last, Brown Shaping Lasts," central image of Buster Brown/Tige with shoe form, cobalt border, red horizontal panel, white text, 1-1/4" dia.................................................. 128.50

Shoe stretcher, plastic, spring-loaded, figural Buster Brown/Tige on exposed end, white, cond. G, 5" h, 9" l.................................................................. 13.75

Sign

Cloth, silk-screened, cushioned/mounted on die-cut wood, 2 pcs put together, Buster Brown and Tige 20" h, 24" w .................................................. 385.00

Plastic, lightup, metal frame, "Buster Brown, America's Favorite Children's Shoe," Buster Brown/Tige at left, blue text, white ground, 6-1/4" h, 14-1/2" w .................................................. 225.50

Tin over cardboard, string/easel-back, "Buster Brown, A Brown Bilt Shoe, For Boys, First Because of the Last, For Girls," circa 1910s-1920s, cond. 7.5-8, 6" h, 13" w .................................................. 132.00

## Butterfly Bread

Door bar, porcelain, die-cut, "Butterfly Quality Breads" in blue/red diagonal text/edges, white ground, 1930s, cond. 9.5 .......................................................... 385.00

## Butter-Nut Bread

Door bar, porcelain, "Butter-Nut Bread" in white on red ground, flanked by "Jaeger's" ovals, 1930s-1940s, cond. 7.5 .......................................................... 176.00

Sign

Porcelain, white text in red oval, cobalt ground, 1940s-1950s, cond. 8.25, 12" h, 29" w...................... 99.00

Tin, embossed, "The Quality Makes You Like Butter-Nut Bread, Rich as Butter, Sweet as a Nut," yellow text/border, cobalt ground, cond. G, 5-7/8" h, 13-3/4" w .................................................. 132.00

**Thermometer, tin, "Ask Your Grocer for...Butter Nut Bread, Rich As Butter, Sweet As A Nut," light paint loss, 6" h, 9-1/2" w, $125.**

# C

## Cadillac

Box, litho tin, "Cadillac Bulb Kit for all Cadillac-LaSalle Motor Cars," oval logo of "Cadillac Motor Car Co., Detroit, Mich.," red/blue on white, with contents, cond. 8, 1-3/4" h, 3-1/2" w, 2-1/2" d ................................................. 148.50

Doorknob, brass, cloisonné Cadillac symbol, 1 complete set with 2 door plates, cond. 8 ......................... 181.50

## Cadillac Beverage

Carrier, cardboard, holds 12 bottles, "Cadillac" oval logo with Cadillac shield, 12 glass bottles with same logo, various flavors, Cadillac Beverage, Detroit MI, cond. VG ................................................................. 137.50

## Calabash

Tin, vertical pocket, litho tin
    Flat top, "Calabash Smoking Mixture," multi-color design, cond. 8 ............................................. 372.00
    Flip/roll top, "Calabash Smoking Mixture," multi-color design, dents, cond. 7.5-8 ........................... 786.00

## California Perfume Co.

**History:** In 1886, David H. McConnell began recruiting independent sales representatives for door-to-door sales of his California Perfume Company products.

**Tin, litho tin, "Elite Powder, California Perfume Co., Kansas City, New York, Montreal, San Francisco," 4-1/8" h, $34.**

The first item sold by the New York-based company was Little Dot, a set of five perfumes.

A new product line called Avon was added in 1928 after it was decided that "California" in the name might hinder expansion. By 1936, all of the company's products were sold under the name Avon.

Sample set, Natoma talc tin, toothpowder tin, Violet toilet water bottle, Savona Bouquet soap bar in cardboard gift box, shows boy/girl with products, 1-1/8" h, 6-1/4" w, 5-1/2" d ................................................................. 797.50

Tin, litho tin
    "Jack and Jill Jungle Jinks," suitcase form, held samples, boy/girl on path to house, cond. 8.5, 3-3/4" h, 5-7/8" w, 1-1/4" d ......................................... 148.50
    "Natoma Rose Pink, California Perfume Co., New York," Indian princess over string of roses, widens toward bottom, cond. 7.5+, 5-1/4" h, 3" w, 1-1/2" d ....... 196.00

## Calso Gasoline

Sign, pump, porcelain, "Calso Gasoline, The California Oil Co.," white/black text, red ground, white border, cond. 8, 11" dia ................................................. 302.50

## Calumet Baking Powder

**History:** In 1889, William M. Wright, a food salesman in Chicago, began experimenting to develop a better baking powder. George C. Rew became his partner in kitchen science in 1890, and they named their new product Calumet. Understanding the importance of a memorable moniker, Calumet was chosen because several areas of Chicago incorporated the word in their names and it would be readily recognized.

General Mills purchased the Calumet Baking Powder Company in 1928 and continued to use the original company's packaging and trademarks.

Table, wooden body/legs, porcelain top, "The Kind Mother Uses," Calumet baby at left, red can at right, blue text/alphabet/numbers/border, white ground, cond. G, 18" h, 20" w, 16" d ............................... 720.50

## Camel Cigarettes

**History:** After R.J. Reynolds split from the American Tobacco Company, it needed a memorable figure to represent its new entry into the cigarette market in 1913. Because the cigarette was a blend of American and Turkish tobaccos, the name Camel was chosen to suggest the product's Middle East origins, and Old Joe

**Sign, tin, "Camels, For More Pure Pleasure!," NOS, 12" h, 32" w, $55.**

of Barnum and Bailey's Circus became the model for the package illustration.

A massive advertising campaign catapulted the brand to success, with Camel accounting for half of the industry's sales in 1921, the same year that the "I'd walk a mile for a Camel" slogan was introduced.

**References:** Douglas Congdon-Martin, *Camel Cigarette Collectibles, The Early Years 1913-1963*, Schiffer Publishing, 1996; ___, *Camel Cigarette Collectibles 1964-1995*, Schiffer Publishing, 1997.

**Collectors' Club:** Camel Joe & Friends, 2205 Hess Dr., Cresthill, IL 60435

Sign, cardboard die-cut, easel-back, "Camels, So Mild - and they taste so good!," brunette in yellow dress with cigarette, also shows pack of Camels, 1950, minimal wear, cond. 9.5+, 30" h, 20" w ............................ 99.00

## Camel Cigars

Tin, vertical box, litho tin, "Camel 5¢" in red at top, "Camel Brand Cigars" in white in blue triangle, shows man on running camel, yellow ground, 5-1/2" h, 4-1/2" w, 2-3/4" d................................................. 89.00

## Cameron's Tobacco (See Photo)

## Campbell's Coffee

Pail, litho tin, yellow/red design of man with camels, Campbell Holton & Co., Bloomington, IL, cond. 7.5, 4 lb, 8" h, 7-3/4" dia ..................................................... 121.00

**Tin, litho tin, "Cameron's Finest Smoking Tobacco, Cameron & Cameron Co.," 1/2-lb, 3-3/8" h, 6-1/4" w, 4" d, $125.**

## Campbell's Horse Foot Remedy

Tin, litho tin, hand-soldered, horse logo on front, directions/ endorsements on other sides, James B. Campbell Co., Chicago, 1890s, cond. 7, 7" h, 3-1/4" sq.................. 93.50

## Campbell's Soup

**History:** Joseph Campbell and Abram Anderson started a canning plant in Camden, N.J., in 1869, but it wasn't until 1897 that the facility began producing soup. The red-and-white Campbell label was introduced in 1898, and the gold medallion that graced the company's cans until just recently was awarded in 1900.

Advertising has been diverse, with trolley signs first used in 1899 and magazine ads in 1905. The pudgy, round-faced Campbell Kids were introduced in 1904, but their contemporary physiques are slimmer and trimmer. The Campbell Kids' dolls were first sold in 1910, the same year that souvenir postcards were introduced.

**References:** Doug Collins, *America's Favorite Food: The Story of Campbell Soup Company*, Harry N. Abrams, 1994; David and Micki Young, *Campbell's Soup Collectibles from A to Z*, Krause Publications, 1998

**Collectors' Club:** Campbell Kids Collectors, 649 Bayview Dr., Akron, OH 44319; Campbell Soup Collector Club, 414 Country Lane Ct., Wauconda, IL 60084

Display, box, "Campbell's Soups, Tomato Juice, Pork and Beans, Franco-American Spaghetti," shows can on 2 sides, Campbell Kids on ends, 1920s-1930s, cond. 9, 27" h, 27" w, 17" d............................................. 412.50
Pennant, felt, pair, "Campbell's Soups," white text, red ground, 1 shows child in rocker, other shows child with pail, cond. 8+, 21" h, 8" w, pr ........................... 253.00

**Bank, tin, "125th Anniversary, Campbell's Condensed Tomato Soup," 4" h, $5.**

Tin, litho tin, "Campfire White Marshmallows, Made By The Campfire Co. Milwaukee, U.S.A.," wear/scratches, 5 lb, $35.

Poster, paper
  Campbell's Kids behind board promoting weekly grocers' specials (P&G Soap, Camay Soap, Chipso), can of soup in lower-left corner, 22-1/4" h, 16-3/8" w ......................................................... 154.00
  Campbell's Kids behind board promoting weekly grocers' specials (Stokely's Grapefruit Juice, Pillsbury Pancake Flour), can of soup in lower-left, creases/edge tears/stains, frame 30" h, 23" w ........... 121.00
Sign
  Cardboard, trolley, "Pepper Pot, What a soup for hungry men, 12¢, Made from a famous Colonial Recipe, Campbell's Pepper Pot," shows can/bowl of soup/Colonial men outside inn, stain/tear/minor scuffs, 12" h, 20-1/2" w .................................... 88.00
  Porcelain, curved, die-cut, can motif, "Campbell's Condensed Vegetable Soup," cond. VG, 22-1/2" h, 13" w ......................................................... 4,895.00

## Campbell's Tomato Juice

Pot, enameled metal, "Campbell's Tomato Juice," red text/handle/rim, white ground, 9" h, 10" w ........... 99.00

## Campfire Marshmallows

Tin, litho tin, slip lid, "Campfire Marshmallows Supreme," campfire scene outside tent, cond. 8, 7-3/4" dia ..... 43.00

## Canada Dry

**History:** After J.J. McLaughlin of Toronto, Canada, formulated Canada Dry Pale Ginger Ale in 1906, he wanted a trademark that would symbolize the company's heritage. To that end, he designed a logo that incorporated a crown and a map of Canada. Some of the early advertising also included a beaver.
Clock, lightup, glass face/cover, metal case, "Canada Dry," red text in shield showing North America, crown on shield, black design/numbers, Pam Clock Co., lights but doesn't run ......................................... 180.00
Cooler, picnic style with tray ................................. 191.50

Sign, porcelain, "Canada Dry Beverages," edge chips/wear, 7" h, 24" w, $40.

Sign, metal, flange, "Drink Canada Dry" in white shield with crown, chips, scratches, 14-1/2" h, 17-1/2" w ........ 100.00
Sign, tin, embossed, green tilted "Canada Dry" bottle, white ground, rounded corners, 54" h, 19" w ....... 138.50

## Canadian Explosives (See Photo)

## Canadian Straight

Can, litho tin, slip lid, "Canadian Straight Cut Plug Pipe Tobacco, 25¢," shows beaver, white text on red/cobalt bands, cond. 8, 3" h, 4-1/4" dia ........................... 27.50

## Cannon's Slice Plug

Tin, vertical pocket, litho tin, "Cannon's Irish Sliced Plug Flake Smoking Blend," blue text, white ground, diagonal "Aromatic" in red, cond. 8.5 ......................... 133.00

## Capital Peanuts

Can, litho tin, "Imported And Domestic Salted Nuts A Specialty, Capital Brand Salted Peanuts, Fresh Taste, Crispy And Nutritious," shows capitol dome on 1 side, bowl of peanuts on other, yellow/white text, dark ground, red/yel-

Tin, "Canadian Explosives, Limited, Snap Shot," The Thomas Davidson Mfg. Co. Ltd., Montreal, CXL Trademark, 4-1/2" h, $165.

low trim at top/bottom, Empire State Nut Co., Albany, N.Y., cond. 8, 10 lb, 9-3/4" h, 8-1/4" dia ................ 214.50

## Capitol Motor Oil

Can, tin, "Capitol Motor Oil, SAE 30" in red, "Paraffine Base" in white on blue band, white capitol dome in blue circle, dome in red circle on sides, white ground, Atlantic Refining Co., Philadelphia, cond. 7+, 2 gal, 10-5/8" h, 8-1/2" w, 5-5/8" d .................................................... 77.00

## Captain John Orderleys

Tin, litho tin, hinged, "Captain John Orderleys will put you in order for constipation, biliousness, dyspepsia, The Owl Drug Co., San Francisco, Cal.," cartoon owl with rifle at left, red/black/yellow text, blue ground, red border, cond. 8, 1/2" h, 2-1/2" w, 1-3/8" d ................ 66.00

## Captain's Coffee

Can, keywind, litho tin, "Captain's Fancy Brown Coffee" in black oval, small round image of sailing ship, cond. 9-, 1 lb ................................................................ 132.00

## Caraja Coffee

Tin, paper label, sample, "All Coffee, Good Coffee," shows house through palm trees, Dwinell Wright Co., not marked "sample," cond. 8, 1/4 lb, 3-1/2" h, 2-5/8" dia ....................................................... 187.00

## Carborundum

Display, countertop, brass with sharpening stone inset on top, "Carborundum, Niagara Falls, Saves Time, Saves Money," Indian logo, soiling, 3" h, 11-1/4" w, 3-3/4" d .............................................................. 330.00

## Cardinal

Tin, vertical pocket, litho tin, "Cardinal Cut Plug," cardinal on branch against light-blue ground, gold otherwise, cond. 7.5, 4-1/2" h ......................................... 1,538.00

## The Cardui Calendar

Calendar, 1911, paper, complete, full sheet featuring "M.A. Theoford's Black Draught Liver Medicine and McElree's Wine of Cardui Woman's Relief Medicine," cond. 8.5 ............................................................. 39.00

## Cargray

Sign, porcelain, "Cargray Gold," yellow/black with winged logo, cond. 10, 10" dia ...................................... 357.50

## Carhartt

Door push, porcelain, embossed, "Push, Carhartt Union Made Overalls," red text, white ground, cond. 8+, 7" h, 3-1/2" w ........................................................... 660.00

## Carlton Club

Tin, vertical pocket, litho tin, "Carlton Club Mixture, Perfect Blend of Choicest Tobaccos For The Pipe," crest with lion/unicorn, white ground, matte finish, cond. 8+ ......... 206.00

Sign, porcelain, die-cut, "Carnation Fresh Milk," 1940s-1950s, cond. 9, 15" h, 14" w, $330. (Photo courtesy of Gary Metz, Muddy River Trading Co.)

## Carnation

Container, milk glass, tin lid, "Carnation Malted Milk" in fired-on text, minor dents to lid, 8-1/2" h, 6-1/2" dia ........ 231.00

Sign

    Aluminum, shield-shape, "Carnation Ice Cream," shows sundae in stemmed glass, white/black text, red over white ground, yellow border, 1940s, cond. 9.5+, 3' h, 3' w ................................................................ 357.50

    Porcelain, die-cut, "Carnation Ice Cream," pedestal dish of product, red over white ground, yellow border, scratches/chips, 23" h, 22" w ................. 357.50

## Carte Blanche

Tin, litho tin, "Natural Virginia Cut Cavendish, Carte Blanche," round landscape image with house upper-left over leaves, text in 3 banners/panels, cond. 9-, 2" h, 5" w, 3" d ............................................................. 132.00

## Carter Carburetor

Display, tin, 4 drawers, blue text on yellow drawer fronts, blue cabinet, 10 cardboard divider boxes, cond. VG, 7-1/2" h, 35-1/2" w, 7-1/2" d ............................... 44.00

## Carter's Guardian Typewriter Ribbon

Tin, litho tin, round, shows 3 bombers, Boston, cond. 8 ............................................................. 27.50

## Carter's Little Liver Pills

**History:** Dr. John Carter founded Carter Medicine Company in Erie, Pa., around 1840. He and his brother eventually built their own store and began selling a variety of compounds, extracts, and other medic-

Bottle, glass, paper label, "Carter's Little Liver Pills," cork top, 36 pills, 2-1/8" h, $5.

inal products. Sometime in the 1880s, they introduced Carter's Little Liver Pills, advertised as a cure for headaches, dizziness, constipation, and sallow skin, among other assorted ailments.

Booklet, 31 pgs, cover loose, 5-3/4" h, 3-1/2" w........ 6.50
Bottle, glass, cork-top, red paper label, "Laxative Aiding Bile Flow" beside Carter's logo, 100-count, 2-1/4" h..........7.50
Trade card, paper
   "Presented by the Makers of Carter's Little Liver Pills," girl in bed sleeping with doll, white palette on black ground, reverse with "Sick Headache Positively Cured By Carter's Little Liver Pills...," cond. EXC, 5-1/2" h, 4" w .................................................. 12.50
   Same as above, 2 kittens playing in snow, cond. EXC, 5-1/2" h, 4" w .................................................. 12.50

## Cascarets

Pocket mirror, round, "All Going Out, Nothing Coming In, Cascarets Did It," cherub on chamber pot, red logo, white ground, cond. 8.5........................................ 49.50
Sign, paper, "Best For The Bowels, Cascarets Candy Cathartic, Regulate The Liver, Annual Sales 6,000,000 Boxes, They Work While You Sleep," C in Cascarets forms hammock for woman, red/yellow text, black ground, new frame, edge wear/soiling, 28" h, 41" w .............................................................. 368.50

## Case

Sign, neon on 2 porcelain die-cut signs, metal housing, "CASE" in white vertical text, black trim, letter "E" of neon broken, cond. VG, 72" h, 20" w, 12-1/2" d ............. 885.50

## Castle Hall Cigar

Sign, tin, "D.S. Erb & Co's Castle Hall Cigar," blue text/ border, yellow ground, crazing/minor scratches, 13" h, 37-1/2" w .......................................................... 203.50

## Castrol

Cap badge, cloisonné, porcelain inlaid, "Castrol" in red on white ground, remainder green/black, "Qualified Operator Lubrication Service," with name, pinback with wear, cond. NM, 1-5/8" h, 1-1/4" w ............ 770.00
Thermometer, porcelain, red name on white circle, green ground top/bottom, white center, "ESTP Brux. 4-54-71" at bottom, no tube, cond. 8, 32" h, 6" w ........ 66.00

## Caswell's Coffee (See Photo)

Can, litho tin, "Caswell's Coffee, Yellow & Blue Brand, Geo. W. Caswell Co., San Francisco, U.S.A.," 3 lb, $185.

## Cattaraugus

Sign, cardboard, die-cut, keyhole shape
   "For the Man who really appreciates Quality, there is nothing quite so pleasant as a Cattaraugus Knife," man sharpening knife on workbench, knife in foreground, newer frame, Cattaraugus Cutlery Co., Little Valley, NY, framed, cond. G, 15" h, 12" w..........121.00
   "No Tool so useful to the growing boy as a Cattaraugus Knife," boy in suit/bow tie at work, knife in foreground, Cattaraugus Cutlery Co., Little Valley, NY, framed, bottom corner missing/creases, 15" h, 12" w ...........99.00

## Cavalier Diesel Fuel

Gas globe, 2 glass lenses, glass body, arched red/blue text, white ground, lens cond. 8.5/7, body cond. 9, 13-1/2" dia........................................................ 357.50

## Cen-Pe-Co Motor Oil

Can, litho tin, "Cen-Pe-Co Two Cycle Motor Oil, Central Petroleum Company," unopened, 1 qt, $10.

# Centlivre

Sign

Paper, "C.L. Centlivre Brewing Co. Brewers & Bottlers of Lager Beer, Fort Wayne, Indiana" under colorful factory/street scene, portrait in oval at left, soiling, 29"h, 42" w.................................................... 709.50

Paperboard, "The Centlivre tonic, Builds up the system, gives strength and enjoyment to life! For sale here," shield-logo in upper-right of panel with nurse holding tray/product on table, framed, cond. 9, 10" h, 20" w.................................................. 247.50

# Central Hudson Line

Poster, "Central Hudson Line, Newburgh/Poughkeepsie/Kingston," shows man and woman with binoculars at railing, "B.B. Odell" on life preserver, with trip dates, cond. NM, 45-1/2" h, 29-1/2" w ........................ 715.00

# Central Union

Lunch box, litho tin

Rectangular version, "Central Union Cut Plug, The United States Tobacco Co., Richmond, Virginia," moon face (woman's face in crescent moon), gold design/text, red ground, cond. 7.5 .................. 61.00

Tall version, moon face on red ground, single handle on top, cond. 8, 6" h, 6" w, 4" d..................... 127.50

Tin, vertical pocket, litho tin, "Central Union New Cut Smoking, Ready For Use In Pipe Or Cigarette," woman's face in crescent moon, red ground, cond. 8+ ............................................................ 337.00

# Century Tobacco

Tin, flat pocket, litho tin

"Century, P. Lorillard & Co.," oval portrait of man flanked by 2 male characters in top hats over "Century," black on red ground, under oval opening is spin dial showing 4 candidates, back shows factory, cond. 8.5...................................................... 414.00

"Century" in centered circle, white text on black ground, surrounded by red/white flowers/embellishments, black ground overall, cond. 7.5-8, 3-1/2" x 2-1/4" ...................................................... 324.50

# Ceresota Flour

**History:** Ceresota Flour was first sold in 1891, a product of the Northwestern Consolidated Mill Company. The well-known trademark of a boy slicing a loaf of bread has been in use since 1912.

Pinback button, celluloid, "For Young or Old - The Best Flour sold, Ceresota," trademark boy on stool, cond. 9.5, 1-1/2" dia...................................................... 55.00

Pocket mirror, round, "Prize Bread Flour of the World, Ceresota Flour," trademark boy on stool, white text on black border, cond. 7.5 ........................................ 60.50

Match holder, hanging, litho tin, "Ceresota Prize Bread Flour of the World," trademark boy on stool above 3-D barrel, orig box, like new, 5-3/8" h, 2-1/4" w ........880.00

Rolling pin, stoneware, "D.F. Gerardo, Groceries & Queensware, Sole Agents Ceresota Flour, Phone 20, Toluca, Ill.," blue text, pumpkin-color stripes, wooden handles, 15" l, 3" dia ...................................... 1,100.00

**Doll, cloth, "Ceresota Flour, The Northwestern Consolidated Milling Co.," 13" h, $185.**

**Match holder, litho tin, "Ceresota Prize Bread Flour of the World," 5-1/2" h, $180.**

Dispenser, wooden keg, 4 "Challenge Root Beer" tag signs, 1940s-1950s, cond. 8-8.5, 20" h, $330. (Photo courtesy of Gary Metz, Muddy River Trading Co.)

Sign, litho tin, "More Power, More Speed, Champion Spark Plugs," spark plug in center, "Champion" in white on black bowtie design, yellow ground, 1940s-1950s, cond. 9.5-9.75, 14" h, 30" w, $495. (Photo courtesy of Gary Metz, Muddy River Trading Co.)

## Champion Spark Plugs

Clock, plastic clock with glass lens in center of die-cut steering wheel, spark plug over Champion logo, French, cond. 8 ................................................. 379.50

## Charter Oak Coffee

Can, paper label on cardboard, metal top/bottom, pry lid, "Williams' Charter Oak Coffee, the Williams & Carleton Co.," shows Connecticut's famous historical tree, cond. 8+, 5" h, 4-3/4" dia ................................. 550.00

## Chase & Sanborn Coffee

**History:** After James S. Sanborn, a purveyor of coffee and spices, met Caleb Chase, it wasn't long before they decided to create Chase & Sanborn in 1878. Their Seal Brand coffee was the first roasted coffee to be sold in a sealed container and became nationally known as a result of heavy advertising.

Chase & Sanborn joined Standard Brands in 1929, being purchased and acquired several times since then.

## Certified Gasoline

Gas globe, 2 different lenses, glass body, "Certified 70 Octane Gasoline" in blue/red under black LOGCo, red border, white ground; "Certified Gasoline" in red/blue text under blue LOGCo, blue border, white ground; lens cond. 9/8, 13-1/2" dia ............................... 357.50

## Cetacolor

Banner, canvas, "Not a Soap - Cetacolor, Prevents Washed Goods from Fading, 10¢ Package," woman in oval at left, white/yellow text, black ground, 1900-1910, cond. 8, 24" h, 36" w .................................. 66.00

## Challenger Cigars

Tin, square corner, litho tin, convex top/bottom, hinged lid, "Challenger, This Box Contains Five Invincibles for 5¢, These Cigars are made and Packed under Sanitary Methods," knight on horseback, white ground, W.K. Gresh & Sons, cond. 8+, 5-1/2" h, 3-1/3" w ........... 148.50

## Challenge Root Beer (See Photo)

## Champagne Velvet Beer

Sign, litho tin over cardboard, "Champagne Velvet Beer" in oval, "The Beer With The Million Dollar Flavor" near bottom, scene of 2 fishermen on shore with 3rd in water, Terre Haute Brewing Co., Terre Haute IN, cond. VG, 14-1/2" h, 19-1/2" w .................................... 176.00

## Champion Implements

Calendar, paperboard, 1902, "Champion Binders, Mowers and Rakes, The Warder, Bushnell & Gessner Co., Springfield, Ohio, Chicago, Ill., U.S.A.," 3 scenes of horse-drawn equipment, pad begins with May, cond. 9, 6-1/4" h, 3-1/2" w .......................................... 214.50

Can, keywind, litho tin, "Chase & Sanborn Coffee," 1 lb, $10.

Bin, store display, litho tin, "Chase & Sanborn's Standard Java, The Best Coffee in the World, Warranted Strictly Pure and the Finest Quality," detailed images all four sides, green ground, cond. 7.5-8, 21-1/2" h, 13" sq .............................................................. 770.00

## Chase's Tea

Bin, countertop, litho tin, roll front, smaller size, Oriental woman with cup, "The cup that cheers but not inebriates," E.M. Chase Tea Co., Manchester NH, cond. 8, 9" h, 7" w, 6" d...................................................... 181.50

## Chateau Frontenac Brand Coffee

Can, litho tin, "Coffee" in red banner surrounded by leaves with chateau in background, Kearney Bros. Limited, Montreal & New York, tall with original knob to slip lid, cond. 8.5 ............................................... 165.00

## Chautauqua

Can
Paper label over cardboard, "Chautauqua Select Blend Coffee, Steel Cut," oval image of ship with American flags, scattered chips, large paper tear, 6" h, 4-1/4" dia .............................................. 149.50
Tin, pry lid, "Swell Blend Chautauqua Brand Coffee, Steel Cut," oval image of ship in cobalt medallion, light-blue ground, cond. 8, 1 lb, 6" h, 4-1/4" dia ................ 275.00

## Checker Jam

Can, litho tin, round, "Checker Pure Raspberry Jam," moon smiling at 2 bearded elves playing checkers on toadstool, raspberries on back, black/white checkered ground, red band top/bottom, Canadian, cond. 8.25+, 4 lb ..................................................................... 308.00

## Checkers Pop Corn

Pocket mirror, round, "Eat Eat Eat, A Nice Prize In Each Package, Shotwell Mfg. Co., Chicago," shows red/white product box flanked by "Wonderful," black ground, red/white text, red/white checkered border, cond. 8.25 ......................................................... 88.00

## Checkers Tobacco

Tin, vertical pocket
Sample, paper label over cardboard, tin top/bottom, "Checkers Tobacco, Manufactured by Weisert Bros. Tobacco Co., St. Louis, Mo.," red text on white ground, full, cond. 7 ............................. 215.00
Litho tin, short version, "Checkers Granulated Plug, Weisert Bros. Tob. Co., St. Louis," gold text, checkered red/black ground, cond. 7.5-8 ............... 339.00
Litho tin, "Checkers Plug, Weisert Bros. Tob. Co., St. Louis," white text and top, checkered red/black ground, full, cond. 8 ...................................... 600.00

## Checker Taxi

Sign, cardboard, "Call a Checker Taxi, Dial 2-3434, Extra Passengers Free, Also Cadillac Limousines," green taxi, black text, white ground, cond. 8.5, 7" h, 11" w ..................................................................... 302.50

## Cheer Cup Coffee

Can, keywind, litho tin, cup beside red starburst with "1 Lb. Net," white text, black ground, Epping Smith NY, cond. 8, 1 lb, 4" h, 5-1/8" dia............................. 175.00

## Cheer Up

Clock, round, double bubble, "Drink Cheer Up, Sparkling Lemon-Lime," red/black text, white ground, black numbers, circa 1950s, cond. 8.25-8.5 .................. 1,265.00
Sign, chain-hung, "Drink Cheer Up, A Delightful Drink, A Real Super-Charged Beverage," bottle pouring into glass with ice, possibly cut down from a menu or manufactured as a sign, cond. 9.25, 11" h, 9-1/2" w ...................... 66.00
Thermometer
Pam style, red "Cheer Up" by bottle, cond. 8.75, 12" dia ......................................................... 495.00
Rectangular, dial at top, "Drink Cheer Up" on white ground with red ring lettered "A Delightful Drink, A Real Super Charged Beverage," 1930s-1940s, rechromed frame, cond. 8-8.5, 20" h, 16" w ........................ 687.50

## Chef Coffee

Can, keywind, litho tin, chef in green oval, white text on red band top/bottom, white band in center, Lee & Cady, Detroit, cond. 8, 1 lb................................. 176.00

## Chero-Cola

Sign, cardboard, "Bracing - Cooling, Chero-Cola, Ice Cold - Served Here," baseball player/women in stands with bottles, black/white/red text, framed, cond. VG, 18" h, 12" w....................................................... 319.00

## Cherry Blossoms

Bottle topper, litho tin, die-cut, boy/girl sitting with bottle on each end, name in red at top, circa 1920, cond. 7.5-8, 6-1/4" h, 11-1/2" w......................................... 825.00
Carrier, tin, 6-bottle, "Cherry Blossoms" in red on white panel, red ground, metal handle over top, with six 6-oz green bottles, paper label mkd "Cherry Blossoms" on red panel over blue ground with flowers, label edges peeling, carrier 10-1/2" h, 8-1/2" w, 5-1/2" d ..... 544.50

## Cherry Brand Chocolates

Hand mirror, miniature, celluloid/metal, "Fine Chocolates And Bon Bons, Cherry Brand," 4 cherries on white ground, orange gold handle/rim, Cy Gousset NY, minor soiling/scratches/wear to gold, 4" h, 2" w................. 99.00

## Cherry Rail

Sign, porcelain, "Cherry Rail, Door County's Premium Lager, Cherryland Brewing, Ltd.," train in gray circle on red ground, small chips to edge, 14" h, 19" w ....... 275.00

## Cherry Smash

Dispenser, porcelain, "Always Drink Cherry Smash, The Nation's Beverage" hanging cherries on both sides, "5 cents" on ends, circa 1920, base repaired, stripes enhanced, mismatched pump, cond. 8.5-9 ........1,430.00

Thermometer, litho tin, "Chesterfield, More Than Ever, They Satisfy," embossed cigarette pack, 13-1/2" h, 5-3/4" w, $121.

Postcard, heavily embossed, "Cherry Smash, Our Nation's Beverage," portrait of George Washington, glass of product inset on axe, circa 1910-1915, cond. 9.5 .......................................... 302.50

## Cherry Sparkle

Sign, tin over cardboard, embossed, string-hung, "Exquisite Cherry Sparkle, The Taste Tells The Tale," boy with bottle, yellow ground, cond. 8+, 6" h, 13-1/4" w ......... 687.50

## Chesterfield

Thermometer, tin, rounded corners, "Chesterfield, They Satisfy" on white strip at top/bottom, "Straight Grade A Top Tobacco" in circle beside image of pack, tobacco leaves on black ground, cond. 7.5+, 13" h ........ 132.00

## Chevrolet

**History:** European auto racer Louis Chevrolet provided the name for this automotive company, but he didn't have much to do with its success. Instead of using Chevrolet's designs for big, expensive cars, William Crapo Durant chose to make simpler, cheaper models. Because he was providing the financial backing for the company, Durant's decisions carried some weight. Eventually, he decided to retain the Chevrolet name but merge the company with another of his businesses, Little Motor Company. Durant produced his first car in 1912. The square and parallelogram trademark was copied from wallpaper in a Paris hotel.

Ashtray, plastic, bowtie logo shape, embossed bowtie "Chevrolet" logo in center, NOS, 3-1/2" w ........... 44.00
Clock face, metal, rounded corners, "Super Chevrolet Service" in center using blue ring around bowtie logo, black text, white ground, 15-1/8" sq .................. 341.00
Paperweight, metal, embossed "Chevrolet" bowtie logo, cond. 9, 2" h, 3-1/2" w, 1-1/2" d.......................... 88.00

Sign, porcelain, "Chevrolet," white text, cobalt ground, cond. 8, 12" h, 36" w, $990. (Photo courtesy of Collectors Auction Services)

Poster, paper, "We Airline-Check When We Chevy Tune for Top-Flight Performance," mechanic working on car, black/orange/white text, airplane lower-right, cond. EXC, 44" h, 17" w ............................................. 170.50
Sign, cardboard
    Die-cut, "Chevrolet" bowtie logo, white text/border, blue ground, cond. 7, 10-3/4" h, 30" w ........... 88.00
    Trolley, "Chevrolet, Low in First Cost, Lowest in Upkeep, Ask for a Demonstration," early auto at left under Chevy logo, dealer info at bottom, green/black on orange ground, framed, tear, 12-1/2" h, 22-1/2" w .......................................................110.00
Sign, porcelain, made for neon, "Chevrolet" in white on cobalt bowtie logo on yellow center, "Super Service" in yellow on cobalt border, no neon, cond. 8, 42" h, 48" w ........................................................... 1,650.00

## Chicago Cubs Chewing Tobacco

Can, litho tin, eagle with American flags in oval, red/black text, yellow ground, 1930s, cond. 8+, 3-1/2" h, 6" dia.............................................................. 159.50

## Chicago Daily News

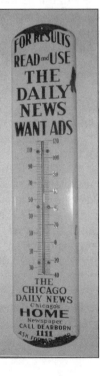

Thermometer, porcelain, "For Results Read and Use the Daily News Want Ads, The Chicago Daily News, Chicago's Home Newspaper, Call Dearborn 1111, Ask For Ad Taker," considerable chipping, 39" h, 8" w, $110.

Tin, litho tin, hinged lid, "Chi-Ches-Ters New Style Diamond Brand Pills, Large Size, 1 dozen $2, Chichester Chemical Co., Philadelphia," 3-1/2" h, 7-1/4" w, 3-1/4" d, $65.

Sign, porcelain, "Eisenlohr's Cinco Cigars," red "Cinco," yellow ground, cond. 8-8.5, 46" h, 30" w, $275. (Photo courtesy of Gary Metz, Muddy River Trading Co.)

# Chicago Motor Club

Sign, porcelain, 2-sided, "Official Service Station, Chicago Motor Club, A.A.A.," yellow top, white circular design with central red star in "C" on black ground, cond. 8.25-8.5, 44" h, 36" w .............................. 467.50

# Chi-Ches-Ters (See Photo)

# Chiclets

Box, store display, cardboard, cloth hinge, orig label on glass top inside, leaf/seal design, cond. 8.5, 10" x 7-1/2" .................................................................. 317.00

# Chief Garden Tractor & Implements

Sign, flange, painted metal, die-cut, "Authorized Sales & Service, Chief Garden Tractors & Implements," Indian in headdress with shield/spear, black/yellow text, yellow over red ground, circular design on black extender, crazing/bubbling/scratches/stains, 13-3/8" h, 17-5/8" w .......................................................... 104.50

# Chi-Namel Paints

Sign, porcelain, 2-sided, "Chi-Namel Paints" in white text on blue vertical panels, Chinaman top-right, cond. NM, 30" h, 9-1/2" w ..................................................... 357.50

# Christian Herald

Calendar, 1905, paper, die-cut, 4 girls and 4 birds, cond. 8+, 29" h, 11-1/2" w ............................................ 302.50

# Christy's Coffee

Can, litho tin, pry lid, oval medallion with plantation workers in fields, white ground, cond. 8+, 1 lb, 6" h, 4-1/4" dia .......................................................... 385.00

# C.H.Y.P. Inter-Collegiate Mixture

Tin, litho tin, square corner, flags/baseball-football gear, yellow ground, cond. 7, rectangular .................. 176.00

# Cinco Cigars

Sign, tin over cardboard, hanging, beveled, "Eisenlohr's Cinco Cigars, Made in Three Sizes," man in uniform in wicker chair, cond. 8.5, 11-1/4" h, 7-1/4" w ....... 605.00

Tin, vertical box, litho tin, "Cinco Londres Cigars," oval medallion of man/woman/ostrich, yellow ground, cond. 8.5, 5-1/4" h, 3" sq ............................................. 44.00

# Circus Club Mallows

Tin, round, slip lid in shape of hat, dog motif, Harry Horne Company, Toronto, cond. 8, 6-1/2" h ............... 149.00

# Cities Service

**History:** Founded as a public utility in 1910, Cities Service was responsible for the operation of various municipal services, including natural gas, lighting, and ice. Around 1914, the company made a foray into the world of petroleum marketing, with a collection of gas stations scattered throughout the East and the Midwest. By the mid-1930s, all of the various concerns were operating under the name Cities Services. In 1946, the company's black-and-white color scheme gave way to green and white.

Ashtray, metal, clear plastic dome-shaped "Cities Service" logo in center, 3 sets of ball-shaped cigarette holders on rim, NOS, 7-3/4" dia ......................... 55.00

Can, tin, "Cities Service Oils, Once-Always, Cities Service Oil Co.," black text, yellow ground, cond. 8.5, 1/2 gallon, 5-1/2" h, 8" x 3-1/4" .............................. 209.00

Clock, twin rolled edges, "Cities Service Petroleum Products" in white at rim, triangle logo in center, green ground, cond. 7.5, 19" dia ................................ 264.00

Gas globe, 2 glass cloverleaf lenses, wide glass body, "Cities Service" under small logo, black text/border,

Can, oil can, litho tin, "Cities Service Utility Oil, If It's Cities Service, It Has To Be Good!," 4 oz, $68.

white ground, lens cond. 8/7.5, body cond. 8.5,
    15-1/2" dia..................................................... 1,100.00
Lighter
    Metal, vinyl grip, "Cities Service" logo on green body,
        orig Paul Sherman box, NOS, 3-1/4" h, 2-1/4" w,
        1-1/4" d ........................................................ 99.00
    Plastic, figural 8 ball, top lifts to expose lighter, "Cities
        Services" logo on base, orig box, NOS, 3" h,
        2-1/2" w....................................................... 77.00
Notepad/pen, metal case, magnetic pen, "Cities Service"
    logo/merchant info in silver on green ground, 2-digit
    phone number, NOS, cond. 9, 5-1/4" h,
    3-1/2" w........................................................... 55.00
Pen/pencil set, "Cities Service" on black with logo, orig
    box, orig presentation form note, NOS .............. 27.50
Sign
    Painted metal, flange, "Cities Service National Charge
        Cards Accepted Here," green/red text, green stripes
        top/bottom, white ground, cond. 7, 12" h,
        21" w........................................................... 104.50
    Porcelain, "Cities Service Oils, Once-Always" triangle
        logo in center, black text/border, white ground,
        cond. 8, 16" dia............................................ 550.00
    Tin, 2-sided, 1 side says, "Refill with Cities Service
        Oils," white/green design, other side says, "Refill
        with Koolmotor, The Perfect Pennsylvania Oil," Cit-
        ies Service logo lower-left, green over black
        ground, cond. 8, 12" h, 20-3/4" w ................. 605.00

## City Club

Tin, vertical pocket, litho tin
    Short version, "City Club Crushed Cubes, The Pride of

Sign, tin, embossed, "Clabber Girl, The Healthy Baking Powder," red/black text, yellow ground, cond. G, 11-3/4" h, 34" w, $66.

    Our Factory," man reclining in wicker chair as he
        reads paper and smokes pipe, red ground,
        cond. 9...................................................... 963.00
    Tall version, "City Club Crushed Cubes, The Pride of
        Our Factory," man reclining in wicker chair as he
        reads paper and smokes pipe, red ground, cond.
        7.5-8, 4-1/2" h, 3" w ...................................... 296.00

## Clabber Girl

**History:** Clabber Baking Powder was copyrighted in 1899 by the Hulman Coffee Company of Terre Haute, Ind. Originally sold only in Indiana and Illinois, the product was distributed nationally in 1923, following a name change to Clabber Girl Baking Powder.
Sign, tin, 2-sided, "Clabber Girl, The Double-Acting Bak-
    ing Powder," red/black text, yellow ground, 2 dented
    corners, cond. EXC, 11-3/4" h, 34" w.................. 99.00

## Clark

Gas globe
    2 glass lenses, wide glass body, "Clark" in black on white
        panel, orange ground above/below, black border, lens
        cond. 8, body cond. 8, 13-1/2" dia.....................456.50
    2 different glass lenses, newer plastic body, "Clark"
        and "Crown Extra," red text, white ground, Clark

Sign, litho tin, "A Happy Thought! Clark's Teaberry Quality Gum, That Mountain Tea Flavor," red/green text, yellow ground, red border, 1930s-1940s, cond. 8.25-8.5, 9" h, 12" w, $495. (Photo courtesy of Gary Metz, Muddy River Trading Co.)

lens cond. 9, Crown Extra lens cond. 8.5, body cond. 8.5, 13-1/2" dia.................................. 209.00

## Clark & Host Coffee

Can, paper label over metal, "Clark & Host My Favorite Brand Coffee, Tempts the Taste," oval image of child sitting on lap of old man, red band with "Coffee" near bottom, green ground, cond. 8+, 3 lb, 9-1/2" h, 5-1/2" dia......................... 187.00

## Clark's Gum

Blotter, cardboard, "The Clark Twins, Highest Quality Great Sellers, The D.L. Clark Co., Pittsburgh, U.S.A.," text flanked by images of girl with boxes of Zig Zag and Clark Gum, unused, cond. EXC, 4" h, 9-1/4" w ............. 247.50

Tin, litho tin, "Clark's Teaberry Pepsin Gum, 5¢," shows pack of gum, yellow ground, cond. 8, 5" h, 7-1/2" w, 6-3/4" d.............................................. 330.00

## Clark's Thread

**History:** In 1813, the Clark family started making cotton thread in Scotland. The Coats family was involved in the same pursuit by 1826, and in 1830, James and Peter Coats were operating the family business under the name J.&P. Coats. The two families continued competing for shares of the thread market, both establishing bases in the eastern United States.

In 1866, George Clark of Newark, N.J., developed a six-cord thread that could be used with Elias Howe's newly patented sewing machine. He called his innovation "Our New Thread," which was later shortened to O.N.T.

After the firms and their affiliates merged in 1896, the conglomerate became known as J&P Coats Ltd., with the American arm of the company becoming Coats & Clark, Inc. in 1952.

Cabinet, wood, 5 drawers with reverse-painted glass fronts advertising product, "Clark's Mile-End Spool," paint loss to glass, minor scuffs to cabinet, 19" h, 30" w, 18-1/2" d........................................... 495.00

Sign, cardboard, beveled edge, "Clark's Mile-End Spool Cotton," outdoor scene of girl in red dress standing with dog, cond. 8+, 17-5/8" h, 12-5/8" w ........... 907.50

## Cleo Cola

Screen door brace, metal, embossed, "Drink Cleo Cola For Goodness Sake," cond. 7.5-8, 6" x 12" ...... 154.00

## Cleo-Tex Condoms

Box, cardboard, woman in yellow dress, blue ground, slide-out center with contents, circa 1930, cond. NM, 9/16" h, 1-3/4" w, 1-5/8" d ................................ 316.00

## Cleveland Superior Baking Powder

Tin, paper label, slip lid, portrait of man, black on red ground, cond. 8+, 3-1/4" h, 2" dia ...................... 30.00

## Clicquot Club

Bank, chalkware, boy in parka holding green bottle, cond. 9, 7" h................................................. 176.00

Clock, lightup, metal case, square, "Time to serve Clicquot Club Beverages," boy in parka holding bottle, red text, green 12/3/6/9, white ground, circa 1959, cond. 8.25-8.5, 15" sq............................................. 187.00

## Climax Peanut Butter

Pail, litho tin, "Climax Peanut Butter, J.W. Beardsley's Sons, Newark, N.J.," cobalt/white text, white oval with red horizontal band, red ground, cond. 8.25+, 1 lb ................................................................ 143.00

## Climax Plug Tobacco

Sign, porcelain, "The Grand Old Chew, Climax Plug Tobacco," white text/border on cobalt circle, red ground, minor edge chips/fading/scratches/missing grommet, 15" sq............................................... 770.00

Tobacco cutter, cast iron, embossed, "Climax" on arched frame, orig paint, cond. 8, 6" h, 19" l, 4" w.......... 69.50

## Clinton Engines

Sign, painted metal, 2-sided, "Authorized Clinton Engines Service Station," arrowhead logo, red/white/black text, white ground, cond. 8/7+, 18" h, 24" w ............... 66.00

## Cloverdale Soft Drinks

Sign, litho tin
  Beveled edge, easel-back/string-hung, "Cloverdale Soft Drinks, Made With Mineral Water," white oval on green ground, silver-embossed dots form text, red "Vitamin B-1 Added" box, 1950s, cond. 8.5, 9" h, 13" w.................................................................38.50
  Die-cut, embossed, bottle shape, "Cloverdale Pale Dry Ginger Ale," yellow label on green, 1940s, cond. 8-8.25, 36" h ................................................... 159.60

Thermometer, black/red text, green 4-leaf clover at top, white ground, cond. 9.25, 12" sq ...................... 275.00

## Clubb's Mixture

Tin, horizontal box, litho tin, lid has red club over "Clubb's Mixture, One Pound, A High Grade Tobacco For Pipe Use, A. Clubb & Sons, Estab'd 1878, Toronto, Montreal," gold text on white ground, trademark image of 3 men on front, cond. 7.5, 4" h, 6-1/2" w, 4" d.................................................................37.50

## Club Lido Smoking Mixture

Tin, vertical pocket, 2 white pipes with smoke raising to top of tin, white over black ground, cond. 8-8.5 ...........101.00

## Clysmic Table Water

Tip tray, litho tin, oval, "Clysmic, King of Table Waters" on gold rim, shows woman at waterside with deer/oversized bottle, cond. 8.5 ...................................... 220.00

## Coach and Four

Tin, vertical pocket, litho tin, "Coach and Four English Pipe Blend," horse-drawn carriage, black/red ground, cond. 8 .......................................................... 244.00

# Coca-Cola

**History:** An Atlanta pharmacist, John S. Pemberton, is credited with first developing the syrup base used for Coca-Cola. He was attempting to formulate a patent medicine for those experiencing headaches, nervousness, or stomach upsets. In 1887, Willis E. Venable mixed the syrup with carbonated water, and the rest, as they say, is history.

George S. Lowndes and Venable bought Pemberton's interests in the company in 1888, and Asa Griggs Candler, owner of a pharmaceutical company, also became a partner. After a number of transactions and a payment of $2,300, Candler became the company's sole owner.

The Atlanta Journal carried the first print ad for Coca-Cola on May 29, 1886. In 1893, a trademark was granted for Coca-Cola written in script, and in 1945, the term Coke was registered.

Over the years, thousands of items ranging from calendars and trays to Christmas ornaments and toys have sported the company's logos to advertise the popular drink. Early items can be dated based on the slogans used. "Deliciously Refreshing" was the campaign in 1900, "Thirst Knows No Season" in 1922, "The Pause that Refreshes" in 1929, and "Things Go Better with Coke" in 1954.

**References:** Gael de Courtivron, *Collectible Coca-Cola Toy Trucks*, Collector Books, 1995; Shelly Goldstein, *Goldstein's Coca-Cola Collectibles*, Collector Books, 1991 (1996 value update); Deborah Goldstein-Hill, *Price Guide to Vintage Coca-Cola Collectibles 1896-1965*, Krause Publications, 1999; Bob and Debra Henrich, *Coca-Cola Commemorative Bottles*, Collector Books, 1998; William McClintock, *Coca-Cola Trays, rev. 2nd ed.*, Schiffer Publishing, 2000; Allan Petretti, *Petretti's Coca-Cola Collectibles Price Guide, 10th ed.*, Antique Trader Books, 1997; Allan Petretti and Chris Beyer, *Classic Coca-Cola Serving Trays*, Antique Trader Books, 1998; Joyce Spontak, *Commemorative Coca-Cola Bottles: An Unauthorized Guide*, Schiffer Publishing, 1998; B.J. Summers, *B.J. Summers' Guide to Coca-Cola, 2nd ed.*, Collector Books, 1999; ___, *B.J. Summers' Pocket Guide to Coca-Cola, 2nd ed.*, Collector Books, 2000; Al and Helen Wilson, *Wilson's Coca-Cola Guide*, Schiffer Publishing, 1997

**Collectors' Clubs:** Cavanagh's Coca-Cola Christmas Collector's Society, 1000 Holcomb Woods Pkwy., Suite 440B, Roswell, GA 30076; Coca-Cola Collectors Club International, P.O. Box 49166, Atlanta, GA 30359; The Cola Club, P.O. Box 158715, Nashville, TN 37215; Florida West Coast Chapter of the Coca-Cola Collectors Club International, 1007 Emerald Dr., Brandon, FL 33511

**Museums:** Biedenharn Candy Company & Museum of Coca-Cola Memorabilia, 1107 Washington St., Vicksburg, MS 39180, phone: (601) 638-6514; Schmidt's Coca-Cola Museum, P.O. Box 848, Elizabethtown, KY 42701, phone: (502) 769-3320 x 237; The World of Coca-Cola Pavilion, 55 Martin Luther Dr., Atlanta, GA 30303, phone: (404) 676-5151.

Badge, hat, bronze, circa 1940s, "Drink Coca-Cola," cond. 8.5+, 3-1/2" ............................................... 38.50
Banner
   "Have a Coke, Compliments of this Store," "Free" in one red circle, hand with Coke bottle in other circle, cond. 8.5, 13" h, 41" w................................ 99.00
   Silk, white with gold fringe, "Things go better with Coke" in red text, 1960s, light soiling, 46" h, 23-1/2" w ......................................................... 55.00
Baseball scorekeeper, perpetual counter, cond. 6.5-7.5................................................................ 121.00
Blotter, paper
   Man on bicycle pausing to enjoy a Coke, green and ivory, soiling/water stains, 3-1/2" h, 7-3/4" w............... 165.00
   Circa 1926, "Refresh Yourself, Drink Coca-Cola, Delicious and Refreshing," flanked by hobbleskirt bottles, framed, cond. 9.75 .................................. 66.00
   1929, "The pause that refreshes," man and woman with Cokes, framed, cond. 9.5+ ..................... 121.00
   1934, "And one for you, The pause that refreshes," woman on blanket, framed, cond. 9.75 .......... 99.00
   1935, "The drink that keeps you feeling fit for duty ahead," cond. 9................................................ 38.50
   1935, "Good with food, Try it," plate of food and 2 bottles, framed, cond. 9 ....................................... 60.50
   1935, "Carry a smile back to work - feeling fit," woman in red outfit, framed, cond. 9.75 ...................... 33.00
   1940, "The greatest pause on earth," clown, cond. 8.25+ .............................................................. 55.00
Bookmark, 1903, "Drink Coca-Cola, 5¢," woman with glass, elaborate floral border, cond. 9.25+, 6" h, 2" w ......................................................................... 907.50
Bottle, salesman sample, amber, straight-sided, embossed "Coca-Cola," Williamstown (NJ) Glass Co.," repro paper label, cond. 9.5+, 3-1/4" h .......... 2,860.00
Bottle holder, wire holder with tin sign on front, holds two bottles, 1950s, "Enjoy Coca-Cola While You Shop, Place Bottle Here," scratches to frame, 4-3/4" h, 5-1/2" w......................................................... 104.50

**Billboard, approx 24 individual paper sheets dry-mounted to linen, 1948, "Drink Coca-Cola, Delicious and Refreshing" button, "The rest-pause that refreshes, Welcome in peace ... more welcome in war work," cond. 8-8.5+, 8' h, 20' w, $1,045. (Photo courtesy of Gary Metz, Muddy River Trading Co.)**

Calendar, paper

1909, "Drink Coca-Cola, Delicious And Refreshing," outdoor scene of woman with glass under Chinese lanterns, orig metal strip at top, pad begins with April, few areas of restoration, cond. 8.5-8.75+, 20-1/2" h, 11" w ...................... 14,300.00

1912, "Drink Coca-Cola, Delicious And Refreshing," woman in long dress/large floral hat drinking glass of Coke, pad begins with June, museum mounted/framed, cond. 8-8.25, 31" h, 12" w ........... 7,150.00

1913, woman in white dress and bonnet with red bows, framed, reproduction calendar page, cond. 8.75, image 18-1/2" h, 15" w ...................... 9,900.00

1914, Betty, woman in pink dress and bonnet, full pad, framed, cond. 8.25-8.5+ ........................... 2,530.00

1918, 2 women on beach, full pad of 13 pages, framed, cond. 8.25-8.5 ........................... 7,150.00

1920, woman in yellow dress with bottle, golfers in background, professional repair to 2" tear, 31-3/4" h, 12" w ...................... 1,705.00

1922, woman in pink dress/hat at ballpark, baseball players in background, orig metal strip, full pad, cond. 9-9.25, 30-1/2" h, 12" w ................... 6,050.00

1937, boy with dog and fishing pole, full pad, framed, cover sheet in poor condition, cond. 8.5-9+ ...... 440.00

**Calendar, 1913, paper, "Drink A Bottle Of Coca-Cola," reproduction December pad, orig. page showing woman in white, framed, cond. 8.75, $9,900. (Photo courtesy of Gary Metz, Muddy River Trading Co.)**

1940, seated woman in red dress with bottle/glass, "the pause that refreshes," button logo, full pad, pad cond. 7-7.5, calendar cond. 5 ......................... 88.00

1946, Sprite boy on cover, complete, cond. 9-9.25+ ....................... 825.00

1954, cond. 7.5 ...............................110.00

1958, cond. 8.5+ ............................... 143.00

1959, cond. 8-8.5 ............................... 192.50

1960, cond. 9.25-9.5 ........................ 22.00

Camera, plastic, miniature, "Drink Coca-Cola" in black on white top, black body, out of focus, cond. 7.5, 2" l ...................... 121.00

Card table, 1930s, bottle logos in corners, Coke tag on back, cond. 7.5+ ...................... 55.00

Carrier, aluminum, 6-pack, circa 1940s, embossed "Coca-Cola," cond. 9...................... 66.00

Carrier, bent wood, "Drink Coca-Cola," red text, circa 1940s, cond. 7 ...................... 93.50

Carrier, cardboard

4-bottle, 1940s, "Drink Coca-Cola, 17¢," cond. 7.5...................... 121.00

6-bottle, box-type, 1920s, "Six Bottles Coca-Cola, Serve Ice Cold, Drink Coca-Cola with Sandwiches, Cheese & Crackers, Cookies and with your floats," unused, cond. 8 ......................110.00

6-bottle, box-type, circa 1930s, "Six Bottles Coca-Cola, Serve Ice Cold, 27¢," unused, cond. 9.5............ 187.00

6-bottle, collapsible, 1939, "Drink Coca-Cola, 25¢," cond. 8.5...................... 93.50

6-bottle, collapsible, Christmas, 1940s, "Season's Greetings, 25¢," holly leaves/berries, cond. 7.5-8 ...................... 121.00

6-bottle, wire handle, "Drink Coca-Cola, 25¢," cond. 6...................... 49.50

Carrier, stadium vendor, metal

Circa 1910s, low round base, central V-shape handle, "Drink Coca-Cola" in red on yellow ground, cond. 6.5-7 ...................... 412.50

Circa 1950s, metal, painted, embossed, Acton 20-bottle carrier/vendor, "Drink Coca-Cola" in white on red ground, cond. 8...................... 275.00

Carrier, wooden, 6-pack

Early 1940s, lift handle, "Drink Coca-Cola in Bottles, Pause...Go refreshed" logo with wings, mkd "new consumer case," red on yellow ground, cond. 8.5-9...................... 231.00

1940s, "Drink Coca-Cola in Bottles, Pause...Go refreshed" logo with wings, cond. 7 ............. 143.00

Change receiver, ceramic, 1890s, "The Ideal Brain Tonic For Headache and Exhaustion, Drink Coca-Cola, Change Receiver, Delightful Summer and Winter Beverage, Delicious Refreshing Invigorating," gold text, white ground, cond. 7, 1" h, 9" dia ................. 5,500.00

Clock, light-up, metal and glass, rectangular, "Drink Coca-Cola," clock face over red text, white ground, cond. 8, 11" h, 12" w ...................... 165.00

Coasters, colored aluminum, circa 1950s, boxed set of 8, orig box, coasters cond. NM, box cond. 8 ......... 66.00

Cooler

Cavalier picnic cooler, 1950s, "Drink Coca-Cola in Bot-

tles," orig box, cond. 7.5-8, 18" h, 18" w,
13" d ............................................................ 440.00
Glascock salesman sample, 1929, with case of sample
bottles, cond. 7+, 10-1/2" h, 8" w, 5" d ........... 4,070.00
Cup, tin, 1930s, "Drink Coca-Cola in Bottles, Coca-Cola
Bottling Co., Greencastle, Ind." lettered inside bottom,
wear/spots ...................................................... 143.00
Cup dispenser, Siphonmix automatic cup dispensing
machine, 1923, "Drink Coca-Cola," restored and with
reproduction sign, sold with orig sign in poor cond., restoration cond. 9.5, 74" h, 26" w, 18" d .................. 17,600.00
Cutout, paper
1927, circus, framed, cond. 7-7.5 ...................... 22.00
1929, store corner, framed, cond. 8.5 .............. 121.00
Dish, pretzel, circa 1935, 3 miniature Coke bottles hold
central round dish, cond. 7-7.5 ........................ 187.00
Dispenser, syrup, countertop, metal, 1940s, "Drink Coca-
Cola, Ice Cold" in oval, end has "Have A Coke" in cir-
cle, with glass stand/mounting hardware, cond. 7+,
14" h, 8" w, 18" d ............................................110.00
Doll, Santa Claus
Black Santa, white boots, cond. 8.5 ................. 154.00
White Santa, 1950s-1960s, stuffed body, black boots,
cond. 7-7.5, 18" h ..........................................110.00
Door bar, tin, adjustable, 1950s, "Refreshing, Coca-Cola,
New Feeling!," red text, yellow ground,
cond. 8-8.5 ....................................................... 330.00
Door handle, metal back, 1930s-1940s, "Delicious Drink
Coca-Cola Refreshing" button above image of bottle,
Bakelite handle with metal band, cond. 5-6,
12" h ................................................................ 121.00
Door push/pull plate, tin
1950s, "Push/Pull" in green on white upper panel,
"Refresh Yourself" in white on green lower panel
with "Drink Coca-Cola In Bottles" red button logo,
cond. 9.5, 6" h, 3" w ................................... 1,375.00

**Countertop light-up signs, 1950s, "Drink Coca-Cola": (top) "Please Pay Cashier," cond. 8.25+, $990; (bottom) "Popcorn," cond. 9.25-9.5, $1,430. (Photo courtesy of Gary Metz, Muddy River Trading Co.)**

1960s, "Push/Pull" in green, "Drink Coca-Cola, Be
Really Refreshed!" in white on red fishtail panel,
white ground, cond. 8-8.5, 8" h, 4" w ............ 880.00
Fan, bamboo and paper, circa 1910, "Drink Coca-Cola,"
Oriental scene with woman drinking from early glass,
cond. 7, 15" h, 9-1/2" w ..................................... 176.00
Festoon, cardboard
1918, "Drink Coca-Cola, Delicious and Refreshing," 3
women with parasols/glasses, adjustable side
pieces show roses/blue ribbons, cond. 8.25-8.5+,
approx 7' l ................................................. 5,060.00
1934, "Ice Cold-Delicious, The Pause That Refreshes,
Cooling-Exhilarating," icicle design, 5 pcs, framed,
orig envelopes, cond. 7-8.5, 12-1/2' l .......... 935.00
Festoon component, cardboard, die-cut, "Drink Coca-
Cola, Delicious and Refreshing," leaf design with man
holding glass, red rectangle at top, 1927, cond. 5-6,
20" h, 12" w ..................................................... 176.00
Glass, clear glass, flare style
Circa 1912, "Drink Coca-Cola," large "5¢,"
cond. 9 ......................................................... 770.00
Circa 1914-1918, "Drink Coca-Cola," syrup line, small
chip, cond. 7.5 .............................................. 77.00
Glass, clear glass, modified flare style
Circa 1910s-1920s, "Coca-Cola," cond. 9 ........... 71.50
1927, "Coca-Cola," C has "Trademark" in tail, cond.
9.5 ............................................................... 121.00
Glass, pewter lined, 1930s, Coca-Cola logo, leather
pouch, cond. 9 ................................................ 990.00
Insert, cardboard, 1950s, "Let us put a case in your car,"
gas station attendant putting product in woman's
trunk, cond. 6.5-7, 15" h, 12" w ...................... 77.00
Jug, syrup, clear glass, embossed, early 1900s, "Coca-
Cola," bail handle with repaired wire, cond. 8.5,
1 gal ............................................................ 2,200.00

**Clock, electric, "Drink Coca-Cola In Bottles," yellow/white text on red circle, yellow numbers on white ground, 1930s, orig case/motor, works, cond. 8-8.5, 17-1/2" h, 14" w, $4,620. (Photo courtesy of Gary Metz, Muddy River Trading Co.)**

Keg, syrup, wooden, paper label on one end
   5 gal, 1930s, "Delicious, Refreshing, Coca-Cola," label
      cond. 5-6, keg cond. 8-9 .............................. 176.00
   10 gal, circa 1940, cond. 7, 21" h. .................... 275.00
Kickplate
   Porcelain, 1950s, "Drink Coca-Cola Fountain Service,"
      cond. 9-9.25+, 12" h, 28" w ....................... 1,540.00
   Tin, 1908, Spanish, "Tomese Coca-Cola, En Botellitas
      6¢ Plata," flanked by straight-sided bottles, framed,
      NOS, cond. 9.5-9.75, 12" h, 36" w ............ 1,375.00
   Tin, 1942, man and woman with bottle, "Drink Coca-
      Cola," red ground, NOS, 9.5-9.75+ ............... 962.50
Kite, paper, Hi-Flier, "Coca-Cola" above bottle, orig sup-
   port/strings/sticks, circa 1930s, cond. 8 ............ 550.00
Magazine advertisement
   1914, "Delicious Coca-Cola, Pure and Wholesome,"
      portrait of woman drinking glass of Coke, back
      cover of The National Sunday Magazine, framed,
      cond. 8.5 ...................................................... 38.50
   1936, "Thru 50 Years, Making a pause refreshing,"
      color image of 2 soda jerks, full page newspaper
      ad, framed, cond. 9.5 .................................. 137.50

**Light fixture, 3-D, orig brass/copper framing with Art Deco
influence, 2 different versions of bottles, one with high-
lighted letters/the other without, acid-etched interiors
stained caramel, NOS gold-colored caps, metal polished/
restored, cond. 9.25-9.5+, 37" h, 17" w, $15,400. (Photo
courtesy of Gary Metz, Muddy River Trading Co.)**

1936, "Thru 50 Years...the pause that refreshes," color
   image of 2 women in bathing suits,
   cond. 8.5 ............................................................ 44.00
Matchbook
   1912, text only, "Drink Coca-Cola In Bottles, Delicious
      And Refreshing," minor bends, cond.
      9.25-9.5 ...................................................... 770.00
   1912, image of woman holding bottle, unused, cond.
      9.25-9.5+ .................................................... 990.00
Matchbook holder, metal, white, circa 1959, full of Coca-
   Cola matchbooks, cond. 9.5 ............................. 330.00
Menu, 1903, 2-sided, Hilda Clark, "Coca-Cola, 5¢" lower-
   right, cond. 8.25-8.5 ...................................... 2,750.00
Menu sign, tin
   1956, "Enjoy Coca-Cola" in white script on red ground
      pointing to right at hobbleskirt bottle, cond. 7-7.5,
      28" h, 20" w ................................................ 143.00
   1958, "Coca-Cola, Sign of Good Taste" in white script
      on red fishtail logo, cond. 8-8.5 .................... 231.00
   1959, "Coca-Cola" in white script on red fishtail logo,
      cond. 7-7.5 .................................................. 198.00
   1960s, "Enjoy Coca-Cola" in red circle logo beside
      "things go better with Coke" slogan, red/white top over
      green board, cond. 9.25-9.5, 28" h, 20" w ........ 330.00
Music box, plastic, cooler shape, circa 1950s, cond.
   8 ....................................................................... 143.00
Napkin, rice paper, "Hot - Tired - Thirsty? Drink Coca-Cola,
   Delicious - Refreshing - Thirst-Quenching," seated
   woman in red dress/blue hat, cond. 9.5, 12" sq ....... 99.00
Napkin holder, 1950s, insert card of Sprite Boy drinking
   from fountain glass, back card features Johnston's Hot
   Fudge Sundae and Beechnut Orange Drops,
   cond. 7 ........................................................... 2,200.00
Night light, circa 1950s, plastic, bottle cap shape, orig
   box, cond. 8.5-9 ................................................. 49.50
Olympics, 1932, event schedule wheel, 2-sided, cond. 9-
   9.5 ..................................................................... 121.00
Pin, service, set of 4, for 5/10/15/20 years,
   cond. 9.5 ........................................................... 154.00
Plate, sandwich, circa 1931, "Drink Coca-Cola" at rim,
   yellow with glass and Coke bottle in center, cond. 6-7,
   7.25" dia ............................................................ 209.00
Playing cards
   1928, "Tastes good!" by woman with straw drinking from
      bottle, green ground, "Coca-Cola Playing Cards,
      Refresh yourself!" on orig. box, complete deck, cards
      cond. 8.75-9, box cond. 8-8.5 ...................... 2,200.00
   1943, airplane spotters, complete with Joker, informa-
      tion card, orig box, box cond. 8, cards
      cond. 9-9.5 .................................................. 275.00
   1943, stewardess in circle, bottle with wings, blue
      ground, box cond. 7.5-8, cards cond. 9.5 ....... 55.00
   1943, woman in circle, bottle/leaves, red ground, box
      cond. 7.5, cards cond. 9.5 ............................. 77.00
   1958, "Refresh," 5 hands/4 bottles, button logo, box
      cond. 6.5, cards cond. 8 ................................ 55.00
Price list, booklet, "Coca-Cola Bottlers' Current Advertising Price List 1933," cond. 7 ............................. 253.00
Rack, wire, folding, circa 1940, for 6-pack storage/display,
   round sign at top, "Take Home a Carton, Coca-Cola, 6
   Bottles 25¢ Plus Deposit," cond. 6.5-7, 56" h ........ 412.50

Record holder, plastic, hi-fi club lazy Susan, 45 rpm holder, red/white, orig cardboard box, box cond. 6.5, holder cond. 8.5 ............................................. 275.00

Sandwich toaster, 1930s, with electric cord, cond. 7 ......................................................... 1,650.00

Seltzer bottle, glass

    Clear, "Property of Cairo, Illinois, Coca-Cola Bottling Co.," red decor of waiter, unmarked chrome top, cond. 8.5 ....................................................... 275.00

    Clear, "Coca-Cola Bottling Company, Cairo, Illinois" in red, unmarked metal top, cond. 8-8.5 ............................................................ 297.00

    Green, fluted, chromed top, "Coca-Cola Bottling Co. R.I., Illinois," cond. 7.5 ................................. 143.00

Sign, cardboard

    1935, 2-sided, "Thirst knows no season," hand with bottle and button logo, ground shows ice-capped mountains on half, palm trees on the other, cond. 9.5-9.75, 13" h, 21" w ............................... 2,970.00

    1938, vertical, woman in white swimsuit on rock, button logo at top, cond. 7-7.5, 50" h, 30" w ............... 770.00

    1940, "The good old pause that refreshes," sailor girl with fishing pole on dock, button logo, orig gold frame, cond. 7.25-7.5, large horizontal ......... 687.50

    1940, "Your thirst takes wings," woman aviator in front of airplane, "Drink Coca-Cola" button logo upper-left, cond. 7.25-7.5, 20" h,36" w ................. 1,980.00

    1941, "Easy to take home," woman in blue dress picking up 6-pack, cond. 8.5-8.75, 27" h, 16" w ......... 1,100.00

    1941, "They all want Coca-Cola," waitress with tray of hamburgers, button logo, cond. 9.5, 20" h, 36" w ...................................................... 1,210.00

    1941, "Refreshment right out of the bottle," woman holding roller skates and drinking bottle of Coke by open cooler, cond. 9-9.25, 27" h, 16" w ........ 770.00

    1942, Canadian, "Thirst knows no season," couple building snowman, button logo, edge nicks, cond.

**Sign, porcelain, 2-sided, red dispenser mkd "Drink Coca-Cola, Ice Cold," orig stainless steel edge band, 1950s, cond. 8.25-8.5, 27" x 28", $1,430. (Photo courtesy of Gary Metz, Muddy River Trading Co.)**

    9.25-9.5, large vertical ................................. 412.50

    1942, "Hello Refreshment," woman in bathing suit, button logo, cond. 8-8.25+, 20" h, 36" w ..................... 440.00

    1943, "Coke time," boy and girl eating lunch from steps, orig gold frame, cond. 7.75-8 ......... 1,540.00

    1944, "For people on the go," soldier and woman in short dress, button logo, cond. 7.5+ ............. 962.50

    1944, "Refreshment you go for," woman on bicycle, button logo, cond. 8.75-9+, large horizontal ........ 1,017.50

    1947, set of 10 sports hangers, tattered orig envelope, cond. 9-9.25+ ........................................... 4,510.00

    1948, "Pause for Coke," baseball player with woman in blue skirt, cond. 9.5, 27" h, 16" w .......... 3,080.00

    1952, "What I want is a Coke," woman in bathing suit lying on stomach in the sand, button logo, framed, cond. 8.75+, large horizontal ...................... 1,760.00

Sign, cardboard cutout

    1913, "North, South, East, West, They All Drink It," 4 women in ovals surrounded by flowers, museum mounted/framed, believed to be the only 1 known, cond. 7.75-8.25, 24" h, 31" w ................. 28,600.00

    1937, "Drink Coca-Cola, Cold Refreshment," shows hobbleskirt bottle, diamond shape, string hanger, cond. 7.25-7.5, 21" sq ................................... 797.50

    1947, "Party Refreshment," tray of hors d'oeuvres by 4 bottles, Coke button logo at top, white text on red strip at bottom, cond. 8.25, 28" h, 36" w ......... 55.00

    1951, "Be refreshed" in banner by button sign, 3 women at table drinking glasses of Coke, cond. 7, 16" h, 24" w .................................................. 165.00

    1954, "Stock up Now...Take Some Home," bottle through ring of food, 4 hangers, cond. 8.5, 4' h, 3' w .............................................................. 302.50

Sign, cardboard, easel-back

    1934, movie stars Johnny Weissmuller and Maureen O'Sullivan, framed, restored to cond. 9-9.25+ .................................................. 3,520.00

    1950, 3 hobbleskirt bottles by 2 trays of food, cond. 8.5-9, 27" h, 16" w ............................................ 220.00

    Playing-card promotional from Piqua OH plant, framed, cond. 8-8.25, 18" h, 12" w ................. 60.50

Sign, cardboard, trolley

    Circa 1907, "Tried Coca-Cola? Relieves Fatigue, Sold Everywhere," soda jerk, framed, cond. 6, 10-1/2" h, 20-1/2" w .................................................. 1,210.00

    1927, "Good Company," couple making a toast, cond. 7+, 9-1/2" h, 20" w ................................... 1,980.00

Sign, celluloid

    Circa 1940s, "Coca-Cola, Delicious, Refreshing," orig envelope, cond. 8-8.5+, 9" dia ...................... 330.00

    1940s, heavily embossed, "Pause...Go Refreshed, Coca-Cola," hand and bottle over wings, red ground, cond. 9.25-9.5, 8-3/4" dia ............. 2,310.00

    1940s-1950s, "Coca-Cola" in script over hobbleskirt bottle, cond. 8-8.5, 9" dia............................. 275.00

Sign, Kay displays

    1930s, wooden laminated triangle with metal filigree and applied bottle, "Drink Coca-Cola," red over yellow, cond. 7.5-8, 20" x 19" ......................... 1,485.00

    1930s-1940s, wooden and wire, set of 4, Sports

Sign, porcelain, die-cut script, "Drink Coca-Cola," 1930s, NOS, mint, 5-1/2" h, 18" w, $1,760. (Photo courtesy of Gary Metz, Muddy River Trading Co.)

Series, features golf/fishing/swimming/badminton, cond. 7-7.5+, 16" dia.................................. 2,420.00
1940s, Masonite and composition, set of 5, features navy ships, 2 with boats intact, one with repaired boat, 1 with partial boat, 1 missing boat frame, cond. 7, 8-1/2" h, 25" w............................ 1,980.00
Plywood and wire-frame, shows U.S. and fountain glass, directionals, green ground, cond. 8.25-8.5, 16" dia....................................................... 1,980.00

Sign, lightup
1940s-1950s, countertop, waterfall motion, "Pause and Refresh, Drink Coca-Cola In Bottles, Have A Coke," restored cond. 9-9.5 ........................ 1,760.00
1950s-1960s, plastic/metal, rectangular, "Drink Coca-Cola" in red/white, cond. 8, 12" h, 24" w....... 209.00
Plastic/metal, round, 2-sided, "Shop Refreshed, Drink Coca-Cola In Bottles," other side with "Have A Coke Here," red arrow points down, halo rings each side, cond. 9.25-9.5, 16" dia............................... 1,265.00

Sign, Masonite, "Take a case home Today! $1.00 Plus Deposit, Coca-Cola," yellow/white text, red ground, yellow border, cond. 9.25-9.5, 14" h, 12" w................ 220.00

Sign, paper
1927, "Pause a Minute, Refresh Yourself," flapper girl with bottle, framed, cond. 7-7.5+, 20" h, 12" w.......... 440.00
1936, Chinatown, Oriental woman in blue dress, framed, cond. 9.75, 22" h, 14" w................ 1,375.00
1941, "Refreshment right out of the bottle," woman in yellow jacket/dark skirt drinking bottle beside open cooler, framed, cond. 3-4, 27" h, 16" w.......... 82.50
1941, "Thirst knows no season," couple building snowman, button sign upper right, cond. 5-6 .......... 99.00
1953, "Take Enough Home," figures pulling wheeled platform with 8 hobbleskirt bottles down winding road ending at cottage, framed, cond. 9.25-9.5, 30" h, 20" w.................................................... 110.00
"I am a Five-Star Coca-Cola Dealer" with hobbleskirt bottle in lower right, framed, cond. 5-6, 18" h, 12" w...................................................... 71.50
"Sweetwater Clifton," pro basketball player in New York outfit, framed, cond. 6-7, 13" h, 11-1/2" w......... 440.00
"Take Along Coke in 12 oz. Cans, Buy a Case," large-diamond can and dock scene, framed, cond. NM, 20" h, 36" w.................................................. 352.00

Sign, porcelain
1950s, hobbleskirt bottle encircled by green "Delicious Refreshing," cond. 9.25, 24" sq .................... 330.00

1950s, red logo with white script, curved ends for building mounting, cond. 8.75, 24" h, 67" w................... 231.00

Sign, porcelain, button,
Late-1940s/early-1950s, 2-sided, orig cutouts at bottom, interior ring frame and 2 key posts, cond. 8.75-9.25, 48" dia .............................................. 550.00
1940s-1950s, "Coca-Cola" over hobbleskirt bottle, cond. 8-8.25+, 24" dia ............................... 522.50
"Coca-Cola In Bottles," cond. 9.5, 36" dia........ 550.00

Sign, porcelain, die-cut
1925, self-framed, "Fountain Service, Drink Coca-Cola, Delicious and Refreshing," scratches/chips to edges, 46" h, 60" w................................... 2,090.00
1930s, script, "Drink Coca-Cola," for attachment to a cooler, NOS, mint, 5-1/2" h, 18" w ............. 1,760.00
1936, shield shape, 2-sided, "Fountain Service, Drink Coca-Cola," yellow/white text, half green/half red (diagonal division), cond. 8.25-8.5, 25" h, 23" w...................................................... 2,200.00
1940s-1950s, hobbleskirt bottle, cond. 8.75, 12" h ...................................................... 231.00

Sign, porcelain, flange, "Have a Coca-Cola" in script, chips to edges/scratches, 19" h, 17-1/2" w....... 467.50

Sign, tin
1926, oval, "Coca-Cola" behind woman with bottle, white text, red ground, gold border, touch-ups, cond. 7-7.5, 7-1/2" h, 10-1/2" w ................. 2,530.00
1941, "Drink Coca-Cola" on red ground, horizontal design of couple with bottle at right, cond. 8.75+, 18" h, 54" w .................................................. 852.50
1948, "Coca-Cola," white script, red ground, folded over orig wood frame, cond. 9.25-9.5, 32" h, 62" l .......................................................... 154.00
1950, "Drink Coca-Cola," Coca-Cola in script, white text on red ground pointing toward hobbleskirt bottle on white ground, cond. 7, 10" h, 28" w .... 165.00
1954, "Pick up 6 For Home Refreshment," green text, central 6-pack on white ground, NOS, cond. 9.5, 16" h, 50" w ............................................... 1,485.00
1950s, "Wherever You Go, Drink Coca-Cola," central scene of skier against background of mountains, attached pine cone, wire accents around central sign, cond. 8-8.5, 18" h, 14" w................... 253.00

Sign, tin, button with arrow
Early 1950s (undated), 2-color arrow, "Coca-Cola," minor marks/wear/spider webbing, 16" dia ............. 1,017.50
August 1951, "Drink Coca-Cola," NOS, cond. 9.5-9.75 ............................................... 1,045.00
February 1952, "Drink Coca-Cola," light scratches/wear, cond. 9-9.25, 16" dia ......................... 770.00

Sign, tin, button, red, "Coca-Cola" over hobbleskirt bottle
October 1950, cond. 7-7.25, 48" dia ................. 440.00
July 1954, NOS, cond. 9.5-9.75, 24" dia........... 907.50
August 1954, cond. 7.75-8, 48" dia.................. 467.50

Sign, tin, button, white
Hobbleskirt bottle only, NOS, cond. 9.25-9.5, 24" dia ...................................................... 742.50
Hobbleskirt bottle only, cond. 8.75-9.25, 36" dia ...................................................... 632.50
Sprite Boy decor, 1950s, cond. 8.5, 16" dia.......... 715.00

Sign, tin, crossing guard, die-cut
  1940s, "Stop School Zone, Courtesy Coca-Cola Bottling Co.," girl in yellow dress holding 1930s-style 6-pack, with base, cond. 6.5-7.25, 48" h, 18" w .......... 3,300.00
  1957, "Slow School Zone," policeman with shield-shaped sign, back with button logo and bottle, with base, cond. 9.25-9.5, 64" h, 30" w ............. 4,290.00
  1962, "Slow School Zone," policeman with shield-shaped sign, back with fishtail logo, bottle and "Thank You, Resume Speed," with base, cond. 9.5-9.75, 64" h, 30" w........................ 4,510.00
Sign, tin, die-cut
  6-pack, 1953, "Delicious and Refreshing," all-red carton, cond. 9.5-9.75+, 11" h, 13" w ............. 1,760.00
  6-pack, 1962, embossed, "King Size," gold highlights on carton, paint chips, cond. 8.25+, 30" h, 36" w ..................................................... 1,430.00
  6-pack, 1960s, embossed, "King Size," blue highlights on carton, fishtail logo, late 1950s-early 1960s, cond. 9-9.25, 30" h, 36" w........................ 1,595.00
  Hobbleskirt bottle, Oct. 1947, cond. 9, 16" h........ 176.00
  Hobbleskirt bottle, 1951, cond. 9.5-9.75+, 16" h ................................................................. 220.00
Sign, tin, embossed
  1934, "Drink Coca-Cola" on red ground, hobbleskirt bottle on green ground to left, "Ice Cold" on black ground at bottom, in 1960s aluminum frame, NOS, cond. 9-9.25+, 20" h, 28" w ......................... 742.50
  1961, "Drink Coca-Cola, Enjoy That Refreshing New Feeling," white text on red fish tail ground on white, clean-cut ends, rolled top/bottom border, cond. 9.25-9.5, 24" h, 36" w .................................. 143.00
Sign, tin, flange
  1954, round, "Enjoy Coca-Cola In Bottles," white text over hobbleskirt bottle, red ground, cond. 8/7.25, 18" dia..................................................... 3,300.00
Sign, tin, rack sign, 2-sided, "Enjoy Coca-Cola At Home, Take Home A Carton, 36¢," yellow/white text, red ground, Canadian, late 1930s-early 1940s, cond. 7.5-8+, 16" h, 11" w....................................... 253.00
Sign, tin, salesman sample, 1920s-1930s, "Serve Yourself,

**Sign, tin, 1960s, "Ice Cold Coca-Cola, Enjoy That Refreshing New Feeling," red fishtail logo, white ground, cond. 9-9.25, 20" h, 28" w, $302.50. (Photo courtesy of Gary Metz, Muddy River Trading Co.)**

Drink Coca-Cola, Please Pay the Clerk," mkd "Stenpho Co., Dayton, OH" on back with list of signs/emblems they make, cond. 7.5-8, 3-1/4" h, 6" w ....................... 2,750.00
Sign, tin, self-framed
  1914, "Drink Coca-Cola, Delicious and Refreshing," Betty sign, woman in pink dress/white hat, cond. 7, 41" h, 31" w ............................................... 6,490.00
  1947, string-hung, Sprite Boy with bottle and button sign, French or French Canadian, cond. 9.5-9.75, 12-3/4" dia ................................................ 1,045.00
  1960s, "things go better with Coke," red text over red button over hobbleskirt bottle, cond. 9-9.25, 54" h, 18" w...................................................... 412.50
  "Drink Coca-Cola" and "Take home a carton," red/yellow with 6 bottles in cardboard carrier priced 30¢, scratches/chips, 53-1/2" h, 17" w ................. 825.00
Sign, tin, spinner sign, 4 button-logo wings, 1950s, orig mounting base missing the suction cups, cond. 9.5+ ..................................................... 2,090.00
Syrup dispenser, ceramic, 1896, base, bowl and lid, no spigot, some repairs to bowl, cond. 5-6 ......... 1,815.00
Thermometer, tin
  1930s, rounded top/bottom, gold hobbleskirt bottle, red ground, cond. 6, 16" h ............................ 143.00
  1940, "Drink Coca-Cola, Delicious and Refreshing," silhouette of girl drinking bottle of Coke, cond. 7, 16" h, 6-1/2" w .............................................. 231.00
  1950s, embossed, rounded top, "Drink Coca-Cola In Bottles" on red button at top, "Quality Refreshment" in red at bottom, white ground, black stripes, NOS, cond. 9.5-9.75, 9" h, 3" w ............................... 825.00
Tip tray
  1903, tin, woman with glass, "Delicious Refreshing," cond. 9.6-9.7, 4" dia ................................... 6,270.00
  1907, "Drink Coca-Cola, Relieves Fatigue 5¢," woman holding up glass, cond. 8.5-8.75................... 742.50
  1909, "Drink Coca-Cola," woman with glass leaning against table, cond. 8.5 .............................. 357.50
  1913, "Drink Coca-Cola, Delicious And Refreshing," woman in wide/dark hat with glass, cond. 9.25................................................................ 357.50
  1914, "Drink Coca-Cola, Delicious And Refreshing," woman in white bonnet, cond. 8.5 ............... 247.50
  1916, "Drink Coca-Cola" on rim, outdoor scene of woman with glass, 2 roses in foreground, cond. 8.25................................................................ 209.00
  1920, "Drink Coca-Cola," outdoor scene of woman in yellow dress/white hat with glass, cond. 8 ............209.00
Toy
  Car, litho tin, Ford taxi, friction, made by Taiyo (Japanese), 1960s, orig box, cond. NM, 3" h, 10-1/2" w .................................................... 302.50
  Dispenser, plastic, with 4 plastic glasses, dispenses from bottle, handle stuck in closed position with bottle attached, cond. 8-8.5 ............................. 121.00
  Roll toy, metal, made to be used with a stick, 1930s, cond. 8-8.5............................................... 193.00
  Truck, Buddy L, model 5426, pressed steel, yellow with 5 cases and 2 hand trucks, orig box cond. 7, truck cond. 9-9.25+, 15" l.............................. 550.00

Writing tablet, "Drink Coca-Cola," unused, 10" h, 8" w, $22.50.

Truck, Marx, model 991, pressed steel, early 1950s, red cab, yellow bed, orig box cond. 8-8.5, truck cond. 9.5+, 20-1/4" l ................................. 1,072.50

Same truck as above, yellow cab/bed, cond. 8-8.25, 20-1/4" l ........................................ 467.50

Truck, Marx, model 1088, tin, yellow stake truck, orig box cond. 8.5, truck cond. 9.5+, 18-3/4" l ............ 1,100.00

Truck, Marx, model 1090, tin, yellow with 12 mini cases of Coke and hand truck, cond. 7.5+, 17-1/2" l .................................................... 632.50

Truck, Marx, model 21, metal, 1954-1956, with 8 cases, orig box cond. 8-8.5, truck cond. 9.5, 12-1/2" l .................................................... 962.50

Truck, Marx, plastic, cardboard side panels picture cases, 6 plastic cases on top, 1956, cond. 9, box cond. 8 .......................................................... 605.00

Trade card

1892, shows woman sitting at soda fountain, framed, cond. 6.5-7, 5-1/2" x 3-1/2" ..................... 2,090.00

1907, folding, "Drink Coca-Cola," shows woman in bathtub when closed, shows same woman with tray serving Cokes to 2 seated gentlemen when open, cond. 8.5-9, 3-1/2" h (closed), 5-1/2" h (open), 6-1/4" w ................................................. 1,265.00

Train

Express Limited #2, 1970s-1980s, NRFB, cond. 9.5 ................................................... 209.00

Lionel, circa 1973-1974, missing some track, train orig box cond. 7, train cond. 9 .......................... 343.00

Tray

1907, large oval, "Drink Coca-Cola, Relieves Fatigue, 5¢," woman in green dress with white trim, glass in right hand, gold border, cond. 7.5-7.75, 16-1/2" h, 13-1/2" w ................................................. 5,060.00

1908, Topless, semi-nude woman, "Wherever Ginger Ale, Seltzer or Soda is Good, Coca-Cola is Better - Try It," few shallow dents/bends, rim with scratches/ chips, cond. 8.25-8.5 ...............................11,000.00

1914, Betty, woman in white shawl and bonnet, "Drink Coca-Cola, Delicious and Refreshing," "Ward Gayden" engraved above bonnet, possibly a presentation tray, chips, cond. 8.5-8.75 ..................... 550.00

1914, Betty, oval, woman in white shawl and bonnet, "Drink Coca-Cola, Delicious and Refreshing," cond. 8.5+, 15-1/4" h, 12-3/8" w ............................ 605.00

1922, Summer Girl, woman in wide-brim hat, cond. 8.5 ................................................... 935.00

1926, Golfing Couple, man pouring drink for seated woman, cond. 9 ........................................ 1,045.00

1927, Curb Service, man and woman in car, cond. 8-8.25+ ................................................... 852.50

1928, Soda Jerk, cond. 6.5-7 ............................ 367.50

1928, Bobbed Hair Girl, girl drinking from bottle with straw, image cond. 9.5, overall cond. 8.75 ........935.00

1931, The Barefoot Boy, boy in straw hat sitting on ground eating lunch, puppy at this feet, cond. 8.5 ................................................... 1,045.00

1932, Girl in Yellow Bathing Suit, girl sitting on deck chair, cond. 8.25 ...................................... 715.00

1934, Maureen O'Sullivan and Johnny Weissmuller, cond. 8.75-9.25 ...................................... 1,815.00

1937, Running Girl, woman in yellow bathing suit, cond. 9.25-9.5 ............................................. 495.00

1938, Girl at Shade, woman in yellow dress and straw hat, blue shade in background, cond. 9.75+ .....577.50

1939, Springboard Girl, woman on diving board, Spanish, cond. 8.75 ........................................... 253.00

1940, Sailor Girl, girl in sailor outfit sitting on dock, cond. 9.25-9.5+ .......................................... 605.00

1941, Skater Girl, woman in skates sitting on log, cond. 9.25-9.5+ .......................................... 412.50

1942, Two Girls at Car, cond. 9.25 ................... 687.50

1953, Menu girl, cond. 8-8.25 ............................ 66.00

Vienna art plate, 1908-1912, woman in white dress and red hat, gold frame and black shadowbox frame, cond. 9.5-9.75 ................................................... 990.00

Whistle, cardboard, pictures straight-sided bottle, circa 1910, framed, cond. 7-7.5, closed measures 6" h, 1-1/2" w .......................................................... 522.50

Window banner

"...And Take Home," shows 6-pack bottle and 1947, cond. 9.5+, 9" h, 25" w ................................. 44.00

"Redeem Coupons Here for Coca-Cola Cartons," shows 6-pack of bottles, 1940s, cond. 9.25, 7" h, 22" w .......................................................... 121.00

Window display, cardboard, Sprite Boy with triangular-shaped 6-pack, "Take Home a Carton" and "Easy to Carry" on 6-packs on each side, 1947, NOS, cond. 9.75 .......................................................... 4,400.00

Window shade, bamboo, "Drink Coca-Cola In Bottles," 1910s-1920s, cond. 6-6.5, 51" x 93" ................. 440.00

Tin, sample, litho tin, pry lid, "Cocomalt, A Delicious Food Drink, Chocolate Flavor," 2-3/4" h, $7.50.

Boxes, cardboard, Colgate's Lilac Imperial (toilet water) and Rapid-Shave Cream, in orig box, each 3" h, $45.

## Coca-Cola Gum

Blotter, "Best Sanitary, Made to Chew, Franklin Card Co., Richmond, Va.," shows 2 packs of gum, mid-1910s, cond. 8.5-8.75, 4" h, 9-1/2" w ............................ 742.50

## Cocoa Coffee

Can, litho tin, sample, "Cocoa Coffee, Roasted and prepared by our exclusive process, Cocoa Coffee Co., Boston," cond. 8, 2" h, 1-5/8" sq ....................... 209.00

## Cocomalt (See Photo)

## Cody Cigars

Cigar box, wood and cardboard, paper label under lid shows Buffalo Bill Cody, cond. 8 ....................... 176.00

## Co-Ed Dresses

Sign, litho tin, "Co-Ed Dresses, Shown Here Exclusively," female graduate on round blue ground/gold border, text in gold on lower banner, chips/scratches/dents, 23-3/4" h, 18-3/4" w ............................................ 55.00

## Coffee House Coffee

Can, keywind, litho tin, "Day'sa Breakin, Ye Olde Bacon, Stickney Coffee House, 1834,"" shows men dining, cond. 8+, 1 lb, 4" h, 5" dia ................................. 231.00

## Coles Bitters

Sign, porcelain, "No More Malaria, Coles Peruvian Bark and Wild Cherry Bitters Will Cure You, The Best Nerve and Blood Tonic," white on blue ground, cond. 8+, 6" h, 16" w ................................................................ 1,705.00

## Colgan's Gum

Display case, oak and glass, wooden top, acid-etched lettering, lists 6 flavors, new shelves/supports/finish/ hardware, cond. 8.5+, 18" h, 9" w, 8" d ............. 660.00

## Colgate

**History:** Having originally sold soaps and candles in

Baltimore in the early 1800s, William Colgate founded William Colgate & Company in New York City in 1806. In 1847, the company was relocated to Jersey City, N.J.

Colgate toothpaste was introduced in 1877. Initially sold in jars, it wasn't until 1890 that the product was marketed in a tube.

Sign, paperboard, "Colgate Talc Powder," shows floral-dec tin of "Violet Talc Powder," white text, black ground, Colgate & Co., framed, cond. 8-, 10" h, 8" w .............. 132.00

Tin, litho tin
"Colgate Eclat Talc Powder," sample, white text on blue ground in yellow/white medallion, white ground with blue horizontal band, gold top, full, cond. 9, 2-1/4" h, 1-1/4" w ......................................... 63.00
"Colgate's Monad Tinted Talc, an Exquisite Violet Perfume," cond. 8.25............................................ 99.00
"Colgate Talc for Men, Invisible, Soothing, Refreshing," blue on white ground, cond. 8, 3-1/4" h, 1" w, 3/4" d ......................................................... 27.50

## College Girl Talc

Tin, litho tin, "Steltex College Girl Talc, Affinity Co., Grand Rapids, Mich.," girl with tennis racket, light-blue ground, circa 1920s, cond. 8.5, 6" h, 1-3/4" w, 1-1/2" d ........................................................... 660.00

## Colonial Club Cigars

Sign, flange, painted metal, "Colonial Club 5¢ Cigars," yellow/red text, dark ground, scratches/chips to edge, 8-3/4" h, 18" w.................................................. 126.50

## Colonial Dame Coffee

Pail, litho tin, "Colonial Dame Steel Cut Coffee, Southern Gateway Corporation Roasters and Packers, Hagerstown, Md.," oval portrait of woman, red floral drape, blue ground, cond. 7.5-8, 5 lb, 8" h, 7-3/4" dia.............. 357.50

## Colonial Gas

Sign, porcelain, 2-sided, "Colonial Gas," green text, white

ground, reverse side painted over, cond. 8/7, 23" h,
49" w ......................................................................... 198.00

## Colonial Ice Co.

Sign, porcelain, die-cut, "Colonial Ice, Ice Co." in red on
white circle, "Health Guard" in green on white horizontal panel, green border, cond. EXC, 11-3/4" h,
21" w ......................................................................... 440.00

## Col-tex

Gas globe, newer plastic body with 2 lenses, "Col-tex" in
white on red diagonal band with stripe above/below,
white ground, "Property of Coltex Refining Company,"
lens cond. 9/8.5, body cond. 9, 13-1/2" dia .......... 242.00

## Colton's Cough Drops

Tin, "Colton's Cough Drops For Coughs & Colds Are
Without A Rival, Will Relieve Dyspepsia & Catarrh,"
fanciful embellished design, green ground, hinged lid,
cond. 8+, 7" h, 5" w, 5-1/2" d ............................ 550.00

## Columbian Coffee

Can, keywind, litho tin, name in black/red in white diamond
over "S&W" in black oval with starburst, plantation
scenes on brown ground, cond. 8-8.5, 1 lb ............. 55.00

## Columbia Veterinary Remedies

Sign, paper litho, shows trotting horse "Nancy Hanks"
with driver, cond. NM, 7" h, 10" w ..................... 165.00

## Comet Tobacco

Lunchbox, paper label, "Comet Plug Cut Tobacco," yellow comet and stars, cobalt ground, 1910 tax stamp,
cond. 7.5-8 ...................................................... 281.00

## Comfort Powder

Tin, litho tin, "Comfort Powder," red text on side with baby,
other side shows nurse, cond. 9-, 3-1/2" h ............ 412.50

## Comrade Coffee

Can, litho tin, "Comrade Steel Cut Coffee," dog's head in
gold oval, gold text, white ground, J.A. Folger & Co.,
Kansas City, San Francisco, no lid, dents/scratches/
stain, 3 lb, 7" h, 6-1/8" dia ................................ 93.50

## Concord Dairy

Sign, porcelain, from milk wagon, "Concord Dairy, Inc.,
Milk, Cream, Pasteurized, Lic. 242," white/red, New
Hampshire, EXC, 22" dia .................................. 275.00

## Conkeys First Aid Products

Sign, painted metal, die-cut, "Conkeys First Aid Products"
beside rooster with hurt foot, "Poultry Service Station" at
bottom, "First Aid" in red circle, rest in black/yellow
design, chips/bubbling, 20" h, 14" w ..................... 165.00

## Conoco

**Reference:** Todd P. Helms, *The Conoco Collector's
Bible*, Schiffer Publishing, 1995

Can, metal,
"Conoco Motor
Oil, Medium,
Continental Oil
Company,"
Minute Man on
white panel,
yellow ground,
cond. 8/7, gal,
11-1/4" h, 8" w,
3" d, $1,375.
(Photo cour-
tesy of Collec-
tors Auction
Services)

Salt/pepper shakers, plastic, gas pump shape, white,
"Conoco" triangular logo, "Conoco" and "Conoco
Super," orig box, cond. 8+, 2-3/4" h, 1" w, pr .... 170.50
Sign, porcelain
"Do Not Oil While In Motion," red text over red triangular logo, black stripes/border, white ground, cond. 8,
8" h, 15" w ................................................. 176.00
2-sided, round, "Conoco Gasoline," Minuteman logo,
black/red text, yellow ground, restored, cond. 9/7,
23" dia ...................................................... 715.00

## Constans Coffee

Can, litho tin, slip lid, "Constans Brand 'Constantly Good'
Coffee," cobalt/gold/red text and gold sunrise on white
panel, blue ground, Consumers Wholesale Supply Co.,
Minneapolis, paint chips/scratches/dents, 9-1/2" h,
5-1/2" dia ....................................................... 22.00

## Continental Cubes Pipe Tobacco

Pocket mirror, celluloid, oval
Portrait of woman with flowing hair, "Latest and Best
Process, Continental Cubes Pipe Tobacco," cond.
EXC, 3" h, 1-3/4" w ...................................... 313.50
Woman in red dress sitting on pocket tin while holding
cards in her hand, some spotting in mirror glass,
otherwise like new, 2-3/4" h, 1-3/4" w ........... 357.50
Tin, vertical pocket, litho tin
Concave, shows standing man in 18th-century attire
reading a paper, cond. 8-, 3-3/4" h, 3-3/4" w ...... 385.00
Shows standing man in 18th-century attire reading a
paper, cond. 8+, 4" h .................................... 466.00
Shows standing man in 18th-century attire reading a
paper, cond. 8.5, 4-1/2" h ............................. 660.00

## Continental Insurance Co.

Sign
Glass, reverse-painted, die-cut lettering, figure

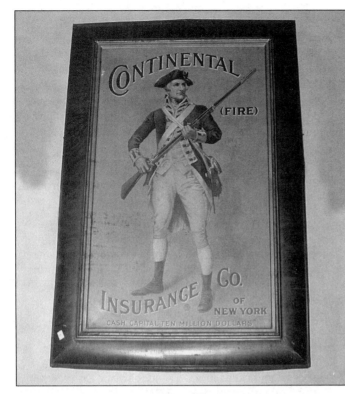

Sign, litho tin, self-framing, "Continental (Fire) Insurance Co. of New York," rust/scratches, 30-1/4" h, 20-1/4" w, $450.

recessed under glass, "The Continental Insurance Company, One of the American Fore Insurance And Indemnity Group," soldier at left, lists cities, cond. EXC, 13" h, 21" w ............................. 82.50

Paper, "Continental Life Insurance Company of New York," early patriot with gun trudging through snow, framed, cond. 9, 27" h, 21-1/2" w .............. 1,017.50

## Cook Book Salt

Box, waxed paper over cardboard, "Cook Book Salt by Texaco," red with Texaco star logo, resembles cookbook, cond. EXC, 3 lb, 8" h, 5" w, 2-3/8" d ...................... 522.50

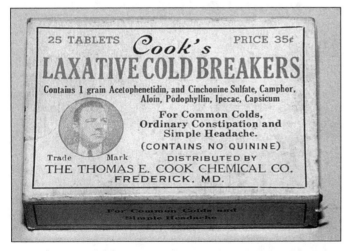

Box, cardboard, "Cook's Laxative Cold Breakers, The Thomas E. Cook Chemical Co., Frederick, Md.," 25 tablets, 1-5/8" h, 2-3/8" w, $3.

## Cook's Goldblume (See Photo)

## Cook's Laxative (See Photo)

## Cooper Beverage

Seltzer bottle, blue glass, fluted, chromed top, "Cooper Beverage, Pittsfield, Mass.," cond. 7-7.5 .......... 143.00

## Cooper's Sheep Dipping Powder

Sign, porcelain, "The King Of Dips, Cooper's Sheep Dipping Powder, A Trump Card Every Time," king of spades motif, fading/touch-ups to chips, 30" h, 20" w ........935.00

## Cooper-Tox (See Photo)

## Co-Op Motor Oil

Sign, tin, embossed, "Use Co-Op Motor Oil, Buy With Confidence," red/blue logo, blue/white/red text, white over black ground, Consumers Cooperative Association, Kansas City, cond. 7+, 10" h, 20" w .......... 143.00

## Coors Malted Milk

Sign, litho tin, wood frame, "Cook's Goldblume Beer, A Quality Cargo in 1853, F.W. Cook Co., Evansville, Ind.," wear/scratches, 23-1/2" h, 29-3/4" w, $125.

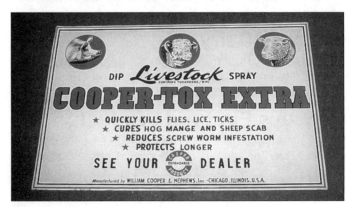

Sign, litho tin, "Cooper-Tox Extra, Livestock Dip Spray, Manufactured by William Cooper & Nephews, Inc., Chicago, Illinois, U.S.A.," 24" h, 36" w, $30.

Can, tin, "Coors Pure Malted Milk" on front, "The Malted Milk With A Distinctive Flavor" on side with round logo of mountains, white ground, Adolph Coors Co., Golden-Denver, CO, stains/soiling/dents, 25 lb, 14-3/4" h, 9-3/8" sq .................................................. 61.50

## Copenhagen

Dispenser, litho tin, "Fresh Copenhagen, It's a pleasure," black/white, red ground, 14-1/2" h, 3" dia .......... 22.00

Door push, celluloid over tin, "Pull, Fresh Here," shows can of snuff, orig envelope/instructions, cond. 9.5+, 8" h, 3" w ........................................................ 132.00

## Copy-Right Typewriter Ribbons

Tin, litho tin, shows Indian in headdress, red ground, blue image on bottom, cond. 8+, 3/4" h, 2-1/2" sq...... 44.00

## Corduroy Tires

Sign, lightup, reverse-painted glass, wood frame, "Replace With Corduroy 'Factory Fresh' tires, Extra Quality," white on red ground, cond. 8, 11-1/2" h, 18" w ..................................................... 203.50

## Cork Town

Tin, vertical pocket, litho tin, "Tobins Cork Town Pipe Tobacco," circular medallion with green top hat in green vertical bar, white ground, cond. 8-8.5 ............... 1,724.00

## Corn Bread

Sign, heavy paper, "Chew Rich and Mellow Corn Bread," shows product on yellow ground, cond. 8+, 18" h, 30" w ........................................................ 28.00

## Corn King Manure Spreaders

Sign, paper, "Corn King Manure Spreaders, International Harvester Company of America," oval farm images of brook scene and horse-drawn manure spreader in field, 2 panels show 2 different models, ©1908, archival backing, cond. G, 25-1/2" h, 20" w .............. 550.00

## Corona Wool Fat

Cabinet, wood, "Corona Wool Fat For Horses & Cows" painted above/below glass-pane door, chips/stains/warping/cracks/worn paint, 23-3/8" h, 14-3/8" w, 9-3/8" d ..................................................... 192.50

## Corylopsis of Japan

Tin, litho tin, shows Japanese woman with parasol, Imperial Perfumery Co., Saint Louis, cond. 8.5+, 4-1/2" h, 2-1/2" w ..................................................... 302.50

## Cough Checkers

Matchsafe, litho tin, hinged flip lid, striker on base, "Cough Checkers, Check Huskiness, Tickling Cough and Sore Throat," white text on red panel, black/white checkered ground, cond. 8.5, 3" h, 1-1/2" w, 1/4" d ...................................................... 44.00

## Country Club Tobacco

Lunch box, litho tin, "Country Club Smoking or Chewing Kentucky Long Cut, The Scotten Tobacco Co., Detroit, Mich.," motif with tobacco leaves, blue/gold, severe rust, cond. 6 ............................................ 75.00

Tin, vertical pocket, litho tin, slide lid, fat version, silver/black text, red ground, cond. 8+, 3-3/4" h, 3-1/2" w, 1-1/4" d ................................................ 506.00

## Cowan's

Sign, paper, "Cowan's Milk Chocolate" in white over girl in red hat/holding product, floral border, red ground, orig "Cowan's" frame, cond. 8.5, 25-1/4" h, 18" w .................................................... 385.00

## Cow Baking Soda

Sign, heavy paper, "Cow Brand Baking Soda, This Is An Enlarged Copy, A Small Card Packed In Each Package," on border, product lower-right, shows "Irish Setter" in field, new frame, ©1903, Church and Dwight co., EXC, 14-1/2" h, 18" w ............................... 176.00

## Cowboys and Indians Cookies

Box, cardboard, covered wagon pulled by 2 running horses, red Nabisco logo in corner, yellow ground, string handle, ©1956, unopened, cond. EXC, 3" h, 5" w, 1-3/4" d ....................................................66.00

## Cow Chow

Scale, hanging, brass, "Cow Chow Makes More Milk, Don't Guess, Use This Purina Milk Scale," metal back, minor wear/scratches, 15-1/2" h, 4-1/2" w........................................................ 66.00

## Cow-Ease

Display with sprayer, metal on footed base, "Spray Your Team Free, Cow-Ease Keeps Flies Off Cattle and Horses," shows man spraying a cow, minor scratches/fading, 34" h, 21" w, 12" d ................................ 825.00

## Cracker Jack

**History:** When Frederick William Rueckheim added molasses to popcorn in 1896, the concoction became known as Cracker Jack. Beginning in 1910, each box contained a coupon that could be redeemed for a prize. It wasn't until 1912 that the prizes themselves were placed in the boxes.

The Cracker Jack sailor boy and his little dog Bingo first appeared in the company's advertisements in 1916 and debuted on the boxes in 1919. Early toy prizes were made of paper, wood, and even lead, with plastic toys introduced after 1948.

**References:** Alex Jaramillo, *Cracker Jack Prizes*, Abbeville Press, 1989; *Larry White, Cracker Jack Toys: The Complete, Unofficial Guide for Collectors*, Schiffer Publishing, 1997

**Collectors' Club:** Cracker Jack Collectors Assoc., P.O. Box 16033, Philadelphia, PA 19114

Collector's tin, 2nd in a series, 8-1/8" h, 5-7/8" d, $5.

**Museum:** COSI Columbus, 280 E. Broad St., Columbus, OH 43215, phone 614-228-2674

Display, cardboard, 2-fold, "The year 'round confections," shows Cracker Jack and Angelus Marshmallows boxes with product spilling out, circa 1920s, 20" h, 27" w .................................................. 242.00

# Crayola (See Photo)

# Cream Dove

Cup, litho tin, "Cream Dove Brand Salted Peanuts," flying dove in round medallion, cond. 8-, 2-1/8" h, 2-1/4" dia.......................................................... 198.00
Tin, litho tin, "Cream Dove Blanched and Salted Whole Peanuts, Prepared By Cream Dove Mfg. Co., Binghamton, N.Y.," white dove in blue medallion on yellow/blue ground, cond. 8, 10 lb ............................. 165.00

# Cream of Wheat

**History:** In 1893, Tom Amidon, a miller working at the Diamond Mill in Grand Forks, Iowa, persuaded the mill's owners to produce a new porridge product that his wife had created. Aptly named Cream of Wheat, the product originally came in boxes made of hand-cut cardboard decorated with an old woodcut of a black chef holding a saucepan over his shoulder.

The new breakfast cereal was quite popular, and in 1897 the company relocated to Minneapolis, Minn. Company legend says that one of the company's owners, Emery Mapes, spotted a black waiter in a Chicago restaurant and asked him to pose for a picture that could be used for the Cream of Wheat chef. It is the only likeness that has been used by the company, although the figure was updated in 1925 and has appeared in several poses.

Advertisement, magazine ads, circa 1920, cond. 9.25, 15-1/2" h, 10-1/2" w, lot of 4 ................................ 49.50
Doll, cloth, uncut, black waiter with bowl of "Cream of Wheat," white jacket/red-white striped pants, circa 1915, cond. 9.5, 17" h, 28" w ............................ 102.50

# Credo Peanut Butter

Pail, litho tin, "Credo Brand Peanut Butter, Cream Dove M'f'g Co. Inc., Binghamton, N.Y.," oval with "Credo" in red on white, "Peanut Butter" in white, red ground, cond. 8+, 1 lb, 3-3/4" h, 3-1/4" dia ................... 142.00

# Crème de la Crème Tobacco

Tin, horizontal box, litho tin, "Crème de la Crème Smoking Mixture," oval portrait of woman, cond. 8.5, 2" h, 5" w, 3-3/4" d............................................................. 181.50

# Crescent Beverages (See Photo)

# Crescent Coffee

Can, keywind, litho tin, "Crescent Vacuum Packed Coffee," white text in white crescent moon, blue ground, cond. 8, 1 lb ...................................................... 27.50

# Crescent Flour

Door push, litho tin, embossed, "Push And Try a Sack of Crescent Flour, Sold Here," shows sack of product

Blotter, paper, "50 Years of Crayola Leadership," 3-3/8" h, 6-1/4" w, $22.50.

Sign, tin, embossed letters, "Crescent Beverages Since 1893," NOS, 14" h, 20" w, $30.

Box, paper, "Cretors Pop Corn," stain and foxing, 10" h, 7" w, $20

Chair, folding, wooden, "Cross-Cut Cigarettes," black motif, shows court- ship front, wedding scene on back, 31" h, $550.

with star in crescent moon, white on cobalt, cond. 8+, 9-5/8" h, 3-3/4" w ...............................110.00

## Crescent Salted Peanuts

Tin, litho tin, pry lid, scroll design with image of boy/girl carrying crescent moon hung from a pole, Crescent Nut & Chocolate Co., Philadelphia, scratches/dents/ scuffs, 10 lb, 9-3/4" h, 8-1/4" d .......................... 302.50

## Cretors Pop Corn (See Photo)

## Cricco Typewriter Ribbon

Tin, litho tin, square, bottom shows warrior/bow&arrow/ headdress, Consolidated Ribbon & Carbon Co., cond. 8 ............................................... 27.50

## Crispaco Salted Peanuts

Can, litho tin, "Crispaco Salted Peanuts, Guaranteed by Crisp Packing Co., Petersburg, Va.," red round emblem in center, white text on flowing green design, red ground, 10 lb, lid cond. 5, can cond. 8........ 247.50

## Cross, Abbott Co.

Box, display, wood, paper label under lid, "Cross, Abbott Company, White River Junction, Vt., Absolutely Pure, Ground Spices, Mustard," shows girl lower-left, black/ red text on yellow ground, cond. 8+, 12" x 14-1/4" x 8-1/4"............................................... 193.50

## Cross-Cut Cigarettes (See Photo)

## Crossed Swords Plug Cut

Tin, litho tin, square corner, shows crossed swords, 2 portraits of women, yellow ground, J.B. Pace Tobacco Co., Richmond VA, cond. 8 ................................. 48.50

## Crossman Bros. Seeds

Poster, litho paper, "Crossman Bros. Seeds, Rochester, N.Y.," woman holding basket of "New Crop, New

Black-Eyed Wax Bean," beans in background, cond. NM, 24" h, 18" w ............................................. 1,072.50

## Crowfoot Typewriter Ribbon

Tin, litho tin, square, "Crowfoot Typewriter Ribbon," spread- wing bird, black text, red ground, cond. 7.5 ............. 82.50

## Crowley's Needles

Cabinet, oak, "Crowley's Needles" decal on long drawer top/bottom, 2 rows of 5 new drawers each in center, porcelain pulls, cond. EXC, 9-1/2" h, 18-3/4" w, 9-5/8" d ............................................. 253.00

## Crown Jewel Peanut Butter

Pail, litho tin, white diamond with red/gold crown in cen- ter, gold ground, F.M. Cobb Co., Cortland NY, cond. 7.5, 14 oz, 3-1/4" h, 3-3/4" dia .......................... 166.00

## Crown Quality Ice Cream

Sign, tin, embossed
"Crown Quality Ice Cream, Andreson & Patterson Mfgrs, Worcester, Mass.," white text on green/red ice cream cooler filled with ice, black ground, dents/scratches, 29" h, 21" w .....................................550.00
"Crown Quality Ice Cream," puffy crown in oval, red/ black text, yellow ground, scratches/stains/dents, 24" h, 18" w ................................................. 170.50

## Crubo Apple Butter

Sign, trolley, cardboard, "Don't be a goose, Get it, Crubo Apple Butter, Crusikshank Bros. Co.," child and 5 white geese, blue/white text, newer frame, cond. EXC, 12" h, 19-1/2" w................................................. 82.50

## Cruiser Motor Oil

Can, tin, "Crusier 100% Pure Pennsylvania Motor Oil" under

ship, panel over black diamond on yellow ground, ©1932, no top, cond. 7+, qt, 5-1/2" h, 4" dia ......... 126.50

## Crystal Flash Motor Oil

Can, metal, "Crystal Flash" in blue on white burst on blue ground, "Tough Film Motor Oil" in red on white panel at bottom, red band top/bottom, unopened, cond. 8+/7+, qt, 5-1/2" h, 4" dia ............................................. 88.00

## Cub Tobacco

Sign, tin, rolled top/bottom edge, "Smoke Cub, Best Tobacco 10¢ Can Buy," "Smoke" in oval at left, bear in oval at right, white ground, cond. G, 1" h, 15" w ................................................................. 121.00

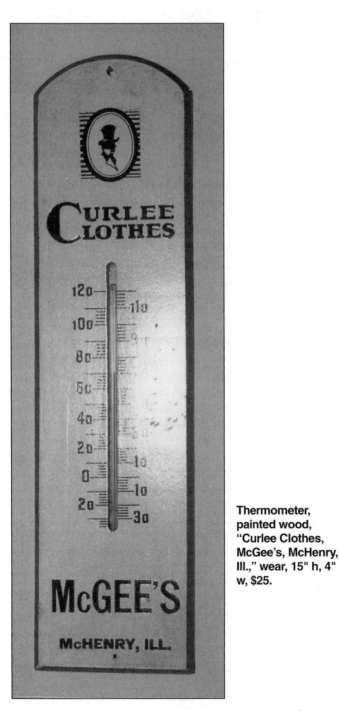

Thermometer, painted wood, "Curlee Clothes, McGee's, McHenry, Ill.," wear, 15" h, 4" w, $25.

Sign, tin, red and white, "Curtiss Baby Ruth Gum," wear, scratches, $150.

## Culture Smoking Tobacco

Pack, paper label, sample, "Culture Crimp Cut Smoking Tobacco, Sure Quality" on yellow medallion on yellow/ black striped ground, opened from bottom, cond. 8, 2-1/4" h ............................................................. 105.00

Tin, vertical pocket, litho tin, "Culture Crush Cut Smoking Tobacco, Super Quality, Scotten Dillon Company, Detroit, Mich." on yellow medallion, yellow/black striped ground, cond. 8 ..................................... 147.00

## Cunningham's Ice Cream

Tray, litho tin, "Cunningham's Ice Cream, Famous For Over 40 Years," ice cream in stemmed dish, circa 1920s, cond. 8+, 10-1/2" h, 13-1/4" w.............. 467.50

## Curlee Clothing

Calendar, paper, 1921, die-cut, easel-back, "Curlee Clothes, Curlee Pantsman" in suit holding calendar area, unused, full pad, 5-3/4" h, 3-1/2" w.......... 198.00

## Curtiss

Displayer, metal rack, 5 round tiers, rotates, round 2-sided tin sign at top, "Play Safe, Curtiss Saf-T-Pops, Safety Handle," white on red ground, scratches/chips, 19" h, 7" dia, sign 5-1/4" dia............................. 187.00

Toy, truck, Curtiss Candy Truck, plastic, Marx, 1950s, cond. 9-9.5, orig box cond. 7.5, 9" l .................. 302.50

## Custom House Cigars

**History:** Custom House brand was created by Jacob Stahl Jr. & Company, but the trademark was transferred to The American Cigar Company in 1902. Labels showed various custom houses where the duty on imported tobacco was collected. Facilities in Boston, Chicago, New York, and St. Louis were represented.

Tin, litho tin, slip lid, "Custom House Club Perfectos," full-can image of building/street traffic, "Custom House" in red at top, cond. 7.5-8, 5-1/2" h, 5-1/2" dia ....... 235.00

## Cuticura Talcum Powder

Tin, litho tin, sample, small top, mother on one side/baby on other, black on red, cond. 8, 2-1/4" h, 1-1/4" w............................................................. 27.50

# D

## D.C.&H. Coffee

Can, litho tin, round medallion shows woman at flax wheel, floral border, white ground, Driscol, Church & Hall, New Bedford MA, cond. 8, 6" h, 4" dia........................ 1,760.00

## Dad's Cookie Co.

Jar, glass, clear, embossed, "Property of Dad's Cookie Co.," Pyrex, 15" h, 10-1/2" dia ......................... 181.50

## Dad's Root Beer

**History:** Before the formula for Dad's Root Beer was developed, the company was called the Original Chicago Distilled Water and Beverage Company. The trademarked image of a smiling boy with upswept hair has been used to promote Dad's Root Beer since the 1940s. The beverage was sold in a 12-ounce "Junior" size, a quart "Mama" size, and a half-gallon "Papa" size.

Can, litho tin, conetop
- 12 oz, "Delicious Dad's, Old Fashioned Root Beer" yellow diagonal box, yellow/white checkered ground, black band at bottom, 1940s-1950s, cond. 7+...................................................... 275.00
- Qt, 1940s-1950s, cond. 7.5-8 ........................... 154.00

Sign, litho tin, embossed
- "Have A Dad's Old Fashioned Root Beer…It's Delicious," wide diagonal yellow band, 2 dark corners, red trim, 1950s, cond. 9.75, 18" h, 46" w......................... 275.00
- Same with cobalt corners, cond. G, 19" h, 27" w.......................................................... 176.00
- "Unbelievable, Dad's Root Beer," "Dad's" in bottle cap at right, red/black text, white ground, 1950s-1960s, cond. 9.5, 12" h, 30" w................................. 275.00

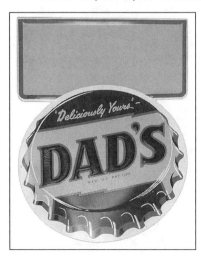

**Sign, litho tin, die-cut, embossed, "Deliciously Yours, Dad's," NOS, 28" h, 20" w, $176.**

Sign, tin, embossed, "Dairy Made Ice Cream, You're sure - It's pure," wood frame, 1920s, cond. 6.5-7, 28" h, 20" w, $825. (Photo courtesy of Gary Metz, Muddy River Trading Co.)

"You'll love Dad's…tastes like Root Beer should!," yellow diagonal panel with "Dad's" in black/red trim, yellow text on cobalt ground, yellow/red border, unused, cond. 9.25, 12" h, 31" w................. 203.50

## Dairy Made Ice Cream

Sign, tin, embossed, "Dairy Made Ice Cream, You're sure - It's pure," seated child holding cone, wood frame, edge wear/scratches, 35" h, 26" w.................... 770.00

## Dairymen's League

Sign, porcelain, "Dairymen's League, Member, Dairymen's League Co-operative Association, Inc.," white/cobalt text, cobalt over white ground, considerable chips at 3 corners, 7" h, 14" w ........................... 44.00

## Daisy Typewriter Ribbon

Tin, litho tin, "Daisy Brand Typewriter Ribbon," daisy in blue square, red text, green ground with red-outlined daisies, cond. 8, 3/4" h, 2-3/8" sq .................... 357.50

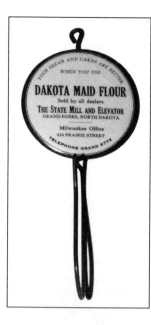

Bill hook, celluloid, "Dakota Maid Flour, The State Mill and Elevator, Grand Forks, N.D.," 2-1/2" dia, $35.

Biscuit cutter, embossed tin, "Davis Baking Powder, None Better," $22.50.

# Dakota Maid (See Photo)

# Dallas Brewery

Tip tray, litho tin, "Dallas Brewery Home Beer, Dallas, Texas," 4-1/4" dia ................................................ 71.50

# Dana's Cut Plug

Tin, paper label, square corner, image of warrior with helmet having bird design, blue ground, 1883 revenue stamp, cond. 7, 1-1/2" h, 4-1/2" w, 3-1/4" d ........... 86.00

# Dan Patch Cut Plug

**History:** The Dan Patch brand was a full line of tobacco, with packages featuring the most famous pacer of all time. A record holder at several distances, the horse died July 11, 1916, and his grief-stricken owner passed away the following day. Roasted coffee was also sold under the Dan Patch name.

Lunch box, litho tin, 2 handles, Dan Patch/sulky/driver on red circle, yellow ground, cond. 7.5-8 ............... 192.50

# Darigold

Tin, litho tin, "Darigold Sweet Cream Butter," cow in gold oval, white ground, gold bands, blue band at bottom, gold/white text, cond. 8+, 1 lb, 2-3/4" h, 4" dia ................................................................ 143.00

# Dauntless Coffee

Can, paper label, "Dauntless Regular Grind Coffee, Roasted and Packed by 'Ye Olden Coffee House,' Hulman & Co., Terre Haute, Ind." warrior logo on both sides, red ground, cond. 8+, 6" h, 4-1/4" dia ................... 121.00

# Davis Baking Powder (See Photo)

# Dayton Peanut Butter (See Photo)

# Dead Shot Powder

Watch fob, brass, celluloid front shows falling duck, "Dead Shot Powder" in border, back advertises Ameri-

Tin, litho tin, "Dan Patch Cut Plug," 6" w, 4" d, $110.

Pail, tin, "Dayton Peanut Butter, The Dayton Nut Products Co., Dayton, Ohio," wear, rust, 7 oz, 3" h, $38.50.

can Powder Mills, scratches to celluloid,
1-1/2" dia........................................................ 198.00

# Deep Rock

Gas globe, 2 lenses, newer plastic body, "Deep Rock" in
blue on yellow panel with blue divider, white ground,
base melted on body, lenses cond. 9, body cond. 7,
13-1/2" dia........................................................ 181.50

# Deep-Rock

Can, tin, "Goes Farther, Deep-Rock, Lasts Longer, Petroleum Products," early "7" racer, "Deep-Rock" in red,
striped ground, Shaffer Oil and Refining Co., Chicago,
cond. 7, gal, 10-1/4" h, 8" w, 3" d ................... 1,045.00
Sign, tin, embossed, "Deep-Rock Prize Oil," red/black text,
black border, cond. 7, 19-1/8" h, 27" w ................... 55.00

# Deerfoot Farm Sausages

Sign, cardboard, "Deerfoot Farm Sausages, Made at the
Farm in Southboro, Mass. of Choicest Materials, For
Sale Here," pig with front hooves over edge of black
circle/white trim, white/black text, red ground, cond. 9,
11" h, 15-1/4" w ................................................. 102.50

# Deering

Calendar, 1906, paper, woman in blue dress on stone
wall, "Deering Harvesters" sign in background, "Deering Ideal Binders" advertised on calendar pad, complete pad, cond. 8.5+, 20-1/4" h, 13" w ............. 302.50

# Deerwood Coffee

Can
Paper label on cardboard, tin top/bottom, color image
of 12-point buck, cond. 8.5, 5-7/8" h,
4-1/4" dia ..................................................... 467.50
Litho tin, keywind, "Deerwood Coffee" in white on red
panel, buck between "Steel Cut/Vacuum Packed"
on white ground, cond. 8.25+, 1 lb ............... 412.50

# Defender Motor Oil

Can, tin, "Defender Motor Oil, 100% Pure Paraffin Base, De-
Waxed," GI at left, white/blue text, red/blue ground, Penn-

**Tin die-cut cow and calf, "De Laval Cream Separators"
advertising on back, bent legs, cond. VG, pr, $176. (Photo
courtesy of Collectors Auction Services)**

sylvania Petroleum Products Co., Philadelphia, cond. 7,
2 gal, 10-3/4" h, 8-1/2" w, 5-1/2" d ......................... 104.50

# Defiance

Tin, litho tin, "Defiance Allspice," knight on horseback, cond.
8.5+, 2 oz, 3-1/4" h, 2-3/8" w, 1-1/4" d ................... 176.00

# Dekalb

Sign, cardboard, die-cut, 2 1-sided signs bolted together,
"Dekalb" in red on yellow ear of corn with green wings,
soiling/edge wear, 16" h, 31-3/8" w ..................... 55.00

# De Laval

**History:** In 1879, Swedish engineer Dr. Carl Gustaf
De Laval invented a machine that could quickly separate cream from milk, thereby avoiding the wait for the
cream to rise to the top. In addition to dairy separators,
the firm also produced butter churns, milk pumps, pas-
teurizers, and emulsifiers by the end of the century.

Based in New York City, the company advertised on
everything from tip trays to match safes, and from catalogs to calendars.

Calendar
1909, paper, "De Laval Cream Separators, Save $10 to
$15 Per Cow Every Year of Use, 1,000,000 Machines
in Use," oval scene of woman in pink dress on rock in
stream, cows wading behind her, full pad, tears/
crease/staining, 19-5/8" h, 12-5/8" w ................. 577.50
1949, paper, "De Laval Separators, Milkers, Food
Freezers, Water Heaters," shows product demon-
stration at fair, full pad, orig mailing tube, 44" h,
17-1/2" w ...................................................... 264.00
Match holder
Litho tin, die-cut, shape of cream separator, unused,
orig box, 6-1/4" h, 4" w ................................. 797.50
Pocket knife, metal, "De Laval Cream Separators,
World's Standard, Nearly 2,000,000 In Use," handle
3-1/2" l ............................................................ 176.00
Sign
Porcelain, flange, "De Laval Authorized Agency," yel-
low/blue design, shows separator with 2 buckets,
circa 1920s-1930s, cond. 9.25-9.5, 26" h,
18" w ............................................................. 1,265.00
Tin, orig gesso frame, "De Laval Cream Separators" 4
vignettes of cows/cream separators, central oval
image of woman with cow, frame mkd "De Laval,"
minor scratches to tin, edge wear to frame, 41" h,
29-1/2" w ...................................................... 1,265.00
Tip tray, litho tin, "De Laval Cream Separators, Over
750,000 In Use" on rim, "Save $10.00 to $15.00 Per
Cow Every Year of Use, The De Laval Separator Co.,
New York, Chicago, Montreal" around cream separator on white ground, cond. 8, 4-1/4" dia ............ 275.00

# Delaware Punch

Dispenser, 3-pc, milk glass body, metal lid/pedestal,
"Delicious Delaware Punch," white on black ground,
circa 1930s, cond. 7, 12" x 10-1/2" ............... 1,017.50

Sign, flange, painted metal, "Replace with a Delco," red over white ground, cond. 7, 18-1/2" h, 22-1/2" w, $154. (Photo courtesy of Collectors Auction Services)

## Delco

Ashtray, porcelain, oblong, "Delco" in white in red triangle, blue ground, cond. 8, 5-1/4" x 3-1/2".............11.00
Sign, painted metal, 2-sided, "Delco Dry Charge" on auto battery, yellow text, white ground, black border, cond. 8.5, 20" h, 26" w................................. 209.00

## Delicious Coffee

Can, litho tin, "Delicious Brand Coffee, McTighe Grocery Company Distributors Binghamton, New York," floral accents, cond. 8+, 1 lb, 6" h, 4" dia.................. 154.00

## Del Monte Mixture

Tin, vertical pocket, litho tin, blue ground,
cond. 6 ............................................................ 264.00

## Denver Sandwich Candy

Sign, litho tin, embossed
   Strip, "New Denver Sandwich Candy 5¢," white/yellow text, red ground, 1940s-1950s, cond. 9.5, 2-1/2" h, 22" w................................................ 121.00
   "New Denver Sandwich Candy 5¢," yellow/white text, red ground, cond. G, 11-3/4" h, 23-3/4" w................ 77.00

## Derbies

Tin, litho tin, "Derbies, Quality Guaranteed" on green band, yellow ground, shows jockey cap and crossed whips, Ess-Jay Labs, cond. 8, 1/4" h, 2-1/4" w, 1-5/8" d.......................................................... 385.00

## Desoto

Sign, porcelain, composition, embossed, helmeted Desoto image in center, missing neon, cond. 7+, 37-1/2" dia...................................................... 335.50

## DeSoto Coffee

Can, small pry top, litho tin, "DeSoto High Grade Coffee," small cup, black/yellow text, wave-like black ground under white, cond. 8.25, 1 lb.................. 38.50

## Detroit Club

Tin, vertical pocket, slide lid, fat version, "Detroit (in banner) Club Plug Cut Mixture Manufactured for Charles J. Holton, Detroit, Mich.," cond. 8+, 3-1/2" h, 5" w ............................................................. 2,938.00

## Detroit-Special Overalls

Display, cardboard, standup, die-cut, pig shape, "Finck's Detroit-Special Overalls, Wear Like a Pig's Nose, For Sale Here, Union Made," text on white pig/green grass, cond. G, 24-1/2" h, 34-3/4" w................ 198.00

## Devoe Paints & Varnishes

Sign, flange, litho tin, die-cut, "The First American Paint Maker, Devoe, Founded 1754," oval medallion shows Indian painting his face, paint chips/scratches, 26" h, 15" w .......................................................... 2,090.00

## De Voe's Tobacco

Tin, vertical pocket, litho tin
   Concave, "De Voe's Sweet Smoke, Manufactured By De Voe Tobacco Co., Stock Owned By United States Tobacco Co., Richmond, Va., U.S.A.," crossed pipe and cigarette with lettering in smoke cloud, red ground, cond. 8.5........................ 495.00
   "De Voe's Makings, Roll Your Own, Manufactured by De Voe Tobacco Co., Stock Owned By United States Tobacco Co., Richmond, Va., U.S.A.," crossed pipe and cigarette with lettering in cloud, red ground, cond. 8.5 ................................... 781.00

## Devotion Coffee

Can, litho tin, snap top, "Page's Devotion Brand Coffee," oval scene of older couple drinking coffee, yellow ground, cond. 9, tall 1 lb ................................. 288.00

## Dial Tobacco

Tin, vertical pocket, litho tin
   "Dial Smoking Tobacco, 100% Burley," orange dial with white "D," red ground, cond. 8+ ............. 91.50
   "Dial Smoking Tobacco, For Pipe And Cigarettes," orange dial with white "D," red ground, cond. 9................................................................ 140.00
   "Dial Smoking Tobacco, Turn To A Real Smoke," orange dial with white "D," red ground, cond. 7.5...................................................... 67.00

## Diamond Dyes

**History:** Diamond Dyes debuted in 1881 and were available in 36 colors suitable for all types of fabrics and feathers.

Cabinet, tin, "Best Results, Diamond Dyes for Dyeing or Tinting, The Blue Package is for Silk or Wool Only..., Easy to Use, Diamond Dyes for Dyeing or Tinting, The White Package Dyes or Tints Any Goods...," white diamond logo on doors, red/yellow diamond logo on side, 2 doors, holder on side, chips/dents/scratches/stains/ rust, 15-5/8" h, 18-1/2" w ................................ 121.00

Matchbook holder, brass, hinged cover, "Dietz Lanterns, A Good Light," 2-1/8" h, 1-5/8" w, $30.

Tin, pocket, litho tin, "J.G. Dill's Best Cube Cut Plug, Richmond, Va.," 4 oz, 2-3/4" h, $55.

Cabinet, wood, litho tin panel
   "Diamond Dyes, The Standard Package Dyes of the World," 5 children playing near steps, house in background, blue/yellow text, opens from front/back, cond. G, 24-5/8" h, 14-3/4" w, 8-1/8" d ..................... 1,072.50
   "The Diamond Dyes, Domestic Fancy Dying," child in diamond-shaped frame surrounded by flowers/feathers, cond. 8+, 20-1/4" h, 16-1/2" w, 9-1/4" d ..................... 3,630.00
   "It's Easy To Dye With Diamond Dyes," woman dying clothes from basin on work table, refinished case, cond. 7, 29-3/4" h, 22-1/4" w, 9-3/4" d ........... 1,375.00
   "It's Easy to Dye With Diamond Dyes," woman/girl with ribbon, other children with ball, chips/scratches/worn finish, 30" h, 23" w, 10" d ..................... 880.00

## Diamond Edge Tools

Sign, tin, embossed, "Diamond Edge Tools," red text below white courtesy panel with merchant info, "DE, Diamond Edge Is A Quality Pledge, Tools And Cutlery" logo at left (red-diamond over yellow circle), blue ground, cond. VG, 9-3/4" h, 27-1/2" w ................ 38.50

## Diamond Matches

Dispenser, metal, coin-op, "3 Books Diamond Matches One Cent," matchbooks flank crank in center, round body, inverted V-shape pedestal, cond. VG, 13-1/2" h, 10-1/2" w, 5-1/2" d............................................. 522.50

## Diamond Stars Chewing Gum

Wrapper, waxy paper, ball player on red star on yellow ground, premium offer to exchange 15 wrappers for Major League photo art pictures of stars, National Chicle Co., cond. EXC, 6-3/8" h, 5" w ..................... 148.50

## Dietz Lanterns (See Photo)

## Dill's Best

Box, vertical pocket, cardboard, sample, "Dill's Best, A Fragrant Smooth Natural Tasting Smoking Tobacco

For Pipes, J. G. Dill Company, Richmond, Va., U.S.A., Sample, Not to be Sold," central oval medallion with woman, yellow ground, cond. 8.5, full size ......... 39.00
Display, tray with 3 pocket tins, cond. 8-8.5, 12" w, 7-1/4" d ............................................110.00
Tin, litho tin
   Flat pocket, "Dill's Best Sliced," girl in red dress, yellow ground, 3/4" h, 3-3/4" w, 2-3/8" d................... 29.00
   Horizontal box, litho tin, "J.G. Dill's Best Cut Plug," oval medallion with woman at left, yellow ground, cond. 9............................................................ 29.00
   Vertical box, litho tin, "J.G. Dill's Best Rubbed Cube Cut, Richmond, Va.," girl motif at left, yellow ground, cond. 8.5, 2-3/4" x 3-1/2" x 2-1/8".................. 38.50
Tin, vertical pocket, litho tin
   Complimentary, "Dill's Best, A Fragrant Smooth Natural Tasting Smoking Tobacco For Pipes, J. G. Dill Company, Richmond, Va., U.S.A.," and white oval with "Complimentary Regular Size Package Free," central oval medallion with woman, yellow ground, full, cond. 8 ................................................... 75.00

Tin, pocket, litho tin, "Dill's Best, J.G. Dill Co., Richmond, Va.," 4-1/2" h, $44.

Sample, "Dill's Best A Fragrant Smooth Natural Tasting Smoking Tobacco For Pipe or Cigarette, J.G. Dill Company, Richmond, Va., U.S.A., United States Tobacco Co. Successor," also "Sample, Regular 15 (Cent) Size, Not To Be Sold," waist-up view of woman in oval, yellow ground, full, cond. 8+ ................ 231.00

Sample, "J.G. Dill's Best Granulated Tobacco," large central oval medallion with woman, yellow ground, cond. 7.5 ...................................................... 253.00

Short version, "J.G. Dill's Best Rubbed Cube Cut Plug, Richmond, Va.," girl motif at left, yellow ground, cond. 8+, 2-3/4" h ............................................ 60.50

Tall version, "J.G. Dill's Best Rubbed Cube Cut, Richmond, Va., U.S.A.," woman in oval at left, black design, yellow ground, cond. 8, 4-1/2" h ............................................................. 85.00

"Dill's Best Smoking Tobacco, Rubbed, J.G. Dill Co., Richmond, Va. U.S.A.," woman in oval in center, yellow ground, cond. 8.5 ............................... 133.00

"Dill's Best, A Fragrant Smooth Natural Tasting Smoking Tobacco For Pipes, J. G. Dill Company," woman in oval in center, yellow ground, full, cond. 8+ ......... 44.00

## Diamond Chewing Gum

Tin, embossed, diamond shape, lift-off lid, cond. EXC, 5/16" h, 2" w, 1-3/8" d ......................................... 366.00

## Dilnorpa Baby Talcum

Tin, litho tin, "Dilnorpa Baby Talcum, Boraxed, The Dill Company, Norristown, Penna.," shows baby, gold text, blue ground, cond. 8.5, 6" h, 2-1/4" w, 1-1/4" d ........................................................... 1,155.00

## Dilworth's Golden Urn Coffee

Can, keywind, litho tin, oval with red lettering and urn, gold flourishes, yellow ground, cond. 8, tall 1 lb ........... 224.00

## Dining Car Coffee

Can, keywind, tin, "Dining Car Coffee, Norwine Coffee Co., St. Louis," 1 lb, $405.

## Dino Gasoline

Gas globe

New Capcolite plastic body with 2 glass lenses, "Dino Supreme" in red under green/red Sinclair logo with dinosaur, lens cond. 8, body cond. 7, 13-1/2" dia ................................................... 198.00

Newer plastic body with 2 lenses, "Dino Gasoline" green/red text under green/red Sinclair logo with dinosaur at top, all cond. 9, 13-1/2" dia ........ 258.50

## Diplomat Whiskey

Sign, litho tin, orig gesso frame, "Diplomat Whiskey, Just Right, Glasner & Barzen Distilling and Importing Co., Kansas City, Mo.," group of dignitaries drinking at table, paint chips/yellowing/scratches, 37-1/2" h, 50" w .............................................................. 605.00

## Dixie Boy

Pack, rice paper, "Dixie Boy Brand Flashlight Crackers, Loi Sze Pau Chuk," black boy in straw hat eating slice of watermelon, unopened, cond. 9, 3-1/4" h, 2" w, 2 packs ............................................................ 110.00

## Dixie Chop Cut Tobacco (See Photo)

## Dixie Cigarettes

Tin, litho tin, farmer and tobacco field in green, Canadian, cond. 8 .............................................................. 94.00

## Dixie Cups

Dispenser, metal with glass cup holder, "Dixie Cup Company, Easton, Pa., Chicago, Ill., U.S.A., Patented Dec. 15, 1913," white paint specks/scratches, 32" h ............. 440.00

## Dixie Gasoline

Gas globe, 2 lenses

Clear ripple body, blue metal bands, "Dixie Oils Gasoline, Power To Pass," "Oils" in red on yellow diamond at center, "Dixie Gasoline" in white on blue

Tin, litho tin, "Allen & Ginter's Dixie Chop Cut Plug Smoking Tobacco, Allen & Ginter Branch of the American Tobacco Co., Richmond, Va.," 1-3/4" h, 4-1/2" w, 3-1/4" d, $195.

oval around "Oils," "Power To Pass" in blue on yellow ground, lenses glued onto body, lens cond. 9/8.5, body cond. 9, 13-1/2" dia .................... 1,100.00

Newer plastic body with "Dixie Premium Gasoline," "Premium" in red on yellow diamond at center, "Dixie Gasoline" in white on blue oval around "Oils," yellow ground, 1 lens cracked, lens cond. 8.5/6, body cond. 9, 13-1/2" dia .............................. 192.50

Wide body, "Dixie Oils Gasoline, Power To Pass," "Oils" in red on yellow diamond at center, "Dixie Gasoline" in white on blue oval around "Oils," "Power To Pass" in blue on yellow ground, lenses glued onto body, lens cond. 8.5, body cond. 9, 13-1/2" dia .................................................... 231.00

## Dixie Kid Cut Plug

Lunch box, litho tin, "He Was Bred In Old Kentucky" on light-blue ground with red and yellow trim, "Dixie Kid Cut Plug, Nall & Williams Tob. Co. Inc., Louisville, Ky.," shows black boy on cotton, cond. 8+, 4-1/4" h, 7-7/8" w, 5-1/4" d................................................................. 357.50

## Dixie Milk

Sign, cardboard, "They All Go For" in black, "Dixie Milk" in red reflective text, text on yellow panel below old man/boy in homemade go-cart, dog racing alongside, cond. G, 22" h, 14" w ........................................ 143.00

## Dixie Queen Tobacco

Can, litho tin, small top, "Dixie Queen Plug Cut," red text, woman in large hat, white ground, cond. 8+, round.................................................................... 333.00

Lunchbox, litho tin
    Basketweave version, cond. 8 ...........................115.50
    "Dixie Queen Plug Cut Smoking Tobacco," round images of woman in large hat, light-blue/white ground, cond. 8+, 4" h, 7-7/8" w, 5-1/4" d ............................... 330.00

## Dixon's Stove Polish

Trade card, paper, Lime-Kiln Club, "Brother Gardner Addresses the Lime-Kiln Club on the Virtues of Dixon's Stove Polish," room full of black men, cond. NM, 5-1/8" h, 6-1/4" w.......................................... 77.00

## Dodge

**History:** Brothers John and Horace Dodge both worked as mechanics in Niles, Mich., before starting their own automotive business in Detroit in 1901. They began by producing automobile engines for companies including Oldsmobile Corporation, and they quickly became one of the largest suppliers in the country. At some point in time, the brothers became stockholders in the Ford Motor Company, but by 1913, that relationship had ended.

Advertisements for the "new Dodge Brothers' car" began appearing in 1914, and in that same year, the company was incorporated as Dodge Brothers Motor Car Company. The early Dodge Brothers emblem consisted of a turquoise-and-white six-pointed star superimposed on a globe.

Bank, tin, barrel-shape, "Economy Barrel, Save Six (55 Gallon) Barrels of Gas A Year With Dodge, Bank the Difference," dents, wear, 4" h, $75.

In spite of the fact that the company was extremely successful, it was unable to meet its payroll in 1928 and was purchased by the Chrysler Corporation.

Bank, tin, barrel shape, "Owners Report, Dodge Saves Up To 6 Barrels Of Gas In A Year, Switch To Dodge And Save Money," white on red ground, cond. 9, 3-3/8" h, 2-1/16" dia ............................................. 55.00

Lighter, metal, pickup over "From Pickups To Diesel Power," other side shows semi over "Dodge Builds Tough Trucks," cond. 7, 2-3/8" h ....................... 33.00

Sign, neon, porcelain, die-cut, "Dodge Plymouth," white text/border, blue ground, no transformer or neon, cond. 7+, 28" h, 60" w....................................... 935.00

## Dog-On Good Cigars

Can, paper label on tin, "A Dog-On Good Cigar," shows dog standing in open box of cigars, circa 1920s, cond. EXC, 5-1/4" h, 5" dia ...................................... 2,310.00

## Dom Benedictine

Sign, porcelain, die-cut, round with extended panel, "Dom Benedictine Liqueur," black text on yellow ground, "Benedictine" in white on blue panel, shows bottle, chips/scratches/cracks, 39" h, 49" w ..............................165.00

## Domestic Sewing Machine

Sign, paper, "The Little Savage, copied from a piece of embroidery done on The Light Running Domestic Sewing Machine," woman in tropical setting, circa 1915, framed, 27" h, 12-1/2" w ........................ 528.00

Bag, sample, paper wrapper, "Sample, Domino Cane Sugar, Granulated, American Sugar Refining Company," 2-1/2" h, $2.50.

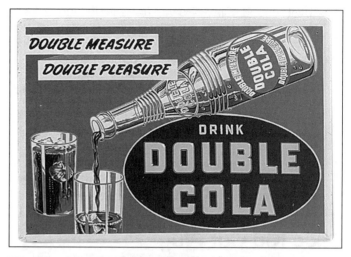

Sign, tin, embossed, "Double Measure, Double Pleasure, Drink Double Cola," bottle pouring into glass, 1 glass already full, text in 2 white bars at top, black oval at bottom, red ground, 1940s, cond. 9-9.25, 20" h, 28" w, $550. (Photo courtesy of Gary Metz, Muddy River Trading Co.)

## Dominion Condoms

Tin, litho tin, "Dominion Transparent, Three For One Dollar," shows woman, brown/tans, cond. NM, 1/4" h, 2-1/8" w, 1-3/4" d............................................ 1,155.00

## Dominion Tires

Thermometer, porcelain, rounded top, "Drive Safely, Ride On Dominion Tires," shows tire, black/white text, red ground, cond. 8, 30" h, 10" w............................ 825.00

## Domino Sugar (See Photo)

## Donald Duck Coffee

Can, litho tin
 Keywind, "Donald Duck High Grade Pure Coffee," cartoon figure on yellow ground, cond. 8+, 1 lb, 3-5/8" h, 5" dia.......................................................... 742.50
 Sample, coin-slot lid, "Free Sample," full-figure Donald Duck on yellow ground, cond. 8.5, 2-1/4" h, 3" dia ............................................. 565.00

## Donald Duck Soft Drinks

Sign, celluloid, pictures head of Donald Duck, 1940s-1950s, cond. 6, 9" dia ......................................... 55.00

## Don-Dé Coffee

Tin, litho tin, keywind, yellow cup on dark panel, yellow/red/blues ground, Weppner-Weil Co., Cleveland, cond. 8, 1 lb .................................................... 149.00

## Donniford

Can, vertical pocket, litho tin, tall version, small pipe on yellow ground, dark stripe at top/bottom, cond. 9, 4" h, 3-3/8" w ........................................................... 121.00

## Double Cola

Chalkboard, tin, "Drink Double Cola" in white on red oval, green ground at top with 3 stripes, blackboard at bottom, chips/edge dents, 28" h, 20" w................... 77.00
Sign
 Painted metal, die-cut, "Drink Double Cola" in white on red oval, green ground with 3 stripes, V shape to stand from wall like flange, minor chips, 20" h, 32" w............................................................... 302.50
 Tin, "Enjoy Double Cola" in red oval, white starbursts at sides, white text, green ground with white stripes, white border, cond. VG, 18" h, 54" w............. 110.00
 Tin, embossed, diamond, "Drink Double Cola" in yellow on black oval over starburst, red ground, rounded inner panel, cond. G, 45" h, 45" w..................... 165.00
Thermometer, tin
 "Drink Double Cola, you'll like it better" red ovals top/bottom, white ground, 1960s, cond. 9.5, 17" h .......................................................... 165.00
 "Drink Double Cola, you'll like it better" red ovals top/bottom, white ground, 1960s, chips/fading, 27" h, 8-1/2" w ........................................................ 88.00

## Douglas Ethyl Gasoline

Sign, tin, embossed, "Douglas Ethyl Gasoline," black/red text on white ground, winged heart at left on dark ground, cond. 8, 10" h, 14" w............................ 385.00

## Dove Meats

Sign, litho tin, "Dove Brand Sugar Cured Family Meats & Leaf Lard, The John C. Roth Packing Co., Cincinnati, O.," woman with doves, sea in background, cond. 8+, 27-3/4" h, 19-5/8" w ....................................... 1,650.00

## Dove Spices

Tin, litho tin, round, "Dove Brand Imported Paprika," white doves facing each other, "Imported Paprika" on

Box, cardboard, "Frank's Dove Brand Whole Caraway Seed, The Frank Tea & Spice Co., Cincinnati, Ohio," 1-1/4 oz, $10.

red panel, white text, dark ground, Frank Tea & Spice Co., Cincinnati, cond. 8+, 3-1/2 oz...................... 93.50

## Dowagiac Grain Drills (See Photo)

## Drake's Cake

**History:** Because his pound cake recipe was so popular with family and friends, Newman E. Drake opened his own bakery, Drake Baking, in 1896. He continued to run the operation even after it was purchased by the forerunner of Nabisco.

In 1900, Newman's sons started Drake Brothers Bakery in Brooklyn in 1900. The two bakeshops began selling Devil Dogs in 1923 and Yankee Doodles cupcakes in 1929, after taking over Yankee Cake Company of Providence, R.I.

Pocket mirror, oval, "Drake's Cake, Pure Food," portrait of woman, light wear, 2-3/4" h, 1-5/8" w............ 742.50

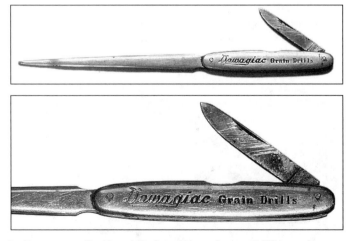

Letter opener/knife, plated metal, embossed "Dowagiac Grain Drills," handle marked "H. Keschner, Germany" and "Antelope," 9-1/8" l opened, 7-1/4" l closed, $157.50.

## Drake's Palmetto Wine

Match holder, hanging, litho tin, duck in flight in yellow circle, medicinal cure, cond. 7.5, 4-7/8" h, 3-5/8" w ......... 412.50

## Dr. Caldwell Syrup Pepsin

Sign, cardboard, die-cut, standup, easel-back
"Dr. Caldwell originator of Syrup Pepsin, A Doctor's Family Laxative," well-dressed doctor holding product, unused, cond. NM, 15" h, 6" w .............. 605.00
"Hey Mom! Where'd Grandpa Put The Syrup Pepsin" in voice balloon by boy in striped pajamas, "He wants the Liquid Laxative" in arched panel, "Dr. Caldwell's Syrup Pepsin combined with Laxative Senna Compound For All Ages," boy stands on stool by open medicine cabinet over bathroom sink, wear to edges/tape repair/minor stain, 37" h, 27" w........................................................... 137.50

## Dr. Daniels

**History:** Started by Dr. A.C. Daniels in 1895 and incorporated in 1899, this producer of veterinary products was out of business by 1916. Because the company was active for only a short time, items related to it are particularly valued by collectors. Dr. Daniels used his own image to advertise his line of products.

Bottle, paper label on amber glass, 12-sided, "Dr. A.C. Daniels' Grape Oil," portrait/chicken, cork top, full, cond. EXC, 3-1/4" h ............................................. 99.00
Pinback button, celluloid, "Dr. A.C. Daniels' Horse Medicines," central close-up image of mad-looking horse, cond. EXC, 7/8" dia............................................. 385.00
Sign, paper, orig cardboard mat
Dogs playing baseball, dogs in stands, stadium billboards advertise product, cond. EXC, 12" h, 15" w....................................................... 1,017.50
"Be honest to your pets, Give them the Best, You know it's Dr. Daniels'," dogs playing poker, circa 1915, orig wrapper, unused, like new, 13-1/2" h, 18" w............................................................. 412.50

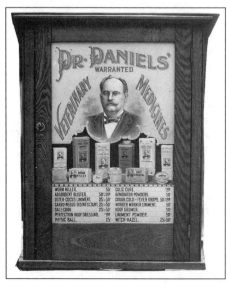

Cabinet, wood, tin front, "Dr. Daniels' Warranted Veterinary Medicines," shows doctor with 12 packages/containers of product over price list, cond. 8+, 27" h, 21" w, 7-1/2" d, $6,710. (Photo courtesy of Wm. Morford)

"Dr. Daniels' Cough, Cold and Fever Drops," 5 horses at fence, by R.A. Fox, cond. 8+, 11" h, 17" w ............................................................... 440.00

"Dr. Daniels', Hoof Dressing, On Guard for the Hoofs," German shepherd in front of 6 horses, cond. 8- , 14" h, 17" w .......................................... 385.00

"Use Dr. Daniels' Dog Medicine, Is The Winner Over Them All," dogs playing football, cond. EXC, 14" h, 20" w ............................................. 605.00

"Use Dr. Daniels', Don't get caught," dogs at game table, cond. NM, 14" h, 18" w ...................... 330.00

"Use Dr. Daniels', For Your Friend When In Need," dogs playing poker, cond. 8.5+, 14" h, 18" w ............ 242.00

"Use Dr. Daniels', For Your Pets," dogs playing cards, cond. 8.5+, 14" h, 18" w ................................ 385.00

Thermometer, painted wood

"Dr. A.C. Daniels' Famous Veterinary Medicines, Home Treatment For Horses and Cattle, Dog Remedies," and advertising for New York merchant, cond. 7, 20-3/4" h, 5" w ................................ 385.00

"Dr. A.C. Daniels' Warranted Horse Remedies/Horse Medicines," lists various horse cures, cond. 7, 21" h, 4-7/8" w, ........................................................ 385.00

Tin, litho tin, hand-soldered, "Dr. Daniels' Hoof Food, Perfection Hoof Dressing," Dr. Daniels on front, hooves in various states of health on back, cork top, cond. 7, 4-3/4" h, 3-1/8" dia .............................................. 305.00

Tip tray, litho tin, "Dr. A.C. Daniels' Horse & Cattle Medicines," shows heads of 3 white horses, scalloped edge, cond. NM, 4-1/4" dia ............................ 1,705.00

# Dr. Hess

Sign, flange, litho tin, banner shape, "Dr. Hess Stock & Poultry Preparations Sold Here," shows horse/cow/pig/sheep/chickens, yellow/blue ground, cond. 7-8, 11" h, 18-1/4" d ..................................................... 880.00

# Dr. Hoffman's Red Drops

Match holder, hanging, litho tin, bottle on blue ground, red trim, rust, 5" h, 3-3/8" w, 1-1/4" d ................ 412.50

# Dr. LeGear's

Tin, litho tin, "Dr. LeGear's Gall Remedy," shows horse/cow, red/black design, Dr. L.D. LeGear Medicine Co., St. Louis, cond. 8.5, 1-1/2" h, 3-1/2" dia ............. 33.00

# Dr. Lesure's

Cabinet, wood, glass front

"Dr. Lesure's Medicines, Warranted, Veterinary," stenciled lettering, 27" h, 20-3/4" w, 6-3/4" d .................. 2,035.00

"Dr. Lesure's Warranted Veterinary Medicines" stenciled on bonnet top, circa 1890s, cond. 8+, 28-1/2" h, 15-3/4" w, 5-3/4" d ....................................... 1,485.00

Cabinet, wooden, litho tin panel, "Dr. Lesure's Famous Remedies," shows horse peeking through oval opening, refinished case, cond. 8+, 26-7/8" h, 20-3/4" w, 6-3/4" d ....................................................... 5,060.00

Pocket mirror, celluloid, "Dr. Lesure's Remedies, Prove their worth by the results they accomplish, Free Pri-

vate Treatment of Domestic Animals, Send for Free Booklet," shows doctor/cow/horse/sheep, cond. 8.5+, 2-1/8" dia ....................................................... 632.50

# Dr. Morse's Indian Root Pills

Display, countertop, cardboard, die-cut

3 sections, "Dr. Morse's Indian Root Pills, Favored for 50 Years for Constipation and Biliousness," shows Indian grinding roots with teepees in background, edge wear/soiling, 27" h, 41-1/2" w .............. 605.00

Shows Indian in canoe hunting fish, creases/soiling, 9-1/2" h, 19-1/2" w ......................................... 187.00

# Dr. Pierce's

Sign, paper, "Used by the First Americans, Dr. Pierce's Golden Medical Discovery," shows Indians scanning horizon, creases/color touchup, 41" h, 27-3/4" w ....................................................... 1,072.50

# Dr. Pepper

**History:** Charles Courtice Alderton is credited with creating Dr. Pepper in 1885. W.B. Morrison coined the name, and R.S. Lazenby, a Waco, Texas, chemist, perfected the drink.

After introducing Dr. Pepper at the World's Fair Exposition in St. Louis in 1904, Morrison and Lazenby made their partnership a formal arrangement and opened the Artesian Mfg. & Bottling Company. In 1923, they relocated the company to Dallas, and in 1924 they renamed the business the Dr. Pepper Company. Early logos contained a period after "Dr," but by 1950, the punctuation had been eliminated.

**Collector's Club:** Dr. Pepper 10-2-4 Collector's Club, 3100 Monticello, Suite 890, Dallas, TX 75205

**Museum:** Dr Pepper Museum, 300 S. 5th St., Waco, TX 76701, phone 254-757-1025 or 800-527-7096

Ashtray, glass, "Dr Pepper," white text in red oval over gold "V," white ground on round interior of square ashtray, 1960s, cond. 8.5 ........................................ 66.00

Badge, name

Enameled, red checkered logo at top, "at 10-2-&4 o'clock" at bottom, 1930s, cond. 9, 1-1/2" h, 2-1/4" w ....................................................... 412.50

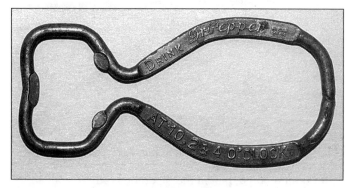

**Bottle opener, metal, "Drink Dr. Pepper At 10, 2 & 4 O'Clock," other side says "Drink A Bite To Eat," light rust, 3-1/2" l, $23.**

Metal, red/white oval logo at top, "at 10-2&4 o'clock" at bottom, 1930s, cond. 7, 1-3/4" h, 2-1/4" w.......................................................522.50

Blotter, paper

"at Ten, Two & Four," white/red/white banner over 3 tilted bottles with 10-2-4 clock logo, "Dr. Pepper" red checkered logo lower-right, green ground, 1940s, cond. 9.5........................................................ 264.00

"Drink Dr. Pepper, King of Beverages, Free from Caffeine and Cocaine, At Fountains and in Bottles," black text, white ground, cond. 8.5 ................110.00

"Plenty Good at 10-2-4," boy with dog, Dr. Pepper logo, 1930s-1940s, cond. 8 ........................... 121.00

Bottle, seltzer, glass, fluted

Amber, Memphis TN, cond. 9.25-9.5 ................ 990.00

Blue, Amarillo TX, small nicks, interior stains, cond. 7.5............................................................. 3,850.00

Dark-green, narrow waist, Shreveport LA, cond. 8.5+..................................................... 935.00

Green, doctor at top, Amarillo TX, stained interior, cond. 7.5.............................................. 3,630.00

Bottle, syrup, clear glass, foil label, "Dr. Pepper, King of Beverages," 1920s, 70% of gold border remains, light edge chipping, no cap, cond. 7.5+ ................. 2,310.00

Bottle opener, metal, embossed "Drink Dr. Pepper," reverse mkd "Little Rock Bottling Co.," spearhead-shaped end with notch for bottlecaps, loop at opposite end, cond. 8.5, 7-1/2" l...................................... 247.50

Box, cardboard

Fountain syrup, held 4 1-gal jugs, circa 1930s, cond. 6.5-7 ........................................................... 55.00

Same as above, 1966, cond. 6.5-7 ...................... 5.50

Button, pinback, celluloid, "Perk Up with Dr. Pepper, Good For Life," red text, red checkered logo, black 10/2/4, yellow border, 1940s-1950s, cond. 9.25-9.5, 4" dia.............................................................. 660.00

Calendar

1935, "Yo! Ho!...Energy Up!" above woman on ship, slanted "Dr. Pepper 5¢" solid-red logo, artwork by Earl Moran, framed, missing metal strip at top, December page only, cond. 7-7.5, 33" h, 16" w......................................................... 6,050.00

Bottle topper, cardboard, "Drink Dr. Pepper, Good For Life" red logo, "Seasons Greetings from Your Dealer," red ground, cond. 9.5, $1,870. (Photo courtesy of Gary Metz, Muddy River Trading Co.)

Calendar, paper, 1943, "Drink Dr. Pepper, Good For Life" red logo, titled "Blackout For Fatigue," artwork by Earl Moran, full pad, cond. 7.25-7.5, 24" h, 13-1/2" w, $1,540. (Photo courtesy of Gary Metz, Muddy River Trading Co.)

1936, woman in white ball gown carrying tray with product, red checkered logo, pad begins with May, orig metal strip, cond. 7.5+, 30" h, 16" w..............1,540.00

1937, woman in white dress, artwork by Earl Moran, complete pad, Wharton (TX) Bottling Works, framed, cond. 7.25-7.75 ........................... 2,310.00

1938, seated woman in yellow dress, tilted red checkered logo upper-right, artwork by Earl Moran, full pad, framed, 33" h, 16" w ........................ 1,210.00

1939, "You'll like it too!," white text upper-left, woman in white dress with bottle in each hand, red checkered logo lower-left, metal strip, full pad, framed, cond. 8.25, 31" h, 15" w............................. 2,750.00

1940, 2 women at Dr. Pepper cooler with red checkered logo, orig metal strip, full pad, cond. 7.25-7.5, 31" h, 15" w ............................................... 1,760.00

1941, woman in white shirt/yellow vest with bottle under red checkered logo and yellow 10-2-4 clock logo, orig metal strip, pad begins with February, framed, cond. 6.5-7, 24" h, 11-1/2" w ........... 770.00

Calendar, paper, 3 months per page

1959, woman with ski poles over shoulder, 10-2-4 bottlecap ....................................................... 192.50

1960, "75 years good, 1885-1960," woman with bottle over vintage image in background, cond. 8.5-9.............................................................. 176.00

1961, "the friendly Pepper-Upper," woman with poodle/ribbons, cond. 9.25-9.5 ........................... 297.00

1962, "the friendly Pepper-Upper," woman/child building snowman, cond. 8+ ............................... 132.00

1963, "It's different...I like it!," skiers, cond. 9.5....................................................110.00

1965, "Dr. Pepper, Distinctively Different...," woman in white dress looking in oval mirror, cond. 9.25-9.5 ..................................................... 88.00

Calendar holder, plastic and aluminum, 3-D bottlecap design, "Dr Pepper" in white on red horizontal panel, red 10/2/4, daily calendar pages hang beneath bottlecap, 1950s, partial pad, cond. 8.5 ..................... 88.00

Carrier

Aluminum, 12-bottle, "Drink Dr. Pepper, Good For Life," red on yellow, 1930s-1940s, cond. 9.5 ............ 495.00

Cardboard, closed top, 24-bottle, "Home Carton, Dr. Pepper, 24 Bottles," red on green on green-striped ground, 1947, cond. 8.5-9 .............................. 99.00

Cardboard, 12-bottle (26-oz), open top, non-divided, "Drink Dr Pepper, the friendly Pepper-Upper," red on yellow ground, cond. 8.5-9 ...................... 242.00

Cardboard, 24-bottle, "Drink Dr Pepper," white on red rectangle on green/white striped ground, 10-2-4 logos on handle, 1952 ................................ 154.00

Cardboard, 24-bottle, "Drink Dr Pepper," white on red rectangle, 1958, cond. 8-8.5 ......................... 220.00

Masonite, with slide/handle, twin 6-pack, "Dr. Pepper, Return Empties In This Carrier, Deposit Required," white on red ground, with 12 embossed bottles, cond. 8 ........................................................ 143.00

Metal, spot-welded, embossed, 6-bottle, "Drink Dr. Pepper, Good For Life," red text, cond. 8+ ............... 440.00

Wire and tin, 6-bottle, "Drink Dr. Pepper, Good For Life," white on red ground, yellow 10-2-4 logos, cond. 6.5-7 .................................................. 687.50

Wire and tin, 6-bottle, "Drink Dr. Pepper, Good For Life," white on red ground, cond. 6.5-7 ...................... 715.00

Wooden, twin 6-pack, "Twin Six, Pick It Up...," red lettering, 10-2-4 logo on ends, with 12 embossed bottles, cond. 6.5-7 ........................................... 990.00

Change receiver, glass, "Drink Dr. Pepper, King of Beverages, At Fountains And In Bottles," red/black text, white ground, 1915, cond. 7.5+, 6" dia ...................... 2,970.00

Clock

**Fan pulls, cardboard, 2-sided, "Drink Dr. Pepper, Good For Life" red logo: (left) Patricia White with autumn leaves, cond. 8.25, $2,640; (right) Woman with squirrel, cond. 9.5, $385. (Photo courtesy of Gary Metz, Muddy River Trading Co.)**

Glass, reverse-painted, orig countertop stand, "Drink Dr. Pepper, Good For Life, Thanks Call Again," red/yellow/black, replaced motor/hands, 1930s, cond. 9-9.25 ................................................. 4,290.00

Neon, octagonal, "Drink Dr. Pepper, Good For Life" solid-red logo, red 10/2/4, other hours black, white ground, glass face with red border, late 1930s, cond. 7, 18" h, 18" w ...................................... 687.50

Neon, round, metal with glass front, metal face with red 10/2/4, "Drink Dr. Pepper, Good For Life," edge wear/rust spotting/scratches, clock works, neon broken, 21-1/2" dia ....................................... 935.00

Neon, square, "Drink Dr. Pepper, Good For Life" red checkered logo, red 10/2/4, other hours black, yellow ground, cond. 7.5-8, 15" sq ..................... 825.00

Pam style, glass face/cover, metal case, "drink a Bite To Eat," red checkered logo over yellow 10-2-4 clock logo, yellow ground, red 10/2/4, other hours black in white border, 1940s, cond. 8.5-9, 15" dia ......................................................... 715.00

Plastic, lightup, bottlecap shape, "Dr. Pepper" on red horizontal bar, red 10/2/4, 1950s, needs cleaned, cond. 7-7.5, 11" dia ....................................... 203.50

Cooler

Airline style, "Drink Dr Pepper" in red, inner tray, cond. 7.5+, 16" h, 18" w, 9" d ................................ 187.00

Glascock style, 2-case size, long sides have "Drink Dr. Pepper, Good For Life" red checkered logo with halo bottle on green ground at left, short sides have same design without bottle, 1930s, no lid, cond. 5.5-6.5 ......................................................... 660.00

Junior style, "Drink Dr. Pepper, Good For Life" solid-red logo sign above double doors, yellow 10-2-4 clock logo decals on side, 1940s, cond. 6-6.5 ................................................. 1,705.00

Picnic cooler, white "Dr Pepper" in red oval, 1950s-1960s, cond. 8, 12" h, 19" w, 10" d ............... 220.00

Cutout, cardboard

"Drink Dr. Pepper" red checkered logo upper-right, Dr. Pepper stadium vendor handing bottle to man/woman in stands, 10-2-4 clock logo lower-right, 1930s-1940s, cond. 6.5, 32" h, 25" w .................. 2,420.00

"Drink Dr. Pepper, 5¢" logo on solid-red panel upper-left, "At 10-2 & 4 O'Clock" beneath woman with glass on blue panel, potted plants in background, 1930s-1940s, cond. 7.5, 18" h, 24" w ........................ 1,650.00

Decal

Applied to glass, "Drink Dr. Pepper, Good For Life," red checkered logo, framed, 1940s, cond. 9-9.5, 10" h, 24" w .................................................. 176.00

"Drink Dr. Pepper, Good For Life, Please Pay Cashier," red checkered logo, green trim, yellow 10-2-4 logo at top, 1930s-1940s, unused, cond. 9, 9" h, 12" w .......................................................... 412.50

Display, bottle, plastic, round "Dr. Pepper" logo with white text on red vertical panel, red 10/2/4, white ground, 1950s, cond. 8-8.5, 4' h ................................... 577.50

Door bar

Aluminum, 1-pc, "Drink Dr. Pepper" red checkered logo flanked by 10-2-4 clock logos, silver ground, cond. 7-7.5 ................................................... 176.00

Porcelain on iron framework, "Drink Dr. Pepper, Good For Life" red checkered logo flanked by 10-2-4 clock logos, 1930s, cond. 8.25 .................. 2,310.00
Tin, "Drink Dr. Pepper" in flattened red oval over yellow "V," "the friendly Pepper-Upper" in red, white ground, red extenders, cond. 8.75................. 440.00
Tin, "Drink Dr. Pepper, frosty, man, frosty!," red text on white ground, red extenders, cond. 6.5-7 .......... 412.50
Door pull, tin, orig Bakelite handle, "Drink A Bite To Eat" over red checkered logo, "at 10-2 & 4" above bottle, red text, white ground, 1930s-1940s, cond. 8.25-8.5, 12" h, 3-1/2" w.................................................... 990.00
Fan, cardboard
    Wooden handle, "Drink a Bite To Eat At 10-2 And 4 O'Clock," red checkered logo over bottle, yellow ground, red logo flanked by bottles on reverse, 1930s, cond. 8.5 ........................................... 412.50
    Wooden handle, "Drink Dr. Pepper" red logo beside woman in yellow dress, artwork by Earl Moran, "With our compliments..." on reverse, man in top hat, front cond. 8.75-9, back cond. 7 ............ 357.50
    "Drink A Bite To Eat At 10, 2 And 4 O'Clock, 3 A Day Keeps Energy up," red checkered logo on reverse, woman on front, 1940s, cond. 7.5 ................. 467.50
    "75 years good, Dr. Pepper, Good For Life," faint image of woman in large hat behind text, cond. 8-8.5.................................................................. 143.00
Festoon, cardboard, 5-pc, "Drink Dr. Pepper, Good For Life" logo, woman with glass, magnolias, 2 glasses at each end, 1930s-1940s, some cardboard missing, medium/heavy bends, cond. 7-7.5, approx. 10' l.................. 8,800
Festoon component, cardboard, die-cut
    4 cowgirls sitting on fence, 1940s-1950s, cond. 8, 25" h, 29" w.......................................................... 1,017.50
    Woman in green hat/holding glass over football, yellow flowers/red ribbon, "Drink Dr. Pepper, Good For Life" red checkered logo, 1940s, water damage/paper loss, 23" h, 38" w............................ 2,750.00
Glass, applied label, "Dr Pepper" in red on white oval over "V," 1960s, cond. 9.5................................. 88.00
Lighter
    "Dr. Pepper" red checkered logo, orig box mkd "No. 350 Fire Fly Flick Model," 1940s, unused, cond. 9.5...................................................... 330.00
Megaphone, heavy cardboard, metal ring at top, "frosty, man, frosty" under cartoon image of dog, "Dr Pepper"

**Kickplate, litho tin, embossed, "Drink Dr. Pepper, Good For Life," red/white logo, yellow ground, 1941, cond. 8.25+, 12" h, 29" w, $577.50. (Photo courtesy of Gary Metz, Muddy River Trading Co.)**

in red on white band, yellow ground, 1950s, unused ............................................................................ 357.50
Menu board, plastic, "Drink Dr Pepper" in white on red oval over gold "V," "Distinctively Different...for today's light'n lively taste," white ground, yellow border, 1960s, chipped corner, cond. 8.25, 1' h, 3' w.................. 66.00
Menu sign, litho tin, embossed
    "Drink Dr Pepper," white text in red oval over gold "V," white ground, green chalkboard area, "Dr Pepper..." in white at lower-left, 1960s, cond. 9.25, 20" h, 14" w............................................................................ 275.00
    "Drink Dr Pepper," white text in red oval, white ground with blue/white bowed design at bottom, black chalkboard area, 1960s, cond. 7.5, 28" h, 20" w............................................................................ 88.00
    "Drink Dr Pepper," white text in red oval with white border, red ground, black chalkboard area, 1970s, cond. 7.5, 28" h, 20" w.................................... 66.00
Mirror/thermometer combo, red checkered logo over "at 10-2-4" in red, bottle-shaped thermometer upper-left, 1930s, cond. 7, 6" h, 8" w .................................. 935.00
Mobile, cardboard, 2-sided, 4-pc, "Drink Dr. Pepper, Wake Up Your Taste, Remember Dr. Pepper (pointing finger)" and bottle/bottle cap, cond. 8+, approx 24" sq.................................................................... 715.00
Pen, celluloid over metal, "King of Beverages" logo, "Free From Caffeine And Drugs," end pulls off to reveal pencil housed inside the barrel, cond. 7-8 .......... 1,100.00
Pencil
    Celluloid cover, bullet-style, "Dr. Pepper, King of Beverages," red logo, white ground, cond. 6.5-7, 3-1/4" l........................................................... 1,100.00
    Celluloid cover, bullet-style/opener combination, "Dr. Pepper, Good For Life" red checkered logo over "You Drink A Bite To Eat," 1940s, cond. 8.5-9, 4-1/2" l....................................................... 1,017.50
Playing Cards
    1930s, child sitting in cabin doorway, complete with bridge card/joker, box cond. 5, cards cond. 9+ ............. 605.00
    1940s, seated woman in blue blouse/skirt holding out bottle, red checkered logo upper left, 10-2-4 logo at right, yellow ground, unopened, box cond. 7-7.5, cards cond. NM ......................................... 495.00
    1946, woman in red dress, red checkered logo over yellow 10-2-4 clock logo upper right, black ground, complete deck, box cond. 8, cards cond. 9-9.5 .......................................................... 385.00
Rack, wire, collapsible, litho tin sign, "pick a pack of (10-2-4 bottle cap)" in yellow/white stripes, 1950s-1960s, cond. 7.5 ................................................................110.00
Radio, transistor, plastic, vending-machine shape, oval logo over "the friendly Pepper Upper, distinctively different," 1960s, cond. 7.5-8, 7" h, 3" w................ 297.00
Ring, gold, "Dr. Pepper, Accredited Route Salesman," 10-2-4 clock logo, cond. 7, man's size 9 .......... 660.00
Rubber stamp, "Drink Dr. Pepper, Good For Life," mounted on wood block with handle, 1930s-1940s, cond. 7, 7-1/2" l................................................ 440.00
Sidewalk marker, brass "Drink Dr. Pepper, Safety First," and 10-2-4 designations, 1930s-1940s, cond. 7, 4" dia.......................................................... 275.00

Sign, aluminum, embossed, 2 pcs, "In" and "Out," white text in blue arrows with red tails on white ground, bottom has "Drink Dr Pepper" in red in white oval on red panel, 1960s-1970s, "In" cond. 8-8.25, "Out" cond. 9.75, pr.................................................. 137.50

Sign, cardboard

2-sided, horizontal, aluminum frame, "A Lift for Life," square dancers, reverse shows cheerleader, 10-2-4 bottle cap, yellow ground, cond. 7 ............... 330.00

String-hanger, "Take Home a Carton of Dr. Pepper, Good For Life, 25¢ (Plus Deposit)," tilted red checkered logo over 10-2-4 clock logo, red text, 1930s-1940s, cond. 8, 18" h, 12" w ........................ 198.00

"Smart lift, Drink Dr. Pepper, Good For Life,"" snow scene with woman/dog, red checkered logo over 10-2-4 clock logo, cond. 9.25, 15" h, 25" w .................. 495.00

Sign, celluloid over tin over cardboard

"Drink A Bite To Eat," tilted "Dr. Pepper, Good For Life" solid-red logo by bottle/10-2-4 clock logo, 1940s, easel-back/string hanger missing, cond. 8.5+, 6" h, 7-1/2" w.......................................................... 935.00

"Please Pay When Served, Drink A Bite To Eat, Dr. Pepper," bottle and clock logo, 1930s-1940s, cond. 8-8.25, 8" h, 11" w...................................... 1,155.00

Sign, paper

"Drink Dr Pepper" repeated in red on yellow upper/lower panels, "frosty, man, frosty!" in black beneath cartoon dog on white ground, 1950s, cond. 9.25, 22" h, 16" w................................................... 357.50

"frosty, man- frosty!" upper left, "the friendly Pepper-Upper" in white on blue band, outdoor scene of man barbecuing in chef's hat, reaching for bottle having "Dr Pepper" 10-2-4 logo, 1950s, cond. 9.5, 15" h, 25" w............................................................ 137.50

"frosty, man- frosty!" upper left, "the friendly Pepper-Upper" lower-right, 2 cartoon dogs with "Dr Pepper" 10-2-4 bottlecap used as a drum, white ground, 1957, cond. 7.5-8, 15" h, 25" w..................... 192.50

"Good With Food," sandwich/glass, red checkered logo, cond. 8, 22" l ....................................... 143.00

**Sign, heavy cardboard, beveled, "Drink Dr. Pepper, King Of Beverages," circa 1910, cond. 8+, $4,070. (Photo courtesy of Gary Metz, Muddy River Trading Co.)**

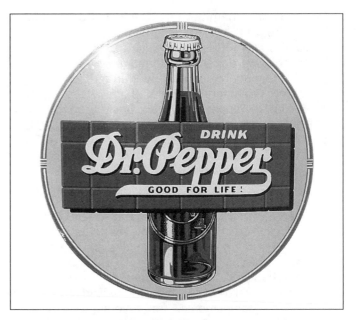

**Sign, tin, 1940, "Drink Dr. Pepper, Good For Life" logo over bottle, yellow ground, cond. 8.25-8.5, 3' dia, $2,640. (Photo courtesy of Gary Metz, Muddy River Trading Co.)**

"Have a Picnic at the New York World's Fair on us!," white/yellow text, "Dr Pepper" in white in red oval over yellow "V," picnic basket with 2 bottles sticking out, 1964, cond. 8.75+, 15" h, 25" w............. 275.00

"It is our Responsibility to be successful under conditions as we find them" in black text, "Forward Faster in 'Fifty" in gold circle upper-left, tilted "Drink Dr. Pepper, Good For Life" checkered logo lower-right, 1950, cond. 7-7.5, 27" h, 21" w .................... 176.00

"New Taste Thrill, Dr. Pepper and Ice Cream," 2 Dr. Pepper glasses with floats, red checkered logo, cond. 6.5-7, 22" l ............................................ 66.00

"Take Home A Carton...," 6-pack in green/white-striped carrier, red checkered logo, 1940s, cond. 7, 22" l ................................................................110.00

"Teens! Make the scene at Dick Clark's TV Celebrity Party," red oval "Dr Pepper" logo over white "V," image of Dick Clark, "Contest details on every carton" at bottom, 1963, cond. 9.75, 18-1/2" h, 12" w.......................................................... 99.00

"Today's Special," hamburger/glass, red checkered logo, cond. 7, 22" l ........................................ 187.00

"We redeem (Dr. Pepper red checkered logo) Coupons," black text, yellow ground, cond. 9.25, 14" h, 15" w............................................................. 176.00

Sign, porcelain

Rounded corners, "Drink Dr Pepper," white text/border, red ground, 1950s-1960s, cond. 9.5, 6-1/2" h, 17" w............................................................... 143.00

Same design as above, some touchups, cond. 8.25, 9" h, 24" w ................................................................ 88.00

"Dr. Pepper, Good For Life," red checkered logo, green border, 1930s-1940s, cond. 9.5, 5" h, 13-1/2" w .................................................... 825.00

"Dr. Pepper, Good For Life," flanked by 10-2-4 logos, red/white ground, 1930s-1940s, cond. 7.75-8, 8" h, 36" w......................................................... 2,420.00

Sign, porcelain, button
"Drink Dr Pepper," white text on red horizontal band, red 10/2/4, red border, white ground, circa 1950s-1960s, cond. 9.25, 10" dia ........................... 220.00
Sign, tin
Sidewalk A-frame sign, 2-sided, oval logo with gold V at top, white ground, 1969, cond. 7.5-8, 36" h, 26" w ................................................................ 385.00
Sign, tin, button
Bottle-cap shape, 10-2-4 logo, "Dr Pepper" in white on red band, white ground, cond. 9.75, 24" dia . 412.50
Flange edge, 10-2-4 logo, "Dr Pepper" in white on red band, white ground, cond. 9.25-9.5, 36" dia............................................................. 440.00
Sign, tin, embossed, rounded corners
"Dr Pepper," white text in red oval on white ground, "Drink" in red in upper-left, red border, 1966, cond. 9.5, 2' h, 4' w ...................................... 247.50
"Drink Dr Pepper," white text in red oval over yellow "V," white ground, "Drink Dr Pepper, Distinctively Different," red text/oval logo over pop-tab can with red oval, white/checkered ground, 1960s, cond. 8.25+, 54" h, 18" w ...................................... 121.00
Sign, tin, flange
Die-cut, "Drink Dr. Pepper, Good For Life" red check-ered logo on green ground, bottle with halo at left, late 1930s, better side cond. 8.25-8.5, lesser side cond. 7.25-7.5, small version, 10" h, 17-1/2" w................................................... 2,090.00
Die-cut, same design as above, 1937, larger size, cond. 7-7.5+, 14-1/2" h, 24" w .................. 1,100.00
Die-cut, "Dr. Pepper" bottlecap, white text on red hori-zontal panel, 10/2/4 in red, yellow ground with white panel at bottom, 1959, cond. 9.5, 18" h, 22" w......................................................... 1,485.00
Sign, tin over cardboard, orig string hanger, "Drink Dr. Pepper, Good For Life" red checkered logo, "Thank You, Call Again" on lower blue panel with yellow 10-2-4 clock logo, 1930s-1940s, cond. 8.5-8.75, 8" h, 13" w ............................................................. 4,950.00
Statue, Perky, figure holding out 2 bottles, wooden base, 7-1/2" h
Bronze, cond. 8.5-9.......................................... 247.50
Gold, cond. 8.................................................... 302.50
Silver, cond. 8.5 .............................................. 330.00
Syrup jug, glass, paper label
"Drink Dr. Pepper, Good For Life" red checkered logo, yellow ground, orig cap, 1940s-1950s, cond. 7, gal............................................................... 170.50
"Dr Pepper," white text in red oval over "Fountain Vending Syrup," red/yellow stripes on white ground, orig cap, 1950s-1960s, cond. 8-8.5, gal ........ 33.00
Thermometer, Pam style
"Dr Pepper" oval logo with white border on upper half, "Hot or Cold" in white on lower half, white numbers, burgundy ground, cond. 9-9.25, 12" dia............ 170.50
Same design as above, cond. 7.5, 18" dia........ 176.00
"Hot or Cold, Dr Pepper," red/blue text, red flattened oval logo, white ground, blue/red numbers cond. 9 .................................................................. 275.00

**Thermometer, porcelain, "Dr. Scholl's Foot Comfort Headquarters, Pain Cramps or Callouses There? Let us take care of your Foot Troubles, Demonstra-tion Free," worn blank for store identifi-cation, chips, 39" h, 8" w, $80.**

"Hot or Cold, Enjoy Dr Pepper," red/green text, red oval logo, white ground, white numbers on green border, cond. 9-9.25 .................................. 1,430.00
Thermometer, tin
"Drink A Bite To Eat At" clock hands pointing to 10/2/4 in clock design at top, "Dr. Pepper, Good For Life, 5¢" in red panel at bottom, bottle at left, tube at right, aqua border, 1930s, cond. 7, 13" h, 4-1/2" w ...................................................... 2,310.00
"Drink Dr. Pepper, Good For Life" red checkered logo at top, "at 10, 2 and 4" on white horizontal panel, bottle with halo on green ground, tube above bottle, rounded bottom, 1930s, cond. 7.5+, 17" h....................2,310.00
"When Hungry, Thirsty or Tired," red checkered logo, 10-2-4 bottle, yellow ground, rounded corners, 1940s, cond. 7.75-8, 26" h, 10" w................. 330.00
Thermometer, tin, rounded top
"frosty cold," 2 red boxes, 10-2-4 logo at top, "Drink Dr. Pepper" in red band at bottom, white ground, cond. 7...................................................... 176.00
"frosty cold," red/black boxes, 10-2-4 logo at top, "Dr. Pepper" in red band at bottom, white ground, cond. 8-8.25 ..................................................... 247.50
"frosty, man, frosty!," 10-2-4 logo at top, "Drink Dr. Pepper" in red band at bottom, white ground, cond. 9.25-9.5, 16" ............................................... 715.00
"Hot or Cold," white text in red band at top, red oval/yellow "V" at bottom, white ground, cond. 8.25.............................................................. 176.00
Tray, tin
Oval, "Drink Dr. Pepper, At All Soda Fountains, 5¢" on rim, outdoor scene with woman reclining on stone bench, 2nd woman standing beside her, circa 1910, cond. 8-8.5, 16-1/2" h, 13-1/2" w .............. 8,800.00
Oval, "Drink Dr. Pepper, King of Beverages, Free

From Caffeine And Drugs," red text, white ground, yellow border, 1906, cond. 7.75-8.25+, 13-3/4" h, 16-1/2" w........................................... 770.00

Round, "Dr. Pepper, King of Beverages" logo at top, red/pink roses, cond. 7.5-8, 10" dia .......... 1,210.00

Watch fob

    Billiken, gold, oval, cond. 8 ............................. 165.00

    Billiken, silver, oval, cond. 8+ .......................... 165.00

    Eagle, larger, rectangle, cond. 9, 1-1/2" h........ 165.00

    Eagle, smaller, rectangle, cond. 8, 1-1/4" h ...... 220.00

## Dr. Pepper's Mountain Herbs

Clock, regulator, wood, reverse-painted glass, "Natures Own Remedy, Dr. Pepper's Mountain Herbs," mountains/horses, circa 1910, cond. 7-7.5 ............. 2,970.00

## Dr. Scholl's

**History:** Early medicine makers certainly did not forget the foot in their quest for fame and market share. One of the most famous of the foot healers was William M. Scholl. His concern for feet developed while he was working at his first job, in a Chicago shoe store in 1899. He enrolled at Illinois Medical College and experimented with foot remedies in his spare time. In 1904, he introduced his first product, an arch-support device.

Display, countertop, metal case with glass front, "Dr. Scholl's, Remedies for All Foot Troubles" over images of products, dents/rust, 23" h, 14-1/2" w, 10-3/4" d.......................................................... 495.00

## Dr. Shoop's Health Coffee

Match holder, hanging, litho tin, shows product, cond. 8+, 4-7/8" h, 3-1/2 w................................................. 357.50

## Dr. Swett's Root Beer

Envelope, "Dr. Swett Root Beer" in return address, shows child with mug of drink in front of silhouette-like image of old man in same pose, cond. 8, 3-5/8" h, 6-1/2" w ................................................................ 33.00

Sign, cardboard, "Dr. Swett's The Original Root Beer, On the Market Sixty Years, From Childhood to Old Age," shows child with mug of drink in front of silhouette-like image of old man in same pose, cond. 8+, 18" h, 13-1/2" w.............................................................. 330.00

## Dr. Wells

Chalkboard, tin, diagonal "Dr. Wells" at top, "The Cooler Doctor" at bottom, green center, cond. VG, 27" h, 18-1/2" w.............................................................. 38.50

Sign, tin, embossed, "The Cooler Doctor, Puts out a hot thirst better than any other doctor," cartoon skier, "Dr. Wells" sign by ski jump, minor scratches, 11-1/2" h, 31" w ................................................................ 104.50

## Dr. White's Cough Drops

Tin, flat pocket, litho tin, hinged lid, "Dr. White's Celebrated Cough Drops, Extremely Pleasant to the Taste…," blue on white ground, cond. 8+, 5/8" h, 3-1/2" w, 2-1/4" d.......................................................... 412.50

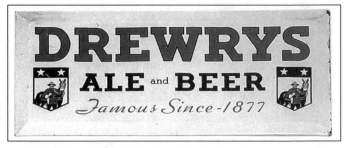

Sign, tin over cardboard, string hanger, "Drewerys Ale and Beer, Famous Since 1877," edge wear, 6" h, 13" w, $105.

## Dream Castle Tobacco

Pack, paper label on heavy cardboard, "Dream Castle, A Mild Aromatic Smoke," silhouette of man with pipe, castle and "Dream Castle" in smoke cloud, white on black ground, full, cond. 9................................... 34.00

## Dreikorn's Bread

Sign, tin, embossed, rolled edges, "Reach For-Dreikorn's Good Bread," yellow/white text, red ground, cond. NM, 16" h, 27-1/2" w ................................. 99.00

## Drewerys (See Photo)

## Driver's Chocolate Club

Bank, litho tin, "Stop for Driver's Chocolate Club," graphic of children in pedal car stopped by officer, English, orig key, cond. 8.5, 6" h, 3-1/2" w, 2-7/8" d .............. 302.50

## Droste's Cocoa

Tin, litho tin, "Droste's Cocoa, Holland," man/woman in train car, Droste & Co, cond. 8.25, 5" h, 2-1/2" sq........................................................... 176.00

## Drug-Pak Condoms

Tin, litho tin, mortar/pestle logo, white lettering on blue ground, with contents, cond. 8.5+, 1/4" h, 2-1/8" w, 1-3/4" d .......................................................... 605.00

## Drumhead Cigarettes

Tin, litho tin, flat 50, "Player's Drumhead Cigarettes, Supplied to crew for personal use only," shows drum, cond. 7.5-8 .......................................................115.50

## Drummond Tobacco Co.

Sign, litho paper, older wood frame, "Compliments of Drummond Tobacco Co., St. Louis, Mo., Manufacturers of Horse Shoe, J.T. and Drummond Natural Leaf Chewing Tobaccos," woman in white nightgown, ©1894, creases/edge tears, 33" h, 28" w ........................176.00

## Duble-Tip

Tin, litho tin, "Three Original Duble-Tip Prophylactics, Distributed by Department Sales Co., New York, N.Y.," woman in bathing suit, yellow ground, cond. 8+, 1/4" h, 2-1/8" w, 1-5/8" d.............................................. 522.50

## DuBois Beer

Sign, litho tin
"Ask For --- Du Bois Export Beer," white on red ground, white border, paint chips/rust spots, 35-1/2" h, 70" w ................................................................ 110.00
"DuBois Budweiser Beer," black/red text, "D" and "B" in white on red panels, white ground, red border, paint chips/rusted edges, 35-1/2" h, 70" w ................ 220.00
Embossed, "Try the Original, DuBois Budweiser, Truly Different, Always Good," shows bottle, black/red text, yellow ground, black border, DuBois Products & Cold Storage Co., DuBois PA, dents/paint loss/wrinkles, 19-1/2" h, 13-1/2" w ........................ 71.50

## Duke's Mixture

Door push, porcelain, "Duke's Mixture, The Roll of Fame, Guaranteed by Liggett & Myers Tobacco Co.," cond. 8+, 8-5/8" h, 4-1/4" w ...................................... 1,017.50
Sign, litho paper, metal strips top/bottom, "Free Presents for Coupons, Duke's Mixture Quality Tobacco," shows product, man holding up coupon, variety of premiums, circa 1913, like new, 29-3/4" h, 20" w ............... 209.00

## Duke's Cameo Cigarettes

Folding chair, wood, stenciled seat back pictures woman in front, cigarette pack in back, cond. 8-, 31" h, 16-1/2" w ........................................................... 632.50

## Duluth Imperial Flour

Sign, tin, beveled edge, "Duluth Imperial Flour, Without A Rival," black chef removing loaf of bread from pan, bag of product on table, water stains/chips/2 nail holes, 25" h, 18" w ............................................ 385.00

## R.G. Dunn Cigars

Strip sign, porcelain, white text, red ground, cond. NM, 3" h, 21-1/4" w ...................................................... 385.00

## Dunlop

Clock, tin face, metal tire with "Dunlop" in yellow plastic text at top, iron mounting bracket at side, cond. 7.5, 36" h, 48" w ......................................................... 770.00

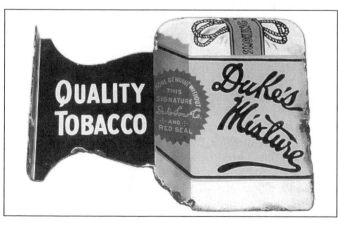

Sign, flange, porcelain, "Duke's Mixture, Quality Tobacco," chips, rust, 11" h, 14-1/4" w, $350.

Sign, tin, embossed, "Dunlop Tires," vertical black text over reverse-type panel, yellow ground, red border faded, cond. 7+, 60" h, 13-7/8" w ...................... 181.50

## Dunnsboro

Tin, vertical pocket, litho tin, "Dunnsboro Mild Pipe Smoking," hunting scene with riders on horseback following dogs, cond. 7.5-8 .......................................... 1,627.00

## Duplex Motor Oil

Can, litho tin, "Duplex Motor Oil No. 1, Manufactured Expressly For Pierce-Arrow Cars & Trucks, Enterprise Oil Company, Buffalo, N.Y.," early auto in oval, yellow ground, 1 side blank, cond. 7, 5 gal, 14-1/2" h, 9" sq ................................................................. 236.50

## Duplex Outboard Special Motor Oil

Can, tin, "Duplex Outboard Special Motor Oil," 2 fishermen in boat, black text, green ground, Quaker State Oil Refining Corp., Oil City PA, qt, cond. 7, 6-7/8" h, 4-1/2" w, 2-1/4" d................................................. 27.50

## DuPont

**History:** Although members of the DuPont family had been clockmakers in their homeland of France, they switched to manufacturing gunpowder once they arrived in the United States.

In 1803, the United States Army placed its first order for a small shipment of gunpowder. After that, the DuPont brothers became major suppliers for the military, even after the U.S. government intervened in 1911 to break up the company's gunpowder monopoly.

Early advertisements showed a hunter surrounded by an assortment of wild animals, perhaps attesting to the power of the product.

Calendar, paper, 1960, "Explosives Department" over red oval "DuPont" logo at bottom, hunting dog in pointing position between 2 trees, full pad/3 months per pg, cond. EXC, 31" h, 15" w.................................... 27.50
Display, cardboard, standup window display, "DuPont Auto Polishes, For a Real Shine," black shoeshine boy looking at reflection in car finish, Duco-Polish shown on left wing, Duco-Wax on right, cond. 8.5+, 37-1/2" h, 45" w .......................................................... 1,705.00
Watch fob, cloisonné-inlaid sterling silver presentation fob, "DuPont" in lower oval, "For Greater Safety" in round medallion with cross, embossed with woman, orig strap/box (no lid), unused, 1-5/16" dia............................176.00

## DuPont Powder Co.

Sign, paper, hunting dog, "Edm. H. Osthalc, Joe Cumming, By Antonio Picciola 1899, copyright 1907 by B.I. Dupont DeNemous Powder Co.," 16-3/4" h, 21" w ........................................................... 412.50

## Durham Mustard

Tin, paper label over tin, cow head, red/black text, yellow

ground, Clawson Co., Philadelphia, cond. 8, 3" h,
2-1/4" w, 1-3/8" d................................................. 34.00

## E.R. Durkee & Co.

Box, wood, paper label on front/inside lid, front label
reads "E.R. Durkee & Co's Selected Spices, Strictly
Pure, Cinnamon" on front, "Warranted Strictly Pure,
E.R. Durkee & Co., N.Y. Trademark" stamped on side,
5" h, 12-3/4" w, 7-1/2" d .................................... 137.50

## Duroc Beaver Ribbons

Tin, typewriter ribbon, litho tin, "Beaver Ribbon, Duroc,
the M.B. Cook Co., Chicago, Ill.," color panel of 2 bea-
vers at tree, cond. 8 ............................................ 60.50

## Dutch Boy Paints

**History:** More than 20 American manufacturers of
white lead joined forces in 1891 to create the National
Lead Company. They turned to advertising manager
O.C. Harn in their search for a symbol that would unite
the various arms of the company as it advertised its
new line of products. Harn liked the idea of a Dutch
boy, because the Dutch were noted for keeping things
clean and whitewashed. A Dutch artist drew the pre-
liminary sketches of Michael Brady, an Irishman, and
Lawrence Carmichael Earle completed the portrait
that would become the company's official trademark.

Figure, papier-mâché, full-bodied
    Dutch boy holding 2-sided cardboard sign showing
        paint can, typical cracking to figure, figure
        15" h .......................................................... 440.00
    Dutch boy holding "Dutch Boy White Lead" brush/can
        in front of him with both hands, cond. 8,
        28" h ............................................................ 715.00
    Dutch boy with hands at sides, cond. 7, 15" h,
        pr ................................................................. 220.00
Match holder, litho tin, die-cut, embossed, figural of
    seated boy with can, paint brush, cond. 8+, 6-3/4" h,
    3-1/2" w....................................................... 1,072.50

**String holder, heavy metal,
die-cut, 2-sided "Lewis
White Lead" sign over
seated boy painting with
bucket of "Dutch Boy All-
Purpose Soft Paste White
Lead," 1920s-1930s, restoration, cond. 7.5-8, 26" h,
14" w, $4,400. (Photo cour-
tesy of Gary Metz, Muddy
River Trading Co.)**

Sign, cardboard, die-cut, standup
    Boy behind "Dutch Boy All-Purpose Soft Paste White
        Lead" can carried by 2 men in white, "A Quick-Mix-
        ing Pure White-Lead for all painting" in white on his
        hat, NRA logo, circa 1930s, cond. 6-6.5, 37" h,
        21" w........................................................ 357.50
    Boy holding up "Dutch Boy White Lead" can and "Holi-
        day Greetings to All, We thank you for your patron-
        age" 1927-1928 calendar, cond. 8.25-8.5, 52" h,
        22" w........................................................ 467.50
    Boy leaning over, dipping brush in "Dutch Boy White
        Lead" can, "Paint With An All-Lead Paint For
        Greater Durability And Lower Cost Per Year" in
        black on white square, circa 1930, part of easel
        missing, cond. 6.5-7, circa 1930s, 45" h,
        32" w........................................................ 880.00
    Boy on ladder with "Dutch Boy White Lead" can, brush in
        right hand, cond. 8.25-8.5, 5' h, 2' w..............3,520.00
    Boy on motorcycle hauling 3 "Dutch Boy White Lead"
        cans, circa 1930s, cond. 7, 8-1/2" h,
        14" w........................................................ 467.50
    Boy with oversized brush/can of ""Dutch Boy All-Purpose
        Soft Paste White Lead," circa 1920s-1930s, support
        detached, cond. 8.25-8.5, 35" x 31" ..................880.00
    Boy with wooden keg, brush in raised right hand,
        1920s-1930s, part of easel back missing, cond. 6-
        6.5, 32" h, 22" w ............................................ 104.50
Sign, porcelain, die-cut, "Dutch Boy Paints" under oval
    design of seated boy with wooden keg of paint, brush
    in raised right hand, circa 1950s, cond. 8.25-8.5, 55"
    h, 30" w ........................................................ 1,430.00
String holder, heavy metal, die-cut, 2-sided, "Atlantic White
    Lead" sign over Dutch boy on swing painting, orig bucket
    string holder, cond. 9, 26" h, 14" w......................5,720.00

## Dutch Masters

Sign, porcelain, "Dutch Masters Paints" in black on white
    border, Dutch man image in center on red ground,
    minor edge chips, 26" dia ................................. 357.50

## D-X

Gas globe, 2 lenses
    Narrow glass body, 2 different lenses, "Diamond D-X
        Lubricating Motor Oil," black/white text, large black/
        white D-X over red diamond outline, V-shaped
        panel at bottom with white text, white ground;
        "Power" in black on red diamond outline, white
        ground; DX lens cond. 8.5, Power lens cond. 9,
        body cond. 9, 13-1/2" dia............................. 412.50
    Plastic body, narrow, DX diamond logo with blue text
        between red triangles, over red "Boron," white
        ground, lenses cond. 8, body cond. 7.5,
        13-1/2" dia .................................................. 187.00
    Plastic body (newer), black "D-X" over red diamond out-
        line, "Ethyl" in white on black back, "Lubricating Gaso-
        line" at bottom, white ground, 1 lens damaged, lens
        cond. 9/6, body cond. 8.5, 13-1/2" dia............... 187.00
    Plastic body (newer), "D-X Boron," diamond "D-X" logo
        with red border at top, "Boron" in red on thin red/
        black L-shaped swoosh, white ground, all cond. 9,
        13-1/2" dia ................................................. 264.00

# E

## E and Z Peanut Butter

Pail, litho tin, black diamond on gold ground, cond. 7, 1 lb, 4" h, 3-7/8" dia ...................................................... 36.50

## Eagle Coffee

Can, litho tin, "Eagle Brand Coffee, George C. Buell & Co. Inc., Rochester & Auburn, N.Y.," spread-wing eagle on mountain in ring of stars, white ground, cond. 8+, 1 lb, 6-1/8" h, 4-3/8" dia .............................. 275.00

## Earl & Wilson

Display, countertop, wood with cardboard inserts advertising different collars, "Earl & Wilson Collar Packet, 3 for $1," 4 collars in display, glass top, circa 1923, 16-1/4" h, 27-1/4" w....................................................... 825.00

## Eastman Kodak

See Kodak

## Easybright Polish

Can, litho tin, "Easybright Polish, Glycerine Paste," round image of girl in bonnet, text on blue/yellow ring, cond. 8+, 1-1/4" h, 2-5/8" dia ....................................... 95.50

## Eatagood Peanut Butter

Pail, litho tin, "Eatagood Brand Peanut Butter, Smith & Son, Inc., White River Junction, Vt.," red text/graphic design, yellow ground, cond. 8, 1 lb, 3-1/2" h, 3-3/4" dia.......................................................... 273.00

## Ebbert

Sign, litho tin, self-framing, "In The Shade Of The Old Apple Tree" under scene of man/woman picking apples by wagon/2 horses, chickens by lane, "Best At The Price, The Ebbert, Owensboro, Ky., And Always The Same" in upper-left, name on frame, cond. G, 23-3/8" h, 34-1/2" w........................................................ 880.00

## Edelweiss Beer

Glass, etched, "Edelweiss Registered, The P. Schoenhofen Brwg. Co., Chicago," 2 with small chips, cond. VG, 3-1/2" h, 2-1/4" dia, set of 4 .......................... 55.00
Tray, litho metal, "Edelweiss Beer" in gold on image of smiling woman, "The Peter Schoenhofen Brewing Co., Chicago" on floral rim, ©1913, cond. G, 13-1/2" dia........................................................ 165.00

## Eden Cube Cut

Tin, vertical pocket, litho tin, "Best In The World, Don't

Bite, Eden Cube Cut, Globe Tobacco Co., Detroit, Mich., U.S.A.," white text, red ground, central leaf with "Eden" in black, cond. 8 ..................................... 711.00

## Edgeworth

Tin, flat pocket, litho tin, small version, "Edgeworth Extra High Grade Sliced Pipe Tobacco," black text, blue ground, full, mint, 5/8" h, 3-1/4" w, 2-1/4" d .............. 33.00
Tin, vertical box, litho tin, 4-sided concave, humidor top, "Edgeworth Extra High Grade Ready Rubbed," black text, central light-blue diamond, lighter blue ground with embellishments, knob finial, cond. 8, 6-3/4" h, 4-1/2" sq...................................................... 55.00
Tin, vertical pocket, litho tin
Sample, "Edgeworth Extra High Grade Ready-Rubbed Smoking Tobacco," cobalt lettering, blue ground, cond. 9........................................................ 82.50
"Edgeworth Ready-Rubbed Extra High Grade, America's Finest Pipe Tobacco," white lettering, blue/ white striped ground, Canadian tax stamp, full, cond. 9, 4-1/4" h, 3" w .................................. 646.00

## Edgeworth Junior

Tin, vertical pocket, litho tin
"Edgeworth Junior Extra High Grade Tobacco for pipe or cigarettes," pipe in blue/white shield, light-blue over cobalt ground, cond. 8.5 ........................ 72.00
"Edgeworth Junior, Light Mild Burley, Pipe-Cigarette, Tobacco," pipe in blue/white shield, blue ground with 2 dark bars, cond. 8.5 .......................... 188.00
Sign, cardboard, trolley, "All Kinds of Talking Machine Repairs Made, W.T. Geltz," shows Edison cylinder phonograph, framed, cond. NM, 13-1/2" h, 23-1/2" w .................................................. 1,155.00

## Edison Mazda Lamps

See also National Mazda Lamps
Calendar, paper
1925, "Dream Light" by Maxfield Parrish over "Edison Mazda" banner/Toledo merchant, complete pad, 19-1/8" h, 8-1/2" w....................................... 473.00
1927, "Reveries" by Maxfield Parrish under "Edison Mazda Lamps" banner, merchant info above full pad, small chip, few white spots, 19-1/8" h, 8-1/2" w ..................................................... 363.00
1929, "Golden Hours" by Maxfield Parrish under "Edison Mazda Lamps" banner, merchant info above full pad, scattered foxing, small piece of tape, 19-1/8" h, 8-1/2" w ....................................... 615.00

**Playing cards, "Edison Mazda Lamps," pictures "The Waterfall" by Maxfield Parrish, complete deck, boxed, $127.50.**

1930, "Ecstasy" by Maxfield Parrish over merchant info over "Edison Mazda Lamps" banner, complete pad, minor scuffing/margin wear, 19-1/8" h, 8-1/2" w....................................................... 881.00

1931, "The Waterfall" by Maxfield Parrish over merchant info over "Edison Mazda Lamps" banner, complete pad with some damage to cover sheet, age toning, 19-1/8" h, 8-1/2" w ..................... 505.00

1932, "Solitude" by Maxfield Parrish over merchant info over "Edison Mazda Lamps" banner, complete pad separated, pad paper loss from tape, minor wear, 19-1/8" h, 8-1/2" w.............................. 473.00

Calendar, pocket, celluloid

1922, "Edison Mazda" in circular design with wings at top, "Egypt" by Maxfield Parrish, cond. 7-, 3-3/4" h, 2-1/4" w.......................................................... 99.00

1931, "Edison Mazda Lamps" in banner at top, "The Waterfall" by Maxfield Parrish, cond. NM, 3-3/4" h, 2-1/4" w.......................................................... 168.50

Tin, litho tin, "Edison Mazda Lamps for your car, The Handy Kit of Spares," bulb on orange ground, Maxfield Parrish "Get Together" design on side and on 2 cardboard boxes containing bulbs (orig contents of tin), cond. 8, tin 1-3/4" h, 3-5/8" w, 2-1/2" d.............. 220.00

## Edison Star Metal Polish

Can, metal, star motif, "Edison Star Metal Polish, Edison

Chemical Co., Boston, Mass.," rust spots/scratches, no cap, 8 oz ...................................................... 22.00

## Edward's Coffee

Can, keywind, litho tin, "Edward's Coffee" in white on green panel, "Fine Grind" in red on yellow band, "5¢ Off Regular Price" in red on white seal on red ground, Safeway Foods, unopened, cond. 9-, 1 lb .......... 93.50

## Edward's Marshmallows

Display box, litho tin, glass see-through lid, "Edward's Sugar Puff Marshmallows," child in cap, white ground, circa 1920s, cond. 8, 4-1/2" h, 13" w, 10" d ................... 440.00

## Effecto Auto Finishes

Sign, flange, porcelain, "We Sell Effecto Auto Finishes And Pratt & Lambert Varnishes," ground in 7 swaths of color, cond. 8, 7" h, 14-1/4" w ........................ 1,072.50

## Eight Ball

Mirror, metal frame, round "Eight Ball" logo upper-right, bottle lower-left, minor scratches/stain, 11-3/4" h, 3-5/8" w............................................................ 82.50

Sign, button, celluloid over cardboard, "Here's Your Cue, Drink Eight 8 Ball, The Big Favorite," pictures bottle top and 8 ball, cond. NM, 9" dia........................ 275.00

## EIS

Sign, tin, octagonal, "Stop Here for Brake Service, For Best Stops We Use EIS Parts Fluid," green/white/orange design, cond. 8, 15" h, 15" w .................. 16.50

## Electomatic Typewriter Ribbon

Tin, litho tin, round, shows Electomatic typewriter, International Business Machines, Rochester NY, cond. 8.5+................................................................. 41.00

## Electric Mixture

Tin, litho tin, square corner, "Pace's Electric Mixture," street scene with 4 women, cond. 7.5, 2" h, 4-1/2" w, 3-1/2" d ........................................................... 212.00

## Electrolux

Salesman sample, refrigerator, plastic, front door removes to reveal food cards, back removes to reveal glass tube bubbler, bottom bubbler tube broken, orig presentation box, 7-1/2" h, 4" w, 1-3/4" d.......... 242.00

## Elephant Coffee

Can, litho tin, hinged lid, "The Renowned Elephant Java Coffee, 3 lbs. Net Weight, General Depot, 7 Vesey St., New York, Jos. Stiner & Co., Importers," black graphic of elephant/tropical trees, green ground, cond. 8, 5-1/4" h, 7-3/4" w, 5-1/2" d ............................. 1,650.00

## Elgin Watches

Clock, neon, tin face, metal housing, reverse-painted glass cover, "Elgin Watches" in white, white numbers, lights white, cover cracked, 22-1/2" dia, 5-1/2" d ................................ 280.50

Sign, glass, reverse-painted, "Full Bodied Jeweled Elgin Watches, The World's Standard" under winged statue holding pocket watch, framed, minor pieces missing from face, 29-1/2" h, 23" w ................................ 522.50

## Elite Powder

Tin, litho tin, "Elite Powder, A Perfect Foot Powder," cond. 8-8.5, 4-1/8" h, 2-1/8" w ..................................... 34.00

## Elizabeth Park Coffee

Can, keywind, litho tin, garden scene with gazebo/flowers, cond. 8, 4" h, 5" dia ..................................... 797.50

## El Moriso Cigars

Sign, cardboard, standup, "El Moriso 5¢ Guaranteed Hi-Grade Cigar, Cellophane Wrapped," red/black text, yellow ground, front separating from cardboard, cond. G, 10-1/8" h, 13-5/8" w ......................................... 33.00

## El Paxo Cigars

Can, litho tin, Indian princess, cond. 8+, 5-1/2" h, 5" dia ................................................................. 187.00

## El Producto Cigars

Can, litho tin, woman on stone bench, peacock/cliff/water, blue ground, held 50 cigars, cond. 8+, 5-3/4" h, 5-1/2" dia ......................................................... 176.00

## Embassy Cigarettes

Tin, vertical pocket, litho tin, hinged lid, name in red on all sides/top, crest flanked by lions/"20 Cigarettes"/star emblem, W.D. & H.O. Wills, cond. 8.5, 3" h, 3-3/4" w, 3/4" d .................................................................. 218.00

## Emblem Motorcycle Co.

Pocket mirror, celluloid, "Strength and Power, Emblem Mfg. Co., Angola, N.Y.," shows 2-seat motorcycle, cond. EXC, 1-3/4" h, 2-3/4" w ........................... 687.50

## Emerson

Clock, lightup, glass face/front, metal case, "Emerson Television and Radio," white/yellow text, red ground, round clock face at left, "Emerson" logo in center, window with "Better Style, Performance, Value...Emerson Is Your Best Buy" on spinner, cond. EXC, 10-1/4" h, 14" w ................................................................ 385.00

## Empire

Pinback button, celluloid over metal, "I Chirp For The Empire Because It Makes The Most Dollars For Me" and "Empire Cream Separator Co., Bloomfield, New Jersey," pictures cream separator, 1-1/4" dia ........................ 44.00

## Empress Coffee

Can, keywind, litho tin, "Empress Coffee, New Pressure Pack," queen at bottom, "Drip Grind" in red crown at

Can, oil can, tin, "Enco Handy Oil, Humble Oil & Refining Company, Houston, Texas," plastic neck and spout, 4 oz, $28.50.

top, white circle with gold/orange/red bands, cond. 8.25, 1 lb ................................................................. 38.50

## Empson's

Sign, cardboard, die-cut, tomato/leaves shape, "Use Empson's 'Preferred Stock' Ketchup," white text on red tomato, "Empson's" in black on white card, framed, cond. VG, 10" h, 14" w ...................................... 159.50

## Enco (See Photo)

## Ensign Perfection Cut

Tin, vertical pocket, litho tin
"Ensign Perfect Cut Tobacco," Yale, blue/yellow/red flags on white ground, cond. 7.5-8.5 ........... 385.00
"Ensign Perfection Cut Tobacco," Amherst on rear, blue/yellow/red flags on white ground, cond. 7.5 ..................................................... 442.00
"Ensign Perfection Cut Tobacco," Washington and Lee, blue/yellow/red flags on white ground, cond. 8-8.5 ........................................................ 1,210.00

## Enterprise Cash Market

Bill hook, celluloid/metal, oval, "Enterprise Cash Market, Homer W. Schrack, 218 W. Main St., Alhambra, Phone 441 J, We Deliver," hand-colored image of men behind meat counter, Alabama, cond. EXC, 6-3/4" h, 2" w ................................................................. 154.00

## Epicure Tobacco

Tin, vertical pocket, litho tin, "Epicure Shredded Plug Tobacco," rectangle shows person in red shirt sleeping on ground, red ground, full, cond. 8.5 .............. 285.00

## Erzinger's No. 1 Smoking Mixture

Tin, horizontal box, litho tin, text in black banners, circular of shock of grain, floral design on red ground, J. Erzinger, cond. 8, 3" h, 5" w, 3-5/8" d ....................... 91.00

Sign, porcelain, "Esso Elephant Kerosene," cond. 8+, 24" h, 12" w, $660. (Photo courtesy of Collectors Auction Services)

## Esser's Paints

Clock, lightup, Pam style, "Esser's Paints, Yessir! It's Esser's Glass," red outline of painter with 2 cans on yellow center, red text, white border, 15" dia .............. 165.00

## Esso

**Reference:** J. Sam McIntyre, *The Esso Collectibles Handbook: Memorabilia from Standard Oil of New Jersey*, Schiffer Publishing, 1998

Banner, canvas, "World's Finest Choice" in red over "Esso" Happy figure, cond. 7, 83" h, 6" w.......................... 132.00
Calendar, paper
 1933, color images at top of each month, Jan/Feb missing, cond. 8, 12-3/4" h, 8-3/4" w .............. 97.00
 1947, baby with "1947" tag receiving globe from old man with scythe, Tennessee merchant info, newer frame, NOS, cond. EXC, 16" h, 9-3/4" w ........................ 33.00
Display, cardboard box, die-cut, "Handy Oil" in white beside "Esso" oil-drop figure, blue ground, 20 plastic figural bottles, full, "Esso Handy Oil code no. 8355," bottles 5-1/2" h, display, 10" h, 15" w ............... 385.00
Football team roster, cardboard, 1938 Army-Navy game, sliding insert, 3-1/2" h, 5-3/4" w .......................... 42.00
Gas globe
 2 lenses, high-profile metal body, "Esso" in red over black triangular "Ethyl" logo, white ground, all cond. 9, 15-1/2" dia ............................................... 363.00
 Milk glass, 1-pc, fired-on text, black "Esso" in oval, foreign, paint loss, cond. 7/6, 14"h, 14" w, 5" d .............................................................. 302.50
Pen/pencil set, "Esso" in oval, pencil shows Happy, pen shows girlfriend, NOS, cond. 9, 5" l .................... 110.00
Pins, enameled metal, die-cut, Happy/girlfriend with red bow in hair, oval "Esso" logo on outfits, he salutes, she waves, NOS, 1-1/8" h, 1/2" w, pr........................ 93.50
Plate, ceramic, oval "Esso" logo under cartoon image of dog, black on white ground, cond. 8, 8" dia, pr................. 55.00
Pocket knife
 Metal, engraved, visible gas pump shape, "Essolube" on

body on both sides, "Standard" on globe on 1 side, "Esso" on globe on other, cond. 9, 3" l .............. 121.00
 Stainless steel, gasoline pump shape, 2-sided, "Esso" at top of pump, cond. 8/7+, closed 2-1/4" l, extended 4-5/8" l ........................................... 82.50
Sign, porcelain
 Individual letters, black, spells out "Esso Service," mounting hardware, NOS, cond. 9, 13-5/8" h ............. 231.00
 "Esso Royal Raylight Paraffin," oval logo, red/black text, red over white over red ground, cond. 7, 18" h, 22-1/4" w ...................................................... 137.50

## Estey Organ Works

Sign, paper, "Estey Organ Works, Brattleboro, Vt., U.S.A.," red/black text lower-right, bird's-eye view of factory/surrounding area, gesso frame, stains/repaired frame, 21" h, 17" w.............................................. 121.00

## Ethyl Gasoline Corp.

Gas globe
 2 glass lenses, high-profile metal body, "Refiners" in black over "Power Distributors" in yellow on black bar over "Ethyl Brand of Anti-Knock Compound" in black triangular Ethyl logo with black rays, white ground, lens cond. 8/7.5, body cond. 7, 16-1/2" dia ................................................ 1,210.00
 2 lenses, newer plastic body, "Imperial Refineries" in red on white border, center with "Ethyl Brand of Anti-Knock Compound, Ethyl Corporation" in black triangular Ethyl logo with yellow rays, lens cond. 9, body cond. 8, 13-1/2" dia.............................. 209.00
Sign, porcelain, 2-sided, round, "Derby's Flexgas" in white on red border, yellow/black Ethyl triangular logo in center on white ground, cond. 8, 30" dia.......................... 473.00

## Eureka Harness Oil

Can, tin, "Eureka Harness Oil, for oiling, blacking and preserving the leather of harnesses, carriage tops, etc.," white text, cond. G, 9-1/2" h, 5-1/2" sq.................. 176.00
Sign, tin, embossed, "Eureka Harness Oil, Makes Old Harness Like New," black text, yellow ground, framed, small chips/paint specks, 5-1/4" h, 20-1/4" w .................. 154.00

## Eureka Stock Food

Sign, paper, "Eureka Stock Food, The Great Flesh Producer, Manufactured by Shrader Drug Co., Iowa City, Iowa," 3 girls in winter coats/hats, black text, large stain lower-left/some edges loss, 20-1/4" h, 15-3/8" w..................................................... 88.00

## Eve

Tin, vertical pocket, litho tin, "Eve Cube Cut, Globe Tobacco Co., Detroit" nude woman with tobacco leaf at waist, cond. 8+............................................. 566.00

## Eveready

Sign, paper
 "Broadcasting Studio" on clubhouse with 5 boys/dog, red "Eveready Radio Batteries" logo, artwork by Jackson, 1930, cond. G, 32" h, 24" w .............................. 242.00

Bank, plastic, "Save With the Cat, Eveready, ©1981, Union Carbide Corp," $5.

"The difference between Day and Night," red "Eveready Flashlights & Batteries" logo, 2 children watching man in library shine flashlight on globe, artwork by Frances Tipton Hunter, archival backing, cond. VG, 32-1/2" h, 22-1/4" w ..................... 192.50

## Everpure

Sign, porcelain, 2-sided, "Everpure Safe Water," silhouette of nude at spring, cond. 8-8.25, 12" h, 9" w............110.00

## Eversweet Deodorant

Tip tray, litho tin, rectangular, "A Toilet Necessity For Refined People," woman in long white dress with upstretched arms holding flowers, cond. 9.25 ........................... 577.50

## Evinrude

Clock, lightup, double bubble, glass face/front, metal body, "Authorized Evinrude Parts & Service," blue/red text, blue/yellow triangular design in white border with blue numbers, cond. 8+, 15" dia ................... 1,045.00

Pin, metal, oversized, shape of outboard motor, "Evinrude" in blue on white, red oval logo, 3-1/4" h, 2" w, 1" d ............................................................. 80.00

Sign, hardboard, "Dependable Home Remedies, Ex-Lax, The Chocolated Laxative," NOS, 10" h, 15" w, $15.

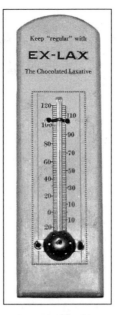

Thermometer, painted wood, "Keep 'regular' with Ex-Lax, The Chocolated Laxative," near-mint, orig box, 6-1/8" h, 2" w, $38.50.

## Excelsior Beer

Tray, litho tin, oval, "Compliments of The Excelsior Brewing Co., Brooklyn, N.Y.," on lower rim, woman in sailor outfit with glass, flanked by beer bottles, cond. G, 13-3/4" h, 16-3/4" w ............................................................. 396.00

## Exide

Sign

Metal, flange, die-cut, battery-shape, "Exide" in red on battery front, red circle on side, black ground, cond. 8.5/8, 13" h, 14" w ........................................ 258.50

Tin, embossed, "Exide Batteries," white text, red trim, black ground, red border, cond. 7, 16" h, 48" w ............................................................. 143.00

## Ex-Lax

Door push, porcelain, "Push, Get Your Box Now, For Relief of Constipation, Ex-Lax, The Chocolated Laxative," shows red/white/blue box, cobalt ground, cond. 8+, 8" h, 4" w.................................................... 357.50

Door push/pull, porcelain, "Push, The Happy Medium Laxative," shows red/white/blue box on yellow panel, cobalt ground, "Pull" sign with same design, both with chips/scratches/rust, each 8" h, 4" w, pr ....................... 269.50

Thermometer, porcelain, square corners, "Ex-Lax, the chocolated laxative, millions prefer Ex-Lax," red/white/blue/cobalt, 1930-1940s, cond. 9.25, 36" h, 8-1/8" w ........................................................... 275.00

# F

## Fairbanks-Morse

Sign, porcelain

"Fairbanks-Morse Sales & Service" in yellow on black border, yellow center with "FM" logo of hand holding weight, scratches/chips/stain, 20" dia ............ 66.00

"Fairbanks-Morse Scales," white text, cond. 9.25, 9" h, 50" w................................................................. 66.00

## Fairbanks Soap

Trade card, complete set of 8, Fairbanks Twins preparing for/taking bath in wooden tub, circa 1885, N.K. Fairbanks & Co., corner breaks on 2 cards, cond. 8.25, 5" h, 3-1/4" w, set ........................................... 344.30

## Fairmont Creamery Co.

Pot scraper, litho tin, "Use this scraper to keep many things clean and to get the best price sell Fairmont, your cream, The Fairmont Creamery Co., Established 1884," red/orange, cond. 7.5+, 2-7/8" h, 3-3/8" w .................. 143.00

## Fairmount Ice Cream

Can, tin, "Fairmount Imperial Bulk Ice Cream, Guaranteed To Satisfy," white/green text, white over light-green ground, Fairmount Foods Co., Parkersburg WV, cond. VG, 32 oz ...............................................11.00

## Fairmount Tobacco

Tin, vertical pocket, litho tin

"Fairmount Mixture, Manufactured By Weisert Bros. Tob. Co., St. Louis," scroll lettered "Turkish Virginia Perique Havana" in white box on red/white latticed ground, no "10¢" cond. 8 .............................. 327.00

"Fairmount Tobacco, 10¢, Manufactured By Weisert Bros. Tob. Co., St. Louis," scroll with "10¢" in white box on red/white latticed ground, white lid, creamier color, cond. 8+ ............................................. 309.00

"Fairmount Tobacco, 10¢, Manufactured By Weisert Bros. Tob. Co., St. Louis," scroll with "10¢" in white box on red/white latticed ground, gold lid, whiter color, cond. 9, tall version ............................ 538.00

## Fairy Soap

**History:** Fairy Soap was produced by the N.K. Fairbanks Soap Company and was one of several popular brands sold by the firm. First marketed in 1897, its oval shape separated it from the rectangular bars of its competitors. Early advertisements showed a child sitting on a cake of Fairy Soap, and the company's slogan was, "Have You a Little Fairy in the House?"

Advertisement, magazine ad, fairies on honeybees flying with a bar of soap, promotes "1900 Fairy Calendar Free," from The Cosmopolitan, 9-1/2" h, 6-1/2" w.............................................................. 15.00

Tip tray, litho tin, round, "Have you a little 'Fairy' in your home?," girl sitting on oval cake of Fairy soap, cond. 9 ...............................................................110.00

## Fairy Tree

Tin, litho tin

"Lucie Attwell's Fairy House Biscuit & Money Box," round base/domed top, cartoon images of fairies with wheelbarrow on base, silver top, William Crawford & Sons, coin slot added to top, cond. 8, 8" h, 8" dia ....................................................... 253.00

"Lucie Attwell's Fairy Tree Biscuit Money Box," round base/cone-shape top, cartoon images of squirrel and fairies on base, baby surrounded by fairies on top, William Crawford & Sons, English, cond. 8, 14" h, 5-1/2" dia ............................................. 467.50

## Falke Mercantile Co.

Bin, litho tin, Cinnamon, "The Falke Merc. Co., Denver, Colo." on lift-up lower door, round image of battleship, cond. 7+, 12-1/2" h, 9" w, 9-3/8" d ................... 715.00

## Falk Tobacco Co.

Tin, litho tin, "Highest Grade Smoking Tobacco Manufactured by Falk Tobacco Co., New York and Richmond, Va.," double lids, 5-1/2" h, 7" w, 4-1/2" d, $148.50.

**Wall display, "Falstaff, Premium Quality Beer," metal background, plastic half bottle and logo, wooden frame, 19" h, 8" w, $22.50.**

# Falstaff

Tin, vertical pocket, cardboard, tin top/bottom, "Falstaff Granulated Plug," round image of Falstaff, dark ground, cond. 8 ............................................. 1,099.00

# Famous Mainsprings

Tin, litho tin, "One Dozen Famous Mainsprings, Every Spring Warranted, W.P. Hitchcock, Syracuse, N.Y.," portrait of Indian in headdress on animal skin, cond. 7.5-8, 1" h, 3" w, 3-3/8" d ...................................110.00

**Lunch box, litho tin, "Fashion Cut Plug Tobacco," shows man and woman in formal attire, cond. 8.5, 4-1/5" h, 7-1/2" w, 5" d, $385.**

# Fan Taz

Watch fob, celluloid center, "R.U.A.(fan symbol)? I Am, Drink Fan Taz, Drink of the Fans, A Hit," baseball theme with ball/bat, back has baseball score keeper, orig leather strap, cond. NM, 1-7/8" dia ......... 1,320.00

# Far-go Machine Oil

Can, tin, name in body of cartoon man with hat, yellow ground, Fargo Oil Co., Denver, cond. 8.5, 1 oz, 3" h, 2" w ................................................................. 88.00

# Farmers Pride Coffee

Can, paper label, "Farmers Pride Brand Steel Cut Coffee," girl holding doll beside farmer with coffee cup, Hulman & Co., Terre Haute, Ind., NOS, 6-1/8" h, 4-1/8" dia......................................................... 275.00

# Fashion Cut Plug Tobacco (See Photo)

# Fast Mail Tobacco

Can, paper label
"Bagley's Fast Mail Fine Cut" around side, no graphics on top, cond. 8+, 2" h, 8" dia ........................ 143.00
"Fast Mail Light Chewing Tobacco," colorful train, circa 1910, cond. 8, 5" h, 5-1/2" dia .................. 2,420.00
Pail, litho tin, "Fast Mail Fruit Flavored Tobacco...Dark But Not Strong," train image, red/black design, gold-tone lid, cond. 9, 5" h, 5-1/2" dia ................... 2,447.50

# Father Christmas Toffee (See Photo)

# Fatima Turkish Cigarettes

Box, display, cardboard, pictures pack of cigarettes showing woman behind veil, flanked by symbols, opened cigarette pack on back, cond. 8+, 17-1/4" h, 13-1/2" w, 4" d.................................................. 385.00
Match holder/ashtray, ceramic, "Fatima Turkish Blend Cigarettes" and "Cameron & Cameron Co., Richmond, Va., Liggett & Myers Tobacco Co. Successor," scratches/crazing, 3" h, 4" w, 3" l..................... 176.00

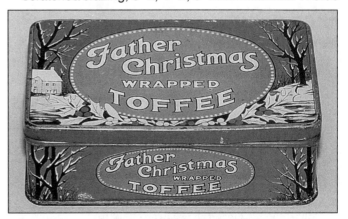

**Tin, litho tin, "Father Christmas Wrapped Toffee," red and blue, 1-7/8" h, 5-1/2" l, 3-1/4" w, $49.50.**

Printer's proof, cardboard, pictures pack of cigarettes showing woman behind veil, flanked by symbols, red ground, cond. NM, 22" h, 18" w ........................ 143.00

## Fatoco

Tin, vertical pocket, litho tin, "Fatoco Crushed Plug For Pipe and Cigarette, Falk Tobacco Co., Richmond, Va.," green ground, cond. 8 .............................. 143.00

## Faultless

Display jar, clear glass, 2-pc, embossed "Faultless Wonder Nipples," nipple-shaped glass lid in amber satin finish, cond. EXC, 13" h, 5-7/8" dia ................ 3,080.00

## Faultless Pepsin Chips

Sign, cardboard, die-cut, standup, "Chewing Gum, Faultless Pepsin Chips, Delicious and Fragrant," girl in blue dress at corner chair, a finger to her lips, circa 1890s, restored to cond. NM, 15-3/4" h, 12" w .............. 660.00

## Favorite Tube Patch

Tin, cardboard sides, tin top/bottom, "Favorite Self Vulcanizing Tube Patch, Sticks and Stays Stuck," woman driving horseless carriage, 4" h, 2-1/4" w, 1-1/4" d .............................................................. 935.00

## Fayette's Ice Cream

Sign, porcelain, die-cut, 2-sided, "Fayette's Ice Cream," cobalt text/trim, orange ground, cond. VG, 20" h, 28" w ................................................................. 346.50

## Federal Judge

Sign, tin, embossed, "Judge For Yourself, Federal Judge, 5¢ Cigar," red/white, circa 1930s, cond. 8-8.25, 9" h, 20" w .................................................................. 66.00

## Federal Tire

Calendar, 1926, cardboard, die-cut, "There's a Federal at the end of your phone - call up," flapper woman with candlestick phone behind Federal Balloon Cord tire, full pad, cond. 8-, 5-1/2" h, 3-1/4" w .................. 165.00

## Feen-a-mint

Display case, tin, wooden base, mirror top center, back with shelf, "Feen-a-mint, The Chewing Laxative, Chew It Like Gum, No Taste But The Mint, Children Like It," scratches/paint chips/dents, 16-1/4" h, 7-1/2" w, 5-1/2" d .................................................................. 500.00

Sign, porcelain, "Feen-a-mint for Constipation," shows box and product on orange background, touch-ups/fading/rust, 7" h, 29-1/4" w ................................ 715.00

## Fergus Rolled Oats

Box, cardboard, round, "Fergus Brand Quick Cooking Rolled Oats," waterfall scene, yellow text, white ground, Beall & McGowan Co., Ferfus Falls MN, cond. 8-, 3 lb ................................................................. 66.00

## Ferndell

Calendar, cardboard, 1903, "Calendar for 1903, Ferndell Pure Foods," woman reading book, 6 months per left/right border, advertises Ferndell Coffee on back, cond. 9, 8-1/2" h, 7" w ................................................. 27.50

## Ferndell-Remus Tea

Tin, litho tin, "Ferndell-Remus Brand Tea," Oriental scene with bridge over stream, distributed by Spague, Warner & Co., Chicago, cond. G, 1/2-lb, 5" h, 3-1/8" sq ................................................................. 27.50

## D.M. Ferry & Co. Seeds

Seed box, oak, litho paper label under lid, "Choice Flower Seeds From D.M. Ferry & Co., Detroit, Mich.," shows 3 children in flower garden, cond. 8.5, 6-3/4" h, 11-1/2" w, 9-3/4" d ................................................................. 440.00

## Festive Pop Corn

Tin, cardboard, tin top/bottom, shows circus performers, unopened, 5-1/4" h, 2-5/8" dia ........................ 330.00

## Field & Stream

Display, cardboard, wood base, die-cut, "Field & Stream Outdoor Clothing," cartoon winter scene of dog chasing rabbit past hunter in red coat, red text in yellow panel, also black text, 3 pcs mounted for 3-D effect, Gordon & Ferguson, St. Paul MN, cond. EXC, 11-3/4" h, 15-3/4" w ................................................................. 82.50

## Filtered Gasoline

Gas globe, pierced tin-sanded/painted metal inserts, painted-metal collar, heavily weathered, needs restored, 17-1/2" dia ........................................ 715.00

## FI-NA-ST Peanut Butter

Pail, litho tin, "FI-NA-ST First National Peanut Butter," round image of man in white coat, white text, red ground, cond. 9, 1 lb ............................................ 143.00

## Fiore 100

Gas globe, Capcolite plastic body with 2 lenses, "Fiore 100" in black, orange ground, lens cond. 9/8+, body cond. 7, 13-1/2" dia .......................................... 187.00

## Fire Brigade

Cigar box, "Fire Brigade" in red over cartoon image of firemen fighting house fire, circa 1901, 50-count, Rochester Litho Co., cond. 9- .......................... 522.50

## Fireman's Fund Insurance Co.

Sign, cardboard, "Agency Of the Automobile Department, Fireman's Fund Insurance Company," scenes of "Fire, Property Damage Collision, Theft," framed, Young & McCallister, L.A., cond. 8, 12-1/2" h, 22-1/2" w ................................................................. 550.00

# Firestone

Ashtray, rubber tire with glass insert, "Century of
Progress, Firestone, Chicago 1934," orig box, cond.
8+, 5-3/4" dia........................................................ 242.00

Blotter, "Firestone Gum-Dipped Motorcycle Tires, Most
Miles Per Dollar," man on early motorcycle, small "F"
shield logo, merchant info mentions Harley-Davidson,
cond. 8+, 3-1/8" h, 6" w.........................................110.00

Display, tire rack, cardboard, "Firestone, Most Miles Per
Dollar," orange/white text, cobalt ground, orange border, G, 5-1/8" h, 17" w, 9-1/8" d........................... 44.00

Pin, lapel, oval cloisonné enameled metal pin with "Firestone" on white bar between blue bands, "Firestone 1915
Picnic" in gold on blue ribbon, cond. NM, pin 1/2" h,
3/4" w, ribbon 3" l.................................................. 36.50

Sign

Cardboard, die-cut, round, pr, fit in tires, "Firestone
Oldfield Type 4-40-21 $5.95, The Tire That Taught
Thrift To Millions" and "$3.60 4-40-21, Firestone
Courier Type, Low Priced Mileage, Good Quality,"
cond. G, 22" dia, pr.........................................115.50

Metal, 2-sided, "Firestone" in white on red panel, white
ground, red border, cond. 7, 10" h, 24" w .......... 38.50

Porcelain, flange, die-cut, oval, "Firestone" in orange
on black panel with "F" shield logo, tilted tire
ground, cond. 7, 36" h, 28" w...................... 825.00

Porcelain, "Firestone" in orange, black ground, wood
frame, NOS, cond. 9, 20" h, 74" w................ 467.50

Porcelain, "Firestone, Ground Grip Farm Tires,"
orange/white text, cobalt ground, wood frame,
cond.8 ............................................................ 550.00

Tin, "Firestone" red/white bowtie logo, white ground,
cond. 7, 10" h, 25" w...................................... 22.00

# First American Life Insurance Co.

Sign, litho paper, wood frame, name in white on black
border around image of Indian brave, creases/soiling,
17-1/2" sq......................................................... 220.00

# First National Bank

Sign, glass, reverse-painted "First National Bank," black
3-D text, gold ground, framed, minor flaking,
24" sq............................................................... 544.50

# First Pick Coffee

Tin, keywind, litho tin
"First Pick Coffee," 2 yellow chicks in grass/flowers, back
pictures coffeepot, cond. 8.5+, 1 lb ................ 2,035.00
"High Grade Vacuum Packed First Pick Coffee,"
shows coffee cup and two white chicks on white/
cobalt ground, cond. 8, 1 lb ........................... 216.00

# B. Fischer Coffee

Bin, store display, litho tin, "B. Fischer & Co., Importers,
New York, Nectar Java," shows racing yachts, cond.
8+, 22" h, 13" sq.............................................. 467.50

# Fisher's Peanuts

Can, litho tin,
"Fisher's Salted in
the Shell Peanuts,"
pry lid, dents, 10 lb,
$82.50.

# Fishmuth' Cube Mixture

Tin, vertical pocket, litho tin, concave front, flat back,
"Fishmuth's Cube Mixture," portrait of woman, yellow
ground, cond. 8, 4" h, 3-1/4" w....................... 3,003.00

# Fisk

Calendar, cardboard
1926, die-cut, "Fisk Balloon Tires Absorb The Shock,"
boy sitting on tire, framed, pad begins with May,
5-1/2" h, 3-1/4" w ............................................ 71.50
1927, embossed, "Time to Re-Tire, Get a Fisk," boy
with tire/lamp, white on blue ground, full pad,
framed, 6-1/8" h, 3-1/2" w............................... 60.50

Display, figural, composition, boy with pair of newer paja-
mas/rubber tire/candle, boy incomplete, cond. G,
22" h....................................................................110.00

Can, litho tin, "Fisk Gas
Line Anti-Freeze," screw
top, 12 oz, $15.

Sign, litho tin over cardboard, "Five Brothers Plug, Toothsome as Honey," 5 bears with product, red ground, yellow trim, cond. 8.5, 16" sq, $6,050. (Photo courtesy of Wm. Morford)

Poster, litho paper, "Flexible Flyer" brand skis, "Ski Pico Peak, Long Trail Lodge, Rutland, Vt.," $1,000.

## Sign

Litho tin, clock design with moveable hands, "Fisk Tires" on shield in front of boy with tire/lamp, black shield/border, yellow ground, cond. 8, 6-1/8" dia ..................................................... 330.00

Litho tin, clock design with moveable hands, "Time to Re-tire Get Fisk Tires," boy with tire/lamp, blue shield, yellow ground, blue trim with white numbers, cond. 8, 6-3/4" dia........................................... 176.00

Wood, framed, 2-sided, "Fisk Tires Tubes Service Station," blue shield over boy with tire/lamp, black text, yellow ground, cond. 7, 41-1/2" h, 30-1/2" w..................................................... 825.00

## Five Brothers Plug (See Photo)

## Five-O

Sign, litho tin, embossed, "Five-O Chocolate Flavor," bottle at left, yellow ground, red band at bottom, red border, 1940s, cond. 8.75+, 12" h, 24" w ................110.00

## Fleet-Wing Petroleum Products

Gas globe, 1 lens, wide glass body, "Fleet-Wing" in blue over red bird, white ground, cond. 8, 14" dia ................. 357.50

Thermometer, painted metal, rounded top/bottom, "Fleet-Wing Petroleum Products, Tailored to the Season," red bird at top, red/black text, white ground, cond. 7, 38-1/2" h, 8" w..................................................... 60.50

## Fleischmann's Yeast

Calendar, paper, 1905, "On Hand The Year Round," man outside storefront with horse/Fleischmann's buggy on street, pad begins with June, framed, cond. 8, calendar 14-3/8" h, 10-1/8" w ..................................... 83.50

Sign, glass, reverse-painted "Fleischmann's Compressed Yeast," hand holding product in red circle mkd

"Special Attention Is Invited To Our Yellow Label Which Is Affixed To Every Cake Of Our Yeast And Of Which The Above Is A Fac-simile, The Only Genuine, Beware Of Imitation," framed, some loss of image, 27-3/4" h, 21-1/4" w................................................110.00

## Flexible Flyer (See Photo)

## Flick and Flock

Tin, vertical box, litho tin, both sides show 2 dogs on brown ground, cond. 7.5, 6" h, 5-1/2" w, 4" d...................659.00

## Flite

Gas globe, 2 lenses, narrow glass body, "Flite" in black on white ground, lens cond. 8, body cond. 9, 13-1/2" dia........................................................ 165.00

## Flor de Franklin

Tin, vertical box, litho tin, held 25 cigars, shows Benjamin Franklin holding kite string, cond. 7.5, 5-1/2" h, 3" w .................................................................110.00

## Florida Chewing Gum

Display, store box, cardboard, "Florida Chewing Gum, 3 Flavors, 5¢," shows woman reclining with 3 packs, 20 full packs, no cover, cond. EXC, 5-1/4" h, 6-3/8" w, 4-3/8" d ......................................................... 2,530.00

## Flying A

Also see Tydol

Gas globe

"Flying A Gasoline," 1 lens, newer plastic body, winged "A," red on white ground, body chipped, lens cond. 9, body cond. 7, 13-1/2" dia.......................... 203.50

"Flying A Super Extra," 2 lenses, newer high-profile metal body, winged "A," white on red ground, lenses scratched/chipped, 13-1/2" h ........................ 269.50

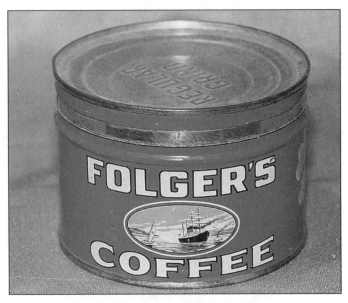

**Can, keywind, tin, "Folger's Coffee," 1/2-lb, $75.**

Gas pump top, shoebox form, milk glass, 2-sided, "Flying A Gasoline," winged "A" logo, red on white ground, cond. 8, 6-1/4" h, 14-1/2 w, 6-1/2" d.................. 825.00

# Folger's Coffee (See Photo)

# Forbes (See Photo)

# Force Wheat Flakes

Doll, cloth, stuffed, depicts man holding box of cereal, hat reads "Sunny Jim," 16-1/2" h .............................. 45.00

**Tin, litho tin, "Forbes Pure Ground Cream Tartar, The Woolson Spice Co., Toledo, Ohio," 1-1/2 oz, $5.**

## Ford Gum and Gumball Machines

Gumball machine, glass dome, chromed base, "Branded Ford Gum 1¢, Branded Ford For Your Protection" decal, cond. G, 12" h, 8" dia .............................110.00
Plate, black milk glass, fired-on images of vending machines, orig gift box, mint, 10" dia ................ 253.00

## Ford Motor Co.

**History:** Henry Ford began experimenting with internal combustion engines during the early 1890s and completed his first car in 1896. Ford and a number of associates filed incorporation papers in 1903, and the Ford Motor Company was born.

The two-cylinder Model A debuted on July 23, 1903. From 1903 to 1908, the first 19 letters of the alphabet were used to name the cars, although some models were experimental and never reached the production stage. The first Model T was introduced in 1908 and was an immediate success, due to the number of improvements made over previous models. The company built the first moving automobile assembly line in 1913, and on May 26, 1927, the 15-millionth Model T rolled out of the plant.

In 1942, the company halted automobile production and began manufacturing aircraft engines, tanks, and other machinery of war to assist in the European theater. Ford even produced 8,600 B-24 (Liberator) bombers.

Postwar efforts centered around revitalizing the financially strapped company. The Thunderbird was introduced in 1954, the Continental Mark II in 1955, and the Falcon in 1959. The oft-maligned Edsel debuted on Sept. 4, 1957, and the company announced it was dropping the line on Nov. 19, 1959.

The much-loved Mustang hit the road in 1964, following one of the most innovative advertising campaigns in history. First, reporters viewed the car at the Ford Pavilion of the New York World's Fair. Then they were provided with a set of road rally instructions and given Mustangs for the 750-mile trip to Detroit. Naturally, all of the major newspapers covered the event. Time and Newsweek published cover stories on the

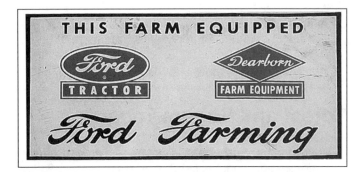

**Sign, tin, "This Farm Equipped, Ford Tractor, Dearborn Farm Equipment, Ford Farming," wear, dents, scratches, 11" h, 22" w, $30.**

rally, and the Ford sponsored simultaneous programming on the three major television networks. As a result, Mustang was catapulted into position as the third- best selling car in America in just two years.

Banner, cloth, 1942 "Ford Six, 90 Horsepower, America's Most Modern Six," white text, red center, blue top/bottom, fading/creases, 60" h, 40" w ...................... 187.00

Lock, brass, "Ford" script logo in oval, guard for key slot, 2 "Ford" keys, cond. 8, 2-7/8" h, 1-3/4" w .......... 77.00

Sign
   Neon, oval, "Genuine Ford Parts," green neon, works, 18" h, 30" w........................................ 539.00
   Paper, "1946 Ford, Smart New Interiors, The Smartest Ford Car Ever Built!," 3 scenes of interior, cond. 7, 35" h, 46" w........................................ 88.00
   Porcelain, "Ford" in blue script in white oval on blue ground, cond. 7, 25-1/2" h, 40" w ................. 357.50
   Porcelain, 2-sided, die-cut, oval, "Genuine Ford Parts," oval logo in center, cond. 8/7+, 16-1/2" h, 24" w........................................ 335.50

Slide, glass, "The New Ford Town Sedan, Beauty of Line and Mechanical Excellence," red/white text under auto, "The Weir Supply Co.," cond. 8, 3-1/4" h, 4" w ............................................110.00

Smock, cloth, "Bay Shore Motors" in red embroidery around blue "Ford" oval, cond. 8, size 42 ........ 357.50

## Ford Motor Co., Misc. Retailers

Calendar, cardboard
   1920, scene of child in car, Rochester NY dealership, cond. 8.5, 13" h, 10" w...................................110.00
   1949, "Your Ford Dealer" with oval logo, Douglas MacArthur portrait, Pennsylvania merchant, Jan. page missing, cond. VG, 25-5/8" h, 16" w ............... 22.00

Matchbox, celluloid/metal, "Simsbury Garage Co., Repairing and Auto Supplies, Tires and Accessories, Gas, Mobiloils, Ford Sales and Service," shows 2 different early autos, black on white, Connecticut Ford/ Lincoln dealer, 1-1/2" x 2-3/8" x 7/8" ................. 111.00

Sign, tin, embossed, "Ford, Service Station, Sales Agency," white on black ground, "Schenck Manufacturing & Supply Co., Parkers Landing, Pa."" in white arrow, cond. 7, 11-1/2" h, 35-1/2" w .................. 385.00

## Foremost

Sign, tin, embossed, die-cut, shape of a milk carton
   "Foremost Churned Butter Milk," scratches, 30" h, 15" w ........................................ 88.00
   "Foremost Homogenized Vitamin D Milk," dents, 22" h, 11" w ........................................ 132.00

## Forest and Stream Tobacco

Canister, litho tin
   Round image of fisherman in stream, red ground, striped domed lid, cond. 8+, 5-1/2" h, 4" dia ................ 962.50
   Screw top, "Forest And Stream Pipe Tobacco," red ground, duck flying from white oval, white text on black bands, red ground, cond. 8+ ................ 47.50

Clock, light-up, "Fort Pitt Special Beer," aluminum frame, convex glass, cond. VG, 15" dia, $104.50.

Tin, vertical pocket tin, litho tin, fisherman motif
   Creel top, "Forest and Stream Tobacco," round image of fisherman in stream, red ground, full, cond. 8........................................ 248.50
   Cut-down sample, "Forest, Stream" in white on black banners, red ground, cond. 7.5-8 .................110.00
   "Forest and Stream Tobacco," round image of fisherman in stream, red ground, cond. 8+, 4-1/4" h ........................................ 259.00

Tin, vertical pocket tin, litho tin, duck motif
   "Forest and Stream Pipe Tobacco," duck flying from white oval, red ground with black banners, cond. 8+........................................ 138.50
   "Forest and Stream Pipe Tobacco, 10¢" duck flying from white oval, red ground with black banners, gold version, cond. 9.5 ................................ 231.00

Tin, vertical pocket tin, litho tin, men/canoe motif, "Forest & Stream Tobacco" in white, central image with 2 men in canoe, one hauling in fish, red ground, cond. 8, 4-1/4" h, 3" w........................................ 394.00

## Fort Pitt Beer

Clock, tin face, lightup, glass cover, metal housing, "Fort Pitt Special Beer" reverse-painted in white on upper rectangular panel, "Fort Pitt Special" in red on white round clock face, black numbers, cracked paint/dents/ scratches, 16" h, 25" w ......................................110.00

Sign
   Metal, light-up, glass face, counter/wall mounts, "Fort Pitt Special Beer, Choicest Malt, Finest Hops, Fort Pitt Brewing Co., Pittsburg 15, Pa.," shows fort in red circle, scratches, 14-1/2" dia .................. 330.00
   Painted metal, embossed, wood frame, "Thanks To Our Courageous President and Sound Thinking Members Of Congress And U.S. Senators for this Delicious Fort Pitt Beer, Pittsburgh, Pennsylvania -

Tin, litho tin, 1 lb, "Fountain Fine Cut Tobacco, Lowell & Buffington Tob. Co., Covington, Ky.," 8-1/4" d, $100.

Sharpsburg Suburb," shows couple dining in formal attire, nail holes/touch up/rust spots, 22-3/4" h, 26" w........................................................... 990.00

## Fort Western Coffee

Can, litho tin, oval scene of fort, Indian in canoe, blue over red ground, 1 lb, 5-5/8" h, 4-1/4" dia ......... 264.00

## C.B. Foster & Co. General Hardware

Postcard, paper, Indian adages, set of 4, "Wise Man Listen Well, Good Hunter Always Welcome, Peace Pipe All Agree Get Together, A Brave Prepared is Never Afraid," Ransomeville NY, Phone 36, cond. 8.5, each 3-1/2" h, 6" w, set ..................................................11.00

# Fountain Tobacco (See Photo)

# Four B.B.B.B. Tobacco (See Photo)

## Four Roses Smoking Tobacco

Tin, vertical pocket, litho tin
 Flat top, design of four roses on silver ground covering entire front, cond. 8.5, 4-1/4" h ...................... 541.00
 Flip top, embossed design of 4 red roses on silver panel on red ground, cond. 8.5..................... 332.00
 Short flat top, embossed design of 4 red roses on silver panel on red ground, full, cond. 9 ........... 484.00
 "Four Roses special Cut Plug Smoking Tobacco,"oval medallion of 4 red roses, green ground, cond. 8.5.................................................... 600.00

## Fox's Bread

Calendar, paper, 1913, "Eat Fox's Bread" on straw hat worn by boy at stone fence, girl in white dress picking flowers, pad begins with July, cond. 8............... 121.00

## Frank Fehr Brewing Co.

Tray, litho tin, "Fehr's Famous F.F.X.L. Beers, None Purer None Better" on rim, outdoor scene of classic couple in flowing robes embracing, company name at bottom, Frank Fehr Brewing Co., Louisville KY, ©1910, minor scratches/nail hole, 13" dia .............................. 451.00

## Frank Jones Ales

Match scratcher, porcelain, top third with "Frank Jones Portsmouth Ales" in white on red shield, blue ground, wear to scratching surface on bottom third, 6" h, 4" w................................................................. 330.00

## Franklin Caro Co.

Jar, clear glass, ground glass lid with "Franklin Caro Co."

Tin, paper label, "Four B.B.B.B. Brand Tobacco, John Blaul's Sons Co., Burlington, Iowa," 11-1/2" h, $950.

Sign, corner, porcelain, "Frank Fehr Brewing Co. Lager Beer, Louisville, Ky.," mint, 30-1/4" h, 18-1/4" w, $5,700.

Sign, porcelain, "Worlds Highest Standard, The Free Land Overalls, Union Made Guaranteed, Trousers, Shirts, Triple Stitched," red/white text, blue ground, small central shield, 1930s, cond. 9.5, 10" h, 30" w, $302.50. (Photo courtesy of Gary Metz, Muddy River Trading Co.)

embossed on flat-sided finial, "Franklin Caro Co., Richmond, Va." embossed on lower part of front panel, rim chips, cond. VG, 11-3/4" h, 5" dia ................ 77.00

## Franklin Cigars

Playing cards, deck of 52, "Franklin 5¢ Cigars," Franklin holding kite string, no jokers, orig box with soiling, most cards EXC cond. ........................................ 55.00

## Frank's Choice

Sign, tin, polished, embossed, diamond, "Smoke Frank's Choice, The Boss, 5¢ Cigar, F. Stoessiger, Freeport, Ill.," clock face/"We Close This P.M. At" in center with moveable hands, black text, silver ground, cond. 8+, 6-1/2" h............................................................. 209.00

## Free Land Overalls (See Photo)

## Freeman

Sign, light-up, metal housing with glass front, "Freeman shoes for men," lights white/yellow on red pinstripe background, works, 9" h, 20" w.......................... 88.00

## Freihofer's

Display, tin, glass front and half of sides, metal shelves with wood frame, "Freihofer's Quality Cakes, A Cake for every taste, Pound, Sponge, Fruit," dents/rust/scratches, 27-1/2" h, 14-3/4" w, 17" l ................ 660.00

## French Auto Oil

Can, litho tin
"Marshall Oil Co. Standardized French Auto Oil, Keeps Your Motor Young," early race cars on dirt track, cond. 7.5, 1/2 gal, 8-1/2" h, 6-1/8" w, 2-3/4" d ....................................................... 742.50
"Marshall Oil Co. Standardized French Auto Oil, the Remedy for 90% Of Your Motor Troubles," early race cars on dirt track, white ground, cond. 7/6, gal, 10-1/4" h, 8" w, 3" d ..................................... 385.00

## French Bauer Ice Cream

Display, lightup, figural milk glass ice cream cone mounted in wooden base, lettering redone, 1930s-1940s, cond. 8, 17" h ..................................... 2,420.00

Pail, tin, "French Market Coffee and Chicory, American Coffee Company, Inc., New Orleans, La.," 3 lb, $175.

Globe, glass, "French Bauer Ice Cream" in blue/red, soiling/water stains to lenses, crack to base, 13-1/2" dia....................................................... 467.50

## French Market Coffee (See Photo)

## Frescodor Borated Talcum

Tin, litho tin, "Frescodor Borated Talcum De Luxe," $525.

# Freshpak Coffee

Can, keywind, litho tin, "Drip Grind Freshpak Brand Savory & Satisfying Coffee," shows cup of coffee, "Freshpak" in red beside "Grand Union" symbol, light-blue over cobalt ground, cond. 9, 1 lb ................. 75.00

# Freund's Bread

Sign, porcelain, "Freund's Old Tyme Bread, White or Rye, Makes Sandwiches Better," red/black on white ground, the back marked "Fishing Worms For Sale," 1940s-1950s, cond. 8.25-8.5+, 12" h, 17" w ....................... 99.00

# Frictionless Metal Co.

Sign, litho tin, self-framing, "The Metal That Never Fails, Frictionless Metal Co., Richmond, Va., U.S.A.," naked child holding up metal, open crate behind him, woodgrain border, ©1903, cond. 7, 22-1/4" h, 16" w ................................................................. 302.50

# Friends Smoking Tobacco

Sign, tin, "Friends Smoking Tobacco 10¢, Heavy Foil Pocket Pouch," man/dog in round blue circle at left, red/blue text, yellow ground, cond. G, 10-1/4" h, 21-1/4" w ....................................................... 99.00

# Frigidaire

Sign, porcelain, "We Cool Our Milk with Frigidaire, Product of General Motors," shows cow, white text, cobalt ground, cond. EXC, 13-3/4" h, 19-1/2" w .......... 550.00

# Frigidtest Anti-Freeze

Can, litho tin, soldered seam, "Frigidtest Permanent Anti-Freeze, Ethylene Glycol Type," shows 2 polar bears on icebergs, airplane in sky, red/white, cond. 8+, 1 qt., 5-1/2" h, 4" dia ................................................. 143.00

# Fritz Bros' Best

Sign, reverse foil on glass, framed, "Smoke Fritz Bros' Best, Five Cent Cigars," restored to cond. 9+, 6" h, 17-1/4" w ........................................................ 250.00

# Frontier

Gas globe
  "Frontier Double Refined Gasoline," 1 glass lens, new metal holder, cond. 9, 13-1/2" dia ................. 495.00
  "Frontier Ethyl," 2 lenses, narrow glass body, blue/red text, white ground, all cond. 9, 13-1/2" dia ......... 302.50
  "Frontier, Rarin'-To-Go," 2 vintage lenses on new body, white text on red ground (lower half), silhou-

ette of man on rearing horse at top, white ground, cond. 8.5-9 .................................................. 1,100.00

# Frosty

Sign, embossed cap, "Drink Frosty Root Beer," bottle cap motif with bearded character holding bottle, circa 1940s, cond. 8.75-9.25, 12" dia ........................ 396.00

# N. Frudden Son

Pitcher, yellowware, Red Wing Saffron, rust and white stripes, ink stamp advertising "N. Frudden & Son, Lumbermen Since 1889, Nora Springs, Iowa," base ink-stamped "Red Wing Saffron Ware," spout chips, 6 1/2" h ................................................................. $100.

# Fry

Sign, pump sign, porcelain, 2-sided, badge shape, "Fry" in red on black circle at center, "Guarantee, Visible" in white on red ground at top/bottom, white border, metal clamp, cond. 7, 8" h, 5" w ................................ 412.50

# Full Dress

Tin, vertical pocket, litho tin
  Flip top, full-figure man in tuxedo in red oval, gold ground, Patterson, cond. 8 ........................... 193.00
  "Full Dress Selected Burley-Roll Cut Pipe and Cigarette Tobacco, Made Exclusively For Sears, Roebuck and Co., Chicago, Seattle, Dallas," waist-up image of man in tuxedo in white rectangle, red ground, cond. 8 ........................................ 1,331.00

# Fuller's Christmas Candy

Tin, litho tin, scene of Santa and reindeer, octagonal, 3" h, 6-1/2" w ...................................................... 27.50

# Fun-To-Wash Washing Powder

**History:** Manufactured by Hygienic Laboratories, Inc., of Buffalo, N.Y., packaging for Fun-To-Wash washing powder featured a smiling black woman wearing a red bandanna on her head. Because there was a large community of Germans in upstate New York, where the product was primarily sold, instructions on the packages were also written in German.

Box, cardboard, "25 Cents, Fun-To-Wash Washing Powder Manufactured Only By The Hygienic Laboratories Inc,. Buffalo, N.Y.," shows mammy on front/back, sealed to display, cond. 9, 7-1/2" h, 5" w ............ 55.00

# G

## Gainer Feeds

Sign, tin, rolled edge, "Gainer Feeds, More Gains Per Dollar," yellow scale arm/weight on red ring with blue center, lower blue panel, white text, yellow ground, minor scratches/soiling, 20" sq ..........................110.00

## Galaxy Coffee

Milk pail, tin, "Galaxy Java Blend Roasted Coffee, Aragon Coffee Co., Richmond, Va.," gold stencil, blue ground, cond. 8, 2 lb, 8-3/4" h, 5-1/2" dia............................ 577.50

## Galaxy Soft Drink Syrup

Bottle, glass, figural, "Galaxy" fired-on label, orig. cardboard box, 12 empty bottles, different colored labels for flavors, box tattered, bottles cond. EXC, 8-1/2" h, case of 12 ........................................................ 269.50

## Gale Manufacturing Co.

Match holder, hanging, litho tin, "Gale Manufacturing Co. Makers of Agricultural Implements, Albion, Mich., Gale Means Good," oval image of factory, cond. 8+, 4-7/8" h, 3-3/8" w, 1-3/8" d................................................ 687.50

## Galena Signal Oil Co.

Match case, metal, embossed, "Compliments of Galena Signal Oil Co., Franklin, Pa." in oval, floral ground, gold, cond. 7, 3" h, 1-1/2" w ................................ 99.00

## Gallaher's Honeydew

Tin, litho tin, "Gallaher's Rich Dark Honeydew," 2 men smoking by fireplace in parlor/maid in background, yellow text, cond. 9, 1-3/4" h, 6-1/2" w, 3-1/2" d.......................... 198.00

## Game Tobacco

Bin, countertop store bin, litho tin, "Game Fine Cut, Manufactured by Jno. J. Bagley & Co., Detroit, Mich.," shows game birds on both sides, cond. 8, 7-1/2" h, 11-1/2" w, 7-3/4" d ............................................... 770.00

## Garcia Grande

Display/cigar lighter, tin slant-front/footed display holding "Garcia Grande" paper litho over cardboard cigar box, paper cigar fronts inside, some labels missing, case mkd "Light A Garcia Grande, Just Mild Enough," no plug, name scratched on case, box with tears/writing, cond. G, 8" h, 9-1/4" w, 8-3/4" d........................ 121.00

## Garcia y Garcia Cigars

Tin, paper label, held 50 cigars, "Garcia y Garcia, Fine Mild Cigars, 15¢," shows building in ring of 12 medallions, white ground, label also on lid, cond. 8.5, round.................................................................. 71.50

## Garcia y Vega Cigars

Sign, pressed fiberboard, "Garcia y Vega, Est. 1882, The Bonded Havana Cigar," woman carving "GYU 1882" on tree, chips/cracks............................................. 27.50

## Garden of Allah Coffee

Can

Keywind, litho tin, "Garden of Allah Hotel Blend Coffee, Delano, Potter & Co., Inc., Boston, Mass.," palm trees on red/yellow ground, cond. 8, 1 lb...................... 94.00

Slip lid, paper label, "Garden of Allah Coffee," camel's head in rounded panel, black text, soiling on back, cond. 7, 1 lb.................................................... 66.00

## Gardner Salted Peanuts

Jar, clear glass, "Always in Good Taste, Gardner Salted Peanuts, 5¢," red text, glass lid, rim chips/crack, 7-3/4" h, 7" dia ................................................................ 154.00

## Garland Stoves (See Photo)

## Gebhardt's Chili Con Carne

Soup pot, electric, "Gebhardt's Eagle Chili Con Carne" slug plate, eagle design, aluminum pot, domed lid, chips/rust/stains ............................................... 165.00

**Pocket mirror, celluloid, "Garland Stoves and Ranges, The Michigan Stove Company, Detroit, Chicago, Largest Makers of Stoves in the World," 2-3/4" h, 2" w, $35.**

Oil can, "Gebhart's, 100% Pure Pennsylvania, Gold Comet Plus Motor Oil, 200 Neutral, Gebhart Stores, Inc.," red ground, scratches, rust, 2 gallons, $35.

## Gebhart's Motor Oil (See Photo)

## Gem City Ice Cream

Sign, sidewalk sign, heavy metal, 2-sided, "Gem City Ice Cream, Supreme Since 1901," black text, yellow ground, cond. 7.5-8.5, 20" h, 28" w ................... 143.00

## General Porcelain Enameling & Mfg. Co.

Sign, porcelain, "It Can Be Done" and company name in white on cobalt ground, possibly a salesman sample, 1930s, cond. 9.25+, 3" h, 9" w ......................... 302.50

## Gen. Steedman Cigars

Sign, cardboard, embossed, gesso frame, "Gen. Steedman 5¢ Cigar 5¢, Hettermann Bros. Co., Makers, Louisville, Ky.," flowers with central picture of man helping woman from coach, frame chips, 16-1/2" h, 13" w ............. 440.00

## George Washington Cut Plug

Lunch box, litho tin, large size, wooden handle, "Smoke, Chew, George Washington Great American Cut Plug," oval portrait in black/white, red text on light-blue ground, red trim, cond. 8.5+ ............................. 194.00

## Ghostley Pearl

Sign, tin, embossed, "Our Choice...The Ghostley Pearl, Assured Poultry Profits, The Gem of the Poultry Industry," shows chicken over pearls, scratches/chips, 12" h, 18" w .................................................................. 176.00

## Giant Coffee

Pail, litho tin, "Giant Brand Roasted Coffee," shield logo over crossed ferns on white ground, red/blue/cobalt bands top/bottom, C. Lenning, Brown, Duluth MN, cond. 7+, 5 lb, 8-1/2" h, 7-1/2" dia..................... 157.50

## Giant Salted Peanuts

Tin, litho tin, shows giant with club over shoulder and castle in background, green text, red ground, cond. 8+, 10 lb., 11-1/4" h, 7-1/2" dia ......................... 357.50

## Gibbs

Sign, flange, porcelain, die-cut, "Gibbs" in red on white circle beside tilted red/white/blue barber pole, cond. VG, 24" h, 20" w................................................. 467.50

## Gilbert Paper

Clock, light-up, Pam clock, "Gilbert Quality Papers," hand with pen and paper, works, cond. 8.5, 15" dia............................................................ 187.00

## Gillette

**History:** King Camp Gillette was a frustrated inventor until he began designing a safety razor with disposable blades in 1895. After partnering with MIT graduate William Nickerson, Gillette formed the American Safety Razor Company in 1901. The name was changed to Gillette Safety Razor Company in 1902, and production finally began in 1903. Sales were slow at first, but by 1905 the company had established both a sales office and a manufacturing facility overseas.

The trademark signature and photo of Gillette appeared on the outer wrappings of the blades and razors. Seeing that the mark was too large for some packages, in 1908 the company adopted a diamond trademark with an arrow-pierced "Gillette" in the center.

Gillette was adept at using premiums to increase product recognition and generate customer loyalty. At one point, dealers who purchased a box of Wrigley's gum were given a Silver Brownie razor set. Banks used "Save and Shave" promotions to offer Gillette razors to new depositors, and all manner of busi-

**Sign, flange, porcelain, pictures safety razor and box of Gillette Blue Blades, cond. 8-8.25, 19-1/2" h, 21-1/2" w, $3,080. (Photo courtesy of Gary Metz, Muddy River Trading Co.)**

nesses gave away razors on opening day.

Company chemists developed Brushless shaving cream in 1936, with the product debuting in 1937, and lather shaving cream was first sold in 1940. Because of manufacturing restrictions during the war, Gillette did not release any new products from 1930 to 1945. Instead, the company concentrated on switching its focus from price to quality.

Pocket mirror, round, "Shave Yourself, Gillette Safety Razor, No Stropping, No Honing," yellow/white text, black round, red/white border, cond. 7.75.........110.00

## Gillett's Vanilla Extract

Door push, metal, raised finish, "Push and Remember," shows product box with owl sitting on crescent moon, Sherer-Gillett Co., Chicago, black on white, cond. 8, 6-1/2" h, 2-1/2" w ............................................. 264.00

## Gimlet Coffee (See Photo)

## Ginger-Mint Julep

Dispenser, stoneware, fired-on lettering, "Drink Ginger-Mint Julep" in orange oval, "2599 Property of Emerson Drug Co. Baltimore Maryland" on bottom, white glazed body, metal dispenser, cond. VG, 14" h, 8" dia .............. 770.00

## Gladiator Coffee

Bin, store size, litho tin, "Gladiator Blend Fancy Roasted Coffee, Brewster, Crittenden & Co., Rochester," stenciled gold text, black ground, door at top, cond. 8, 21-1/2" h, 13-1/4" sq ...................................... 1,540.00

## Gland-O-Lac (See Photo)

Can, paper label, "Gimlet Ground Coffee and Chicory, H&K, St. Louis, Hanley & Kinsella Coffee and Spice Co.," rust and soiling, 8 oz, $45.

Clock, light-up, "The Gland-O-Lac Company, Omaha, Nebr., Quality Medicines," metal frame, glass front, 14-1/2" sq, $150.

## Glendora Coffee

Can

    Keywind, litho tin, "Eternized Fresh, Glendora Coffee, Vacuum Packed," name in white on red oval, cobalt ground, cond. 8-, 1 lb...................................... 38.50

    Pry lid, paper on cardboard, sample, "Sample, Glendora Brand Coffee," "Glendora" in white, "Coffee" in cobalt in white oval, cobalt ground, gold band top/bottom, cond. 8.5+, 3-1/2" h .......................... 49.50

## Globe Casket Mfg. Co.

Paperweight mirror, celluloid, "Globe Casket Manufacturing Co., Manufacturers of Bronze, Copper, Armco Metal, Hardwood & Cloth Covered Caskets, Burial Garments & Casket Hardware, Kalamazoo, Mich. -- Denver, Colo.," cracked, 3-1/2" d, $25.

Bookmark, paper, "This Is The Place, Compliments of The Globe-Wernicke Co., Cincinnati, Sectional Bookcases," 6-15/16" h, 2-1/16" w, $17.50.

## Globe Ginger Ale

Tray, litho tin, "Globe Pale Dry Ginger Ale, Compliments of Globe Beverage Co.," shows flapper on globe pouring drink, cond. EXC, 13" dia ........................... 264.00

## Globe Seal Motor Oil

Sign, tin, "Globe Seal Motor Oil, Seals the Pistons, The Globe Refining Co., Cleveland," central seal with man adding oil to engine over globe, cond. 7, 14" h, 10" w ................................................................ 187.00

Sign, cardboard, easel back and string hanger, 3-D fish, "Enjoy Goebel Beer," titled "German Brown Trout," also marked "A 1953 Continuation of the Goebel Sports Series originated in 1943," $62.50.

Can, litho tin, "Gold Award Motor Oil," 2 gal, $15.

## Globe-Wernicke (See Photo)

## Glor Bros. & Willis Mfg. Co.

Pocket mirror, celluloid, round, "If you are looking for Sanitary Stable Fixtures, Glor Bros. & Willis Mfg. Co., Attica, N.Y. ...," pictures device, cond. EXC, 2-1/8" dia ....... 66.00

## GMC

Clock, neon, tin face, glass cover, metal case, octagonal, "Sales, GMC Trucks, Service," red/blue text on yellow, blue numbers, white border, red border on cover, white neon, cond. 7 ..................................................... 880.00

## Goebel Beer (See Photo)

## Gold Award (See Photo)

## Gold Bond

Tin, vertical pocket, litho tin
  Short version, "Old Reliable Gold Bond Cross Cut Plug Smoking Tobacco, Pipe or Cigarette," blue ribbon with gold text, white ground, cond. 8, 3-1/2" h, 2-1/2" w ...................................................... 265.00
  Tall/fat version, "Old Reliable Gold Bond Cross Cut Plug Smoking Tobacco, Pipe or Cigarette," blue ribbon with gold text, white ground, cond. 8-8.5, 4-1/2" h, 3-3/8" w ..................................................... 258.50
  "Old Reliable Gold Bond Cross Cut Plug Smoking Tobacco, Pipe or Cigarette," blue ribbon with gold text, white ground, cond. 8, 4-1/2" h, 3" w ............................................................. 231.00

## Gold Crown Gasoline

Gas globe, milk glass, 1-pc, gold trim, metal base, cond. 8, 16-1/2" h, 17" w ............................................. 418.00

## Gold Dust

**History:** Two black children sitting in a tub of water advertised Gold Dust products made by the N.K. Fair-

**Boxes, paper, "Gold Dust Washing Powder," 8 oz; sample, "Gold Dust Washing Powder, Free Home Sample," cond. 9, 2-1/2" h, 1-1/2" w, $35 each.**

banks Soap Company. Although Fairbanks had produced the washing powder since the early 1880s, it wasn't until the twins graced their packaging that the product met with any real success.

Originally drawn by Edward Windsor Kemble, the twins illustrated such slogans as "Fast Colors Warranted to Wash Clean and Not to Fade" and "Let the Gold Dust Twins Do Your Work." The trademark was registered in 1884, and the Gold Dust twins were among the most readily recognized advertising symbols of the 19th century. The brand was discontinued in the 1930s when the company was sold.

Fan, cardboard, 2-sided, Gold Dust twins seated at 1904 World's Fair, children advertising Fairy Soap on back, wooden handle, 12" h, 7-1/2" w ........................ 150.00

Sign
    Cardboard, trolley, "Gold Dust, For Spring House-cleaning," woman at doorway, Twins at right with bucket/product, 1920s-1930s, repairs, cond. 8-8.5, 11" h, 21" w .................................................. 302.50
    Litho tin, embossed, black on yellow ground, shows Gold Dust twins at left, cond. 8-, 3" h, 12" w ............. 495.00

## Golden Age Coffee (See Photo)

## Golden Bear Cookies

Pail, litho tin, cartoon animals, giraffe's neck being used as a slide, orig lid, cond. 8, 3 lb, 8-1/2" h, 7-3/4" dia ......................................................... 176.00

## Golden Cup Coffee (See Photo)

## Golden Dream Coffee

Can, keywind, litho tin, "Vacuum Packed Golden Dream Coffee," woman picking coffee beans, white/dark text in red panel, cond. 8, 1 lb .................................. 49.50

## Golden Guernsey

Sign, porcelain, "Shamrock Dairy, Golden Guernsey, America's Table Milk," leprechaun in green hat at left in yellow sunburst with shamrocks, green/yellow/black text, white ground, 1940s-1950s, cond. 8.5, 22" h, 56" w ............................................................. 1,100.00

## Gold-en Girl Cola

See also Sun-Drop
Sign, tin, embossed, die-cut, bottlecap shape, "Gold-en Girl Cola" in white on red ground, white edge, chips/yellowing/scratches, 33" dia............................. 396.00

**Can, keywind, tin, "Golden Age Coffee, Bunn Capitol Grocery Co., Bloomington/Springfield, Ill.," 1 lb, $40.**

**Can, keywind, tin, "Golden Cup Coffee, Carpenter Cook Company, Menominee, Michigan," orange and red ground, 1 lb, $15.**

Crate, wooden, "Goldenmoon Fruits & Sirups," $110.

# Goldenmoon (See Photo)

# Golden Morn Coffee

Can, litho tin, twist lid, red sun/gold rays on black ground, gold band at bottom, gold/black text, R.C. Williams Co., NY, cond. 8.5, 1 lb, 6" h, 4-1/4" dia.............. 89.00

# Golden Rod Baking Powder

Tin, paper label, shows girl, cond. 7.5, 3-1/4" h, 2" dia............................................................. 43.00

# Golden Rod Tobacco (See Photo)

# Golden Rule

Gas globe lens, 2 glass lenses, fired-on text/design, "Golden Rule" in red on yellow center, white border, cond. 8/7.5, 13-1/2" dia.................................... 280.50

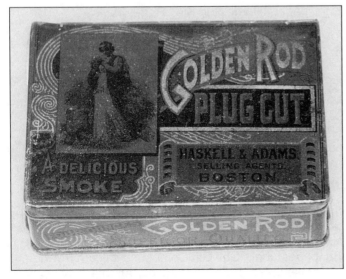

Tin, litho tin, "Golden Rod Plug Cut, Haskell & Adams, Selling Agents, Boston," 1-3/8" h, 4-3/8" w, 3-3/8" d, $40.

Poster, paper, "Golden Shell Motor Oil," black ground, archival backing, cond. 8, 55" h, 39-1/4" w, $132. (Photo courtesy of Collectors Auction Services)

# Golden Sceptre

Tin, litho tin, sample, "Surbrug's Golden Sceptre, Depot-159 Fulton St., N.Y.C.," arm holding sceptre, red drape, gold text, cond. 8, 1-5/8" h, 1-5/8" w, 1-1/4" d ............................................................. 495.00

Tin, litho tin, vertical pocket,
Short version, "Golden Sceptre," rounded corners, white panel shows arm holding sceptre, cond. 8.5..................................................... 251.00
Short version, "Surbrug's Golden Sceptre, Perfection For The Pipe," arm holding sceptre, red drape, cond. 8, 2-3/4" h, 3-3/8" w ......................... 184.00
"Floss Cut, Surbrug's Golden Sceptre, Burley," arm holding sceptre, red drape, white ground, cond. 7.5-8 .................................................... 270.00
"Surbrug's Golden Sceptre, Burley Floss Cut," arm holding sceptre, yellow ground, cond. 7.5 .... 265.00

# Golden Seal Cut Plug

Tin, horizontal box, litho tin, embossed, central seal with JL&S in red, red text, crossed red bands, 4 feathers, J. Lemesurier & Sons, Quebec, cond. 7.5.............. 38.50

# Golden Shell Auto Oil

See also Shell
Can, litho tin, embossed
"Golden Shell Auto Oil," gold shell logo, yellow text, red ground, Shell Company of California, cond. 8/7, gal, 10-1/2" h, 8" w, 2-3/4" d ......................... 825.00
"Golden Shell Auto Oil, Heavy," gold shell logo on red panel, orange/white checkered ground, cond. 7, gal, 11-1/8" h, 6" w, 3-1/2" d ......................... 440.00
Sign, cardboard, "Time to Change, Summer Golden Shell Motor Oil 25¢," face of crying baby beside diaper on clothesline, cond. VG, 58" h, 40" w................... 137.50

# Golden Standard Tea

Tin, litho tin, blown-out rounded corners, "Golden Standard Tea," crossed flags behind medallion, scenic panels, cond. 8+, 9" h, 7" w, 5" d ............................. 27.50

Tin, litho tin, "Golden Sun, Cayenne Pepper, The Woolson Spice Company, Toledo, Ohio," wear, light rust, 2 oz, $18.50.

## Golden State Ice Cream

Tray, litho tin, Palmer Cox's Brownies and a dish of ice cream, cond. 8.5, 13-1/4" h, 10-1/2" w .............. 550.00

## Golden Sun (See Photo)

## Golden Wedding

Can, keywind, litho tin, snap top, "Golden Wedding Brand Improved Vacuum-Packed Coffee," small oval silhouette of older couple at left, gold text, white ground, gold trim top/bottom, cond. 8+, 1 lb ................................................................. 75.00

Spice rack, wire rack, 12 red litho-tin cans of "Golden Wedding" spices, circa 1920s, 4-1/2" h, 11" w, 4" d ............................................................. 242.00

Tin, paper label, "Gold Label Baking Powder," 12 oz, $25.

Sign, porcelain, large strip sign, "Gold Medal Flour," white text, red ground, 1910s-1920s, cond. 9.5, 10" h, 60" w, $550. (Photo courtesy of Gary Metz, Muddy River Trading Co.)

## Golden Wedding Tobacco

Tin, litho tin, square corner, "Golden Wedding Extra Fine Flake Cut," red wedding bell, yellow ground, some litho off, cond. 8 ................................................. 60.50

## Golden West Peanut Butter (See Photo)

Can, paper label, Western scene with covered wagons, white text, dark ground, Golden West Products, Los Angeles, cond. 7.5, 8 oz, 2-7/8" h, 3" dia ............ 72.50

## Gold Label Baking Powder (See Photo)

## Gold Medal Flour

**History:** Caldwallader C. Washburn erected his first flour mill in Minneapolis in 1866. After partnering with John Crosby in 1877, the two formed the Washburn Crosby Company. Three brands of the company's flour were entered in the 1880 Miller's International Exhibition, with one awarded the gold medal. The winning flour was then aptly named Gold Medal, and the Washburn Crosby Company went on to become General Mills.

Sign, paper, "A Kernel of Wheat, Gold Medal Flour," white/yellow text over dissected wheat, "Washburn-Crosby Co. Gold Medal Flour" logo, archival backing, cond. G, 42" h, 28" w ........................................ 154.00

## Gold Mine Icicle

Sign, paper, "Home Run King Roger Maris Says...Refresh with Gold Mine Icicle, Buy 'em Here, ...in delicious Frozen Fruit Flavors," shows Maris at bat, cartoon character and product, 1960s, cond. 9, 11-1/4" h, 17-1/2" w .......................................... 385.00

## Gold Seal (See Photo)

## Gold Shore Tobacco

Lunch box, litho tin, handleless, "Gold Shore Cut Plug Tobacco, Smoking or Chewing, Jno. J. Bagley & Co., Detroit, Mich.," winged horse, red text, white ground, columns at corners, missing clasp, cond. 8, 4-1/4" h, 7" w, 4-1/2" d ................................................... 104.50

## Golf Girl Talcum

Tin, paper label, "Golf Girl Compound Talcum Powder, Blankenbaker Bros., Distributor," full image of woman golfer with boy on one knee watching behind her, cond. 8+, 5-1/2" h, 2-1/2" dia ......................... 2,200.00

**Thermometer, porcelain, "Gold Seal 99 90/100 Pure Crop Seed, Seedtown Chicago, Nitragin, The Original Legume Inoculator," chips, 27" h, 7" w, $150.**

# Gollam's Ice Cream

Sign, heavy metal, 2-sided, "We Serve Gollam's Lebanon Ice Cream," child with oversized ice cream cone, white text, black ground, 1941, cond. 8 ...................... 550.00

# Goodell Auto Oil

Can, tin, "All Lubrication, No Waste, Goodell Auto Oil," green text in black circle on green tree, white ground, H.S. Goodell, Hancock, MI, no lid, cond. 7+/7, 1/2-gal, 6-1/4" h, 8" w, 3" d............................................. 308.00

# Good Friends Whiskey

Pocket mirror, oval, barrel motif, shows settler/Indian, cond. 8.75 ....................................................... 143.00

# Good Humor Ice Cream

Sign, porcelain, blue text above/below ice cream bar missing 1 bite, white ground, blue border, 1940s, cond. 7.5+, 26" h, 50" w ................................... 577.50

# Good Luck Baking Powder

Can, paper label over tin, round, "Good Luck Baking Powder," downturned horseshoe, white text, red ground, unopened, cond. 9+, 8 oz ...................... 77.00

# Good Luck Service

Sign, porcelain, oval, red/green text, green horseshoe/ border, white ground, 1930s, cond. 8.25, 19" h, 31" w ............................................................... 522.50

# Good Luck Tobacco

Sign, cardboard, diamond shape, "Good Luck, Four Leaf Clover, Drummond Tobacco Co.," shows woman in swamp, 4-leaf clover at top, framed, 15-3/8" h,

15-1/4" w.......................................................... 852.50

# Goodrich

Box, litho tin, "Repair Outfit, Goodrich Tires, Best In The Long Run," silhouette of car/trees, cond. 7, 2-1/2" h, 6-1/2" w, 2" d.............................................. 44.00

Display, tire rack, litho tin, "Goodrich Silvertowns," white text under 2 red diamonds, cobalt ground, small "G" logos on sides, cond. 7, 7-1/2" h, 15-1/4" w, 10-1/2" d .......................................................... 341.00

Sign, curb sign, tin on iron stand, 5-sided, "Goodrich Tires" in white under red "G" with wreath/diamond logo, black ground, repainted base, cond. 7, 48" h, 28" w ................................................................. 550.00

Sign, flange

Metal, die-cut, round, "Goodrich Tires" in white around edges, red "G" with green wreath in center, black ground, cond. 7, 18" h, 18-1/2" w ................. 522.50

Porcelain, die-cut, round, "Garage" across center, "Goodrich Tires" around edges, cobalt/white, cond. 8+, 18" h, 18-3/8" w ...................................... 880.00

Porcelain, die-cut, round, "Free Air" in cobalt on white horizontal bar, "Goodrich Tires" at border in white on cobalt, cond. 7, 18" dia ........................... 522.50

Sign, porcelain

"Goodrich Silvertowns" under tire in red panel, white text, dark ground, cond. 7, 40" h, 27-1/2" w .............. 467.50

"Goodrich Tires," white horizontal/vertical text, red/ green "G" with wreath/diamond logo, black ground, cond. 8+, 78" h, 18" w.................................... 522.50

2-sided, pentagraph, "Goodrich Tires" under red "G" with wreath/diamond logo, white text, dark ground, green border, cond. 7.5, 17" h, 28" w .......... 385.00

**Sign, porcelain, die-cut, oval, "Goodrich Silvertowns" over red "G" wreath/diamond logo, white text, black ground, green border, cond. 8/7, 19" h, 23-1/2" w, $357.50.**

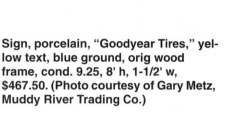

Sign, porcelain, "Goodyear Tires," yellow text, blue ground, orig wood frame, cond. 9.25, 8' h, 1-1/2' w, $467.50. (Photo courtesy of Gary Metz, Muddy River Trading Co.)

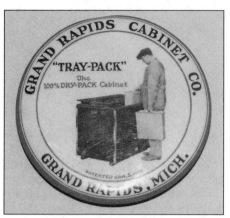

Paperweight mirror, celluloid, "Grand Rapids Cabinet Co., 'Tray-Pack,' The 100% Dry-Pack Cabinet, Grand Rapids, Mich.," 3-1/2" d, $15.

# Goodyear

**History:** After accidentally discovering vulcanized rubber in 1839, Charles Goodyear applied for patents and made several unsuccessful attempts at starting a business before he died in a Paris debtors' prison in 1860. In 1898, brothers Frank and Charles Sieberling resurrected Goodyear's process and began using it to manufacture bicycle tires. They named their company The Goodyear Tire & Rubber Company and adopted Mercury's winged foot as their trademark.

As a company, Goodyear was responsible for a number of industry firsts: the tubeless tire in 1903, pneumatic tires for aircraft in 1909, rubber tires in 1926, and synthetic rubber tires in 1937.

To ship raw material and finished products, Goodyear relied on Wingfoot Express, the country's first interstate trucking fleet. Their first slogan of note, "More people ride on Goodyear than on any other kind," debuted in 1916. Presently, the company manufactures tires for almost every type of vehicle. Ironically, bicycle tires are not included in that impressive array.

Plaque, brass, embossed, "Ten Years of Friendly Relations, GoodYear," busy street scene with factory, blimp, tire with flag, name written in marker, cond. 8, 17" h, 12" w ....................................... 82.50
Pocket mirror, litho metal, "Goodyear Balloon" tire around earth, blue ground, light scratches, 2-1/4" dia... 231.00
Sign, paper, "Workers Are Never Late because of tire trouble when they ride Goodyear Akron Bicycle Tires," 2 men with bikes, cond. 8, 21" h, 13" w ............ 495.00

Sign, porcelain
Die-cut, blimp shape, "Goodyear, #1 in tires," yellow/blue text, white/blue blimp, possibly a prototype, cond. 8, 18-1/2" h, 40" w .......................... 3,300.00
Die-cut, winged foot, blue/white, 1930s-1950s, cond. 9.25-9.5, 46" w ............................................. 715.00
Flange, oval, "Goodyear" in yellow on blue panel with red winged foot outline, tire ground, cond. 7, 34" h, 21-1/2" w ..................................................... 797.50
"Goodyear Service Station, Good Wear," Goodyear Balloon tire around earth at left, winged foot logo, yellow/blue text, cobalt ground, cond. 7.5+, 2' h, 6' w ................................................................. 357.50
2-sided, lightup, "Goodyear Tires" with winged foot logo, tire at left, white text, cobalt ground, most text replaced with flat milk glass, restored, cond. 8+, 28-3/4" h, 72" w ......................................... 2,640.00
Sign, tin, die-cut, embossed, gold winged foot, cond. 8+, 19" h, 61" w............................................... 286.00

# Gordon's Potato Chips

Can, tin, slip lid, "Gordon's Fresh Potato Chips" in red under early Gordon's delivery truck, white ground, red band at bottom, red lid, Gordon Foods, cond. VG, 11-1/2" h, 7-1/2" dia ........................................... 71.50

# Graham Motor Cars

Ashtray, brass, embossed, "Graham Motor Cars" at rim, profile of 3 knights, cond. 8, 4" dia................... 143.00

# Grain

Tin, vertical pocket, litho tin, early slide closure, "Grain Plug Cut, Fragrant and Delicious Pipe or Cigarette, The Surbrug Co., Richmond-New York," red band, yellow ground, cond. 9 ......................................... 367.00

# Grand Prize Beer

Clock, wood/metal, "Enjoy Grand Prize BeerE" arched top, plastic cover over wood, white clock/red border, black/red text, gold ground, cond. 9-, 14-1/2" h, 12-1/2" w, 3-1/2" d........................................... 264.00

# Grand Rapids Cabinet Co. (See Photo)

## Grand Union Hotel

Sign, porcelain, "Grand Union Hotel, Opposite Grand Central Depot, New York City...Rooms $1.00 Per Day and upward," shows hotel and busy street, French-made, 1870s-1880s, cond. 8+, 4" h, 5-7/8" w................... 522.50

## Grand Union Tea Co.

Calendar, 1905, cardboard, die-cut, fold-down, shows 4 girls flanked by flags and flowers, cond. 8+, 29" h, 9-3/4" w............................................................. 412.50

## Granger

Tin, vertical pocket, litho tin, "Granger Rough Cut Pipe Tobacco," single tobacco leaf with "Rough Cut" in white, "Granger Pipe Tobacco" in yellow, dark ground, cond. 8.5 ....................................................... 1,590.00

## Granulated 54

Tin, vertical pocket, litho tin
Sample, "Granulated Sliced Plug 54, Free Sample, Made By John Weisert Tob. Co., St. Louis, U.S.A.," "54" on tobacco leaf, blue panel, yellow ground, cond. 7.5-8................................................. 138.00
Sample, fat version, "Granulated Sliced Plug 54 Sliced Plug, Free Sample, Made By John Weisert Tob. Co., St. Louis, U.S.A.," "54" on tobacco leaf, blue panel, yellow ground, cond. 8, 3" h, 2" w, 1" d ............................................................. 261.00
Sample, tall/thin version, "Granulated Sliced Plug 54 Sliced Plug, Free Sample, Made By John Weisert

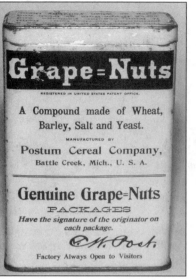

Tin, litho tin, "Grape Nuts, Postum Cereal Co., Battle Creek, Mich.," 14 oz, $25.

Tob. Co., St. Louis, U.S.A.," "54" on tobacco leaf, blue panel, yellow ground, cond. 8.5 ............ 287.00
Short/fat version, "Graulated Slice Plug 54, Made By John Weisert Tob. Co., St. Louis, U.S.A.," yellow "54" on rectangular plug, light-blue ground, yellow sides/top, cond. 7-7.5 ..................................... 88.00
"Grandulated Sliced Plug 54, Made By John Weisert Tob. Co., St. Louis, U.S.A.," "54" on tobacco leaf, blue panel, yellow ground, back with writing only, cond. 8.5-9.................................................. 221.00
"Granulated Sliced Plug 54 Tobacco Made By John Weisert Tob. Co., St. Louis, U.S.A.," "54" on tobacco leaf, blue panel, yellow ground, leaf on front and back, cond. 8.5 ............................. 212.00

## Grape-Crush

Dispenser, purple glass, barrel shape, metal lid and dispenser, embossed "Grape-Crush" and bunches of grapes, scratches and minor rust spotting, 12-1/2" h, 6-1/2" dia...................................................... 3,300.00

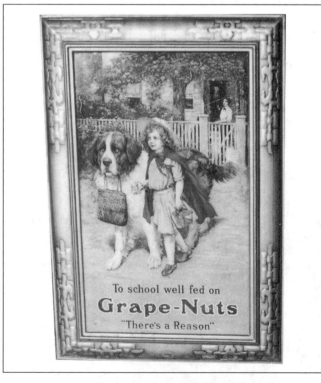

Sign, litho tin, self-framed, "To school well fed on Grape-Nuts, There's a Reason," girl with St. Bernard, circa 1915, cond. 7.5+, 30-3/4" h, 20-3/4" w, $2,200. (Photo courtesy of Gary Metz, Muddy River Trading Co.)

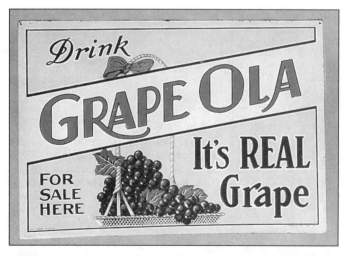

Sign, tin, embossed, "Drink Grape Ola, It's Real Grape, For Sale Here," yellow ground, 1920s-1930s, cond. 8-8.25, 14" h, 20" w, $143. (Photo courtesy of Gary Metz, Muddy River Trading Co.)

Sign, cardboard, "Thirsty or Not! Enjoy Grapette Soda, Imitation Grape Flavor," woman with trowel, NOS, 20" h, 32" w, $55.

## Grape-Nuts (See Photo)

## Grape Ola (See Photo)

## Grape Sparkle

Sign, litho tin over cardboard, embossed, "Drink Grape Sparkle, A Snappy Wine Flavor," girl in yellow with bottle, white/yellow text, cobalt ground, cond. 8+, 6" h, 13-3/8" w .......................................................... 962.50

## Grapette

**Collectors' Club:** Grapette Collectors Club, 2240 Highway 27N, Nashville, AR 71852

Sidewalk marker, brass, round, embossed "Enjoy Grapette, Walk Safely," circa 1940s-1950s, cond. 9-9.5 .................................................................... 49.50
Sign, porcelain, "Grapette Soda, Imitation Grape Flavor," white/red text, dark ground, red rim, 1940s-1950s, cond. 7-7.5, 10" h, 26" w ................................... 132.00

Sign, tin, die-cut, Grapette, edge rust/ paint chips, 1930s-1940s, cond. 6.5, 41" h, $467.50. (Photo courtesy of Gary Metz, Muddy River Trading Co.)

## Great American Insurance Co. (See Photo)

## Great Blend Flake

Carton, paper label, "C. Peper Tob. Co., Great Blend Flake," white ground, red/blue stripes at top/bottom, sticker on side says "One Aim - Victory," U.S. War Bond and stamp, full, cond. 8.5, 8 oz, 4-5/8" x 3-3/4" .................................................................... 80.00
Tin, vertical pocket, litho tin, "C. Peper Tob. Co., Great Blend Flake," fancy "B" in red on white ground, black text, cond. 8.5 .................................................. 242.00

## Great Slice Plug

Tobacco cutter, cast iron, "Great Slice Plug" in red on head, figural floral base, cond. 7.5, 6" h, 16" l ................... 198.00

## Great West

Lunch box, litho tin, red medallion with product, black text on red ground, canted lid, cond. 7.5-8 .............. 133.00

## Great Western

Sign, litho tin over cardboard, self-framed, "The Great Western Line, Smith Manufacturing Co.," farm scene with horse-drawn manure spreader, gas engine, woman at cream separator, dents/nail holes, 19" h, 27" w .......................................................... 1,870.00

## Greenfield Gasoline

Gas globe, glass insert lenses, metal collar, "Greenfield Gasoline, Service," heavy flaking, 18" dia ........ 264.00

## Green Goose Tobacco

Tin, vertical box, litho tin, "Green Goose Cut Plug Smoking And Chewing Tobacco," red text, yellow ground, goose at left, cond. 6.5, 6" x 4" x 4-1/4" ............ 354.00

Sign, tin over cardboard, "Great American Insurance Company, New York," Uncle Sam by 1917 financial statement, cond. 8.25+, 25" h, 17" w, $302.50. (Photo courtesy of Gary Metz, Muddy River Trading Co.)

# Green River

Dispenser, trophy design, clear glass with landscape logo, mounted on chrome base with 2 urn-type handles, circa 1930s-1940s, no lid, cond. 7 ........... 220.00

Display, countertop, cardboard with "Green River" bottle, "First for Thirst" on red arrow at top, "Green River, the Favorite of Millions, 5¢ a bottle plus deposit," cond. 9-, 11-1/4" h, 7-12" w ................................................. 71.50

# Green Seal Sliced Plug

Tin, horizontal flat pocket, litho tin, gold text in black seal on vertical red band, red/white design otherwise, The Surbrug Co., New York, cond. 8+ ........................ 82.50

# Green Turtle Cigars

Lunch box, litho tin, oval image of turtle, green ground, cond. 8 .............................................................. 357.50

# Greyhound Lines

Poster, paper, "Pioneers of Highway Travel, 1835 and 1935," image of stagecoach driver at top/bus at bottom, framed, cond. 7.5, 26" h, 20" w ................. 132.00

Salt/pepper shakers, metal, bus shape, rubber tires, cond. 8+, 1" h, 3-1/4" w ......................................... 93.50

Sign, porcelain, 2-sided, oval, "Greyhound Lines" in orange, blue ground, running greyhound in center, cond. 7, 20-1/2" h, 36" w .................................. 522.50

# Grit

Calendar, 1905, heavy paper, girl in hat/coat hugging dog, calendar pages at border, framed, Grit Publication Co., cond. VG, 15-1/4" h, 11-1/2" w ........... 132.00

# Griffith & Boyd Co. Fertilizers

Sign, paper, embossed, "Griffith & Boyd Co. Fertilizers" upper-left, framed, tears/repaired tear/scuffs, 24-1/4" h, 19-3/4" w .............................................................. 302.50

# Gripwell Tires

Sign, wood, "Gripwell Tires, Guaranteed 6000 Miles, None

**Can, cardboard, tin top/bottom, "Guardian Service Cleaner," 8 oz, $10.**

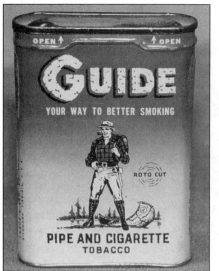

**Tin, pocket, litho tin, "Guide Pipe and Cigarette Tobacco, Your Way to Better Smoking, Larus & Bro. Co., Richmond, Va.," 4-1/4" h, $335.**

Better Made," shows tire, triangular "Gripwell Triangle NonSkid" logo with shaking hands, cond. 7, 16" h, 12" w ................................................................... 467.50

# Gruen

Clock, glass face, plastic sides, metal rim, "Gruen Watch Time" in center, red text/numbers, white ground, merchant info around blue border, wiring/plug need replaced, cond. G, 17" dia ................................. 60.50

# GSU Power Center

Sign, porcelain, triangular with rounded corners, "GSU Power Center," pictures Reddy Kilowatt, porcelain chips/scratches, 33" h, 44" w .............................. 55.00

# Guaranteed Measure

Gas globe, pierced-tin sand-painted metal inserts, painted metal collar, 19-1/2" h, 17-1/2" dia ........................632.50

# Guardian Service Cleaner (See Photo)

# Guide (See Photo)

# Gulf

**Reference:** Charles Whitworth, *Gulf Oil Collectibles*, Schiffer Publishing, 1998

Badge, celluloid over metal, pinback, "Get More Gas Mileage, Ask Me," black on orange ground, blue border, 1920s ..................................................... 55.00

Can, litho tin
  "Gulf" oval logo over "Experimental Racing Oil (LS-1320)," unused experimental can, cond. VG, 9-1/2" h, 6-1/2" w .............................................................38.50
  "Gulflube Motor Oil" over orange logo, white/blue text, blue over white ground, unopened, dents/scratches, 5-1/2" h, 4" dia............................. 49.50
  "Gulflube Motor Oil, Parafine Base" over orange logo, white text, blue (blue/white checkered on back) over

**Poster, paper, "Happy New Year, Gulf," orange logo, blue ground, archival backing, circa 1940, cond. 8+, 42" h, 27-3/4" w, $93.50. (Photo courtesy of Collectors Auction Services)**

white ground, "Tamper-Proof" repeats at top/bottom, unopened, NOS, 5-1/2" h, 4" dia ........................ 159.50

"Gulfpride, The World's Finest Motor Oil, H.D., High Detergency" over orange logo, white/orange text, blue over white ground, unopened, NOS, 5-1/2" h, 4" dia............................................................. 121.00

"Gulfpride Motor, The World's Finest Motor Oil" over orange logo, white/orange text, blue over white ground, early cars under top rim, unopened, minor rust/scratches, 5-1/2" h, 4" dia...................... 121.00

"Gulf Supreme Motor Oil" over orange logo, white text, blue over white ground, dotted band at center, "Tamper-Proof" repeats on orange band at top/bottom, unopened, 5-1/2" h, 4" dia .................... 159.50

"Gulf Supreme Motor Oil" over orange logo, white text, orange over white ground, unopened, minor scratches/rust, 5-1/2" h, 4" dia...................... 121.00

Display, tin, "Cruisemaster" beside "Gulf" logo on white sign at top, blue cabinet, 2 shelves, 13 full pt cans of Valvetop Oil, NOS, cond. 9 .............................. 198.00

Gas globe

"Gulf," 2 lenses, milk glass Gill body, blue/white text, orange ground, all cond. 7, 13-1/2" dia......... 330.00

"That Good Gulf Gasoline," 1-pc, embossed, black text, orange borders, restored text, cond. 9.5.......... 990.00

Photograph, color, family in white car with attendant pumping gas, late 1950s-early 1960s, framed, cond. 8+, 22-3/4" h, 41" w ............................................ 159.50

Sign, porcelain

Die-cut, "Gulf" in blue on white panel overlapping orange circle, cond. VG, 41-3/4" h, 47" w ...................... 170.50

Flange, "That Good Gulf Gasoline, Gulf Refining Company," "Gulf" on red circle, blue text, white ground, cond. 8, 18" h, 22" w...................................... 330.00

2-sided, "Gulf" in blue/white shadows on orange ground, white border, cond. 7, 30" dia .......... 302.50

"Gulf" in blue/white shadows on orange ground, cond. 8, 20" dia .................................................... 143.00

"That Good Gulf Gasoline," black text, "Good Gulf" in orange panel, white ground, black border, cond. 8, 10-1/2" dia .................................................... 220.00

"There is More Power in That Good Gulf Gasoline," central round logo, blue/white text, white triangle on blue ground, cond. 7, 30" h, 72-1/2" w ......... 330.00

Sign, pump plate, porcelain

Gulf logo over blue "Marine," white ground with blue border, cond. EXC, 8-1/2" h, 11-1/4" w ......... 275.00

Round, "Gulf Kerosene," blue/red text, white ground, blue border, cond. EXC, 10-1/2" dia ............... 82.50

Thermometer, dial-type, "Gulfpride, The World's Finest Motor Oil," Gulf logo, aluminum frame/back, glass front, cond. EXC, 12-1/4" dia ........................... 385.00

## Gulflex

Display, porcelain, embossed, "Gulflex Registered Lubrication" under Gulf logo, 7 sets of hooks labeled, white ground, cobalt border, cond. 8, 50" h, 32" w ................................................................ 330.00

Sign, tin, embossed, "Your Car Needs Gulflex, Registered Lubrication," round Gulf logo, black/white text, diagonal "Gulflex" in shadowed text, orange over black ground, black/white border, "A.A.W. 3-52," cond. 7, 24" h, 48" w...................................................... 264.00

## Gurd's Distilled Water

Sign, tin, embossed, "Be Good To Your Battery, Use Gurd's Distilled Water, We Sell It!," radios/autos in corners, white text, red ground, cond. 8, 6" h, 21-1/2" w......................................................... 385.00

# H

## Hadensa

Sign, porcelain, "Piles Radically Cured, Hadensa, Stops
Bleeding, Cures Piles At Any Stage, No Need Of
Operation," shows tube of product under red
"Hadensa," white text/border, cobalt ground, cracking/
chips/touchup, 12" h, 18" w.............................. 214.50

## Hales Leader Coffee

Can, keywind, litho tin, "Hales Vacuum Packed Coffee,
Drip Grind," 2 blue bands with white text, red/white
checkered ground, Hale-Halsell Co., McAlester OK,
cond. 8, 1 lb .................................................... 155.00

## Half and Half Tobacco

Tin, vertical pocket, litho tin, sample, "Lucky Strike" in red
circle in upper-left, "Half and Half" in white horizontal
stripe, "Buckingham Cut Plug Tobacco" in lower-right,
green ground, cond. 7.5-8.................................. 82.50

## Hall's Chocolates

Calendar, paper, 1917, "Hall's Chocolates, Tease The
Taste," woman in dress leaning against seated man in
suit with pen/paper, plate of product on table, December
pad only, framed, cond. G, 30" h, 16-3/4" w .......... 121.00

## Hambone Tobacco

Pouch, cloth, paper label, "Hambone Smoking Tobacco,
The Piedmont Tobacco Co., Danville, Va.," shows

Plate, painted china, "J. Palleys Hambone Sweets Above All
Five Cent Cigars," mkd "Buffalo" on back, 10-1/4" d, $90.

black man holding ham bone, 1917 tax stamp,
unopened, cond. EXC, 3" h, 2" w, 1" d ............ 467.50

## Hamilton Brown Shoe Co.

Sign, litho paper, "Compliments of Hamilton Brown Shoe
Co., St. Louis, U.S.A." upper right, "The Prettiest
Woman In America" under woman in white dress,
framed, creases/tears/stains, 31" h, 22" w .........302.50

## Hamm's Beer

Display, lightup, keg motif, changing split paperboard
including "Brewed Natural... For Natural Drinkability"
with bear at billboard, "Hamm's Beer" lightup, cond.
9+, 9" w............................................................ 121.00

## Hand Made Tobacco

Canister, litho tin, small top, "Hand Made Flame Cut,
Globe Tobacco Co., Detroit, Mich.," woman's hand
with ring holding product, blue ground, pre-1901,
cond. 8.5, 6-1/2" h, 5" dia.................................. 434.50
Tin, vertical pocket, litho tin
    "Hand Made Flake Cut, Globe Tobacco Co., Detroit,
    Mich.," globe medallion shows woman's hand with
    ring holding product, red trim, cond. 9 .......... 495.00
    "Hand Made Flake Cut, Globe Tobacco Co., Detroit,
    Mich.," globe medallion shows woman's hand with
    ring holding product, red trim, cond. 8+, 4" h, 3-1/2" w,
    1-1/4" d ........................................................577.50

## Handsome Dan Mixture

Pack, heavy paper, "Handsome Dan Mixture, Granule
Cut" in 3 panels/banner, round panel with "Yale Mas-
cot" bulldog, black ground, Phillip Morris Co., cond.
8.25+................................................................ 55.00

## Hanes

Display, composition figure of yawing child with dog, advertises "Merrichild Sleepers," with box of Hanes underwear
and box of Knit underwear (missing end), cracking and
crazing to display, denting/wear .............................71.50

## Hanover Coffee

Pail, litho tin, "Hanover Brand Fresh Roasted Coffee,
C.D. Kenny Co.," green ground with yellow/black
stripes, 3 lb, 8-3/4" h, 6" dia ............................. 198.00

## Happy Hollow Coffee

Can, litho tin, small top, white on red ground, semi-circular country club scene, back shows rectangular golfing scene, Olson Coffee Co., Omaha NE, cond. 7.5, 3 lb, 9-1/2" h, 5-3/4" dia ........................................... 990.00

## Happy Home Coffee

Can, paper label on tin, "Happy Home Coffee," round image of woman serving coffee, house on reverse, red text, yellow over black ground, stained, cond. 7, 1 lb ...................................................................... 27.50

## Happy Hour Coffee

Can, litho tin, shows steaming cup of coffee, pink ground, cond. 8, 6" h, 4" dia.......................................... 253.00

## Harbor

Gas globe, 2 glass lenses, new plastic body, red/black Harbor flag logo on white ground, "Trademark" on 1 lens, all cond. 9, 13-1/2" dia.............................. 209.00

## Hard-A-Port Tobacco

Playing cards, deck of 52 cards, circa 1890s, different graphics show risqué images of Victorian women, slight wear and creasing, no joker or box, 3-3/4" h, 2-1/4" w ..................................................... 522.50

## Harley-Davidson

Can, tin, "Genuine Harley-Davidson Motor Cycles Oil For Two Cycle Motors," shield logo, white/orange text on black panel, orange ground, contents, cond. 8, 8 oz, 4" h, 2-1/2" dia .................................................. 148.50

Clock, alarm clock, "Harley-Davidson" under soldier on motorcycle/War Bonds logo, orig box mkd "Waralarm, A One Day Alarm Clock" and "Compliments Harley-Davidson Motor Co.," cond. 8.25+, clock 4-1/2" dia.......................................................... 242.00

Hat, cloth, plastic visor, "Harley-Davidson" logo stitched on front, black ground, white braid above white visor, cond. 7, size 6-3/4............................................... 99.00

Sign
    Neon, wood, embossed text, "Harley-Davidson Motor Cycles," shield logo, new neon, cond. 9, 30" h, 40" w.............................................................. 935.00
    Porcelain, die-cut, can shape, "Genuine Harley-David-son Motor Cycles Oil, Refinery Sealed," shield logo, white/orange text on black panel, orange ground, cond. 8, 11" h, 8" w ..................................... 1,760.00

## Harmony Coffee

Can, small top, cardboard, tin top/bottom, square, "Harmony Blend Coffee," families at restaurant in shield-shaped panel, yellow/black/red text, floral trim, green ground, cond. 8, 3 lb ........................................ 506.00

## Harmony Pipe Tobacco Co.

Tin, 3" h, 2-3/4" d.................................................. 27.50

## Harp Plug Cut

Tin, vertical pocket, paper label, "Harp Plug Cut, Manu-factured by Jno. Weisert Tobacco Co., St. Louis," harp

Sign, painted milk glass, detailed scene of early hunting cabin with dog, guns, bearskin, "I.W. Harper Whiskey" on deer rack, gold frame with chips, 29-1/2" h, 23-1/2" w, $1,485. (Photo courtesy of Gary Metz, Muddy River Trading Co.)

and "Trade Mark" in red circle, "Harp Plug Cut" in white text, cond. 9 ....................................................... 165.00

## I.W. Harper Whiskey (See Photo)

## Harrison's Heart O' Orange

Sign, tin, embossed, "New Big Size Harrison's Fresh Fruit Heart O' Orange, 5¢, Not A Pop," 2 oranges drinking from bottle, cond. 9.5, 28" h, 8" w ................................................................ 2,090.00

## Hartford Tires

Sign, flange, metal, die-cut, "Hartford Tires Give Tire Insurance" in orange on cobalt panel with winged logo, panel passes thru center of "Hartford Rubber Works Co." tire, cond. 7/6, 19-1/2" h, 13" w .............. 1,320.00

Sign, tin, embossed, "Harrison's Heart O' Orange Sold Here," 1930s-1940s, cond. 7, 14" dia, $330. (Photo courtesy of Gary Metz, Muddy River Trading Co.)

# Harvard

Tin, "Harvard Jumbo Peanuts, Educate the Taste," peanut dressed as Harvard student waving banner, 10 lb, cond. 7.5, 10" h ................................................ 138.00

# Harvilla's Beverages

Display, cardboard, die-cut, "Have Harvilla's Handy" in yellow circle on red square atop green triangle with man's hand, slot for bottle, with glass "Harvilla's Beverage" 7-oz bottle, display with tear/bends/wear, bottle cond. G .................................................... 44.00

# Haserot's Senora Coffee

Can, keywind, litho tin, taller version, "Drip Grind," black/red/white text, yellow ground, black lower band with silhouetted coffee cups on top, cond. 8+, 1 lb .................. 46.00

# Havoline Motor Oil

Sign, porcelain, 2-sided, "In Sealed Cans For Your Protection, Havoline Motor Oil, Waxfree," red/blue bull's-eye, white over blue ground, "Waxfree" in red, cond. 8/7.5, 11" h, 21" w ................................................. 308.00

Sign, tin, 2-sided, "New and Improved, Keeps Your Engine Clean, Havoline Motor Oil," bull's-eye logo, red/white text, white over black ground, NOS, cond. 9/8+, 18-1/2" h, 21-1/2" w ............................. 275.00

# Hawaiian Kona Coffee

Can, keywind, litho tin, lime-green version, "Hawaiian Kona Coffee" in white/yellow text on black diamond over "S&W" in starburst oval, yellow ground with palm trees, considerable wear to lid, body cond. 8+, 1 lb ..................................................................... 93.50

# Hawkeye Incubator Co.

Tray, tin, "Compliments of the Hawkeye Incubator Co., Newton, Iowa" at top, "One Minute Washer" on bottom, seated woman in red dress with glass leaning against fireplace, ©1905, cond. VG, 17-1/4" h, 12-1/4" w .......................................................... 352.00

# Headlight

Sign
Metal, embossed, wood frame, "Headlight Work Clothes, Union Made Headlight Overalls," small train logo, orange ground, frame repainted, cond. 8+ ......................................................... 302.50
Porcelain, "Agency For Headlight Union Made Overalls," train at right, white text, "Headlight Union Made" in cobalt on white light beam, cobalt ground, red border, cond. 7.75-8.25, 10" h, 32" w ........................... 302.50

# Heath & Milligan Paints

Tip tray, litho tin, "Heath & Milligan Paints, Sunshine Finishes," 2 girls/dog on hardwood floor, white text on red border, orig. "Compliments of" paper label on back, cond. 8.25, 4-1/4" dia ........................................ 231.00

# Heccolene Oils

Can, tin
"Heccolene Oils, Hecco, (blank), H. Earl Clack Co.," orange ground, cond. 8/7, gal, 11-1/4" h, 8" w ................................................................. 167.00
"Heccolene Oils, Hecco, (blank), H. Earl Clack Co.," orange ground, cond. 8, 5 gal, 15" h, 9" sq .......... 55.00

# Heineken

Sign, porcelain pillow, "Heineken, Let meest getapt!" and "Heineken bier," shows beer glass/waiter with 2 glasses of beer on a tray, minor scratches, 23-1/2" h, 16" w ................................................................. 275.00

# Heinz

**History:** In 1869, Henry Heinz, who had been mixing, bottling, and selling his own horseradish for some time, joined forces with L.C. Noble to start Anchor Brand Food Company. The name was later changed to Heinz, Noble, and Company. The firm went bankrupt in the mid-1870s and was re-established in 1876 as the F. and J. Heinz Company, with the final name change to H.J. Heinz Company occurring in 1888.

Contrary to popular belief, the term "57 varieties" did not refer to the number of products produced by the company. Rather, the phrase was used simply for its advertising effect.

The well-known Heinz pickle symbol was used as early as 1910.

Jar, glass, plain base, ground lid with Keystone finial embossed key/logo on front, key on back and "H" on 2 sides, Pittsburg spelled with the "h," cracked base, cond. 9-, 12" h, 5" sq ........................................ 110.00
Sign
Cardboard, embossed, "Heinz Preserved Sweet

**Jar, glass, paneled, paper label, "Heinz Apple Butter, H.J. Heinz Co., Pittsburgh, Pa.," no lid, 1 lb, 14 oz, $45.**

Mixed Pickles, Keystone Brand," keystone logo at left, cond. NM, 4-1/8" h, 11" w ...................... 522.50

Tin, rolled lip on 3 edges, "Heinz Home-style Soups, 2 Minute Service, Large Bowl 15¢," shows 5 bowls, lists 10 varieties, white/yellow/cobalt text, cobalt ground, red band at top, white band at bottom, cond. VG, 10-1/2" h, 27-1/2" w ...................... 302.50

Soup machine, metal and Fiberglas, slots for storing cans, with 2 metal cups and can opener, electric, minor wear, 32" h, 25" w ................................... 165.00

Toy, truck, litho tin body, rubber tires, "Heinz Food Products" red logo with green pickle, "Rice Flakes, Baked Beans, Bottled Vinegars" on white truck, working lights, orig box, cond. 8+, box 5" h, 12" w, 3" d .............................. 605.00

# Helmar Turkish Cigarettes

Sign

Flange, porcelain, die-cut, "Helmar Turkish Cigarettes, Quality Superb, 10¢" top has Helmar cowgirl in straw hat, small images of product/pointing hand, white text, red ground, cond. 8, 23" h, 16" w .................. 1,246.00

Paper, framed, "Helmar Turkish Cigarettes," outdoor scene of woman in pointed straw hat/leather jacket, product shown lower-right, fading/edge wear/water marks, 42-1/2" h, 33" w................................. 737.00

# Heptol Splits

Tip tray, litho tin, "Heptol Splits, For Health's Sake," cowboy on bucking horse, gold text on black rim, cond. 7.25 ................................................................. 121.00

# Herald Square Typewriter Ribbon (See Photo)

# Hercules Condoms

Tin, litho tin, "Hercules Latex Prophylactic Sheaths, Robert J. Pierce, New York," Hercules holding globe, red over black ground, cond. 8.5, 1/4" h, 2-1/8" w, 1-5/8" d................................................................. 935.00

Tin, litho tin, "Herald Square Typewriter Ribbon," 2-5/8" sq, $4.

# Hercules Gasoline

Gas globe lens, 2 lenses, "Hercules Gasoline" in white on black border, "Ethyl" in red across white center, cond. 8.5, 13-1/2" dia.................................................. 275.00

# Hercules Powder Co.

Calendar

1915, metal strips top/bottom, "E.C. Smokeless Shotgun Powder, Easy on the Shoulder, Grand Prize, Smokeless Shotgun Powder, Panama Pacific Exposition Awarded to Hercules Powder Co.," shows black-breasted plovers on shore, others landing, cond. 8+, 25-3/4" h, 15" w ........................... 852.50

1940, "Pioneers" artwork by N.C. Wyeth shows man, woman and boy in a covered wagon, framed, minor creases/soiling, unused, 31-1/2" h, 14-1/2" w ...................................................... 357.50

1943, "Not This Trip, Old Pal," shows World War I soldier with dog, framed, unused, 31-1/2"h, 14-1/2" w ...................................................... 253.00

1940s, top only, "Stowaways," Walter Beach Humphrey artwork shows boy and puppy in car with father figure and hound dog in background, cond. 9.5................................................................. 132.00

1940s, top only, N.C. Wyeth artwork of 3 hunters walking down road with 2 hound dogs, cond. 9.5 ............44.00

Sign, paper

"Hercules E.C. & Infallible Smokeless Shotgun Powders, L.&R. Orange Extra Black Sporting Powders, Hercules Powder Co.," titled, "I'se done lost de lunch," winter scene with black father/son hunting with dog, metal strips top/bottom, 1923, cond. 8, 25-1/8" h, 15-1/2" w........................................................1,430.00

"The Game Bird of the Future," shows 2 pheasants with "For the Field, the Marsh, or at the Traps, Use 'Infallible' or 'E.C.'," framed, minor creases/soiling, 23-1/4" h, 20-1/4" w ...................................... 770.00

**Rack, flavors sign, metal, "Hershey's Ice Cream, Famous For Quality Since 1894," 26" h, 11" w, $95.**

Sign, cardboard, "Thirsty or Not! Enjoy Grapette Soda, Imitation Grape Flavor," NOS, 20" h, 32" w, $60.

Can, tin, paper label, twist lid, "Red Cow Coffee, Jos. Strong & Co., Terre Haute Coffee & Spice Mills, Terre Haute, Ind.," 1 lb, $400.

Sign, cardboard, die-cut, counter-sitter, "Look New Sunbeam Is Better," with display loaf, 1950s, cond. 9.25, 27" h, 12" w, $1,760. (Photo courtesy of Gary Metz, Muddy River Trading Co.)

Tin, vertical pocket, litho tin, "Buckingham Bright Cut Plug Smoking Tobacco, John J. Bagley & Co.," unopened, 4-1/2" h, $130.

Coca-Cola 1913 cardboard cutout, medallions of 4 women, "North, South, East, West, They All Drink It," museum mounted/framed, believed to be the only 1 known, cond. 7.75-8.25, 24" h, 31" w, $28,600. (Photo courtesy of Gary Metz, Muddy River Trading Co.)

Calendar, 1909, paper, orig metal strip at top, "Drink Coca-Cola, Delicious And Refreshing," pad begins with April, few areas of restoration, cond. 8.5-8.75+, 20-1/2" h, 11" w, $14,300. (Photo courtesy Gary Metz, Muddy River Trading Co.)

Display, cardboard hanger, die-cut, 3-D, 1944, "Have A Coke," Sprite Boy with Coca-Cola hat, orig easel back, cond. 8.75-9, 18" h, 14", $4,730. (Photo courtesy of Gary Metz, Muddy River Trading Co.)

Signs, tin, die-cut: (left) 1958, 6-pack with "Regular Size" dot on carton, cond. 9.5-9.75, 11" h, 13" w, $2,970; (right) 1950, 6-pack, "6 for 25¢," shows wire handle, edge nicks, cond. 9.5, 11" h, 13" w, $1,760. (Photo courtesy of Gary Metz, Muddy River Trading Co.)

Thermometers, porcelain, Canadian, "Drink Coca-Cola, Thirst knows no season," silhouette of girl: (left) red/green version, 1939, tube ties missing, cond. 8.75+, 18" h, $1,870; (right) red version, circa 1940, cond. 9.5+, 18" h, $2,530. (Photo courtesy of Gary Metz, Muddy River Trading Co.)

Change receiver, ceramic, 1890s, "The Ideal Brain Tonic For Headache and Exhaustion, Drink Coca-Cola, Change Receiver, Delightful Summer and Winter Beverage, Delicious Refreshing Invigorating," cond. 7, 1" h, 9" dia, $5,500. (Photo courtesy of Gary Metz, Muddy River Trading Co.)

Calendar, 1912, paper, "Drink Coca-Cola, Delicious And Refreshing," pad begins with June, museum mounted/framed, light stains/wrinkling, cond. 8-8.25, 31" h, 12" w, $7,150. (Photo courtesy of Gary Metz, Muddy River Trading Co.)

Seltzer bottles, fluted, mkd "Coca-Cola Bottling Co.," metal tops, $143 each. (Photo courtesy of Gary Metz, Muddy River Trading Co.)

Sign, cardboard, 1906, Lillian Nordica, "Coca-Cola, At Soda Fountains, 5¢," few light stains/small tears, period frame, cond. 7.5-8, 46" h, 26" w, $15,400. (Photo courtesy of Gary Metz, Muddy River Trading Co.)

Sign, tin, 1933, receding "Ice Cold Coca-Cola Sold Here" panel by 1923 bottle, cond. 9.25-9.5+, $1,485. (Photo courtesy of Gary Metz, Muddy River Trading Co.)

Tin, "Light Hiawatha Fine Cut, Absolutely The Best," cond. 7.5-8, round, 2" h, 8" dia, $212.

Tin, litho, "Monarch Teenie Weenie Super Quality Toffies, ©RM&Co 1928," 1 lb, unopened, $225.

Box, paper, "Fresh Tuxedo Tobacco," full, 4-3/8" h, $25.

Sign, flange, metal, "Winston tastes good," 13" h, 11-1/2" w, $85.

Sign, porcelain, "Sweet-Orr Overalls," red/cobalt graphic on white panel, circa 1940s, cond. 9.75+, 9-1/2" h, 27" w, $467.50. (Photo courtesy of Gary Metz, Muddy River Trading Co.)

Display, cardboard, "Hickman's Silver Birch Chewing Gum 5¢, R.H. Hickman Co., Pittsburg, Pa., ©1927," with 17 packets (3 missing), 6-1/4" w, 4-1/4" d, $325.

Thermometer, painted wood, beveled edges, "Clark 4 P.M. 'Clark Bar O'Clock,' Clark Bar, Join the Millions In This Mid-Afternoon Candy Delight," wear, light paint loss, 19" h, 5-1/2" w, $385.

Pocket mirror, celluloid, "Yellow Cabs, Main 4941," 3-1/2" dia, $175.

Festoon, cardboard, 5 pc, "Drink Dr. Pepper, Good For Life" logo, 1930s-1940s, some cardboard missing, medium/heavy bends, cond. 7-7.5, approx. 10' l, $8,800. (Photo courtesy of Gary Metz, Muddy River Trading Co.)

Sign, aluminum, string-hung, 1940s, "Drink Dr. Pepper, Good For Life": (left) "Energy Up! At 10-2 And 4," missing orig string, cond. 8+, 10" dia, $1,210; (right) "At 10-2 And 4, 5¢," orig string, cond. 8.5, 10" dia, $1,485. (Photo courtesy of Gary Metz, Muddy River Trading Co.)

Sign, cardboard, small horizontal, "Tops!" with "Dr. Pepper, Good For Life" logo and "Drink A Bit To Eat" with 10-2-4 logo, orig wooden frame with 10-2-4 logo at top, partial 1946 calendar pad, cond. 8.25-8.5, $1,485. (Photo courtesy of Gary Metz, Muddy River Trading Co.)

Thermometer, litho tin, "Drink Dr. Pepper," bottle with halo, 1930s, cond. 7.5+, 17" h, $2,310. (Photo courtesy of Gary Metz, Muddy River Trading Co.)

Sign, tin, flange, die-cut, small version, late 1930s, "Drink Dr. Pepper, Good For Life," better side cond. 8.25-8.5, lesser side cond. 7.25-7.5, 10" h, 17-1/2" w, $2,090. (Photo courtesy of Gary Metz, Muddy River Trading Co.)

Fan pulls, cardboard, 2-sided, "Drink Dr. Pepper, Good For Life!": (left) "10-2-4 Or When You're Hungry, Thirsty Or Tired," bather with ship's wheel, cond. 7.5, $2,200; (right) "Drink A Bite To Eat at 10-2-4 O'clock," woman in director's chair, cond. 7, $1,870. (Photo courtesy of Gary Metz, Muddy River Trading Co.)

Pin trays, tin, each mkd "Drink Dr. Pepper, At All Soda Fountains, 5¢" (clockwise from upper left): round, 2 dogs, cond. 7, $1,430; oval, black boy with watermelon, cond. 7.5, 3-1/4" h, $2,530; round, 2 cats, cond. 8.5-9, 2-1/2" dia, $1,210; oval, single dog, cond. 8-8.5, $1,650. (Photo courtesy of Gary Metz, Muddy River Trading Co.)

Sign, tin, 1940s, "Take Home A Carton," striped 6-pack carrier mkd "Pick Up Your Energy, Drink Dr. Pepper, Good For Life," cond. 9.25-9.5, 28" h, 20" w, $1,045. (Photo courtesy of Gary Metz, Muddy River Trading Co.)

Sign, tin over cardboard, orig string hanger, 1930s-1940s, "Drink Dr. Pepper, Good For Life, Thank You, Call Again," cond. 8.5-8.75, 8" h, 13" w, $4,950. (Photo courtesy of Gary Metz, Muddy River Trading Co.)

Tray, porcelain, circa 1900, "Drink Dr. Pepper, Bracing, Healthful, Invigorating, Ideal Beverage," central image of 1900 marble-based syrup dispenser is faint, cond. 7.5-8, 15" dia, $3,410. (Photo courtesy of Gary Metz, Muddy River Trading Co.)

Kickplate, porcelain, 1940s, "More Bounce To The Ounce," bottle breaking through background by "Pepsi-Cola" bottle cap, cond. 9.5-9.75+, 14" h, 36" w, $5,720. (Photo courtesy of Gary Metz, Muddy River Trading Co.)

Door push, tin, 1930s, "Drink Pepsi-Cola, 5¢, Worth Twice Its Price," detailed image of bottle with "Pepsi-Cola, Refreshing, Healthful" label, raised border, cond. 9.25+, 13-1/2" h, 3-1/2" w, $1,155. (Photo courtesy of Gary Metz, Muddy River Trading Co.)

Sign, tin, die-cut, bottle cap shape, "Pepsi-Cola," crazing, 14" dia, $140.

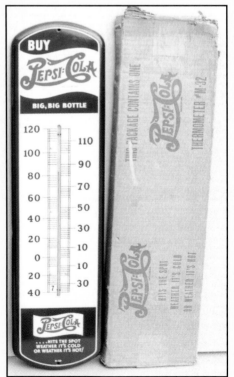

Thermometer, tin, "Buy Pepsi-Cola, Big, Big Bottle, Pepsi-Cola ...Hits The Spot Weather It's Cold Or Weather It's Hot!," NOS, orig box cond. 6-7, thermometer cond. 9.5, 27" h, 7" w, $1,595. (Photo courtesy of Gary Metz, Muddy River Trading Co.)

Sign, tin, die-cut, bottle-shape, "Pepsi-Cola 5¢ Sparkling, Satisfying, Pepsi-Cola, Made Only By Pepsi-Cola Company, Long Island City, N.Y., Bottled Locally by Authorized Bottlers From Coast to Coast, 12 Ounces," 29-1/2" h, 8-1/4" w, $560.

Dispenser, countertop, porcelain/stainless steel, "Drink Orange-Crush Fruit Flavored Drink, Ice Cold," Crushy finial, 1930s, cond. 8.25-8.5, $1,430. (Photo courtesy of Gary Metz, Muddy River Trading Co.)

Sign, porcelain, "Drink Orange-Crush," unused, 1938, cond. 9.25-9.5, 3' h, 5' w, $6,050. (Photo courtesy of Gary Metz, Muddy River Trading Co.)

Tin, paper label, "Sea Gull Baking Powder, The Sea Gull Specialty Co., Baltimore, Maryland," 4 oz, $90.

Can, tin, "Watkins Baking Powder, Purity Guaranteed, J.R. Watkins Co., Winona, Minn.," full, 1 lb, $58.

Can, litho tin, twist lid, "Gold Bond A1 Coffee, Jewett & Sherman Co., Milwaukee, Wis.," 3 lb, $145.

Can, tin, "Hills Bros Coffee, Red Can Brand, The Original Vacuum Pack," cond. 8+, 1 lb, $121.

Thermometer, chalkware, embossed, "any time... any weather... Thirsty? Just Whistle," 1930s-1940s, cond. 8.25-8.5, 12" sq, $907.50. (Photo courtesy of Gary Metz, Muddy River Trading Co.)

Sign, litho tin, die-cut, embossed, bottle shape, NuGrape Soda, 1950s, cond. 9.25, 17" h, $220. (Photo courtesy of Gary Metz, Muddy River Trading Co.)

Sign, tin, embossed, "Enjoy Hires Root Beer, Healthful, Delicious," circa 1930s, cond. 9.25-9.5, 27" h, 10" w, $275. (Photo courtesy of Gary Metz, Muddy River Trading Co.)

Sign, tin, embossed, self-framed, "Say! Drink A Bottle Of Hires," circa 1908-1916, 13" h, 9" w, cond. 8-8.5, $25,300. (Photo courtesy of Gary Metz, Muddy River Trading Co.)

Sign, cardboard, "Drink Nesbitt's California Orange," Andrew Loomis artwork of girl/boy with bottles talking to clown in white, circa 1940s, cond. 9.25+, 2' h, 3' w, $385. (Photo courtesy of Gary Metz, Muddy River Trading Co.)

Thermometer, tin, bottle shape, "Sun Crest," 1940s, 17" h, 5" w, $214.50.

Door push, plastic, "Ex-Lax, Get
Your Box Now," 8" h, 4" w, pr, $90.

Tin, litho tin, "Ex-Lax, Fig Flavor, A Pleasant
And Effective Laxative," 2-3/8" x 3-7/8", $10.

Box, wood, "White Fawn Biscuit, The Geo. Young
Bakery, Utica, N.Y.," 10" h, 12-1/2" w, 13-1/2" d, $190.

Sign, tin over cardboard, beveled, "Stoneware,
The Best Food Container, We Sell All Sizes,"
19" h, 13" w, $1,650.

Thermometer, tin, "NR All Vegetable Laxative, Come In If You Get It Here It's Good, Tums Quick Relief for Acid Indigestion," patriotic motif, wear, scratches, 27" h, 7-1/4" w, $160.

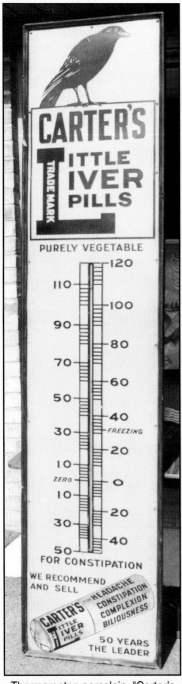

Thermometer, porcelain, "Carter's Little Liver Pills...50 Years The Leader," 1910s, cond. 8-8.25, 8' h, 21" w, $990. (Photo courtesy of Gary Metz, Muddy River Trading Co.)

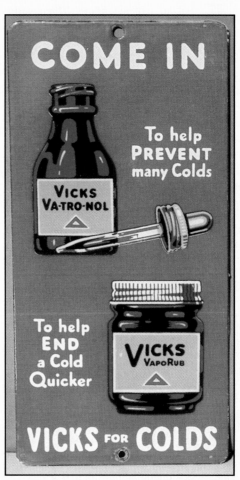

Door push, porcelain, "Come In, To help Prevent many Colds, To help End a Cold Quicker, Vicks For Colds," cobalt bottles/dropper of Vicks Va-Tro-Nol and Vicks VapoRub, 1940s, cond. 9.5, 8" h, 4" w, $467.50. (Photo courtesy of Gary Metz, Muddy River Trading Co.)

Can, metal, paper label, "Cressler's Antiseptic Tooth Powder, Burk's Medicine Co., Chicago," orig box, $145.

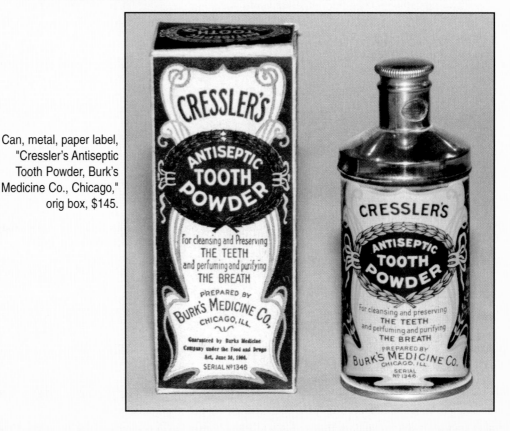

Tip tray, " 'Quick Meal' Ranges, Ask Your Dealer," cond. NM, 3-3/8" h, 4-5/8" w, $159.50.

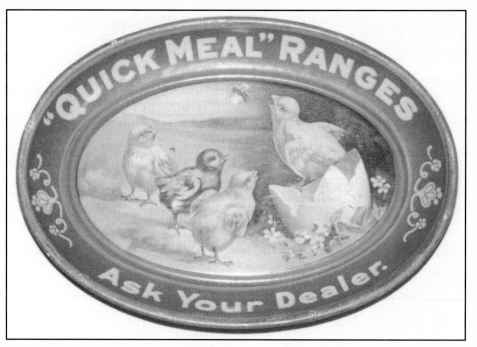

Tin, vertical pocket, litho tin, "Bull Dog Cut Plug DeLuxe," 1910 tax stamp, unopened, 4-5/8" h, $725.

Container, paper, tin top/bottom, "Gold Dust Scouring Cleanser, Lever Brothers Co., Cambridge, Mass.," 14 oz, $77.

Tin, paper label, "Wigwam Cream Tartar, Carpenter Cook Co., Menominee, Michigan," 1-1/2 oz, $40.

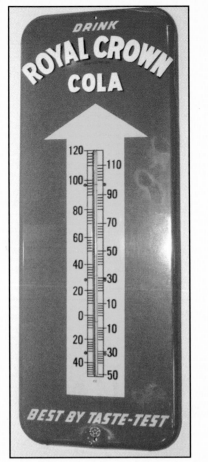
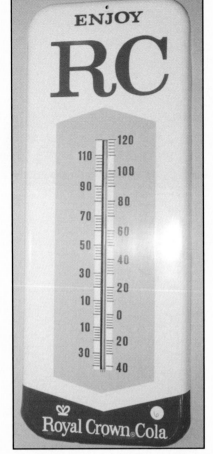
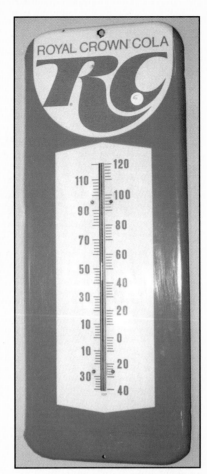

Royal Crown thermometers, tin, each 25-1/2" h, 9-3/4" w, $125 each.

Sign, paper, fold-out cardboard, self-framed, "We're a 'Fresh Up' family,
You like it ... it likes you! 7Up," NOS, 13-1/2" h, 23-1/2" w, $32.50.

Sign, tin, crossing guard, "Slow, School Crossing, 7Up," policeman motif, orig metal base, 1950s, cond. 7-8, 5' h, 2' w, $2,190.
(Photo courtesy of Gary Metz, Muddy River Trading Co.)

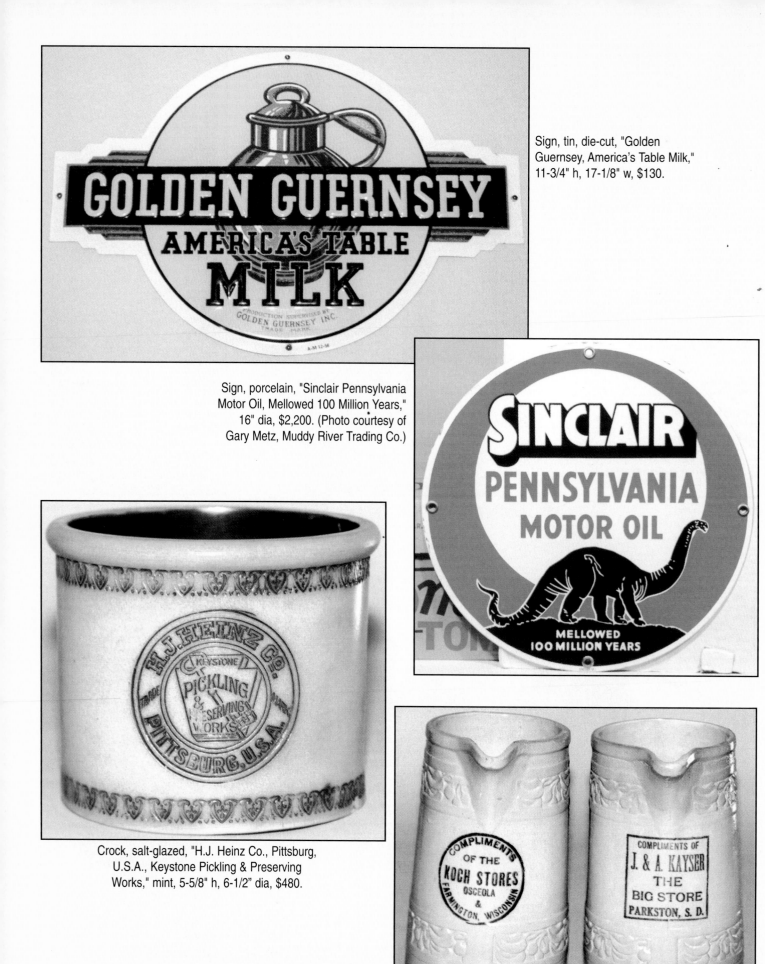

Sign, tin, die-cut, "Golden Guernsey, America's Table Milk," 11-3/4" h, 17-1/8" w, $130.

Sign, porcelain, "Sinclair Pennsylvania Motor Oil, Mellowed 100 Million Years," 16" dia, $2,200. (Photo courtesy of Gary Metz, Muddy River Trading Co.)

Crock, salt-glazed, "H.J. Heinz Co., Pittsburg, U.S.A., Keystone Pickling & Preserving Works," mint, 5-5/8" h, 6-1/2" dia, $480.

Red Wing stoneware pitchers, Cherry Band pattern, blue/white, ink stamp advertising, 9" h, each, $550.

# Hershey's

**History:** For more than 20 years, Milton Hershey struggled to become a success as a candy maker. For more than 20 years, he failed. Then, after purchasing the chocolate-making machines he had seen at the Columbian Exposition in Chicago in 1893, he began covering his caramels with chocolate. The candy was an instant success, and in 1903 Hershey began building a chocolate factory in Derry Church, Pa. The town honored him by changing its name to Hershey in 1906.

At one time, the company trademark included a cherub sitting on a cocoa bean while holding a cup of cocoa. Although the mark was printed on company correspondence and letterhead, it was never used on any product packaging. Interestingly enough, Hershey enforced a no-advertising policy for his company, believing that a good product, a good display, and a good value were the most important factors in selling an item.

## Herz Plug

Tin, litho tin, oval image of early sparkplug, blue/red/white striped ground, circa 1910, cond. 8.5, 2-1/2" h, 1-5/8" sq............................................................. 220.00

## Heverly's Cough and Distemper Powder

Crock, glazed ceramic, paper label, "Heverly's Cough and Distemper Powder," horse design, unopened, chipping to underside, 3-3/4" h, 3-1/2" dia.............................. 198.00

Tin, paper label, hand-soldered, "Heverly's Powder," shows horse, blue on white ground, H.C. Porter & Son, Towanda, Pa., cond. 7.5, 4-1/4" h, 2-1/4" sq............................................................. 55.00

## H.F. Coffee Co.

Measure, coffee, wooden, "H.F. Coffee Co., St. Louis, Mo.," 3" h.................................................... 33.00

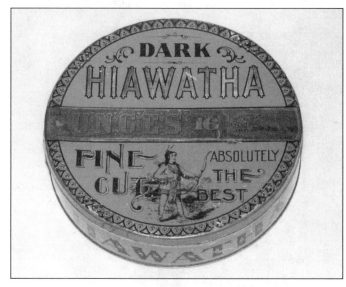

Tin, litho tin, 1 lb, "Dark Hiawatha, Spaulding & Merrick, Chicago," 8-1/4" d, $120.

# HGF Coffee

Can, keywind, litho tin, "HGF Brand Coffee" in white circle over scene of men picking coffee beans, white ground, brick-type band, H.D. Lee Mercantile Co., St. Louis/Selena KS, cond. 8.25+, 1 lb.................. 104.50

## Hiawatha

Box, cardboard, "Genuine Hiawatha Fine Cut Chewing Tobacco," red text and image of Indian, contains 12 unopened paper label foil packs with 1917 tax stamps, cond. EXC, 5-1/2" h, 4-3/4" w, 4" d.................. 412.50

Tin, round, "Light Hiawatha Fine Cut, Absolutely The Best," full-figure Indian with bow, orange ground, cond. 7.5-8, 2" h, 8" dia ............................................. 212.00

## Hickory

Tin, vertical pocket, litho tin, recessed lid, "Hickory Extremely Mild Pipe Mixture," central design with crossed pistols on white medallion, red ground, full, dent to rear, cond. 9+....................................... 121.00

## Hi-D

Thermometer, Pam style, tin face, glass cover, "CSC Hi-D Ammonium Nitrate," oval logo at top, red/black text, white ground, white numbers on black border, Chemical Solvents Co., cond. VG, 12" dia.................... 88.00

## High Art Coffee

Can, keywind, litho tin, overall scene of fishing village, cond. 8+, 1 lb, 4" h, 5" dia................................. 253.00

## High Compression Supertest

Gas globe, 2 lenses, narrow glass body, "High Compression H-C Supertest," black/white/red text, "H-C" on fire burst above spark plug, lens cond. 8, body cond. 9, 13-1/2" dia........................................................ 825.00

## High Grade

Tin, vertical pocket

Blue version, "High Grade Smoking Tobacco," central image of 2 men, Ilsey tin maker (pre-1901), cond. 7.5................................................................. 446.00

Green version, "High Grade Smoking Tobacco," central image of 2 men, Ilsey tin maker (pre-1901), cond. 7......................................................... 341.00

## High-Park Coffee

Can, keywind, litho tin, plantation scenes, plants and red coffee cup on yellow ground, cond. 9+, 1 lb ..........121.00

## Hills Bros. Coffee

**History:** Austin H. Hills and his brother Reuben were certain they did not want to work in the San Francisco shipbuilding business of their father. Instead, they decided to open a small retail grocery store in a stall at the Bay City Market. They soon established a store named Arabian Coffee and Spice Mills and began selling roasted coffee beans, tea, spices, and extracts.

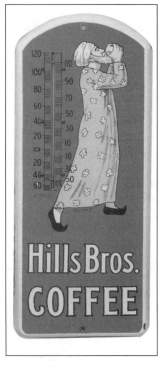

**Thermometer, porcelain, rounded top, "Hills Bros. Coffee" in white at bottom, man in turban/yellow robe drinking upper-right, tube upper-left, red ground, white border, cond. 8.25, 21" h, 9" w, $825. (Photo courtesy of Gary Metz, Muddy River Trading Co.)**

Following Edwin Norton's 1903 patent of a machine that used a vacuum to can foods, the brothers felt certain the technology could be used to improve their business. That same year they became the first to sell coffee in vacuum-packed cans, which prolonged freshness.

At that point, they thought it would be prudent to apply for a trademark for the Hills Bros. name. Ironically, the trademark letter from Washington arrived shortly after both the store and its contents were destroyed during the San Francisco earthquake of 1906. The brothers rebuilt the store, changing the product name to Hill Bros. Highest Grade Coffee.

In a continual quest for improvement, the company's product was packaged in a keywind can beginning in 1926 and a keyless can in 1963. Although there have been several redesigns, the original trademark image of an Arab drinking coffee from a cup is still in use.

Can, litho tin
"Hills Bros. Coffee, Blue Can Brand," circa 1910, cond. 8+, 3-5/8" h, 5" dia ........................................ 522.50
"Hills Bros. Coffee, Red Can Brand, The Original Vacuum Pack," man in turban/yellow robe drinking, red ground, circa 1920s, cond. 8+, 2-1/2 lb, 8-1/4" h, 5" dia ............................................................. 121.00
Display, automated, "Issassee, Give yourself a Coffee Break! Treat Yourself To The Finest, Hills Bros. Coffee," paper behind glass in base, composition figure of cross-legged Arabic boy with pot/cup, boy pours coffee/drinks, pot taped to hand, cond. VG, 41" h, 21" w, 18" d ............................................................. 3,025.00
Puzzle, cardboard, die-cut, "Where's The Fire? It's Under A Pot Of Hills Bros. Coffee, No One Can Resist That Marvelous Aroma," shows red keywind can/cartoon characters on large coffee kettle over flames, orig box, ©1933, framed, cond. VG, 16" h, 14" w .............. 99.00

## Hindoo Smoking Tobacco

Tin, vertical pocket, litho tin, litho top, "Hindoo Granulated Plug Smoking Tobacco" .................................... 355.00

## Hi-Plane Tobacco

Sign, tin, embossed, rounded corners, "Hi-Plane Tobacco, 10¢, For Pipe And Cigarettes," 1-prop plane on red vertical pocket tin at left, black/white text, green over black ground, small scratches/chips, 11-5/8" h, 35-1/8" w .......................................................... 154.00
Tin, vertical pocket, cardboard
"Hi-Plane Shredded Tobacco," white 4-engine plane on red ground, with Zip code, full, cond. 8, 1 oz ............................................................. 138.00
"Hi-Plane Smooth Cut Tobacco For Pipe And Cigarette," 4-engine sea plane on red ground, cond. 8 .......................................................... 314.00
Tin, vertical pocket, litho tin
Cut-down sample, "Hi Plane Smooth Cut," 1-engine plane on red ground, cond. 8 ........................ 147.50
"Hi Plane Smooth Cut Tobacco For Pipe And Cigarette," 1-engine plane on red ground, cond. 8 .......................................................... 126.50
"Hi Plane Smooth Cut Tobacco For Pipe And Cigarette," 2-engine plane on red ground, full, cond. 8.5 ......................................................... 184.00

## Hires Instant Coffee

Can, sample, paper label on tin, pry lid, "Hires Instant Soluble Coffee," Charles E. Hires Co., cond. 7, 2" h, 2-3/8" dia ............................................................. 577.50

## Hires Root Beer

**History:** Philadelphia druggist Charles E. Hires experimented with mixtures of roots and herbs until he invented a beverage which he called root beer because he thought the name would appeal to laborers and other working men. Hires sold the drink at his drugstore, and the mixture of herbs, barks, and berries was sold at

**Tin, litho tin, "Hi-Plane Tobacco, Larus Bro. Co., Richmond, Va.," 6-1/4" h, $220.**

Dispenser, Hires, Munimaker syrup dispenser, heavy marble base with copper, brass and glass dispenser, rust stains and scratches and closed crack to marble, Hires ID plate enhanced with new paint, brass and copper spigots polished, stains to text on glass globe, cond. 8, $4,620. (Photo courtesy of Gary Metz, Muddy River Trading Co.)

Door push/pull, metal, "Drink Hires" light-blue/white striped ground, cond. VG, 13-1/2" h, 2-5/8" w, 1-3/8" d, $198. (Photo courtesy of Gary Metz, Muddy River Trading Co.)

grocery stores and soda fountains and was exhibited at the Philadelphia Centennial Exposition in 1876.

The drink did have a drawback. Consumers had to boil the ingredients, strain the mixture, add sugar and yeast, ferment the brew, and then bottle the end product. It wasn't until 1880 that Hires introduced a liquid version of the mixture that didn't require boiling and straining.

The attire of the Hires boy seen in much of the company's advertising can be used to help date the piece. From 1891 to 1906, the lad wore a dress; from 1907 to 1914, he donned a bathrobe; and from 1915 to 1926, he modeled a dinner jacket.

Barrel, wood and metal, "Ice Cold Hires R-J Root Beer, With Real Root Juices" and "Loaned by Charles E. Hire's Co., Philadelphia U.S.A. No. 16870" on slug plate above spigot, scratches/dents/paint loss, 23-1/4" h, 14" d .................. 220.00

Baseball score keeper, celluloid, "Hires, The Put-Out Route For Thirst," cartoon image of Josh Slinger, circa 1920s, 3" h, 2" w .................. 357.50

Dispenser, ceramic, hourglass shape, orig metal pump marked "Hires," dispenser lettered "Drink Hires, It is Pure," 1920s, cond. EXC, 13-1/2" h, 8" d .......... 1,485.00

Dispenser tag, painted stainless steel, "Hires R-J Root Beer, with Real Juices," cond. 8+, 6" h, 4" w .................. 110.00

Display

Cardboard, die-cut, "Hires Root Beer, Cools and Refreshes," orange boat speeding on water, 1930s-1940s, cond. 7.75+, 10" h, 12" w .................. 231.00

Paper over cardboard case, glass cover, "Ingredients of Hires, A Good Pure Drink" under lid, 14 compartments showing ingredients, lid shows Hires boy/2

early dispensers, edge wear/tears/soiling, 9" x 10-1/2" .................. 698.50

Menu sign, tin, embossed

Rolled edges, "Drink Hires," name in yellow on diagonal cobalt panel, tilted bottle with bull's-eye logo at right, light-blue/white-striped ground/border, chalkboard at bottom, cond. VG, 29-1/2" h, 15-1/2" w .................. 99.00

"Drink Hires," name in red on diagonal yellow panel, tilted bottle with bull's-eye logo at right, light-blue/white-striped ground/border, chalkboard at bottom, cond. 8.25, 29-1/2" h, 15-1/2" w .................. 71.50

"Hires R-J Root Beer With Real Root Juices, Ice Cold 5¢ Bottles," white text/red panel on red/black bull's-eye, blue ground, chalkboard at bottom, 29-1/4" h, 15-1/4" w .................. 187.00

Mug, creamware

"Drink Hires Rootbeer," pictures child pointing, cracked handle, cond. 8.5 .................. 143.00

Mettlach, "Join Health and Cheer, Drink Hires Rootbeer," shows child in blue suitcoat, 1/2" hairline on back lip, 5-1/8" h, 4-1/4" dia .................. 330.00

Photograph, albumen, cardboard mount, shows general store with large Hires poster with owl, cond. 9 .................. 104.50

Sign, cardboard

Die-cut, standup, "Hires Root Beer since 1876, With Roots-Bark-Herbs," shape of foaming root beer glass, 2-1/4" tear, cond. 8, 30" h, 14" w .................. 440.00

Embossed, string-hung, "Drink Hires Rootbeer" beside round medallion of Hires kid, faint crease line, restored, cond. 8+, 6" h, 10-3/4" w .................. 5,280.00

Bottle of Hires outside frosted window with fireplace scene inside, framed, 1950s, cond. 9.75, 18" h, 12" w .................. 154.00

Sign, flange, tin, "Hires, So Refreshing," light-blue ground, 1940s-1950s, cond. 8.5, 12" h, 14" w, $385. (Photo courtesy of Gary Metz, Muddy River Trading Co.)

"Birch Bark from America, One of the sixteen ingredients, Drink Hires," round portrait of Indian woman, ground shows birch tree, glass, cond. EXC, 21" h, 15" w........................................... 3,630.00

"Drink Hires," Haskel Coffin artwork of woman and tray holding bottle and glass, framed, cond. 7.25-7.75, 20" h, 15" w................................................. 1,017.50

Sign, lightup, round, "Drink Hires, Made with Roots,-

Sign, celluloid, "Say! Drink Hires," circa 1905, cond. 7.25-7.75, 8" h, 6" w, $2,860. (Photo courtesy of Gary Metz, Muddy River Trading Co.)

Barks-Herbs, Here," bull's-eye with white/blue/black/red, 1940s-1950s, cond. 8-8.25, 16" dia........ 2,530.00

Sign, heavy paper, "Drink Hires in Bottles," oval Haskell Coffin portrait of woman with glass, bottle in corner, 1910s, cond. 7-7.5, 21" h, 15" w...................... 660.00

Sign, litho tin

Die-cut, embossed, bottle shape, bull's-eye logo, 1950s, cond. 9.75, 57" h............................. 522.50

Die-cut, oval, "Drink Hires," 2 women drinking from glasses with straws, 1910s-1920s, cond. 6-6.5, 20" h, 24" w................................................440.00

Embossed, round, "Hires R-J Root Beer With Real Root Juices," red/black bull's-eye, white text, 12" dia .......................................................... 82.50

Embossed, "Enjoy Hires, it's always pure," woman in red hat and tip of bottle, blue ground with green border, cond. 8+, 9-3/4" h, 27-3/4" w ................. 907.50

Embossed, "Hires R-J Root Beer With Real Root Juices," bull's-eye logo in center, "In Bottles" lower left, "Ice Cold" lower-right, orig paper cover, NOS, 9-3/4" h, 27-3/4" w ........................................ 137.50

Embossed, "Hires R-J Root Beer With Real Root Juices, A Toast to Good Taste," red/black bull's-eye on blue triangle, white ground, "With Real Root Taste" in red bar, 1940s-1950s, cond. 8.25-8.5, 13" h, 19" w .................................................. 121.00

Rolled frame, "Have A Hires And Refresh, Made with Roots Barks Herbs," white checkmark in red/black bull's-eye logo, red bar near bottom, white/black text, light-blue ground, 8-1/2" h, 17-1/2" w .................93.50

"Drink Hires Root Beer," slanted bottle, black/orange text in white explosion, blue ground, 1940s-1950s, cond. 9-9.25, 42" h, 13" w ........................... 440.00

"Hires to your Health," standing boy with mug, white text between legs, black ground, circa 1910, cond. 6-6.5, 28" h, 20" w ....................................... 687.50

Sign, tin over cardboard, beveled edge, string-hung, "Got a Minute, Have a Hires, Your Invitation to Refresh," bull's-eye logo at top, invitation motif, 1940s, cond. 8+, 8-1/2" h, 6" w..................................................... 66.00

Sign, tin, 2-sided, "Hires R-J Root Beer For Real Juices," 10" h, rust, $65.

Trade card
    Die-cut, "It Pops. Effervescent too. Exhilarating. Appe-
        tizing. Hires Rootbeer," Hires kid behind box/glass,
        1890s, cond. 8-8.5 .......................................... 49.50
    "Say You 'Auto' Drink Hires Rootbeer," Hires kid on
        horseless carriage, 1900, cond. 8-8.5, 7" h,
        5" w ........................................................... 82.50
Tray, litho tin, round
    "For Thirst And Pleasure (at border), Hires since 1876
        Root Beer, With Roots, Barks, Herbs," red/black/
        blue bull's-eye design, black/white text, circa 1950,
        NOS, cond. 9.25-9.5, 41" dia ........................ 577.50
    "Hires 5¢, Things is getting higher, but Hires are still a
        nickel a trickle," shows "Josh Slinger" soda jerk,
        1915, cond. 5.5-6, 12" dia ............................ 137.50
    "Say! 5¢, Drink Hires Refreshing," child with mug logo
        in center, white to gold to red ground, black rim,
        circa 1905-1910, cond. 6.5-7, 12" dia ........... 198.00

# Hi Tower

Gas globe, newer plastic body with 2 lenses, "-Hi- Tower"
    in yellow, "Tower" on green band, black outline behind
    "-Hi-," black triangular "Ethyl" logo at bottom, white
    ground, cond. 8.5/8, body 8, 13-1/2" dia .......... 467.50

# HL Black Cigars

Cigar store Indian, carved wood, painted, "HL Black
    Cigars" in red on black base, Indian in headdress hold-
    ing staff/cigars, paint chips/wood cracking/figure loose
    at base, 73" h, base 20" sq .......................... 14,300.00

# Hoffmann's Old Time Coffee

Can, litho tin, "Hoffmann's Old Time Blended Coffee,"
    white-haired woman with cup, cond. 8+, 1 lb, 4-1/4" h,
    5-1/4" dia ..................................................... 302.50

# J.G. Hoffmann & Sons Co.

Sign, paper, "J.G. Hoffmann & Sons Co., Manufacturers
    of Celebrated Star Oak Harness Leather, Wheeling,
    W.VA., U.S.A.," under round star logo, detailed factory
    scenes, oval portrait upper-right, black/red text,
    framed, cond. G, 36" h, 48-1/2" w ..................... 445.50

# M. Hohner

Box, metal and wood, 3 tiers, paper label on top and
    inside of box lid, "M. Hohner, The Finest Harmonica
    Made," shows man, woman and child with harmoni-
    cas, scratches, 6" h, 10-3/4" w, 9-1/2" d .......... 143.00

# Holiday Tobacco

Pack, vertical pocket, heavy paper, "Holiday Smoking
    Mixture, Mild, Mellow," tropical scene with palm trees,
    green ground, full, cond. 9 ................................ 48.00
Tin, vertical pocket, litho tin, recessed lid, "Holiday Pipe
    Mixture, Aromatic in the Pack, Aromatic in the Pipe,"
    steamer ship with palm branches, cond. 8+ ........ 43.00

# Hollingsworth Candies

Sign, porcelain, "Hollingsworth Unusual Candies, For

Tin, litho tin, hinged lid, "Honest Labor Cut Plug, R.A.
Patterson Tobacco Co., Richmond, Va.," 1" h, 4-5/8" w,
2-3/4" d, $30.

Those Who Love Fine Things," white on red ground,
    "My Hobby Box" logo at top, circa 1940s, cond. 7.5+,
    12" h, 29" w .................................................. 286.00

# Holsum

Door bar, litho tin on tubular chrome frame, adjustable,
    "the bread to buy," shows loaf of bread, white ground,
    cond. 8.5 ...................................................... 143.00
Sign, paper, metal strips top/bottom, "To My Valentine" on
    green ribbon at top, "Holsum Bread, Miller Patton Bak-
    ing Co." at bottom, girl in pink sweater reading valen-
    tine, boy in suit, cherub/floral trim, unused, cond. 9.25,
    35" h, 11-3/4" w ............................................ 104.50
Sign, tin, embossed
    "Buy Holsum," yellow text in corners, loaf of "Holsum"
        bread in canted white panel, cobalt ground, cond. VG,
        13" h, 27" w ................................................ 220.00
    "Buy Holsum Bread," pictures loaf in wrapper, cond. 9-
        9.25, 13" h, 27" w ........................................ 220.00

# Home Brand Coffee

Can, inset lid, litho tin, "Home Brand Coffee" in red text,
    "Vacuum Sealed, Roasted Granulized" in black, small
    round design, yellow ground, cond. 8.5, 1 lb ........... 38.50

# Home Comfort Ranges

**History:** Because Home Comfort Ranges were obvi-
ously too heavy to be carted around the countryside,
traveling salesmen carried scaled-down versions in
the backs of their wagons.

Sign, curved porcelain, detailed factory scene, cond. 8+,
    4-3/4" h, 5-7/8" w ........................................... 440.00

# Honest Labor Cut Plug (See Photo)
Sign
    Cardboard, "Honest Scrap, An Everday Scrap," out-
        door scene of startled dog/cat, product in center,
        "Honest Scrap" on orig frame, cond. VG, 10-1/4" h,
        30" w ......................................................... 632.50

Tin, "Honest Scrap, A Pleasing Chew," muscular arm with hammer on red ground, dents/wrinkles, 8-3/4" h, 6-3/4" w .......................................... 203.50

## Honest Tobacco

Pack, paper, "Honest Long Cut Smoking and Chewing Tobacco," man in hat lighting pipe on 1 side, man with trolley driver on other, poem on side, cond. 9.25 .............................................. 121.00

## Honest Weight Tobacco

Pack, "Honest Weight Tobacco, Weyman & Bro.," shows hand holding scale weighing baby in cloth wrap, red/blue text, white ground, red border, full, cond. 9.5 .................................................. 155.00

## Honey-Bear Pipe Mixture

Pack, paper, foil-lined, "Honey-Bear Rum and Honey Pipe Mixture, Mild and Fragrant," drawing of 2 bear cubs at beehive in tree, white ground, empty, cond. 9 ............................................... 38.50

## Honey Bee Snuff

Sign, tin, embossed, shows can of "Honey Bee Sweet Snuff, Sweet As Honey," brown/red text, hive design, newer wood frame, ragged edges with rust, paint bubbling, 19-1/4" h, 13-1/2" w ................................... 66.00

## Honey-Moon Gum

Clock, figural, cast iron, bronze finish, king's squire with extended trumpet, circa 1890s, 12" h ............ 2,860.00

## Honey Moon Tobacco

Sign, litho tin, embossed, shows vertical pocket tin with man and woman sitting on yellow crescent moon with stars on dark-blue ground, cond. 8+, 9-3/4" h, 6-3/4" w ............................................. 327.00
Tin, vertical pocket, litho tin

**Tin, pocket, litho tin, "Honey Moon Tobacco, Penn Tobacco Co., Wilkes-Barre, Pa.," man sitting on crescent moon, cond. 8+, 4-1/2" h, $185.**

Cut-down sample, "Honey Moon" upper part of circle with man's head/face in sky, cond. 8 ........... 126.50
Version with man on crescent moon, "Honey Moon Rum-Flavored Tobacco, 10¢," stars on dark-blue sky, red ground otherwise, cond. 8 .............. 331.00
Version with man/woman on crescent moon, "Honey Moon Tobacco, Penn Tobacco Co., Wilkes-Barre, Pa.," stars on dark-blue sky, red ground, cond. 7.5 ........................................... 605.00

## Honeysuckle

Can, keywind, litho tin, "Honeysuckle 10¢ Plug Bright Chewing Tobacco," flower with bees, red ground, cond. 8+, 4" h, 5-1/4" dia .................................... 91.00

## Honor Coffee

Can, cardboard, tin top/bottom, "Honor Brand Diamond Cut Coffee," pictures George Washington, cobalt trim, cond. 8, 6" h, 4-5/8" w, 3-1/8" d ....................... 220.00

## Honor Peanut Butter

Tin, litho tin, "Honor Brand Peanut Butter, Honor Brand Is Better," gold text on white ground, other side shows George Washington, Gowan-Lenning-Brown Co., Duluth, Minn., no lid, cond. 7-7.5, 25 lb, 9-1/2" h, 10" dia ............................................. 104.50

## Hood's Ice Cream

Sign, flange, painted metal, round, "Hood's Ice Cream" in white on red border, trademark cow in center, paint loss/rust to flange, 19" dia ............................. 1,320.00

## Hood's Sarsaparilla

**History:** Charles I. Hood opened a drugstore in 1870 and began developing his own line of medicines several years later. It wasn't long before Hood's Sarsaparilla and Hood's Pills were being sold on the national level. Hood used a plethora of items to advertise his products, with attractive women and cherubic children featured on many of them.

Calendar
1889, cardboard, die-cut, "Hood's Sarsaparilla Calendar 1889," girl in white bonnet, pad begins with July, paper loss/stains/tears/thumbtack holes, 9-7/8" h, 5-1/2" w ...................................... 44.00
1892, paper, "Hood's Sarsaparilla Calendar 1892," circular scene of 8 children around full pad, blue ground outside circle, product info on back, cond. 9+, 7" sq .......................................... 60.50
1900, heavy paper, die-cut, "Hood's Sarsaparilla Calendar 1900" on bonnets of 2 girls in pink/blue dresses, pad begins with April, cond. VG, 6-1/2" h, 5" w ............................................... 38.50
1901, heavy paper, "Hood's Sarsaparilla Calendar 1901" upper-right, "Hood's Sarsaparilla Calendar" cover on full pad, girl in white dress sitting with hands together, titled "Patience" lower-left, framed, small creases/tears, 9-3/4" h, 6-3/4" w .................... 110.00

1903, paper, "Hood's Sarsaparilla Calendar 1903" upper-right, titled "Four Friends," girl in red dress with terrier/St. Bernard/donkey, full pad less cover sheet, framed, fold/edge wear/tears, 16-1/2" h, 6" w ................................................................... 99.00

## Hood Tires

Sign

Litho tin, "Neighborhood Tire Experts, Hood Tires," blue/white text, white over blue ground, trademark man in red coat and flag, advertises hardware store, ©1916, unused, cond. 8.5, 11-3/4" h, 23-1/2" w ...................................................... 825.00

Porcelain, rounded top, "Tires" in white under round image of man in red with flag, cobalt ground, cut down from larger sign, cond. 8.5, 24" h, 16" w .......... 440.00

## Hoody's Peanut Butter

Pail, litho tin, "Hoody's Famous Peanut Butter," boy/girl seesawing on peanut mkd "Hoody's Goodies," white text, red ground, cond. 7.5, 1 lb ...................... 154.00

## Hoppe's Gun Cleaning Patches

Display, "7 sizes, 3 Shapes, Use Hoppe's Patches to Clean All Firearms," round logo, with 12 cardboard boxes, 1940s, cond. NM ...................................... 55.00

## Hoppingtot Peanut Butter

Pail, "Hoppingtot Brand Fancy Peanut Butter, Wentworth, Corporon Co., Haverhill, Mass.," white medallion shows peanut-shaped cow, outer yellow oval band

**Calendar, paper, "Hood's Sarsaparilla Calendar 1894," pad begins with April, 8-3/4" h, 5-1/2" w, $35.**

with blue text, blue ground, cond. 7, 1 lb, 3-7/8" h, 3-5/8" dia ............................................................ 715.00

## Horace Peanut Butter

Pail, litho tin, oval label in English and French, red ground, Canadian, cond. 8+, 3-3/8" h, 3-7/8" dia ............... 242.00

## Horlicks

**History:** In 1873, James and William Horlick began producing Horlicks Food, an infant cereal made from bran and malt. The product was reformulated in 1883 and patented as Horlicks Malted Milk, first made by William and Arabella Horlick in Racine, Wis.

A combination of malted barley, wheat flour, and milk, it could be easily reconstituted and was nutritious and easily digested. Both the American and British armed forces included malted milk products in their ration kits during the Spanish American War, World War I, and World War II.

Appropriately enough, the product's slogan was "The Original Food Drink," and much of the advertising showed a girl with a cow and a package of Horlicks. During the 1930s, the company sponsored radio's Lum and Abner programs.

Pocket mirror, round, "The Original Malted Milk, Ask For Horlicks, Avoid Substitutes," girl in white/cow, white border, cond. 8.5 ................................................. 66.00

## Hornet Gasoline

Gas globe

2 glass lenses, plastic body, "Hornet Gasoline," black text/double-box design, orange ground, lens cond. 9, body cond. 7, 13-1/2" dia .......................... 357.50

Newer plastic body with 2 lenses, "Hornet Gasoline," black text/double-box design, orange ground, all cond. 9, 13-1/2" dia .................................... 330.50

## Horse Shoe Tobacco

Sign, flange, porcelain, "We Sell Horse Shoe Tobacco,"

blue on orange ground, chips/touch ups/fading, 8" h, 18" w ................................................................. 220.00

## Horton's Ice Cream

Sign, porcelain, "Horton's Ice Cream, Established 1851, The Premier Ice Cream of America," man in chef's hat cranking ice cream inside dark ring, chips/fading/ stains, 28" h, 20" w .......................................... 302.50

## Hostess

Box, litho tin, "Hostess Holiday Fruit Cake, Hostess Cake" in red/white text on white 5-sided panel on front, "United Bakeries Corporation UBC" on side, fruit/ leaves ground, cond. EXC, 3" h, 6-1/2" w, 3-1/4" d.............................................................. 44.00

## Hostess Coffee

Can, twist lid, "Hostess Brand Coffee" in cobalt, "In a class by itself" on white panel, orange ground, cobalt band top/bottom, cond. 8+, 1 lb .......................... 27.50

## Hotel Tuller

Pocket mirror, celluloid, oval, "Hotel Tuller, In The Heart of Detroit," shows hotel/street, cond. NM, 2-3/4" h, 1-3/4" w ............................................................. 144.00

## Hour-Glass Semolina (See Photo)

## The Household

Match striker, litho tin, hanging, "Your Credit Is Good, The

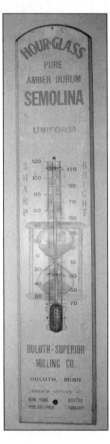

Thermometer, painted wood, "Hour-Glass Pure Amber Durum Semolina, Uniform, Sharp, Bright, Duluth-Superior Milling Co., Duluth, Minn., Branch Offices At New York, Boston, Philadelphia, Chicago," beveled edges, some fading, 36" h, 7-1/4" w, $150.

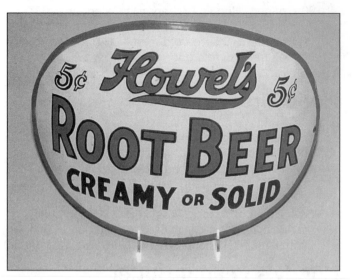

Sign, porcelain, curved oval, "Howel's Root Beer," $385.

Household, Manchester, N.H.," pointing man in suit-coat/tie, red text, white ground, yellow border, circa 1915, cond. 8.25+, 7-1/2" h, 4-3/4" w .............. 143.00

## Howdy

Sign, tin, embossed, "The Way to Howdy, The Friendly Drink," arrow points right, circa 1940s, cond. 9-9.5, 3" h, 9" w......................................................................198.00

## Howel's

Dispenser
  Ceramic, orange globe shape on white base, metal dispenser with porcelain knob, "Drink Howel's Original Orange-Julep 5¢," scratches/wear, 15" h, 9" dia ....................................................... 1,760.00
  Wooden barrel, 2 taps, attached curved porcelain sign, "Howel's 5¢ Root Beer, Solid or Creamy," red/ blue text, white ground, circa 1920s, 16" h, 17" dia ......................................................... 440.00

## Howertown Sanitary Dairy

Tray, metal, "Howertown Sanitary Dairy, Wm. H. Kleppinger Prop., Clarified and Pasteurized Milk and Cream, Grade A Guernsey, Butter and Cottage Cheese," shows plate of cottage cheese, bottle of milk and stick of butter on table, chips/scratches/dents, 13-1/4" sq ...........................71.50

## Hoyts Baby Talcum (See Photo)

## Hrobak's Beverages

Sign, tin, embossed, rolled edges, "Drink Hrobak's Delicious Beverages, Triple Action Lithiated Lemon, Falcon Pale Dry," orange/black text, white ground, cond. VG, 9-1/4" h, 20" w ............................................. 55.00

## Huck & Yogi Bath Soap

Box, cardboard, "Huck & Yogi Bath Soap, Baths Are Fun For Everyone," Huck standing in red bathtub with scrub brush, pink oval on yellow ground, Yogi lower-

Tin, litho tin, "Hoyt's Baby Talcum, Hoyt Brothers Inc., Newark, N.J.," 4-3/4" h, $125.

Container, wooden, "Witker, Halsted & Co.'s Hunkidori Chewing Tobacco, Toledo, Ohio," 12-1/2" h, 12" d, $110.

right, early 1960s, with soap, cond. NM, 3" x 4-1/2" x 1-3/8"................................................................ 38.50

## Hudepohl

Sign, cardboard, "Hudepohl Beer and Ale," outdoor scene of seated man with glass, resting dog, bottle/pretzels on table, red text, framed, crease/scratches, 38" h, 29-1/2" w.................................................. 357.50

## Hudson Motor Car Co.

Lock, metal, embossed, Yale, "Hudson Motor Car Co." in tri-angle logo, with key, cond. 9, 3" h, 2-1/8" w ........... 121.00

## Hugh Campbell's Shag

Tin, vertical box, litho tin, "Hugh Campbell's Shag Smoking Tobacco for Pipe, for Cigarette," profile of man smoking pipe with larger silhouette, yellow ground, cond. 8.5, 4-1/2" h, 6-1/4" w, 4" d...................... 333.00
Tin, vertical pocket, litho tin
   Variation without "Hugh," "Campbell's Shag Smoking Tobacco for Pipe and Cigarette," profile of man smoking pipe with larger silhouette, yellow ground, cond. 8......................................................... 424.00
   "Hugh Campbell's Shag Smoking Tobacco for Pipe and Cigarette," profile of man smoking pipe with larger sil-houette, yellow ground, cond. 8+ ...................... 575.00
   "Hugh Campbell's Shag Smoking Tobacco for Pipe and Cigarette, 10¢," profile of man smoking pipe with larger silhouette, yellow ground, cond. 7.5, 2 oz............................................................. 423.50

## Hully-Gee Pepsin Gum

Wrapper, paper, "Hully-Gee Pepsin Gum, Licorice, Ten 10 Chews One Cent," "Say all de fellos chu's dis gum.

See!" on Yellow Kid at left in red oval, red/green text, white ground, Buckeye Gum Co., Salem OH, cond. 9.25, 3-1/2" ...................................................... 632.50

## Humble Oil Co.

Tie clip, metal, embossed, delivery truck design, cond. EXC, 3/8" h, 1-5/8" w .......................................... 77.00

## Humphrey's

Medicine kit, wooden box with paper advertising label inside, stamped metal plaque on lid, hardcover Hum-phrey's vet manual, 3 bottles, stains to label, 10" h, 9-3/4" w, 6" d.................................................. 253.00

## Hunkidori Chewing Tobacco (See Photo)

## Hunter Cigars

Can, litho tin, large scene of horse and fox hunter in red jacket jumping fence, cond. 8, 5-1/4" h, 3-5/8" w, 1-1/2" dia........................................................ 385.00

## Huntley & Palmer

Tin, litho tin
   Christmas biscuits, scene on lid of Santa and toys, 4" h, 8" dia................................................................27.50
   Shows birds on flowering branch, raised panels, top with handle and left/right opening lids, flange bot-tom, cond. 8 ............................................... 92.50

## Hunt's Economy Ice Cream

Sign, flange, metal, "Enjoy Economy Ice Cream, Best for Less," shows ice cream cone, 1940s-1950s, cond. 9-9.5, 9" h, 15" w.................................................. 165.00

## Hupmobile

Sign, porcelain, 2-sided, "Hupmobile Service," white text/border, black ground, piece missing at grommet hole, cond. 7, 16" h, 30" w......................................... 302.50

## Husky

Bucket, tin, "Husky Brand Grease," Western Oil & Fuel Co.,

Sign, porcelain, die-cut, 2-sided, "Husky Service," yellow/white text on black ground, red sun, yellow rays, cond. 8+, 48" h, 38" w, $7,150. (Photo courtesy of Collectors Auction Services)

Minneapolis, cond. 8, 25 lb, 9-1/2" h, 12" dia ......... 357.50

Can, litho tin, "Husky Mid-Continent Motor Oil," Husky on snow, Northern Lights on yellow ground, Western Oil and Fuel Co., Minneapolis, cond. 8, qt, 5-1/2" h, 4" dia ................................................................. 467.50

Sign, porcelain, "Husky Hi-Power Inc." in white circle around dog, "Husky Hi-Power" in cobalt panels under dog, orange ground, cond. 8, 14-3/4" sq .................... 1,017.50

Pail, litho tin, "H. Earl Clack Inc., Husky," dog in white ring, "Husky" in white on black panel, cond. 8, 10 lb, 9" h, 7-1/2" dia ................................................. 154.00

Jug, stoneware, unmarked Red Wing, ink stamped "Hydro Clean Toilet Cleaner, Manufactured Only By Plunkett Chemical Co., Chicago, Ill., To Be Returned When Empty," Bristol glaze, 5 gallons, $175.

Figure, "Mr. Hygrade's Hot Dog" on badge, left arm reattached at elbow, 1940s-1950s, cond. 8, 3' h, $1,265. (Photo courtesy of Gary Metz, Muddy River Trading Co.)

## Hyde Propellers

Sign, porcelain, "Hyde Propellers Sales and Service, Hywinco," pictures propeller, restored, 26" h, 18" w ................................................................. 990.00

## Hydro Clean (See Photo)

## Hy-Gee Condoms

Tin, litho tin, shows Eastern man in red/blue in palace with plants/pillars, NM, 1/4" h, 2-1/8" w, 1-5/8" d ........... 258.50

## Hygrade's Hot Dogs (See Photo)

## Hy-Quality Coffee

Sign, ceiling-hanger, cardboard, die-cut woman with cup on swing suspended beneath sign, "Try Our Suggestion, Roth's Hy-Quality Coffee, Delicious to the Last Sip" on top sign showing product box, cond. 8.5, 37" h, 16" w ................................................................. 1,419.00

# I

## Icy Pi

Cabinet, metal, reverse-painted glass at top, "Icy Pi, Crisp, Sweet, Fresh, 5¢," shows woman with product, glass door, glass/metal tray inside, cond. VG, 18" h, 10-1/2" w, 7-1/2" d............. 440.00

## Ideal

Box, shell box, 2-pc, paper over cardboard, "Ideal Non-Rusting Smokeless Shotgun Shells," shows shell on side, red text, white ground, blue border, 12 gauge, Hibbard, Spencer, Bartlett & Co., Chicago, fading/soiling/edge wear, 2-5/8" h, 4-1/4" sq..................... 121.00

## Ideal Towel, Coat & Apron Co.

Pocket mirror, celluloid, "Call Cedar 1800 For Service, Ideal Towel, Coat & Apron Co., The Ideal Home of the Ideal, Frank B. Ninness, President, Pittsburgh, Pa.," office building with men beside company trucks, cond. VG, 3-1/2" dia.....................115.50

## Idle Hour Tobacco

Tin, litho tin
Flat pocket, "Idle Hour Cut Plug," winged hourglass, cond. 8.25, 3/4" h, 4-1/2" w, 2-1/2" d ............. 71.50
Horizontal box, "Idle Hour Sliced Cut Plug," portraits of Jefferson/Napoleon, cond. 8, 2-1/2" x 5-1/2" x 3" ............. 242.00

## Impala

Sign, cardboard, "Impala Convertible," man/woman with red convertible, license plate "Impala 4-4-63 Chevrolet," cond. 8, new frame, 20-1/2" h, 34-1/2" w ............... 38.50

## Imperial Airways

Sign, paper
Cutaway shows interior of seaplane, sea/mountains background, text/"Imperial Airways" in white on lower black band, archival backing, foreign, cond. EXC, 28" h, 43" w ......................... 797.50
"28 New Empire Flying Boats, 200 M.Ph.H., Imperial Airways, Europe, Africa, India, The Far East, Australia," 2 lines of seaplanes in flight, 1937, archival backing, cond. EXC, 43" h, 28" w ................. 880.00

## Imperial Copper Polish

Tin, paper label, shows rotund policeman with nightstick, Imperial Products, Philadelphia, unopened, cond. 8-, 5" h, 3-1/3" d .................................................. 231.00

## Imperial Gasoline

Gas globe, 1 lens
High-profile metal body, "Imperial Gasoline" in red at edges, black triangular "Ethyl" logo in center with yellow text/rays, white ground, cond. 8, body cond. 7......................................................... 440.00
Newer plastic body, "Imperial Gasoline" in black on yellow/orange shield, white ground, lens cond. 9, body cond. 7.5, 13-1/2" dia........................... 132.00

## Imperial Ice Cream

Sign, porcelain, 2-sided, shield-shape, "Imperial Ice Cream, Of Course," crown over black text, yellow ground, cond. 9.25, 30" h, 50" w...................... 385.00

## Imperial Polarine

Can, tin
"Imperial for Ford Cars Use Polarine Friction Reducing Motor Oil For Motor Cars And Motor Boat Lubrication, Will Feed At Zero Temperature," polar bear in white shield, red banner at bottom, red/blue text, The Imperial Oil Co., cond. 7, 1/2 gal, 7-1/4" h, 8" w, 3" d ............................................................ 770.00
"Imperial Polarine Friction Reducing Motor Oil, for Motor Car, Motor Boat, and Tractor Lubrication, Heavy," polar bear in white shield, red banner at bottom, red/blue text, Imperial Oil Co., cond. 7+, gal, 12" h, 8" w, 3" d.................................... 550.00

## Inca Maiden Coffee (See Photo)

**Pail, litho tin, "Inca Maiden Coffee, The McAfee Newell Coffee Co., Bloomington, Ill.," rusted through, 4 lb., $350.**

## Independent Public Telephone

Sign, flange, porcelain, blue/white with lettering and telephone graphic in center circle, dents/chips/rust, 18" sq ..................................................................... 82.50

## Indian Cylinder Oil

Can, tin, embossed, "Indian Cylinder Oil, Put Up Specifically For Use In Indian Motorcycles," round "Indian Motorcycles" logo with Indian silhouette, black text, green ground, Hendee Manufacturing Co., Springfield MA, handle bent, cond. 7, gal, 11" h, 6" w, 3-1/2" d ............ 715.00

## Indian Gas

Gas globe, 2 lenses, wide glass body, "Indian Gas" on white border, red circle in center, lens cond. 8.5/8, body cond. 8.5, 13-1/2" dia ............................... 935.00

## Indian Head Brake Fluid

Can, tin, "Indian Head (Castor Oil Base) Hydraulic Brake Fluid," shows "Chief Permatex" in headdress, red text, blue over black ground, Permatex co., Kansas City & Brooklyn, cond. 8+ ................................................ 49.50

## Indian Head Overalls

Sign, porcelain, "Indian Head Union Made Overalls, Pants-Shirts, Made by Morotock Manfg. Co., Danville, Va., For Sale Here," oval portrait upper-left, white text, blue ground, cond. VG, 10" h, 14" w ................ 935.00

## Indian Motorcycles

Book, vinyl cover, Indian Record Book 1929-1930, cond. VG, 4-1/4" h, 2-3/4" w ......................................... 99.00
Catalog, 1913, 24 pgs, cond. 8.5+ ....................... 385.00
Cigar cutter, metal with embossed Indian head, "Indian Motorcycle, Powerplus Motor," Hendel Manufacturing Co., Springfield, Mass., 1" h, 2-1/2" w .............. 440.00
Pin, metal, early 3-D logo of Indian bust/wings, cond. 8.5, 1/2" h, 2" w ...................................................... 302.50

## Industrial Supplies Corp.

Calendar, paper, 1953, metal strips top/bottom, "Sure Will" under woman in 2-pc bikini, artwork by Joe Mozart, complete pad, Industrial Supplies Corp., Appleton WI, 33-1/2" h, 16" w .............................. 33.00

## Ingram

Gas globe, new Capcolite plastic body with 2 glass lenses, "Ingram" on white band on orange ground, lens cond. 9/7, body cond. 9, 13-1/2" dia .......... 352.00

## Insurance Company of the State of Pennsylvania

Sign, porcelain, "The Insurance Co. of the State of Penna. 1794," crest with 2 horses, bent corners/scratches, 16" sq............................................... 187.00

## Interlux

Sign, porcelain, "Have The Smartest Boat In The Fleet With... International" at top, "Marine Paints.. Choice of Master Painters Everywhere," shows can of "Interlux" paint in yellow circle, "20 Striking Colors" in red circle, shows boats being painted at left, white/black text, purple over black ground, International Paint Co., cond. G, 14" h, 24" w ...................................... 440.00

## International

Thermometer, painted wood, "International Stock Food and Veterinary Preparations, Guaranteed," shows harness horse, rounded top, cond. 8+, 24" h, 6" w.............. 935.00

## International Business Machines (IBM)

Tin, litho tin, typewriter ribbon, typewriter on green ground, cond. 8+, 3/4" h, 2-5/8" dia ................... 42.00

## International Harvester

**History:** Cyrus Hall McCormick, whose mechanical reaper revolutionized farming, merged his business with four other firms to become the International Harvester Company in 1902.

By World War I, Harvester had established itself as a leader in the production of power tractors. Its 1922 Farmall introduced what would ultimately become the standard tractor configuration—two closely set front tires to fit between the rows and two large rear tires to provide traction while clearing low crops.

The company's trademark was created in 1946, and the lowercase "i" superimposed on the uppercase "h" resembles the image of a farmer sitting on a tractor. (The dot is the operator's head.)

Clock, neon, tin face, glass cover, metal body, "International Harvester" in black under large red/black "IH" logo, black numbers, white ground, yellow trim, neon lights white, 15-1/2" sq..................................... 715.00
Sign, porcelain
   "International Motor Trucks, C.I. Laudenslager & Sons, Valley View, Pa.," white/black text, green over white ground, cond. 8, 10-1/8" h, 27-1/2" w ............ 49.50
   "International Trucks, Zacherl Motor Truck Sales," white text, cobalt ground, cond. G, 36" h, 61" w ........... 55.00

## International Varnish

Sign, litho tin over wood, self-framed, "The Man Who Knows The Best Finishes, International Varnish Co. Limited, Toronto, Can.," black painter with 7 containers of product, restored to cond. 9, 10-1/2" h, 16-1/2" w ............... 385.00

## Interwoven

Display, cardboard, standup, "He Wants Interwoven Socks" banner on Christmas tree, Santa on ladder, dog on ground over "Interwoven Socks," Interwoven Stocking Co. 1934, cond. VG, 21" h, 14" w ......................... 500.50
Sign
   Cardboard, die-cut, "At the Sign of Interwoven Socks for Christmas" on street sign, gentleman in red coat with horn/luggage, 1935 Interwoven Stocking Co., cond. G, 36" h, 18" w..................................... 60.50

**Box, cardboard, "Interwoven Socks," 1930s, $35.**

Paper with archival backing, "Interwoven Socks for Christmas," vintage Christmastime street scene, artwork by Rudolph Zirm, scratches, 17-1/4" h, 49-1/2" w .................................................... 104.50

# Invader Motor Oil

Can, litho tin, black semi-circle with knight on horseback, black text, yellow ground, Chas. F. Kellom & Co., Philadelphia, full, cond. 8, qt, 5-1/2", 4" dia .............. 49.50

# Iris Coffee

Can, keywind, litho tin, "New Iris coffee, Coffee Pot or Percolator," white "Iris" in black oval flanked by irises, red ground, lighter band, cond. 8.5+, 1 lb ........... 49.50

# Ironbrew

Sign, Glo-glas, reverse glass, metal frame, stands or hangs, "We Serve Ironbrew In Bottles Ice Cold, bottled By Blakeslee Bros., New Haven, Conn., Non-Alcoholic," bottle at right, white text, black ground, circa 1930s, cond. 8.5-8.75, 10" h, 12" w .................. 440.00

# Iron Horse Tobacco

Pack, paper, "Iron Horse Tobacco," train engine, orig cellophane wrapper intact, cond. 9.25+ .................... 66.00

# Iroquois

Clock, lightup
  Double bubble, glass/metal, "Iroquois Beer-Ale" under profile of Indian in headdress, red/white text, ground resembles end of wooden keg, 3/6/9/12 in white, 15" dia ................................................. 880.00
  Molded embossed plastic with metal back and hands, "Iroquois Beer-Ale, Since 1842," embossed Indian in full head dress, paint chips to hands, 17" dia .......................................................... 440.00
Tip tray, litho metal, "Iroquois Brewery, Buffalo," shows Indian in multi-colored headdress, edge wear/scratches, 4-1/4" dia ........................................... 71.50

Tray, litho tin, "Iroquois Indian Head Beer, Iroquois Ale," portrait of Indian in headdress in center, black/red text, white ground, text repeats on inside rim, scratches/chips/bubbling-rust to bottom, 12" dia ................. 60.50

# Irwin-Hodson Co.

Sign, tin, embossed, "The Irwin-Hodson Co. Enameled Steel Road Advertising Signs, Built to Endure, Portland, Oregon," black on yellow ground, cond. 8.5, 9-3/4" h, 19" w ................................................. 121.00

# Islay's

Sign, porcelain
  "Islay's," cond. 9.5, 22" h, 40" w .......................... 93.50
  "Islay's Milk Cream," cond. 8.75, 16" h, 12" w ......... 49.50

# Iten Biscuit Co.

Tin, litho tin, held animal cookies, swing handle, animals/toy soldiers/clown, 2-1/2" h, 4-3/4" w, 3" d ........ 126.50

# Ithaca Gun Co.

Display, cardboard, die-cut
  "Ithaca Featherlight Repeaters," shows Canada goose against round simulated-wood plaque, 14-1/2" h, 16-1/2" w ..................................................... 209.00
  "Ithaca Featherlight Repeaters," shows ring-neck pheasant against round simulated-wood plaque, 14" h, 21" w .................................................. 115.50

# Iver Johnson Bicycles

Pinback button, "Iver Johnson Cycles," central image of woman in straw hat, tire-motif border, cond. NM, 7/8" dia ............................................................. 357.50
Sign, litho cardboard, "Iver Johnson, Going Strong, Get Yours Now, J.N. Harry, Berwick, Pa.," shows boy on bike with feet on handlebars over "Iver Johnson Agency," red/blue text, white ground, soiled/tears, 11" h, 22" w ................................................................. 77.00

# Ivory Soap

**History:** Founded in 1837 by brothers-in-law William Procter and James Gamble, the Procter & Gamble company made candles and soap in Cincinnati, Ohio. Their unusual white soap was given its special name by Procter's son, Harley, after hearing the 45th Psalm read during a church service.

The ability to float was also a unique characteristic of Ivory, one which the company capitalized on once they realized its sales potential. "99 44/100% Pure, It Floats" became synonymous with the product following a barrage of outdoor advertising, as well as newspaper and magazine ads.

Sign
  Paper, "A Busy Day," girl by wooden tub hanging doll clothes on line, Maude Humphrey artwork, gesso frame, cond. EXC, 22-1/2" h, 20" w ............. 258.50
  Porcelain, strip, white text, blue ground, cond. EXC, 3-1/4" h, 21" w ............................................. 330.00

## J&P Coats

Cabinet, wood, spool shape, "J&P Coats" over 4 drawers, plaster cord around sides, 1 slat missing, 22" h, 18" dia ............................................................ 1,045.00

Sign, paper on cardboard/composition card mount, "J.&P. Coat's Spool Cotton Is Strong!," woman watching man catch fish, product on ground, framed, extensive repairs/fading/varnish lifting, 19" h, 24" w .......... 88.00

## Jack Sprat

Tin, black-eyed peas, litho paper label, unopened, 6 lb 12 oz, 7" h .................................................... 50.00

## Jacob Hoffmann

Sign, paper, wood frame, "Compliments of Jacob Hoffman Brewing Co., Oriental Brewery...Canada Malt Ales and Porter," shows stemmed glass/cigar/vase of flowers, creases/tears, cond. VG, 32" h, 25" w ....................110.00

## J.A. Harps

Kerosene can, metal, paper label, "The Never-Fail For Kerosene," gives directions/guarantee, red/yellow/blue design, has pump/spigot, J.A. Harps Mfg. Co., Greenfield, OH, label sealed with contact paper, cond. 7, 5 gal, 15" h, 11-1/2" dia ......................................... 16.50

## James Logan Cigar (See Photo)

## Janney Best Paints

Clock

Electric, metal housing, bottom lights up with advertising for "Hansen Hardware, Authorized Dealer, Janney Best Paints" and can of paint, clock face shows 12 paint cans, minor scratches/soiling/rust, clock runs but doesn't light, 18-1/2" h, 26" w ......... 385.00

Lightup, metal body, reverse-painted glass decal on face, "Whenever you paint, Whatever you paint,

Tobacco hammer, metal, "James Logan 5¢ Cigar," 4-1/2" l, $30.

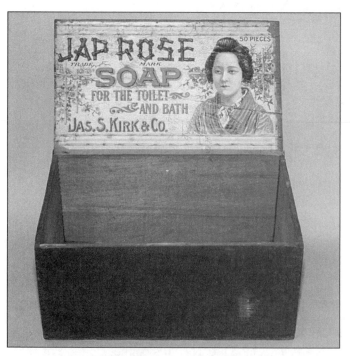

Box, wooden, machine dovetails, olive paint, litho paper label under lid, "Jap Rose Soap for the Toilet and Bath, Jas. S. Kirk & Co., 50 pieces," lid broken and glued in 2 places, litho torn, 6-3/4" h, 13-5/8"w, 9" d, $25.

Always use Janney Best Paints Varnishes Enamels" in white on black panel, "There's Nothing Better" in red seal, black numbers, new wiring, decal loose in places, 15-1/2" sq ............................ 88.00

## Jantzen

Sign, countertop, celluloid, mounted to wooden base, "The suit that changed bathing to swimming," shows woman in red suit stretched out in dive, cond. 8+, 3-5/8" h, 10" w, 1-1/2" d .................................................... 550.00

## Jap-A-Lac

Banner, cloth, "Use Jap-A-Lac New Wood Finish, Wears Like Iron," man applying finish to floor at left, product can at right, red text, white ground, Glidden Varnish Co., Cleveland, stains/soiling/creases, 24" h, 61-1/2" w ......................................................... 302.50

## Jap Rose Soap

Shipping box, paper label on wood, machine dovetails, "Jap Rose Soap For The Toilet And Bath," Oriental woman at right, branded image on ends, paper loss, cond. 8- ............................................................ 44.00

## Japp's Hair Rejuvenator

Display, metal over cardboard, easel-back/hung, "Restores Gray Hair Instantly, Japp's Hair Rejuvenator, Prepared In Seven Different Colors," white panel with space for samples, oval image of women/man in upper corners and at right, additional text, white/red text, brown ground, J.P. Japp Toilet Requisite Co., Cincinnati, minor scratches/yellowing, 9-1/4" h, 13-1/4" w .................................. 49.50

## Jay-Bee Motor Oil

Can, tin, hand-soldered, round medallion with "JB," red ground, The James Bailey Co., Portland ME, scuffs, cond. 8-, approx 1 qt., 6" h, 8-1/2" w, 2-3/4" d ............................................................. 121.00

## J.B. Lewis

Sign, litho tin, "J.B. Lewis Shoe-Maker, Boston, Working for You" on crates beside shoemaker, "Wear Resisters" on his apron, 4 nail holes/minor chips/scratches/dents, 19-1/2" h, 13-1/2" w ............................... 412.50

## JBM Mixture

Tin, vertical pocket, paper label, "Hugunin's JBM Mixture," white text in dark rectangle, cond. 7.5 ................... 266.00

## J.C. Norris & Co.

Label, paper, for barrel, "J.C. Norris & Co's Biscuit, Concord, N.H.," round image of child/dog, detailed graphics include flowers/banners, black ground, red border, cond. NM, 16" dia ............................................. 315.00

## Jell-O

**History:** Feeling the urge to hone his culinary skills, Peter Cooper, the creator of the Tom Thumb locomotive, patented a gelatin dessert in the mid-1840s. His creation apparently languished in obscurity until a cough syrup maker in Leroy, N.Y., discovered the product and adapted it in 1895. Given the name Jell-O, it was first marketed in 1897 and met with a largely unenthusiastic response. Francis Woodward, owner of Genesee Pure Food Company, bought the patent in 1899, and sales improved thereafter.

The four flavors originally advertised in 1902 were lemon, orange, raspberry, and strawberry. Cherry and chocolate were added in 1904, peach in 1911, and lime in 1930. The peach-flavored version was short-lived, being discontinued shortly after its introduction, while chocolate was finally dropped in 1927.

Jell-O pudding and pie filling was first sold in 1932, and, to the delight of homemakers, the instant variation made its entry in 1953.

Sign, paper, roll-down, metal strips top/bottom, "Jell-O, America's most famous dessert," shows plates of lemon and cherry Jell-O, opened box of product, circa 1920, 40-1/4" h, 15" w ...................................... 302.50

## Jennie Lind Cigars

Sign, cardboard, insert "Jennie Lind" cigar label, "Smoke Jennie Lind Hand Made Havana 5 Cents, Manufactured By The National Cigar Co., Bristol, Ind." on sign, cond. 8-, 8-1/4" h, 14-1/2" w ........................... 132.00

## Jenny Aero Gasoline

Gas globe, 2 lenses, milk glass body, "Jenny Aero Gasoline," blue/red text, Jenny Mfg Co., Boston, all cond. 9, 13-1/2" dia ...................................................... 440.00

Tip tray, litho tin, "Four Extra Pounds of Fuel In Every Ten Gallons Of Jenny Aero Gasoline, More Weight Means More Power," black/white text, image of airplane, orange ground, "Hy-Power Valvoline Aero Jenny Oil" in white on black rim showing 4 cars, cond. 8, 4-1/8" dia .......................................................... 110.00

## Jersey Lane Ice Cream

Sign, porcelain, 2-sided, "Agency, Jersey Lane Ice Cream, Lorain Creamery," red/green text, white medallion on green ground, edge chips/water stains, 20" h, 28" w ....................................................... 357.50

## Jim Beam

Decanter
China/plastic/rubber, 1929 Model T police car, unopened, white film on roof, 15-1/2" l ........... 66.00
China/plastic/rubber, 1935 Duesenburg Roadster, unopened, cond. EXC, 18-1/2" l ................... 121.00
China/plastic/rubber, 1956 Thunderbird, top lifts, unopened, cond. G, 14" l ............................... 66.00
Plastic, Western & Atlantic railroad baggage and express car, bottle under roof, unopened, 16-1/2" l .......................................................... 55.00

## Jim Hogg Cigars

Sign, paper, "New Governor Size Jim Hogg Cigars, Back to 5¢, Corona Size 3 For 20¢," portrait of "James Stephen Hogg" at left, black/red text, yellow ground, red border, cond. 9+, 9" h, 20" w ........................ 33.00

**Sign, hanging, brass, "John Deere, He Gave to the World the Steel Plow" and "John Deere Centennial, 1837-1937," joined in the middle, each 8" d, $950.**

# John Deere

**History:** A blacksmith from Vermont, John Deere relocated to Grand Detour, Ill., in 1825. There he designed a new style of steel plow blade which was quite popular with the farmers. Deere moved his company to Moline, Ill., in 1848, and the trademark of a leaping deer was registered in 1876, although it was used as early as 1873.

Sign, porcelain, "John Deere Farm Implements," centered shield shows yellow deer leaping log on red ground, yellow/red text, black ground, cond. VG, 24" h, 72" w .............................................. 1,155.00

Tape measure, pocket, celluloid, "John Deere, He Gave To The World The Steel Plow," white on black panel under oval portrait, red border, running deer logo on back, cond. EXC, 1-3/8" dia ............................. 176.00

## John Drew Cigars

Sign, litho tin, "John Drew 5¢ Cigar" in black at border, triangle logo, shows portrait of man with mustache, dents/scratches/paint chips/nail holes, cond. VG, 18-1/2" dia ....................................... 440.00

## John Middleton's Club Mixture

Tin, vertical pocket, litho tin, brown text in yellow medallion on brown ground, cond. 8+ ...................... 1,348.00

## John Ruskin Cigars

Can, litho tin, "John Ruskin Cigar 5¢," portrait of man with leaf/berries wreath, light-blue ground, cond. 8, 5-1/2" h, 3-1/2" sq........................................... 121.00

Crock, stoneware, white glaze, ink-stamp mark, "Home Made Preserves, Manufactured By H.A. Johnson & Co., Boston, Mass.," orig lid/bail handle, 6-1/4" h, 5-3/4" dia, $110.

Sign, tin, embossed
   "John Ruskin" in red, "Best and Biggest" in white on black oval, cigar lower-right, yellow ground, minor edge chips, 9-3/8" h, 29-1/2" w.................110.00
   "John Ruskin, Best and Biggest" on yellow ground, cigar, edge wear/scratches, 9-1/2" h, 29-3/4" w ................................................ 176.00

# H.A. Johnson & Co. (See Photo)
# Johnson's Powdered Wax

Can, tin, "Johnson's Powdered Wax for dancing floors," couple dancing, yellow/blue design, white ground, rusted top/bottom, S.C. Johnson & Son, Racine WI, round, 14 oz, 5-5/8" h ....................................... 22.00

# Johnston

Sign, glass, bullet-shape, 1930s-1940s, "We Serve Johnstons Hot Chocolate, Rich In Chocolate Flavor," orig box, cond. 9.75, 13-1/2" h, $1,045; "We Serve Johnstons Hot Fudge, Genuine Milk Chocolate," orig box, cond. 9.75, 13-1/2" h, $1,210. (Photo courtesy of Gary Metz, Muddy River Trading Co.)

Box, paper, "Jolly Time Brand Pop Corn, American Pop Corn Co., Sioux City, Iowa," copyright 1918, 1930, 10-1/4" h, 7" w, $35.

## Jolly Time Pop Corn

Pail, litho tin, "Jolly Time Hulless Pop Corn" in white/yellow, "Guaranteed to Pop" in white cloud, boy/girl on red ground, Good Housekeeping seal, ©1927, no lid, cond. 7.5, 1 lb, 4-1/2" h, 3-1/4" dia ...................... 46.00

## Juicy Fruit

See Wrigley's

## Jumbo Bread

Sign, litho tin, die-cut, elephant, "Brown's Jumbo Bread" in white on red banner on elephant, 1940s-1950s, cond. 9.5, 13" h, 15" w ...................................... 550.00

## Jumbo Peanut Butter

Pail, litho tin, round image of elephant head, ground in vertical stripes, Frank Tea & Spice Co., Cincinnati, no lid, cond. 8+, 3-3/8" h, 3-3/4" dia .................... 1,650.00

## Jumbo Pop Corn

Can, tin, "Burch Best Jumbo Pop Corn," blue/red text in shield, elephant on hind legs, popcorn ground, red band at top, blue at bottom, Burch Mfg. Co., Kansas City, soiling/watermarks/rusted top-bottom, 10 lb, 9-1/2" h, 6-1/2" dia ............................................. 60.50

## June Kola

Sign
Painted metal, embossed, "June Kola, Now in Quarts! 6 Full Glasses" shows bottle of product, green ground, minor scratches, 35-1/4" h, 23" w ..................... 170.50
Tin, "June Kola, Now in Quarts! 6 Full Glasses" shows bottle of product, green ground, minor scratches/ chips, 11-1/2" h, 23-1/2" w .............................. 71.50

## Junior Shell

Can, tin, "Junior Shell, Specially Prepared for Cleaning and Automatic Lighters," black panel on yellow shell logo, red ground, "Shell" in vertical text on side, foreign, Shell Mex BP Ltd, cond. 7, 5" h, 3" w, 1-3/4" d ........................ 77.00

Lunch box, litho tin, "Just Suits Cut Plug," 4-1/2" h, 8" w, $70.

## Junket Mix Ice Cream

Pot scraper, litho tin
Shows box of Junket Chocolate Powder on one side, Junket Ice Cream Mix on other, wear, cond. 7.5-8, 2-5/8" h, 3-1/4" w ........................................... 495.00
Shows girl with doll and bowl on one side, product box on reverse, unused, cond. 8.5+, 2-5/8" h, 3-1/4" w ......................................................... 522.50

## Just Suits

Canister, litho tin, small top, "Just Suits Cut Plug" on red ground, gold central medallion with "BL, Buchanan & Lyall Manufacturers, New York, N.Y.," cond. 8.5, 6-1/2" h, 4-7/8" dia ............................................................253.00
Door push or match striker, porcelain, "Just Suits Cut Plug, The Amer. Tob. Co. Succ'r," round "BL" logo of "Buchanan & Lyall of New York, U.S.A.," yellow text, red ground, cond. 8, 6" h, 3" w.......................... 242.00
Sign, porcelain, die-cut, pipe shape, "Suits Millions, Will Just Suit You, Just Suits Cut Plug," red/white, restoration to chips, 6-3/4" h, 16-1/2" w .................... 1,320.00

## Kadee Smoking Tobacco

Tin, vertical pocket, litho tin, "Kadee Smoking Tobacco, Truly Yours, Christian Peper Tobacco Co., St. Louis, Mo.," white text, dark ground, red stripe, cond. 8-8.5, 4-1/2" h, 3" w.................................................. 2,420.00

## Kamels

Tin, litho tin, "Kamels 1/4 Doz. Latex Prophylactics, Distributed by Frank Aardnoff, New York, N.Y.," man with camel, Mideast village in background, with contents, cond. 8, 1-5/8" x 2-1/8" ...................................... 302.50

## Kamo

Jar, glass, paper label, "Kamo Brand Curry Pwd.," shows duck on water, cond. 8+, 3" h, 2" dia................... 55.00

## Kanotex

Gas globe
  1 lens, wide glass body, arched red name over star at top, black triangular Ethyl Gasoline Corporation logo at bottom, white ground, lens cond. 8, body cond. 7.5, 15" dia.......................................... 555.50
  2 lenses, 1 Kanotex lens, red name over star design, white ground, cracked, blank lens other side, broken metal rim, Kanotex lens cond. 6, body cond. 8.5, 14-1/2" dia ........................................... 275.00

Menu board, tin, "Tops in Taste, Kayo, It's Real Chocolate Flavor, Specials Today," edge paint chips, rust, 26-3/4" h, 13-1/4" w, $70.

2 lenses, glass Gill ripple body, red "Kanotex" over black star, "Bondified" in white on red panel, white ground with 2 red lightning bolts, orange body, lens cond. 8.5, body cond. 9, 13-1/2" dia.......... 1,842.50
2 lenses, glass red ripple body, red name over star design, white ground, all cond. 9, 13-1/2" dia ............................................... 1,705.00

## Kar-A-Van Coffee

Can, pry lid, litho tin, "Vacuum Packed Drip Grind Kar-A-Van Famous Coffee," small mosque, white/red/black text, yellow over black ground, cond. 8-, 1 lb ......................27.50

## Kayo

Sign, tin
  Embossed, "Tops in taste, Kayo, It's real Chocolate Flavor," boy running with bottle below voice balloon, yellow over black ground, cond. VG, 27-3/8" h, 13-7/8" w ....................................................... 253.00
  "K-O your thirst with Kayo," cartoon boxer in hat at left, bottle at right, yellow/white text, orange ground, chips/bubbling paint/rust, 9" h, 25" w........... 137.50

## KC Baking Powder (See Photo)

## Kellogg's

**History:** In 1876, Dr. John Kellogg was named the manager of the Battle Creek Sanitarium in Battle Creek, Mich. The Seventh-Day Adventists had established the institution as a health-cure emporium, and Kellogg was

Can, litho tin, pry lid, "KC Baking Powder, Double Acting," 5 lb, $15.

zealous in his attempts to create healthful foods for breakfast. He and his brother, Will Keith Kellogg, made their first wheat flakes in 1894.

John Kellogg started his own company, the Sanitas Food Company, and by 1899 he was in a partnership with his brother. Together they created corn flakes in 1898, but it wasn't until 1906 that The Battle Creek Toasted Corn Flake Company came into existence. The name was shortened to Toasted Corn Flake Company in 1907 and changed to Kellogg Toasted Corn Flake Company in 1909, finally becoming simply Kellogg Company.

Both Krumbles and Pep reached grocers' shelves in 1912, 40% Bran Flakes were introduced in 1915, and Rice Krispies were first heard from in 1928.

Display, cardboard, standup, "Always look for this signature, W.K. Kellogg" red text on black lower border, woman with armful of corn stalks, shows early "Kellogg's Toasted Corn Flakes" box, mounted to additional backing, 1920s, cond. 7.5, 41" h, 22-1/2" w ................................................. 1,052.00

Puzzle, cardboard, "keep going with Kellogg's" below boy on scooter beside racing dog, dated 1933, framed, minor fading/scuff, 8" h, 6" w ............................... 71.50

Watch fob, metal, die-cut, box shape, "Kellogg's Toasted Corn Flakes," red/black text, early box design, vinyl band worn, fob EXC cond., 1-1/2" h, 1-1/4" w .................. 66.00

# Kelly

Sign, painted metal, "Kelly Builds Quality, Quality Builds Kelly," white on green ground, cond. 7, 8" h, 24" w .............................................................. 495.00

# Kemp's Root Beer

Sign, litho tin, "Drink Kemp's, The Old Fashioned Root Beer And Ginger Ale, Pure and Unexcelled," bottle at left over "In Bottle Only," black text, yellow ground, circa 1920s, cond. 9.5, 14" h, 20" w .................. 253.00

# Ken-L

Door push, litho tin, "Ken-L Meal, Ken-L Ration, Ken-L Biskit," yellow dog face at top, white/yellow text, blue ground, cond. 9.5 ............................................. 330.00

# Kendall

Can, litho tin
"Kendall Chassis Lube," white text on red circle, white ground, vehicles on black band at bottom, Kendall Refining Co., Bradford PA, cond. 8, 1 lb, 4-1/2" h, 3-1/4" dia ...................................................... 27.50

"RU Glyde, Kendall Clear Rubber Lubricant," white text in red circle, lists uses, white ground, Kendall Refining Co., Bradford PA, cond. 7, gal, 10-1/2" h, 6-1/2" w, 4-1/4" d ............................................. 11.00

Clock, spinner lightup, tin face, glass cover
"Kendall, The 2000 Mile Oil," white text on red ground, top has hand with 2 fingers, black numbers on white border, lights white, rewired, cond. 9, 20" dia ...................................................... 1,100.00

Sign, tin, embossed, "Ask for Kendall Motor Oils," white text on red ground, cond. 7+, 9-3/4" h, 12" w, $412.50. (Photo courtesy of Collectors Auction Services)

Sign, tin, self-framing, "Do Your Engine a Favor... Kendall Motor Oil," round red logo at right with hand showing 2 fingers, white text, cobalt ground, cond. 8, 36" h, 72" w .............................................................. 55.00

# Kennebec Cigars

Counter display, litho tin, "Kennebec" in silver over oval portrait of Indian flanked by tomahawks/bow and arrows, woodgrain ground, image repeated inside lid, cond. 7.5, 2-1/4" h, 8-1/2" w, 5" d ...................... 28.50

# Kenney Bros. Cigarettes

Playing cards, transparent, deck of 52 cards, "Hold to the Light, Read Your Fortune, Kenney Bros. High Class Cigarettes," 2-7/8" h, 1-1/2" w ........................... 605.00

# C.D. Kenney Tea

Sign, litho tin, embossed, "Compliments of C.D. Kenney Co.," portrait of George Washington under eagle flying with flag, fancy gold border, cond. 8.5, 7" h, 5" w ................................................................. 71.50

Tin, litho tin, "C.D. Kenney Co. Importers of Fine Teas, Baltimore," small medallion of boat on front, also woman's portrait/flowers, cond. 8, 7-1/2" h, 4" sq ................. 330.00

# Kent

Display, pair, lightup, figural cigarette packs, 1 near-mint, 1 with slight discoloration on side from warmth of bulb, 12" h ................................................................ 132.00

# Kentucky Club Mixture (See Photo)

# Kentucky Fried Chicken

Display, litho metal, die-cut, 2-sided, shape of Col. Sanders holding cane in the air, pipe in center to mount on a base, edges bent/scratches/dents, 55-1/2" h, 24" w, 38" w with cane ............................................... 412.50

Tin, litho tin, "Aromatic Kentucky Club Mixture," plaid ground, 14 oz, 6-1/2" h, 4-3/4" w, 3-3/4" d, $10.

Globe, milk glass, tall, bucket shape, shows Col. Sanders between red panels, 1960s, cond. 9.5 .............110.00
Sign, molded plastic, portrait of Col. Sanders, white ground, fading/scratches/2 pieces missing at corners/ cracks, 36" h, 32-1/2" w ...................... 55.00

# Kentucky Power Co.

Sign, porcelain, "Kentucky Power Company" in white on blue ground, "Helping You Live Better...Electrically" in blue at bottom, red Reddy Kilowatt with hardhat at left, white ground, cond. G, 36" h, 48" w.................. 253.00

# Kern's Bread

Sign, tin, embossed, rounded corners, "Take Home Kern's Bread," black/red text, yellow ground, mkd "Robertson 8-59," cond. EXC, 8" h, 42" w .......... 71.50
Thermometer, litho tin, rounded corners, "Kern's Bread, Take It Home," tube at left, red/black text, yellow/white swirled ground, cond. 8-, 13-1/2" h, 5-3/4" w ...................... 121.00

# Kernstown Rye

Pocket mirror, round, "Ralph Savage, Winchester, Va., All Drink Kernstown Rye, No Swelled Head," sow nursing piglets, cond. 8.25............................................. 302.50

# Kerr View's Ice Cream

Sign, porcelain, die-cut, 2-sided
Ice cream cone, "Serving Kerr View's Sweet Cream Ice Cream, Made Fresh Daily," 1930s-1940s, cond. 9.25-9.5+, 54" h, 24" w ............................. 3,520.00
Milk bottle, "From Our Own Herd, Use Kerr-View's Raw & Pasteurized Milk And All Other Dairy Products," red text, white ground, 1920s-1930s, cond. 8.5-8.75, 48" h, 19" w ............................... 1,760.00

# Key Klips Cigars

Canister, display, litho tin, embossed, hinged lid with "Key Klips 5¢" on glass, oval medallion with key over 3 tobacco leaves, cond. 7.5+, 6-1/2" h, 5-1/2" dia......................................................110.00

# Keynoil Motor Oil

Can, metal, "Keynoil Motor Oil," eagle at left, red/black text, white ground, black lower border, White Eagle Oil and Refining Co., Augusta KS, Fort Worth TX, Casper WY, cond. 7, 6-1/2" h, 8" w .............................. 522.50

# Keystone Brand Pure Lard

Tin, litho tin, "Keystone Brand Pure Lard, The Lima Packing Co., Lima, Ohio," red with Keystone logo, wire side handles, 50 lb ...................................................... 45.00

# Key System

Sign, porcelain, die-cut, "Key System" in cobalt on white ring around green/blue image of tree, winged key logo in yellow/black, cond. VG.................................. 825.00

# Kibbe's Peanut Butter

Pail, litho tin, "Kibbe's Peanut Butter, Smooth As Velvet," red/black text in oval, yellow ground, Kibbe Bros. Co., Springfield MA, cond. 8.25, 1 lb........................ 88.00

# Kim-Bo

Tin, vertical pocket, cardboard, tin top/bottom, "Kim-Bo Cut Plug Tobacco, 5¢ The Can," woman in dress, green ground, cond. 8.5.................................... 220.00

# King Albert Cigars

Sign, litho tin, embossed, "King Albert High Grade Cigars, Moebs-Walsh Co. Makers, Detroit, U.S.A.," round medallion of king flanked by soldiers/ship, cond. 7.5-8, 9-3/4" h, 13-3/4" w ................................. 550.00

# Kingan's

Printer's proof, litho paper, "Kingan's Hams and Bacons," 4 fairies lifting platter of ham, circa 1920s, like new, 28" h, 42" w...................................................... 132.00

# King Cole

Can, keywind, cardboard, tin top/bottom, "Regular Grind, For Coffeepot, For Percolator, King Cole Coffee," small circular image of king with cup at bottom, white text, brown ground, white band at bottom, cond. 7.5+, 1/2 lb ................................................................. 50.50
Door bar, porcelain, "The Cafe, King Cole, Tea Coffee," red/black text, yellow ground, chips, 3" h, 31-1/2" w .................................................................115.50
Sign, porcelain, die-cut, "King Cole Tea and coffee," yellow/white text in cobalt panel under oval image of King with cup, cond. VG, 15" h, 9" w...................... 1,430.00

# King Edward

Tin, vertical pocket, "King Edward Crimp Cut Smoking

**Sign, porcelain, "King Kard Overalls," 1920s-1930s, 10" h, 32" w, $2,310. (Photo courtesy of Gary Metz, Muddy River Trading Co.)**

Tobacco," king's portrait in crest-type design with lion and unicorn, red ground, cond. 8.5 ................ 1,252.00

# King George

Tin, vertical pocket, litho tin, "King George Cross Cut, Frishmuth Bro. & Co. Inc., Philadelphia, U.S.A.," red oval medallion with 2 rampant lions on white ground, full, cond. 8+ ...................... 303.00

# King Joy Coffee

Can, keywind, litho tin, taller version, king with cup, white text, red ground, black band at bottom, Morgar Coffee Co., Inc., Brooklyn NY, cond. 8.5, 1 lb .............. 101.00

# King Kard Overalls (See Photo)

# King Midas Flour

Pot scraper, litho tin, "King Midas Flour, The Highest Priced Flour in America, And Worth All It Costs," back view of child in bonnet, blue ground, cond. 8, 2-7/8" h, 3-5/8" w .............................................. 385.00

# Kingsbury Beer

Sign, tin, embossed, "Kingsbury Pale Beer, Manitowoc Products Co., Manitowoc, Wis.," bottle in black oval at left, white text, red ground, scratches/dents/creases, 19-1/2" h, 27-1/2" w .......................................... 143.00

# Kingsbury Mixture

Tin, vertical pocket
  Cardboard, "Kingsbury Mixture" in black, "Free Sample," red seal on yellow ground, full, cond. 8.5............ 45.00
  Litho tin, "Kingsbury Mixture," seal with lions flanking shield marked "CPTCo" on yellow ground, Christian Peper Tob. Co., St. Louis, Mo., cond. 8.5, 4-1/2" h ......................................................... 755.00

# Kingsford's Starch

Box, wood, paper labels on ends, "Kingsford's Starch" with color image of 2 people, "Kingsford's Silver Glass Starch, Corn Products Refining Co.," on sides, with lid, cond. 8.25, 11" x 7" ............................................. 44.00

# King's Puremalt

Tip tray, litho tin, oval
  "King's Puremalt, Strengthening, Good For Insomnia, Healthful," shows bottle, cond. 8.75 ............... 77.00

"King's," shows nurse with "King's Puremalt" tray holding bottle, "Panama Pacific International Exposition" in ribbon by 2 medals, cond. 8.5 ..................... 77.00

# Kirkland Garage

Sign, tin, die-cut, embossed, arm with pointing finger, "Kirkland Garage, 24 Hour Service," black on white ground, "No. 67" on hand, cond. 7, 6-1/2" h, 28" w ............313.50

# Kirkman's Borax Soap

Sign, paper, "Why Not Use the Best? Kirkman's Borax Soap," sepia-tone photo of 5 women, orig mat board, framed, 13" h, 17" w.......................................... 440.00

# Kis-Me Chewing Gum

Trade card, moon face with walking legs, cond. 8-, 4-3/4" h, 3-1/4" w .................................................................154.00

# Kiss Me Kisses (See Photo)

# Kist

Door pull, litho tin, missing the handle, "Enjoy Kist Beverages, Here's Refreshment," cond. 8.75 .............. 66.00
Sign, cardboard, "For 5¢ Only!! plus deposit Six Bottle Carton Kist Root Beer with the purchase of every cart on of Kist Orange, limited time only...," large bottle at left, 6-pack lower-right, orange/white/black text, diagonal white-black-white ground, cardboard bubbling/separating, 18" h, 27-1/2" w...................................... 27.50
Sign, paper, blonde in black dress posing with "Kist" bottle, signed "Elvgren," cond. VG, 17-1/2" h, 13-1/2" w......................................................... 231.00

# Kiwi

Sign, porcelain, foreign, "Kiwi, The Quality Boot Polish, Renowned in Black & Tans," pictures bird and product, 4 colors, chips/scratches, 18" h, 12" w ............. 467.50

**Container, paper, "Glick's Kiss Me Kisses 5¢, The Max Glick Co., Cleveland, O.," yellow and red, dated 1906, $110.**

**Display, wall-hung, 3-D plastic, "Knickerbocker, New York's Famous Beer," $20.**

## Klorofil Dandruff Cure

Bottle, enameled label, shows woman whose long hair forms "K" in name, cond. EXC, 7-5/8" h, 2-1/2" dia.......... 253.00

## Knickerbocker Beer (See Photo)
## Geo. H. Knollenberg & Co.

**Egg carrier, wooden, red paint with black stenciling, 3 sides mkd "The Geo. H. Knollenberg & Co., Dealer in Dry Goods Carpets Furniture, Richmond, Ind.," 4th side mkd "Reliable Egg Carrier, Mfd by The Reliable Incubator & Brooder Co., Quincy, Ill., Pat. Nov. 16, 1897," no lid, broken handle, 10-3/4" h, 13-1/2" w, 12-1/4" d, $85.**

## Knox

Sign, litho on canvas paper, product box by nanny/girl topping desert with strawberries, artwork by Harry Roseland, gesso frame, cropped, cond. 9-, 16" h, 20" w ................................................................ 473.00

## Kodak Film

**History:** While planning a trip to the Caribbean in the 1870s, George Eastman discovered that he would not be able to carry all of the photographic equipment necessary to preserve his vacation memories. After reading all that he could on photography, he invented dry plates in 1880 and rolled film in 1884.

In 1888, Eastman began merchandising his newly invented "disposable" camera in Rochester, N.Y. (Both camera and film were sent to Eastman's factory to be processed.) He chose Kodak as the brand name because he liked its distinctive sound.

Clock, lightup
    Metal, glass face/lens, "Use Kodak Film" in red under box of film, red text, black 3/6/9/12, dots for other hours, white ground, cond. EXC, 15-1/4" sq ..................................................... 132.00
    Plastic, "Kodak, America's Storyteller" in black over film box, black 3/6/9/12, dots for other hours, yellow border, new wiring, cond. VG, 19" dia ............ 49.50
Display
    Cardboard, die-cut, "Stop Here for... Kodak Verichrome Film," woman in red/white Hawaiian-pattern bikini top/wrap with 2 boxes film/camera, black/red text on yellow panel, scratches/wear/bent/stains, 5' 4" h, 21" w ....................................... 115.50

**Sign, metal, 2-sided, triangular form with "Developing, Printing, Enlarging" at top, illust of "Kodak Verichrome Film" box, edge wear/rust/scratches, 17" h, 17" w, $330. (Photo courtesy of Collectors Auction Services)**

Metal, "Don't forget...Kodak Film" at top, blue front shows Ed Sullivan with voice balloon, "Hold it! Got film?," also "See the Ed Sullivan Show, Buy 2 and have enough!," 2 each slots for 620/127 film, fading/chips/scratches/rust inside back, 15" h, 12-1/2" w, 7-1/2" d ........................................................ 55.00

Sign
Porcelain, European, "Produits, Kodak, En Vente Ici," vertical red text, yellow ground, cond. 6.5-7, 52" h, 12" w.............................................................. 253.00

Porcelain, raised finish, 2-sided, "Developing & Printing" over Verichrome film box, blue ground, yellow/black border, cond. NM, 14" h, 20" w........... 742.50

Window display, cardboard foldout, 3-D, "Kodak as you go," man/woman in red canoe, made to hold No. 1 Kodak in woman's hands, orig shipping carton, 30" h, 38" w, 17" d .................................................. 1,650.00

# Kodak Tobacco

Tin, horizontal box, litho tin, "Kodak Cut Plug Smoking Tobacco," scene of building/sea, cond. 8, 1-1/2" h, 5" w, 3-1/2" d...................................................... 236.50

# Kohl's Superfine Coffee

Can, slip lid, "Kohl's Superfine Steel Cut Coffee," woman over triangle, red/dark text, white ground, same image on back, cond. 8-, 1 lb...................................... 605.00

# Koldpruf (See Photo)

# Ko-Nut

"On Ice, Long Green, Ko-Nut, Red Rock, In Bottles, 5¢, Red Rock Co.," red/green text, white ground, green

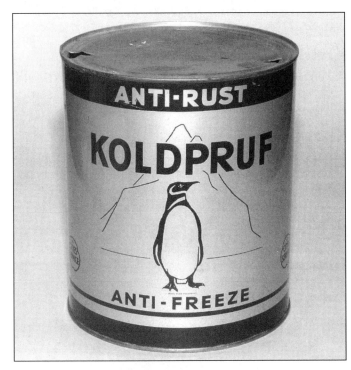

Can, litho tin, "Anti-Rust Koldpruf Anti-Freeze, Cities Service, Cities Service Oil Co.," 1 gal, $20.

Display, litho tin, "They're So Refreshing! Kool Cigarettes," 8" h, 7-1/8" w, 4-1/8" d, $25.

border, dents/scratches/chips/yellowing, 27-1/2" h, 19-1/2" w.......................................................... 104.50

# Kool Cigarettes

Salt/pepper shakers, plastic, figural, Millie/Willie penguins, soiling/wear, 3-1/4" h, pr.......................... 55.00

Sign, tin
Embossed, penguin with pack of Kools, "Smoke Kools" in voice balloon above penguin with product, cond. 8, 16-3/4" h, 8-1/2" w ........................... 83.00

Flange, rounded outer corners, "We Sell Cigarettes, Smoke Kool," Willie lighting cigarette beside "Kool" pack, red/white text, white over green ground, chips/rust to edges and flange, 13-1/2" h, 10-1/2" w .................................................... 154.00

Tin, flat 50, litho tin, "Cork Tipped Kool Mild Menthol Cigarettes," green rectangular Kool logo, small penguin in lower-right corner, white ground, cond. 9 ............................................................. 160.00

Sign, tin, "We Sell Cigarettes, Only Kool gives you real Menthol Magic," NOS, light rust, $45.

## Koolmotor

Gas globe, 2 glass lenses, newer high-profile metal body, "Koolmotor" in black on white central panel, "High Test Anti Knock Gasoline" in black on green border, all cond. 9, 15-1/2" dia .......................................... 374.00

Sign, tin, 2-sided, 1 side with "Refill with Koolmotor, The Perfect Pennsylvania Oil," Cities Service logo lower-left, green over black ground, reverse with "Refill with Cities Service Oils," white/green design, cond. 8, 12" h, 20-3/4" w ...................................................... 605.00

## Kotex

Display, countertop, base with 2 uprights/4 support rods, ends show nurse in white holding Kotex box at her hip, 13-1/2" h, 14" w, 8-1/2" d ................................. 335.50

## Ko-We-Ba Rolled Oats (See Photo on Cover)

**History:** The name Ko-We-Ba is a combination of the first two letters of the last names of the owners of Kothe-Wells & Bauer Company. Based in Indianapolis, Ind., the company sold grocery products. The company's logo consisted of a red diamond containing a colorful orange and blue butterfly and the phrase "Ko-We-Ba Means the Best."

## Kramer's

Door push, litho tin, "Drink Kramer's, All Flavors," green bottle, red/white text on black band at top, white ground, green border, cond. 8.75, 12-1/2" h ......................... 49.50

## Krane's Baby Talc

Tin, litho tin, "Krane's Baby Talc, A talc which meets the highest medical standards for the care of infants," blonde child, red border forms ribbon, cond. 8, 4-3/4" h,

Sign, tin, "Kramer's Full Flavored Beverages, Kramer's Bottling Works, Mt. Carmel, Pa.," 9" h, 20" w, $30.

Sign, flange, porcelain, "Kurfees Paints, Good Paint since 1897, Louisville, Ky.," near-mint, 14" h, 20-1/4" w, $30.

2-1/4" w, 1-3/4" d ................................................ 333.50

## Kreso

Display, litho tin, "Kreso Dip No. 1, Protects All Livestock From Parasites And Disease," marquee with die-cut cow/sheep/pigs/chickens, roughness to marquee/worn text, cond. 8-, 18" h, 12" w, 6-1/4" d .................. 852.50

Sign, tin, embossed, "Kreso Disinfectant, Kills Germs Everywhere," red/black text flanked by "Kreso Disinfectant, A Guard Against Disease" on armor, merchant info at top, yellow ground, black border, cond. G, 12" h, 23" w ........................................................ 38.50

## Krisp Peanut Brittle

Can, litho tin, slip top, "Delicious Appealing Krisp Peanut Brittle, the old fashioned kind, Lummis & Co., Philadelphia, Established 1852, Suffolk, Va.," yellow ground, cond. 8+, 10 lb, 8-1/2" h, 12" dia ........................ 48.50

## Krout's Baking Powder

Tin, paper label, "Krout's Baking Powder, Made from Grape Cream Tartar," flying eagle with banner and American flag, cond. 8.5+, 6" h, 3-1/8" dia ............................ 577.50

## Kuragon

Door push, litho tin, "Kuragon Has Given Satisfactory Results In Treatment of Gonorrhoea & Gleet Luzerine Products Co., Hunlock Creek, Pennsylvania," 1920s, cond. 8, 5-7/8" h, 3-7/8" w ................................. 110.00

## Kurfees Paints (See Photo)

# L

Sign, flange, tin, "Buy L&M Filters Here!," opposite side advertises Chesterfield, NOS, 15" h, 12" w, $70.

## L&M Cigarettes

Thermometer, tin, embossed, rounded corners, "Check Today's Change (red checkmark)...To Modern L&M, Sold Here," yellow/red text, embossed red/white pack lower-left below tube, blue ground, cond. EXC, 13-1/4" h, 5-3/4" w .............................................................. 121.00

## Labatt Beer (See Photo)

## La Corona Cigars

Tin, litho tin, slip lid, classic scene with woman, cond. 8, 6" h, 2-1/4" dia .................................................. 266.00

## Ladyfair Talcum

Tin, litho tin, bulbous shape, flat-sided, shows well-dressed woman each side, cond. 8.5, 4-1/2" h, 2-3/4" w ........................................................... 187.00

## Lady Hellen Coffee

Can, pry lid, paper label on cardboard, tin top/bottom, "Lady Hellen Brand Coffee," shows woman, white text, green ground, gold band top/bottom, cond. 9+, 1 lb .......... 88.00

## LaKreem Coffee

Can, sample, litho tin, "LaKreem Pure Coffee, Montgomery

Sign, pressed paper, blue felt with gold letters, "Imported Canadian Labatt Beer," $2.

Mills, Jersey City, N.J., Free Sample," coffee cup, black on gold ground, cond. 8, 2-1/2" h, 2" dia ................ 154.00

## T.G. Lancey & Co. (See Photo)

## Land O' Lakes

Thermometer, litho tin, rounded top/bottom, "When The Flour Really Counts, Make The Butter Land O' Lakes

Tip tray, tin, "T.G. Lancey & Co., Everything in Hardware," $170.

Sweet Cream Butter," trademark Indian squaw at bottom under billowing clouds, black/red/blue text, small scratches/chips, 27" h, 8" w ............................ 258.50

## Lark Coffee

Can, paper label on cardboard, "Lark Brand Steel Cut Coffee," lark on branch, red/black text, yellow ground, Newmark Brothers, Los Angeles, cond. 8.25, 1 lb ....... 412.50

## Latakia Tobacco

Tin, vertical pocket, paper label, "Finest Improved Latakia, Cut From The Best Syrian Leaf, Falk Tobacco Co.," cond. 7.5, 4-1/4" h, 3-1/4" w ....................... 34.00

## Latch-String Rolled Oats

Box, cardboard, shows child with basket on both sides, H.J. Hughes Co., Omaha NE, Red Oak IA, faint staining, cond. 8.5, 9-1/2" h, 5-1/2" dia.................. 1,155.00

## Lava Soap

Sign, cardboard, string-hung, diamond, "Leaves the skin absolutely clean and soft, Better than a Turkish bath, Instantly removes all dirt grease and grime," bar of "Lava Chemical Resolvent Soap" with open box, blue/yellow/blue ground, fading/small hole, 8" h, 8" w ............... 27.50

## Lavine

Sign, paper roll-down, metal strips at top/bottom, "Mail us 12 Lavine front labels or 30 cents in cash or postage stamps and get this picture without the printing on it, Hartford Chemical Company, Hartford, Conn.," Victorian woman at table with box of product, circa 1890, cond. 8+, 28-1/2" h, 13" w ................................ 687.50

## Lawrence

Sign, cardboard in metal frame, "Lawrence Tiger Brand

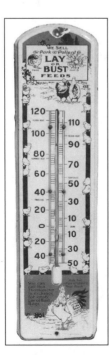

**Thermometer, porcelain, "We Sell Park & Pollard Co. Lay or Bust Feeds," red panels on yellow ground, cond. 7-7.5, 27" h, 7" w, $770. (Photo courtesy of Gary Metz, Muddy River Trading Co.)**

Paints & Varnishes, Paints-Enamels-Varnishes," tiger's head in center oval, scratches/warping, 42" h, 30" w .................................................................. 176.00

## Lay or Bust Feeds

Chalkboard, tin, rolled edges, "Fresh Eggs, Lay or Bust Feeds," black text by round red logo, yellow ground, chalkboard mkd "Large, Medium, Small" with blank and "Per Doz." for each, larger blank space at bottom, cond. VG, 26" h, 20" w...................................... 385.00

## L.B. Silver Co.

Pinback button, celluloid over metal, "There Can Be But One Best, L.B. Silver Co. 400 Grand Arcade, Cleveland, Ohio," shows pig lettered "O.I.C." and ribbon design, stain/fading, 2" dia................................. 27.50

## LCV Talcum

Container, Kewpie figural, composite, orig labels, cond. 8-, 7" h .............................................................. 132.00

## Leaf Chewing Gum

Sign, tin, "Leaf" in white on red panel, "The Flavor Lingers Longer" in red on lower white ribbon, shows pack of "Leaf Spearmint Chewing Gum," yellow ground, cond. G, 8-7/8" h, 25-1/8" w................................ 88.00

## Lee

Sign
Neon, "Lee" jeans label motif, "jeans" in neon script, lights orange, cond. EXC, 24" h, 36" w......... 412.50
Tin, embossed, "Lee Union-Alls Overalls, Whizits, Union Made," carpenter lower left, logo lower right, black/red text, yellow ground, cond. 8.25+, 13" h, 27" w........................................................... 412.50

## Lee Coffee

Can, keywind, litho tin, coffee plants on mountainside, white ground with wide cobalt band, H.D. Lee Co., Kansas City MO, Salina KS, cond. 8+, 1 lb ........ 44.00

## Leinenkugel's

Double bubble clock, glass and metal, "Leinenkugel's" in red oval followed by "Made with Chippewa Water from the Big Eddy Springs," shows Indian head in yellow circle, scratches, 15" dia ................................... 533.50

## Lemon-Crush

Dispenser, ceramic, figural lemon on floral base, embossed "Ward's Lemon Crush" on both sides, orig ball pump mkd "Lemon" on porcelain knob, some wear, cond. EXC, 13" h, 9" w ........................ 1,760.00

## Leonard

Gas globe, newer plastic body with 2 lenses, "Leonard" in black on white stripe, red ground, lens cond. 9/8.5, body cond. 9, 13-1/2" dia ................................. 170.50

## Leonard, Crosset & Riley

Bill hook, celluloid and metal, oval, "Leonard, Crosset & Riley, Ocala, Fla, Thomasville, Va., Macon, Ga., Charleston, Md.," hand-colored image of giant watermelon on flatbed railroad car, 6-3/4" h, 2" w .......................... 150.50

## LePage's

Rack, metal, litho tin marquee, "The Russia Cement Co., LePage's Gold Medal Mucilage," red/yellow/black, cond. 7.5+, 12-1/2" h, 8" w, 8-1/4" d ................. 330.00

## Levi Strauss & Co.

**History:** Levi Strauss made his fortune during the California Gold Rush, but instead of panning for glittery rocks, he used brown tent canvas to develop a line of pants that were both tough and durable. Designed with copper-riveted seams to withstand the rigors of western life, the pants soon became popular with easterners who had visited dude ranches and wanted the same clothing for leisure wear. After switching to a blue French fabric called "serge de Nimes," the term denim was coined. The French word for cotton trousers was "gene," hence the term jeans. In 1936, the company began sewing a red tag into the seam of the back right pocket. Zippers weren't used until 1955.

Display, blue jeans, 501 Button Fly, cond. NM, 76" waist, 45" l ................................................................. 264.00
Sign, neon, 1-pc, round, "Levi Strauss & Co., SF, Cal" in round borders, neon lights red, cond. EXC, 26" dia .............................................................. 385.00

## Lewis Lye (See Photo)

## Life

Tin, vertical pocket, litho tin, "Life Pipe Tobacco, Ken-

Pocket tape measure, celluloid, shows can of "Lewis' Lye," Pennsylvania Salt Mfg. Co., Philadelphia, 1-1/2" dia, $20.

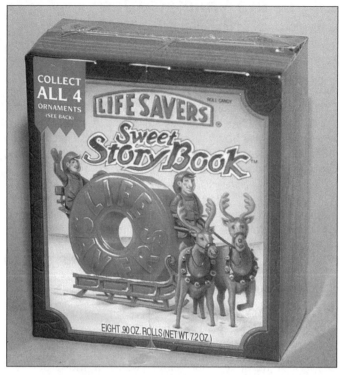

Box, cardboard, "Lifesavers Sweet Story Book," contains 8 rolls of candy, $5.

tucky White Burley," yellow tobacco leaf on red ground, cond. 8.5 ......................................... 1,070.00

## Lifebuoy Soap

Sign, cardboard
2-sided, string-hung, "Lifebuoy Soap, A Life-Saver," bearded seaman in rain hat, reverse with "Cleans and Disinfects" and woman on lifesaver, crease/fading, 5" dia .................................................... 687.50
Trolley, "Teachers and Mothers Know that Lifebuoy Health Soap Protects Family," teacher with 3 students, yellow/white text, red ground, framed, cond. EXC, 12" h, 22-1/4" w .................................... 132.00

## Life Savers

Display, countertop, metal, glass dividers, decal, "Life Savers" logo with black text on arched ground on divider, cond. G, 5-1/4" h, 6-1/4" w, 7-1/2" d ........................ 33.00
Sign, porcelain, "Real Life Savers, Always Good Taste," open roll of product with S-shaped red arrow, red/white text, black ground, 1920s-1930s, cond. 8, 60" h, 27" w ............................................................. 1,100.00

## Lift Beverage

Sign, tin, embossed, "Drink Lift Beverage, It's Good For You," shows green bottle with airplane on label, mountains in background, red text, white ground, chips/rusted back/corner bent, 12" h, 7" w ................ 126.50

## Liggett's Cherriade

Bottle, backbar syrup bottle, clear with white/red label, heavy chrome over metal cap, circa 1920s, cond. 8-8.5 .............................................................. 165.00

## Lily of the Valley Coffee

Can, litho tin, red medallion with white flowers/green leaves, white ground, gold trim, cond. 8, 1 lb, 6-3/8" h, 4-1/8" dia.......................................................... 220.00

## Lily White Flour

Pocket mirror, celluloid, oval, "Lily White Flour, The Flour the Best Cooks Use, Valley City Milling Co., Grand Rapids, Mich.," shows boy/girl with bag of flour, plate of biscuits, foxing at edge, 1-5/8" h, 2-3/8" w........................... 385.00

Sign, tin, embossed, self-framed, curved, "Ask for Lily White Flour, The Flour The Best Cooks Use, Made Only By Valley City Milling Co., Patent Roller Process, Lily White, Grand Rapids, Mich.," factory on flour bag, wheat, blue band with red border/text, red/dark text on white ground, oak-grain frame, cond. 8-, 35-1/2" h, 19" w............................................................. 5,280.00

## Limberlost Fish Supply Co. (See Photo)

## Lime-Crush

Dispenser, ceramic, figural lime, "Ward's Lime-Crush, Color Added," ball pump mechanism frozen, scattered paint wear, cond. 8.5+, 13" h, 9" w.................. 3,190.00

## Lime-Julep

Sign, cardboard, string-hung, "Lime-Julep" in black over couple using 2 straws to drink from 1 bottle, "It's Julep time" in white at lower-right, cond. 8.25, 11" h, 8" w ...................................................................... 170.50

## Lincoln Club Coffee

Pail, slip lid, paper label on tin, "Lincoln Club Fresh Roasted Coffee," portrait of Lincoln over white circle, white text, red ground, Andresen, Ryan Coffee Co., Duluth, MN, paper loss/darkening, cond. 7.5+, 5" ........................ 82.50

## Lincoln Coffee

Can, pry lid, paper label on tin, "Lincoln Brand Steel Cut Coffee," oval portrait of Lincoln, red/white/blue ground, cond. 8+, 1 lb, 5-1/2" h, 4-1/4" dia .................... 330.00

## Lincoln Flour

Sign, paper, metal strips top/bottom, "Lincoln Flour, Its sound integrity & absolute purity make Lincoln Flour distinctly a Quality product, Ask Your Grocer," shows Lincoln, white/black text, orange ground, cond. 9, 22-1/4" h, 16" w................................................. 231.00

## Lindley's Motor Coffee

Can, keywind, litho tin, "Lindley's Motor Brand Coffee," motor with round red border, bold text, dark ground, red panels, cond. 7.5, 1 lb ................................ 121.00

## Lion Coffee

**History:** Lion Coffee was the principal brand of the Woolson Spice Company of Toledo, Ohio. In fact, when the company was founded in 1882, Lion Coffee represented its entire business. Woolson would eventually add spices and other brands of coffee to its line.

Can, keywind, litho tin, "Lion Coffee," lion's head in circle, white text, red ground, Woolson Spice Co., cond. 8+, 1 lb ....................................................................... 33.00

## Lion Head Motor Oil

Can, tin, "Monarch Of Oil, Lion Head Motor Oil," white text, "Lion Head" in black on white diagonal with lion's head, red ground, Gilmore Oil Co., Los Angeles, cond. 7+, qt, 5-1/2" h, 4" dia ...................................... 176.00

## Lions Stock Remedy

Can, litho tin, "Lions Stock Remedy, Manufactured by

Tin, cardboard, tin top/bottom, "Goldfish Food, Limberlost Fish Supply Co.," 3 oz, $12.50.

Thermometer, porcelain, "Listerine the safe Antiseptic for Coughs-Colds, Sore Throats, Bad Breath," bottle on blue ground, cond. 8+, 30" h, 12-1/2" w, $880. (Photo courtesy of Gary Metz, Muddy River Trading Co.)

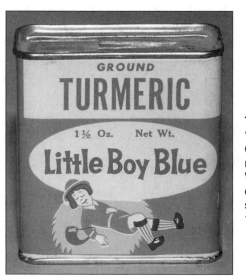

Tin, paper label, "Little Boy Blue Ground Turmeric, Lansing Wholesale Groceries Co., Lansing, Mich.," 1-1/2 oz, $40.

Live Stock Remedy Company," round image of fierce lion face, yellow/red ground, cond. 8-, 9-1/2" h, 6-1/4" dia ........................................................ 154.00

## Listerine

Toothbrush holder, litho tin, die-cut, Skeezix comic character, orig box, cond. NM, 6" h, 3" w ................. 440.00

## Little Boy Blue (See Photo)

## Little Giant Farm Equipment

## Little Giant Stock & Poultry Food

Pail, litho tin, wood handle, oval design shows farm animals at border, pig in center mkd "5 Feeds For One Cent," yellow ground, Little Giant Food Co., Newark, NJ, cond. 8, 25 lb, 12-1/2" h, 10-1/4" dia .......... 121.00

## Little Mozart Cigars

Tin, litho tin, oval, shows draped frame picturing Mozart, cond. 8+, 4-1/2" h, 6-5/8" w, 4-1/4" d ................ 209.00

## Little Van Dam

Tin, litho tin, 25-count, "Little Van Dam" over bearded

Sign, painted steel, "Little Giant Elevators, Little Giant Farm Equipment, Portable Elevator Mfg. Company, Bloomington, Ill.," 10-1/2" h, 17" w, $55.

man in hat, red text, brown ground, Tunis Cigar Co., Grand Rapids MI, cond. 8.25, 5" h, 3" sq ............ 88.00

## Lloyd's Condoms

Tin, litho tin, "1/4 Dozen, Lloyd's, Made From Liquid Latex, Distributed by World Merchandise Exchange, New York, N.Y.," black text, gold ground, cond. 7.5+, 1/4" h, 2-1/8" w, 1-3/4" d ................................... 577.50

## Lloyd's Premium Coffee

Can, keywind, litho tin, neck-up scene of flying woman with wings, blue/red text, yellow ground, cond. 8, 1 lb ......................................................................... 77.00

## Log Cabin Coffee

Can, keywind, litho tin, "Log Cabin Brand Coffee," log cabin scene between yellow panels with red text, dark ground, restored, Shaffer Stores, Altuna PA, cond. 8.25, 1 lb ........................................................... 990.00

## Log Cabin Syrup

**History:** P.J. Towle of St. Paul, Minn., first sold Log Cabin syrup, a mixture of corn syrup and flavorings, in 1887. Originally, the product was packaged in rectangular tins with paper labels, but the namesake cabin-shaped tin was patented in 1897. The paper labels used from 1909 to 1914 showed a stretched animal skin covering the back door of the cabin; the labels used from 1914 to around 1918 depicted a child standing at the door. Beginning in 1919 the tins were decorated with a lithographed picture.

As part of the home-front war effort, the tins were not used during World War II, but by 1948, brown log cabins with red-and-white labels were available. Beginning in 1949, the syrup was sold in bottles, although a set of Frontier Village tins was offered in the 1950s, and a variety of special tins have been used periodically.

Tin, litho tin, "Towle's Log Cabin Ready-Spread Confection Butter, The Towle Maple Products Co.," overall log-cabin motif, litho label with vignette of log cabin on red ground, cond. 8+, 3-3/8" h, 4-1/4" d ............ 907.50

Display, cardboard, litho paper, "Towle's Log Cabin Syrup," back bows, 22" h, 28-1/2" w, 8" d, $400.

Tin, litho tin, cabin-shaped

"Blacksmith" scene, cond. 8, 5" h, 4-3/4" w,
2-7/8" d ...................................................... 330.00

"Frontier Inn," western scene, cond. NM, 5 lb., 6" h,
6-1/2" w, 4" d ............................................... 385.00

"Frontier Jail" scene, cond. 7.5-8, 12 oz, 4" h, 3-3/4" w,
2-1/2" d ...................................................... 165.00

"Towle's Log Cabin Syrup," girl in doorway, red/brown
ground, cond. 8, 12 oz ................................. 104.50

Toy, pull toy, litho tin, cabin shape, "Towle's Log Cabin Syrup,
Log Cabin Express," girl in doorway, red metal wheels,
cond. 8, 5-3/4" h, 4-3/4" w, 3-3/4" d ......................... 522.50

# Log Cabin Tobacco

Tin, horizontal box, litho tin, "Log Cabin Flaked Gold Leaf
Cavendish, Lambert & Butler, England," log cabin scene
with hunters/fishermen, cond. 8, 1-1/4" h, 4-3/4" w,
3-1/8" d ........................................................... 33.00

# London Dry

Door push, litho tin, "Ask for London Dry Beverages, The
Topper of all Drinks," round image of man in top hat,
white text on red diagonal band, black diagonal bands
with flavors, unused, cond. 9, 10" h, 4" w ......... 170.50

# London Sherbet

Tin, vertical pocket, litho tin

Block text, "London Sherbet Mixture, A Rare Combination For Pipe And Cigarettes, Falk Tobacco Co.,"
cocktail glass in red rectangle, green ground, cond.
7.5 ............................................................... 256.00

Block/script text, "London Sherbet Mixture, A Rare
Combination For Pipe And Cigarettes" in block text,
"Falk Tobacco Co." in script, cocktail glass in red
rectangle, green ground, cond. 8+ ................ 294.00

# Long Green

"On Ice, Long Green, Ko-Nut, Red Rock, In Bottles, 5¢,
Red Rock Co.," red/green text, white ground, green
border, dents/scratches/chips/yellowing, 27-1/2" h,
19-1/2" w ..................................................... 104.50

# Longhorn Typewriter Ribbon

Tin, litho tin, round, blue circle with long-horn steer, yellow over blue ground, American Carbon Paper Mfg.
Co., Chatham VA, Ennis TX, cond. 8 .................. 38.50

# Long Tom Smoking Tobacco

Tin, horizontal box, litho tin, black man standing at left,
white ribbon on yellow ground, cond. 7.5, 2" h, 5" w,
3-5/8" d ........................................................... 73.00

# Look Out

Can, litho tin, oval small top, "J.G. Dill's Look Out Extra
Mild, Rough & Ready Tobacco, Prepared Especially
For The Pipe, J.G. Dill Inc., Richmond, Va.," life pre-
server/rescue scene, gold rope trim, gold/red text, 2-
tone green ground, tin cond. 7.5, lid cond. 6, 6" x 4" x
5" ................................................................. 586.00

Tin, litho tin, scene titled "Hiawatha's Wedding Journey," mkd
Loose-Wiles Biscuit Co., with handle, 2 lb, 8 oz, 9-1/2" w, $75.

Tin, litho tin

Flat pocket, "J.G. Dill's Look Out Cut Plug Extra Mild,"
rescue image of ship at sea, lighthouse, lifesaver,
anchor and oars, green and red text on green
ground, hinged lid, wear, cond. 8-, 7/8" h, 4-1/2" w,
2-3/4" d ...................................................... 242.00

Vertical pocket, "J.G. Dill's Look Out Rough & Ready
Tobacco," shows life preserver/anchor/rope,
cond. 8 ....................................................... 1,214.00

# Loose-Wiles Biscuit Co. (See Photo)

# Lord Kenyon Tobacco

Tin, vertical pocket, litho tin, "Lord Kenyon Blend Super-
Mild Tobacco," man with pipe, street lamp, black/white
ground, cond. 8-8.5 ....................................... 432.00

Tin, litho tin, "Allen & Ginter's Genuine Louisiana Perique,
Grown in St. James Parish, Louisiana, Mfg by A&G Branch
of the Am. Tobacco Co., Richmond," 1-3/4" h, 3-7/8" w, 2-5/
8" d, $176.

## Lost Spring Whiskey

Sign, litho tin, rolled edge, embossed, "Lost Spring Whiskey, B.S. Greil & Co., Cincinnati, O.," nude woman at falling stream of water, primarily red lettering, black ground, circa 1905-1915, cond. 6-6.5, 22" h, 17" w .................................................. 385.00

## Louisiana Perique (See Photo)

Tin, litho tin

Horizontal box, "Genuine Louisiana Perique," round image of graduate smoking pipe, black/yellow design, Marburg Bros., Baltimore, American Tobacco Co. Successor, cond. 8+, 1-3/4" h, 3-1/2" w, 2" d ............. 82.50

Vertical pocket, paper label, "Finest Genuine Louisiana Perique, Cut From Carrot, Falk Tobacco Co.," white text, dark ground, cond. 7.5, 4-1/4" h, 3-1/4" w............................................................ 53.00

## Lovell & Covel

Pail, candy, litho tin

Little Red Riding Hood, Boston.......................... 165.00

Independence Hall, Valley Forge, cond. 8+, 2-7/8" h, 2-7/8" dia ......................................... 522.50

## Loving Cup

Tin, vertical pocket, litho tin, "Loving Cup Flake Cut, Highest Grade Leaf Tobacco," 2-handled cup in yellow medallion, red ground, cond. 8 ....................... 3,509.00

## Lowe Brothers Paint

Sign, neon, metal/glass, "Lowe Brothers Paint," lights orange, rust marks, 11" h, 30" w, 7" d ............... 308.00

## Lowney's Cocoa

Chalkboard, wood frame, 2-sided, "Lowney's Cocoa" repeated 3 times on frame, lower portion shows box, cond. 8, 33" h, 14-1/2" w................................... 495.00

## Lucky Cup Coffee

Can, keywind, litho tin, taller version, "Steel Cut, Lucky Cup, Richest flavor Coffee," shows cup in horseshoe,

**Pail, litho tin, Lovell & Covel, nursery rhyme, "This Little Pig" and "The Queen of Hearts," 2-7/8" h, each $200.**

white text, ground in bands of red/white/blue, cond. 9, 1 lb ......................................................115.50

## Lucky Curve Tobacco

Tin, vertical box, litho tin, "Lucky Curve Plug Cut Tobacco," white image of pitcher/baseballs, yellow text/bats on red ground, cond. 7, 4-1/4" h, 6-3/4" w, 4-1/2" d ........................................................... 586.00

## Lucky Star

Tin, vertical pocket, litho tin, "Von Eichen's Toasted Mild Lucky Star Cut Plug Smoking Tobacco" in gold, small flag in gold oval, dark diagonal bar on red ground, cond. 8 .......................................................... 1,452.00

## Lucky Strike

**History:** The name Lucky Strike was used for cut plug tobacco as early as 1871. American Tobacco Company began marketing cigarettes by that name in 1917. Because the moniker was a reference to the Gold Rush days, the trademark consisted of a muscular arm with a hammer in the hand.

"Reach for a Lucky Instead of a Sweet" was the advertising slogan used in 1928, with "LSMFT" (Lucky Strike Means Fine Tobacco) relied on in later years. The slogan "Lucky Strike Green has gone to war" was used after the company eliminated green from its packaging during World War II so that the metal base used to make the coloring could be converted to bronze for the war effort.

Canister, litho tin, dome top, shorter version, "Genuine Lucky Strike Roll Cut Smoking Tobacco," red circle with "Lucky Strike" shown 3 times on body, also on lid, remainder has green text on green ground, flange bottom, cond. 7.5-8, 5-1/2" h, 5" dia ...................... 302.50

Display, cardboard, die-cut

Easel-back, "This Year Give The Best" in wreath by Santa with Christmas-motif Lucky Strike carton, red/white "Lucky Strike" pack lower-left, cond. VG, 13-1/4" h, 8-1/4" w ......................................... 154.00

3-D pop-out figures, "Lucky Strike Cigarette" round logo by "Lucky girls, Lucky boy" panel, "The mildest cigarette you ever smoked because - 'It's toasted'"

**Tin, pocket, litho tin, "Lucky Strike Roll Cut, R.A. Patterson Tob. Co.," 4-1/4" h, $91.50.**

at bottom, terrace scene of 3 seated women in blue/red/black dresses reaching for open pack held by man in suit, orig box, stains/scratches/bent corners, 34" h, 24" w................................................ 478.50

Sign, heavy cardboard, easel-back, "Luckies - a light smoke of rich, ripe-bodied tobacco, It's Toasted" in red/black text, woman with cigarette in port hole, man outside, red/green pack of Lucky Strike Cigarettes lower-left, edge wear/fading, 36" h, 27-1/2" w ................................ 170.50

Tin, horizontal box, "Lucky Strike, R.A. Patterson Tobacco Co., Rich'd, Va." in red circle on green ground, cond. 8, 8 oz, 2-1/8" h, 4-3/8" w, 3-1/4" d................................................................ 44.00

Tin, vertical pocket, litho tin, red/green variation

Sample, "Genuine Lucky Strike Roll Cut For Pipe Or Cigarette," red circle on green ground, "Lucky Strike" in red circle, along with "R.A. Patterson Tobacco Co., Rich'd Va.," cond. 7.5-8, 3-1/4" h, 2-1/2" w...........................................................118.00

"Genuine Lucky Strike, It's Toasted, Roll Cut Tobacco For Pipe Or Cigarette," red circle on green ground, cond. 7.5, 4-1/2" h ................................ 101.00

"Genuine Lucky Strike, Prepared For The Pipe," red circle on green ground, cond. 7.5, 4" h, 3" w................. 79.00

"Lucky Strike, R.A. Patterson Tobacco Co., Rich'd Va., Genuine Roll Cut, For Pipe or Cigarette," red circle on green ground, cond. 7-7.5, 4" h ................. 43.00

Tin, vertical pocket, litho tin, red/white variation

Recessed lid, "Genuine Lucky Strike Roll Cut Tobacco," red circle on white ground, cond. 9 ................... 932.00

"Genuine Lucky Strike Roll Cut Tobacco," red circle on white ground, cond. 9 ................................ 1,025.00

# Luden's Chewing Gum

**History:** After realizing that cough drops were made from many of the same ingredients he used in making candy, William H. Luden set out to produce his own cough drops. Together with a local pharmacist in Reading, Pa., the two formulated a menthol cough drop that they colored amber in order to distinguish it from the red lozenges made by other companies.

Can, "Luzianne Coffee and Chicory, Wm. B. Reily & Company, Inc., New Orleans," 1 lb, 5-1/2" h, $95.

Felt, painted-on design of 3 packs of gum/3 red roses, brown ground, cond. 8+, 11" dia ...................... 330.00

# Lusterlite Kerosene

Sign, cardboard, "Lusterlite Kerosene, Highest Quality For Lighting Heating And Cooking, For Sale Here," central orange logo for "Gulf Refining Company Lusterlite Kerosene," white ground, cond. 8.5, 14" h, 22" w ................................................ 49.50

# Luxury Tobacco

Pack, paper, foil-lined, "Luxury Cut Plug Smoking Tobacco," basket of fruit, white ground, cond. 9 ................................................ 27.50

Sign, cardboard, die-cut, easel-back, "10¢ Luxury Tobacco," fruit-dec pack over image of seated man in suit with pipe, cond. 9.25, 11" h, 9" w .............. 357.50

# Luzianne Coffee

Salt/pepper shakers, plastic, figural, nannies in green/red skirts, cond. 8.5, 5" h ........................................ 187.00

# Lyceum Little Cigars

Tin, flat pocket, litho tin, square corner, "Mild Quality" in wreath, "Lyceum" on gold diagonal band, red ground, 1/2" h, 3" w, 1-3/4" d ........................................ 27.50

# Lydia Pinkham

**History:** A staunch advocate of women's rights and a fierce opponent of slavery, Lydia Estes Pinkham made her first batch of medicine on her own kitchen stove. After losing their money in an economic downturn in 1873, the family began peddling Lydia Pinkham's Vegetable Compound, said to treat those ailments of womanhood that male members of the medical profession chose to ignore.

In 1879, Pinkham's face was added to the bottle and the company's advertising, resulting in a twofold increase in sales.

Pinkham died in 1883, and one of her sons took over the business. By 1898, Lydia Pinkham's Compound was the most heavily advertised product in America.

Calendar, paper, "Bringing You Health" over image of biplane, "Lydia E. Pinkham's Vegetable Compound" under oval image of Pinkham flanked by banners, "Facts" cover sheet to full pad, framed, edge stains, 22-3/4" h, 15" w.................................................. 121.00

Tatting shuttle, celluloid, portrait of Pinkham, cond. NM, 2-7/8" l, 3/4" w...................................................... 50.50

# Lykens Dairy

Sign, tin, "Lykens Dairy, Pasteurized Milk and Cream, For Mothers Who Care," white text on red ground, reversed panel at bottom, cond. VG, 14" h, 30" w.................77.00

# Lyons' Tea

Sign, flange, porcelain, "Lyons' Tea Sold Here" in white, dark ground with yellow trim, probably British, cond. 9.5, 12" h, 18" w................................................ 550.00

# M

## Maas & Steffen

Calendar, paper, 1941, "Maas & Steffen, Inc., Direct Receiver of Furs, St. Louis, U.S.A.," otter/waterfalls, titled "Otter Playground," yellow/white text on lower cobalt ground, calendar pad missing, framed, cond. G, 23-1/2" h, 17" w ................................................. 99.00

## Mac Cigars

Sign, tin, "Smoke Mac Cigars, Manufactured by Celestino Fernandez Company, Milwaukee, -Wis.," blue "M" diamond logo, blue text/border, white ground, cond. G, 10" h, 14" w ......................................................... 88.00

## MacGregor's Ice Cream

Sign, porcelain, 2-sided, "We Serve MacGregor's Ice Cream, The Cream Of The Town," white "MacGregor's" in diagonal blue band, vertical red/white checkered band, blue band with "The Cream..." at bottom, rounded top, 1940s-1950s, cond. 7.5, 22" h, 17" w .......... 187.00

## Madison Cigar Manufacturing Co.

Sign, heavy paper, "Madison Cigar Manufacturing Co....Philadelphia" over risqué image of Indian maiden with feather in her hair, 1906, cond. 9.25+, 30" h, 15" w ........................................................... 1,320.00

## Magnet Coffee

**Can, keywind, tin, "Millar's Magnet Brand Coffee, E.B. Millar & Co., Chicago, Denver," 1 lb, $44.**

## Magnolene Petroleum

Can, tin
"Magnolene Brand," white magnolia center in green leaves, white ground, yellow trim, Magnolia Petroleum Co., Beaumont, TX, cond. 7, gal, 11" h, 6" w, 3-1/2" d ........................................................ 357.50
"Magnolene Brand Motor Oil," white magnolia/green leaves, black text, white ground, Magnolia Petroleum Co., Beaumont, TX, cond. 7, 1/2-gal, 6-3/4" h, 8" w, 3" d .................................................... 572.00
Watch fob, metal, round, embossed on both sides, "Use Magnolene Brand Oils And Grease," flower in center, wear/oxidizing, 1-3/4" h, 1-1/2" dia ................... 401.50

## Magnolia Metal Co.

Pocket mirror, celluloid, round, "Magnolia Metal Company" under flower/metal bars, black border, scratches/spotting, 3-1/2" dia ............................. 66.00

## Magnus California Pure Orangeade

Dispenser, syrup, box-shape, image of orange/children on teeter-totter, circa 1920s, cond. 7, 13" h, 17" w, 12" d ........................................................... 1,705.00

## Mail Pouch

**History:** Samuel and Aaron Bloch began producing cigars and plugs of tobacco in 1879 in Wheeling, W.Va. Experimenting with a new type of chewing tobacco, they mixed left-over cuttings of tobacco with water, molasses, licorice, sugar, and salt. Sold in paper bags printed with "Chew Mail Pouch," the product was a success. As demand for the chew increased, the availability of cuttings decreased, and by 1932 whole leaves were being used, even though the package continued to be labeled scrap.

The company advertised in a number of ways, but perhaps the most famous icons of rural America were the Mail Pouch painted barn signs.

Sign, cardboard, standup, "Mail Pouch, The Real Man's Choice" over scene of Indian man/boy in boat, "The Boat of the Prairies" in lower band, cond. G, 21" h, 14" w ............................................................. 154.00
Sign, porcelain
"Chew Smoke Mail Pouch," white/yellow text, dark ground, cond. 9.25, 3-3/4" h, 18" w ............. 231.00
"Chew and Smoke Mail Pouch, The Quality Tobacco," "Mail Pouch" in yellow on diagonal blue ground,

remainder blue on white ground, cond. 8+, 12" h, 42" w...................................................... 577.50

Sign, tin, embossed, "Chew Smoke Mail Pouch," white/yellow text, cobalt ground, paint chips/bends/bubbling, 3-3/8" h, 14" w................................. 99.00

Thermometer
Metal, rounded top/bottom, "Chew Mail Pouch Tobacco" in cobalt/white/red bull's-eye design at top, "Treat Yourself to the Best" at bottom under packs of Mail Pouch and Mail Pouch Sweet, blue/yellow text, cobalt ground, white border, cond. G, 39" h, 8" w................................................................ 126.50

Porcelain, rounded top/bottom, "Treat Yourself To The Best, Chew Mail Pouch Tobacco," white/yellow text, cobalt ground, white border, minor scratches/chips, 38-1/2" h, 8" w ............................................. 231.00

Porcelain, orig wood frame, "Chew Mail Pouch Tobacco, Treat Yourself To The Best," white/yellow text, blue ground, no tube, 1920s-1930s, cond. 8.25, 74" h, 19" w.......................................... 632.50

## Main Brace Tobacco

Lunch box, litho tin, "The Main Brace Cut Plug, J.G. Dill, Richmond, Va.," red on yellow basketweave ground, cond. 8+ .............................................................. 93.50

## Majors China Cement

Push plate, porcelain, "Pull, Majors China Cement Is Good for Repairing Glassware, Furniture, Etc.," oval medallions and scales holding 250 lb, red ground with blue band, cond. NM, 7-7/8" h, 3-3/8" w ........ 1,100.00

## The Makins

Tin, vertical pocket, cardboard, tin top/bottom
Center slide top, round image of man smoking, red ground, Globe Tobacco Co., cond. 7.5 ......... 440.00

## Malco

Sign, pump sign, porcelain, "Malco" in black under bird logo, yellow trim, white ground, NOS, cond. 9, 12" dia ......................................................... 1,430.00

## Maltby's Cocoanut

Tin, litho tin, small top, "Maltby's Patent Prepared Cocoanut," round red image of coconuts/palm trees, gold/black/red ground, cond. 8, 5-7/8" h, 3-3/4" sq.................. 111.00

## Malt-Nutrine

**History:** Anheuser-Busch introduced Malt-Nutrine in 1895, one year before the company debuted Michelob.

Sign, tin over cardboard, beveled edge, "A Hurry Call" in white, "Malt-Nutrine" on lower border, white horse pulling doctor's buggy, stork flying with 2 bottles, chips/scratches, 7-3/4" h, 12-5/16" w ......................... 82.50

## Malto Rice

Doll pattern, cloth, "My Name Is Miss Malto-Rice," instructions at side, ©1899, The American Rice Food

and Mfg. Co., Matawan, NJ, cond. EXC, 34-1/2" h, 17-1/2" w........................................................ 143.00

## Mamma's Choice Rolled Oats

Box, paper label over cardboard, "Mamma's Choice Brand Rolled Oats, Packed For Samuel Mahon Company, Ottumwa-Ft. Madison, Iowa," cond. 8+, 7-5/8" h, 4-1/4" dia........................................................ 412.50

## Mammoth Peanuts

Can, litho tin, pry lid, "Mammoth Brand Jumbo Whole Blanched Salted Peanuts, The Kelly Co.," large oval with mammoth, white ground, cond. 7.5-8, 10 lb, 11" h, 7-1/2" dia.......................................................... 847.00

## Mammy's Favorite Coffee

Pail, litho tin, "Mammy's Favorite Brand Coffee, C.D. Kenny Co., Buffalo, N.Y.," shows mammy holding tray, floral border, orange ground, dents, scratches, cond. 8-, 4 lb., 10-5/8" h, 6" dia ................................. 467.50

## Manco

Tin, vertical pocket, litho tin, "Manco Handi-Cut for Pipe and Cigarette," central shield with banners above/below, red ground, cond. 7-8+ ...................... 1,680.00

## Mandeville & King Co.

Sign, paper
"Mandeville & King Co., Superior Flower Seeds," Dutch lady watering flowers with water can, windmill in background, framed, soiling/fading, 35-1/2" h, 23" w................................................................302.50

"Superior Flower Seeds, Mandeville & King Co., Rochester, N.Y.," different colors of mums, newer frame, creases/tears, 27-1/2" h, 15-3/4" w ...............110.00

## Manhattan Cocktail

Tin, vertical pocket, litho tin, "Manhattan Cocktail, Modern Cut, Falk Tobacco Co.," small images of rooster and cocktail glass, gold text, green ground, central stripe reversed, cond. 7.5-8 ............................ 242.00

## Manhattan Coffee

Can, keywind, litho tin, taller version, "Manhattan Vacuum Packed Coffee," silhouette of skyline against red ground, cond. 8.5-9, 1 lb.................................... 111.00

## Manhattan Fire & Marine Insurance Co.

Clip, litho tin, "Cash Capital $1,000,000, The Manhattan Fire & Marine Insurance Co.," round image of Indian in headdress, red ground, New York, cond. 7.5, 2-3/4" h, 2-1/4" w............................................................. 82.50

## Manitowoc Canning

Tin, litho tin, "Manitowoc Canning" in red banner over black/white image of ship, yellow ground, Albert Landreth Co., Manitowoc, WI, cond. 8- ................... 55.00

## Manru & Nilo

Sign, litho tin, self-framing, "Manru & Nilo, King and Queen of Bottled Beers," oval image of woman with glass, A. Schreiber Brewing Co., Buffalo, scratches/dents/rust spots, 24" h, 20-1/2" w ...................... 143.00

## Mansfield Sanitary Pottery Co.

Salesman sample, pottery toilet, 2-pc, embossed "Mansfield," orig paper label, 6" h .............................. 231.00

## Mansion Inn Coffee

Can, keywind, litho tin, "Mansion Inn Coffee" in red text on white block, "All Method Grind" in white text on red block, black ground with white vertical stripes, shows cup of coffee, Stop & Shop, Boston, cond. 7.5-8, 1 lb ..................................................................... 60.50

## Maquoketa

Pinback button, celluloid over metal, "Maquoketa Cuban Hand Made Cigars, All Genuine Maquoketa Cigars Have O. McCaffrey & Co., Maquoketa, IA., Printed On Labels," shows early open car, minor soiling, 1-3/4" dia ............................................................. 82.50

## Marathon

Can, litho tin, hand soldered, "Marathon Motor Oil, Best in the Long Run, Transcontinental Oil Co.," outstretched runner, yellow text, green ground, cond. 8, 1 gal, 6" h, 8-1/2" w, 5-1/2" d.............................. 632.50

Gas globe, 1 lens, narrow glass body, "Marathon Premium Super-M," logo over blue text, white ground, lens cracked/glued, lens cond. 6, body cond. 8, 13-1/2" dia........................................................ 104.50

Marathon sign, porcelain, "Best In The Long Run," white on cobalt banner under runner, red ground, white/red border, cond. 8+, 72" dia, $550. (Photo courtesy of Collectors Auction Services)

## Marco Rolled Oats

Can, cardboard, round, "Marco Rolled Oats" under sheaf of wheat, white text, red ground, H.A. Marr Grocery Co., cond. 8-, 3 lb .............................................. 27.50

## Marguerite Cigars

Calendar, cardboard, 1903, "Marguerite Havana Cigars, Fritz Bros. Co. Makers, Cin. O," hand-applied lettering, oval cameo center with paper inset image of woman, full pad, cond. 8-, 15" h, 12" w ........................... 62.50

## Marigold Dairy Products

Clock, lightup, double bubble, glass face/cover, metal body, "Marigold Quality Chekd Dairy Products," blue Q with red checkmark in center, blue/red text, blue numbers, white ground, 15-1/2" dia ........................ 660.00

## Marine Cigars

Can, paper label, "The Marine Cigars," maritime theme, cond. 8, 4-1/2" h, 5-1/4" dia ............................. 209.00

## Marine Ethyl

Sign, pump sign, porcelain, "Marine Ethyl," red text, "Marine" on wavy white bar in cobalt oval, white ground, cond. 8+, 15" h, 14" w......................... 412.50

## Market Coffee

Can, keywind, litho tin, "Market Brand Coffee, Drip Grind," man with cup/pot at left, white/black text, red ground with white band/yellow stripes, cond. 8.25+, 1 lb ..................................................................... 27.50

## Mark Twain Cigars

**History:** "Mark Twain, known to everyone—liked by all" was the slogan used for this brand of cigars. Twain's image was flanked by scenes from Huckleberry Finn and Tom Sawyer on packaging for the popular smokes.

Sign, litho tin, embossed, "Liked by All, Mark Twain 5¢ Cigars 5¢," black/red text, yellow ground, red border, 1930s-1940s, cond. 7.5 ..................................... 82.50

## Marlin

Banner, cloth, gold trim, "Marlin Rifles & Shotguns, One Hundred Years of American Gunmaking," shows "Marlin 1870 1970" token, red/black text, white ground, stains, 29" h, 20" w .............................................. 60.50

## Marquette Club Ginger Ale

Sign, cardboard, die-cut, "Mixes Best For Your Guests," man in suit/hat holding out bottle, applied glass eyes, cond. 9.25+, 12" h, 8" w................................ 38.50

## Marshall Field Cigars

Tin, horizontal box, litho tin, "Marshall Field Distinctive Cigars, Very Mild Regardless of Color," image of framed portrait, emblem on each side, black/gold text, red ground, cond. 8, 1-3/8" h, 5-1/4" w, 3-3/4" d ............. 60.50

Display, cardboard, die-cut, standup, "Keep A Bottle On The Ice, Marquette Club Pale Dry Ginger Ale," woman at icebox, with bottle with orig label, 1920s-1930s, cond. 9.25, 26" h, 22" w, $187. (Photo courtesy of Gary Metz, Muddy River Trading Co.)

## Marsh Wheeling Stogies

Decals, black text on orange ground, approx 150, cond. 9 ............................................... 44.00

## Martin Dawson Co.

Cup, tin, "The Martin Dawson Co., Chicago, U.S.A.," 1-5/8" h, 2-1/2" d, $7.50.

Can, litho tin, "Martin Incubator Range Oil, Martin Oil Service, Inc., Blue Island, Illinois," plastic bail handle, 5 gal, $15.

## Martin Oil

Gas globe

Newer plastic body with 2 lenses, "Martin Super Regular," red "Martin" on blue "M" logo over 8 red stripes, blue/red text, white ground, all cond. 9,
13-1/2" dia .................................................. 209.00

Plastic body with 2 lenses, "Martin Xtra Special Ethyl," red "Martin" on blue "M" logo over 8 blue stripes, red text, white ground, lens cond. 8.5, body cond. 7,
13-1/2" dia .................................................. 319.00

2 different lenses, plastic body, "Martin Purple Martin

Tin, litho tin, "Marvel Mystery Oil," orig top, ©1928, 1 pt, $50.

Thermometers, tin: "Worth Crowing About, Marvels, Quality Cigarettes," light-blue border, 12" h, 3-3/4" w; "Worth Crowing About, Marvels, the Cigarette of Quality," dark-blue ground, cond. EXC, 12" h, 4" w, $135 each.

Ethyl," Martin logo over purple stripes, purple/red text, shows purple martin, white ground; "Martin Super Regular," Martin logo over red stripes, Ube/red text, white ground, lens cond. 9/8, 13-1/2" dia.......... 467.50

## Marvello Typewriter Ribbon

Tin, litho tin, "Sold only by Sears Roebuck," zig-zag pattern of blue/black on white, round, cond. 9 ................... 88.00

## Marvel Mystery Oil (See Photo)

## Marvels (See Photo)

## Marvin's Biscuit

Tin, litho tin, hinged, "Marvin's Superior Fancy Biscuits, Pittsburgh," oval medallion with child in sailor suit on larger design with flowers and tiles, 2-1/2" h, 6" w, 4" d .................................................................... 275.00

## Maryland Beauty Raw Oysters

Tin, litho tin, "The oyster you love to eat, Maryland Beauty Brand Raw Oysters, Fresh from the shell for discriminating people," round portrait of woman, white text, white panels, red ground, cond. 8.25+, pt, 3-3/4" h, 3-1/2" dia............................................................ 99.00

## Maryland Club Coffee (See Photo)

## Maryland Club Tobacco

Tin, vertical pocket, litho tin
    Flat top, "Maryland Club Mixture," building in circle on red ground with white "MC," cond. 9............. 617.00

Can, keywind, tin, "Maryland Club Coffee," gold and brown ground, wear, rust, 1 lb, $15.

    Flip top, "Maryland Club Mixture," building in circle on red ground with white "MC,"cond. 8.5........ 1,026.00

## Ma's Beverages

Sign, tin
    Die-cut, bottle shape, "Old Fashion Ma's Root Beer, The Kind That Mother Used To Make" in white oval label having oval image of grandmother, cond. G, 9-3/4" h, 6" w ................................................ 137.50
    Embossed, rolled edges, "Ma's Cola, 16 oz. bottle," tilted bottle with white label having oval image of grandmother, red/blue text, white ground, dents/ scratches/nail holes, 31" h, 22-1/2" w............. 66.00

## Mascot Baking Powder

Tin, paper label, bulldog in oval medallion, floral accents, unopened, cond. 8, 5-3/8" h, 3" dia................... 231.00

## Mascot Crushed Cut Tobacco

Pocket mirror, round, dog in center on white, white text on red border, cond. 8.75................................... 88.00

## Mason & Hamlin Pianos

Sign, tin, embossed, "Mason & Hamlin Grand & Upright Pianos, Boston, New York, Chicago," shows grand piano, white on black ground, framed, cond. VG, 24" h, 32" w .................................................................192.50

## Mason's Root Beer

Sign
    Tin, embossed, "Foam-topped...Refreshing, Mason's Root Beer," name in "M" logo, bottle filling glass at right, red/yellow text, white ground, red/yellow border, cond. VG, 32" h, 56" w .........................110.00
    Tin over cardboard, round, "Enjoy Mason's Root Beer,

ice cold," bottle at right, "Mason's" in black "M," yellow strip near bottom, yellow/black text, 1940s-1950s, cond. 8, 9" dia ................................... 110.00

Thermometer

Pam style, tin face, glass cover, "Enjoy Mason's Root Beer" on yellow center, "Bold refreshing flavor" on white border, black text/numbers, cond. EXC, 12" dia........................................................ 203.50

Tin, embossed bottle, rounded corners, "Enjoy Mason's Root Beer" at top, "Foam-Topped Refreshment" on yellow panel at bottom, red "M" logo, tilted bottle at left, tube at right, white ground, circa 1960, cond. 8-, 25" h, 10-1/4" w ............................... 99.00

## Massachusetts Bonding and Insurance Co.

Sign, litho tin, self-framed, "Massachusetts Bonding and Insurance Company, Capital $1,500,000, Fidelity and Surety Bonds, Automobile, Property Damage, Elevator and General Liability, Accident & Health, Burglary & Theft, Plate Glass, Insurance, Agencies Throughout the United States," upper-left seal with Indian in headdress/"Our Contract, Your Security," cond. 7.5, 19" h, 27-1/4" w ........................................................ 192.50

## Massasoit Coffee

Sign, linen, "Massasoit Coffee, Fine Aroma, Delicious Flavor," round portrait of Indian in headdress in center, white text, elaborate frame, 34" h, 27" w .......... 907.50

## Massatta Talcum

Tin, litho tin, sample, small top, Oriental motif, cond. 8+, 2-1/4" h, 1-1/4" ................................................... 39.50

## Massey-Ferguson

Sign, metal, self-framed, "World Famous Farm Equipment, Massey-Ferguson," 3-triangle logo, dents/scratches, 20" h, 40" w ..................................... 154.00

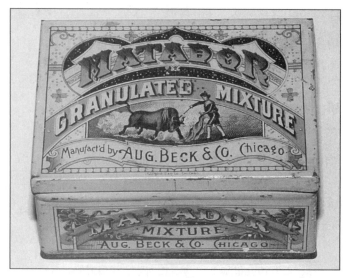

Tin, litho tin, "Matador Granulated Mixture, Aug. Beck & Co.," 2" h, 4" w, 3" d, $55.

**Poster, cardboard, cutout, easel-back missing, "Drink Mavis, Real Chocolate Flavor," woman with bottle/feet dangling in water, 1920s-1930s, cond. 8.75+, 30" h, 18" w, $825. (Photo courtesy Gary Metz, Muddy River**

## Masterpiece Fertilizers

Sign, tin, embossed, "Masterpiece Fertilizers, Geo. W. Uhr - Azusa," cond. G, 13-1/2" h, 20" w .............. 33.00

## Master Mason

Tin, vertical pocket, litho tin, "Master Mason Ready Rubbed Smoking Tobacco," oval color image of man with product and "A Square Deal," cond. 8............................1,664.00

## Master Workman

Tin, flat pocket, litho tin, large version, "J. Wright Co., Genuine Master Workman, Richmond, Va.," central white circle with name in red/black, dark ground with product, cond. 8+, 3/4" h, 4-1/2" w, 2-3/4" d ........................82.50

**Sign, flange, tin, "The Sign Of Good Coffee, We Serve Maxwell House, Good to the Last drop," blue ground, 1950s, cond. 8.25-8.5, 27" h, 14" w, $1,100. (Photo courtesy of Gary Metz, Muddy River Trading Co.)**

## Matador Granulated Mixture (See Photo)

## Matoaka

Tin, vertical pocket, litho tin, "Matoaka Blue Ribbon Smoking Tobacco," oval portrait on yellow ground, cond. 7.5 ....................................................... 1,650.00

## Mauser Mill Co.

Towel holder, metal, hanging, shows bag of flour, white finish, orig box (separated flap), 7-3/8" h, 2-7/8" w ............................................................. 75.00

## Mavis (See Photo)

## Max-I-Mum Coffee (See Photo)

## Maxwell House Coffee

**History:** After several years as a traveling salesman for a wholesale grocery in Nashville, Tenn., Joel Cheek became a partner in the business, but his real dream was to make and sell a better coffee. Much of his spare time was spent experimenting with different blends until, in 1882, he felt confident enough to start his own business. In 1884, he took his coffee to a Nashville hotel called the Maxwel House, where it was so well received that it was soon known as Maxwell House Coffee.

Although slight changes have been made to the mixture over the years, the trademark logo of the tilted cup with the phrase "Good to the Last Drop" has remained unchanged. A comment by Theodore Roosevelt is thought to have been the basis for the advertising slogan.

Can
    Keywind, litho tin, red version, "Drip Grind Maxwell House Coffee," cup with "Good To The Last Drop" slogan, red ground, cond. 9, 1 lb .................... 54.00

Can, keywind, tin, "Max-I-Mum Coffee, Max-I-mum Coffee Co., Oakland, Calif.," 1/2 lb, $60.

Slip lid, paper label on tin, "Maxwell House High Grade Coffee," shows building, red text, blue ground, cond. 8-, 1 lb ................................................... 27.50
Sign, cardboard, "A Rich Delicious Blend for the Best Tables, Maxwell House Coffee," can at left, "Good to The Last Drop" logo upper-right, white/red text, black ground, yellow/white checkered border, 1920s, cond. 8+, 8-3/4" h, 12-3/4" w ................................... 221.00

## May-Day Coffee

Tin, paper label, slip lid, "Millar's May-Day Brand Coffee," white ground, yellow trim, E.B. Millar & Co., Chicago, cond. 9, 1 lb, 3-1/2" h, 5-1/2" dia ........................ 61.00

## Mayo's Tobacco

Lunch box, litho tin, "Mayo's Cut Plug For Smoking And Chewing," in gold on cobalt ground, reversed central rectangle with "Mayo's Tobacco, It's Always Good," cond. 8 ............................................................. 55.00
Sign
    Cardboard, "Mayo's Plug, Light and Dark," crowing rooster on 3 blocks of tobacco, edge wear, framed, 31" h, 18-1/2" w ........................................... 220.00
    Porcelain, "Mayo's Plug, Light and Dark, Smoking Cock O' The Walk," shows crowing rooster on product, cond. EXC, 13" h, 6-1/2" w ................. 1,705.00
Tin, Roly Poly, litho tin
    Dutchman, light wear, cond. 8-, 7" h ................. 495.00
    Mammy, cond. 7.5, 7" h ..................................... 496.00
    Man from Scotland Yard, cond. 8+, 7" h ........ 1,124.00
    Satisfied Customer, cond. 8, 7" h ...................... 847.00
    Singing Waiter, cond. 7.5-8, 7" h ...................... 715.00
    Storekeeper, faded, cond. 7, 7" h ..................... 224.00
Tin, paper label, "Mayo's Cut Plug for Smoking and Chewing, Mayo's Tobacco Is Always Good," gold text, cobalt ground, cond. 8+, 4" x 6" ......................... 77.00

## Maytag

Can, fuel mixing, litho tin, with handle and spout, 8" h................................................................ 60.00

Tin, litho tin, "Mazola, A Pure Salad and Cooking Oil From Corn," no lid, 1 qt, $40.

# Mazda Lamps

Display, countertop, lightup, "Westinghouse/W" in white on red circle with black border over base with "Mazda Lamps" in red on black, circa 1930s, cond. 8-8.5, 13" h, 15" w ..................................................... 550.00

# Mazola (See Photo)

# McAvoy's Beer

Tray, litho tin, "McAvoy's, Beats 'em All" on green rim, "Malt Marrow" in red by scene of boy with dog/bottle, crazing/paint chips, 12" dia .............................. 242.00

# McCormick & Co.

**History:** Root beer flavoring extract and fruit syrups sold under the names Bee Brand and Silver Medal were among the first items sold by McCormick and Company, started by Willoughby M. McCormick in Baltimore in 1889. The company also sold Iron Glue, with "Sticks Everything But the Buyer" as its slogan. Some sources credit the company with being the first to market tea in gauze pouches, the forerunner of the modern tea bag.

After 1934 the spoon-or-sift top was used on all McCormick ground spice tins, and the large MC trademark was added to the company's products in 1938.

Tin, litho tin, "Bee Brand Teas, McCormick & Co.," native woman outdoors with table set for tea, cond. 8+, 1-1/2" h, 3" dia ................................................ 330.00

# McCormick-Deering

Sign, tin, embossed, "Notice We Use Only Genuine Parts in Reconditioning McCormick-Deering Machines," yellow text, blue ground, cond. VG, 12" h, 16" w.............. 231.00

**Bottle opener/milk cap lifter, litho tin on metal, "Milk & Bee Brand Vanilla Is Delicious, McCormick & Co. Balto., Bee Brand Extracts - Spices, Banquet Teas," 4-3/4" l, 1-5/8" d, $55.**

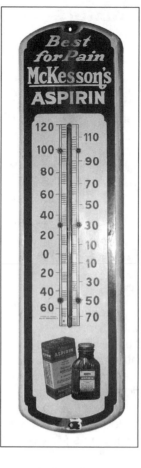

**Thermometer, porcelain, "Best for Pain, McKesson's Aspirin," chips, wear, 27" h, 7" w, $150.**

# McDonald's "Pilot" Tobacco

Tin, litho tin, slip lid, "For Pipe and Cigarette," white heart medallion with pilot at ship's wheel, red ground, cond. 8, 4" h, 4" dia ................................................... 28.00

# Walter McEwan

Tin, spice, store size, litho tin, "Walter McEwan, Albany, N.Y.," round medallion with stag, also flowers/embellishments, yellow ground, cond. 7.5+, 10 lb, 11" h, 7" sq ............................................................ 522.50

# McFadden's Electric Coffee

Tin, paper label, slip lid, "McFadden's Electric Brand Coffee, McFadden Coffee & Spice Co., Dubuque, Iowa," white text and bolts of electricity, dark ground, cond. 8-8.5, 1 lb, 3-1/2" h, 5-1/2" d ................................. 72.00

# McKesson's

Tin, litho tin, "McKesson's Baby-Powder," 2 naked children at fireplace, cond. 8.5, 6-1/2" h................. 192.50

# McLaughlin's Coffee

Bin, litho tin, roll top pictures cup and saucer, front with leaves and flowers, green ground, red sides, wear, scuffing, cond. 7, 22-1/2" h, 18" w, 12" d ......... 660.00

Can, litho tin, snap top, tall version, "McLaughlin's Steel Cut Columbia Coffee," sailing ship on sides, "Columbia" in red band, white ground, cond. 8, 1 lb .............. 165.00

Figurine, composition, "We Serve Meadow Gold Dairy Products," lettering on both sides, 1 leg glued at break, 1 teat missing, paint chipping, crazing, 13" h, 21" l, $95.

## Meadow Gold (See Photo)

## Medaglia D'Oro Caffe

Can, keywind, litho tin, central medallion flanked by gold medals, ground in red/white/green bands, S.A. Schonbrunn & Co., New York, unopened, cond. 8.5+, 12 oz (but 1 lb size can) ................................................. 34.00

## Meier's Ice Cream

Sign, porcelain, 2-sided, "We Serve Meier's Ice Cream, Waukesha," red text/border, yellow ground, chips, 24" h, 35-3/4" w .................................................................... 357.50

## Mellor & Rittenhouse Co.

Tin, litho tin, glass front, hinged lid, "Mellor & Rittenhouse Co. Licorice Lozenges," cottage scene on lid, cond. 8+, 7" h, 5" sq ...................................................... 264.00

## Melo-Crown (See Photo)

## Melrose Photo Studio

Pocket mirror, celluloid, round
 Baby portrait, hand-tinted, New York City, cond. EXC, 2-1/4" dia .......................................................... 44.00
 Bride, black/white, New York City, cond. EXC, 2-1/4" dia .......................................................... 33.00

## Mennen Talcum

**History:** Gerhard Mennen already owned his own drugstore in Newark, N.J., when the 22-year-old pharmacist began experimenting with new products. Mennen's Sure Corn Killer was introduced in 1878 and was widely advertised. Mennen's Borated Talcum Infant Powder was added to the line in 1889, but the cardboard containers leaked, so Mennen quickly switched to tin cans with shaker tops.

Beginning in 1892, a small picture of Mennen's head was printed on the shoulder of the cans and served as a trademark; a larger picture of Mennen as a baby graced the front of the cans.

Thermometer, porcelain, "Pollack Wheeling Stogies, Smoke Melo-Crowns," dents at bottom, light soiling, 38-3/4" h, 8-1/4" w, $175.

Tin, litho tin
 "Mennen Baby Talcum," child in sailboat, blue/white stripes, cond. 8-8.5, 5" h, 1-1/2" sq ............... 38.50
 "Mennen Medicated Powder," small image of man, green/white stripes, cond. 8+, 1/4 oz, 2" h, 1" dia ............................................................. 31.00
 "Mennen Talcum For Men, Use After The Bath," green/white stripes, cond. 7.5, 5-1/2" h, 2-1/2" w, 2-1/2" d ......................................................... 29.00

## Mercantile Cigars

Jar, amber glass, fired-on text, tin lid, "Mercantile Cigars, 5¢" around "The DWG Corp." shield logo, yellow design, minor rust on lid, cond. EXC, 5-1/2" h, 4-1/2" dia ............................................................. 16.50

## Mercedes Benz

Sign, porcelain, convex, "Mercedes Benz" in gray with leaves on border, logo in center, blue ground, cond. 8, 23-1/2" dia ......................................................... 533.50

## Merck

Sign, glass, reverse-painted, "Prescriptions Carefully Compounded, We Use Merck's Chemicals" in gold, white Merck cross logo at left, black ground, framed, 11-1/4" h, 17-1/4" w ........................................... 302.50

## Mercury Outboard Motors

Clock, lightup, metal body, glass face "Sales, Service" in black on yellow ground, shield logo at bottom, new wiring, 15" dia ...................................................... 209.00

## Merita Bread

Sign, tin, embossed, "Merita Enriched Bread, It's

Enriched, buy Merita Bread," Lone Ranger/Silver over loaf of bread, black/white text, wear/soiling/stains/rust, 36" h, 24" w ............................................ 412.50

## Messer's Charcoal Gum

Tin, litho tin, 2-pc, worn/chip, 1/2" h, 2-5/8" w, 7/8" d ..................................................... 742.50

## Metco Typewriter Ribbon

Tin, litho tin, round, red oval on black, cond. 8 ........ 33.00

## Metro

Sign, pump, porcelain, die-cut, shield shape, "Metro" under red Pegasus, white ground, top corners repaired, 13" h, 12-1/2" w .................................. 561.00

## Meyer Pumps

Calendar, paper, 1944, metal strips top/bottom, "Take off your hat to the Myers Pumps," barnyard scene of boy/girl pumping water, shows numerous pumps/accessories, full pad, cond. 8.25+, 51" h, 17" w ............. 302.50

## M-F-A Gasoline

Gas globe

2 glass lenses, narrow plastic body, blue "M-F-A Gasoline" in red/white/blue shield with stars over stripes, white ground, body broken, lens cond. 9, body cond. 7, 13-1/2" dia ............................. 176.00

New plastic body with 2 lenses, blue "M-F-A" in red/white/blue shield with stars over stripes, "Gasoline, Motor Oils, Greases" in blue at edge, white ground, 1 lens cracked, lens cond. 8/7, body cond. 9, 13-1/2" dia .................................................. 412.50

## Michelin

**History:** Since 1896, the Michelin Tire Man has been the trademark of the Michelin Tire Company. Originally designed by cartoonist Maurice Rossillon, the character is also known as Bibendum, derived from a French word on one of the company's early advertising posters. The muscle-bound figure was portrayed lifting a champagne glass filled with nails and broken glass, and a portion of the text read, "The Michelin tire drinks all obstacles."

Ashtray, ceramic, full-figured Michelin man, 4-1/4" h, 4-1/4" dia ......................................................... 88.00
Display, cardboard, standup, die-cut, Michelin man, yellow "Michelin" on blue drape from shoulder to waist, blue ground at base, cond. 8, 71-1/2" h, 35" w ............... 99.00
Toy, rubber, figural Michelin man wearing blue bibs embossed "Michelin," holding Michelin Man doll, cond. G, 7" h ........................................................................ 137.50

## Michigan Propellers

Thermometer, Pam style, tin face, glass cover, "Outboard, Inboard, Stern Drive, Michigan Propellers," yellow propeller in center, blue text/numbers, white ground, cond. 8, 12" dia .................................... 385.00

## Mickey Mouse Clothing

Box, cardboard, 2-pc, "Mickey Mouse Undees Make Children Happier," pie-eye Mickey/Minnie watching girl lifting dress to show underwear, cond. 7.5-8, 10-1/2" h, 7-1/4" w ............................................................. 330.00

## Mid-West

Gas globe, 1 glass lens, wide glass body, "Mid-West" in black on white diagonal of red shield, 3 stars at bottom, white ground, cond. 8.5, 13-1/2" dia ......... 143.00

## Milady Coffee

Can, keywind, litho tin, black/white text, single red rose in slender holder, yellow ground, lower black band, H.P. Lau Co., Nebraska, cond. 9, 1 lb ..................... 137.50

## Milady Decoletee Gillette

Box, cardboard, safety razor, "Milady Decoletee Gillette Safety Razor," oval image of woman in purple with upstretched arms, floral accents, blue ground, Gillette Safety Razor Co., top flap separated, 2-5/8" h, 1" sq ................................................................... 16.50

## Mil K Botl

Display, countertop, cardboard, die-cut, "Mil K Botl" bottle on blue circle, "Double Size, 5¢" in yellow, black base, sides fold back, cond. 9.25+, 10" h, 8-1/2" w ................... 60.50

## Milking Shorthorns

Sign, tin, die-cut, arched top, holds license plate holder, "Milking Shorthorns, The Breed That Fills Every Need," cow on green landscape/yellow sky, black/yellow text, cond. G, 5-1/4" h, 10-1/4" w ................. 55.00

## Miller Beer

**History:** After German brewmaster Frederick Miller moved to the United States in 1854, he began producing beer in wooden barrels in a brewery he purchased in Milwaukee, Wisc. Charles Henning first bottled the beer in 1879, but by 1883 Miller was bottling it himself. Miller's son, Ernest, took over the company following his father's death in 1888.

Beginning in 1889, an eagle above a circle mark was used to identify the company's products. Use of the symbol was discontinued in the 1940s, although it was subsequently reinstated in 1985. Among the company's many advertising slogans: "The Best Milwaukee Beer" (1903), "Champagne of Bottle Beer" (1906), and "Enjoy Life with Miller High Life" (1938).

Playing cards, complete deck, "The Champagne of Bottle Beer" slogan at bottom, Girl on Moon logo over red "Miller High Life" logo, orig box, used, 1950s ............................................................. 16.50
Sign, litho tin over cardboard, "Miller High Life Crew, Milwaukee," shows beer bottle, trademark image of woman in pointed hat sitting on crescent moon, circa 1920s, cond. 8, 17" h, 11" w ............................ 825.00

## Miller Tires

Sign, porcelain, "Miller Tires, Geared-To-The-Road," white text, yellow border, cond. 8, 20" h, 74" w .............. 605.00

## Milward's Needles

Needle case, wooden, 3 drawers, reverse-painted glass labels, "Milward's Celebrated Needles," cond. 8, 10-3/8" h, 14-3/4" w, 8-3/4" d ......................... 880.00

## Milwaukee Crane

Sign, porcelain, "The Milwaukee Crane," red/blue text, circle with curved horizontal panel, red top/bottom of circle, cobalt ground, cond. VG, 18" sq ............. 220.00

## Milwaukee Harvesting Machines

Match holder, hanging, litho tin, "Milwaukee Harvesting Machines, Always Reliable, Light Draft," farmer holding basket with company logo, cond. 8.5+, 5-1/2" h, 3-3/4" w ............................................. 742.50

## Milwaukee Sentinel

Sign, porcelain, barber pole, bowed front, "Read the Milwaukee Sentinel, First News of the Day, A.C. Backus Publisher" in cobalt on white panel at top, red/white/blue diagonals, cond. G, 48" h, 10" w .............. 247.50

## Minneapolis Universal Farm Motor

Pocket mirror, celluloid, "The Great Minneapolis Line, Minneapolis Universal Farm Motor, Eats Only When Busy, The Machine That Will Keep The Boy On The Farm," shows early steel-wheel tractor, cond. EXC, 2-1/8" dia ......................... 412.50

## Miscellaneous

Box, cardboard, clothing box, lid has large color image of Santa reaching into bag over "and a Merry Christmas," artwork by Guy Arnoux, 1930s, cond. 7.5+, 1-1/5" h, 10" sq ............................................................. 440.00
Calendar, sample, paper, patriotic motif with American flag, planes, ships, lettered "Dominate Your Market! 1944 Super Jumbos, Spotlight Your Message, Impressively, Effectively, 'A Big Value in the Finest Kind of Advertising,'" 1944 calendar pad, creased corner, folded, 44" h, 30" w ............................................. 55.00
Display
  Bronze with wood base, spread-wing eagle on globe, 26" h, 21" w ................................................... 825.00
  Tin, "Keys" in white vertical text on brown ground, hooks for blanks (Chrysler, Dodge, Studebaker, Nash, Ford, Lincoln), cond. 7 ......................... 22.00
Fan, folding, wooden and paper, Café Martin, New York City, shows woman and dog on early airplane, speed boats in water below, scattered foxing, cond. 8-, 9-1/2" h, 17-3/4" w ............................................... 143.00
Gas globe
  "Diesel," newer plastic body with 2 lenses, text in black

Box, tin, "Twas the Night Before Christmas," single handle, 2-1/4" h, 4-3/4" l, 2-7/8" d, $357.50.

on white band, red ground, lens cond. 9, body cond. 8.5, 13-1/2" dia ............................................. 176.00
  "Gasoline," milk glass, 1-pc, etched text in black with oversized "G," curved border line top/bottom, cond. 8, 13" h, 11" dia ......................................... 1,001.00
  "Kerosene," low-profile metal body, 2 lenses, text in red, white ground, repainted body, lens cond. 9/8.5, 15" dia ................................................ 258.50
  "Smokeless Kerosene Odorless," plastic body with 2 lenses, red/blue text, white ground, lens cond. 9, body cond. 8, 13-1/2" dia............................ 247.50
Globe, milk glass
  "Auto Hotel," glass, etched, 1-pc, cond. 7, 16" dia ............................................................ 385.00
  "Barber Shop," milk glass, fired-on design, triangular, text in black, red/blue stripes at edges, cond. VG, 12" h, 9-1/2" w ............................................... 825.00
  "Beauty Shoppe," milk glass, 1-pc, etched design, text in black, portrait of woman in center, fading/paint chips, 12-1/2" h, 11" dia................................ 467.50
  "Say it with Flowers, Fellow Society of American Florists," glass, high profile metal body with 2 lenses, minor fading, repainted body, 16-1/2" dia ......................... 429.00
Hanger, support arm and wall bracket for Colonial outdoor sign, gray porcelain, late 1940s, cond. 7-7.5, 6-1/2' l ............................................................. 605.00
Napkin ring, celluloid, "Compliments of Corner Cigar Store," hand-colored image of woman.............. 145.00
Pail
  Metal, "Pure Canadian Honey," yellow beehive/2 bees under yellow "Honey," blue ground, rust to lid/bottom, 8 lb, 6-1/2" h, 6-1/4" dia ........................115.50
  Tin, "Compliments of Santa Claus, Wishing You Merry Christmas and Happy New Year," colorful St. Nick

**Figurine, chalkware, "We Grind our Hamburger Fresh Daily," ears detached, chips to horns and feet, paint chips to back side, 15" h, 19" l, $135.**

Sign, porcelain, "Barber Shop," curved, $200.

in holly wreath, back shows Santa in sleigh and church scene in sepia colors, turn of the century, cond. 8.5, 3-1/2" h, 3-1/2" dia ...................... 907.50

Poster, paper, "Automobile Needs" in white over family picnic scene with mother/father/daughter/son, cond. G, 37" h, 23-1/2" w ............................... 88.00

Rack, wood/wire, tombstone shape, "Daily News" in white on dark paint at top, repairs/fading/cracked paint/stains/nail holes at top, 62" h, 15-1/2" w .......................... 715.00

Sign

"5¢," porcelain, oval, white text, red ground, edge nicks, cond. 9-9.25, 7" h, 5-1/2" w ................ 165.00

"5¢" and "Drink," porcelain, white on red ground, 1930s-1940s, cond. 8.25, 8" h, 18" w, pr...................... 660.00

"10¢ Men's Size Handkerchief, Ready For use, Soft Laundered, Sanitarily Packed," porcelain, triangular, white handkerchief, red/white text, red ground, 1930s, cond. 9.25-9.5, 13-1/2" h, 6" w.......... 302.50

"Barber Shop," porcelain, flange, white on cobalt panel, red/white/blue diagonals slant toward center, cond. EXC, 12" h, 24" w .............................. 258.50

"Bus Station," porcelain, 2-sided, iron frame, silhouette of people boarding bus, water stain/chips/frame rusted, 20" h, 16" w........................................ 390.00

"Bus Stop," porcelain, 2-sided, 3 hangers at side, white vertical text, dark ground, cond. 7, 29-1/2" h, 6" w............................................................. 159.50

"Clean Rest Rooms," porcelain, 2-sided, white text/border on mottled black-green ground, cond. 9.25-9.5, 1' h, 5' w................................................. 357.50

"Do Not Clean with Gasoline," tin, man cleaning at left, man/explosion at right, red text, white ground, cond. 7, 6" h, 24" w.................................................. 71.50

"Drugs," neon, 2 repairs to tube/transformer, needs new wiring, 10" h, 31-1/2" w .......................... 82.50

"Enjoy Ice Cream, A Refreshing Healthful Treat, Ice Cream Manufacturers," hanging, diamond shape, red with white text, 1940s-1950s, near-mint, 10" sq.......................................................... 275.00

"Entrance," glass, reverse-painted, gold-colored tin backing, white text, rust spotting, paint running on some text, 3-3/4" h, 18" w............................... 22.00

"The Housatonic Inn," wooden, white text, blue reflective sand finish, circa 1900, 28" h, 42" w.................. 660.00

"Ice Cold Water," porcelain, 2-sided, black ice-capped text on white ground, 1950s-1960s, cond. 9.25-9.5, 20" h, 10" w .................................................... 121.00

"Ladies & Gents Manicuring From 10 A.M. To 7 P.M.," glass, reverse-painted, framed, cond. G, 11" h, 22" w................................................................ 99.00

"Ladies Rest Room Equipped With Sanitary Seat Covers," porcelain, flange, green text, white ground, NOS, cond. 9, 9-3/4" h, 10-1/4" w ............... 330.00

"Look Better, Feel Better," porcelain, curved, barber pole, red text top/bottom, red/white/blue V-shaped stripes, white ground, William Marvy Co., St. Louis, orig box/hardware, NOS, cond. EXC, 48" h, 7-7/8" w ........................................................ 159.50

"Manicuring," porcelain, curved, rounded corners, 1920s, cond. EXC, 2-1/2" h, 9-7/8" w ............ 110.00

"Men" and "Women," porcelain, 2-sided, red text, white ground, cond. 9.5, each 7" h, 20" w............... 110.00

"Money Orders," brass, recessed text, frame with embossed floral motif, scratches, 2-3/4" h, 15" w............................................................... 55.00

"No Autos Filled While Engines Running, Oil Or Gas Lights Burning Or Occupants Smoking," porcelain, white on red ground, NOS, cond. 9, 12" h, 18" w ................................................................ 605.00

"Notice, Filling Service Will Not Be Rendered While Motors Are Running, Occupants Smoking or Lamps Burning," porcelain, filling station sign, text only, cond. 8+, 18" h, 22" w.................................. 797.50

"Official Vehicle Safety Inspection Station," tin, die-cut, 2-sided, bear holding sign, yellow ground, metal frame between signs, cond. 7, 43" h, 28-1/2" w .................................................... 192.50

Sign, porcelain, "Serve It And You Please All," bowl of Neapolitan ice cream, white text on blue border, circa 1910s-1920s, cond. 9-9.25, 18" dia, $577.50. (Photo courtesy of Gary Metz, Muddy River Trading Co.)

"Please, Noise Annoys," metal, heavy gauge, embossed, hospital zone, nurse with finger to lips, blue ground, white border, 1956, cond. 8-8.25, 24" h, 18" w .................................................. 275.00

"Pony Express Trail, 1860 1861," porcelain, silhouette of rider on horseback, minor chips to edges, minor water stain, 14" dia ........................................ 830.50

"Pop Corn," lightup, plastic and metal, fluorescent light, text between 2 bags of popcorn, circa 1950s-1960s, cond. 8.5, 9" h, 26" w ........................ 198.00

"Safety First, No Cards Filled While Motor Is Running, Or Occupants Smoking, Thank You," porcelain, white text/border, cond. 8.5, 17-3/4" h, 12" w ............. 412.50

"School Drive Slowly," tin, die-cut, crossing guard in red uniform/hat and tall black boots, black text on yellow ground, dents/scratches, 15" dia metal base, 60" h, 18" w.................................................. 1,045.00

"Send Your Telegrams Here" porcelain, flange, cobalt text on white shield, "Postal Telegram, The International System," white on cobalt ground, 1930s-1940s, cond. 8+, 15-1/2" h, 14" w.................. 330.00

"Spectacles Properly Fitted," glass, reverse-painted, 2 eyes over white text, black ground, framed, paint chips, 17-3/4" h, 33-3/4" w............................ 275.00

Sign, wooden, "Rooms With Garage," silver text on blue-gray ground, 11-1/2" h, 34" l, $220.

"Stop Your Motor," porcelain, red on white ground, cond. 8.5, 6" h, 23-1/2" w .............................. 71.50

"Telephone Bills May Be Paid Here," porcelain, flange, white on blue ground, chips to flange, 8-1/4" h, 12" w.......................................................... 302.50

"Telephone Pay Station," porcelain, flange, white text on cobalt ground, "Independent Local and Long Distance Telephone" in white/cobalt on red/white/cobalt shield in white circle, cond. EXC, 18" sq..................... 330.00

"Tractors With Lugs Prohibited," painted metal, embossed, black text, yellow ground, cond. 8, 8" h, 12" w.............................................................. 66.00

## Miss America Coffee

Can, keywind, litho tin

"Miss America Coffee, Regular Grind," small portrait of woman in circle of stars/over banner, blue/white text, ground is bands of blue/white/red, cond. 8.5, 1 lb................................................................. 102.50

Same as above, "Drip Grind, Vacuum Packed," cond. 8.5, 1 lb......................................................... 82.50

## Mission Orange

Cans, display cans, tin, "Mission Orange Drink, Dextrose Enriched," blue oval on orange/white striped body, orig box, NOS, case of 48.......................................... 77.00

Dispenser, porcelain, cylindrical shape, metal spigot, "Drink Mission Orange" slug plate, orange ground, black lid/base, scratches, 25-1/2" h, 13-1/2" dia........................................................ 247.50

Pocket mirror, round, "Insist on Mission Brand, It's Real Juice, Made in Los Angeles, Mission, It's Pure Quality, California Orange & Grapefruit Juice, William Stoffel Co.," smiling sun/oranges/grapefruit on white ground, black border, cond. 9 .......................................... 66.00

Sign, litho tin, embossed, "Drink Mission Orange, California Sunshine Flavor," sun with halo of oranges, "Mission" on black flag, yellow ground, orange border, circa 1950s, cond. 9.25, 2' sq ........................... 247.50

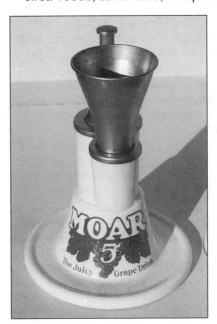

Syrup dispenser, ceramic/nickel-plated metal, "Moar 5¢, The Juicy Grape Drink," 1916, cond. 8.5, 11-1/2" h, $4,400. (Photo courtesy of Gary Metz, Muddy River Trading Co.)

## Missouri-Kansas-Texas Lines

Sign, porcelain, shield shape, "M-K-T" in white, "Missouri-Kansas-Texas-Lines" in black on white diagonal, black leaf design, red ground, scratches/chips, 24" h, 27" w ................................................................. 550.00

## Moar (See Photo)

## Mobil

**History:** Mobil started out as Vacuum Oil Company in 1886, and was part of John D. Rockefeller's Standard Oil conglomerate when the Supreme Court declared the Rockefeller holdings a monopoly in 1911. Vacuum Oil joined forces with Socony in 1931 and began selling both oil and gasoline products under the flying red horse symbol. The company's name was changed to Socony-Mobil in 1935 and shortened to Mobil in 1966.

For many years, Mobil gas stations displayed only the red Pegasus on their signs. After it was discovered that the public did not associate the logo with a particular brand or company, the signs were redesigned to include the company's name.

Pump sign, porcelain, "Mobilgas Special," 12" h, 13" w, $98.

Ashtray, Pegasus, bronze finish, 3-D horse logo, engraved "Fred Pennington 1923," 6" h, 7" w .......................... 385.00
Bookends, pair, metal, bronze finish, 3-D horse logo on each, hairline or repair to one leg, circa 1920s, 5-1/2" h, 4-1/2" w .................................................................. 412.50
Flag, cloth, red Pegasus on white ground, blue borders top/bottom, possibly 1940s, unused, cond. NM, 12-1/2" h, 18-1/2" w .......................................... 117.50
Gas globe, 2 glass lenses, narrow plastic body, "Mobilfuel Diesel" in black/red under large red Pegasus, white ground, lens cond. 9, body cond. 8, 13-1/2" dia .................................................. 467.50
Lighter
    Barlow, "Aviation Products" under red Pegasus, orig box, mint, 2-1/4" h, 1-1/2" w ........................... 82.50
    Zippo, "Magnolia Pipe Line Co." under red Pegasus, orig box, mint, 2-1/4" h, 1-1/2" w ..................... 77.00
Oiler, tin, "Mobil Handige Olie," back side in English, red Pegasus logo, blue/red text, white over red ground, made in U.S. for South African market, 5-3/8" h ................. 44.00
Sign, cardboard, "New, Keeps Engines Clean 3 Times Longer," gold/blue can of "Mobil Super Mobiloil" at left, cond. 8, 22" h, 43" w .......................................... 16.50
Sign, neon, plastic, embossed, die-cut, left-facing red Pegasus outlined in neon, not old, cond. 8+, 53" l ................................................................ 797.50
Sign, porcelain
    Die-cut, "Mobil" in blue over Pegasus, blue upper border, red arrow-shaped lower border, white ground, cond. 7, 41" h, 81-1/2" w ............................... 357.50
    2-pc, "Correct Fuel Oil For Home Heating," white text, blue ground, 5" h, 13-3/4" w, and "Mobilheat," blue letter, white ground, red Pegasus, 14-1/2" h, 15" w, orig hanging hooks/shipping box, both cond. NM ...................................................... 1,815.00
Thermometer
    Painted wood, "Mobil Products," Lancaster, Pa., distrib-

utor, lists products, shows Pegasus, red on white ground, cond. 8.5+, 8-1/2" h, 3" w .................. 176.00
Pam style, tin face, glass cover, "Mobil Car-Care At All Temperatures" under red Pegasus, black text/numbers, white ground, cond. 8, 11-3/4" dia ........... 324.50

## Mobilgas

Badge, hat, cloisonné, shield shape, "Mobilgas, Mobiloil" in blue/black under black Pegasus, white ground, cond. 8, 1-3/4" h, 1-1/2" w .............................. 231.00
Calendar, paper, single page, Sept 1934, "Follow the Magnolia Trail...Hills Are Just Scenery With Mobilgas Ethyl," 22" h ..................................................... 165.00
Gas globe
    Newer Capcolite plastic body with 2 lenses, "Mobilgas Special" in under red Pegasus, white ground, all cond. 8, 13-1/2" dia ...................................... 308.00
    2 lenses, high-profile metal body, "Mobilgas" under red Pegasus, white ground, body repainted, all cond. 8, 15-1/2" dia ................................................. 385.00
Gas globe lens, 2 glass lenses, "Mobilgas Special" in black/red and "Mobilgas" in black, each under red Pegasus, white ground, cond. 8, 16" dia ......... 495.00
Sign, porcelain, 2-sided, black "Mobilgas" under red Pegasus, "Product of a Socony Vacuum Company" below in red, red border, white ground, cond. 8/7+, 30" dia ............................................................. 660.00
Sign, tin, large red Pegasus over "Mobilgas," white ground, cond. 7, 24" h, 30" w ........................... 143.00

## Mobiloil

Cabinet, metal, 3 orig porcelain signs, repro globe, new electric, tin repro interior chart over orig inside front door, restored, 84" h, 24" sq ......................... 1,540.00
Can
    Metal, "Make the Mobiloil Chart Your Guide, Gargoyle Mobiloil Marine (Heavy Medium)," red gargoyle,

black/red text, white ground, unopened, cond. 8+, gal, 9-1/2" h, 5" sq ............................ 93.50

Tin, "Gargoyle Mobiloil," red gargoyle, black text, white ground, red lower band with small Pegasus in shield, Socony Vacuum Oil Co., cond. 8, qt, 5-1/2" h, 4" dia.............................................. 88.00

Tin, "Mobiloil Outboard Special" under red Pegasus, blue/red text, white ground, blue wave-like band at bottom, unopened, cond. 8, 5-5/8" h, 4" dia.................... 176.00

Rack, wire rack

Porcelain sign on front, "Authorized Service, Genuine Gargoyle Mobiloil" with red gargoyle, black/red text, white ground, under smaller "Property of Vacuum Oil Co." sign, cond. 8, 27" h, 32" w, 19-1/2" d ......... 550.00

2-sided tin sign at top, "Mobiloil Special, For All Cars All Year 'Round," red Pegasus, mkd "A-M 2-54," tubular frame, cond. 7................................... 154.00

Sign, porcelain

2-sided, "Gargoyle Mobiloil" in black on white ground with red gargoyle logo, "Nafta Texaco" on red ground with star logo in white circle, diagonal divider, cond. 7, 36" dia ............................ 3,025.00

Cookie-cutter type, die-cut, right-facing Pegasus, red, cond. 8+, 8' l ................................................ 3,630.00

Die-cut, embossed, left-facing Pegasus, red, 1940s-1950s, cond. 6.5+, 2' h, 3' w ...................... 1,100.00

Die-cut, embossed, left-facing Pegasus, red, cond. 7+, 35" h, 45" w.................................................. 1,567.50

Flange, "Gargoyle, Mobiloil Vacuum Oil Company," red gargoyle, black text on white, cond. 8-, 15-1/2" h, 24" w.............................................................. 440.00

Lubster 2-sided, "Make the chart your guide, Gargoyle Mobiloil A," red gargoyle, black text, white ground, red border, cond. 7, 8-3/4" dia ...................... 209.00

Rack sign, "Authorized Quart Service, Gargoyle Mobiloil," black text, red gargoyle, handle cut-out at

**Sign, porcelain, "Gargoyle, Mobiloil 'AF' Certified Service," black/red text, red gargoyle at top, white ground, cond. 9.5-9.75, 8" dia, $825. (Photo courtesy Gary Metz, Muddy River Trading Co.)**

**Tin, litho tin, "Roasted Mocha & Java Coffee, Packed and Fully Warranted by the Woolson Spice Co., Toledo, Ohio," elaborate design, 2 lb, $75.**

top, arched cut-out at bottom, restored, cond. 8, 23" h, 20" w ....................................................... 203.50

"Ask for Gargoyle, Mobiloil, Authorized Service, Vacuum Oil Company," black text on white ground, red gargoyle, cond. 8.5+, 24" h, 19-1/2" w.......... 522.50

"Authorized Service, Genuine Gargoyle Mobiloil," red "Genuine"/gargoyle, black text, white ground, cond. 8, 10-3/4" h, 13-1/2" w ................................ 522.50

"Gargoyle Mobiloil 'D' Recommended for All Motor Cycle Engines, Vacuum Oil Company Ltd.," silhouette of man on motorcycle, red gargoyle logo upper left, black/red text, white ground, cond. 8, 9" h, 11" w ................................................................. 2,007.50

"Let us Mobiloil your car, Engine, Chassis, Gears," black/white text, red ground, cond. 7, 36" h, 60" w.............................................................. 385.00

## Mocha & Java Coffee (See Photo)

## Model

Can, litho tin, slip lid, round, "United States Tobacco Company's Model Smoking Tobacco, Extra Quality For Pipe Or Cigarette," round image of crossed pipe/cigarette on gold ground, white text on red ground, gold border/trim, cond. 7.5, 6-1/4" h, 4-3/4" dia ..............................52.00

Sign

Porcelain, "Yes, I said Model Smoking Tobacco," bald man in suit at left, black text, yellow ground, edge chips/scratches/chips, 12" h, 36" w ............. 302.50

Tin, "Did you say 10¢? Model Smoking Tobacco," bald man at right, white text, red ground, scratches/dents/torn mounting hole, 11-1/2" h, 34-1/4" w ...................................................... 165.00

Tin, vertical pocket, litho tin

Sample, full size, "Model, For Pipe Or Cigarette, Mild-

Mellow, Extra Quality Smoking Tobacco, United States Tobacco Co.," centered yellow oval with cartoon face of balding man with long white moustache smoking pipe, red ground, cond. 8 .............. 182.00

Sample, full size, "Model, For Pipe Or Cigarette, Mild-Mellow, Extra Quality Smoking Tobacco, United States Tobacco Co.," also "Sample, Regular 10¢ Size, Not To Be Sold," centered yellow oval with cartoon face of balding man with long white moustache smoking pipe, red ground, cond. 7.5................ 86.00

Sample, "Model Smoking Tobacco For Pipe or Cigarette, Complimentary Package, 15¢ Size," red band near top with white text, price in red circle near bottom, full, cond. 8, 4-1/4" h, 3" w.................... 522.50

Silver version, "Model Smoking Tobacco For Pipe or Cigarette, Complimentary Package, 15¢ Size," red band near top with white text, price in red circle near bottom, full, cond. 9 ............................... 99.00

"Extra Quality Model Smoking Tobacco, For Pipe Or Cigarette, United States Tobacco Co., Richmond, Va., U.S.A.," lower-left yellow oval with cartoon face of balding man with long white moustache smoking pipe, red ground, cond. 8.5............................ 97.00

"Model Smoking Tobacco For Pipe or Cigarette, Complimentary Package, 15¢ Size," red band near top with white text, price in red circle near bottom, full, cond. 8.5 ......................................... 29.00

"Model, For Pipe Or Cigarette, Mild-Mellow, Extra Quality Smoking Tobacco, United States Tobacco Co.," centered yellow oval with cartoon face of balding man with long white moustache smoking pipe, red ground, cond. 8.5 .................................. 101.00

"Model Smoking Tobacco, For Pipe or Cigarette," small image of smoking pipe and cigarette overlapping cream circle on white latticed ground, cond. 9......................................................... 636.00

## Mohawk Chieftan Motor Oil

Can, litho tin, blue/red text on white upper band, Indian with single feather in red circle on blue band, red strip at bottom, Mohawk Refining Corp, Newark NJ, cond. 8/7, qt, 5-1/2" h, 4" dia ...................................... 253.00

Tin, litho, "Monarch Peanut Butter," 1 lb, $300.

## Mona Motor Oil

Can, litho tin

"Mona Motor Oil, For All Motor Vehicles" separator, shows car/motorcycle/tractor on blue ground, cond. 8+, 1/2 gal, 6" h, 8-3/4" w, 3-3/8" d ......................................................... 330.00

"Mona Motor Oil, For All Motor Vehicles" separator, shows car/motorcycle/tractor/speedboat/airplane on blue ground, Monarch Mfg. Co., cond 7+, gal, 10-1/2" h, 8-3/4" w, 3-3/8" d.......................... 412.50

## Monarch Foods

Can, keywind, litho tin, "Monarch Coffee" round lion's-head logo, black/gold uppercase name, white ground, cond. 8-, 1 lb ....................................................... 49.50

Tin, litho tin, "Monarch Cocoa," lion logo on white panel, blue ground above/below, upper-case cobalt text, minor chips/scratches, 6" h, 3-1/4" sq................ 71.50

## Monarch Ribbon

Tin, litho tin, square, typewriter ribbon, shows Monarch Visible Typewriter, cond. 7.5 ............................ 132.00

## Monogram Oil (See Photo)

Sign, porcelain, 2-sided, "Mona Motor Oil, Best Because Purest," bowed in center, porcelain cracking, cond. 7, $302.50. (Photo courtesy of Collectors Auction Services)

Sign, litho tin, embossed, "Stands Up! Monogram Oil," repeating image of soldiers to horizon, black/white text, white/yellow/red ground, wood frame, 1940s, cond. 8.25-8.5, 2' h, 5' w, $962.50. (Photo courtesy of Gary Metz, Muddy River Trading Co.)

Tip tray, tin, "Monticello, It's All Whiskey," pictures fox hunters on horseback, $140.

## Monogram Tea

Sign, porcelain, "Delicious Monogram Tea," white text, cobalt ground, 1920s-1930s, cond. 7.5-8, 12" h, 36" w ................................................................. 187.00

## Monroe Shock Absorbers

Clock, lightup, double bubble, metal body, glass face/cover, "Monroe-Matic Shock Absorbers, Monroe Load-Levelers," blue on white ground, white border, blue numbers, cond. 9, 15" dia ................................. 467.50

## Monticello Coffee

Tin, keywind, litho tin, oval with mansion, cobalt ground, Colonial Stores, Norfolk VA, unopened, cond. 7+, 1 lb, 3-3/4" h, 5-1/8" dia .......................................... 196.00

## Monticello Whiskey

## Moon Shine Tobacco

Tin, vertical pocket, litho tin
"Moon Shine Tobacco Prepared for Pipe and Cigarette, Highly Excellent Qualities," back says, "The Evil Is Removed," round medallion with white crescent moon, red ground, cond. 8+ .............. 2,130.00
"Moon Shine Tobacco Prepared for Pipe and Cigarette, Highly Excellent Qualities," round medallion with white crescent moon, red ground, cond. 7+ .................................................... 1,375.00

## Moorman

Display, cast aluminum, standing pig box with handle, hinged back opening to reveal skeleton and internal organs "Property of Moorman Manufacturing Co., Quincy, Ill.," 15" l ........................................... 1,300.00

## Morman Elders Damtana Wafers

Tin, litho tin, semi-nude woman standing on globe, red ground, cond. 7.5-8, 5/8" h, 1-7/8" w, 3" d ............ 852.50

## Morning Dew Tobacco

Tin, horizontal box, litho tin, "Morning Dew Cut Flake Tobacco," black text, "Cut Flake" in white banner, B. Houde & Co., Quebec, cond. 8, 1" h, 5" w, 3-5/8" d ............................................................. 115.50

## Morris' Supreme Peanut Butter

Pail, litho tin, name in yellow-over-dark oval, shows children at beach, Morris & Company, cond. 9, 1 lb, 4"h, 3-1/2" dia............................................................ 373.00

## Morses

Box, candy gift box, shape of standing Santa, 1920s, cond. EXC, 16-3/8" h, 7-3/4" w ........................ 330.00

## Morton Salt

**History:** When Joy Morton reorganized an existing salt company in 1910, the name Morton Salt Company was chosen. One of the new products introduced was a free-pouring salt sold in a round box with a patented pull-up spout. By 1911, the company's containers featured a smiling girl carrying an umbrella and an emptying container of salt, but it wasn't until later that the phrase, "When It Rains It Pours," was added to the trademark. The blue round container with the girl was first sold in 1914, and the logo has been redesigned many times since then. The possessive ('s) was dropped from the name Morton's Salt in 1948.

Sign
Paper, 1940s-1950s, "What's a potato without Morton's?" shows salt/3 raw and 1 baked potato, girl logo lower left, framed, cond. 8, 18" h, 36" w.............................................................. 187.00

Pencil clip, celluloid, "Morton Salt, It Pours," 1-5/8" l, $20.

Sign, porcelain, die-cut, 2-sided, "Mother Penn All Pennsylvania Motor Oil," white/cobalt/red, 1930s, 6" h, 8-1/2" w, $522.50. (Photo courtesy of Gary Metz, Muddy River Trading Co.)

Tin, embossed, "Morton's Salt" over "It Pours" in narrow border, white on cobalt ground, cond. VG, 9-3/4" h, 27-1/2" w ........................................ 88.00

Tin, "Morton T-M Salt, Trace-Mineralized with Iodine, Cobalt, Copper, Zinc, Iron, Maganese," black/red text beside product box/bag, white ground over black chalkdboard area, unused, cond. 8.25, 30" h, 24" w ............................................................. 60.50

## Mother Jackson's Jiffy Popping Corn

Can, cardboard, tin top/bottom, oval portrait of woman at top, bowl of popcorn at bottom, black/red text on yellow ground, cond. 8, 4-3/4" h, 3-3/4" w, 2-1/2" d ............ 56.00

## Mother Penn Motor Oil (See Photo)

## Mother's Oats

Sign, paper, "Today - The Dionne Quints Had Mother's Oats" in yellow on black strip at top, "Free" in red on black strip at bottom having special offer, portraits of the 5 as babies, framed, cond. VG, 17-3/4" h, 35" w ................................................................. 93.50

## Mother's Worm Syrup (See Photo)

## Motley's Best (See Photo)

Tin, litho tin, "Motley's Best Wave Cut, Absolutely The Finest Smoking," shield-shape medallion of man in lower-left corner, floral design overall, cond. 8+, 2" h, 4-1/2" w, 3-3/8" d ................................................. 467.50

## Motorola

Clock, neon spinner, tin face, metal body, "Motorola Radio For Home and Car," red text, white ground, black numbers, white neon, 21" dia .................. 715.00

Match holder, tin, "Mother's Worm Syrup, Agents For The Six Gooch Remedies," 6-3/4" h, $1,045.

Sign, tin, embossed, "Motorola, America's Finest Car and Home Radio," yellow text, black ground, red border, wood frame on back, cond. 7, 18" h, 72" w ...........280.50

## Motor Seal Motor Oil

Can, litho tin, "Motor Seal Highly Refined Motor Oil," Indian head in headdress at top of green panel, white text/ground, small holes, cond. 8, 2 gal, 11-3/4" h, 8-1/2" w, 5-1/2" d................................................. 82.50

## Mountain Coffee

Sign, tin, "Reeves, Parvin & Co.'s Strong Mountain Coffee," mountain range, red/yellow ground, cond. 8-, 15-5/8" h, 9-7/8" w ...............................................................226.50

## Mountain Dew (See Photo)

Sign, litho tin, embossed, "Ya-hooo! Mountain Dew, It'll tickle yore innards!," red/green lettering on horizontal wood on vertical fencing, mountaineer with jug lower-right, 1966, cond. 8.5-8.75, 17" h, 35" w, $632.50. (Photo courtesy of Gary Metz, Muddy River Trading Co.)

## Mount Cross Coffee

Can

Keywind, litho tin, "Mount Cross" in red text over "Brand" in black, "Coffee" in white on red strip, shows mountain range, J.S. Brown Mercantile Co., Denver, Colo., cond. 8, 1 lb ......................... 147.00

Pry lid, J.S. Brown Mercantile Co., Denver, stains/soiling/fading, 3 lb, 9-1/2" h, 5-1/2" dia.............. 132.00

## Moxie

**History:** Originally called Moxie Nerve Food and intended to be taken with a spoon, Moxie was first sold in Salem, Mass., in 1876. Created by Augustin Thompson, the mixture was one of a number of patent medicines Thompson sold to supplement the income from his medical practice. Several years later, wanting to capitalize on the popularity of soft drinks, Thompson modified his medicine. By 1884, Moxie was being sold in a carbonated form, and it is still sold today.

Over the years, Moxie used some innovative advertising campaigns. The Moxie Bottle Wagon, an 8-foot replica of a Moxie bottle that was pulled by a horse, debuted in 1899. After attracting a crowd, a salesman could enter through a door in the back of the bottle and dispense and sell cold drinks to customers. Around 1915, Frank Archer created the first of the Moxiemobiles, also known as Moxie Horsemobiles because they were an automobile with the figure of a horse mounted on the back.

From 1957 to 1962, the image of Hall of Fame baseball player Ted Williams in his Red Sox uniform was used to promote the beverage. The phrase, "It's My Favorite," accompanied the illustration.

**Collectors' Club:** Moxie Enthusiasts Collectors Club of America, Route 375, Box 164, Woodstock, NY

**Display, cardboard, die-cut, Moxie, orig bottle with paper label, bottle neck repaired on display, cond. 7-7.5, 28" h, 11" w, $187. (Photo courtesy of Gary Metz, Muddy River Trading Co.)**

12498; New England Moxie Congress, 445 Wyoming Ave., Millburn, NJ 07041.

Display, wooden, Moxie Maid, orig straight-sided bottle with paper label, advertising in 3 places, 1920s-1930s, cond. 7, 29" h.................................................... 302.50

Fan, cardboard, oversized, "Drink Moxie, Clean Wholesome Refreshing," close-up of woman, back shows couple in canoe, Moxie Man by fingerhold, circa 1915, cond. 8+, 11-3/4" h, 10-1/4" w........................... 77.00

Glass, clear, embossed, "Moxie," 5-1/2" h, pr ........ 49.50

Match holder, hanging, litho tin, "Learn to Drink Moxie, Very Healthful," shows bottle of Moxie Nerve Food, crate-motif holder, unused, cond. 8.5+, 7-1/4" h, 2-5/8" w, 7/8" d.............................................. 1,265.00

Sign, cardboard, die-cut, easel back, "It's a Hit says Ted Williams," shows "Moxie" bottle, pop-out die-cut image of Ted Williams, circa 1950s, unused, orig mailer, 11" h, 13-1/2" w ....................................................... 1,925.00

Sign, litho tin

Die-cut, 2-sided, Moxie Man over "Drink Moxie," 1920s-1930s, cond. 8.25-8.5+, 6-1/4" sq .....................577.50

Die-cut, "Moxie, I like it," die-cut woman with glass in circular border, cond. 7.5-8, 6-1/8" dia ...... 1,072.50

Embossed, "Drink Moxie, Distinctively Different," white text, red oval with yellow border, black ground with red border, 1930s-1940s, cond. 9.25+, 20" h, 28" w.......................................................... 440.00

Litho tin over cardboard, string-hung, "Moxie will make you Eat Better, Sleep Better, Feel Better," black text, white ground, red seals at corners, cond. 8-, 4-5/8" h, 6-1/2" w..............................................................231.00

Thermometer, litho tin

"Drink Moxie, It's Always A Pleasure To Serve You," Moxie man, white text, oval at top, glass at right, 1952, cond. 7.5+, 26" h, 10" w..................... 495.00

"Drink Moxie, Take home a case tonight, Drink Moxie,

Fan, paper, "Drink Moxie," back mkd "Read the T.N.T. Cowboy," 8-1/4" h, $25.

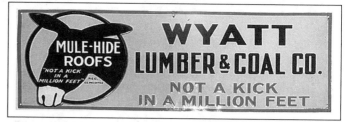

Sign, tin, embossed, "Mule-Hide Roofs, Wyatt Lumber & Coal Co., Not a Kick In A Million Feet," yellow ground, NOS, 10" h, 28" w, $70.

## Mulford's Toilet Talcum

Tin, litho tin, small top, oval, portrait of woman in oval, white ground, front cond. 8, back cond. 6.5, 4-1/2" h, 2-1/2" w .............................................................. 67.00

## Munyon's

Cabinet, wood, tin front/back, "Doctor Yourself, Munyon's Homeopathic Remedies," rust/scratches/stains, orig contents, 23-3/4" h, 17" w, 8" l ........................ 990.00

## Murad Cigarettes

Sign, paperboard, "Everywhere - Why? Murad, The Turkish Cigarette," colorful product box, white text, black ground, cond. 8.5, 3" h, 21" w ............................ 77.00

## Muriel Cigars

Tin, litho tin, "Muriel, The Cigar of Quality," image of Mideast woman in red headcover, brown ground, slide at top/bottom to open vent, scratches/dents, 6" h, 5-3/4" dia ......................................................... 33.00

## Murray Hill Coffee

Tin, paper label, sample, "Sample Murray Hill Java Coffee," round red medallion for Austin, Nichols & Co., blue ground, cond. NM, 2-1/8" h, 1-7/8" w, 1-3/8" d ........................................................... 231.00

Tin, litho tin, "Austin, Nichols & Co's Murray Hill Roasted Java Coffee," shows horse-drawn wagons being loaded, black design on yellow ground, cond. 8, 3 lb., 8-1/2" h, 5" w, 5-1/4" d .................... 577.50

## My Boy's

Box, litho tin, rectangular with rounded corners, "My Boy's American Chewing Gum" and portrait on top, Dutch or European, cond. 7-7.5 ......................... 60.50

Good At Any Temperature," Moxie man at bottom, bottle at top, ground in red and 2 shades of green, 1930s-1940s, cond. 9.75+, 26" h, 10" w .................................................. 3,960.00

"It's Always A Pleasure......To Serve You, Moxie" at top, "Moxie Original" bottle with small logo of Moxie man, light-blue panel behind bottle top, glass tube at right, black/red text, white ground, tube taped in, stains/chips/scratches, 12-1/8" h, 6-3/4" w ................. 187.00

Thermometer, litho tin over wood, "Drink Moxie," Moxie man at top, Moxie crate at bottom, varying temperatures noted (Fever Heat, Blood Heat, etc.), cond. 7.5+, 38-1/4" h, 12" w .............................................. 6,930.00

Tip tray, litho tin

"I Just Love Moxie, Don't You?," white on woodgrain border, center shows blonde with "Moxie" glass, 1910s-1920s, cond. 8.25, 6" dia ................... 176.00

"Drink Moxie, Very Healthful," red/white text, white ground, gold border, 1905-1920, cond. 7.5-8, 6" dia ....................................................... 99.00

## Mr. Cola

Sign, tin, embossed, diamond, "'Mr.' Cola 16 Oz.," red on yellow ground, cond. EXC, 18" h, 18" w ............. 66.00

## Mrs. Baird's

Sign, porcelain, "Mrs. Baird's Sliced Bread," blue ribbon with red/blue lettering, red/blue trim at sides, white ground, 1940s-1950s, cond. 8.75-9.25, 9" h, 19" w ................................................................. 176.00

## Mt. Pleasant Peanut Butter

Pail, litho tin, "Mt. Pleasant Peanut Butter, A quality product made from highest grade materials," mountain on yellow ground, white/black text, Mt. Pleasant Products Co., Lowell MA, cond. 8-, 1 lb ............................ 93.50

## Mule-Hide Roofs (See Photo)

Sign, porcelain, strip, "Everywhere-Why? Murad, The Turkish Cigarette," shows pack in color, white text, cobalt ground, 1910s-1920s, cond. 9.5-9.75, 3-1/2" h, 22" w, $797.50. (Photo courtesy of Gary Metz, Muddy River Trading Co.)

Tray, litho tin, "Gangway For Gansett! Famous Narragansett Lager & Ale, Too Good To Miss," shows Chief Narragansett on cart by cat, artwork by Dr. Seuss, scuff/scratch, 12" dia, $115.50.

## Nabisco

See National Biscuit Co.

## Naphey's Leaf Lard

Pail, miniature, litho tin, made for 1876 Centennial, Philadelphia, 2-1/2" h, 2-1/2" dia................................ 22.00

## Narragansett (See Photo)

## National Auto Club

Sign, porcelain, 2-sided, octagonal, "Official Service Station, National Auto Club, NAC," black/white design, cond. 7, 20" h, 20" w .........................................110.00

## National Bank of London

Tip tray, litho tin, shows collie, children playing marbles, other kids at play, cond. 8+, 3-3/8" h, 5" w ........ 302.50

## National Biscuit Company (Nabisco)

**History:** Adolphus W. Green, among the first to package crackers and sell them under a brand name, helped found the National Biscuit Company in 1898.

Red seals with the words "Inner" or "NBC Uneeda" printed on them were introduced in 1900 and are still in use today, with the logos having undergone several changes in form.

The National Biscuit Company was responsible for a wide variety of products, many of which can still be found on store shelves today. Breakfast staple Shredded Wheat was introduced in 1893, and Cream of Wheat debuted in 1895. Fig Newtons, the original un-cookie, were added in 1891 and Uneeda Biscuits in 1898, while Barnum's Animal Crackers roared onto the scene in 1902. Fun-in-the-middle Oreos were first sold in 1912.

**Collectors' Club:** Inner Seal Collectors Club, 6609 Billtown Rd., Louisville, KY 40299; Pow-Wow, 301 E. Buena Vista Ave., N. Augusta, SC 29841 (Nabisco Straight Arrow Promotion 1948-1954)

Box, litho tin, hinged lid, "Welsh Rabbit Biscuit," oval dining scene on floral ground, cond. 8+, 2" h, 10" w, 4-1/4" d ........................................................... 187.00
Sign, paper, "National Biscuit Company Does My Baking," shows woman holding plate of cookies on green

Tin, litho tin, "Famous Ginger Wafers, National Biscuit Company," twist lid, yellow/white/brown, 9-1/2 oz, $27.50.

Bin, litho tin and glass top, "National Biscuit Company, Uneeda Bakers," plain metal base, wear/scratches, 6" h, 13-1/2" dia, $75.

ground, framed, from the estate of Diana Allen who posed for the piece, minor tears/fold, 27" h, 20" w ........................................... 1,650.00

Table, wooden, detachable sq legs, decal name flanked by red logos, 1910s-1920s, cond. 6.5-7, 30" h, 3' w, 2' d ................................... 440.00

Window card, "Don't miss the new 1937 edition of 'Twin Stars' every Friday night... National Biscuit Company" beside red NBC logo in lower blue panel, pictures Helen Broderick, Victor Moore, Buddy Rogers, cartoon jester, yellow ground, litho missing at edges, 16-1/2" h, 11-1/2" w .......................................... 16.50

# National Cash Register

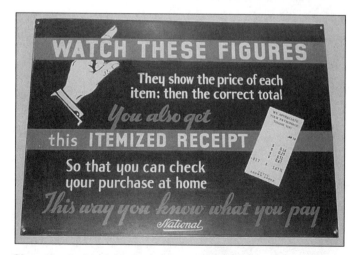

Sign, tin, 1-sided, National Cash Register, "Watch These Figures, They show the price of each item then the correct total, You also get this Itemized Receipt, So that you can check your purchase at home, This way you know what you pay, National," scratches, wear, 12-3/4" h, 17" w, $20.

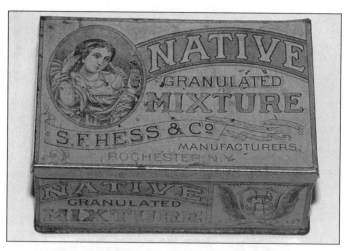

Tin, square corner, litho tin, "Native Granulated Mixture, S.F. Hess & Co., Rochester, N.Y.," 1-5/8" h, 3-7/8" w, 2-5/8" d, $12.50.

Bill spike, pressed metal, silver finish, embossed "National Cash Register," cond. EXC, 6-1/2" h, 3-1/4" dia ........................................... 159.50

# National Life and Accident Insurance Co.

Calendar, 1939, cardboard, Walt Disney's Three Little Pigs playing music, radio tuned to WSM, wolf seen leaving out the window, company shield logo on wall, 14" h, 11" w ............................................. 187.00

# National Mazda Lamps

Display, litho tin, electric, arched top shows blue box of "National Mazda Lamps" over scrolled ornamentation, "National Mazda Lamps" lettered on wood base, cond. 8, 13" h, 27" w, 6" d .......................................... 662.00

# National Transportation Co.

Fan, cardboard, "When in New York, Do As New Yorkers Do, Choose the Cab You Ride In, 5 Can Ride for the Price of 1," shows yellow cab, back has bird's-eye

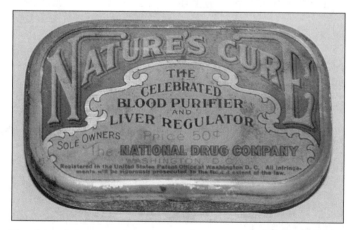

Tin, litho tin, "Nature's Cure, The Celebrated Blood Purifier and Liver Regulator, National Drug Company," wear to edges, 3-3/8" w, 2-1/8" d, $30.

Thermometer, round, brass frame, glass cover, "Feel like a Million, Nature's Remedy, The SAFE Dependable All Vegetable Laxative, Get a 25¢ Box," 9-1/4" d, $75.

map of 1939 World's Fair, cond. 8, 9-3/4" h, 10-1/2" w .............................................................. 94.50

## Nation-Wide

Sign, porcelain, die-cut, self-framed, "Nation-Wide Food Stores," shows North America in red stripes with United States in solid black, scratches/chips, 36" h, 32" w .............................................................. 121.00

## Native Granulated Mixture (See Photo)

## Nature's Cure (See Photo)

## Nature's Remedy

Thermometer, porcelain, Nature's Remedy, "NR To-Night Tomorrow Alright, feel like a million, Get a 25¢ box, Safe Vegetable Laxative," white letters, blue ground, small chips, 27" h, 7" w, $250.

Thermometer, porcelain, rounded top/bottom, "NR To-Night, Tomorrow Alright, Nature's Remedy, NR-Tables-NR, Better Than Pills For Liver Ills, Get a 25¢ Box, Come In, If you get it here, It's good," white/red text, cobalt ground, 1920s-1930s, cond. 8.5+, 27" h, 7" w ................... 412.50

## Navy Tobacco

Can, litho tin, small top, "Smoke, Chew Navy Smoking Tobacco, G.W. Gail & Ax, Baltimore, Md.," black text, green ground, diamond logo, cond. 7, round ...... 42.00

## Nebraska Blossom Cigars

Can, litho tin, large image of cowgirl, 25 count, cond. 8+, 5-1/4" h, 4" dia ............................................. 2,420.00

## Nehi

Kickplate, litho tin, embossed, "Drink Nehi Beverages," bottle boxed in at right, black/red text, yellow ground, 1940s, cond. 8.25-8.5, 11-1/2" h, 29" w ............ 192.50

Sign

Cardboard, "Drink Genuine Nehi in all popular flavors, Watch For This Bottle," bottle at left, green skirt/woman's legs at right, yellow oval on green ground, circa 1940s, cond. 8.75-9, 13" h, 20" w ........... 198.00

Paper, 1920s woman in hat with "Nehi" bottle, signed Armstrong, framed, edge tears/spotting, 23-5/8" h, 16-7/8" w ...................................................... 66.00

## Nerve Fine Cut

Tin, litho tin, round, shows sailor on flagpole, "Nerve" on red flag, Globe Tobacco Co., cond. 7, 3/4" h, 2-3/4" dia ............................................................. 89.00

Calendar, paper, 1935, "Drink Nehi," Rolf Armstrong artwork of woman in yellow dress with white stole, Aug-Dec pages, cond. 8.5-7.75, 24" h, 11-1/2" w, $550. (Photo courtesy of Gary Metz, Muddy River Trading Co.)

Thermometer, tin, "Don't Say Orange, Say Nesbitt's, a soft drink made from real oranges," near-mint, orig cardboard box, 22-3/4" h, 6-1/2" w, $325.

## Nesbitt's

Sign, cardboard, "Drink Nesbitt's California Orange," family of 4 cooking hotdogs outside at brick grill, EXC, 25" h, 36" w ........................................ 154.00

Sign, litho tin, embossed, "Drink Nesbitt's California Orange," tilted bottle at right, yellow/white/orange text, black ground, 1940s, cond. 8.75, 5" h, 12" w .................. 198.00

Tin, litho tin, "Nestle Morsels, Toll House Cookies," collector's tin, 6-3/8" h, 4-1/2" sq, $5.

Sign, litho tin, flange, oval, "Nesbitt's California Orange Sold Here," tipped bottle/"5¢" at right, white/orange on black ground, 1940s, NOS, cond. 8.5-9.5, 13" h, 18" w ................................................................ 990.00

## Nestle

Appliance, metal container, ball finial on lid, "Nestles Hot Fudge" on base, "Nestles" repeated around lid, white/red text, brown ground, silver container/lid, 12" h, 9-3/4" dia ...................................................... 132.00

## Nestle Permanent Waving

Kay display, die-cut, "Nestle Permanent Waving, Licensed Nestle Shop," shows woman's head at top, white/black text, tan/yellow ground, detachable feet, orig paper tag on back, cond. 8-8.5, 18" h, 15" w .......................................................... 1,265.00

## Newbro's Herpicide

Sign, aluminum, chain-hung, "Newbro's Herpicide, 10 cts Extra, A Delightful Hair Dressing, Kills Dandruff Germ," cond. 8.5, 4" h, 8" w ........................... 126.50

## New Factory Smoking Tobacco (See Photo)

## New York Cigars (See Photo)

## New York Coachoil

Can, tin, "New York Coachoil, Once Used, Always Used, The Best Oil For The Purpose," show coach, ornate border, white/blue text, blue ground, Marshall Oil Co., with contents, cond. 8, 6-3/4" h, 3" w, 1-3/4" d ............. 104.50

Tin, "New Factory Smoking Tobacco," light-blue ground, wear, scratches, $25.

Tin, litho tin, "Haynie's New York Hand Made Quality Cigars, 5¢," wear, scratches, 5-1/2" h, 4-1/8" d, $58.

## New Yorker Beverages (See Photo)

## New York Sunday Journal

Poster, paper, "Around the World with the Yellow Kid in the Great New York Sunday Journal, The Yellow Kid Sails Jan. 17," cartoon characters on a boat, cond. 8.5+, 15" h, 20" w ........................................... 4,950.00

## Niagara Fire Insurance Co.

Sign, porcelain, "Safety - Fund Policies, Niagara Fire Insurance Company, New York," falls scene at left,

Sign, litho tin, embossed, "New Yorker Beverages," 1930s-1940s, cond. 7-7.5, 32" h, 56" w, $330. (Photo courtesy of Gary Metz, Muddy River Trading Co.)

Sign, tin, "Nichol Kola," 11-3/4" h, 29-1/2" w, $104.50.

white text, cobalt ground, circa 1910-1915, cond. 9.5, 11" h, 21" w .................................................... 2,970.00

## Niagara Shoes

Sign, tin over cardboard, beveled edge, "Niagara shoes for youthful feet, Watch the way they wear," red/white text under oval scene of falls, black ground, fading/minor scratches, 19" h, 9" w ............................ 209.00

## Nichol Kola (See Photo)

## Nickel King Cigars

Sign, cardboard, "Smoke Nickel King Cigars," silver/black text, red ends to black banner, embellished silver ground, soiling/minor chips, 6" h, 18" w ............. 27.50

## Nigger Hair Tobacco

Pail, litho tin
  Caramel variation, "Smoke or Chew Nigger Hair Smoking Tobacco," each side shows African woman with ring in nose and ear, cond. 8-, 6-1/2" h, 5-1/4" dia............................................................605.00
  Yellow version, "Smoke or Chew Nigger Hair Smoking Tobacco," each side shows African woman with ring in nose and ear, cond. 7+, 6-5/8" h, 5-3/8" dia ..................................................... 192.50

## Nine O'Clock Washing Tea

Sign, tin, embossed, "We Sell Nine O'Clock Washing Tea, Premium Tickets in Every Package For a Limited Time," pictures Victorian woman at grandfather clock, framed, cond. 8-, 13" h, 13-1/2" w ................. 1,980.00

## Nitro Club

See also U.M.C. Nitro Club
Box, shell box, 2-pc, paper label on cardboard, "Nitro Club Loaded Paper Shells, Smokeless Powder," round red "Remington UMC" logo over flying duck, side shows shell, 12 gauge, Remington Arms Co., Bridgeport CT, fading/wear/side labels loose, 2-1/2" h, 4-1/8" sq............... 27.50

## None-Such

Display, cardboard, self-framed die-cut figure, "For Delicious Mince Pies, Fruit Puddings and Fruit Cakes, Use None-Such New England Mince Meat, Like Mother Used To Make," woman in apron with mincemeat, cond. 8, 11" h, 8-3/4" w .................................... 550.00

Coffee grinder, litho tin, "None-Such, The Bronson Walton Co., Cleveland, O." wooden base, cast-iron arm with wooden knob, extensive wear, 11" h, 5-1/4" sq, $310.

Pail, litho tin, blue text on orange ground, cond. 8, 1 lb, $88.

## Norco Feeds

Sign, tin, "Cut Costs With Norco Feeds," pig in dress sharpening knife at left, black/red text, white ground, scratches/stains/dented corners, 12" h, 24" w ........................ 242.00

## Normans' Inks

Sign, porcelain, convex, "Normans' Inks, Unrivalled," bottle of ink spilling on bulldog by table, cat at window, white/red text, yellow ground, restored, cond. EXC, 37-1/2" h, 21" w ................................... 990.00

## North American Savings Company

Calendar, paper and cardboard, 1902, pictures Indian, framed, missing January-June calendar pages, corners missing to calendar pad, creased top corner/nail hole/tear, 17-1/2" h, 14" w ................................ 302.50

## North American Van Lines

Toy, truck, tin keywind, Marx, 1940s-1950s, orig box, light wear/scratches, cond. 9-9.25, box cond. 8.5+ with minor warping, 14" l .......................................... 275.00

## North Pole Cut Plug

Canister, horizontal with oval top, litho tin, "North Pole Cut Plug, The United States Tob. Co., Richmond, Va.," shows 2 polar bears attacking a walrus with the sun on the horizon, Masker & Marcuse, cond. 9, 1 lb. ................ 1,398.00

## North Pole Tobacco

Pack, paper label, sample, "Smoke United States Tobacco Co.'s North Pole Chew," red/white/blue shield, white ground, full, cond. 8, 2-1/2" h, 1-3/4" w.................. 212.00

## North Star Tobacco

Tin, flat pocket, "North Star Fine Cut Tobacco, Cotterill Fenner & Co., Dayton, O.," shows woman/cherubs in clouds in front of star, cond. 9.25+, 3-3/4" h, 2-3/8" w ......................................................... 825.00

## Norva Peanut Butter (See Photo)

## Noxie-Kola

Sign, tin, embossed, "For 'Goodness Sake' Try A Glass, Noxie-Kola 5¢," white text/border, black ground, cond. G, 3-1/16" h, 13-3/4" w........................................ 71.50

## NRA (ammunition)

Sign, cardboard, die-cut, easel back, "Winner of 1924 Olympic Championship, The deadly little cartridge," shows outdoor scene of gopher standing on hind legs beside 2 boxes of bullets," circa 1925, unused, cond. NM, 13-5/8" h, 11" w .......................................... 660.00

## NuGrape

Calendar, 1949, 2 months on each page, cond. 9.5+ .......................................................... 77.00
Clock, lightup, glass face, metal body, "NuGrape Soda" in yellow oval over bottle, white face chipped, glass cover missing, 16-1/2" h, 13-1/2" w ................... 93.50
Kickplate, litho tin, embossed, "Drink NuGrape-Soda, Imitation Grape Flavor, A Favorite With Millions," bottle boxed off at left, white ground, 1930s, cond. 8, 12" h, 30" w .............................................................. 198.00
Sign, cardboard
    Die-cut, laminated, "NuGrape Soda, A Flavor You Can't Forget" beside bottle, possibly a cash register topper or stand-up counter sign, cond. 9-9.5, 6" h, 11" w................................................................ 77.00
    "Everybody likes a Change, Everybody likes NuGrape Soda," boy/girl with 6-pack in cardboard carrier at left, oval yellow logo lower-right, white ground, late 1940s, cond. 9.5, 13" h, 26" w........................ 99.00
Sign, porcelain, oval, "You Need a NuGrape Soda, Imitation Grape Flavor," black text, yellow ground, 1940s-1950s, cond. 9.75, 6" h, 12" w .......................... 253.00
Sign, tin
    Embossed, bottle of "NuGrape Soda," cond. 8-, 21-3/4" h, 8" w ....................................................... 126.50
    Embossed, raised edge (self-framing), "You Need A" in yellow on black ribbon at top of bottle of "NuGrape

**Sign, plastic, vacuum-formed, "Fun, Fun, More Fun with refreshing NuGrape Soda, Imitation Grape Flavor," 14" h, 12" w, $25.**

    Soda," green ground, 1940s, cond. 8.5-8.75, 44" h, 18" w ......................................................... 550.00

    Embossed, "Drink NuGrape Soda," bottle on yellow ground, circa late 1930s, framed, cond. NM, 12" h, 4-1/2" w ......................................................... 165.00

    Flange, "NuGrape Soda, A Flavor You Can't Forget," black/red text, yellow oval, hand with bottle, 1930s-1940s, cond. 7-8, 13-1/2" h, 20" w ............... 467.50

Thermometer, tin

    Die-cut, 1940s, "NuGrape Soda," glass below yellow label, cond. 9.25, 17" h ............................... 302.50

    Die-cut 1950s, "NuGrape Soda," glass below yellow label, cond. 8.25+, 16" h ............................... 99.00

    Rounded corners, "If you only knew what goes into NuGrape you'd never drink anything else," text at top, bottle on left, glass on right, white ground, 1950s-1960s, cond. 7.75, 16" h ...................... 66.00

    Round top/bottom, "Drink NuGrape Soda, A Flavor You Can't Forget," shows 6 bottles, black/white text, white over red ground, soiling/dents/chips, 16" h, 6-3/4" w ......................................................... 99.00

## Nustad's Pointer Coffee

Can

    Keywind, litho tin, "Nustad's Pointer Brand Coffee, N. Nustad Company, La Crosse, Wis.," hunting dog, dark text, "Coffee" in white text on red band, yellow ground, cond. 8-8.5, 1 lb ............................... 93.50

    Paper label over tin, "Nustad's Pointer Brand Coffee," hunting dog, dark text, yellow ground, cond. 8-, 1 lb, 6" h, 4-1/4" dia ............................................. 412.50

## Nut-Brown Coffee

Can, keywind, litho tin, taller version, "Millar's Nut-Brown Brand Coffee, Just-Rite," text in medallion, woman

**Tin, litho tin, "Nu Way Cod, Nu-Way Cod Laboratories, Ft. Wayne, Ind.," 4-1/2" w, 2-1/2" d, $25.**

    with cup in upper-right oval, blue ground with white stripe, E.B. Millar & Co., Chicago/Denver, cond. 8+, 1 lb ...................................................... 104.50

## Nutex Condoms

Tin, litho tin

    "Rolled Nu-Tips by Nutex," white text, red ground, blue/white logos, cond. 8-, 1/4" h, 2-1/8" w, 1-11/16" d .................................................. 632.50

    "Rolled Transparent Nutex," red/blue text, band logo, cond. 8.5+, 1/4" h, 2-5/8" w, 1-7/8" d ........... 440.00

    "The White Nutex, Get Next to Nutex," 2-tone green, central round green medallion with white "plus" logo surrounded by larger outline of logo, 1/4" h, 2-1/4" w, 1-5/8" d ......................................................... 687.50

## Nutrine Candies

Tin, store can, litho tin, "Nutrine Higher Quality Candies, Nutrine Candy Co., Chicago, U.S.A.," also "N Candies of a Higher Quality" seal, colorful design with knight in armor holding red flag, circa 1920s, 14" h, 10" dia ............ 412.50

## Nuvana

Door push, aluminum, embossed edges/lettering, "Nuvana Cigar 5¢" on red ground, "Pull" on black ground, paint loss/scratches, 6" h, 2" w ............. 88.00

## Nu Way Cod

## Nyal

Sign, porcelain, oval, "Nyal" in yellow on orange ground over white winged logo, "Service Drugstore" in yellow on red border, edge chips/scratches/ stains, 23-1/2" h, 36" w ................................................................. 165.00

## Nylotis Talcum

Tin, litho tin, 3-sided, shows peacock, white text, red ground, Nyal Co., Detroit, cond. 8+, 6" h, 1-5/8" w ......................................................... 98.00

## O-Baby Gum

Display box, cardboard, die-cut, standup back shows girl in blue dress holding oversized stick of O-Baby Gum, 1¢, Canadian, cond. 8.5+, 6-3/4" h, 4-5/8" w...................................................... 440.00

## Occidental Fire Insurance Co.

Match holder, hanging, litho tin, "Compliments of The Occidental Fire Insurance Co.," black/white text in blue horizontal/white curving bands, holder shows various flags, cond. 7.5+, 4-1/2" h, 3-1/4" w .................. 295.00

## O'Connor's Mocha & Java

Can, keywind, litho tin, "Regular Grind, O'Connor's Vacuum Packed Coffee, Genuine Mocha & Java," white text, shows map of trade routes, cond. 8, 1 lb.................. 44.00

Sign, litho tin, embossed, "Odin 5¢ Cigar" on suitcase carried by cartoon character smoking "Odin" cigar, "5¢ Cigar" at bottom, black text with red "Odin," yellow ground, 1920s-1930s, cond. 7.5+, 27-1/2" h, 19-1/2" w, $522.50. (Photo courtesy of Gary Metz, Muddy River Trading Co.)

## Odin Cigars

Sign, litho tin, embossed, "Odin 5¢ Cigar" on suitcase carried by cartoon character smoking "Odin" cigar, "5¢ Cigar" at bottom, all-black text, yellow ground, chips/scratches/soiling, 27-1/2" h, 19-1/2" w............. 418.00

## O.F.C. Rye

Sign, paper, framed, "O.F.C. Rye" in lower-right corner, black butler with bottle on tray over "Massa's Favorite," edge wear/fading, damaged frame, 30-1/4" h, 26" w ................................................................. 121.00

## Off 'N' On Tire Chains

Display, cardboard, stand-up, "Off Without Tools, On Without Tools, On Without Effort, Stays Locked, Pyrene, Makes Safety Certain," shows 2 men installing tire chains, circa 1920s, cond. 8.5+, 12-1/2" h, 22" w ................................................................. 440.00

## Ogburn, Hill & Co.

Sign, cardboard, "We Sell Ogburn, Hill & Co.'s Natural Leaf 'Rich and Waxy' Tobaccos," Indian maiden in canoe with flowers, framed, cond. 8-, 14" h, 10-3/4" w ............ 176.00

## O.H. Cow's Relief

Tin, litho tin
    Large "O.H." in red on lid with other text, cow image on side over "Read Our Guarantee On Cover," cond. 7.5, 2-3/8" x 3" x 2" ......................................... 71.50

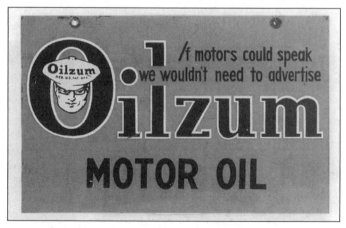

Sign, metal, 2-sided, "If motors could speak we wouldn't need to advertise, Oilzum Motor Oil," black text, orange ground, cond. 7, 10" h, 15-1/2" w, $280.50. (Photo courtesy of Collectors Auction Services)

Additional red text on lid, cow image on side under/ over "Cow's Relief, Price 50 Cents," cond. 8, 2-3/8" x 3" x 2" ................................................. 55.00

## Oilmax Cement

Sign, tin, embossed, "Oilmax Cement for cementing oil wells," red/black text, black border, yellow ground, cond. 7.5, 13-3/4" h, 27" w .................................. 60.50

## Oilzum Motor Oil

Cuff links, metal, oval, molded head of Oilzum man, cond. 8, 3/4" w .......................................... 203.50
Sign, tin, "Oilzum Motor Oil, choice of Champions," red triangular logo with face at left, black/white text, white ground, blue band at bottom, NOS, orig box, cond. 9, 15" h, 36" w ........................................................ 313.50

## OK Gum

Pinback button, celluloid, "OK Perfect Gum," shows clown in red, cond. EXC, 7/8" dia ....................... 220.00

## Old Andy Coffee

Can, paper label on cardboard, shows President Andrew Jackson, cond. 7+, 1 lb, 3-5/8" h, 5-1/4" dia .......... 231.00

## Old Barbee Whiskey

Tray, litho tin, oval, "Jno. T. Barbee & Co., Louisville, Ky.," on rim, log cabin scene with 2 women tasting Old Bar- bee Whiskey, sign on cabin, minor scratches/chips, 13-1/2" h, 16-1/2" w ........................................... 176.00

## Old Boston Coffee

Tin, keywind, litho tin, shows horse-drawn stagecoach and 6 male attendants helping female passenger, yel- low/black ground, ©1941, cond. 8+, 1 lb ........... 242.00

## Old Charter Distillery

Tray, litho tin, "Wright & Taylor, Old Charter Distillery" on red border, "Distillers, Louisville, Ky." at top of scene of 2 women at water's edge/product at left/factory back- ground, cond. VG, 12" dia ................................. 363.00

## Old Colony Lemonade

Sign, celluloid, round, "Old Colony Lemonade," pictures patriot with drink, minor stains, light soiling, cond. 7.5-8, 9" dia ................................................................. 33.00

## Old Colony Tobacco

Sign, polished tin, "Old Colony" in red over Colonial couple walking outdoors, "Bagley's Old Colony Mixture Smok- ing Tobacco" with red oval of woman in blue scarf at left/ right, cond. 8.5, 5" h, 15-1/4" w ........................... 71.50
Tin, vertical pocket, litho tin
  Concave/taller variation, "Bagley's Old Colony Mixture Smoking Tobacco," red oval with woman in blue scarf, silver ground, cond. 8.5, 4-1/2" h, 3" w ............ 259.00
  Concave/taller variation, "Bagley's Old Colony Mixture Smoking Tobacco, John J. Bagley & Co., Detroit,

Mich." red oval with woman in blue scarf, gold trim, silver ground, cond. 9.5, 4-1/2" h, 3" w ......... 451.00
  Flat, "Bagley's Old Colony Mixture Smoking Tobacco," red oval with woman in blue scarf, silver ground, cond. 8, 4-3/8" h ........................................... 253.00
  Sample, "Bagley's Old Colony Mixture Smoking Tobacco," red oval with woman in blue scarf, gold ground, cond. 8.5-9 ..................................... 726.00

## Old Company's Lehigh

Sign, porcelain, circular top over 5-sided base, "Old Company's Lehigh, Anthracie, It lasts longer!," fading/ chips, 12" h, 12" w .......................................... 220.00

## Old Dad

Tin, paper label, "Old Dad" over large oval portrait of man, image flanked by cherubs, ©1910, held 25 cigars, cond. 8+, 5-1/2" h, 4" dia ...................... 294.00

## Old Drum Whiskey

Clock, tin face on wood drum, "Old Drum" in red text around edges in place of numbers, drummer and "Old Drum Brand Blended Whiskey" in center, Calvert Dis- tillers Corp., New York City, hands rusted/rim cracked, wiring/plug worn, 12" dia .................................. 231.00

## Old Dutch

**History:** Even though Michael and Edward Cudahy owned a meatpacking company, they produced many products of the non-edible variety. Old Dutch Cleanser was introduced around 1906 and, by 1938, was recog- nized around the world. At one point, an ad agency convinced executives with the company to drop the word "old" from the name and to refrain from using the logo of the Dutch girl chasing dirt. Both were rein- stated when it became obvious consumers were unhappy with the change.

Sign, litho tin over cardboard, "Use Old Dutch it's Thrifty, A little goes a long way, Safe and Sanitary," shows can of product with Dutch woman logo, blue ground, cond. 8-, 8" h, 9-3/4" w .............................................. 253.00

**Sign, litho tin over cardboard, beveled, "For Healthful Cleanliness, There's nothing like Old Dutch," back of Dutch woman in bonnet at left, yellow ground, 1930s- 1940s, cond. 9, 9" h, 18" w, $935. (Photo courtesy of Gary Metz, Muddy River Trading Co.)**

Transom, Dutch woman logo flanking "115," decal on glass, wood frame, 14-1/2" h, 35-1/2" w ............ 38.50

## Old Dutch Root Beer

Sign, litho tin, embossed, "Old Dutch Root Beer," windmill upper right, black/white text, white over black ground, 1950s, cond. 8, 18" h, 36" w ............................ 176.00

## Old English Tobacco

Playing cards, "Old English Curve Cut Pipe Tobacco," man in red jacket, red/black text, green ground, complete, unused .................................................... 77.00

## Old English Wax

Tin, litho tin, chauffeur polishing early auto, yellow ground, Boyle Co., Cincinnati, 1920s, cond. 7.5+, 1-5/8" h, 3-3/4" dia .............................................................. 44.00

## Olde Tavern Coffee

Can, keywind, litho tin, white text in red box under image of tavern/horse & buggy, yellow ground, Lee & Cady, Detroit, Mich., cond. 8+, 1 lb .............................. 71.50

## Old Fitzgerald

Lamp, motion lamp, "Fritz' Mist" in red/green text under snow-covered "Old Fitzgerald" bottle, cylinder shade, cond. 9, 14" h ...................................................... 88.00

## Old Fort Feeds

Sign, porcelain, die-cut, "Old Fort Feeds, Old Fort Mills Inc., 'Famous for Feeds,' Marion, Ohio, Harrisburg, Pa.," shows wagon wheel/wagon/pioneer with gun, scratches/repairs/touch-ups, 47-1/2" h, 40" w ........................ 467.50

## Old German

Door inserts, fired-on glass, pr, "Old German Premium Lager" in white on red banner, one says "For Men" and pictures man in German garb, other "For Women," shows woman, cond. EXC, 5" h, 11" w ............ 137.50

## Old Gold Cigarettes

Display, countertop, cardboard, "Old Gold Cigarettes, You Can't Improve on Nature," 3-D truck motif with image of woman walking dog, open top for holding packs, with 3 packs, wheels worn/bent, cond. 8, 5-3/4" h, 11" w ...................................................................... 412.50

Sign, porcelain with self-framing edge, "Old Gold Cigarettes, Not a Cough in a Carload" in red on yellow ground, chips, 12" h, 24" w ................................ 357.50

## Old Green River

Canister, paper, "Old Green River Smoking, A real old-fashioned nature flavored smoke. Made from Kentucky's best nature-cured tobacco just ground up ready for your pipe, Green River Tobacco Co., Owensboro, Ky.," silhouette of trees and river under shield-shaped design, cond. 8 ...................................... 83.00

## Old Hickory Bourbon

Thermometer, tin over cardboard, "Old Hickory, Amer-

Ashtray, litho tin, can-shaped, "Old Judge Coffee, David G. Evans Coffee Co., St. Louis," 3" h, $35.

ica's Most Magnificent Bourbon," tilted bottle at left, round thermometer face at bottom, red/white text, blue ground, Old Hickory Distillers Co., Philadelphia, 8-7/8" dia ............................................................ 44.00

## Old Hickory Typewriter Ribbon

Tin, litho tin, close-up of typewriter keys with skyscrapers in background, 2-tone green ground, cond. 8.5, 7/8" h, 2-1/2" sq .......................................................... 132.00

## Old Judge Coffee

Can, litho tin, slip top, "Percolator Steel Cut Old Judge Coffee, Settles The Question," owl on branch in round medallion flanked by leaves, white/blue text, red ground, cond. 7.5, 3 lb ...................................... 82.50

## Old Kentucky

Sign, paper, framed, "In Old Kentucky...Outside the Race Track," red text, blacks at fence, white couple at tree, ©1896, 38" h, 47" w .......................................... 616.00

## Old Mansion Coffee

Can, keywind, litho tin
Oval medallion shows mansion, blue ground, unopened, cond. NM, 1 lb, 3-1/2" h, 5" dia ........................ 220.00
Small oval medallion with mansion, white text, "Old Mansion" on wide red band, "Coffee" beside oval on narrow blue band, cond. 8, 1 lb ...................... 38.50

## Old Master Coffee

Tin
Litho tin, snap top, oval medallion of man with white hair/beard and red cloak, gold/cobalt ground, round, cond. 8+, 3 lb, 9-1/2" h ................................ 138.00

Paper label, oval medallion of man with white hair/ beard and red cloak, gold over green ground, cond. 8+, 1 lb, 6" h, 4" dia ......................................... 99.00

## Old Mr. Boston

Clock, embossed metal, shaped like a flask with "Old Mr. Boston, Fine Liquors" on obverse and reverse, scratches, 21-1/4" h, 10" w, 5-1/2" d ................. 137.50

## Old Philadelphia Coffee

Can, keywind, litho tin, shows historic Philadelphia landmarks, unopened, cond. 8-, 1 lb, 3-1/2" h, 5" dia ............................................................... 231.00

## Old Ranger

Clock, lightup, metal frame, round, "Old Ranger Beer and Ale, Hornell Brewing Co. Inc., Hornell, N.Y.," shows ranger with musket/coonskin cap, red/black text, white ground, black numbers, cond. EXC, 15" dia ...................................................................318.00

## Old Reliable Coffee

Pocket mirror, celluloid over metal, "Old Reliable Coffee, Always Good," shows man smoking while leaning on an Old Reliable coffee can, scratches/chips, 2" dia ...................................................................... 93.50

Sign, tin, "Always Good, Old Reliable Coffee," shows product in lower right and man in red jacket and hat, yellow ground, 1920s-1930s, cond. 9, 9-1/4" h, 6-1/2" w, $660. (Photo courtesy Gary Metz, Muddy River Trading Co.)

Sign
Litho paper, "Old Reliable Coffee, Always the same, Always good," trademark man at top, box of product at bottom, yellow/white text, blue ground, water stains, 21-1/2" h, 11-1/2" w ........................... 104.50
Tin, embossed, "Always Good, Old Reliable Coffee," black on yellow ground, chips/scratches/bent corners, 6-1/2" h, 13-3/4" w ............................... 88.00

## Old Rip

Tin, vertical box, "Old Rip Long Cut Smoking Tobacco, Allen & Ginter, Richmond, Va.," shows aging man with cane hobbling toward town, red ground, circa 1895 Ginna tin, cond. 7-1/4" h, 5" w, 3" d .................. 303.00

## Oldsmobile

Clock, neon, metal body, "Oldsmobile Service" around shield logo, white neon at inner border, case repainted, glass cracked, cond. 8, 21" dia, 6" d .....................660.00
Sign, porcelain, 2-sided, "Oldsmobile Service," gold globe in silver border, white text on cobalt border, yellow trim, cond. 8+/7, 60" dia............................. 550.00

## Old Squire

Tin, vertical pocket, litho tin, short version, "Old Squire Pipe Tobacco, A Rich Mellow Blend For Cool Smoking, 10¢," round black/white image of squire with pipe, red ground, cond. 8.5...................................... 237.00

## Old Style Lager

Vendor, wood, backbar point-of-sale vendor, "We don't aim to make the most beer: only the best, Old Style Lager, America's Quality Beer," Musketeer-looking man at right, 8 compartments for cigarette packs, front panel flips up, cond. 9+, 12-3/4" h, 21-1/2" w, 4" d.................................................................. 60.50

Clock, glass face/cover, metal body, Oldsmobile logo at 12-o'clock position, white ground, cond. 8+, 15-1/2" sq, $522.50. (Photo courtesy of Collectors Auction Services)

Sign, graniteware, cobalt, "Genuine Austrian Omega Enameled Ware For Sale Here, Best, Purest, Fred. W. Morse, Omega," 16" h, 21" w, $150.

## Old Town Typewriter Ribbon

Tin, litho tin, round, "Old Town Hermetic Secretarial Typewriter Ribbon, Self Renewing, Air Tight, Factory Fresh," silhouette of woman at typewriter, red/black text, yellow ground, unopened/with key, cond. 9 ......................... 43.00

## Omar Cigarettes

Sign, litho paper, "Omar Turkish Blend cigarettes, the joy of life, 20 for 15¢," 2 men smoking, pack in lower-left, frame mkd "Omar Turkish Blend Cigarettes," framed, water marks/soiling, 2" h, 18-1/2" w .................. 445.50

## Omega Enameled Ware
## (See Photo)

"One Night Corn Cure," cast-iron, $1,200.

## Ondoca Fruit Drinks

Pocket mirror, celluloid, oval, "Ondoca Delicious Fruit Drinks, At Fountains, Grocers, Druggists," woman in bathing suit with beach ball, umbrella, cond. EXC, 2-3/4" h, 1-3/4" w...................................................... 357.50

## O'Neill Creamery

Sign, porcelain, die-cut, 2-sided, cream-can shape, "O'Neill Creamery, Cash For Cream," black on red ground, loss of luster/fading/scratches/chips, 27" h, 15" w .............................................................. 660.00

## One Night Corn Cure (See Photo)

## Opaline

Can, tin, "Sinclair Opaline Motor Oil," black/red text over "Sinclair Oils" logo, striped ground, Sinclair Refining Co., Chicago, cond. 8/7, gal ............................. 330.00

## OPM (Our Private Mixture)

Tin, vertical pocket, litho tin, "The Perfect Pipe Tobacco, OPM, Our Private Mixture," white text in white panel, cobalt ground, cond. 8-8.5 ................................ 333.00

## Orange-Crush

Calendar, paper, 1946, girl in green dress with black/white teddy bear, framed, cond. 8.75-9.25, 30" h, 15" w ................................................................ 412.50

Calendar top, paper, circa 1920s, woman under umbrella on rock on shore, mentions all 3 flavors, bottle lower-right, cond. 6.5-7, 20" h, 12" w .......................... 605.00

Chalkboard, tin, embossed
"Discover Orange Crush," hand on tilted bottle at left, oblong orange logo at right, light-blue ground at top, blackboard at bottom, white border, minor scratches/rust, 26-7/8" h, 18-3/4"w ................. 66.00
"Drink Orange-Crush," black/white text on orange ground at top, blackboard at bottom, orange border, ©1935, cond. G, 19" h, 13" w ...................... 214.50

Can, tin, "Opaline Motor Oil, Sinclair Refining Company, Chicago," early race car with Sinclair symbol on radiator, cond. 8, 1 gal, 11" h, 8" w, 3" d, $1,760. (Photo courtesy of Collectors Auction Services)

**Kickplate, litho tin, embossed, "Drink Ward's Orange-Crush, also Ward's Lemon-Crush and Ward's Lime-Crush," bottle in black oval at left, white/black text, orange ground, 1920s-1930s, cond. 9.25-9.5, 9" h, 20" w, $797.50. (Photo courtesy of Gary Metz, Muddy River Trading Co.)**

**Sign, litho tin, "drink Orange Crush, refreshing delicious," winter scene, tilted bottle at right, orange/white oblong logo in center, black text, 1950s-1960s, cond. 7.5-8, 32" h, 56" w, $275. (Photo courtesy of Gary Metz, Muddy River Trading Co.)**

Clock, lightup, plastic face, metal case, "Discover Orange Crush," oblong logo, black 6/12, white ground, hands bent/face soiled, 15-1/2" sq............................... 159.50
Dispenser
  Ceramic, figural orange on floral base, orig metal dispenser, base embossed "Ward's Orange-Crush," navel above "Ward's" on 1 side, mkd "Orange" on porcelain knob, cond. EXC, 13-1/2" h, 8" dia................. 2,530.00
  Glass, embossed white glass orange, black glass pedestal with decals, stainless lid with stirring mechanism, 1930s-1940s, cond. 7.5 ...................... 550.00
Door push, embossed tin, "Come in, Drink Orange-Crush" over slanted bottle, 1920s, cond. 9.25, 12" h, 3" w ................................................................. 495.00
Fan, hand, 1920s, cond. 9.5, 7" h, 10" w .............. 440.00
Jar, amber glass, "Orange Crush" embossed on upper rim, overall embossed decor, plain area for label, metal lid/bail, cond. G, 11" h, 6-3/4" dia .............. 27.50

**Sign, Masonite, "Rush! Rush! for Orange-Crush Carbonated Beverage," Crushy at bottom holding up bottle onto white circle, yellow/white letters, orange ground, 1942, cond. 8.5-8.75, 48" h, 18" w, $825. (Photo courtesy of Gary Metz, Muddy River Trading Co.)**

Kick plate, "Take Home A Handipack, Orange-Crush Carbonated Beverage, 6 bottles for 25¢," 6-pack of bottles in white insert at left, orange ground, 1930s-1940s, cond. 9.25+, 12" h, 28" w............................. 1,705.00
Menu board, litho tin, embossed, "Drink Orange Crush," small Crushy with titled bottle over leaves, black/white text, orange ground/border, "Orange-Crush" in white at bottom, circa 1930s, cond. 8.25-8.5, 28" h, 20" w ................................................................. 467.50
Sign, cardboard
  Die-cut, heavily embossed, blue shield "Refreshment for Workers and Fighters" over "Orange-Crush Carbonated Beverage," gold eagle on cobalt ground, 1940s, 9.5+, 10" h, 7" w................................. 88.00
  Self-framed, "Naturally - it Tastes Better! Orange-Crush," couple on beach, 1940s-50s, cond. 8.75, 20" h, 26" w .................................................. 143.00
  String-hung, "Drink All Fruit Crushes, Orange, Lemon, Lime," woman in straw hat picking oranges, 1940s, printed in England, cond. 9.25, 13-1/2" h, 9-1/2" w ......................................................... 60.50
Sign, celluloid, button-type
  "Discover Orange Crush," orange lower half with ruffled top, on white, cond. 8-8.5, 9" dia ............ 71.50
  "Enjoy Orange Crush," straight orange band on white, 1940s, cond. 8.5, 9" dia................................. 60.50
  "Enjoy Orange Crush," orange band with ruffled top on white, Parent's Magazine seal, cond. 9.25-9.5, 9" dia........................................................... 209.00
  "Enjoy Orange Crush, Naturally - it Tastes Better," orange ground, cond. 8.5, 9" dia ................... 82.50
  "Ask for a Crush, Carbonated Beverage" over Crushy figure, orange ground, dated 1946, cond. 8.5+, 9" dia ......................................................... 176.00
  Crushy figure over "Orange-Crush, Carbonated Beverage," orange ground, cond. 8.25-8.5, 9" dia ......................................................... 165.00
  Crushy figure over "Orange-Crush, Fruit Flavored Drink," orange ground, cond. 8.5-9, 9" dia ................... 176.00
  Crushy figure over "Orange-Crush, It Tastes Better," orange ground, cond. 8.25-8.5, 9" dia ......... 357.50
Sign, Masonite, "Feel Fresh! Drink Orange-Crush Carbon-

**Sign, litho tin, embossed, "Take Home A Handipack, Orange-Crush, Carbonated Beverages, 6 Bottles for 25¢," shows 6-pack in cardboard carrier on white square at left, yellow/white text, orange ground, 1940, cond. 9.25+, 12" h, 28" w, $1,650. (Photo courtesy of Gary Metz, Muddy River Trading Co.)**

ated Beverage," Crushy at left, yellow/white text, orange ground, wood frame, 1943, cond. 8.25-8.5, 14" h, 40" w ............................................................ 467.50

Sign, metal, die-cut, embossed, "The New Flavor Guarding Bottle," bottle shape, cond. 8, 54" h, 13" w ............ 495.00

Sign, plastic, embossed, shows boy/girl sharing a bottle of Orange Crush in ice cream parlor setting, 1950s-1960s, cond. 9.5+, 12" h, 10" w .......................... 38.50

Sign, reverse-painted glass mirror sign, orig frame, "Thank You, Please Pay When Served, Orange-Crush, 5¢," 1920s-1930s, cond. 8.25-8.5, 15" h, 23" w ......... 1,320.00

Sign, tin

"Ask for a Crush Carbonated Beverage, flavor sealed in the brown bottle," Crushy holding bottle on "C" of "Crush," orange ground, black trim at bottom, white trim overall, 1940s, cond. 9.5, 20" h, 28" w ........................................................... 440.00

"Take Home A Handipack, Orange-Crush, Carbonated Beverages, 6 Bottles for 25¢," shows 6-pack in cardboard carrier on white square at left, yellow/white text, orange ground, 1940, cond. 9.25+, 12" h, 28" w .......................................................... 1,430.00

Crushy and "Feel Fresh! Drink Orange Crush Carbonated Beverage," white over orange ground, rounded corners, 1943, cond. 9-9.25, 16" h, 12" w ..... 286.00

Round, "There's Only One Orange-Crush Carbonated Beverage," orange ground, 1939, cond. 8.25-8.5, 16" dia.......................................................... 187.00

Sign, tin, embossed

"Ask For...Orange-Crush Carbonated Beverage," 1940s, cond. 9, 12" h, 20" w ........................ 165.00

"Drink Orange-Crush Carbonated Beverage," amber bottle at left, Crushy upper-right, yellow/white text, white courtesy panel at top, orange ground, late 1930s-early 1940s, cond. 8, 3' h, 5' w .......... 330.00

"Drink Orange Crush Carbonated Beverage," bottle in white insert at left, orange ground, silver border with rounded corners, 1939, cond. 9-9.25, 14" h, 40" w ........................................................ 687.50

"Feel Fresh! Drink Orange-Crush Carbonated Beverage" Crushy beside bottle in white insert at left, orange ground, 1940s, cond. 8.5-8.75, 17" h, 48" w .......................................................... 385.00

"There's Only One Orange-Crush Carbonated Beverage," orange ground, silver trim, rounded corners, 1939, cond. 8.5+, 20" h, 28" w ..................... 242.00

"Thirsty, Crush that Thirst!" in black over orange logo, "Orange Crush, delicately carbonated" with white text, tilted bottle at right, light-blue ground, 1950s-1960s, cond. 8.75, 12" h, 30" w ................... 176.00

Sign, tin, embossed, diamond shape

"Drink Orange-Crush, Carbonated Beverage," Crushy at bottom, orange ground, yellow/white text, 1940s, cond. 8.5-8.75, 41" sq ................................. 632.50

"Drink Orange-Crush Carbonated Beverage, Natural Flavor, Natural Color," orange ground, silver edge, 1940s-1950s, cond. 8.75-9, 20" sq............... 242.00

"Drink Orange-Crush, Naturally - It Tastes Better!," orange ground, 1940s-1950s, cond. 9.25-9.5, 40" sq ......................................................... 253.00

"There's Only One Orange-Crush Carbonated Beverage," Crushy at bottom, orange ground, 1941, cond. 8.75-9, 16" sq .................................... 385.00

Sign, tin, flange

Bottlecap design, "Enjoy" on one side, "Sold Here" on the other, dark ground, 1950s, minor edge rust, slight paint loss, light scratches/wear, cond. 8-8.25, 14" h, 18" w ............................................... 220.00

Embossed, strip, rolled edges, "Ask for A Crush, Natural Flavor! Natural Color!," yellow/white text, orange ground, cond. G, 3-1/4" h, 26-1/2" w ............. 82.50

"Drink Orange-Crush Carbonated Beverage" in yellow/white on orange octagon, "Sold Here, Ice Cold" in white on black at side, late 1930s, cond. 8.5-9.5, 14" h, 18" w ................................................. 715.00

Embossed, diamond shape, "Feel Fresh! Drink Orange-Crush Carbonated Beverage," Crushy at bottom, orange ground, 1939, cond. 8.5, 16" sq ......................................................... 275.00

"There's Only One Orange-Crush Carbonated Beverage, Sold Here - Ice Cold," orange ground, black trim at bottom, 1942, cond. 8-8.5, 13" h, 18" w ............ 330.00

**Thermometer, dial, round, aluminum frame, "Crush," 12" d, $30.**

Sign, tin over cardboard, "Drink Orange-Crush," black text, orange ground, Canadian, circa 1930s, hanger missing, cond. 9.25, 5-1/4" h, 7-3/4" w ............. 440.00

Syrup dispenser

Glass, heavily embossed, orange form lettered "Orange-Crush," metal clamp and spigot, no lid, cond. 8.5, 7" h................................................ 522.50

Porcelain, orange form, "Ward's Orange Crush," 1920s, orig marked ball pump, cond. 7.................... 1,265.00

Thermometer

Pam style, bottle-cap logo, black ground, cond. 8.25 ............................................. 275.00

Pam style, "Drink (in banner) Orange Crush" and flowers on orange ground, 1950s, cond. 9.25-9.5......... 209.00

Tin, die-cut, bottle shape, 1950s, cond. 5, 29" h .............................................................. 66.00

Tin, rounded corners, "Orange Crush" white/orange bottle cap at top, light-blue ground, cond. G, 16" h, 6" w................................................................. 93.50

Tin, rounded top/bottom, ""Naturally - It Tastes Better! It's That Natural Fresh Fruit Flavor" and bottle on white ground, 1930s-1940s, cond. 8.75-9, 15" h, 6" w................................................................. 319.00

## Orange-Julep

Backbar bottle, clear, label under glass, "Drink Orange-Julep," white, gold border, 1910s-1920s, cond. 7.5 ............................................................. 143.00

Tray, litho tin, "Drink Orange-Julep" on top/bottom border, woman with glass in green swimsuit under parasol, cond. VG, 13-1/4" h, 10-1/4" w .......................... 165.00

## Orange Kist

Cooler, metal, embossed tin sides, "Drink Orange Kist, Enjoy Kist Beverages In All Flavors," 3 bottles at right, "Orange Kist" in white on black arch, orange ground, cabriole legs, scratches/dents/paint loss, 31" h, 31" w, 22" d.................................................................. 385.00

**Menu board, tin, "drink Orange Kist, Special Today," wear, scratches, 19" h, 13" w, $50.**

## Orcico Cigars

Tin, litho tin, "Orcico, 2 For 5¢," portrait of Indian, camp scene background, cond. 8, 5-5/8" x 6-1/8" x 4-1/8" ............................................................. 360.00

## Oriental Ethyl Gasoline

Gas globe, newer plastic body with 2 lenses, blue text, white ground, all cond. 9, 13-1/2" dia................ 198.00

## Ormo Coffee

Can, keywind, litho tin, taller version, shows cup of coffee, "Ormo" in white, "Coffee" in orange on black band, blue ground, Bursley & Company, cond. 8.5, 1 lb ........... 60.50

## Oronite Lighter Fluid

Container, metal, shaped like a visible gas pump, glass cylinder, "Oronite Lighter Fluid for pocket lighters," Standard Oil Co. of California, missing spout, cond. 7, 15-1/2" h, 5-1/2" dia .......................................... 528.00

## Ortlieb's

Sign, tin, self-framing, "Ortlieb's Lager Beer-Ale," woman with pilsner glass over black ground with yellow/white text, yellowing/scratches/paint chips, 14" dia.......... 110.00

## Oshkosh B'gosh

Sign, porcelain, "Oshkosh B'gosh Union Made Overalls," white on red ground, black border, 1930s-1940s, cond. 9.25-9.5, 10" h, 30" w........................................ 412.50

## Osterloh's Mixture

Can, litho tin, "Osterloh's Mixture, 100 Per Cent Fine," round medallion with dollar sign, red ground, cond. 8, 4-3/4" h, 6" w, 4" d ............................................ 220.00

## Oster

Clock, lightup, plastic, "Enjoy Oster Electric Scalp Massage with your favorite tonic, Make an appointment for your next haircut Now!," barber using massage on cli-

**Wagon, wood, original paint, metal spokes and wheels, hand brake, "Spring Coaster, OVB, Our Very Best," $750.**

**Shaker, plastic, mkd Ovaltine, shows Little Orphan Annie, 5" h, $65.**

ent, Oyster logo in oval, panel for price, red/cobalt text, cobalt border, white ground, scratches/crack/doesn't light, 16" sq ....................................................... 88.00

## O'Sullivan's

Door push, porcelain, "Ask For O'Sullivan's Heels of New Live Rubber," shows bottom of man's shoe, orange ground, cond. NM, 9" h, 4-1/4" w ................... 1,210.00

## Our Mutual Friends

Cigar box, wooden, litho paper labels, 3 blacks at fence, soiling/tears, cond. G, 2-1/4" h, 8-1/2" w, 5" d............. 187.00

## Our Nine

Cigar box, "Our Nine" over image of circa-1900 baseball game, inner label, cond. 8................................. 660.00

## Our Private Mixture

See OPM

## Our Very Best (See Photo)

Pocket mirror, celluloid, oval, "Cutlery & Tools" in ring, OVB logo in center, white ground, cond. NM, 1-3/4" h, 2-3/4" w .............................................................. 66.00

## Ovaltine (See Photo)

## Overholt Whiskey

Sign, tin, ornate wood frame, "It's Old Overholt" on metal plate, scratches/chips, 27-1/4" h, 36-1/2" w ...................................................... 1,100.00

## Overland

Sign, tin, rounded corners, blackboard motif, "We use an Overland Motor Car," white text, black ground, woodgrain/red-striped border, cond. 8, 9-3/4" h, 13-3/4" w.......................................................... 187.00

## Overland Route

Sign, porcelain, 2-sided, die-cut, shield-shape, "Bus Depot, The Overland Route," white/blue text, cobalt top of shield, cobalt diagonal stripe with "Overland" in white over red/white-striped ground, cond. 6, 27" h, 26" w .............................................................. 440.00

## Owens Bottle Machine Co.

Paperweight, glass, white bottom, milk bottle shape, "Owens Automatic Bottle Machine, Compliments of The Owens Bottle Machine Co., Toledo, Ohio," dated 1917, cond. NM, 4-1/8" h, 2-7/8" w................... 495.00

## Oxford Ties

Pocket mirror, celluloid, "The Hit of the Season, Our Oxford Ties, Hanan-Tiedemann Co., Plankinton House Block, Milwaukee, Wis.," woman in short red dress/black stockings/hat, cond. EXC, 2-3/4" h, 1-3/4" w.......................................................... 467.50

## Ox-Heart

Door push, porcelain, "We Sell Ox-Heart Brand Dutch Process Cocoa," cherry in circle, white text, green ground, cond. 8+, 6-1/2" h, 4" w ...................... 577.50

Pail, litho tin, "Long's Ox-Heart Peanut Butter," heart-shaped cherry on brown panel, yellow ground, cond. 8.25+, 1 lb....................................................... 121.00

Sign, cardboard, 2-sided, "We Sell Long's Ox-Heart Brand Chocolates, Name Ox-Heart On Every Piece," cherry/leaves in center, blue/red text, white ground, blue/white striped border, framed, creases/stains, 11-1/4" dia........................................................ 22.00

## Ozonite Detergent

Sign, paper, framed, "Ozonite, The Complete Detergent, Use It For Everything," red banner at top, "Wm. Waltke & Co., St. Louis, Ozonite" barrel on its side in red oval ring, gray panel on yellow ground, white text, tears/slight paper loss, 19-3/4" h, 22-3/4" w ............... 44.00

# P

## Pabst

**History:** In 1844, in Milwaukee, Wis., Philip Best and his sons founded what would ultimately become one of the largest breweries in the world. Originally named for themselves, the operation was run by two sons-in-law, Frederick Pabst and Emil Schandlein, beginning in 1866.

In 1889, the company's name was changed to Pabst, but the original trademark of a B in a circle (for Best) is still used today. The words "Blue Ribbon" were first used on the label in 1895.

Clock, molded plastic, "Pabst Blue Ribbon Beer," white text, blue/white ground, red border, hours in white, 17" dia, 5" d ............................................................... 88.00

Sign
Cardboard, die-cut, bottle shape, "Pabst Blue Ribbon Beer," diagonal label with small red logo, blue ribbon under logo on neck, easel back missing/neck repaired, cond. 7, 32" h, 9-1/2" w ................... 27.50
Sign, neon, glass with plastic protector, red "Pabst," border is blue ribbon, 19" h, 21" w.................. 88.00

## Packard Motor Car Co.

Clip, brass, embossed, shows "Packard" on radiator, floral edges, cond. 8.5, 3-1/4" h ............................ 363.00
Tin, "Packard Bulb Kit" on lid, "Safety First, Carry Spare Bulbs," on side, yellow panels, red ground, contains 6 bulbs, NOS, cond. 8+, 1-3/4" h, 4" w, 2-1/2" d ........................................................ 302.50

Mug, creamware, "Pabst, Milwaukee, 1847 1897," pictures Brigham Young, 4-1/4" h, $295.

Container, cardboard, litho paper, "Padlock Baking Powder, HP Coffee Co., St. Louis," unopened, 12 oz., $80.

## Packard Motor Oil

Can, litho tin, soldered seam, "Packard Special Motor Oil," red hexagon in blue circle, white over red ground, unopened, cond. 8.5+, 1 qt, 5-1/2" h, 4" dia...........................................................275.00

## Padlock Baking Powder (See Photo)

## Page Baby Talc

Tin, litho tin, woman in yellow dress holding infant in white, cond. 8.5, 4-1/2" h, 2-1/2" w, 1-3/8" d....................962.50

## Pal Ade

Sign, strip, litho tin, "Real Orangeade, Pasteurized Not Carbonated," yellow/white text, blue ground, "Drink Pal Ade" heart at left, 1949, cond. 9.25, 4" h, 18" w ................................................................. 93.50

## Palm Cigars

Sign, tin, embossed, "Palm cigars, That different Smoke! 3 for 5¢, De Nobili Cigar Company, Long Island City, N.Y.," 3-pack cigars over crossed palm leaves at left, green/blue/white text, white over cobalt ground, cond. VG, 6-1/2" h, 19-1/4" w ...................................... 88.00

## Palmolive (See Photo)

Sign, tin, "Drink PAL Ade," 12" h, 3" w, $60.

## Palmy Days Tobacco

Tin, vertical pocket, litho tin
"Palmy Days Tobacco, Every Puff a Pleasure, For Pipe and Cigarette, L. Warnick Brown & Co.," white triangle with red "Palmy Days" on green ground, cond. 7.5 ..................................................... 242.00
"Palmy Days Tobacco For Pipe And Cigarette, I. Warnick Brown & Co., Utica, N.Y.," gold text, green ground, cond. 8, 4-3/8" h, 3-3/8" w ............... 264.00

## Pal Tooth Powder

Tin, litho tin, "Police Your Teeth, Pal Tooth Powder," police officer motif, blue uniform, gold ground, cap is officer's head, cond. 8-, 5-1/8" h, 1-5/8" w, 1" d .................. 687.50

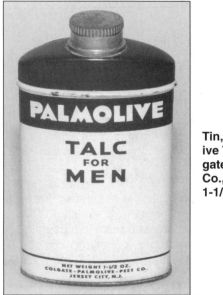

Tin, litho tin, "Palmolive Talc for Men, Colgate-Palmolive-Peet Co., Jersey City, N.J.," 1-1/2 oz, $7.50.

## Pan-Am

Blotter, "Keep pace with Pan-Am Gasoline" under seaplane, round "Pan-Am Gasoline, Motor Oils" logo at right, cond. G, 3" h, 6-1/4" w ........................... 176.00
Gas globe, 2 lenses, wide glass body, oval red/white/blue logo with torch, white ground, lens cond. 7, body cond. 7.5, 12-1/2" dia ................................................. 550.00
Sign, porcelain
2-sided, "Pan-Am Motor Oils" in black around edge, "Stand Up Under Fire" in white on red center with soldier carrying rifle, red border, cond. 7, 29-3/4" dia ................................................. 3,052.50
"Pan-Am Motor Oils," white text on bluish border, "Pan-Am" also in white circle in red ring, cond. 8.5, 15" dia ...................................................... 880.00

## Pappoose Whiskey

Sign, litho tin, "Pappoose Straight Whiskey," shows Indian woman with feathers in hair, restoration to outer frame area, replaced hanger, 14-3/8" h, 11-7/8" w ....................................................... 412.50

## Paramount Typewriter Ribbon

Tin, litho tin, round, red/black/white Deco design, Frye Manufacturing Co., Des Moines, Iowa, cond. 8 .............. 27.50

## Par Coffee

Can, keywind, litho tin, taller version, silhouette of cup on red semi-circle, yellow ground, black band at bottom, General Food Sales Company, cond. 8+, 1 lb ....................... 34.00

## Pare's Drops

Door push, celluloid over tin, "Blue Boy Brand Pare's Drops," shows boy with jar of product, blue/white text, blue over black ground, Dutch, cond. 7.5-8, 9-1/2" h, 3-1/4" w ......................................................... 440.00

## Par-Ex Beer

Tray, litho tin, entire tray is image of woman wearing straw hat, "Par-Ex" at top rim, cond. 8+, 12" dia .............. 302.50

## Parker

Display case
Glass on oak base, hinged wooden back door, "Parker Pens, Lucky Curve, Sell because they Excel," cond. 8+, 4-1/4" h, 17-1/2" w, 9-1/2" d .................... 880.00
Metal, "Parker Quink Contains Solv-X" in white on black panel at top, 7 colors listed at bottom, mkd "Parker Display No. 950," with 28 2-oz bottles in orig boxes, cond. EXC, 14" h, 18" w, 5-1/4" d ...................... 176.00

## Parke's Newport Coffee

Tin, litho tin, snap top, large medallion shows sprawling factory, cond. 8-8.5, 1 lb, 6" h ........................... 179.00

## Parrot and Monkey Baking Powder

Can, litho tin, round, "Parrot and Monkey Baking Powder," monkeys in tree, white text, red ground, unopened, cond. 8.25, 8 oz ................................ 77.00

# Parry Mfg. Co. (See Photo)

## Pastime Tobacco

Box, litho tin, "Pastime Plug Tobacco, The Essence of Excellence," exterior shows hunting scene in red/black, under lid shows jockey/horse jumping fence, circa 1890s, cond. 7.5+, 4" h, 13" w, 12-1/2" d...........................357.50

## Pat Hand

Tin, vertical pocket, litho tin
"Pat Hand, Cube Cut Granules, Price Five Cents, Globe Tobacco Co., Detroit, Mich.," flesh-colored hand on red ground, cond. 8 ........................147.00
"Pat Hand, Cube Cut Granules, Price Five Cents, Globe Tobacco Co., Detroit, Mich.," red hand on red ground, cond. 7.5-8 ........................99.00

## Patterson Seal

Lunchbox, litho tin, seal emblem, basketweave motif, cond. 8.5 ............................................................38.50

## Paul Jones Tobacco

Tin, vertical pocket, litho tin
Blue version, central design of Paul Jones in blue jacket, blue ground, cond. 7.5 .....................935.00
Red version, "Paul Jones Clean Cut Tobacco," oval image of Paul Jones, white text on red ground, cond. 7.5...................................................1,959.00

## Paul Jones Whiskey

Sign, wood, "Paul Jones & Co., Louisville, Ky.," titled "The Temptation of St. Anthony," outdoor scene of black family, mother with watermelon, father with whiskey, boy in middle, cond. 8, 13-7/8" h, 20" w ...........................962.50

## Paxton & Gallagher Co.

Bin, painted and stenciled tin, "Paxton & Gallagher Co.

Tin, pocket, litho tin, "Peachey Double Cut Tobacco, Scotten Dillon Co., Detroit," 4-5/8" h, $221.

Gas Roasted Coffee," roll-up door, red/gold text and design on black ground, scuffs/rust-through pitting underneath and on back side, 19" h, 18-1/2" w, 16-1/2" d ......................................................1,072.50

## Paymaster Cigars

Can, litho tin, "Paymaster Cigar, 2 for 5¢," shows paymaster with cigars, cond. 7.5+, 5" h, 5-1/8" dia..................242.00

## Peachey

Box, store display, cardboard, full, "Peachey Ribbon Cut Scrap Chewing Tobacco," shows peach/leaves, red text on yellow ground, with 12 full packs of product, cond. 8.5-9, 8-1/2" x 5-1/2" x 5" ........................231.00

Thermometer, round, brass frame, glass cover, "Parry M'F'G Co. High Grade Buggies, Indianapolis, Ind.," 9-1/4" d, $105.

Tin, litho tin, "Peacock Brand Certified Food Colors, Wm. J. Stange Co.," unopened, wear/rust, 6" h, 7" sq, $10.

## Peacock Food Colors (See Photo)

## Peacocks Condoms

Tin, litho tin, "Dean's Peacocks, Reservoir Ends, Tested and Rolled," color image of peacock, "To Open Press Here" at top, Dean Rubber Co., cond. NM, 1/4" h, 2-1/8" w, 1-5/8" d.............................................. 60.50

## Peak Frean & Co.

Tin, litho tin, biscuit, sample, lettered "With Compliments of ...," woman with pottery jar on her head, cond. 8+, 3-3/8" x 1-3/4" x 1-1/4" ....................................... 49.50

## Pearl Beer

Clock, neon, octagonal, "Pearl Lager Beer," white text, red oval with "XXX" in circle, black numbers, white ground, red border, lights blue, paint chips/scuffs, 18-3/8" h, 18-3/8" w.............................................. 385.00

## Pedro

Lunch box, litho tin, "Pedro Cut Plug Smoking Tobacco," product in round medallion set in leaves and banner, corncob/peace pipes on sides, red/black text, yellow ground, cond. 8.5 ............................................... 121.00

Sign, cardboard, complete set of 6, "Smoke Pedro Cut Plug," cartoon scenes of blacks in barnyard with cow, circa 1890, 9" h, 10-3/4" w, set ...................... 1,122.00

## Peg Top Cigars

Sign, litho tin, embossed, oval, "The Old Reliable, Peg Top 5¢ For Sale Here," cigar with "Peg Top" in white, yellow ground, darker zig-zag border, cond. 8+, 5-3/4" h, 8-3/8" w ................................................................ 133.00

## Pemco

Gas globe, newer plastic body with 2 glass lenses
   "Pemco Regular Gasoline," red text top/bottom, blue text in center panel, white ground, lens cond. 9/8.5, body cond. 8, 13-1/2" dia............................... 231.00
   "Pemco Regular Gasoline" on 1 lens, "Pemco Premium Gasoline" on other lens, red text top/bottom, blue text in center panel, white ground, lens cond. 9, body cond. 8, 13-1/2" dia........................... 231.00

## Pe-Ne-To

Tray, litho tin, "Pe-Ne-To Peerless Nerve Soda, Serve Cold, Peerless Soda Works, Woonsocket, R.I.," tilted bottle in center, blue ground, red trim, circa, 1905, cond. 9.25-9.5+, 12" dia..................................... 632.50

## Penfold

Display, composition, figural smiling man in golf attire and smoking cigar, "He Played A Penfold" on base, restoration to oversized golf cap, face possibly repainted, 20-1/2" h................................................................ 495.00

## Peninsular Stove Co.

Pocket mirror, oval, "Home of Peninsular, Stoves, Ranges Furnaces, The Peninsular Stove Co., Detroit, Chicago

Buffalo," shows factory/logo, cond. 8.75 .................. 77.00

## Penn-Bee Motor Oil

Can, litho tin, "Pure Pennsylvania Penn-Bee 'Perfection Lubrication' Motor Oil," 2 bees on hive, yellow ground, Thermoil Lubricants Corp, Elk City, OK, qt, 5-1/2" h, 4" dia.................................................................. 148.50

## Penn-Drake Motor Oil

Chalkboard, tin, "Your Equipment Deserves The Best, Always Use Penn-Drake Oils Greases Gear Lubricants, Products of Pennsylvania Refining Company," well logo at left, white/black text, red ground over blackboard, cond. 7, 27-1/2" h, 19-3/8" w.............................. 143.00

Sign, tin, embossed, "Use Penn-Drake Motor Oil," well logo at left, white/red text, red border, black ground, cond. 7, 9-1/2" h, 28" w.................................... 231.00

## Penn-Harris (See Photo)

## Penn Leader Motor Oil

Can, tin, "Penn Leader 100% Pure Superior Quality Pennsylvania Motor Oil" in red/black text under 3 horses/chariot, shield design on white triangle on red ground, Pittsburgh-Penn Oil Co., Pittsburgh, cond. 8/7+, 2 gal, 11-1/2" h, 8-1/2" w, 5-1/2" d ............. 110.00

## Penn-O-Lene

Sign, porcelain, 2-sided, oval, "Penn-O-Lene Straight Gas," bird logo in center, black design/border, orange ground, cond. 7, 36" h, 48" w......................... 1,815.00

Thermometer, celluloid, rounded top/bottom, oval "Penn-O-Lene Motor Oils" black/gold logo over "Superblend Straight Gas, The Island Export Co., Baltimore, Md." in gold/black on white, gold/black border, no hanging hook, cond. EXC, 6-1/2" h, 2" w....................... 137.50

## Penn-Rad

Oil can, tin, embossed, "Penn-Rad 100% Pure Pennsyl-

Tin, litho tin, "Penn-Harris Brand Allspice, Evans-Burtnett Co., Harrisburg, Pa.," 1-1/2 oz, $15.

vania Motor Oil," spout perpendicular to body, handled, cond. 8+, 11" h, 5" dia ............................... 22.00

## Penns Tobacco

Pack, paper, "Penns Long Cut Smoking and Chewing Tobacco," portrait of general on 1 side, muskets/drum/saber/bedroll on other, black on white ground, full, cond. 8.5 ............................................................ 27.50

## Pennsylvania Railroad

Calendar, paper, 1937, new/old trains at station, red ground, metal strips top/bottom, Dec. sheet only, cond. 8, 28-1/2" sq ........................................................ 77.00

## Pennsylvania Vacuum Cup

Sign, porcelain, 2-sided, "Pennsylvania Vacuum Cup, 6000 Mile Tires," white text under tire/tire print, cond. 7+, 22" h, 16" w ................................................ 467.50

## Penny Post Cut Plug

Lunch box, brass clasp, red/black/white design, Strater Brothers Tobacco Co. Branch, Burley Tobacco Co., Louisville, Ky., one edge rough, rest is cond. 8-8.5 ................................................................ 221.00

## Pennzoil

**Reference:** Scott Benjamin and Wayne Henderson, *Gas Globes: Pennzoil to Union and Affiliates*, Schiffer Publishing, 1999

Bottle, glass, fired-on label, "Pennzoil Outboard Motor Oil," red bell logo, black text, red text block, yellow ground, cond. VG, qt, 8" h, 3-1/2" dia ................. 22.00
Can, litho tin
   "United Air Lines Uses Pennzoil Exclusively" at bottom, shows 2-prop airplane, owls by oval "Pennzoil Self Lubrication" logo with red bell, black images on yellow ground, 1 qt, full, cond. 8, 5-1/2" h, 4" dia ........ 137.50
   Same as above, opened from bottom, 5 qt, cond. 8, ........................................................ 137.50
Chalkboard, tin, "Ask for...Pennzoil, America's Favorite Motor Oil," oval yellow logo, black/red text, white ground over chalkboard, cond. 8, 24" h, 17-1/2" w ............ 137.50
Display, wooden base, plastic can-shaped shade over bulb, "Pennzoil Saves Money Motor Oil," shade rotates from heat of bulb, orig box, cond. 9, 8-1/2" h ............................................................ 187.00
Sign
   Hardboard, oval, "Safety System, Pennzoil Lubrication," red bell in center, black text, orange ground, red/black border, circa World War II, cond. 7, 10" h, 16-1/2" w ...................................................... 49.50
   Painted metal, "Pennzoil, Sound Your Z," black over yellow over black ground, large red "Z," oval "Sound Your Z, Pennzoil" logo at bottom, cond. 7, 60" h, 12" w .............................................................. 93.50
   Painted metal, flange, "Pennzoil Courtesy Cards honored here," black text (some with red shadows) on yellow ground, red stripe top/bottom, cond. 7, 14" h, 18" w .............................................................. 60.50

Can, metal, "The Pep Boys Lighter Fluid," 1934, cond. 8, 5" h, $132. (Photo courtesy of Collectors Auction Services)

Tin, "Welcome to our service department, ask for Pennzoil with Z-7," oval logo at bottom, red/blue/white text, white panel on blue ground, cond. 8, 18" h, 24" w .............................................................. 66.00

## Pensupreme Ice Cream

Sign, porcelain, die-cut, curved bottom, "Pensupreme Ice Cream," round image of Ben Franklin at bottom, red/white text, white over green ground, fading/scratches/edge chips, 13" h, 24" w ................................... 330.00

## Pep Boys

Bank, replica of 1923 Chevy delivery van, "1921-1966 45 Years" on one side, cond. 8.5, 3-1/2" h, 6-3/4" l .............................................................. 11.00
Can, tin, "Put Pep In Your Lighter, The Pep Boys Lighter Fluid," 1934, Manny/Moe/Jack marching in red jackets with rifles over their shoulders, white ground, black band at bottom, cond. 8/7, 5-1/4" h, 2-1/2" dia ........................................................ 203.50
Playing cards, Pinochle deck, complete, Pep Boy images on face cards, orig red box, cond. EXC .............. 71.50

## Pepsi-Cola

**History:** The name Pepsi-Cola written in script was registered as a trademark in 1903, although druggist Caleb Davis Bradham of New Bern, N.C., claimed it had been used as early as 1898 for the drink that he invented. A simplified version of the logo was registered in 1906, and the addition of a hexagonal frame and the words "A Sparkling Beverage" was registered in 1937. Although the name Pepsi was used as early as 1911, the block-lettered logo wasn't actually trademarked until 1966.

**References:** James C. Ayers, *Pepsi-Cola Bottles Collectors Guide*, self-published (P.O. Box 1377, Mt. Airy, NC 27030),1995; Everette and Mary Lloyd, *Pepsi-*

*Cola Collectibles*, Schiffer Publishing, 1993; Bill Vehling and Michael Hunt, *Pepsi-Cola Collectibles*, *Vol. 1*, 1990 (1993 value update), *Vol. 2*, 1990 (1992 value update), *Vol. 3*, 1993 (1995 value update), L-W Book Sales

**Collector's Clubs:** Ozark Mountain Pepsi Collectors Club, 9101 Columbus Ave. S., Bloomington, MN 55420; Pepsi-Cola Collectors Club, P.O. Box 817, Claremont, CA 91711

Advertisement, litho on cardboard in metal frame, "Pepsi ... it's got a lot to give," shows smiling couple with bottle of Pepsi, scratches/warping/water stain, 25-1/2" h, 37-1/4" w ............ 121.00

Blotter, "Pepsi and Pete, The Pepsi-Cola Cops," Pepsi bottle with 2 cartoon characters, 1930s, cond. 8.75-9 .................. 60.50

Bottle opener, metal, bottle shape, "America's Biggest Nickel's Worth," rust, 2 3/4" l ............... 44.00

Carrier, 6-pack, wooden, "Buy Pepsi-Cola," red/blue, 1930s-1940s, cond. 8-8.5 ................... 93.50

Cash register topper, cardboard, embossed, die-cut, "Pepsi-Cola" in red on white ground, "Purity.../...In The Big, Big Bottle" in white on blue upper/lower panel, 1940s, orig shipping box, NOS, cond. 9.5 ........ 770.00

Clock

    Bottlecap shape/design, plastic, "Drink Pepsi-Cola, Ice Cold," white ground, cond. 7.75-8, 11" dia ......... 165.00

    Rectangular, plastic face, metal case, "Drink Pepsi" beside angled bottlecap logo at top, square clock face,

**Cooler, salesman sample, heavy cast-aluminum, oval "Pepsi-Cola" logo on light-blue ground, 1940s, restored to cond. 9-9.5, 11-1/2" h, 12" w, 7" d, $2,970. (Photo courtesy of Gary Metz, Muddy River Trading Co.)**

**Matchbook, "Pepsi-Cola, Bigger Drink, Better Taste, 5¢," NOS, mint, $5.**

    cracks/chip, 1950s, cond. 6, 19" h, 14" w ......... 275.00

Clock, lightup, glass face/cover, fiberboard case

    "Drink Pepsi-Cola" bottlecap, nearly fills entire face, yellow ground, 1950s, cond. 9.25 ................. 522.50

    "Pepsi-Cola" round script logo, nearly fills entire face, white ground, 1940s, cond. 8-8.5 ................. 357.50

    Same design as above but smaller logo/larger numbers, cond. 8.5+............................................. 357.50

Clock, lightup, glass face/cover, metal case, "say Pepsi please" in black at top, "Pepsi-Cola" over bottlecap at bottom in panel with yellow border, white face, numbers on edge of metal case, cond. VG, 16" sq ......................................................... 209.00

Clock, lightup, double bubble

    "Be sociable, Have A Pepsi" in upper-left, angled bottlecap logo in lower-right, yellow ground, black numbers in white border, 1950s, cond. 8-8.5 ............... 1,870.00

    "say Pepsi, please" at top-center, "Pepsi-Cola" in black across bottlecap at bottom-center, yellow ground, black numbers in white border, 1950s, cond. 8.5-9............................................... 1,265.00

    "say Pepsi, please" in upper-left, angled bottlecap logo in lower-right, yellow ground, black numbers in white border, 1950s, cond. 8.5-9 ............... 1,100.00

    "say Pepsi, please" in upper-left on white V-shaped panel, angled bottlecap logo in lower-right on yellow/white striped ground, black numbers in white border, 1950s, cond. 9.25-9.5, 15" dia ..................... 1,980.00

    "think young - Say 'Pepsi, please!'," centered over angled bottlecap, yellow ground, white border, cond. 8.5-9................................................... 907.50

Cooler

    Picnic cooler, metal, "Drink Pepsi-Cola" in white, blue ground, cond. VG, 18-1/2" h, 18" w, 13" d ........... 88.00

    Salesman sample, cast aluminum, 1940s, cond. 7.5-7.75, 11-1/2" h, 12" w, 7-1/2" d .................. 2,860.00

Dispenser, barrel, wood, metal staves, painted red/blue,

2 attached signs read "Pepsi" over bottlecap, 2 taps, stainless interior, stains/rust spotting inside, 30" h, 21-1/2" dia .......... 456.50

Display, cardboard, "Pepsi-Cola, Double Size, Bracing-, Refreshing-, 5¢, Ice Cold, Famous for over 30 years," blue/white text, red ground, NOS, cond. 9.75, 13-1/2" h, 6-1/2" w .......... 209.00

Door push, tin, 1930s, "Drink Pepsi-Cola, 5¢, Worth Twice Its Price," detailed image of bottle with "Pepsi-Cola, Refreshing, Healthful" label, raised border, cond. 9.25+, 13-1/2" h, 3-1/2" w .......... 1,155.00

Fan pull, heavy cardboard, die-cut, Pepsi policeman carrying 6-pack of product, "Pepsi-Cola, Bigger, Better" on carrier, circa 1940, cond. 9.5+, 7-1/2" h, 4" w .......... 1,155.00

Festoon, cardboard, die-cut, 7 pieces, "Buy Pepsi Cola Today, Bottle Tall, Liked By All, Hey Hey, Clear the Way, Cost Small," Pepsi and Pete, 6-pack with 2 figures, other 6 pieces with individuals, 1930s, cond. 8.5-9.25, 8' l .......... 1,540.00

Festoon component, die-cut, Pepsi policeman in blue on red circle, "Drink Pepsi-Cola Today," in speech balloon, 1940s, cond. 8.5-9.5 .......... 198.00

Flag, fabric, red "Pepsi-Cola" on white band, blue bands at top/bottom, 1930s-1940s, soiling/fabric loss, cond. 6.5-7, 42" h, 70" w .......... 99.00

Glass, clear with syrup line, 1930s-40s, two-color decor, cond. 9, 10 oz .......... 13.00

Kickplate, porcelain
"Enjoy a Pepsi" in white panel beside angled bottlecap, yellow ground, circa 1920s, cond. 8.5+, 10" h, 30" w .......... 660.00
"More Bounce To The Ounce," bottle breaking through background by "Pepsi-Cola" bottle cap, blue ground, 1940s, cond. 9.5-9.75+, 14" h, 36" w .......... 5,720.00

Menu sign, "Have a Pepsi" beside bottlecap, "Pepsi-Cola, the Light Refreshment" at bottom, black chalkboard area, yellow/white striped ground, 1950s, cond. 6.5-7, 30" h, 20" w .......... 71.50

Mirror/thermometer combination, "Drink Pepsi-Cola, Bigger And Better" on white octagon at top, "Refreshing, Healthful" on 2 vertical panels at sides, tube to the right of woman at bottom, circa 1938, orig frame/box, NOS, cond. 8+, 18" h, 8" w .......... 3,190.00

Printer's proofs, paper
1908-1909, for serving tray, shows woman in green dress and hat, framed under glass, cond. 8.5-9, 17" h, 13-3/4" w .......... 1,155.00
1967 tray, 22 pgs, cond. 7.5, 23" h, 29" w .......... 11.00
Bottle over valley, bottle cap at right, 7 pgs, cond. 7, 28" h, 32" w .......... 110.00
Couple in surf on rocks, bottle cap with Oriental writing in upper right, cond. 9.5, 30" h, 23" w .......... 275.00
Couple on rocks in surf, bottle cap in upper right, 8 pgs, cond. 7.5, 29" h, 22" w .......... 88.00
Girl at rail with camera, bottle cap at right, cond. 9.25, 20" h, 28" w .......... 385.00
Girl in dotted dress with table of food, bottle cap at right, 9 pgs, cond. 8, 34" h, 24" w .......... 33.00
Girl in green skirt at table with chilling bottles, bottle cap at right, 11 pgs, cond. 7.5, 29" h, 22" w .......... 33.00
Girl in red holding bottle, bottle cap/foreign language at top, cond. 9.25, 28" h, 20" w .......... 38.50
Girl in striped sleeveless dress at table, bottle cap at right, 10 pgs, cond. 7.5, 29" h, 22" w .......... 44.00
Girl under tree on mountain top, 9 pgs, cond. 9, 22" h, 29" w .......... 55.00
Girl under tree on mountain top, bottle cap with foreign language/bottle at right, cond. 9.25, 21" h, 28" w .......... 82.50
Girl with camera at rail, bottle cap at right, 14 pgs, some with different language mockups, cond. 7-8, 22" h, 29" w .......... 154.00
Sailboat, bottle cap/bottle at right, 1 pg, cond. 8.5, 29" h, 22" w .......... 22.00
Stream, bottle cap/bottle at right, 29 pgs, cond. 8, 29" h, 22" w .......... 55.00
Stream, bottle cap with foreign language/bottle at right, cond. 9.25, 28" h, 20" w .......... 11.00

Salt/pepper shaker, plastic, 1-pc, "The Light Refreshment" under bottlecap logo, 1950s, orig. box, cond. 9+ .......... 66.00

Screen door brace, tin, embossed, "Drink Pepsi-Cola, Ice Cold" bottlecap over "Take Home Six Bottles," white text, red/white/blue ribbon, blue ground, 1940s, cond. 8.75, 10" h, 10" w .......... 577.50

Sign, aluminum, rounded corners, "tops..." in black on lower white panel, line of "Pepsi-Cola" bottlecaps disappearing into the horizon, landscape ground of blue skies/white clouds over yellow plain, 1940s, 14" h, 36" w .......... 990.00

Sign, cardboard, flange, "Drink Pepsi-Cola, Ice Cold" over dangling bottle with oval label, Canadian, tape repair holding string on, cond. 9.25, 16" h, 9" w .......... 357.50

Sign, celluloid, button-type, "Ice Cold Pepsi-Cola Sold Here," red name, white text, blue/white/blue ground, 1940s, orig string hanger, cond. 8.25-8.5+, 9" dia .......... 330.00

Sign, celluloid over metal and cardboard, easel-back, "Drink Pepsi-Cola" bottlecap logo, edge stains, 9" dia .......... 110.00

Sign, lighted, plastic, rolling-motion light, "Pepsi" rectangular logo, 1972, 17" h, 24" w .......... 385.00

Sign, Masonite
"Drink Pepsi-Cola" on bottlecap on yellow ground, circular with flat bottom, 1954, cond. 8.25-8.5, 4' h, 5' w .......... 192.50

Sign, porcelain, "Enjoy Pepsi-Cola, 5¢, Hits The Spot," red name, white text/musical notes on blue ground, chips, 32" h, 56" w .......... 770.00

Sign, tin
2-sided, rounded corners, "Take Home A Carton, 12 Full Glasses, Pepsi-Cola, Finer Flavor - Better Value," name in red, text in white, red/white/blue ground, 1940s, cond. 8.5/7.75, 10" h, 15" w .......... 440.00
"Drink Pepsi-Cola" bottle cap at top under tilted embossed-style bottle with oval label, 1950s, cond. 9.25-9.5, 48" h, 18" w .......... 522.50
"Have a Pepsi" at top over bottle with white oval label/

swirled design, angled bottlecap lower-right, yellow ground, 1960s, cond. 9.5-9.75, 48" h, 18" w .............................................................. 247.50

"say 'Pepsi, please,'" at bottle under bottle with white oval label/swirled design beside angled bottlecap, yellow ground, 1960s, cond. 8.75, 48" h, 18" w ........... 176.00

Sign, tin, die-cut

Bottlecap shape, "Pepsi-Cola," crazing, 14" dia ..... 140.00

Bottlecap shape over rectangular courtesy panel, "Drink Pepsi-Cola, Ice Cold," 1940s, cond. 8.25, 50" h, 42" w .................................................................... 385.00

Bottle shape, similar to above design, small 5¢ in circle, arrow pointing to octagonal label on smooth bottle, 1936, cond. 8.25-8.5, 29" h ................. 577.50

Bottle shape, small 5¢ in circle, arrow pointing to octagonal label on smooth bottle, 1936, cond. 8.75, 45" h ............................................................... 1,210.00

Bottle shape, large 5¢ in circle, no arrow, octagonal label on embossed-style bottle, 1940s, cond. 7.25-7.5, 45" h ........................................................ 687.50

Bottle shape, oval label, embossed-style bottle, 1940s, cond. 9.25+, 45" h ............................. 962.50

Curb sign, boy holding blank octagonal sign over his head, "Pepsi" button on his yellow/white striped shirt, blue shorts, gym shoes, round metal base, touchups, cond. VG, 50-1/2" h, base 24" dia .................... 495.00

Sign, tin, embossed

Bottlecap shape, "Drink Pepsi-Cola," fading/rust, 30" dia ..................................................................... 275.00

"Curb Service, Pepsi Cola, Ice Cold, Bigger-Better, 5¢," red name, white text, price in red circle, blue/white/blue ground, circa 1939, cond. 8.25-8.5+, 28" h, 20" w .................................................................... 577.50

"Drink Pepsi-Cola 5¢, America's Biggest Nickel's Worth," yellowing/scratches, 12" h, 40" w ...................... 660.00

"Drink Pepsi-Cola, Delicious Delightful," white name with blue text in tails of letters, blue ground, red border, circa 1910-1915, cond. 9.25+, 3-1/2" h, 10" w ...................................................................... 522.50

"Have a Pepsi," black text, "Pepsi-Cola" bottlecap at right, yellow ground, cond. 9.25, 12" h, 31" w ...................................................................... 187.00

Sign, tin over cardboard, beveled, "say, 'Pepsi, please'," black text, swirled bottle with oval logo at right, angled bottlecap on white square bottom-center, yellow ground, cond. VG, 9" h, 11" w ........................... 99.00

Sign, light-up, metal and embossed plastic, "The Light refreshment," woman in pink blouse with glass beside Pepsi logo, yellow ground, unused, orig box, circa 1950s, cond. 8.5+, 9" h, 19" w, 6-1/2" d ............ 797.50

Thermometer, Pam style

"Drink Pepsi-Cola, Ice Cold," red name, white letters, red/white/blue ground, numbers in white border, cond. 9.5, 12" dia ......................................... 1,072.50

"Pepsi-Cola" rectangular logo at bottom, white ground, cond. 8.75-9, 18" dia ...................................... 137.50

Thermometer, tin

Straw Girl, "Weather Cold or Weather Hot, Pepsi-Cola Hits This Spot," woman drinking from bottle, straw is thermometer tube, 1941, cond. 8.25-8.5, 27" h, 7" w ................................................................... 1,017.50

"Buy Pepsi-Cola, Big, Big Bottle, Pepsi-Cola ...Hits The Spot Weather It's Cold Or Weather It's Hot!," NOS, orig box cond. 6-7, thermometer cond. 9.5, 27" h, 7" w ...................................................... 1,595.00

Thermometer, tin, rounded corners

"Have a Pepsi" at top, bottle cap/"The Light refreshment" at bottom, yellow with V-shaped white area, 1950s, cond. 8, 27" h .................................... 231.00

"Have a Pepsi" at top on white V-shaped panel, angled bottle cap over "The Light refreshment" at bottom, yellow ground, 1950s, cond. 8, 27" h .......... 231.00

"The Light refreshment" at bottom, bottle cap at top, yellow ground, 1950s, cond. 8.5, 27" h, 7" w ......... 198.00

Thermometer, tin, rounded top/bottom

"Pepsi-Cola" bottlecap logo at top, "More Bounce To The Ounce" at bottle with red/white/blue ribbon, white ground, cond. VG, 27" h, 8" w ............. 275.00

Thermometer, tin, square corners

"Have a Pepsi" at top, bottle cap at bottom, yellow ground, 1960s, cond. 8.5, 27" h .................... 99.00

"Pepsi" rectangular logo at top/bottom, white ground, cond. EXC, 28" h, 7" w .................................... 49.50

"say 'Pepsi, please'," at top, "Pepsi" over bottlecap on lower white panel, thermometer's numbers in blue circles, yellow ground, cond. VG, 28" h, 7-1/4" w ....................................................... 99.00

Tip Tray, tin

1909, woman in green dress holding glass by table with bottle, cond. 9-9.25+ ........................... 1,320.00

## Pepsi, Diet

Thermometer, outdoor, dial-type, rectangular metal frame, plastic cover, 1960s-1970s, cond. 7.5-8, 32" h, 46" w, 3" d ...................................................... 99.00

## Pepto-Bismol

Display, cardboard, die-cut, "Pepto-Bismol For Upset Stomach," boy with green apple/cores sitting with cocker spaniel, bottle lower-left, white/black text, red banner over white ground, creases/edge wear, 31-1/2" h, 32" w ...................................................... 121.00

## Peretti's Cuban Mixture

Tin, vertical pocket, paper label, central crest, black text/upper-lower stripe, yellow ground, cond. 8+, 4" h, 3-3/8" w ...................................................... 112.00

## Perfect Circle

Sign, litho tin

Embossed, "Don't Drive an Oil Hog, Install Perfect Circle, X-90 Piston Rings, Piston Expanders," cartoon image of pig guzzling oil on car's hood at service station, 3 men watching, cond. 7.5+, 25-1/4" h, 19" w ...................................................... 660.00

"Look out, oil hog! I've got X-90 piston rings now, Perfect Circle Piston Rings, Piston Expanders," cartoon scene of pig and early auto, scuff, dents, cond. 7.5-8, 25-1/2" h, 19" w ...................................... 1,100.00

## Perfection Heater Co.

Pocket mirror, celluloid, round, "Syracuse Heater Co.,

Syracuse, N.Y., Perfection Fireless Cooker," shows cooker, cond. EXC, 2-1/4" dia ............................ 48.50

## Perfection Motor Oil

Can, litho tin, "Crew Levick Perfection Motor Oil, Lubricates Longer, Crew Levick Co., Philadelphia," black diamond at top, black/white text, red ground, cond. 7, gal, 9-3/4" h, 9" w, 3" d ........................................ 55.00

## Perfection Tires

Sign, flange, painted metal, die-cut, "Perfection Asbestos Protected Tires, Eliminates Tread Separation," black/red/white text, yellow ground, tire loops around outer edge, Perfection Tire Rubber Co., Ft. Madison, IA, cond. 7/6, 23-1/2" h, 16-1/8" w ...................... 1,221.00

## Perrine Batteries

Sign, tin, embossed, "Perrine Polar Bear Batteries," polar bear on ice, white text in black panel, red border, white ground, cond. 8, 14" h, 19-1/2" w ...................... 319.00

## Pet

Sign, metal, heavy gauge, "Pet, Dairy Division," 1963, cond. 9.75, oblong, 16" h, 20" w ........................ 121.00
Sign, tin
    Heavily convexed, "Pet Homogenized Milk," white text, blue ground, red border, 2-tier flat border frame with rounded corners, 1961, cond. 9-9.25, 2-1/2' h, 3' w .............................................................. 176.00
    Heavily convexed, "Pet Ice Cream," white text, blue ground, red border, 2-tier flat border frame with rounded corners, 1961, cond. 9-9.25, 2-1/2' h, 3' w .............................................................. 176.00
    "Pet Ice Cream," white text, blue ground, red border, 1959, cond. 8.75+, 42" h, 54" w .................... 121.00

## Peter Pan Ice Cream

Sign, tin, embossed, "Demand Peter Pan Ice Cream, Take Home a Pint," Peter Pan at left, red text, silver/white ground, fading/scratches/chips, new frame, 32" h, 23-1/2" w ............................................................. 385.00

## Peters Cartridge Co.

Box, shell box, 2-pc, paper label on cardboard, "Peters Target Paper Shot Shells, Loaded With Bulk Smokeless Powder," grouse in flight lower-right, red text, white panel, brown ground, slight edge wear/fading, 2-1/2" h, 4-1/4" sq ............................................... 77.00
Calendar, 1915, paper, hunting dogs in field, orig mailing tube, cond. 8+, 20-1/4" h, 15" w ........................ 825.00
Crate, wood, "Steel Where Steel Belongs, Small Arms Ammunition, The Peters Cartridge Co., Cincinnati, O. U.S.A., Loaded Paper Shells, Metallic Ammunition, Primers, Gun Wads," red/black text, dovetailed, small piece missing, 9-1/8" h, 14-1/2" w, 9-1/2" d ........................ 71.50
Sign, cardboard, 2-sided, "Peters Ammunition" in red/white at top, "Peters Packs the Power" at bottom, bull's-eye design shows sporting rifle cartridges/revolver and pistol cartridges/rim fire cartridges in actual size, prod-

Sign, countertop, reverse-painted glass, metal frame, "Peters Shoes, Peters Shoe Co.'s Diamond Brand, St. Louis," rusted frame, 5" h, 12" w, $110.

uct box in center, ballistic chart on back, separating at edges, cond. EXC, 20-1/8" h, 13" w ..................... 66.00

## Peterson's Rose Butter

Sign, litho cardboard, standup, "We're Happy to Recommend Peterson's Rose and Country Roll Style Butter and we know You'll Like It, Too!," 2 boxes of product at left, red/yellow text, yellow over black ground, Galva Creamery Co., cond. VG, 13" h, 20-1/4" w ......... 44.00

## Peters Shoes

**History:** Around 1839, Claflin-Allen Shoe Company, based in St. Louis, was in the business of manufacturing shoes and boots for individuals heading west with the wagon trains. The company's successor, Peters Shoe Company, obtained a copyright in 1907 for the name Weather-Bird, which was used for their line of children's shoes.

Thermometer, porcelain, rounded top/bottom, "Peters Weatherbird, Peters Diamond Brand Shoes, Solid Weather Footwear," bird figure at top, cond. 8+, 27" h, 7" w ................................................................. 687.50

## Pevely Dairy Co. (See Photo)

## Pex

Sign, painted metal, embossed, die-cut, "I Get the Milk-

Beater jar, yellowware, "Pevely Dairy Co." black ink stamp, 2 raised brown stripes, interior glaze flaking, 4-3/8" h, 4-3/4" dia, $80.

Bank Boost From Pex," red/black text on yellow chicken, "Kraft" logo on green base, cond. VG, 19-1/2" h, 14-1/4" w ............................................................... 121.00

## Phillies

Sign, tin, embossed, rolled edge, "Phillies, America's No. 1 cigar," white text on red oval, yellow ground, cigar upper-left, good, 13" h, 20-1/4" l ......................... 71.50

## Phillip Morris

Display, cardboard, standup, die-cut, "No Cigarette Hangover Means More Smoking Pleasure, Call for Phillip Morris" at base, bellhop with oversized pack, gloved hand to mouth, white/red text, cond. G, 44" h, 16-1/2" w .......................................................... 187.00

Sign
Cardboard, die-cut, "Call for Phillip Morris," shows bellhop with product, circa 1940s-1950s, cond. 8+, 14" h, 5" w ..................................................... 198.00
Porcelain, strip, "Do You Inhale? - If So... Call For Phillip Morris, Smoking Pleasure Without Smoking Penalties," pack at left, white text, cobalt ground, 1930s-1940s, cond. 8-8.25, 4" h, 26" w ...................... 825.00

## Phillips 66

Can, tin
"Inflammable, Phillips 66 Aviation Gasoline, Model Motor Blend," winged shield logo on white circle, red ground, small top, cond. 9/8+, 5-1/2" h, 3" dia ................................................................ 110.00
"Phillips 66 Aviation Engine Oil," winged red/black shield logo, various aircraft encircling top, red/black text, blue/white banded ground, Phillips Petroleum Co., full, cond. 8.5, qt, 5-1/2" h, 4" dia ............ 77.00
"Phillips 66 Motor Oil," shield logo in white circle, orange ground with white stripes, "Motor Oil" in black on white band at bottom, cond. 7+, 5 gal, 14-3/4" h, 9-1/4" sq ......................................... 77.00

Clock, double bubble, light-up, "Phillips 66" shield logo,

Can, oil, tin, "Phillips 66 Motor Oil, Phillips Petroleum Company," unopened, 1 quart, $22.

"Tires Batteries" in black on white ground, cond. 8, 15" dia ...................................................................... 990.00

Gas globe
Newer plastic body with 2 lenses, "Phillips 66" orange/black shield logo on white ground, lens cond. 9, body cond. 7, 13-1/2" dia .................................. 330.00
Wide plastic body with 2 glass lenses, shield-shape, "Phillips 66" orange/black logo, 1 lens cracked, lens cond. 9/6, body cond. 8, 13" h, 12-1/2" w .................... 418.00

Lighter, metal, "Greater Houston Division" in black on top, "Phillips 66" shield logo on base, "Vulcan #446 Wee Liter Japan" on bottom, orig box, cond. 8, 1-3/4" h, 3/4" w ................................................................ 16.50

Pen/pencil set, Cross, 12 KT gold-filled, "Phillips 66" shield logo on pocket clasp, engraved, ©1975, orig box, cond. 8 ...................................................... 27.50

Salt/pepper shakers, plastic, gas pump shape, orange, "Phillips 66" shield logo, flat top, cond. 8, 2-3/4" h, 1" w, pr ........................................................................ 82.50

Seat belt, "Phillips 66" shield logo in silver on buckle, one green, one blue, orig boxes, NOS, cond. 7+, pr .......................................................................... 44.00

Sign
Neon, porcelain, embossed, die-cut, "Phillips 66"" in black/orange shield, lights white, new neon, cond. 8, 48" h, 46" w ............................................... 935.00
Paper, "Phillips 66, Flite-Fuel for Your Car," red airplane at bottom, red/black text, yellow ground, framed, cond. 8, frame size 21" h, 17-1/2" w ............................ 27.50
Porcelain, 2-sided, die-cut, shield-shape, "Phillips 66" in shield logo, orange/black, restored, cond. 8.5, 30" h, 29" w ..................................................... 242.00

Tin, litho tin, "Livestock Spray / for Cattle, Horses and other Livestock," farm scene on blue ground, Phillips 66 shield logo, Phillips Petroleum Co., Bartlesville, OK, overall rust/scratches, 14" h, 9" sq .............. 77.00

## Phillips Coffee

Can, keywind, litho tin, farm scene with barn and fields, red ground, cond. 8+, 1 lb, 4" h, 5" dia ............. 330.00

## Phillips Soups (See Photo)

## Phillips Trop Artic Motor Oil

Can, litho tin, green Phillips shield flanked by palm trees, igloo in background, green-to-red ground, Phillips Petroleum Co., full, cond. 8, qt, 5-1/2" h, 4" dia .............. 715.00

## Phoenix Brewery

Match safe, metal, hinged lid, rounded corners, "Phoenix Brewery, St. Louis," eagle/crossed wheat design, cond. 9-, 2-3/4" h, 1-1/2" w .............................. 269.50

## Piccadilly Juniors

Tin, vertical pocket, litho tin, oval, "Piccadilly Juniors, Virginia," emblem at top in white, "Juniors" in red, black ground, English, cond. 8+, 3" h, 2-7/8" w ........... 62.50

## Pickwick Coffee

Tin, litho tin, oval medallion of man in hat flanked by crest-

Sign, card stock, "The World's Fare, Phillips Delicious Condensed Soups, truly Delicious," image from 1939 New York World's Fair, stains/folds, 21" h, 27" w, $220.

type lions, back pictures coffee plantation and mansion, plaid band, 1 lb, 3-3/4" h, 5-1/8" d .......................... 88.00

# Picobac

Match striker, cardboard, "For Your Pipe - Good For Cigarettes too" at bottom, shows vertical pocket tin with hand holding tobacco leaves, "10¢" in red circle, cond. 8, 8-3/8" h, 4" w .................................................. 133.00

Tin, vertical pocket, litho tin

"Picobac, The pick of Tobacco, Very Mild," hand holding tobacco leaves, brown angled stripe on orange/white mottled ground, cond. 8 ...................... 48.00

"Picobac, The pick of Tobacco, Very Mild, 10¢," hand holding tobacco leaves, brown angled stripe on orange/white mottled ground, darker browns, cond. 8 .............................................. 48.00

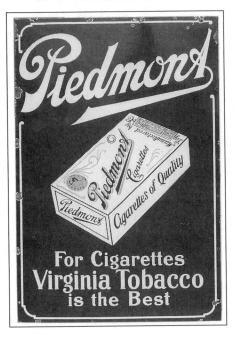

Sign, porcelain, "Piedmont, For Cigarettes, Virginia Tobacco is the Best," blue ground, 1920s-1930s, cond. 8.25+, 46" h, 30" w, $275. (Photo courtesy of Gary Metz, Muddy River Trading Co.)

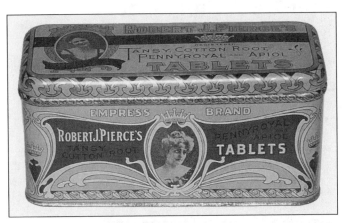

Tin, screw lid, "Picobac, The pick of Tobacco, Imperial Tobacco Co. of Canada Limited," 1915 tax stamp, 1/2-lb, 4-1/2" h, $35.

Short version, "Picobac, The pick of Tobacco, Very Mild, 10¢" 4 tobacco leaves rising from brown angled stripe on orange/white mottled ground, cond. 8+, 4" h, 3" w........................................ 72.50

Tall version, "Picobac, The pick of Tobacco, Very Mild" 4 tobacco leaves rising from brown angled stripe on orange/white mottled ground, "Quality Guaranteed"" mark, cond. 8-8.5, 4-1/2" h, 3" w .................... 140.00

# Piedmont

Chair, wooden folding chair, porcelain panel in back, 2-sided, "For Cigarettes, Virginia Tobacco is the Best, Piedmont, The Virginia Cigarette," white on cobalt ground, chair repainted, sign with stains/fading/chips.................. 137.50

Sign, cardboard, orig Piedmont frame, woman in red dress/hat, "10 for 5¢, Piedmont, The Cigarette Of Quality," shows pack upper-left, circa 1910-1915, cond. 7-7.5, frame 29" h, 15-1/2" w .................. 605.00

# Piel's Beer

Straw/napkin dispenser, bar-top, aluminum, "Piel's Beer" in red at base, 2 elves drinking from keg, 6" x 7" x 6-1/2" ................................................... 33.00

# Robert J. Pierce (See Photo)

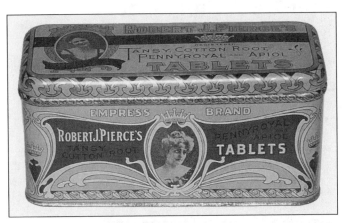

Tin, litho tin, hinged lid, "Robert J. Pierce's Empress Brand Tansy Cotton Root, Pennyroyal And Apiol Tablets," 1 dozen," 3-1/2" h, 7-1/4" w, 3" d, $50.

Tin, "Pinex Laxatives, The Pinex Company, Fort Wayne, Ind., 36 Tablets, 25¢," yellow ground, 3-7/8" w, 2-3/8" d, $5.

## Pieters' Baby Powder

Tin, paper label, "Pieters' Antiseptic Baby Powder (Non Irritating), C. Pieters, 112 Paterson Avenue, Paterson, N.J.," shows baby with product, cond. 8+, 4-3/4" h, 2" w ............................................................... 385.00

## Pigeon Brand Ribbon

Tin, litho tin, round, "Pigeon Brand Ribbon for Corona Automatic," yellow text, white pigeon on black ground, Corona Typewriter Co., Groton, N.Y., cond. 7.5, 1-5/8" dia ......................................................... 34.00

## Piggly Wiggly

Can, litho tin, "Sanitary and Piggly Wiggly Stores," capitol building on yellow ground, cond. 8+, 1 lb, 6-1/4" h, 4" dia ..................................................... 1,485.00
Sign, porcelain, yellow pig face with white "Piggly Wiggly" hat, blue ground, 1940s, cond. 9.5+, 42" dia ......................................................... 1,045.00

## Pilot Chewing Tobacco

Can, keywind, litho tin, small red plane with exhaust spelling "Pilot" over red "Chewing Tobacco," also "10¢ Plug" in circle, W.C. McDonald, 2-1/2" h, 5" dia ...................... 55.00

## Pilot Typewriter Ribbons

Tin, litho tin, "Pilot Brand, Ace of Ribbons," 4-prop airplane on red/white/black ground, cond. 8.5, 7/8" h, 2-5/8" dia ...................................................... 176.00

## Pinex Laxatives (See Photo)

## Pinkerton

Sign, tin, "Caution, K-9 Patrol Pinkerton's Inc.," security guard with German shepherd, red/white letters, cobalt panel at bottom, white reflective ground, chips/crease/rust, 14" h, 12" w ................................................ 60.50

## Pinkussohn's Potpourri

Tin, vertical pocket
  Litho tin, scarce variation without paper label, "Pinkus-

Sign, tin, "Ray's Paint & Floor Service, Edgar, Wisconsin, Pittsburgh Paints," light wear, edge dents, 18" h, 24" w, $25.

sohn's Potpourri Smoking Tobacco, Prepared Expressly For J.S. Pinkussohn Company, Savannah, Ga.," white text, red ground, cond. 8.5, 3-1/2" h ................................................. 323.00
  Paper label, "Pinkussohn's Potpourri Smoking Tobacco, Prepared Expressly For J.S. Pinkussohn Company, Savannah, Ga.," white text, red ground, full, mint, 3-5/8" h, 3" w ............................... 338.00

## Pipe Major

Tin, vertical pocket, litho tin
  "Pipe Major English Smoking Mixture," seated Scottish man being served by man in kilt, yellow ground, dark variation, cond. 8.5 ............................. 302.50
  "Pipe Major English Smoking Mixture," Sea Stores stamp on lid, "For consumption outside U.S. ...," seated Scottish man being served by man in kilt, yellow ground, light variation, cond. 8+ ............... 248.00

## Pippins Cigar

Tin, vertical box, litho tin, embossed, "5¢ Cigars, Pippins, H. Traiser & Co. Inc., Boston," large motif with apple and two smoking cigars, cond. 8.5, 5-3/8" h, 3" sq .............. 300.00

## Pirelli

Sign, tin, embossed, "Pirelli" under colorful image of child in red cap coasting on bike with legs sticking out, black ground, white border, foreign, dents/scratches/rust, 27-1/4" h, 19-1/4" w ...................................... 3,520.00

## Pittsburgh Ice Cream Co.

Tray, woman watching 5 children at a table, green trim, yellow banners, 1920s-1930s, cond. 8-8.25 ............ 1,210.00

## Pittsburgh Paints (See Photo)

## Planet Jr.

Poster, cloth with grommets, "Garden Tools, buy Planet Jr. it pays! Farm Implements," scratches, 11" h, 23-1/2" w ...................................................... 275.00

## Planters House Coffee

Can, litho tin, "Planters House Brand Steel Cut Coffee," shows Planters House Hotel/street traffic, red ground, cond. 8, 5-3/4" h, 4-1/4" dia ............................... 176.00

## Planters Peanut Bars

Box, waxy cardboard display box, die-cut foldup, "Planters Jumbo Block, The Peanut Bar, Winter and Summer, Planters Peanut Bars, Dry and Crisp for Hot Summer and Winter," sweating boy in hat eating peanut bar under mean-looking sun, with orig lid, circa 1930s, cond. 7.5-8, 8" h, 10-7/8" w, 7" d ...................... 1,705.00

Candy bar, wax wrapper, "Planters Peanut Jumbo Block 5¢," Mr. Peanut at left, white text, peanuts ground, free watercolor book offer on wrapper, unused, cond. 8, 2 oz, 2-1/4" h, 4-1/2" w .......................................... 109.00

Display, cardboard, "Planters Peanut Bars, 1¢" on end label, box lid with Mr. Peanut circus images, cond. 7.5+, 3" h, 5-1/4" w, 11-1/4" d ............................. 577.50

## Planters Peanut Butter

Pail, litho tin, pry lid, "Planters High Grade Peanut Butter, Guaranteed Absolutely Pure, Planters Nut & Chocolate Co., Suffolk, Va.," oval medallion with Mr. Peanut, red ground, 25 lb, 9-1/2" h, 10" dia ................... 797.50

Tin, litho tin

"Homogenized Planters Peanut Butter, Beurre De Peanuts," Mr. Peanut logo, peanuts ground, recipe for peanut butter cookies on back flanked by image of boy/girl eating peanut butter sandwich, Canadian, cond. 7.5+, 24 oz, 3-5/8" h, 4-1/4" dia............. 385.00

"Planters High Grade Peanut Butter, Guaranteed Absolutely Pure, Planters Nut & Chocolate Co., Suffolk, Va.," oval medallion with Mr. Peanut, circa 1918, cond. 8-, 1 lb, 4" h, 3-1/8" dia .......... 5,170.00

"Planters High Grade Peanut Butter, Guaranteed Absolutely Pure, Planters Nut & Chocolate Co.,

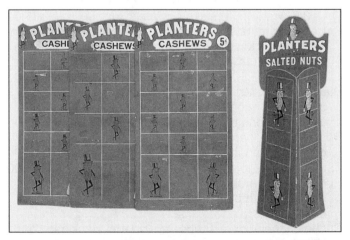

**Point of purchase display, cardboard, easel-back, "Planters Cashews," orange with Mr. Peanut, cond. 7-7.5 to 8.5-9, lot of 3, $2,090. Pyramid display, cardboard, 4-sided, "Planters Salted Nuts" in white at top, orange ground, circa, 1950s, cond. 7.5, 15" h, $1,760. (Photo courtesy of Gary Metz, Muddy River Trading Co.)**

Suffolk, Va.," oval medallion with Mr. Peanut, red ground, cond. 8+, 5 lb ............................... 3,850.00

## Planters Peanuts

**History:** Wilkes-Barre, Pa., was the home of the Planters Nut and Chocolate Company, founded in 1906 by Amedeo Obici and Mario Peruzzi. The debonair peanut with the spindly limbs, top hat, and monocle was in use by 1916.

**Reference:** Jan Lindenberger, *Planters Peanut Collectibles Since 1961*, Schiffer Publishing, 1995

**Collector's Club:** Peanut Pals, P.O. Box 652, St. Clairsville, OH 43950

Bank, plastic, figural Mr. Peanut, 8-1/2" h

   Clear ................................................................. 273.00

   Gold wash finish ............................................. 2,750.00

   Lime-green, minor foot blemish, cond. EXC........385.00

   Set of 4, solid colors, red, cobalt, green, tan, cond. 9.5.................................................... 176.00

   Silver wash finish, orig "Souvenir of Salem, Mass." decal on hat, cond. NM.............................. 2,640.00

   Tan body, black arms/legs/hat........................... 176.00

Box, display, cardboard

   Die-cut, 2-pc, "Planters Peanuts, Defend America, For A Victorious America Buy U.S. War Bonds and Stamps," shows eagle in "V," top also with war bonds verbiage, 1940s, 3/4" tear, stains/fading, 8-3/4" h, 8-1/2" w, 3" d ................................ 632.50

   Die-cut, lift-off lid, round medallion shows woman with bag of peanuts, "Planters Always Hits The Spot, Planters Nut & Chocolate Company, Fresh, 5¢," 1940s, cond. 8.5+, 9-3/4" h, 9" w, 6-3/8" d .................... 440.00

   "Planters Roasted Peanuts" in red/black on white ground, oval red medallion shows peanut lettered "The Peanut Store," also Mr. Peanut, cond. 8+, 10" h, 6-1/4" sq ............................................. 143.00

   "Planters Salted Nuts, fresh, Roaster To You," shows bowl of peanuts, white ground, yellow top/bottom border, 1940s-1950s, cond. 7.5 ....................... 11.00

Box, product, cardboard

   "Planters Salted Peanuts, Red Skin Spanish," Mr. Peanut standing by dish of nuts, red ground, early, cond. 7.5+, 5 oz, 3-5/8" h, 2-7/8" w, 1-3/4" d............2,200.00

   "Planters Spanish Peanuts," Mr. Peanut in oval at left, orange ground, black trim, cond. 7.5-8, 3" h, 3-1/8" w, 2-3/4" d ....................................... 2,145.00

Box, shipping, cardboard, shipping box to Mr. Peanut Vendor toy, "Mr. Peanut Vendor" over image of toy, black on yellow ground, 1950s, cond. NM, 6-3/4" x 8-1/4" x 4" ..........................................................115.50

Can, litho tin

   Pry lid, salesman sample, "The Planters Pennant Brand Salted Peanuts," red pennant on blue medallion, miniature version of 10 lb Pennant Brand store can, cond. 8+, 2-1/2" h, 2-3/8" dia ............. 8,580.00

   "The Planters Clean Crisp Brand Luscious Golden-Meated Salted Peanuts," red/gold text on yellow oval, red ground, circa 1918, cond. 7, 9-5/8" h, 8-3/8" dia ................................................... 412.50

"Planters Pennant Brand Salted Peanuts," red pennant with Mr. Peanut, red/blue text, light-blue ground on darker-blue ground, "This tin Contains 5 Jumbo Peanut Bars" on red top border, cond. 6.5, 10 lb ................................................................ 55.00

"Planters Pennant Brand Salted Peanuts," red pennant with Mr. Peanut, red/blue text, light-blue ground on darker-blue ground, cond. 8, 5 lb, 8" h, 6-1/4" dia .......................................................... 55.00

"The Planters Salted Peanuts, Mother's Brand," round image of mother/child, red text, yellow ground, cond. 8, 10 lb, 9-5/8" h, 8-1/4" dia .......... 12,430.00

"Planters Unblanched Spanish Salted Peanuts,"" shows Mr. Peanut, silver text, red ground, dated 1936, lid opened but attached, cond. 7.5, 8 oz, 3" h, 3-3/8" dia ......................................................... 55.00

Can, litho tin, keywind, "Planters Salted Virginia Peanuts, Table Package," shows playing cards/cocktail glasses, ©1938, cond. 8+, 1 lb, 3-3/4" h, 4-1/4" dia ........... 77.00

Costume, Halloween, Mr. Peanut, plastic mask, plastic/cloth peanut-body, orig shipping box, 1960s, mint ............................................................................ 99.00

Dish, nut, pink fluorescent, compartmented, standing figural Mr. Peanut in center, cond. EXC, 4-1/2" h, 5-1/4" dia .................................................................. 357.50

Dish, covered, metal, nut shape, 2-pc, embossed, "Planters" on top, Mr. Peanut logo embossed inside bottom, 1-3/4" h, 4" w, 2" d .......................................... 1,210.00

Display rack, countertop, litho tin, Z-shaped, "Planters Peanut Specialties," back shows packages of Chocolate Peanuts, Peanut Jumbo Block, Salted Peanuts, cond. 8.5, 4-3/4" x 14" x 7-3/4" ...................... 2,090.00

Fan, cardboard, handheld, "Planters Peanuts, Always Speeding Ahead," Mr. Peanut in peanut-shaped car, semi-circle shape, circa 1940, cond. 8, 5-1/4" h, 8" w ............................................................ 467.50

Figure
  Plastic, lightup, white, like bank but on stand, 1950s, cond. 9.25 .................................................. 412.50
  Wooden, jointed, Mr. Peanut, tan body, black arms/legs, gray "Mr. Peanut" hat, holds cane, cond. 8, 8-1/2" h .................................................... 121.00

Glass
  Cocktail glass, figural Mr. Peanut stem, U-shaped bowl, cond. EXC, 5-1/8" h ........................... 550.00
  Drinking glass, enameled images of Mr. Peanut doing circus acts, mint, 5" h, 2-3/4" dia ................. 154.00

Jar, glass, countertop
  4-Corners Peanut jar, bottom mkd "Made in U.S.A.," cond. 8.5 ............................................................ 209.00
  6-Sided jar, yellow printing on all sides, bottom mkd "Made in U.S.A.," cond. 9.5 ........................... 264.00
  8-Sided jar, 1 side plain for label, 7 sides embossed, chips, bottom mkd "Made in U.S.A.," cond. 7.5 ............................................................. 60.50
  8-Sided jar, embossed on all sides, cond. 8-8.5 ............................................................. 121.00
  Barrel form, embossed figures, "Planters Salted Peanuts," red on black with 70% paint, bottom mkd "Made in U.S.A.," cond. 8.5 ...................... 577.50

Fired-on enamel label, "Planters Peanuts 5¢," and Mr. Peanut, red and blue, embossed back, orig red tin lid, circa 1940, 9" h, 5" w, 7-5/8" d ............... 198.00

Fish bowl shape, decal with Mr. Peanut/"Planters Salted Peanuts, Only Genuine When Sold In Our Trademark Bag, 5¢" decal 95% complete, questionable lid, bottom mkd "Made in U.S.A.," jar cond. 8.5-9 ...................................................... 242.00

"Lady" design, paper label, "Planters Peanuts" in yellow text, round image of woman with package of peanuts, orig green lid, circa 1937, 9-1/4" h, 5" w, 7-1/2" d ........................................................ 550.00

Square jar, embossed "Planters Peanuts," bottom mkd "Made in U.S.A.," cond. 8-8.5 ........................ 60.50

Letter opener, metal, inlaid cloisonné porcelain Mr. Peanut on front of peanut handle, circa 1929, chips, 9" h, 1-3/8" w ............................................... 1,210.00

Lighter, peanut shape, "Planters" in black, unused orig box, 2-5/8" l ........................................... 203.50

Mask, cardboard, unused, smiling peanut face with monocle, 7-3/4" x 8-1/4" ..................................... 232.00

Matches, book, "Planters, Nuts of Distinction" on cover, Mr. Peanut at left, can in center, peanut at right, red/black text, yellow ground, each match shows Mr. Peanut, 1930s, cond. 8+ ............................ 132.00

Mug, ceramic, figural Mr. Peanut, 1 arm is handle, rhinestone monocle, unused, orig sticker on bottom, 3-7/8" h ............................................................ 412.50

Pin, service
  10 years, cloisonné inlaid 14 kt gold, "10" at bottom, Mr. Peanut design, pre-1961, cond. NM, 1-1/4" h ............................................................ 110.00
  15 years, same design as above, "15" at bottom, cond. NM ................................................................... 132.00
  20 years, same design as above, "20" at bottom........................................................................ 132.00
  25 years, cloisonné inlaid 14 kt gold, diamond chip, Mr. Peanut design, 1-1/4" h ........................ 231.00
  25 years, oval, 10 kt gold, diamond chip at right, Mr. Peanut at left, post-1961 design, 5/8" h, 3/8" w ............................................................. 156.00

Pin, Victory, metal/plastic, metal "V" in red circle between wings over "Mr. Peanut," plastic tan Mr. Peanut figure, bend-down tab, World War II era, cond. EXC, 3" h ...................................................................... 66.00

Playing cards, Mr. Peanut paddling peanut-shaped canoe with female passenger, circa 1920s, complete with joker, orig box, cond. 7+ ...................... 1,375.00

Pop gun, cardboard, "Bang! For Planters Peanuts," blue gun, Mr. Peanut in oval medallion on grip, circa 1940, unused, age toning/chips, 4-1/2" h, 9" w ............ 198.00

Punchboard, cardboard, "Planter's Peanuts 5¢ Sale," red/white with blue lettering, unused, 7-1/4" h, 6" w ...................................................................... 154.00

Puppet, hand puppet, rubber, cream with black hat, cond. NM, 6-1/2" h ...................................................... 1,210.00

Radio, transistor, plastic, yellow Mr. Peanut design, unused, orig box/mailing carton, mint, 10" h, 5" w ...................................................................... 110.00

Toy, plastic, windup, Mr. Peanut figure walker, 1950s, 8-1/2" h

Tan body, black arms/legs/hat, works .............. 412.50
Green, works.................................................. 440.00
Red, works ................................................... 550.00
Yellow, works................................................ 605.00
Toy, plastic
Car, light-blue, Mr. Peanut in peanut-shaped car, circa 1950s, 2-3/4" h, 5" w............................... 522.50
Mr. Peanut Vendor, tan Mr. Peanut pushing red cart with green hood/yellow wheels, small break on geared strip, 1950s, 5" x 6" x 3-1/4" ............. 462.00
Train car, clear plastic "Planters" embossed peanut on red car, orig decal "Souvenir of Allentown," 1950s, hairlines under base, 2-1/2" h, 5-1/8" l.......... 165.00
Truck, "Mr. Peanut's Peanut Wagon," red cab, yellow back, unused, mint, 5-3/8" l ............................ 522.50
Vending machine
Metal, enameled, wall-mounted, "Planters Fresh Salted Peanuts, 10¢," large image of Mr. Peanut, white ground, 1940s, cond. 8.5+, 36" h, 7" w, 7-1/4" d ...................................................... 1,815.00
Plastic, red figural Mr. Peanut head, clear hat holds peanuts, circa 1950s, stressing to hat, 8-3/4" h ..................................................... 412.50
Plastic, white figural Mr. Peanut head, clear hat holds peanuts, circa 1950s, corrosion on lid, no coin trap, 8-3/4" h ..................................................... 577.50

## Plantista Cigars

Pocket mirror, celluloid, "Plantista, That Good Havana Cigar, 5¢ to 15¢, Detroit at Home 1911, Detroit Abroad 1911," Detroit Tigers baseball schedule for 1911, small dent, 2-1/4" dia................................................. 440.00

## Plenty Copy Typewriter Ribbon

Tin, litho tin, round, shows cornucopia/banner, Mittag & Volger, Parkridge, N.J., one edge rough, else cond. 8 ............................................................. 27.50

## Plug Crumb Cut

Tin, vertical pocket, litho tin, "Plug Crumb Cut, Extra Fine, Will Not Bite The Tongue," gold text, cond. 9 ......... 444.00

## Plume Motor Spirit

Sign, porcelain, hand-lettered, "Please Shut The Gate, Use Plume Motor Spirit," red text/border, white ground, NOS, cond. 9, 4-1/4" h, 14" w ........................... 176.00

## Plymouth

Sign, neon, porcelain, die-cut, "Dodge Plymouth," white text/border, blue ground, no transformer or neon, cond. 7+, 28" h, 60" w ...................................... 935.00

## Poker Cut Plug

Tin, horizontal box, litho tin, embossed, The Rock City Tobacco Co. Limited, poker scene, cond. 7-8, 2" h, 5" w, 3" d.................................................... 91.50

## Polarine

Can, tin, oil

"Polarine, A Frost and Carbon Proof Oil, For Motor Car and Motor Boat, Will Feed at Zero Temperature," polar bear, white ground, Standard Oil Co., cond. 7, gal, 11" h, 8" w, 3" d.................................... 478.50
"Polarine for 'F' Fords, Seals pistons against loss of power, maintains corrector body at any speed or temperature, Standard Oil Company," red logo, white ground, rust on top, else cond. NM, 1/2 gal, 7" h, 8" w, 3-1/8" d ........................................ 187.00
"Polarine, The Perfect Motor Oil, Consult Chart, Medium," logo in red circle around diamond, white ground, Standard Oil Co., cond. 8, 1/2 gal, 7" h, 8" w, 2-3/4" d ................................................110.00
"Polarine, The Perfect Motor Oil, Maintains Correct Body At Any Motor Speed Or Temperature, Seals Pistons Against Loss Of Power," early auto in countryside, yellow ground, Standard Oil Co., cond. 7, 1/2 gal, 6-1/2" h, 8" w, 3" d.................................................286.00
Can, tin, other, "Polarine Cup Grease," Standard Oil Co. (Indiana), red text in triangle, white ground, cond. 8, 25 lb, 10-1/4" h, 9-1/8" sq ......................................... 99.00
Pocket mirror, celluloid, "Polarine, A Frost and Carbon Proof Oil for Lubrication of Motor Cars and Motor Boats, Standard Oil Co. Incorporated," cond. EXC, 2-1/8" dia.................................................. 231.00
Sign, flange, painted metal, "Polarine, The Perfect Motor Oil, Consult Chart," red/black triangle/circle logo, white ground, cond. 7, 14" h, 18" w........................... 286.00
Thermometer, porcelain, "Saves The Motor, Does Not Thin Out," red logos of "Polarine, The Perfect Motor Oil, Consult Chart" and "Iso-Vis Motor Oil, Standard Oil Company (Indiana)" at top/bottom, directions by tube, faded, not working, cond. 7, 72" h, 18" w ............368.50
Watch fob, metal, embossed, "Socony Polarine," trademark polar bear, cond. 7.5, 1-3/8" dia.............. 121.00

## Polaris

Sign, tin, "Polaris Sno-Traveler, Hunt, fish and just fun for the entire family, Authorized Sales," person on early snowmobile, cond. 7, 35" h, 28" w .................... 533.50

## Polar Tobacco

Pack, paper, large, "Polar Chewing & Smoking Tobacco, Luhrman & Wilbern Tobacco Company," full, cond. 8.5 ......................................................... 154.00

## Polk's Milk

Sign, porcelain, 2-sided, "Polk's Milk, Always Ahead," cow's head on blue ground, white trim, 1930s-1940s, minor chips, 22" dia ...................................... 4,510.00

## Poll Parrot Shoes

Display, hanging, revolving, "Poll Parrot" in white on red oval sign, plastic parrot on perch in center, cage-like wire frame/holders for 6 shoes, separate motor unit/ case/cardboard cover, chips, 33" h, 20" w...................................................... 159.50
Lamp, metal base with "Quality speaks for itself" decal, wood die-cut with decal of "Poll Parrot Shoes" in green

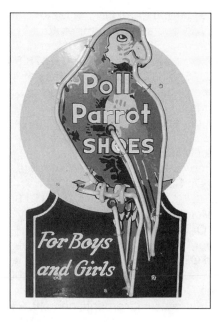

Neon on porcelain, "Poll Parrot Shoes for Boys and Girls," sign shows parrot on circular yellow ground, orig green neon, repro can/cord/transformer, small chips, 1930s-1940s, cond. 8.75-9.25, $2,640. (Photo courtesy of Gary Metz, Muddy River Trading Co.)

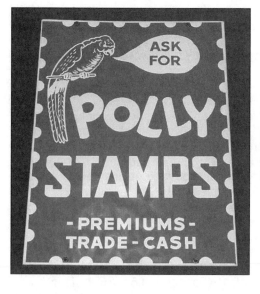

Sign, tin, 2-sided, "Ask For Polly Stamps, Premiums, Trade, Cash," NOS, 28" h, 20" w, $25.

oval under parrot, "Poll Parrot Shoes" on plastic shade in stained glass motif, 19" h, 8" dia ..................... 77.00

Radio, battery-op, composition figural parrot, plastic base, "Poll-Parrot Shoes" at base of parrot, "Poll-Parrot Shoe For Boys And Girls, Quality Speaks For Itself" on cube-shaped General Electric radio, cond. G, 11" h, base 3-3/4" sq ................................................. 104.50

Sign

Paper, "Poll Parrot Shoes, Happy Shoes For Happy Feet," boy in jester's costume holding parrot, framed, cond. EXC, 24-1/2" h, 16" w ........... 242.00

Glass, reverse-painted, "Poll Parrot Shoes for Boys and Girls," Art Deco design with parrot in upper-left on ring, text lower-right/bottom, framed, soiling, 27" h, 14-1/2" w ....................................................... 616.00

## Polly Prim Cleaner

Sign, cardboard, "Polly Prim Cleaner, When things are dim use Polly Prim," white on black upper/lower border, woman with product on red ground, N.K. Fairbanks Co., older frame, tears/touchups/cracked glass, 28-1/2" h, 20-1/2" w ......................................... 203.50

## Polly Stamps (See Photo)

## Polo Cigarette Tobacco

Pack, paper, polo game scene, Rock City Tobacco Co., Quebec, open but full, cond. 8, 4" h, 2-3/4" w ................................................................. 64.00

## Pond Peanut Butter

Can, litho tin, pry lid, "Pond Brand Peanut Butter, H.C. Derby Co.," on yellow oval, cond. 8, 2-3/4" h, 4" dia ................................................................. 39.50

## Pontiac

Banner, cloth, "Prepare Your Car For Winter Now...," Indians butchering buffalo over "Winter Preparation" at

left, "Pontiac Service" logo lower right, fading/stains, 34" h, 90" w ........................................................ 55.00

Printer's block, metal, Indian head silhouette, mounted on heavy piece of metal, cond. 7, 13-1/4" h, 21" w ................................................................. 27.50

Sign, neon, glass, "69 Pontiac," outline of Indian profile in circle, few repairs, 28" h, 38" w ........................ 242.00

## Pop Kola

Sign, tin, embossed, "Drink Pop Kola, 12 Ounces of Pep, 5¢," red text, black panel lower-left, price lower-right, yellow ground, black border, cond. VG, 5" h, 14" w ................................................................. 121.00

## Poppy Marshmallows

Tin, litho tin, poppy decor, cond. 8-8.5, 4 oz, round ................................................................. 220.00

Tin, litho tin, "Possum," with cardboard display "3 for 10¢," (lid not shown) 5" h, $300.

## Porsche

Sign, porcelain, "Porsche, Stuttgart" shield logo, white on red ground, foreign, NOS, cond. 9+, 35" h, 25" w .......................................................... 4,125.00

## Possum Cigars (See Photo)

## Post-Standard

Sign, flange, metal, "Sunday Daily Post-Standard Branch, News Boys Supplied Here," dark text/border, white ground, chips/scratches/rust, 9-3/4" h, 13" w.................................................. 137.50

## Post Toasties

**History:** A visit to the Battle Creek Sanitarium during the time that Dr. John Kellogg was experimenting with cold breakfast cereals in the early 1890s reaffirmed C.W. Post's belief that a healthy body was the direct result of eating healthful foods. To that end, he opened his own home, La Vita Inn, near Battle Creek.

Because Kellogg and his staff did not permit morning coffee, Post worked to develop an acceptable alternative. He created an extremely popular caffeine-free, "pure food drink" that he called Postum.

When Post first introduced Grape-Nuts in 1898, he focused on the product's nutritional value, referring to it as a health food rather than a breakfast cereal. Creating it required a repetitive baking process that reduced the ingredients to grape-sugar, and the nuggets tasted like nuts, hence the name. Elijah's Manna, Post's own brand of corn flakes, debuted in 1906, but a religious outcry resulted in a name change to Post Toasties in 1908.

Festoon, cardboard, 2-sided, 12-pc, individual red letters spelling out "Post Toasties" over design of product box, cond. 9.25+, each approx 9" h, 4" w................. 3,520.00
Sign, cardboard, "How Cereals Are Processed, Flaked And Toasted, Post Toasties," factory scene, 4 bowls at top, 1927, cond. 8-8.25, 21" h, 27" w ............... 247.50

## Wm. Powell Co.

Match holder, hanging, litho tin, rounded top/bottom, "We Match And Beat All Competitors, Compliments of The Wm. Powell Co., Cincinnati, Ohio," holder shows shutoff valve on star, cond. NM, 4-1/2" h, 1-5/8" w ........... 220.00

## Power-lube Motor Oil

Sign, porcelain, 2-sided, "Power-lube Motor Oil, Smooth As The Tread Of A Tiger," tiger on orange panel over oval logo "Guaranteed 100% Pure Pennsylvania Oil," orange text, black ground, white border, cond. 8, 20" h, 28" w ................................................................ 1,677.50

## Prairie Farmer

Sign, paper, "Two dollars in the currency of the United States will pay for the weekly Prairie Farmer one year..." Miss Liberty/shock of wheat/"2" in circle/cow on green ground, "Subscriptions Received Here"" on lower border, black text, archival backing, cond. G, 24-1/2" h, 32-1/4" w .......................................... 121.00

## Pratt & Lambert Varnishes

Sign, flange, porcelain, "We Sell Effecto Auto Finishes And Pratt & Lambert Varnishes," ground in 7 swaths of color, cond. 8, 7" h, 14-1/4" w ........................ 1,072.50

## Pratt's

Display, cardboard, countertop standup, "Stop Losses! Bloody Coccidosis, Pratt's C-Ka-Gene," white/red text, cobalt panel on red ground, shows 5 chickens, folds out to hold 3-1/2 lb box, unused, cond. EXC, 18-1/4" h, 11-1/2" w ......................................................... 166.00

## Preferred Stock Coffee

Can, keywind, litho tin, "Preferred Stock Vacuum Packed Coffee," white cup, white text on red ground, General Grocery Company, Portland OR, lid rough, body is cond. 8.5+, 1 lb .................................................. 60.50

## Preferred Stock Tobacco

Can, litho tin, red/black design shows early stock ticker on side and embossed on lid, cond. 8-, 1-5/8" h, 2-5/8" dia............................................................. 60.50

## Prestone

Thermometer, porcelain, "Prestone Anti-Freeze" in white on blue panel at top, "You're Set Safe Sure" in white on red oval at bottom, gray body, edge chips, 36" h, 9" w ................................................................. 176.00

## Prexy Tobacco

Tin, vertical pocket, litho tin, "Prexy Tobacco For Pipe & Cigarette, B. Payn's Sons Tobacco Co.," central

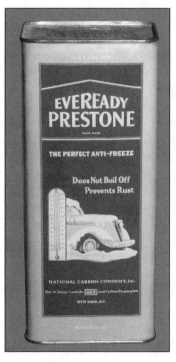

Tin, "Eveready Prestone, The Perfect Anti-Freeze, Does Not Boil Off, Prevents Rust, National Carbon Company," wear, scratches, 1/2-gallon, 9-1/2" h, $110.

medallion with man in black/red graduation outfit, white text, red ground, cond. 7.........................425.00

## Primley's

Box, cardboard, "Primley's California Fruit Chewing Gum," round medallion of lake and "Mt. Shasta," also grapes/cherries, bottom possibly replaced, cond. 8+, 9-1/2" h, 4" w.......................................79.00

Showcase, curved front, glass, oak trim, cond. 7, 12" x 18".............................................550.00

Sign, cardboard, die-cut, bear shape, "Primley's California Fruit Chewing Gum, The Sweetest Thing On Earth," white/red text on brown bear, cond. 8.5, 2-3/4" h, 6-1/2" w.........................................335.50

## Prince Albert Tobacco

Sign

Paper, "Prince Albert - the national joy smoke" in yellow, shows man saying "Swell Flavor And So Easy To Roll," vertical pocket tin at right, new frame, 1937, cond. EXC, 15" h, 29" w.......................115.50

Litho tin, "Prince Albert, the national joy smoke," portrait of Chief Joseph, small image of vertical pocket tin, black ground, framed, cond. 9.25+, 25-1/2" h, 19" w...........................................3,822.50

## Princess Pat Coffee

Tin, keywind, litho tin, portrait of woman in cobalt at top, white ground otherwise, cond. 8, 1 lb, 4" h .............................................240.00

## Principe Alfonso

Sign, litho tin, "S. Ottenberg and Bros Principe Alfonso Clear Havana, 5 In Bundle 25¢," pack of cigars/medallions on white diagonal panel, framed, white/red text, black ground, cond. 9+, 10" h, 13-1/2" w.........275.00

## Providence Washington Insurance Co.

Sign, tin, "Providence Washington Insurance Company of Providence, R.I." in black panel under oval portrait of George Washington with leaves at bottom, wood frame, cond. EXC, 26-1/4" h, 20-1/2" w............363.00

Tin, litho tin, "Cameron's Private Stock, Cameron & Cameron Co., Richmond, Va.," 1-1/2" h, 6-1/4" w, 3-3/8" d, $25.

## Private Stock (See Photo)

## Puck Cigarettes

Tin, litho tin, "Puck 25¢, Virginia Cigarette Tobacco," 2 hockey players, black on yellow ground, cond. 8, 3-1/4" h, 4" dia......................................221.00

## Puck Spices

Tin, cardboard, tin top/bottom, "Puck Brand Pure Ground Black Pepper, Worth the Money," shield medallion shows man leaning against apple tree, red ground, cond. 8.5+, 2 oz, 4-1/8" h, 2-1/4" w, 1-1/4" d...........220.00

## Pulver

Vending machine

Litho tin, embossed, "Pulver's Chocolate Cocoa Gum, Sweet Chocolate Gum, One Cent," shows hand pointing and packet of gum, tins on 3 sides, works, no key, composition Buster Brown figure inside machine, cond. 8, 26" h, 10-1/2" w, 7" d.................7,590.00

Porcelain, "Pulver Chewing Gum in Popular Flavors, Once Cent Delivers a Tasty Chew," red ground, advertising on 3 sides, metal Yellow Kid figure inside, works, frame weathered and worn, some chips to porcelain, 24" h, 10-1/2" w, 5-1/2" d ...............2,970.00

## Pulver's Cocoa

Tip tray, tin, "Pulver's Cocoa, Purity Itself," green text on gold rim, green box of "Pulver's Cocoa" on red ground, cond. VG, 4-1/2" dia.........................137.50

## Punch Bowl Smoking Mixture

Tin, vertical pocket or vertical box, paper label over tin, red text, central image of pedestal-type punch bowl, white ground, unopened, cond. 8 ....................128.00

## Pure As Gold Motor Oil

Can, tin, "Pure As Gold Guaranteed Motor Oil," shows "The Pep Boys, Manny, Moe & Jack," red/black/yellow Art Deco design, ©1933, cond. 8+, 2 gal, 11-1/2" h, 8-1/2" w, 5-3/4" d..............................110.00

## Pure Oil Co.

See Purol

Sign, flange, metal, "Puretest Oils, Insure Motor Life," marked "American Art Works Inc., Coshocton, Ohio," yellow ground, 12" h, 22" w, $275.

Tin, pocket, litho tin, "Puritan Crushed Plug Mixture, Philip Morris & Co. Ltd., NY, London," unopened, 4-1/2" h, $300.

# Pure Stock Cigars

Tin, litho tin, "Pure Stock Quality Cigars 5¢," red banner, floral accents, white ground, cond. 7.5-8.5, 5-1/4" h, 5-1/2" dia............................................................ 82.50

# Puretest Oils (See Photo)

Sign, painted metal, "Puretest Oils Insure Motor Life," black on yellow ground, cond. 8, 11-1/2" h, 22" w .................................................................. 187.00

# Puritan

Tin, vertical pocket, litho tin, "Puritan Crushed Plug Mixture," Continental Tobacco Co., circular portrait of Puritan man in hat smoking pipe, cond. 9 ............... 266.00

# Puritan Baking Powder

Tin, sample, paper label, round medallion shows woman, black ground, yellow border top/bottom, cond. 8-, 2-1/2" h, 1-3/8" dia ............................................. 88.00

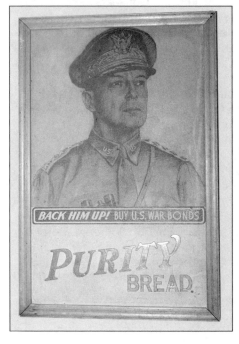

Sign, cardboard, wooden frame, pictures 5-star general, "Back Him Up! Buy U.S. War Bonds, Purity Bread," light stains, 18-1/4" h, 12" w, $15.

# Puritan Cut Plug

Tin, litho tin, round, sailing ship, D. Ritchie & Co., Imperial Tobacco Co. Successor, Montreal, cond. 8, 3" x 3-1/4" ................................................................ 107.00

# Purity Bread (See Photo)

# Purity Ice Cream

Tray, litho tin, "Purity Ice Cream, Deliciously Different," name in black text on red band, dish of ice cream with chocolate sauce/cherry on blue ground, Canadian, cond. 7.5, 12" h, 15-3/4" w .................................. 46.00

# Purity Sugar Butter

Pail, litho tin, "Purity Brand Sugar Butter, A Mixture Made By E.E. Post Co., Utica, N.Y.," round MLB logo, large "ML," shows 2 women, black text, blue ground, fading/chips, 3-1/2" h, 4-1/2" dia................................... 55.00

# Purol

Gas globe
  Low-profile metal body, 2 lenses, 1979 reproduction, "Purol Gasoline" in blue with blue arrow in center, white ground, body repainted, cond. 9 ......... 330.00
  High-profile metal body (new), 2 glass lenses, "Purol-Pep, The Pure Oil Company, U.S.A.," blue text, red curved decor above/below name, blue zig-zag border, all cond. 9, 15-1/2" dia .......................... 852.50
  Plastic body with 2 lenses, "Pure" in blue, blue zig-zag border, white ground, lens cond. 8.5, body cond. 7, 13-1/2" dia ................................................... 203.50
  Wide glass body, 1 glass lens, "Products of The Pure Oil Company" at zig-zag border, larger "Pure" in center, blue design, cracked body, lens cond. 7.5, body cond. 7, 13-1/2" dia............................. 121.00
Matchbox, tin, divided image on lid, "Purol Gasoline" in white with arrow on red ground; "Tiolene Motor Oil" with bull's eye in black on yellow ground, cond. 7, 1-1/2" h, 2-1/4" w .................................................................88.00
Sign, porcelain
  "Pure-Pep, Be sure with Pure," oval "Pure" logo in center, black text, red "sure"/border, white ground, cond. 9-, 12" h, 10" w ...................................110.00
  "Purol-Pep, The Pure Oil Company, U.S.A.," black text, red curved decor above/below name, black zig-zag border, cond. 8, 15" dia .................... 825.00

# Q

Tin, pocket, "Qboid, Finest Quality, Granulated Plug," double concave, 4" h, $66.

Tin, "Quaker Rolled White Oats, The Quaker Oats Company," directions in 6 languages, unopened, 20 oz, $65.

## Q-Boid

Tin, vertical pocket, litho tin
   Fat version, "Qboid Cube Cut Pipe Tobacco," shows tobacco plant in foreground and cabin in background, cond. 9 .............................................. 250.00
   Flat version, "Qboid Finest Quality Granulated Plug, No Rubbing Required, Guaranteed Not To Bite The Tongue," cond. 8.5 ........................................ 103.00
   Oval version, "Q-Boid Finest Quality Cube Cut, No Rubbing Required, Guaranteed Not To Bite The Tongue," tobacco plant on yellow ground, cond. 8, 4-1/2" h ........................................................ 167.00

## Quail Rolled Oats

Paperweight, glass, "Flavor Unequalled, Parched Rolled Oats, Quail Brand, Nebraska City Cereal Mills, Nebraska City, Neb. U.S.A.," pictures quail on ground, cond. NM, 4" h, 2-1/2" w .................................. 302.50

## Quaker Oats

**History:** Sometime during the 1870s, Henry Seymour and William Heston began milling oats in Ravenna, Ohio, using the image of a Quaker man as their logo. At some point, the company was sold and in 1877, the Quaker Mill Company appropriated the symbol, the first use of a registered trademark for a breakfast cereal.

Match striker, cardboard, "Eat Quaker Oats, The World's Breakfast," Quaker Oats man in center, black on white, red rim, unused, 1920s, 6-1/4" h, 3-5/8" w ............. 98.00

Sign, litho tin, round, flat, Quaker Oats man on red ground, 1940s-1950s, cond. 7.5-8, 24" dia ........................ 121.00

## Quaker State

Gas pump insert, glass, reverse-painted, "A Quaker State Product," green text, rounded top, cond. 7, 12" h, 15" w ......................................................... 71.50
Rack, metal with 2-sided tin sign, "Quaker State Motor Oil, Certified Guaranteed" in white on green, rounded top, "Property of Quaker State Oil Refining Corporation AM-4 40" at bottom, 1 tin replacement rack added at bottom, cond. 7.5, 50" h, 22" w, 15-1/2" d .......................... 187.00
Sign
   Painted metal, tombstone design (rounded top), "Quaker State Motor Oil, Certified - Guaranteed," oval "100% Pure Pennsylvania Oil" logo at top, white on green ground, cond. 8, 29" h, 26-1/2" w ..................................................... 143.00
   Porcelain, 2-sided, "Use Quaker State Cold Test Oil For Winter Driving," white text/border, green ground, cond. 7, 6" h, 26-1/2" w .................. 247.50
   Tin, 2-sided, "100% Pure Pennsylvania Oil, Quaker State Duplex Outboard Oil For Outboard Motors - Power Lawn Mowers - Chain Saws," Q logo at left, white/green text, green over white ground, cond. 7, 12" h, 24" w ................................................... 60.50

## Quaker Tea

Sign, flange, porcelain, "Agent 'Quaker' Tea," standing

Can, oil, tin, "Quaker State Racing Motor Oil," unopened, 1 quart, $30.

Quaker man at left, white on cobalt ground, foreign, chips/fading, 9-1/2" h, 18" w ............................ 412.50

## Quality Inn Coffee

Tin, keywind, litho tin
  Early/tall version, shows stagecoach outside Quality Inn, black/white image on yellow ground, Sorver McEvoy & Co., Philadelphia, cond. 8, 1 lb ..................... 172.00
  Shows stagecoach outside Quality Inn, blue on yellow ground, cond. 8.5+, 1 lb, 4" h, 5-1/8" dia............ 209.00

## Queed Tobacco

Tin, vertical pocket, litho tin
  Tall/thin version, "Luxurious Quality" and "Yours Truly..." in black at top/bottom, central diamond with "Queed" in red on white, green ground, cond. 8, 4-3/8" h, 3" w, 7/8" d ..................................... 244.00
  "Luxurious Quality, Queed, Yours Truly, Patterson Bro. Tobacco Inc., Richmond," red text in white diamond, green ground, cond. 8, 4-1/2" h ................... 147.00

Tin, litho tin, "Queen Hair Dressing, Newbro Mfg. Co., Atlanta, Ga.," unopened, 3-3/4 oz, $20.

## Queen Cola

Sign, tin, "Ask For (shows 'Queen Cola' bottle), It's Different And Better," white text, dark ground, Atlantic Beverage Corp., Petersburg, VA faded/chips/paint cracks/bent corners, 19-7/8" h, 7" w ............................. 104.50

## Queen Dairy

Dispenser, porcelain, "Queen Dairy 5¢ Chilled Churned Buttermilk," white with black lettering, 1920s-1930s, complete except for water valve, cond. 9.5, 34" h, 15" dia.......................................................... 2,310.00

## Queen Hair Dressing (See Photo)

## Queen of Virginia

Tin, litho tin, square corner, "Queen of Virginia Perique Mixture," round portrait, black text, red ground, cond. 7-7.5, 2-1/4" h, 4-1/2" w, 3-1/2" d ...................... 88.00

## Queen Quality

Tip tray, litho metal, portrait of woman, "Queen Quality Incandescent Mantles, The Lockwood Taylor Hardware Co. Proprietors Cleveland," rust/scratches, 4-1/4" dia............................................................. 44.00

## Quick-Flash

Gas globe, 2 lenses, 1 pc narrow glass body, "Quick-Flash Hi-Grade" in red, blue eagle in center, white ground, blue border, cond. 8 .......................... 1,870.00

## Quick Meal Ranges

Tip tray, litho tin scene of chicks and bee, cond. NM, 3-3/8" h, 4-5/8" w ............................................. 159.50

## Quicky

Thermometer, tin, rounded top/bottom, "Quicky" in red on yellow oval, "Grapefruit Kissed with Lemon, Tart Tangy Terrific," thermometer glass on design of green bottle, red numbers, white ground, dents/small tear, 16-1/2" h, 8" w.................................................................. 165.00

Match holder, litho tin, "Quick Meal Steel Ranges," 3-3/8" h, 4-7/8" w, $220.

# R

## Racing Sta Lube Motor Oil

Can, tin, soldered seam, "Finest Quality Pennsylvania Oil, Racing Sta Lube Premium Motor Oil," early racer on dark ground, unopened, cond. 7.5-8, qt, 5-1/2" h, 4" dia ................................................................ 275.00

## Radiana Mixture

Tin, vertical pocket, paper label, "Radiana Mixture" in white, "A Sublime Blended Exquisite" in central yellow circle with rays on black ground, "Falk Tobacco Co. Inc.," at bottom, full, cond. NM, 4" h, 3-1/4" w .................... 586.00

## Railway Express Agency

Sign
    Porcelain, chips, 5" h, 120" w ........................... 357.50
    Porcelain, diamond, "Railway Express Agency," black/white text, red ground, edge chips/scratches, 8" h, 8" w ................................................................. 132.00
    Tin over cardboard, "For Fast Dependable Thorough Service, Order and Ship by Railway Express Agency Incorporated," scene at top with train/cart/early truck, black text, white ground, minor scratches/dents/paint chips, 13-1/4" h, 19-1/4" w ........................... 1,017.50

## Rainbow Dyes

Cabinet, countertop model, wood, paper decals, "Rainbow Dyes Beautifully Brilliant, One Dye For All Fabrics," scratches/stains/front edge of base missing, orig contents, 16-3/4" h, 6" w, 12-1/2" d .............................. 825.00

## Raleigh Cigettes

Sign
    Cardboard, easel-back, "Proof Positive, Try the New Raleigh, Plain or Tipped," Douglas Fairbanks Jr. upper-right, pack lower-left, "Less Nicotine, Less Throat Irritants" text box, red/blue text, stain/small tears, 30" h, 20" w .............................................. 55.00
    Paper, "Raleigh" over image of woman, "Union Made, Save New Coupon" in lower banner, pack at right over "Plain Or Cork," red ground, framed, minor soiling/tape residue, 21-1/2" h, 16-1/2" w .............. 77.00

## Ramon's

Jar
    Glass, "Ramon's, The Little Doctor," yellow metal lid, 1930s-1940s, cond. 9.0+ ............................... 60.50
    Heavy glass, clear, embossed "Ramon's Pills" front-center, glass lid, jar with rim chip/nicks, 11-1/2" h, ................................................ 55.00

## Ramses

Tin, litho tin, name in white on black elliptical medallion, blue/red trim, winged accents on cream ground, "Three Genuine Transparent Ramses Rubber Prophylactics," cond. NM, 1/4" h, 2-3/4" w, 1-7/8" d ........................ 66.00

## Rawleigh's Cocoa

Tin, litho tin, sample, "Free Sample, Rawleigh's Good Health Cocoa," round portrait, outdoor scene ground, cond. 9, 2-1/4" h .................................................. 60.50

## Raybestos (See Photo)

## RCA

Puzzle, cardboard, 30 pc, "All that the Victrola gives to others it will give to you," couple seated in parlor, numerous miniature people, Nipper logo lower-left, 1920s, cond. EXC, 8" h, 8-3/4" w .................................... 138.50
Sign
    Porcelain, oval, "His Master's Voice" under classic scene of Nipper listening to phonograph, white text, black ground, yellow border, rust spots/scratches/touchup, 21-1/2" h, 27" w .............................. 770.00
    Pressed metal over composition, classic scene of Nipper listening to phonograph, 16" dia ............ 148.50
Toy, truck, plastic, RCA Television Service Truck, 1950s, Marx, orig box, cond. 9.5, box cond. 9, 8" l ........... 275.00

**Sign, flange, litho tin, "Stop Here for Silver Edge Raybestos Brake Service," black/white/red text, yellow ground, red border, cond. 8.25/7.5, 14" h, 18" w, $385. (Photo courtesy of Gary Metz, Muddy River Trading Co.)**

## Record's Ale

Globe, 2 lenses, high-profile metal body, "Record's Ale" in white on cobalt 4-leaf clover with waterfall center, light-blue ground, lenses taped in, 15-1/2" dia .......... 1,100.00

## Red Bell Coffee

Can, keywind, litho tin, early/tall version, "Drip Grind Red Bell Vacuum Packed Coffee," red bell in black circle with black/white rings and 2 red wing-like strips at top, white over red ground, The Euclid Coffee Co., Cleveland, Ohio, cond. 8+, 1 lb .................................................. 97.00

## Red Belt

Tin, vertical pocket, litho tin, "Bagley's Red Belt, Pipe or Cigarette, Five Cents," red belt, white ground, cond. 8 ............................................................. 124.00

## Red Bird Cigars

Cigar box, "Red Bird, Straight Hand Made" in red, male cardinal on gold medallion, lake-scene ground, circa 1898, cond. 8.25+ ............................................. 143.00

## Red Bird Matches (See Photo)

## Red Cap

Sign, tin, embossed, "Eat Red Cap, Everybody's Candy Bar Choice, 5¢," red text, white ground, 1930s-1940s, cond. 9.5, 10" h, 28" w .......................................... 55.00

## Red Coon

Sign, heavy paper, red raccoon with pack of tobacco on black log, yellow ground, "Sun Cured Red Coon Chewing Tobacco," cond. 8-8.5, 18" h, 12" w .................... 55.00

## Red Cross

Tin, litho tin, "Red Cross Antiseptic Foot Powder, Red Cross Powder Co., Providence, R.I.," foot on large red cross, shell, berries and red crosses on ground, cond. 8+, oval, 4" h, 2-1/2" w ........................................ 121.00

## Red Cross Shoes

Sign, neon, composition, embossed text, metal body, "Red

**Box, cardboard, "Red Bird Matches, Every One Lights," stick matches, unused, 1-1/2" h, 5-1/8" w, 2-3/4" d, $10.**

**Tin, litho tin, "Red Cross Complexion Powder, Pink, Price 20¢, H.S. Peterson & Co., Chicago," 2-3/4" d, $30.**

Cross Shoes" in red, white neon at border, paint chips/dents/composition cracked, 7" h, 21" w ................ 203.50

## Red Cross Tobacco

Sign, porcelain, "Smoke and Chew Red Cross" in black, red cross on each side, white ground, cond. 8+, 3-1/2" h, 21" w ...................................................................... 577.50

## Red Crown Gasoline

Gas globe
Glass body, 2 glass lenses, "Crown" in red on white ground, red border, lens cond. 9/8.5, body cond. 9, 13-1/2" dia ................................................................. 225.50

**Sign, porcelain, 2-sided, "Red Crown Gasoline," red text/crown, white ground, cond. 8/7+, 42" dia, $715. (Photo courtesy of Collectors Auction Services)**

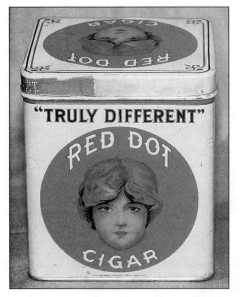

Tin, "Red Dot Cigar, Truly Different, Federal Cigar Co., Red Lion, Pa.," 5-3/4" h, 4-7/8" sq, $58.

High-profile metal body, 2 lenses, "Red Crown Gasoline" in red between blue double borders, red/blue crown in center, white ground, 1 lens cracked, lens cond. 9/6, body cond. 7, 16-1/2" dia ............. 632.50

Milk glass, 1-pc, cond. 8, 16-1/2" h, 17" dia .......... 440.00

Milk glass, 1-pc, "Red Crown" near base, repainted, cond. 7.5, 16-1/2" h, 17" dia ............................ 467.50

Sign, porcelain, red crown in center, red text around border, white ground, orig iron frame/bracket, 1920s-1930s, cond. 8.25-8.5, 42" dia ........... 467.50

# Red Dot Cigar (See Photo)

# Red Goose Shoes

**History:** The Gieseke-D'Oench-Hayes Shoe Company was founded in St. Louis in 1869. Needing a trademark for his company, Herman Gieseke used a goose with a key as a pictorial rendition of his last name. Originally, the goose was white and held a large key in its mouth. In 1907, a metamorphosis occurred, with the fowl becoming a Red Goose and the key disappearing from its beak. The symbol was registered in that same year.

Clock, lightup
    Fiberboard case, round, red goose with yellow lettering, black hours except 12/6, 1940s-1950s, cond. 8.75-9.25 ..................................... 522.50
    Plastic face, wood/wire mesh frame, "Red Goose Shoes" under goose logo, white ground, brass balls at 3/6/9/12, 18" h, 19-1/2" w ........................ 143.00
Clock, neon, metal face, octagonal, "Red Goose Shoes For Boys For Girls," red goose on yellow band, glass with green edge, 1930s, cond. EXC, 18" h, 18" w ........................................... 1,760.00
Figure
    Chalkware, painted, cond. 8, 12" h .................. 198.00
    Composition, goose, embossed "Red Goose Shoes" on front, cond. EXC, 11-1/2" h.............................. 313.50
Mirror, wood frame, metal handle at top with metal stand on sides that lets mirror stand up on counter, Red Goose logo over "Friedman-Shelby All Leather Shoes," minor

cracking of paint to goose, mirror cond. EXC, 21-3/4" h, 15-1/2" w ...................................................... 302.50

Sign, neon, porcelain in 2 pc, goose figure, orig neon, old transformer possibly replaced, 1930s-1940s, cond. 8.25-8.5........................................................ 1,155.00

# Red Head

Box, shell box, 2 pc, paper label on cardboard, "Red Head Shot Shells," 2 Canada geese in flight, round landscape scene with solid blue center, red ground, shell/duck on side, 12 gauge, Montgomery Ward Co., Chicago fair cond., 2-1/2" h, 4-1/8" sq ................ 33.00

# Redicut Tobacco

Lunchbox, litho tin, "Lorillard's Redicut Tobacco, Just Break Off A Piece To Fit," hands holding product, rust, cond. 7 ................................................................. 31.00

# Red Indian

Can, litho tin
    "Red Indian Aviation Motor Oil," Indian in headdress in red, red/blue/white text, white over blue ground, red stripe at top/center/bottom, no bottom, cond. 8, Imperial qt, 6-1/2" h, 4" dia ........................................... 99.00
    "Red Indian Motor Oil," Indian in headdress in red, white text, white over red/black ground, stripes at center/base, McColl-Frontenac Oil Co., Canadian, cond. 8, Imperial qt, 6-1/2" h, 4" dia ............... 71.50
Gas globe
    High-profile metal body (newer), 2 lenses, "Red Indian" in black, central portrait of Indian in headdress, white ground, all cond. 9, 13-1/2" dia ......................... 605.00
    Wide glass body, 2 lenses, "Red Indian" in black, central portrait of Indian in headdress, white ground, 1

Tin, vertical pocket, "Red Jacket Smoking Tobacco," oval, light wear, 4-1/2" h, $137.50.

lens/body cracked, lens cond. 9/6, boy cond. 7,
13-1/2" dia ................................................... 236.50

## Red Indian Tobacco

Canister, litho tin, "Red Indian Cut Plug, The American
Tobacco Co.," Indian in headdress, gold on black
ground, cond. 8+, 6-3/4" h, 5" dia .................... 990.00

## Red Jacket Bitters

Sign, broadside, cloth-finish, board-mounted, "Lewis' Red
Jacket Bitters, The Celebrated Fever & Ague and Malaria
Cure, Lewis & Co.," pictures Indian with head feathers
and paint on face, red ground, cond. 8+, 14-1/2" h,
11" w ................................................................ 2,035.00

## Red Jacket Tobacco (See Photo)

## Red Label Coffee

Can, keywind, litho tin, "S.S. Pierce Co. Red Label Coffee," shield logo with eagle/3 lions, red/dark text, white
band on red ground, S.S. Pierce Co., Boston, cond.
8.25+, 1 lb .......................................................... 27.50

## Red Man Tobacco

Sign, porcelain, "Red Man Scrap Tobacco," white text,
red ground, center is blue ellipse, cond. NM,
12" dia ................................................................ 660.00

## Red Owl Coffee

Can, keywind, litho tin, 'Red Owl Harvest Queen Coffee,
Finest Quality, Regular Grind," red cartoon owl head at
top, blue lower ground in arched panels, white upper,
Red Owl Stores, Minneapolis MN, cond. 8.5+,
1 lb ...................................................................... 46.00

## Red Raven

Tray, litho tin
Rectangular, "Red Raven Splits, Ask The Man" on brown
rim, "Please hurry up Welsh Rabbit..." with image of
rabbit by lobster, red raven in grass, scratches/soiling/
chips, 10-1/2" h, 13-3/4" w .............................. 258.50
Round, "Red Raven, For High Livers' Livers" on black
rim, shows red raven and bottle, cond. 9-,
12" dia ............................................................ 484.00

## Red Ribbon Beer

Tray, litho tin, full scene of bear and case of beer bottles,
cond. 8-, 13-1/4" sq ............................................ 522.50

## Red Rock Cola

Door pull, metal, plastic handle, "Enjoy Red Rock Cola,"
white text, red ground, scratches/chips, 3" h,
24" w .................................................................. 104.50
Sign, tin, embossed
"Drink, Enjoy Red Rock Cola," bottle on red ground,
1939, cond. 9.5, 32" h, 8" w .......................... 275.00
"On Ice, Long Green, Ko-Nut, Red Rock, In Bottles, 5¢,
Red Rock Co.," red/green text, white ground, green

border, dents/scratches/chips/yellowing, 27-1/2" h,
19-1/2" w ............................................................ 104.50

## Red Rooster Coffee

Tin, keywind, litho tin, "New and Improved," drip grind,
red cartoon rooster on red/white ground, cond. 9,
1 lb ...................................................................... 72.00

## Red Rose Coffee

Can, keywind, litho tin, snap top, taller version with
recessed lid, "Vacuum Packed Red Rose Brand Coffee," "Red Rose Coffee" in white text on black banners, oval image of red rose, Western Grocer Mills,
Marshalltown IA, cond. 8+, 1 lb ........................ 137.50

## Red Rose Tea

Door push, porcelain, die-cut, "Red Rose Tea is good tea,"
white on red ground, Canadian, cond. 8.25+, 9" h,
3" w .................................................................... 467.50

## Red Seal Battery

Sign, flange, porcelain, die-cut, battery-shape, rounded
top/bottom, "Guaranteed for all Open Circuit Work,
Red Seal Dry Battery, A Battery Suitable For Every
Use, The Guarantee Protects You," text on red battery,
cond. 8/7.5, 24-1/2" h, 13" w ............................ 990.00
Thermometer, porcelain, rounded top only, "Guaranteed
for all Open Circuit Work, Red Seal Dry Battery, A Battery Suitable For Every Use, The Guarantee Protects
You," text on red battery at top, white text at bottom,
blue ground, 1915 patent date, cond. 7.5, 27" h,
7" w .................................................................... 198.00

## Red Star Cleaning Powder

Box, paper label on cardboard, color scene of mother at
window, girl at stand, young child in Red Star wagon
behind horse pull toy, circa 1880s, cond. 8, 5" h, 3-1/2" w,
1-1/4" d .............................................................. 357.50

## Red & White Coffee

Can, keywind, litho tin, taller version, "Red & White Vacuum
Packed Coffee," cup of coffee on white band, white text,
red ground, cond. 8.5, 1 lb .................................... 54.00

## Red Wolf Coffee

Can, keywind, litho tin, red wolf in black oval, red text, white
ground, dark lid/band at bottom, cond. 7, 1 lb, 3-7/8" h,
5" dia .................................................................. 144.00

## Reed Mfg. Co.

Sign, tin over cardboard, "Guaranteed Against Breakage,
Reed Manufacturing Co., Erie, Penna., U.S.A.," vise in
white oval, white text, red ground, black border, cond.
G, 13-1/4" h, 19-1/4" w .................................... 170.50

## Reel Man

Tin, litho tin, "Reel Man After Shave Talc," man catching
fish mid-stream, blue top/bottom, cond. 9-,
4.75" h ................................................................ 187.00

## Regal Smoking Tobacco

Tin, vertical pocket, flip top, litho tin, crest with 2 lions in circular wreath, cream ground, "Regal Cube Cut Smoking Tobacco," cond. 8................................ 484.00

## Reid, Murdoch & Co.

Dispenser, stoneware, "Reid, Murdoch & Co., Chicago, New York, Boston, Pittsburg" in blue on white glaze, octagonal plate-glass cover with cutout for ladle, from freestanding tin display for pickles, minor chips to glass, chips-cracks to crock, cond. VG ............. 176.00

## Reid's Ice Cream

Sign, porcelain, die-cut, 2-sided, seal-shape, "Certified Dealer, Reid's Special Ice Cream," white/black text, red ground, minor chips/water stain, 30" dia................ 412.50

## Reliance Adv. Co.

Sign, porcelain, "Reliance Adv. Co., Chicago, Milwaukee, New York, Porcelain Enameled Advertising Signs," white/blue text, cobalt/red/white ground, cobalt border, 1940s-1950s, cond. 8.5, 13" h, 24" w ............... 231.00

## Remington Arms Co.

**History:** In 1845 the United States government contracted with Eliphalet Remington for 5,000 rifles. With the assistance of his sons, Philo, Samuel, and Eliphalet, Jr., Remington formed the company of E. Remington & Sons and went on to develop and produce a variety of guns. The business went into receivership in 1886, but by 1888 it had been reorganized as the Remington Arms Company.

Box, paper over cardboard, "Remington Shur Shot Shells, Sure, Safe, Speedy, Smokeless Powder," red "Remington UMC" logo at top, shell on side, 20 gauge, wear/fading/scrape, 2-1/4" h, 3-5/8" sq............... 38.50
Sign, cardboard, die-cut, easel-back
    "Get the Break with Kleanbore Shot Shells," man shooting skeet, 2 boxes of shells, circa 1940s, cond. 8.25, 20" h, 13" w............................... 192.50
    "Remington Kleanbore Hi-Speed 22's, Longer Range, Higher Velocity, More Power... Greater Accuracy," 3

**Sign, metal, "Remington Chain Saws," white letters on red ground, rounded corners, NOS, 10" h, 15" w, $15.**

boys with rifle/target on fencepost, also shows bag/ 2 boxes of shells/rifle/bird/squirrel, circa 1940s, cond. 7.75+, 20" h, 13" w.............................. 577.50

## Remington Chain Saws (See Photo)

## Remrandco Typewriter Ribbon

Tin, cardboard, round, shows woman in flowing yellow dress, orig sq cardboard "Remtico, Office Machine Ribbon" shipping box, 1951 cancellation, Remington Rand, cond. 7.5-8 .............................................. 60.50

## Repeater Tobacco

Tin, litho tin, "Repeater Mild Smoking Tobacco, Fine Cut," man in red jacket on horseback, black text, red trim, cond. 7.5, 4" x 6" ................................................. 36.50

## Reposed

Tin, vertical pocket, litho tin, green text on white medallion, green ground, "Reposed Chipped Plug, John Middleton, Phila. Pa.," cond. 8, 5" h, 3-3/8" w ........................................................ 977.00

## Revelation

Tin, vertical pocket, litho tin, sample
    "Revelation Smoking Mixture, The Perfect Pipe Tobacco, It's Mild and Mellow," red/black text, white ground, red top, cond. 8.5 .............................. 39.00
    "Revelation Smoking Mixture, The Perfect Pipe Tobacco, It's Mild and Mellow" also "Trial Size," red/ black text, white ground, red top, cond. 8.5........................................................ 27.50

## Revenge Lice Destroyer

Can, litho tin, "Revenge Lice Destroyer, Disinfectant, Germicide, Deodorizer," shows rooster before/after, I.D. Russell Co., Kansas City MO, cond. 7.5, 3" h, 4" dia................................................................. 38.50

## Rev-O-Noc Sporting Goods

Sign, litho tin over cardboard, "H.S.B.& Co. Rev-O-Noc, Firearms, Sporting Goods, Fishing Tackle," vignettes with duck hunter, fisherman, baseball players, also fishing, golf, baseball illustrations, circa 1915, cond. 8+, 13-1/4" h, 19-1/4" w..........................................2,970.00

## Rex

Door push, porcelain, "It's In The Blend," green vertical pocket tin on white ground, cond. 8+, 6-1/2" h, 3-3/4" w............................................................ 440.00
Tin, vertical pocket, litho tin, "Rex Mild Cool Burning Pipe And Cigarette Tobacco," portrait of Greek man with wreath on head in oval medallion flanked by torches, dark ground, cond. 8+..........................................265.00

## Rexall

Sign
    Paper, "Rexall Foot-Bath Tablets, For Foot Comfort,

Sold Only At The Rexall Stores," woman in blue dress with feet in bowl of water, holds product in hand, white/light-blue text, blue ground, cross-corner frame, cond. VG, 47-1/4" h, 22" w .................. 341.00

Porcelain, 2-sided, rounded corners, "McFarlin" in cobalt on orange panel mounted over oval panel with Rexall in white on cobalt ground, orange border, in metal housing, iron hangers, chips, 30" h, 72" w ............................................................ 440.00

Tin, litho tin

"Rexall Antiseptic Tooth Powder," oval image of girl with toothbrush, blue/gold text, light-blue ground, cond. 7, 4-3/4" h, 2-1/4" w, 1-3/4" d ............. 166.00

"Rexall Baby Talcum, Comfort for the Little One," oval portrait of blonde infant girl, floral trim, cond. 7+, 4-1/2" h, 2-1/2" w, 1-3/8" d .......................... 231.00

## Rex Coffee

Can, keywind, litho tin, "Regular Grind, Rex Oven Toasted Modern Vacuum Pack Coffee," red/black text, 2 crowns, white ground, red band at bottom, Hulman & Co., Terre Haute IN, opened with can opener, no lid, cond. 8, 1 lb ........................................................ 44.00

## Rex-Ton

Tin, litho tin, "Rex-Ton False-Teeth Cleanser" in shield with red crown/upper dentures, "Cleans, Deodorizes and Removes Smoke Stains on False Teeth" at bottom, blue ground, cond. 7.5, 4-1/2" h, 2-1/4" w, 1-1/4" d............................................................. 248.50

## Rhinelander Butter

Sign, tin over cardboard, beveled edge, "We Sell a Lot of Rhinelander Butter, pound & 1/2 pound cartons," 2 sizes shown, blue ground, cond. 8+, 9" h, 13" w ............ 187.00

## Rice Crispies

Counter sitters, cardboard, die-cut, 3 separate characters, Snap, Crackle, Pop with boxes, each 2-pc, framed, 22" h, cond. 8.75, set of 3 ................................................ 880.00

Dolls, cloth, uncut patterns, Snap, Crackle, Pop, 1948, cond. 9.25+, set of 3 ........................................ 132.00

## Richardson Root Beer

Barrel tag, aluminum, slightly curved, shield shape, "Richardson Root Beer 5¢," circa 1940s, cond. 8.5 ............................................................. 60.50

## Richelieu Cut Plug

Tin, litho tin, slip lid, round, "Richelieu Cut Plug Smoking Tobacco, The Standard Tobacco Co., Quebec," round portrait of bearded man, white diagonal band, blue outer ring, cond. 8+, 2-3/8" x 3-1/2" .................... 82.50

## Richfield

Calendar, paper, 1937, "Going Places with Richfield," policeman stopping traffic for 2 girls/dog on homemade racer, merchant info, unused, cond. EXC, 15" h, 7-1/2" w ....................................................... 137.50

Gas globe, 2 lenses, low-profile metal body, "Richfield Ethyl" in blue/red under flying eagle, white shield, yellow/blue border, lens cond. 8, body cond. 7 ........................ 880.00

Salt shaker, plastic, gas pump shape, yellow, "Richfield Ethyl" eagle logo, cond. 7+, 2-3/4" h, 1" w ............... 44.00

Sign, porcelain, 2-sided, "Richfield" under flying eagle on yellow shield, white/cobalt trim, chips/stains/touchups, 58" dia................................................................. 440.00

## Richheimer's Coffee

Shipping box, wooden, "Richheimer's" on diagonal panel, "Coffee Roasted, Own Process" on red ground, cond. 8.25, 17" h, 30" w, 18-1/2" d .................................... 49.50

## Richlube Motor Oil

Can, tin, "Richlube Motor Oil, The Wonder Oil For Motors, Pennsylvania's Purest," early auto over yellow shield, yellow/blue/white text, blue ground, Richfield Oil Co., Los Angeles, CA, cond. 7, 1/2-gal, 6-1/2" h, 8" w, 3" d .......................................................... 440.00

Sign, tin, 2-sided, "1/4 More Heat Resistance, Richlube Motor Oil, 100% Pure Pennsylvania," yellow/blue text, black ground, yellow border, cond. 7+, 24" dia................................................................. 825.00

## Richmond Gem

Tin, litho tin, "The Richmond Gem Curly Cut For Cigarettes & Pipes," red ground, mentions Paris/Philadelphia awards, 2-1/4" h, 4-1/2" w, 3-1/4" d......................... 66.00

## Riley Bros. Oil

Can, litho tin, "Riley Bro's That's Oil (blank) Oil, Riley Penn Oil Co., Burlington, Iowa," cond. 8, gal, 11-1/2" h, 8" w, 3" d ............................................................ 170.50

## Riley's

Pail, litho tin, embossed, slip lid, "Riley's Rum & Butter Toffee," orange with silhouettes of children at play with kite, cond. 8, 4 lb, 7-1/2" h .................................. 50.00

## Ring Seal Motor Oil

Can, litho tin, soldered seam, "Tankar Ring Seal Motor Oil, Carbon's Natural Enemy," shows tanker car, white/red on blue ground, rust, cond. 8+, 5-1/2" h, 4" dia............................................................... 880.00

## Rinso

Sign, porcelain, 'Soak the Clothes-That's All! Saves Coal Every Wash-Day," red oval, blue ground, chips, 18" h, 24" w ................................................................ 715.00

## Ripple

Cigarette case, litho tin, "Ripple Cigarette Case, Fine Rich Taste," shows cigarette/starburst medallion, cobalt over white ground, cond. 8+ ........................................... 69.00

## Rit

Cabinet, tin

Peaked top, "Never say 'dye' say Rit" on top, front

shows woman with product/dyed garment over "Cake or Flake 10¢," round medallions of Rit/Flaked Rit boxes, woodgrain ground, 6 drawers in back, labels loose/3 handles missing/minor stains, 16-1/4" h, 10" w .............................................. 148.50

Slant-front, "New Improved Rit, Guaranteed To Fast Dye Or Tint, Washes as it Dyes," blue/yellow text, woodgrain ground, 3 drawers in back, cond. G, 8-1/4" h, 11-1/4" w, 14" d ............................... 88.00

## Ritz Crackers

Sign, cardboard, "Ritz" in 3-D text by box of "Ritz" crackers, "America's Favorite Cracker" in blue on black panel with red "NBC" logo, red ground, newer plastic frame, cond. G, 14" h, 26" w.......................................................... 44.00

## River Front Coffee

Can, paper label, cardboard sides, tin top/bottom, "River Front Blended Coffee, Reeves, Parvin & Co., Philadelphia," detailed port scene, red ground, cond. 8-, 1 lb, 6" h, 4-1/4" dia ...................................................... 577.50

## Robin Hood Flour

Sign, flange, porcelain, red text, white ground, 1940s-1950s, cond. 9.5-9.75, 9" h, 18" w......................... 143.00

## E. Robinson's Sons

Tray, litho tin, round, "E. Robinson's Sons Pilsener Bottle Beer" on red rim, factory scene with trains/wagons, cond. VG, 13-1/8" dia...................................... 253.00

## Rob Roy Coffee (See Photo)

## Rob Roy Tobacco

Pack, paper, "Rob Roy Kentucky," Scottish bagpipe

**Can, paper label, "Rob Roy Coffee, Roasted & Packed by The Donald Company, Grand Island, Nebr." 1919 copyright, wear and tears to the label, 3 lbs, $145.**

player over "For Auld Lang Syne," red on orange ground, unopened, cond. 9.25+.......................... 77.00

## ROC

Gas globe, 1 lens, wide glass body, oval "ROC" in black behind red eagle, lens cond. 8, body cond. 9, 13-1/2" dia....................................................... 990.00

## Rochester Root Beer

Globe, milk glass, fired-on red lettering, "Rochester Root Beer," cond. 9, 8" ................................................ 99.00

## Rock Castle

Tin, vertical pocket, litho tin, "Rock Castle Chip Plug," round concave image of castle on rock on both sides, green ground, narrows at bottom, cond. 7.5 ................... 531.00

## Roger Bean Cigars

Can, litho tin, "Roger Bean Cigars 5¢," black/white cartoon illustration of Roger Bean and friends, cond. 8-, 5-3/8" h, 6" w, 4" d ............................................ 522.50

## Rogers Bros.

Sign, paper, "In the year 1847 in asking for Rogers Silver Plate...1847 Rogers Bros.," Victorian woman with house in background, border has 8 pcs of silverplate, merchant info at bottom, archival backing, cond. VG, 45" h, 31" w.......................................................... 110.00

## Romeos Condoms

Tin, litho tin

"1/4 Doz. Rubber Prophylactics Romeos," shield logo in upper left, yellow ground, 1/4" h, 2-1/8" w, 1-3/4" d ................................................................ 302.50

"Reservoir End, 1/4 Doz. Rubber Prophylactics Romeos," shield logo in upper left, violet ground, 1/4" h, 2-1/8" w, 1-3/4" d ............................... 687.50

"Romeos, 3 Rubber Prophylactics, Reservoir Ends," red oval with white text/shield at top, gray ground, cond. 8+, 1/4" h, 2-1/8" w, 1-3/4" d .............. 143.00

"Romeos Reservoir Ends Rubber Prophylactics," red oval with shield logo, tan ground, 1/4" h, 2-1/8" w, 1-3/4" d ........................................................ 198.00

## Ronson Motor Oil

Can, litho tin, triangle design with car/train/airplane, blue with yellow highlights, unopened, cond. 8+, 1 qt, 5-1/2" h, 4" dia .............................................................. 1,375.00

## Roosevelt

Tin

Metal with paper label, "Roosevelt Ginger, Distributed by Karasick Brothers Co., Chicago, Ill.," oval image of Teddy Roosevelt, green can, cond. 8+, 2 oz, 3-1/2" h, 2-3/8" w, 1-1/4" d.......................... 385.00

Litho tin, "Roosevelt Brand Allspice, Distributed by Karasick Brothers Co., Chicago, Ill.," oval image of Teddy

Roosevelt, cream ground, cond. 8+, 2 oz, 3-3/4" h, 2-1/4" w, 1-1/4" d................................................ 825.00

## Rose

Gas globe, older plastic body with 2 lenses, "Rose, Premium MMP," "Rose" in yellow on black circle at center, other text in red on white border, lens cond. 8.5, body cond. 8, 13-1/2" dia........................................... 231.00

## Rose Lawn

Sign, porcelain
   "Rose Lawn Milk, That Good Ice Cream," white/red text, shows milk carton/3 roses, yellow over red ground, 1950s, cond. 7.75, 40" h, 15" w......................... 231.00
   "Rose Lawn Milk, That Good Ice Cream," white/brown text, shows milk carton/3 roses, brown over yellow ground, chips/water stains, 40" h, 15" w ........... 192.50

## Rose Leaf Tobacco (See Photo)

## The Rose of Kansas Coffee

Can, litho tin, pry lid, round image of sunflower, green ground, cond. 7.5+, 3-3/4" h, 5-1/4" dia.............. 1,017.50

## Jesse L. Ross & Co.

Tray, metal, oval, "Jesse L. Ross & Co., Druggists, Waynesburg, Pa.," under classical scene of woman/cherub, minor rust/chips, 13-3/4" h, 16-3/4" w.................... 247.50

## Rosy Morn Coffee

Pail, litho tin, "Rosy Morn Brand Steel Cut Coffee," "Rosy Morn" in white on black bar, "Coffee" in red at bottom, 2 different colorful pastoral scenes, The McAtee Newell Co., Bloomington, Ill., cond. 8-8.5, 4 lb, 7-1/2" h, 7-1/2" dia.......................................................... 419.00

## Rothenberg's Mixture

Tin, vertical pocket, short version, oval image of gentleman, red ground, cond. 7.5, 3" h....................... 333.00

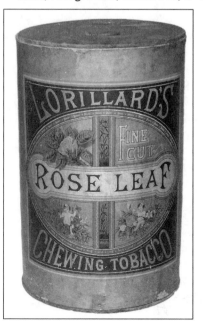

**Container, cardboard, paper label, wooden lid, "Lorillard's Rose Leaf Chewing Tobacco," 14-1/4" h, $400.**

**Can, paper label, "Rough Rider Baking Powder, The Southern Manufacturing Company, Richmond, Va.," tears to label, 5-1/2 oz, $175.**

## Rough Rider Baking Powder (See Photo)

## Round Trip Smoking Tobacco

Tin, horizontal box, litho tin, square corner, "Round Trip Cut Plug Smoking Tobacco," round scene of battleship with rope border, white text on red ground, "Cut Plug" in gold text on black ground, cond. 8.5-9 ......... 533.50

## Roundy's Coffee (See Photo)

## Rowntree's Gums

**Can, keywind, tin, "Roundy's Coffee," cream and brown ground, 1 lb, $12.50.**

**Can, litho keywind, tin, taller version, "Royal Blue Stores Coffee, Chicago," 1 lb, $115.50.**

Jar, clear glass, tin lid embossed "Rowntree's Gums" on front/back of rim, surface rust on lid/jar chipped-cracked, 7" h, 5-1/2" dia ............................ 88.00

# Royal Baking Powder

**History:** "Absolutely Pure," the slogan for Royal Baking Powder, was one of the first to be used on more than just a local basis. It was so instrumental in generating business that, by the 1890s, reliance on advertising slogans had become commonplace.

Tin, sample, paper label, "Free Sample," embossed lid, round medallion shows can, red ground, unopened, no contents, 2-1/4" h, 1-1/2" dia ................................ 33.00

# Royal Blend Coffee

Can, keywind, litho tin, taller version, "Royal Blend Brand High Grade Coffee," red text, crown in red seal with ribbon, red/blue/gold/cream band at top/bottom, Granger & Co., Buffalo, N.Y., cond. 8+, 1 lb ........................... 121.00

# Royal Blue Stores Coffee (See Photo)

# Royal Crown Cola

**History:** Claude Hatcher developed a line of flavored drinks as well as Royal Crown Ginger Ale to sell from his wholesale grocery, Hatcher Grocery Company of Columbus, Ga. Sales convinced him he had a future in the business, and he and his father opened Union Bottling Works in 1905. After reorganization, the company was renamed the Chero-Cola Company in 1912. Nehi debuted in 1924, and the company became the Nehi Corporation in 1928. Royal Crown Cola was introduced in 1934, with loyal customers soon referring to the drink simply as RC. The advertising slogan "Best by Taste Test" was adopted in 1940, and the company became Royal Crown Cola Company in 1959.

Clock, glass face/cover, cardboard body, "Drink Royal Crown Cola, Best By Taste-Test" in yellow/white text on red center, white border, black numbers, 15" dia ............................ 302.50
Menu board, litho tin, embossed, "Royal Crown Cola,

Best By Taste-Test, Menu," white/yellow text flanked by bottles, red top, 1940s-1950s, cond. 9.25+, 28" h, 20" w .................................................................. 357.50
Mirror/thermometer, metal frame, red rectangular logo upper left, glass lower right, 1940s-1950s, cond. 8.5, 12" h, 9" w .................................................... 330.00
Napkin holder, metal, "Drink Royal Crown Cola, Best by taste-test," red body, yellow ends, white/red text, circa 1940s, cond. 8.5, 5" h, 7" w .................................. 660.00
Sign, cardboard
   Trolley, "RC...best way to wish friends Merry Christmas," seated Santa with bottle at left, rectangular red logo lower-right, white ground, circa 1950s, cond. 8.75, 11" h, 28" w .................................... 49.50
   "Shirley Temple says: 'It does taste best!'" over "Royal Crown Cola, Best By Taste-Test" in red panel, shows Shirley Temple holding bottle with pyramid logo, promotes "Since You Went Away" in upper-left, newer frame, 1" pc loose at bottom edge, 12-1/4" h, 29-1/2" w ........................................ 247.50
   "Yes... bring RC!," woman on telephone/holding bottle with pyramid logo, "Royal Crown Cola, Best By Taste-Test" red panel at right, cond. EXC, 11" h, 28" w ............................................................. 82.50
Sign, tin
   2-sided, sidewalk sign, "Relax and Enjoy, Royal Crown Cola, Best By Taste-Test" white top/bottom, bottom with rounded yellow under red ground, tilted bottle on central white circle, 1940, cond. 8.25-8.5, 16" h, 24" w ............................................................. 1,045.00
   Same design as above, open courtesy panel at top, cond. 7.75-8 .................................................... 687.50

**Clock, double bubble, round, "Royal Crown Cola" in red on white diamond, "RC" diamond/crown at top/bottom, red ground, blue border with numbers 12/3/6/9 and crowns in white, orig box, 1963, cond. 9.5-9.75, $1,650. (Photo courtesy of Gary Metz, Muddy River Trading Co.)**

Convex, "Royal Crown Cola, RC," rounded corners, 1960s-1970s, cond. 9.25+, 32" h, 48" w ............. 55.00

Sign, tin, die-cut, 2-sided
  "Relax and Enjoy Royal Crown Cola, Best by Taste-Test," shows bottle, yellow/red ground, orig hanging bracket, cond. 9.25-9.5+, 16" h, 24" w .......................... 1,595.00
  "Take Home A Carton, Six Big Bottles 25¢ Plus Deposit," shows 6-pack in yellow/red carton, green ground, circa 1940, cond. 9.25-9.5, 16" h, 24" w .................................................... 1,540.00

Sign, litho tin, die-cut, embossed
  Bottle shape, pyramids label, cond. 9.25-9.5, 12" h ........................................................ 275.00
  Bottle shape, red over yellow label without pyramids, cond. 8.25, 12" h................................110.00
  Bottle shape, red over yellow square label, 1952, cond. 9.25-9.5, 59" h .......................... 522.50
  Bottle shape, red over yellow square logo with no central design, 1940s, cond. 8.25+, 5' h ........................ 302.50

Sign, tin, embossed
  "Drink Royal Crown Cola," white diamond logo with red crown/text, red ground, cond. VG, 11-1/2" h, 29-1/2" w ............................................................ 66.00
  "Drink Royal Crown Cola, Best By Taste-Taste," yellow/white text, red ground, 1952, orig wood frame on back, cond. 7.5-8+, 22" h, 34" w .................................. 198.00
  "Drink Royal Crown Cola, Best By Taste-Test," name in arch, yellow/white text, red ground, NOS, minor dents to corners, 10-1/4" h, 21" w................... 66.00

Thermometer, painted metal, rounded corners, "Drink Royal Crown Cola, Best By Taste-Test," all-white text, tube on panel with yellow arrow pointing up, red ground, cond. G, 25-1/2" h, 9-1/2" w .................. 93.50

Thermometer, tin, rounded corners
  "Drink Royal Crown Cola, Best By Taste-Test," red rectangular logo at top, glass at left, bottle at right, white ground, 1950s, cond. 7-7.5, 14" h......................110.00
  Red diamond logo at top, glass at left, bottle with diamond logo at right, 1960s, cond. 8, 14" h ......................................................... 143.00

## Royal Daylight Lamp Oil

Sign, porcelain, "Royal Daylight Lamp Oil, Anglo American Oil Co. Ltd., Best American Lamp Oils," oval image of 2 horses hitched to oil wagon, fading/scratches/water stain, 14-1/2" h, 21" w............................................. 880.00

## Royal Pancake Flour

Thermometer, painted wood, "Royal Pancake Flour, Just Try It Today," king eating pancakes, 15" h, 4" w .......... 302.50

## Royal Scarlet Coffee

Can, keywind, litho tin, "Royal Scarlet Regular Grind Coffee," red/white text, potbelly waiter at right, white over red ground, R.C. Williams & Co., New York, cond. 8+, 1 lb ................................................................ 44.00

## Royal Scot Feeds

Sign, tin, embossed, "Royal Scot Feeds," blue text with yel-

low leaves in white border around round image of Scotsman, red/blue/white plaid ground, scratches/dents/nail hole in each corner, 23-1/2" h, 16" w ...................... 66.00

## Royal Triton Motor Oil

Sign
  Porcelain, die-cut, 2-sided, ax-head shape, "America's Finest, Royal Triton Motor Oil," black/white text, white over black ground, cond. 8, 30" h, 25" w........................................................ 181.50
  Tin, die-cut, can shape, rounded top/bottom, "Royal Triton 10-30, Union Oil Company of California," small Union 76 symbol, black over white ground, pinstripes, cond. 8, 30" h, 19" w ........................................176.00

## Royal Typewriter

Sign, paper on cardboard, "Joy for All in this one gift, a Royal Portable," red typewriter in Christmas setting, cond. VG, 27-1/2" h, 21-1/2" w............................... 110.00

## RPM Motor Oil

Sign, porcelain, 2-sided, white "RPM" on swirling orange circle, "Motor Oil" in black at bottom, white ground, cond. 8/7+, 28" dia............................................ 286.00

## Rum and Maple Pipe Mixture

Box, store display, cardboard, "18 Sample Packages, Original Rum and Maple Pipe Mixture, Blend No. 53, These Samples, If Used With Discretion Will Benefit Both Of Us" in red on white, with 12 unopened sample cardboard boxes/matchbook advertising trial packages, cond. NM.............................................................. 152.00

## Runkel's Cocoa

Tin, paper label
  Sample, "Runkel's Pure Cocoa, Sample," woman logo in center, cond. 8, 1-5/8" h, 1-1/4" w, 1" d .............. 66.00
  "Runkel's Pure Cocoa, Prepared From The Choicest Cocoa Beans," woman in red dress with product in red ring, green ground, white/red/black text, cond. 8, 4-1/4" h, 2-3/4" w, 1-1/4" d.......................... 66.00

## Rush Park Seed Co.

Box, display, wood with litho paper on front and inside lid, "Seeds from Rush Park Seed Co." on front decal, having considerable wear, "Rush Park Seed Co., Independence Iowa, Celebrated & Reliable Seed, Grown From Selected And Choice Seed Stock, Are Absolutely Fresh and Can Be Depended to Give Entire Satisfaction, Iowa Grown Seed Are The Best Try Them" on inside decal with edge chipping, 5-1/2" h, 28" w, 13-1/2" deep .................................................. 176.00

## Russian Cigarette Tobacco

Tin, litho tin, square corner, larger size, shows Russian emblem, Aug. Beck & Co., Chicago, cond. 8, 4-1/2" ............................................................ 91.00

## S.&H. Green Stamps

Sign, porcelain, sidewalk, 2-sided, "We Give S.&H. Green Stamps," white on green ground, white border, circa 1950s, cond. 8-8.5, 28" h, 20" w .............. 121.00

## Saf-T-Way

Tin, litho tin, "Air Tested, Saf-T-Way Prophylactics, Made from Liquid Latex," round design, blue and white, hinged lid, cond. 8-, 1/4" h, 2-1/4" w, 1-5/8" d.................... 275.00

## Saint Paul-Mercury Indemnity Co.

Sign, litho under glass on wood, "Saint Paul-Mercury Indemnity Company, Saint Paul, Minn.," shows Mercury behind diagonal "Saint Paul," cond. 9.25+, 12" h, 20" w ...................................................................110.00

## Saint Paul Shoes

Shoehorn, metal, "A.H. Schultz, Sutherland, Iowa" on handle, red oval logo, hand in center, cond. 8.5, 4-3/4" h, 1-3/4" w ............................................... 148.50

## Salada

Door bar, porcelain, 2-sided, "Delicious Salada Tea Flavor," back says "Thank You, Call Again," red text, white ground, cond. EXC, 3-1/4" h, 32" w....................... 77.00
Sign, porcelain, die-cut
    Shape of a box, "Salada Tea, In Metal Packets Only," chips/fading/scratches, 10" h, 19" w ............. 412.50

**Lighter, "Menthol Fresh, Salem Filter Cigarettes," green/ white ground, mkd Zenith, 1-7/8" h, 2-1/8" w, $15.**

    Shape of a coffee tin, "Salada Coffee," chips, 12" h, 12" w............................................................ 495.00

## Salem Cigarettes (See Photo)

## Sampson Baking Powder

Can, paper label over tin, panel shows Sampson holding globe, white text, red/blue ground, circa 1910, part of label missing in back, front cond. 8+, 5-1/2" h, 3" dia............................................................... 163.00

## Sana-Dermal Talcum

Tin, paper over cardboard, oval image of mother/infant, cond. 8+, 2" h, 1-1/4" w, 7/8" d......................... 253.00

## San Antonio Brewing Association

Sign, paper, "The Famous Judge Roy Bean Horse Thief Trial, San Antonio Brewing Association," ©1945, newer frame, wrinkles/stain/bottom piece missing, 21-1/4" h, 26" w.................................................................121.00

## San Antonio Machine & Supply Co.

Calendar, tin over cardboard sign, chain-hung, pictures factory, "San Antonio Plant, SAMSCO, San Antonio Machine & Supply Co., Branches Corpus Christie-Harlingen-Austin-Waco," cardboard calendar months/ dates/days included, minor scratches, 19" h, 13" w ................................................................. 148.50

## San Blas

Tin, litho tin, small top, "San Blas Preserved Cocoanut," monkeys on all sides, black/blue design, cond. 8.5, 5-1/2" h, 2-3/4" sq ............................................... 71.50

## Sandusky Gold Bread

Bag holder, tin, 2-sided, "Sandusky Gold Bread, Radiant Baked," black/red text, white ground, wire hangers, cond. G, 13-1/2" h, 36-1/2" w, 3-1/2" d ............. 104.50

## San Felice Cigars

Sign
    Cardboard, wood frame, "San Felice Cigars, For Gentlemen of Good Taste," man/woman looking at painting, vase with flowers on table in foreground, Deisel-Wemmer Co. Lima, OH, stains to text, 23-1/4" h, 18-1/4" w........................................................187.00
Tin, embossed, "San Felice Cigars, 5¢, For Gentlemen

Sign, tin, "San Felice Cigars 5¢ For Gentlemen of Good Taste," also "Robertson-Dualife-Springfield, Ohio," 13" h, 39" w, $175.

Can, keywind, litho tin, "Sanka Coffee, General Foods Corporation, Hoboken, N.J.," yellow and black ground, unopened, 1 lb, $15.

of Good Taste," shows box of cigars, yellow ground, circa 1930s, cond. 6.5-7, 28" h, 20" w ............ 60.50

## Sanford's Ink

Cabinet, wood, "Sanfords Inks" in white on 4 sides, 4 open-sided shelves over 1 door on encased base, paint loss/cracking to finish, 57" h, 18" w, 14" d ..................... 555.50

## Sanico Coffee

Can, litho tin
Keywind, taller version, "Drip Sanico Coffee Method" in black diamond, "Drip Coffee" in red band, repeated pattern of capitol domes and tree line at bottom, Sanitary Grocery Co., Washington, D.C., cond. 8+, 1 lb ............................... 128.00
"Sanitary and Piggly Wiggly Stores," capitol building on yellow ground, cond. 8+, 1 lb, 6-1/4" h, 4" dia ........................................ 1,485.00

## Sanitary

Clock, lightup, glass face/cover, metal body, "Sanitary Farm Dairies Ice Cream And Milk," red/blue text, blue numbers, white ground, does not light, cond. VG, 15" dia ............................................ 143.00

Bottle, amber glass, paper label, "Sanford's Premium Writing Fluid," orig top, $55.

## Sanka Coffee (See Photo)

## Santa Fe

Tin
Litho tin, keywind, Indian leaning on Sante Fe logo, landscape ground, Midwest Coffee Co., Arkansas City, Kansas, cond. 9, 1 lb, 3-1/2" h, 5" d .................209.00
Paper on cardboard, rectangular, "Santa Fe Brand Pure ground Pumpkin Pie Spice," Indian with red blanket leaning against "Santa Fe" logo, Santa Fe Foods, Arkansas City KS, cond. 8.5, 1.5 oz ....................49.50

## San-Tox

Tin, litho tin
"San-Tox After Shave Talcum," shows nurse, DePree Co., Holland, MI, cond. 8+, 4-5/8" h, 2-1/2" w, 1-3/8" d ........................................ 440.00
"San-Tox Foot Relief," nurse in white panel flanked by columns, blue ground, DePree Co., Holland MI, cond. 7.5+, 4-1/2" h, 2-1/4" w, 1-3/4" d ........... 77.00

## Sapolin

Sign
Die-cut, man at stove pipe, "Sapolin Stove Pipe Enamel, A Gloss Black Finish That Serves, Saves, Satisfies," 1910s-1920s, cond. 8.75+, 8" h, 6-1/2" w ........................................ 88.00
Tin over cardboard, easel/string back, "Sapolin Stove Pipe Enamel," pictures stove/boiler/range top, cond. 9.25, 25" h, 18" w ............................... 522.50

## Satin Finish Confections (See Photo)

## Satin Finish Typewriter Ribbon

Tin, litho tin, "Since 1888, Satin Finish, A.P. Little," oval portrait of black child, red/black ground, unused, cond. 8.5, 1" h, 2-5/8" sq .............................................110.00

Tin, litho tin, pry lid, "Satin Finish Confections, Mfd. By Brandle Smith Co., Philadelphia," orange/black plaid ground, 3 lb, $45.

## Satin Skin Powder

Sign, litho paper, "Satin Skin Powder, 4 Tints, Flesh, White, Pink , Brunet" at top, "Satin Skin Cream" at bottom, woman with fan mkd "Don't you want satin skin," containers of Satin Skin Cream/Satin Skin Powder, black text, yellow ground, archival backing, cond. EXC, 45" h, 30-3/4" w .........................................110.00

## Sauer's Extracts

Cabinet, wood with glass front, orig decal, embossed tin strip sign tacked on each side, 1910s-1920s, cond. 8.8-9, 26" h, 12" w............................................. 990.00
Thermometer, painted wood
　Die-cut, "Sauer's Pure Concentrated Extract Vanilla," shows 3-D box with glass on side, ©1918-19, soiling/scuffs/cracks in paint/faded, 8" h, 3-7/8" w.........................................................110.00
　Rounded top, beveled edge, "Sauer's Flavoring Extracts, None Better, 10 and 25¢, Sixteen Highest Awards and Gold Medals For Purity-Strength And Fine Flavor," shows bottle being removed from "Vanilla" box, red/black text, white ground, tube offset to left, rusted brackets/thermometer not working/fading, 23-1/2" h, 7" w............................. 192.50

## Savage Rifle Powder

Tin, litho tin, "Savage Smokeless Rifle Powder, Savage Arms Co.," black text flanked by rifles, red ground, cond. 8+, 6-1/4" h, 3-7/8" w............................... 715.00

## Savage Tires

Sign, cardboard, silk-screen painted, boy in Indian headdress stopping car, cond. 8, 25-3/4" h, 18-3/4" w.......................................................... 357.50

## Savex Gasoline

Gas globe, 2 lenses, narrow glass body, "Save with Savex Gasoline," black text, "Savex" in white on vertical panel, NOS, all cond. 9, 13-1/2" dia ........... 495.00

## Thos. J. Scanlon

Calendar, litho tin over cardboard, 1906, "Thos. J. Scanlon Dealer In Bar Supplies, Hotel China and Glassware, 14 E. Lacock St. Allegheny, Pa.," woodgrain decor, oval illustration of a girl in a pink dress with 2 roses entitled "A Lady of Quality," each month at the bottom, water stains/warping/dents, 19-1/4" h, 13-1/4" w........................................................ 247.50

## Schaefer Beer

Clock, plastic, electric, barrel form, clock on one end, Schaefer logo on other, "On Tap" on side, 12" h, 9" dia................................................................. 55.00

## Wm. Schellhas Brewing Co.

Sign, litho tin, rolled edges, "Compliments of Wm. Schellhas Brewing Co., Winona, Minn.," central image of beautiful woman, cond. 8-, 14-1/4" sq .............. 825.00

## Schenuit

Sign, flange, painted, "Schenuit Aircraft Tires (star) Tubes," red/black text, white ground, black border, cond. 7, 14" h, 18-1/2" w................................... 137.50

## Schepp's Cocoanut

**History:** During the 19th century, coconut was one of the few sweets that could be stored for any length of time, so it was a popular staple in American kitchens. L. Schepp marketed his Schepp's Cocoanut in New York, relying on clever displays and product premiums to bolster his sales. The Schepp's tins exhibited wonderfully detailed graphics, with many of the containers showing monkeys acting out scenes of family life typical of that period.

Cake box, tin, embossed front/top, various classical scenes by Kaulbach, cond. G, 14" h, 13" sq ......................181.50
Store jar, glass, embossed "Schepp's New Improved Cocoanut," oval "L.S." logo, coconut finial on lid, cond. EXC, 6-1/2" h, 5-1/2" dia................................. 495.00
Pail, litho tin, monkeys/oversized product box, yellow/black, circa 1890, cond. 8+, 4" h, 3-1/4" dia ....................220.00

## School Boy Peanut Butter

Pail, litho tin, "School Boy" in silver, "Peanut Butter" in red/white on blue semi-circle, red ground, Rogers Co., cond. 8+, 1 lb ................................................ 154.00

## Schrafft's

**History:** W.F. Schrafft and his sons started The Boston Candy Company in 1861. The first Schrafft's Candy and Ice Cream Shop opened in New York City in 1898, the brainchild of Frank G. Shattuck, a salesman for the Schraffts. It didn't take long for food to be added to the menu, and, eventually, Schrafft's Restaurants and Motels became a nationwide chain.

Pail, litho tin, pry lid, nursery rhyme images including The

Sign, tin, die-cut, "Schrafft's Chocolate Covered Bars Are Mighty Good," boy in red hat/checkered pants holding bell and sign, 1920s-1930s, cond. 8, 18" h, 12" w, $1,265. (Photo courtesy of Gary Metz, Muddy River Trading Co.)

Old Woman Who Lived in a Shoe, cond. 8+, 9 oz, 3-3/4" h, 3-7/8" dia ............................................ 687.50

# Schwinn

Sign, litho paper, "Ride a Schwinn Lightweight for Health and Pleasure, See the Schwinn-Built," couple with 2 bikes, logo lower-right, Arnold Schwinn & Co., Chicago, newer frame, cond. VG, 39-1/2" h, 24" w .............. 231.00

# Scotch Oats

Box, paper on cardboard, round, "Scotch Brand Oats" in white on black band under Scotsman with bagpipes, "Quick Cooking Style, Cooks in 2-1/2 Minutes," yellow ground, Green Bros. Mercantile, Kansas City MO, cond. 8-, 3 lb ....................................................... 38.50

# Scottie Cigars

Tin, litho tin, "Scotty Cigars," brown/white dog on yellow circle, white text, red ground, 50-count, cond. 8.25, 5" h, 4-1/4" sq .................................................... 357.50

# Scott Tissue Towels

Paper towel holder, litho tin and heavy wire, shows box of product, cond. 8+, 7-1/2" h, 13" w ..................... 522.50

# Scotty Mild Little Cigars

Tin, flat pocket, central image of dog with red scarf, "Scotty" in red at top, "Mild Little Cigars" in black in banner at bottom, white over red ground, red-dotted double border, cond. 9, 5/16" h, 3-1/4" w, 3" d .............................. 101.00

# Seagram's

**History:** After fleeing Russia and settling in Canada in 1889, Yechiel Bronfman started a liquor business. During World War I his sons, Allan and Samuel, ran the enterprise. Although all of the Canadian provinces

Can, paper label, "Seal Brand Coffee, Chase & Sanborn, Montreal," holes and tears to label, 1 lb, $45.

except Quebec were dry, mail order sales were quite good. (Illogical as it seems, such sales were also legal.) After liquor was legalized in 1920, the brothers bought out Joseph E. Seagram & Sons, adopting the name in 1927. Having established themselves with U.S. consumers during Prohibition, the company quickly expanded its market share after the 21st Amendment was ratified in 1933. By 1938, Seagram's had become the largest producer and distributor of liquor.

Clock, electric, metal housing, reverse-painted glass face with 7 Crowns logo/hours mkd by "7" in circle, "Enjoy Seagram's Seven Crown Blended Whiskey," embossed horses, revolving advertisement in glass beneath clock, 14-1/2" h, 16" w .......................... 88.00
Sign, heavy paper, "Endangered Wildlife of North America, Presented by Seagram's Canadian Hunter," shows 10 animals, black/red text, white ground, framed, Joseph E. Seagram & Son, New York, NY, cond. VG, 78-1/4" h, 34-1/2" w .......................... 66.00
Thermometer, round, plastic/glass, "Seagram's VO Imported Canadian," silver text, blue ground, cut-away dial at top under "Temperature," cond. 8.25+, 12" dia ............. 154.00

# Seal Brand Coffee (See Photo)

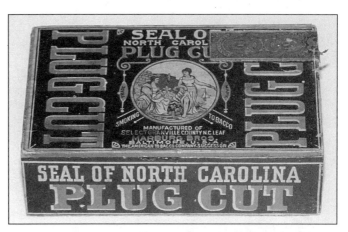

Box, litho paper cover, hinged, "Seal of North Carolina Plug Cut," 2-1/8" h, 6-5/8" w, 4" d, $150.

## Seal of North Carolina Tobacco

Can, litho tin, small top, "Seal of North Carolina Plug Cut," oval scene of 2 women at wall, sea in background, yellow/red text, black ground, cond. 7.5-8, round ................................................................ 244.00

Chair, folding chair, wood, paper label on front shows box of product with 2 women at wall, back shows cardboard pack, cond. 8+ ......................................... 445.00

Sign, cardboard, Victorian woman on pedestal leaning on oversized pack of "Seal of North Carolina Smoking Tobacco, Marburg Bros.," dapper gentlemen watching/ bowing, bottom of orig wood frame lettered "Marburg Bros.," cond. 8, framed size 29" h, 24" w .......... 642.00

## Sealtest

Sign, tin, embossed, "Sealtest Ice Cream," white on red ground, dents/chips/nail holes, 14" h, 30" w ............ 44.00

## Sealy Mattresses

Display, cardboard, die-cut, standup, black boy in bibs with cotton in one hand, hat in other, orig shipping carton, unused, like-new, 39" h, 22" w ................... 880.00

## Seamless Rubber Co.

Home plate, salesman sample, rubber, embossed, beveled edge, "Major League Sav-A-Leg Home Plate, Official," cond. EXC, 4" 3-7/8" ........................... 522.50

## Sea Toast

Can, litho tin, slip lid, "Sea Toast by Keebler," sailboat motif, Keebler-Weyl Baking Co., Philadelphia, cond. 9, 9" h, 3-1/4" dia ................................................ 133.00

## Security Stock Powder

Box, cardboard, "Security Stock Powder, Tonic and Conditioner...," Security Remedy Co., round image of

**Display, cardboard, die-cut, standup, Sealy, black girl with lap full of cotton, orig shipping carton, unused, like-new, 39" h, 22" w, $880. (Photo courtesy of Gary Metz, Muddy River Trading Co.)**

farmer carrying bucket, fence, livestock, Minneapolis MN, unopened, cond. 8+, 10-1/2" h, 7-5/8" w, 4" d ................................................................ 330.00

## Seilheimer's Ginger Ale

Sign, porcelain, red diamond with "So-Da-Licious," black text on white ground, "Seilheimer's Pale Dry Ginger Ale," 1930s-1940s, cond. 9-9.5, 10" h, 18" w ................ 198.00

## Senate Coffee

Can, litho tin

"Senate Brand Drip Grind Coffee," capitol building on yellow ground, blue band at bottom, Tampa Coffee Mills, Tampa, Fla., cond. 7.5, 1 lb ................... 66.00

"Senate Brand Fancy Selected Steel Cut Coffee," capitol building on blue/white striped ground, cond. 8, 1 lb, 6" h, 4" dia ............................................. 302.50

## Sensation Coffee (See Photo)

## Sen-Sen Chewing Gum

Sign, litho tin, embossed, "Sen-Sen Chewing Gum, 5¢, Grown up little Boys like it," street scene with 2 well-dressed men in coats and hats, substantial rust/wear at edges, 6-1/4" h, 6-5/8" w ........................... 1,017.50

## Sentinel Rubbing Compound

Can, tin, "Rubbing Compound" in red over auto in circle, soldier at blue border, white ground, red trim, blue band at bottom, Sentinel Products Co., San Antonio, dents/scratches, gal, 7-1/2" h, 6-1/2" dia ............ 16.50

## Sergeant's Dog Medicines

Cabinet, litho tin, "Sergeant's, Ask For Free Dog Book,

**Can, litho tin, pry lid, "Sensation Steel Cut Coffee, The HD Lee Mercantile Co., Kansas City, Salina, Kan., Waterbury, Conn.," 1 lb., $220.**

Dog Medicines," boy with German shepherd, "The premier dog medicines for 50 years" on side, yellow ground, red/black text, red band at bottom, cond. 7, 14" h, 12" w, 7" d............................................ 632.50

# 7Up

**History:** Charles Grigg worked for a soft drink bottler in St. Louis in 1920, but a quest for independence prompted him to join forces with Edwin Ridgway to start the Howdy Company. Their first drink, a mixture of orange and lemon sold in plain 6 -ouncebottles, was aptly named Howdy.

After a law was passed requiring orange-flavored drinks to contain real orange juice, Grigg developed a lemon-lime mixture that would be cheaper to produce. Originally sold as an antacid under the lengthy name Bib-Label Lithiated Lemon-Lime Soda, the product was later called 7Up and debuted in October 1929. Sensing a declining market for medicinal drinks, the company reduced the carbonation and focused advertising on the refreshing properties of the beverage instead.

Bottle, seltzer, glass, clear, 2-color applied label, "Zetz 7Up Bottling Co., New Orleans, La.," red/black design with black waiter, textured body, cond. 7.5 ....... 495.00

Clock

Lightup, round, red rectangular logo on green circle, green 12/3/6/9/dots for other hours, 1950s-1960s, cond. 9-9.5.................................................. 660.00

Revolving clock/lightup sign, plastic faces, metal frame, "Get Real Action, 7Up (logo), 7Up Your Thirst Away," red/black text, white ground, 1950s, sweep hand inoperable, cond. 7.5+, 14" sq............................................................ 412.50

Display, easel-back, "Seagram's Seven and 7Up, America's Favorite," circa 1950s-1960s, cond. 9-9.5, 10" h, 12" w ............................................................ 18.50

Door bar, porcelain, "Fresh up, Seven-up!," red bubbles logo at left/right, black text, white ground, cond. VG, 3" h, 31" w............................................................ 148.50

Door push plate, white with red 7Up logo with bubbles, made for Bakelite handle (not included), 1940s, cond. 9-9.25, 12" h, 3" w.............................................. 30.00

Kick plate, porcelain, "Fresh Up with 7Up," tilted bottle, 1951, minor edge nicks, cond. 9.5+, 12" h, 30" w ............................................................ 1,650.00

Screen door braces, litho tin

"Fresh Up, 7Up Likes You," other with "It Likes You," black/white with red bubbles logo, 1946, NOS, cond. 9.25+................................................. 275.00

"7Up, Take some home today," red bubbles logo, green/white diagonal stripes, 1940s-1950s, cond. 8.75-9.25, 9" h, 11" w.................................. 440.00

Sidewalk marker, brass, round, embossed "Drink 7Up, Safety First," cond. 6.5-7.5................................. 44.00

Sign, glass, 2-pc, easel-back or hanging, "We Sell 7Up, the Quality Drink," red bubbles logo on black/white ground, 1950s, cond. 9.25, 8" h, 7" w .............. 330.00

Sign, metal, school zone, 2-sided, round metal base, jolly policeman in blue uniform holding yellow and orange "Slow, School Zone" sign, rust/scratches/crease, 61-1/2" h, 24" w.............................................. 1,100.00

Sign, neon

4-color rainbow, "7Up" in red with borders of green/blue/orange, orig frame, 1950s-1960s, cond. 8.5-9, 15" h, 17" w .................................................. 522.50

Neon and plastic, 2-color, "Drink Un" on red/white striped ground over "7Up" neon over "Anytime" on blue ground with white stars, 1960s-1970s, cond. 8.5, 32" h, 24" w .......................................... 440.00

Sign, porcelain, "Fresh Up with" in green over tilted bottle, red/white logo at right, white ground, green band at bottom, 1951, cond. 8.25-8.5, 15-1/2" h, 40" w .............................................................522.50

Sign, tin

Easel-back/string-hung, red 7Up logo, 1950s, cond. 8+, 6" h, 5" w ................................................. 77.00

"Fresh Up! with 7Up," black text over red bubbles logo, white ground, cond. VG, 28" h, 20" w.......... 198.00

Red "7Up" logo (no bubbles), blue/yellow/red flourishes on 3 sides, orange/yellow stripes at bottom, green ground, cond. EXC, 34" sq ................. 137.50

Sign, tin, die-cut, for cooler or rack, "7Up, The Uncola," plain red logo, green text, arched top with sunrise, "No. 34, Made in U.S.A. 1-71," minor scratches, 12" h, 24" w .................................................................. 88.00

Sign, tin, embossed

Curb sign, A-framed mesh body, "7Up" red bubbles logo, sign on each side, cond. VG, 50" h, 28" w................................................................ 165.00

Red 7Up logo at left, "your thirst away" at right, green text on white, ground in elliptical panels of green/light-green/white, 1960s, cond. 8.25-8.5, 12" h, 30" w................................................................ 165.00

Sign, tin over cardboard

Beveled edge, easel-back/string-hung, "The All-Family

**Thermometer, Pam style, "7Up the Uncola," aluminum frame, 12" d, $40.**

Drink" under red bubbles logo, black on white ground, 1960, cond. 9.5, 9" sq......................... 60.50
Easel-back/string-hung, "7Up Smoke Mixer," cond. 7.5-8.25, 7" h, 6" w ...................................... 143.00
Thermometer, Pam style
  Red bubbles logo, green ground, cond. 9.5, 12" dia............................................................ 357.50
  Red bubbles logo over "Fight Against Thirst," black on white ground, circa 1950s, cond. 8.5-9, 12" dia............................................................ 176.00
Toy, rubber figure, bird-like, white shirt with red 7Up logo, black shorts, holds up bottle, 1959, cond. 8-8.5................................................................ 165.00

## Shadows Condoms

Tin, litho tin, 3-pack, "Shadows, As Thin as a Shadow, As Strong as an Ox!," green/white/black, cond. EXC, cond. 8.5, 1/4" h, 2-1/8" w, 1-3/4" d.................. 209.00

## Shamrock

Gas globe, newer plastic body with 2 lenses, "Shamrock" in white on green 3-leaf clover, white ground, lens cond. 8.5, body cond. 8, 13-1/2" dia ................. 231.00
Sign, porcelain, "Shamrock Cloud Master Premium," green clover over blue clouds, cond. 7, 12-1/2" h, 10-1/2" w .......................................................... 165.00

## Shamrock Coffee

Can, litho tin, pry lid, "Shamrock Sani-Fresh Vacuum Coffee," cup and clover, black ground, cond. 8-, 4" h, 5" dia................................................................ 330.00

## Shamrock Dairy

Sign, porcelain, "Shamrock Dairy, Golden Guernsey, America's Table Milk," leprechaun in green hat at left in yellow sunburst with shamrocks, green/yellow/black

text, white ground, 1940s-1950s, cond. 8.5, 22" h, 56" w ............................................................ 1,100.00

## Shamrock Rolled Oats

Box, paper on cardboard, "Shamrock Brand Quick Cooking Rolled Oats," castle design flanked by 3-leaf clovers marked MCC, cond. 8+, 3 lb, 9-1/2" h, 5-3/4" dia...................................................... 253.00

## Shapleigh Hardware Co.

Sign, tin over cardboard, beveled edge, "Hope Inspires, Work Wins, Success Rewards," white "h" in red shield at left, radiating star upper-right, "Shapleigh Hardware Co." on lower border, cond. EXC, 6-1/4" h, 9-1/4" w .......................................................... 44.00

## Sharps Toffee

Tin, litho tin, slip lid, "Sharps Super Kreem Toffee, 6¢ per 1/4 Lb.," shows parrot, cond. 8, 3-1/4" h, 10" dia........... 55.00

## Shasta (See Photo)

## Sheik (See Photo)

## Shell

Badge, cap
  Brass and cloisonné enameled, shell shape, red text/ stripe, screw-on attachment on back, late 1930s-early 1940s, cond. EXC, 1-3/4" h, 1-3/4" w............. 1,430.00
  Metal, inlaid cloisonné porcelain lettering, shell shape with red text, hinged pin/clip on back, cond. NM, 2" sq ............................................................ 797.50
Map, road map, 3-panel, "1929 Shell Road Map, Minnesota," cover shows shell-shaped "Shell Motor Oil" sign over service station, Minnesota dealer, cond. 8+, 9" h, 12" w ................................................................ 99.00
Plaque, etched/painted wood, "The Shell Penguins," pair

**Can, tin, "Shasta Cherry Cola, Shasta Beverages, Consolidated Foods, San Francisco," punch-top, light wear, rust, 12 oz, $28.50.**

**Bucket, litho tin, "Shell, Another Product Developed by Shell Research, Shell Oil Company," wear/ rust, 13-1/2" h, 12" dia, $25.**

**Tin, condom, "Sheik, Reservoir End, Manufactured by Julius Schmid Inc., New York," tan ground, holds 3, full, $40.**

of penguins on ice skates, circa 1930s, 12" h, 9" w .................................................. 231.00
Radiator cover, cardboard, die-cut
    2-sided, "Shell" repeated twice in red vertical lines, red outline of shell logo, yellow ground, cond. 8, 13-1/2" h, 18" w ........................................ 44.00
    "Shell, Starts Quickly," shell logo at top, red text, yellow ground, cond. 8, 11-1/2" h, 19" w ............. 44.00
Salt/pepper shakers, plastic, gas pump shape, "Shell" and "TCP" logos, "Gasoline" and "Premium," yellow/red body, orig box, NOS, cond. 9, 2-3/4" h, 1" w, pr ...................................................................... 192.50
Sign, paper, "Join the Share-the-Road Club here," shell logo with 3 flags, white text, red ground, cond. EXC, 56" h, 39-1/4" w ............................................... 170.50
Sign, porcelain, "Appointed Oil Fired Heating Installer" in black on white ground, shell logo at left, "BP" logo at

**Sign, porcelain, die-cut, 2-sided, "Shell Gasoline," red text, yellow ground, cond. 8, 24-1/2" h, 24-1/2" w, $660.**

right, white ground, red/yellow/orange flames on black ground at top, chips/scratches/stain, 13-1/4" h, 18-1/4" w ........................................................... 231.00
Thermometer, porcelain, rounded top/bottom, "Shell Gasoline, Shell Motor Oil," shell logos top/bottom, red on yellow ground, red trim, 1915 patent date, cond. 8, 27" h, 7" w ............................................... 1,100.00

## Shell Gasoline

Bank, tin, "Super Shell Gasoline" in red on shell logo, "Saves on Stop-and-Go driving," black text, black over yellow ground, "Golden Shell Motor Oil" logo on other side, cond. 7, 3-1/2" h, 2" dia ........................... 110.00
Gas globe, 1-pc, shell-shape
    "Shell" in red, cond. 8, 19" h, 19" w .................. 418.00
    "Super Shell," foreign, cond. 8, 18" h, 18" w .......... 770.00
Sign, painted metal, flange, die-cut, shell-shape, "Shell Gasoline" in red, yellow ground, cond. 8.5, 17-1/2" h, 21-1/2" w ...................................................... 1,595.00
Sign, paper, "Saves on Stop and Go Driving, Super-Shell," cartoon image of unhappy man in car, smiling man getting off train, cond. EXC, 33-3/8" h, 57-1/2" w ......... 77.00
Sign, porcelain
    2-sided, "Shell, Gasoline, State Tax, Total," black area for prices, red text, orange ground, cond. 7, 12" h ............................................................... 396.00
    Die-cut, 2-sided, shell shape, "Shell Gasoline," red text, yellow ground, cond. 7, 25" h, 25" w ................. 423.50

## Shell Motor Oil

Bottle, glass, pyro label, "Shell X-100 Motor Oil," red on yellow ground, foreign, cond. 8, 11-1/2" h ......... 159.50
Can, tin, "Shell Motor Oil" in red ring around yellow shell, orange ground, Roxana Petroleum Corp., cond. 7, 1 gal, 11" h, 8" w, 3" d ...................................... 357.50
Sign, porcelain
    Die-cut, shell-shape, 2-sided, "Shell Motor Oil" in red on yellow ground, cond. 7, 25" h, 24" w ....... 192.50
    Flange, "Shell" in red over red shell logo on yellow ground, "Motor Oil" in yellow on black panel at bottom, cond. 7, 15-3/4" h ................................. 605.00
    Triangular, "Lubricating Always, Shell Motor Oil" in red on yellow ground, foreign, cond. 9, 16-1/2" h, 33" w ............................................................. 770.00
    "Shell Lubricating Oils, Every Drop Tells," square/round cans of Shell Motor Oil, red/black text/border, yellow ground, cond. 7, 31-1/2" h, 24" w ..................... 825.00

## Sheridan Sugar Factory

Pocket mirror, celluloid, rectangular, "Sheridan Sugar Factory, Wyoming's First Plant, Erected 1915," shows plant in oval on sugar bag, blue ground, cond. EXC, 1-3/4" h, 2-3/4" w ............................................. 165.00

## Sherwin-Williams Paint

**History:** Henry Sherwin, owner of Sherwin-Williams Company, designed the company's first trademark, a chameleon sitting on a painter's palette. Ad manager George W. Ford sketched an alternative design in

1895 but kept it hidden, fearful that his attempts at improvement would offend Sherwin. After being uncovered and meeting with approval, Ford's "Cover-the-Earth" design finally became the company's official trademark in 1905.

Sign, porcelain, die-cut
    2-sided, "SWP Cover The Earth, Sherwin-Williams Paint," can pouring red paint over globe, red/white text, name in lower yellow panel, chips, 73" h, 50-3/4" w.......................................................... 313.50
    "SWP Cover The Earth," can pouring red paint over globe, red/white text, cond. G, 45" h, 25" w.................................................................... 451.00
    "SWP Cover The Earth, Sherwin-Williams Paint," can pouring red paint over globe, red/white text, name in brown on lower yellow panel, "Africa, Europe" in white on globe, cond. VG, 63" h, 35-1/2" w................ 368.50
Sign, tin, "Sherwin-Williams Paints" in black on yellow ground at left, ""SWP, Cover The Earth"/can pouring red paint on globe on white ground at right, wood back, cond. G, 34" h, 69-1/2" w .......................... 55.00

## Shot Tobacco

Tin, vertical pocket, litho tin
    "Shot Crushed Plug Cut, Cameron & Cameron Co.," crossed musket/peace pipe, cond. 8, 4-1/2" h, 3" w................................................................. 273.00
    Short version, "Shot Crushed Plug Cut, by Cameron & Cameron Co.," crossed musket/peace pipe, cond. 7.5-8, ........................................................ 124.00

## Shotwell's Marshmallows

Tin, litho tin, shows cake, light-blue ground, blue/red text on white medallion, 1920s, cond. 8, 3-1/2" h, 5-1/2" dia............................................................. 82.50

## Shredded Wheat

Display, glass dome on wooden base, glass embossed "Shredded Wheat" on 2 sides, displays 12 cereal biscuits, cond. EXC, 7" h, 12" w, 8" d .................... 660.00
Sign, paper, "For breakfast -- so easy to prepare, Nourishing," hand pouring milk from creamer onto bowl of prod-

**Tray, tin, "We Serve Shurtleff's Ice Cream," 12" h, 17" w, $65.**

uct, box of "Shredded Wheat" at right, white text, dark ground, newer frame, 10-1/2" h, 16" w .................... 66.00

## Shurtleff's Ice Cream (See Photo)

## Silver Bell

Tin, litho tin, "Silver Bell, A Latex Product Prophylactics," cond. NM, 1/4" h, 2-1/8" w, 1-3/4" d ................. 632.50

## Silver Cup Coffee

Can, keywind, litho tin
    Snap top, early/taller version, "Our Prize," trophy cup in central black oval on gold panel with plants/leaves, red ground, Central Wholesale Grocers, Chicago, cond. 8+, 1 lb................................. 133.00
    Tall version, white trophy cup, white text, ground in red/black diagonal bands, Mogar Coffee Co., Brooklyn NY, cond. 8+, 1 lb .......................... 89.00

## Silver Knight Condoms

Tin, litho tin, "Silver Knight, Disease Preventative," shield in light blue, helmet/name in silver, blue ground, cond. 7.5+, 1/4" h, 2-1/8" w, 1-3/4" d .......................... 797.50

## Silver Latex Condoms

Tin, litho tin, "Silver Latex, Sold For Prevention of Disease Only, Guaranteed Five Years, 3 For 1.00," horizontal band of stripes, vertical band of leaves, black on silver ground, cond. NM, 1/4" h, 2-1/8" w, 1-3/4" d ........................................................... 632.50

## Silver-Marshall Radios

Sign, flange, litho tin, "SM, Authorized Silver-Marshall Service Station," red/blue on white ground, unused, 6-1/4" h, 15-5/8" w .......................................... 154.00

## A.L. Simmons Cigars

Cigar box, wood, color paper label under lid shows A.L. Simmons and gold seals, cond. 8+................... 264.00

## Simonds Saw

Sign, felt, painted surface, "I Tell You It's A Great Saw," carpenter smoking a pipe, like new, 13-3/4" h, 11-3/4" w .......................................................... 143.00

## Simon Pure Coffee

Can, keywind, litho tin, taller version, "Vacuum Packed Simon Pure Coffee," central round medallion with shield, red/blue text, white ground with diagonal blue band, cond. 8.5, 1 lb ......................................... 141.00

## Simplex Tires

Sign, tin, embossed, "Authorized Dealer, Simplex Tires," black tire at right by "Bear Cat Cord," red text over courtesy panel, yellow ground, cond. 7, 9"h, 20" w ................................................................ 242.00

## Simpson Spring Beverages

Charger, litho tin, red text at border, "Purity, Quality" flank image of woman, reddish ground, 1910s-1920s, cond. 7.25-7.5, 17-1/2" dia............................................ 286.00

Sign, litho tin, red text at border, shows woman, reddish ground, 1910s-1920s, cond. 7.5+, 18" sq ............. 132.00

## Sinclair

**Reference:** Scott Benjamin and Wayne Henderson, *Sinclair Collectibles*, Schiffer Publishing, 1997

Gas globe
Narrow glass body, 2 lenses, "H-C" in white on red center, "Sinclair Gasoline" in white on dark border, 1 lens cracked, lens cond. 8/6, body cond. 8.5, 13-1/2" dia .................................................. 275.00

Plastic body, 2 lenses, "Sinclair Power-X, Over 100 Octane," green/red on white ground, all cond. 9, 13-1/2" dia .................................................. 550.00

Plastic body (newer Capcolite) with 2 glass lenses, "H-C" in white on red center, "Sinclair Gasoline" in white on dark border, lens cond. 8+, body cond. 7, 13-1/2" dia .................................................. 412.50

Wide glass body, 2 different lenses, "Sinclair Power-X, The Super Fuel" in green/red/black on white ground, red border; "Sinclair Power-X, Over 100 Octane," green/red text, white ground, red border; all cond. 9, 13-1/2" dia .................................. 363.00

Map, road map, 5-panel, "Florida Sinclair Road Map" in red/blue on 6-sided white panel, cover shows round "H-C Sinclair Gasoline" sign over die-cut dinosaur "Sinclair Credit Cards" sign, Florida on 1 side, U.S. on other, 1934-1936 auto models, cond. 8+, 9" h, 19-1/2" w .............................................................. 60.50

**Doll, Skippy doll in Sinclair uniform, cond. 8.5-9, 13" h, $159.50. (Photo courtesy of Gary Metz, Muddy River Trading Co.)**

Mobile, cardboard, 2-sided, "Sinclair-ize for safety," man in cap holding X-shaped slogan, hanging images of 6 products, NOS, cond. 9, 45" h, 40" w .............. 148.50

Sign, painted metal, 2-sided, "Approved Dealer, Sinclair Credit Cards Honored," white/red text, green over white ground, red border, yellowing/edge chips, 14" h, 23" w ................................................................. 385.00

Sign, porcelain
2-sided, "Sinclair Credit Cards Honored Here," green/red text, green border, white ground, cond. 9, 14-1/4" h, 23" w ................................................................. 330.00

Pump sign, "Sinclair Diesel," dinosaur logo in green, red text, green border around logo, white ground, cond. 8+, 13-1/2" h, 12" w ........................... 264.00

"Sinclair," shadowed white text, green ground, red border, cond. 7+, 6" h, 45" w............................. 330.00

Soap, cardboard box, Dino Soap, soap bar in shape of Sinclair Heating Oils delivery truck, red box with image of green truck, unopened, circa 1960s, cond. NM, 2" h, 4-1/2" w, 1-1/2" d................................................ 55.00

## Sinclair Coal Co.

Thermometer, metal, square corners, "Parade of the Finest, Prepared Super Clean, Sinclair Coal Company," 2 bandleaders by logos for Sinclair Coal, Eagle Coal, Delta Coal, Broken Aro Coal, Mark Twain Coal, Tiger Coal, cobalt/white ground, red top/bottom, paint chips/scratches, 38-5/8" h, 8-1/4" w ........................... 412.50

## Singer Sewing Machine Co.

**History:** Although Isaac Singer had his heart set on a career in the theater, his true calling lay in the world of inventions. After developing a mechanical excavator and making improvements to a machine used for carving wooden printers type, he met Orson C. Phelps, who was making sewing machines. It didn't take long for Singer to improve on the design, and The Singer Manufacturing Company was formed in 1851. By 1852 there were several retail stores, and the Singer sewing machine was eventually sold around the world.

Can, tin, "Singer Oil," white on green ground, "Singer Sewing Machines" red "S" logo with woman at sewing machine, cond. VG, qt, 7-3/4" h, 4-1/2" w, 2" d........................27.50

Sign, flange, porcelain, "Singer Sewing Machines" in red "S" logo with woman at sewing machine, circa 1920s, cond. 8.25-8.5+, 12" h, 20" w............................. 550.00

## Sioux City Nursery & Seed Co.

Box, wood, machine dovetails, paper labels on front/inside lid, "Reliable Seeds, From the Sioux City Nursery & Seed Co. Sioux City, Iowa," chipping to labels, ............................................................. 187.00

## Skagit Maid Ice Cream

Sign, enameled metal, embossed, self-framed, "Enjoy Skagit Maid Ice Cream," round image of Indian woman, cond. EXC, cond. 8.5+, 18" h, 58-1/2" w .............. 302.50

## Skelly

Clock, metal case, diamond shape, "Skelly" in red on white bar over S logo, woodgrain-like ground, cond. 8, 15-1/2" h, 15-1/2" w ........................................... 269.50

Gas globe

"Skelly Fortified Premium," 2 different lenses, wide glass body, red "Skelly" on blue diamond logo in center, "Fortified Premium" at edge in red on white ground on 1 lens, in white on red ground on other lens, lens cond. 8.5, body cond. 9, 13-1/2" dia ................. 302.50

"Skelly Gasoline," 2 lenses, wide glass body, red "Skelly" on blue diamond logo in center, arched "Gasoline" in white over 3 white stars, red ground, lenses epoxied to body, 1 lens cracked, lens cond. 9/6, body cond. 8, 13-1/2" dia ...................... 132.00

"Skelly Gasoline," newer plastic body with 2 lenses, red "Skelly" on blue diamond logo in center, arched "Gasoline" in white over 3 white stars, red ground, blue/white border, all cond. 9, 13-1/2" dia ................. 209.00

"Skelly Keotane," 2 lenses, wide glass body, red text, blue Skelly diamond logo in center, arched "Keotane" over 4 stars, white ground, lens cond. 9/8.5, body cond. 9, 13-1/2" dia ............................... 275.00

"Skelly Motopower Diesel Fuel," 2 glass lenses, newer plastic body, red/blue text, diamond logo in center, white ground, lens cond. 8.5, body cond. 8, 13-1/2" dia ..................................................... 236.50

"Skelly Supreme," 1 lens, narrow glass body, red "Skelly" on blue diamond logo in center, arched "Supreme" in red over 4 red stars, white ground, lens epoxied to body, both cond. 8.5, 13-1/2" dia ................................................. 121.00

"Skelly Supreme," 2 lenses, older plastic body, red "Skelly" on blue diamond logo in center, arched "Supreme" in red over 4 blue stars, white ground, body cracked, lens cond. 8.5, body cond. 7, 13-1/2" dia ................................................. 165.00

Gas pump insert, fired on glass, "Skelly Gasoline," diamond logo, blue-red-blue ground, white text/stars, cond. 8, 4-1/2" h, 10-1/4" w .............................. 49.50

Lighter, Zippo, diamond Skelly logo over double-arrow Hood logo, orig gift box, unused, 1950s ............. 88.00

## Ski (See Photo)

## Sky Chief

Bank, plastic, gas pump motif, "Sky Chief Gasoline" green/red design, "Texaco" star logo, gray ground, tip

Sign, tin, self-framed, "drink Ski, Say Skee-e-e," edge wear, 12" h, 32" w, $60.

Pump sign, porcelain, "Sky Chief Gasoline," name in red on white band, red swoosh, cond. 8+, 18" h, 12" w, $93.50. (Photo courtesy of Collectors Auction Services)

of gas hose broken, cond. 8, 4-3/4" h, 1-5/8" w.............................................................. 302.50

Gas globe, "Sky Chief."

1 lens, narrow glass body, red text on white band, Texaco star logo at bottom on red swoosh, green ground, lens cond. 9, body cond. 8, 13-1/2" dia ..................... 337.50

2 lenses, milk glass Gill body, red text on white band over star logo on red swoosh, green over black ground, lens cond. 8/7, body cond. 8, 13-1/2" dia .................. 302.50

2 lenses, wide glass body, red text on white band over star logo on red swoosh, green over black ground, lens cond. 8.5, body cond. 9, 13-1/2" dia .................. 324.50

Map rack sign, tin, 2-sided, "Sky Chief Gasoline, Localized For You In This Driving Area, Texaco Driving Area #5," green/red/white text, shows Tennessee/surrounding states, white over green ground, cond. 8, 16" h, 15" w ................................................................ 77.00

Sign, porcelain, "Sky Chief Su-preme Gasoline, Super-Charged With Petrox," red/black/white text, 2 white bands, green ground, star logo on red swoosh, "Made in U.S.A. 3-9-64, cond. 9, 18" h, 12" w .............. 99.00

## Sky Maid Coffee

Can, keywind, litho tin, stewardess with cup/4-engine airplane, red/white text, red ground, white band at bottom, cond. 8, 1 lb ............................................... 97.00

## Sky Ranger Aviation Oil

Can, litho tin, "Sky Ranger Flight Tested Aviation Oil," blue/white text, red plane on white ground, red band at bottom, Premier Oil Refg. Co. of Texas, embossed lid, cond. 8.5, qt, 5-1/2" h, 4" dia............................ 302.50

## Smile

Display bottle, "Smile" in black on orange body, circa 1920s-1930s, 1922 patent date, cond. 8.5+, 18" h.............................................................. 825.00

## Smith Brothers (See Photo)

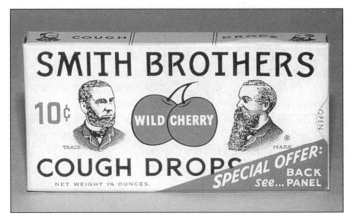

Box, cardboard, "Smith Brothers Cough Drops," back with offer for Ever-Rite ballpoint pen, full, 1-3/8 oz, $5.

## Smith's

Sign, tin, "Smith's Model Dairy Inc. Ice Cream, It's Pleasingly Different," yellow ground, minor scratches, 19-1/2" h, 31-1/2" w .................................................................. 302.50

## Smoker's Nico-Stain

Tin, litho tin, "Smoker's Nico-Stain Tooth Cleanser, Price 75 Cents," reclining woman blowing smoke rings, black ground, cond. 7.5+, 3-5/8" h, 2-1/4" w, 1-1/4" d............................................................... 357.50

## Snoboy

Sign, button, porcelain, cartoon character snowman, 1940s-1950s, cond. 6.5-7, 36" d ......................... 44.00

## Snow Apple Tobacco (See Photo)

## Snowdrift

Sign, porcelain, "For all cooking, Snowdrift, Perfect shortening," white text in blue oval on yellow can, white ground, Southern Cotton Oil Co., chips at edges/upper-right corner missing, 26" sq .................... 154.00

Box, pocket, paper, "John Surrey's Snow Apple Tobacco, Blend No. 549, John Surrey Ltd, N.Y.," 1-1/2 oz, $12.50.

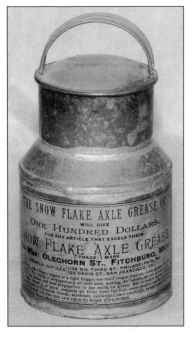

Can, tin, litho label, "The Snow Flake Axle Grease Co., Fitchburg, Mass.," handle on lid and also on back, 7-1/2" h, $195.

## Snow Drift Rolled Oats

Box, paper on cardboard, round, "Snow Drift Special Purpose Rolled Oats," mountains in round panel over oats, red/cobalt text, white over yellow ground, Treger Mill, Sequin TX, cond. 8.25, 14 oz ................... 137.50

## Snow Flake Axle Grease (See Photo)

## Snow Girl

Bag, flour, cloth, "Snow Girl Fancy Patent Phosphated Plain Flour, Reitzel Milling Co., Denton, N.C.," girl on skies in oval, red/blue text, white ground, cond. EXC, 50 lb, 28-1/2" h, 16" w........................................ 49.50

## Snow King Baking Powder

Display, cardboard, die-cut, standup, "Use Snow King Baking Powder, One Trial Convinces," reindeer pulling Santa in sleigh, cond. 8-, 17" h, 28-3/4" w........................687.50

## Society Brand Peanuts

Can, litho tin, "Society Brand Salted Peanuts, Ideal Toasted Nut. Co., Lancaster, Penna.," oval image of couple eating nuts, orange ground, cond. 8.5+, 10 lb, 9-1/2" h, 8-1/4" dia .......................................... 962.50

## Socony

Badge, stamped metal, photo ID, red "SONY Vacuum" and Pegasus stamped in border, hinged pin/clip, small dent, 2" dia...................................................... 132.00

Can, tin, "Socony Dewaxed Paraffine Base Motor Oil" in blue over Socony shield logo in red/blue, white ground, cond. 7+, gal, 10-1/4" h, 8" w, 3" d ........................286.00

Candles, box of 4, snowman with red hat/broom over shoulder, "Tavern Novelty Candles, Snow Boys,

Socony Vacuum Oil Company," box 3-1/8" h, 4" sq ...................................................... 66.00

Gas globe lens, 2 milk glass lenses, "Socony Motor Gasoline" in red on white shield, "Standard Oil Co. of New York" in blue at bottom, blue ground with "SONY" in white at edges, cond. 8, 15" dia ..................... 3,300.00

Gas globe, 2 milk glass embossed lenses, low-profile metal body, "Socony Motor Gasoline" in red on white shield, "Standard Oil Co. of New York" in blue at bottom, black ground with "SONY" in white at edges, cond. 9, 16-1/2" dia ...................... 1,980.00

Plaque, composition, die-cut, embossed, shield shape, "Member, The '300' Club, Socony-Mobil," white text, red Pegasus, stippled ground, cond. 7.5, 16" h, 16-1/2" w ..........................................110.00

Pocket mirror, celluloid over metal, "Socony Motor Oil" in red on white shield, "SONY" in white on dark ground at edges, cond. 7.5, 3-1/2" dia ............................. 71.50

Sign, porcelain, "Socony Motor Oils," white text, blue ground, red/white border, cond. 7, 18" h, 36" w .................................................. 330.00

Sign, porcelain, flange, die-cut, "We Sell Socony Motor Gasoline, Standard Oil Co. of N.Y.," shield logo in circle, white panel at top, white/red text, white/cobalt ground, cond. 8, 24" h, 20" w ........................... 990.00

Sign, porcelain, lubester, 2-sided
"Socony Aircraft Oil No. 1" in red/blue text in white shield on round blue ground, "Medium" in red on white ground at bottom, cond. 8, 9-1/2" h, 8" w ...................................................... 506.00
"Socony Motor Oil" in white shield on round blue ground, "Heavy" in red on white ground at bottom, cond. 8, 11-3/4" h, 8" w ................................ 605.00

Sign, litho tin, concave, "Safety First" on red border, "Socony Motor Gasoline" in shield on blue ground, cond. 8.5+, 8-1/2" d........................................... 577.50

## Sohio

Display, porcelain, "Sohio Recorded Point by Point Lubri-cation," red over white over cobalt ground, brackets for grease gun/lubricants, shelf, cond. 7, 50" h, 30" w .................................................................. 357.50

Sign, porcelain, "Sohio Petroleum Co., S.S. Dozier Lease, Well No. 8 - Part of Ruthy Campbell Sur. No. 50," oval red/blue logo at left, white/blue text, white ground, red border top/bottom, cond. 7, 12" h, 24" w ................................................................. 121.00

## Solitaire Coffee

Can, keywind, litho tin
"Solitaire Coffee," white text, red ground, wavy orange border top/bottom, Morey Mercantile Co., Denver, cond. 9-, 1 lb...................................................... 33.00

## Somerville's Chewing Gum

Tin, "Somerville's Tin Box Chewing Gum, Peppermint," silver text, yellow ground, cond. 7+, 1/2" h, 3-1/8" w, 1-1/8" d ............................................................ 330.00

## Sooner Select Rolled Oats

Box, paper on cardboard, round, "Sooner Select Brand Rolled Oats," 2 oxen pulling Conestoga wagon alongside horse/rider over red band, cobalt ground, Ozmun & Co., Lawton OK, cond. 9-, 1 lb ...................... 467.50

## South Bend Lures

Signs, embossed, chain-hung, "The Angler's Prayer" and "Allah's Proverb,' cond. EXC, 7" h, 5" w, pr ...........264.00

## South Bend Malleable Range (See Photo)

**Can, keywind, tin, "Solitaire Coffee, The Morey Mercantile Co., Denver," 1 lb, $66.**

**Egg separator, tin, "The South Bend Malleable Range, Allways Preferable," 4-1/2" l, 3-3/8" d, $20.**

## Southwestern Associated Telephone Co.

Sign, porcelain, 2-sided, "Southwestern Associated Telephone Company, Telephone," blue/white lettering, shows early phone pole/lines, crazing/chips/scratches, 30" dia .............................................................. 467.50

## Sparrow's Chocolates

Tray, tin, "Sparrow's Chocolates" on top/bottom border, girl crawling on table, sparrow in chocolate box, cond. 8-, 8" h, 6-1/2" w ............................................... 143.00

## Spartan Coffee

Tin, keywind, litho tin, yellow Spartan on red ground, yellow band, cond. 9, 1 lb ........................................ 34.00

## Spear Head Chewing Tobacco

Sign, porcelain, "Hits The Spot, Spear Head Chewing Tobacco," yellow ground with "Spear Head" in red arrow, cond. NM, 6" h, 14" w ............................. 522.50

## Spearior Saws

Sign, tin, embossed, "New Improved Quality, Use Spearior Saws," saw fills entire sign, white text, black ground, dents/scratches/chips, 9" h, 27" w ......................... 231.00

## Speedline

Can, metal, "Speedline High Pressure Grease," shows racing car in oval, yellow ground, black pinstripes, no top, rim dented, 1 lb, 4-5/8" h, 3-3/8" dia .......... 396.00

## Speedway

Gas globe, 2 lenses, wide glass body, "Speedway '79'," blue "Speedway" on white panel, white "79" on red ground, all cond. 9, 13-1/2" dia ......................... 522.50

## Sphinx Condoms

Tin, litho tin, hinged lid, "Three Sphinx, Mfd. By Julius Schmid Inc., New York, N.Y.," Egyptian Sphinx image, 1939, worn edges, 1/4" h, 2-1/4" w, 1-5/8" d .............................................................. 264.00

## Sphinx Mixture

Tin, litho tin, "Sphinx Mixture" upper-right, man/camel in front of Sphinx, black/yellow design, cond. 9-, 1-1/4" h, 4-1/2" w, 3" d ...................................................... 104.50

## Sportsmen Tobacco

Tin, horizontal box, litho tin, horseracing/hunting scenes, white text on blue rectangle, red ground, N. Landry & Co., Montreal, cond. 8+, 3-1/2" h, 5" w, 3-5/8" d .............................................................. 153.00

## Springeez Oil

Can, tin, "Springeez Oil, Lubricant Supreme For Better Protection," white on green ground, spout at top, Halstead Oil Co., cond. 7+, 7-1/2" h, 3" dia ............. 27.50

Sign, litho tin, light-gauge, embossed, "Squeeze, That Distinctive Orange Drink," bottle at left, back view of boy/girl arm-in-arm on bench in front of full moon, orange/yellow text, black over yellow ground, 1940s, cond. 8, $962.50 (Photo courtesy of Gary Metz, Muddy River Trading Co.)

## Sprite

Sign
   Porcelain, button, "Sprite" in green in 6-sided white area, "sprankelfris" in white on green ground, European, 1960s-1970s, cond. 9.25, 16" dia ......................302.50
   Litho tin, "Taste its Tingling Tartness, Sprite," tilted bottle at center, white ground, 1960s, cond. 9.5, 12" h, 32" w ........................................................... 220.00

## Spur

Door push, heavily embossed, "Canada Dry Spur, Big 12 Oz. Bottle 5¢," shows bottle, 1940s-1950s, cond. 7.75-8.25, 12" h, 3-1/2" w ............................................. 40.00
Sign, tin, embossed, "Drink Canada Dry Spur" in shield with crown, "It's A Finer Cola" at bottom, tilted bottle at right, green/red/white text, white over green ground, yellowing/stains/paint loss at edge/dented corners, 22-1/2" h, 26" w ............................................... 148.50

## Squeeze

Sign, litho tin, embossed, "Drink Squeeze, All Flavors," back view of 2 children arm-in-arm on bench, black/red text, white ground, black border, cond. G, 10" h, 28-1/2" w ......................................................... 198.00

## Squib's Nursery Toilet Powder

Tin, litho tin, oval image of child in bathtub over text, white ground, 1920s, cond. 8, 6" h, 2-1/4" w, 1-1/4" d ........................................................... 182.50

## Squirrel Peanut Butter

Tin, litho tin
   "Squirrel Brand Peanut Butter," white oval with squirrel standing on hind legs chewing nut, red ground, cond. 8, 13 oz ............................................... 165.00

Same design, cond. 8+, 27 oz .......................... 156.00
Same design, cond. 8.5-9, 48 oz ....................... 88.00
Same design, cond. 8, 57 oz, 5-1/2" h,
  5-1/8" dia ......................................... 94.00
Same design, made without bail handle, cond. 8.25+,
  4 lb ............................................... 385.00
"Squirrel Brand Peanut Butter," oval with squirrel
  standing on hind legs chewing nut, silver ground,
  red trim, Canada Nut Co. Ltd., Vancouver, B.C.,
  cond. 7.5, 5 lb ...................................118.00

## Squirrel Salted Peanuts

Box, display, cardboard
  Blue, "Squirrel Brand Salted Peanuts, Look For The
    Squirrel And Get The Best," shows squirrel (left)
    watching peanuts spilling from cup, white text, blue
    ground, Squirrel Brand Co., Cambridge, Mass.,
    cond. 8-, 7-1/2" x 9-3/4" x 3-1/2" ..................... 87.00
  Yellow, "Squirrel Brand Salted Peanuts," shows squir-
    rel (right) watching peanuts spilling from box, red/
    black text, yellow ground, cond. 8, 11-3/4" x
    8-5/8" x 3" ................................ 87.00
  Die-cut, "Squirrel Brand Salted Peanuts" in white, "Nut
    Caramels, Peanut Butter, Peanut Bars, Salted
    Nuts" in yellow flanking peanuts can, red ground
    with gray squirrel on top, cond. 9.25, 12" h,
    11" w ................................ 418.00

## Squirt

Calendar, 1949, 3 months per page, different woman on
  each page, also Squirt boy logo, NM .................. 60.50
Door push, embossed, "Drink Squirt," bottle over "Zip In
  Every Sip!," 1941, cond. 9-9.25, 9" h,
  3-1/2" w ................................ 231.00
Glass, boy with "Squirt" bottle, 1948, cond. 9.25,
  4-1/4" h ................................ 77.00
Sign
  Paper, "Drink Squirt, In The Public Eye," red script in
    yellow splash, white text on cobalt ground, newer
    frame, cond. EXC, 30-1/2" h, 39" w ................ 49.50

**Sign, tin, embossed letters, "never an after-thirst, Enjoy Squirt," NOS, copyright 1979, 29" sq, $45.**

**Tin, pocket, litho tin, short/oval version, "Stag Tobacco, P. Lorillard Co.," 3-1/2" h, $101.**

Tin, "Switch To Squirt, never an after-thirst," red/yellow
  logo in center, black band upper-left, boy with oversized bottle on cart at right, red ground, ©1958, bent
  corner, cond. NM, 9-1/4" h, 27-3/4" w ..............198.00
Toy, truck, tin with rubber tires, litho bottles/lettering, friction, "(As?) advertised in Reader's Digest" on side,
  minor scratches/dents, works, made in Japan,
  8" l ............................................. 192.50
Tray, tin, oval, "The drink with the Happy Taste," boy with
  oversized bottle, boy's lasso forms border around text,
  yellow tray border, scratches/worn edges, 14-1/2" h,
  11-1/2" w ............................................. 280.50

## S.S.S.

String holder, cast iron, embossed, kettle shape, "S.S.S.
  For The Blood," missing handles, cond. VG, 4-1/2" h,
  5" dia.................................................110.00

## Stabl Flo

Can, litho tin, red text on gold ground, shows an airplane
  in the shape of a can/thermometer, text at bottom border, ©1956 Chemical Research Laboratories, Superior
  WI, full, cond. 8, qt, 5-1/2" h, 4" dia.................... 82.50

## Stag Chewing Tobacco

Can, keywind, litho tin, "Stag Chewing Tobacco 17¢,"
  shows stag, white/yellow/red text, dark ground, lid
  rust, Canadian, cond. 8+, 5" h, 4-1/2" dia .......... 28.50

## Stag Tobacco

Can, litho tin, "Stag Tobacco, For Pipe And Cigarette,"
  stag in oval, also hunters on horseback, red ground,
  cond. 8, 4-1/2" h, 4" sq..................................... 357.50
Tin, vertical pocket, litho tin, tall/flat version, "Stag
  Tobacco," stag in white oval with landscape, red
  ground, cond. 8.................................................112.00

## Stanavo

Can, tin, "Stanavo Aviation Engine Oil No. 140," white
  image is part eagle/part airplane, red ground, Stan-

dard Oil Co. of California, cond. 7+/6+, gal, 10-1/4" h, 7-1/4" w, 3-1/4" d.................................... 1,320.00

## Standard Lozenges

Tin, litho tin, glass front, "Standard Licorice Lozenges, S.V.&F.P. Scudder," detailed Oriental scene in red/black, cond. 8+, 7-1/2" h, 5-1/8" sq.................. 467.50

## Standard Oil Co.

Calendar, pocket, celluloid, round, "Asphalts-Road Oil-Fuel Oil, Standard Oil Co., Service (Indiana), Asphalt Department...Chicago," round blue torch logo, blue/red on white ground, pocket-mirror design with 23-year rotating dial starting with 1924, cond. EXC, 2-1/2" dia.................................................. 156.00

Decal, paper, red/white/blue oval torch logo, "Standard" in black, NOS, 32" h, 40" w................................ 22.00

Flame topper, plastic, red flame on blue torch, cond. 8/7, 20" h, 18" w.......................................... 99.00

Gas globe

Glass, 1-pc, flame motif, red/white, orig base ring, 1930s-1940s, NOS, orig box from "Advertising Products Inc.," globe cond. 9.75, 21" h.................... 770.00

Plastic/porcelain, 2-pc, red/white plastic flame, blue/white porcelain base, 1940s-1950s, NOS, cond. 9.25-9.5, 29" h.......................................... 577.50

Milk glass, 1-pc, flame shape, red paint, metal base, cond. 7, 13-1/2" dia.................................. 280.50

Manual, paper, stock cover, working drawings/engineering specs for Standard Oil Service Station buildings, NOS, 9" h, 11-1/2" w.................................... 176.00

Pen/pencil combination, oval "Standard" logo on pocket clasp, lead pencil in top, pen in bottom, cond. EXC, 5-5/8" l............................................ 60.50

Sign, porcelain

2-sided, die-cut, oval, "Standard" torch oval, red/white/blue, torch/flame protrudes at top, cond. 9, 54-1/2" h, 58-1/2" w........................................ 990.00

2-sided, "Standard Oil of Texas Products," red/black text, black border, white ground, cond. 8, 33" dia............................................ 412.50

Pump sign, oval torch logo in red/white/blue, white ground, cond. 8, 7-1/4" dia ...................... 55.00

"Standard Red Crown" over oval red/white/blue torch logo, red text, white ground, "50" in circle at bottom corners, "IR 6-51," cond. 8, 15" h, 12" w.......... 66.00

## Standby Tomato Juice

Sign, button, porcelain, shows can of product on dark ground, red/black text over glass/2 tomatoes, 35-1/2" dia........................................ 302.50

## Stanocola

Sign, porcelain, round, "Stanocola Petroleum Products" shield in center, "Standard Oil Company of Louisiana" in white at border, orange/red ground, restored, cond. 8.5, 30" dia........................................ 990.00

## Stanwix

Tin, vertical pocket, "Stanwix Ground Plug, The Ace of

Them All, Scientifically Blended, Falk Tobacco Co., New York, Richmond," white text, blue ground, cond. 8 .................................................... 550.00

## Staple Grain Cut Plug

Tin, vertical pocket, litho tin, slide closure, black 5-arm star with staple in yellow center, black text, yellow ground, cond. 7, 3-1/2" h, 3-1/2" w .................. 550.00

## The Star

Sign, tin, embossed, "Read the Star, Baltimore's Best Evening Newspaper," logo of star flanked by globes, white text, cobalt ground, cond. VG, 9-3/4" h, 13-3/4" w............................................ 71.50

## Star Cup Coffee

Tin, keywind, regular grind, early version, king with cup on red ground, black trim at bottom, Mogar Coffee Co., cond. 9, tall 1 lb.................................. 224.00

## Star Naptha

Door push, porcelain, "Push, Star Naptha Washing Powder," shows box of product, yellow/black, cond. EXC, 6-1/4" h, 3-1/2" w.................................. 412.50

## Star Shoes

Mirror, reverse-painted, "Star Brand Shoes Are Better" in red at top, frame painted black, cond. VG, 21-1/2" h, 15-1/2" w............................................ 110.00

Sign, tin, embossed, "Yes sah! Star Brand Shoes are better, Sold At Best Stores," black shoeshine boy at work, red star logo, red/black text, yellow ground, red/black border, dents/scratches, 18" h, 23" w .............. 550.00

## Star Soap

Sign

Paper, girl in white dress, metal strips top/bottom, 1905, framed, cond. 8.5, 22" h, 15" w ........... 88.00

Porcelain, "Extra Large, Extra Good, Save The Panels," bar of "Star Soap" in center, black text/border, white ground, touchups, 28" h, 20" w .......... 429.00

## Star Tobacco

Sign

Porcelain, "Star Tobacco Sold Here," star logo over plug of tobacco, cobalt text, yellow ground, ragged top edge/rust, 12" h, 24" w .......................... 335.50

Tin, embossed, "Star Tobacco, 10¢, Best for 70 years, Best for you," plug with 2 stars over white star, red/cobalt text, yellow ground, cond. G, 12" h, 23-3/4" w ...................................... 137.50

Tin

Flat pocket, litho tin, "Star Chewing Tobacco, J.G. Flint Jr., Milwaukee," semi-nude woman sitting in chariot, black on red ground, worn bottom, top is cond. 8.5, 1/2" h, 3-5/8" w, 2-3/8" d ...................... 696.00

Vertical pocket, litho tin, stars on red ground, cond. 8............................................ 162.00

Tin, "Star Type Cleaner, Eberhard Faber, New York," 3/4" h, 2-5/8" w, 1-5/8" d, $10.

## Star Safety Razor

Tin, litho tin, "Blade Case, Star Safety Razor, Pat'd & Manufactured By Kampefe Bro's, New York City," central star and stars in upper corners, cond. 8-, 3/8" h, 2-1/4" w, 1-1/4" d .................................. 143.00

## Star Type Cleaner (See Photo)

## Starr Brothers Ice Cream

Sign, porcelain, 2-sided, black text in pentagon over "Starr Brothers Dairy Products" seal with cow in star, yellow/white striped ground, 1930s-1940s, cond. 7.5+, 28 h, 24" w ....................................... 209.00

## Startup's Gum

Tin, litho tin, "Startup's Mountain Mint Gum, keeps Your Teeth White, Mint Fragrance, Lasting Flavor," round medallion of mountains, green ground, cond. 8, 3/8" h, 2" w, 1-1/2" d..................................... 412.50

## State Seal of Montana

Cigar box, wood, ornate brass-tone tin feet/corners, "State Seal of Montana, Old Style Smokers," sea/river/mountain vignettes on paper label under lid, 50-count, cond. 8.5+ ........................................... 93.50

## Steamro

Sign, porcelain, "Spicy 'Steamro' Red Hots," edge chips, 2-1/4" h, 17-1/4" w ................................. 302.50

## Steam Ship Typewriter Ribbon

Tin, litho tin, "Established To Supply All Nations, Steam Ship Brand," detailed image of ship on lid, yellow body, 3-color border, cond. 8, 1-1/4" x 1-3/4" ............. 125.00

## Stegner Beer

Sign, bar sign, reverse painting on glass, "Stegner Lager Beer," blue ground/base, cond. 8.5+, 6" h, 13-1/2" w....................................... 253.00

## Stephens' Inks

Thermometer, porcelain, "Stephens' Inks, For all Temperatures," marks for "Blood Heat, Summer Heat, Tempe Rate, Zero," thermometer glued in/not working, minor chips, 61" h, 12" w ........................................... 385.00

## Stephenson Union Suits

Thermometer, porcelain, rounded top/bottom, "Stephenson Union Suit For All Seasons, Two Piece Underwear, More Wool, More Wear," man shown above and below thermometer glass, red ground, chipping, 39" h, 8-3/4" w.......................................... 577.50

## Sterling Gum

Jar, glass, oval, ground top, tin lid with embossed image of ghost and "Sterling Gum," lid lightly pitted, 7" h, 5" w, 7" d .......................................... 165.00

## Sterling Oil

Pail, litho tin, yellow/white logo, Sterling Oil Company, wear from handle, with lid, cond. 8+, 25 lb, 11-1/2" h, 11" dia ................................................110.00

Thermometer, porcelain, "Sterling Oils" in black on orange ring around red "£" on white ground, round brass thermometer with numbers from -40 to 150 at top, orange/red trim, black ground, chip at base, cond. 8+, 12-3/4" h, 9-1/2" w .................................. 1,100.00

## Sterling Tobacco

Bin, counter, store bin, litho tin, "Sterling Fine Cut Tobacco, Always Good, 5¢ Wax Bags," white/yellow text, red/green/cobalt/yellow plaid ground, cond. 8.25, 7" h, 8-1/4" dia ................................................. 170.50

Can, keywind, litho tin, "Stewarts Private Blend Coffee," 1 lb, $20.

## B. Steubner's Sons

Calendar, paper with archival backing, "Decorated Shaving Cups for the Barber Supply Trade," shows 30 different mugs, edge wear/soiling, calendar missing, 18-3/4" h, 12-1/2" w .......................................... 71.50

## Stewarts Coffee (See Photo)

## Stickney & Poor's

Sign, paper, "Stickney & Poor's Mustards, Spices and Extracts, Yours for Purity and Strength," 3 children with roses/binoculars, minor creases/tear, 24-1/2" h, 19-1/2" w .......................................... 165.00

## St. Laurent's Peanut Butter

Pail, litho tin, "St. Laurent's Brand Peanut Butter, Absolutely Pure and Healthful," silver/cobalt text inside cobalt border with horizontal band, yellow ground, cond. 9, 1 lb .......................................... 93.50

## St. Lawrence Tobacco Co.

Tin, litho tin, "The St. Lawrence Tobacco Co. Ltd., Finest Smoking Tobacco," Canadian flag in wreath, white ground, 4" h, 6" w .......................................... 147.50

## Strawberry Wood Tobacco

Box, dovetailed, paper label, slide lid, carriage scene, cond. 8.5, 5-1/4" x 4-1/4" x 3-1/2" .......................................... 38.50

## Stride Rite

Sign, lightup, glass face, metal body, "The Stride Rite Shoe," tail of oversized "S" underlines name, white light, 3-D effect, NOS, 9" h, 20" w .......................................... 137.50

## Stroh's

Fan, cardboard, wooden handle, waiter with tray serving

**Case, cardboard, "Stroh's Bohemian Style Beer," held 24 bottles, $22.50.**

people at table, "Compliments of..." panel, circa 1910, cond. 8, 14" h, 8-1/5" w .......................................... 277.00

Sign, Kay display, wood, die-cut, "Here's Luck! Fire Brewed Stroh's Bohemian Beer," bowtie-shape orange top over red circle with attached metal horseshoe, cond. 7.75-8, 17" h, 17" w .......................................... 82.50

## Strong-Heart Coffee

Can, litho tin, screw top, oval image of Indian brave, yellow ground, Charles Hewitt & Sons Co., Des Moines, cond. 8, 1 lb, 5-3/4" h, 4-1/4" dia .......................................... 550.00

## Studebaker

Banner, silk, "1954 Studebaker, World's finest performing V-8," yellow/white text, purple ground, gold fringe, cond. VG, 27-1/2" h, 40" w .......................................... 88.00

Can, waxed cardboard, "Special Motor Oil" in blue on yellow panel, round "S" logo, "Studebaker" in yellow at bottom, blue ground, Studebaker Parts and Service Division, South Bend IN, full, cond. 7.5, qt, 5-1/2" h, 4" dia .......................................... 110.00

Sign, hardboard, pr, "Studebaker Authorized Service Parts," wheel logo, white/orange/yellow text, black ground, 1 corner chipped, cond. 7.5, 9-1/4" h, 13" w, pr .......................................... 93.50

## Success

Sign, paper, 1889 calendar, "Success, The Horse's Friend, E.L. McClain Mfg. Co., Greenfield, O.," shows horse writing testimonial letter, cond. 8+, 24" h, 19" w .......................................... 1,210.00

## Successful

Incubator, salesman sample, wooden, orig decals, "Successful, Des Moines Incubator Co.," turned legs, glass doors, brass trim, cond. 8+, 12-1/2" h, 15-1/2" w, 11-1/2" d .......................................... 2,640.00

## Sucrene Feed

Pocket mirror, celluloid, "Happy cow-what makes you laugh? Sucrene Feed and a little calf," cartoon scene of cow/calf by feed bag, cond. NM, 2-1/8" dia .......................................... 412.50

## Suffolk Brand Peanuts

Can, litho tin, "Suffolk Brand Spanish Salted Peanuts, Manufactured by Planters Nut & Chocolate Co., Suffolk, Virginia," banner, blue/white medallion on orange ground, text box on back, cond. 7.5-8, 10 lb .......................................... 7,370.00

## Sultana

Bank, cardboard, tin top/bottom, tall version, girl handing sandwich to boy, yellow ground, cond. 8.5, 4-1/8" h, 3" dia .......................................... 59.50

Fan, cardboard, die-cut, wooden handle, dog in straw hat drinking from "Sultana" cup, advertises Great Atlantic and Pacific Tea Co. on back, cond. 8, 13" h, 6-1/4" w .......................................... 33.00

Pail, tin, "Sultana Peanut Butter, The Quaker Maid Co. Inc., Terre Haute, Ind.," blue ground, wear, scratches, dented lid, 1 lb, $66.

Pail, litho tin

    Orange variation, "Sultana Peanut Butter," girl offering sandwich to boy, red/black text, orange ground, cond. 8.5, 1 lb ................................................. 55.00

    Yellow variation, "Sultana Peanut Butter," girl offering sandwich to boy, red/black text, yellow ground, cond. 8-, 1 lb ................................................. 33.00

## Summer's Worm Powder

Sign, porcelain, "Summer's Worm Powders, Merit Alone Has Made Them Famous, Fed To Over 2000000 Animals Yearly," stamped image of a sheep, cond. 8, 12" h, 18" w ........................................................ 632.50

## Summer-Time Tobacco

Tin

    Paper label on cardboard, tin top/bottom, "Good Old Summer-Time Long Cut Tobacco," seashore scene with woman in red bathing suit, top/bottom soiled, 6" h, 5" dia ...................................................... 71.50

    Litho tin, "Good Old Summer-Time Long Cut Tobacco," seashore scene with woman in red bathing suit, cond. 8-, 8 oz, 5-1/2" h, 4" dia ...................... 132.00

## Sunbeam

Door bar centerpiece, litho tin, die-cut, loaf shape, "Sunbeam Batter Whipped," Miss Sunbeam by red oval, cond. 9.75+, 9" h, 19" w .................................... 412.50

Door push, enameled metal, die-cut, shape of loaf of Sunbeam white bread, white wrapper with Miss Sunbeam, unused, mint, 8-3/4" h, 26-3/4" w ........... 550.00

Screen door, wood, "Reach For Sunbeam, Bread with a Bonus" lettering on screen, oval "Sunbeam" logo, embossed tin door bar, "Reach for Sunbeam Bread," red/white text, blue ground, some wood ornamentation broken/missing, 82" h, 34" w............................. 467.50

Sign, litho tin

    Die-cut, oval, Miss Sunbeam eating buttered bread over yellow text, red ground, yellow border, 1962, cond. 8.25-8.5, 52" h, 35" w......................... 935.00

    Embossed, "Sunbeam Batter Whipped, Compare" wrapped loaf on silver tray beside yellow "Batter Whipped" sign, blue drapes ground, 1962, cond. 9.5-9.75, 12" h, 30" w ................................... 412.50

Sign, litho tin, die-cut, embossed, loaf shape, "Stroehmann's Enriched Bread, Energy-Packed Sunbeam Enriched Bread" label on open loaf, cond. 8-8.25, 31" h, 62" w, $3,520. (Photo courtesy of Gary Metz, Muddy River Trading Co.)

    Embossed, "Sunbeam White Enriched Bread, Stays Fresher Longer" wrapped loaf on silver tray beside yellow sign, red ground, cond. 8.5, 12" h, 30" w............................................................ 220.00

    Embossed, "Reach For Sunbeam Energy-Packed Bread," Miss Sunbeam eating buttered bread at left, white/yellow text, white wheat head, red ground, 1950s-1960s, NOS, cond. 9.75, 18" h, 54" w........................................................ 1,210.00

    Embossed, rounded corners, "Come In! We Serve The Best Made With Sunbeam Rolls," Sunbeam girl with hamburger/hotdog on tray, yellow wheat stalk, yellow/white text, red ground, mkd "A.A.W. 11-53"

Fan, cardboard, die-cut, wooden handle, dog in straw hat drinking from "Sultana" cup, advertises Great Atlantic and Pacific Tea Co. on back, cond. 8, 13" h, 6-1/4" w ...................................................... 33.00

    VG, 54-1/2" h, 18-1/2" w ............................... 1,320.00

    Rounded corners, "Reach For Sunbeam, Energy-Packed Bread," Miss Sunbeam eating buttered bread, white/yellow text, red ground, yellow border, mkd "A.A.W. 3-53," minor scratches/dents, 55" h, 19" w............ 825.00

Thermometer

    Round, Pam style, "Reach for Sunbeam Bread, Let's Be Friends," Miss Sunbeam on white ground with radiating yellow lines, red/blue text, blue border, white numbers, 1950s-1960s, cond. 9-9.25, 12" dia ........................................................ 825.00

    Square, glass front, Miss Sunbeam in red oval over "Sunbeam (in red banner), Enjoy Sunbeam Bread," square inner border, blue on white ground, circa 1970, cond. 7.75-8, 12" sq .......................... 495.00

## Sunbeam Coffee

Can, keywind, litho tin, name in black bands under beaming golden sun, yellow ground, Francis H. Leggett & Co., New York, cond. 8, 1 lb ............................. 60.50

## SunCrest

Clock, glass face, metal case

    "Drink SunCrest Beverages," orange sunrise, paint chips to frame, works, 8" h, 6-1/2" w, 2-1/2" d ...................................................... 110.00

Sign, porcelain, 2-sided, "Sunfreze Ice Cream by Arden," shows boy delivering milk, red text on white, yellow trim, red ground, 1930s-1940s, cond. 9.25/8.25, 32" h, 28" w, $825. (Photo courtesy of Gary Metz, Muddy River Trading Co.)

"SunCrest" bottle on green circle, black numbers on white border, runs but doesn't light, face soiling/scratches/chips to hands, 15-1/4" dia ........... 330.00

Sign, cardboard, "Have a party... Get TingleAted with SunCrest," cartoon image of star-eyed girl with bottle by food tray/dancing in background, wear to edges/paper missing at corner, 17" h, 22" w ................. 27.50

Thermometer, Pam style, tin face, glass cover, "Get TingleAted with Sun Crest, ...all-weather refresher," tilted bottle at center, blue/orange text, blue numbers, white ground, minor soiling/scratches ........................ 209.00

## Sun Cured

Tin, vertical pocket, "Crushed Sun Cured Extra Mild Smoking Tobacco, John J. Bagley & Co., Detroit, Mich., Ready for Pipe," barrel with tobacco leaves, cond. 8 ........................................................ 1,832.00

## Sundown Coffee

Can, paper label over tin, "Sundown Brand Coffee" in white on red band under image of camels/pyramid, yellow ground, cond. 8, 1 lb, 6" h, 4-1/4" dia .................... 198.00

## Sun-drop Cola

Sign, tin

Die-cut, bottle shape, "Refreshing AS A Cup Of Coffee" in white panel over "Gold-en Girl Cola" on teacup, over "Sun-drop Gold-en Girl Cola" red oval logo, green bottle, cond. VG, 60" h, 16" w ................ 533.50

Embossed, "Sun-drop Cola, as you like it, Good to the Last Golden Drop," Golden Cola bottle/logo at left, Diet Sun-drop Cola bottle/logo at right, red/black/blue text, white ground, cond. VG, 12" h, 28" w ........................................................ 176.00

## Sunfreze Ice Cream (See Photo)

## Sun-Kist Tobacco

Can, litho tin, "Sun-Kist Selected Pipe-Mellow Smoking Tobacco, Made Exclusively for Sears-Roebuck And Co., Chicago, Dallas, Seattle," house/tobacco field, yellow ground, domed lid, cond. 8, 5" h, 4-1/4" dia ........................................................ 357.50

Sign, tin, "Need Gas? Sunoco, __ mi. Ahead, Rest Rooms," diamond/arrow logo, yellow/red/cobalt text, cobalt ground, cond. 7, 45" h, 93" w, $220. (Photo courtesy of Collectors Auction Services)

## Sunlight Axle Oil

Can, tin, "Directions For Using Sunlight Axle Oil...," black on white ground, Monarch Mfg. Co., cond. 8, 6-3/4" h, 3" w, 1-1/2" d ...................................................... 77.00

## Sunlight Soap

Poster, paper, "Sunlight Soap, 'I'se Middlin' Proud,' A Morning's Work," cartoon image of mammy with laundry on line, cond. 8+, 29-1/2" h, 19-1/4" w ........................ 302.50

## Sunny Boy Peanut Butter

Pail, litho tin

Shows boy eating sandwich, rays radiating from center, red text/design, white ground, faded, cond. 7+, 1 lb ................................................................ 34.00

Snap top, shows boy eating sandwich, rays radiating from center, blue text/design, white ground, Brundage Bros. Co., cond. 7.5, 25 lb, 9-1/2" x 10" ............ 131.00

## Sunny Brook

Clock, glass face, metal body, "Time to come over on the Old Sunny Brook Brand side! It's From Kentucky, Cheerful as its Name," white/yellow text on green ground, clock to left, plastic bowl behind hands to create illumination, plastic cracked, 10-1/4" h, 17-1/2" w ...................... 143.00

## Sunny Sky Coffee

Tin, keywind, litho tin, "Sunny Sky De Luxe Coffee," shows coffee cup and sunrays over plantation, cond. 8.5+, 1 lb ........................................................ 353.00

## Sunoco

Ashtray, porcelain, round, "Sun Oil Co." on rim, diamond logo in center, yellow on cobalt, cond. NM, 5-1/2" dia ........................................................ 82.50

Banner

Cloth, "Change Now to Summer Type Oil and Grease, Sunoco, Unexcelled Lubrication," Donald Duck in speeding car, text on billboard, ©1939 Walt Disney Productions, cond. 7, 35-1/2" h, 56" w ............. 770.00

Oil cloth, "Keep Your Motor Full Powered! Sunoco Mercury Made Motor Oil, Prevents Power-Killing

Carbon," Mercury running beside red car, white/yellow/red text, black ground, cond. 8+, 36" h, 60" w .................................................... 363.00

Pin, celluloid on badge, "Change Now To Winter Oil and Grease, Sunoco," Old Man Winter blowing, blue/yellow ground, cond. EXC, 3-1/2" dia .................... 160.50

Rack, metal with porcelain sides, "Sunoco Motor Oil" in black on yellow ground, pierced design, bent "Mercury Made" sign at top of 1 side, missing on other side, cond. 7, 28" h, 29" w, 19" d ............................ 341.00

Radiator cover, cardboard, 2-sided, diamond logo on 1 side, "Sunoco Mercury Made Motor Oil" on other, yellow/red on black, cond. 8, lot of 5 ...................... 176.00

Salt/pepper shakers, plastic, gas pump shape, blue, "Blue Sunoco" in yellow diamond, cond. 8+, 2-3/4" h, 1" w, pr .................................................. 231.00

Sign, cardboard, "For Trigger-Quick Starting! Change now to Sunoco Winter Oil and Transep," scene of "Pilgrim" Mickey Mouse shooting at turkey, 1939, framed, cond. 8+, 29-1/2" h, 21-1/2" w ......................... 632.50

Sign, molded plastic, lightup
Die-cut form, metal case, "Sunoco" diamond logo with arrow, blue/yellow/red, cond. 8, 33" h, 47" w, 7-1/2" d ............................................. 242.00
Embossed, metal case, "Sunoco" diamond logo with arrow, blue/yellow/red ground, metal frame, cond. 8, 34" h, 50-1/2" w .................................... 44.00

Sign, porcelain
2-sided, diamond shape, "Gas Sunoco Oil," yellow ground, cond. 8.5/8, 28" h, 42" w ............... 1,050.50
2-sided, pr, "Ladies" and "Men," black text/border, white ground, cond. 7, 6-1/2" h, 17" w, pr ....... 66.00
2-sided, rounded ends, iron hanger, "Rest Rooms" in white, cobalt ground flanked by round silhouettes of woman with umbrella, man with top hat/cane, yellow border, cond. 8/7.5, 14" h, 22" w ............ 825.00
"Mens Rest Room," green text, white ground, cond. 7, 5-1/2" h, 14-1/2" ........................................... 13.75

Sign, tin, "Hopewell, N.J., Texaco, Ahead," white/red text, black/white/black panels, green border, cond. 7+ .................................................. 275.00

Tin, "Sunshine Cheese Wafers," yellow and brown ground, $22.50.

## Sun-Proof Paint

Sign, tin, self-framed, "Satisfaction in Service Since 1855" in gold, shows can of "Pittsburgh Proof Products, Patton's Sun-Proof Paint" at left, 25-1/2" h, 37-1/2" w ........................................... 286.00

## Sunray

Gas globe, 2 glass lenses, newer plastic body, "Sunray Gasoline" in black under beaming sun, orange/green ground, all cond. 9, 13-1/2" dia ...................... 1,320.00

Sign, porcelain, octagonal, "Sunray D-X Petroleum Products," black/white text, "Sunray" bowed under beaming sun on orange/green ground, diamond D-X logo, NOS, cond. 9, 8-3/8" h, 8-3/8" w ............................. 1,210.00

## Sun-Rise Beverages (See Photo)

## Sunshine

**History:** Wanting a change from the standard dark and dank basement bakeshops of the period, J.L. and J.S. Loose of Kansas City opened a baking company founded on the premise that they would produce crackers and cookies in a facility flooded with sunshine. The Loose brothers teamed with industrialist John A. Wiles to create the Loose-Wiles Biscuit Company. Their Sunshine Biscuits were an immediate success.

Buoyed by the popularity of their soda biscuits, sugar wafers, and Hydrox creme-filled chocolate sandwich cookies, the company moved to Long Island City around 1912. Following World War II, the name was changed to Sunshine Biscuits, Inc. By 1955 the corporation had become the world's largest bakery.

Building plate, brass, shield shape, "Sunshine Biscuits" over image of baker, possibly from Kansas City headquarters, cond. G, 21" h sq ............................... 522.50

## Sunshine Cigarettes

Sign, tin, "Twenty for 15¢" in red on yellow ground, pack of "Sunshine Cigarettes" in center, red package with sun rising over trees, homemade wood frame, paint chips/dents, 18" h, 14" w ................................. 192.50

## Sunshine Coffee

Can, keywind, litho tin
2 lions flank beaming yellow sun, red/white text, blue

Sign, tin, "Refreshing Sun-Rise Beverages, Bottled by the Coca-Cola Bottling Company," rust and edge wear, 12" h, 28" w, $50.

ground, red band at bottom, Springfield Grocer Co., Springfield MO, cond. 8, 1 lb .......................... 71.50

King drinking coffee, red ground, black lower border, Mogar Coffee Co., Brooklyn, cond. 8+, 1 lb, 4" h, 5" dia.......................................................... 220.00

## Superior Northwestern

Poster, canvas, "For The Master Painter, For The Home Owner" in 2 black panels, shows professional painter in doorway, man painting his fence, German shepherd holding can of "Superior Northwestern Mixed Paint," yellow ground, Chicago White Lead Oil Co., Chicago, cond. VG, 36" h, 48" w......................................... 88.00

## Superla Cream Separator Oil

Can, tin, "Superla Cream Separator Oil" at bottom, shows cream separators/cows on 3 sides, back has text, Standard Oil Co., cond. VG, 9-1/2" h, 5" w................... 77.00

## Supreme Coffee

Can, keywind, litho tin, "Supreme Coffee, Steel Cut," eagle over blue/gold text, white ground, cond. 8.25+, 1 lb ..................................................................... 126.50

## Supreme Court Coffee

Can, paper label over tin, "Supreme Court Brand Coffee," oval image of courthouse, white text, front cond. 8, back missing section of label, 1 lb, 6" h, 4" dia .............. 181.50

## Supreme Motor Oil

Can, litho tin, hand-soldered, "Low Cold Test, Supreme Motor Oil, Gulf Refining Company," yellow ground, cond. 7, 6-1/4" x 8-1/2" x 5-1/2" ........................ 220.00

## Sure Shot Chewing Tobacco (See Photo)

## Sutter & Miller Hotel

Sign, glass, reverse-painted, gold text on white, scratches, 10" h, 28" w ....................................... 33.00

## Swansdown Coffee

Can, litho tin

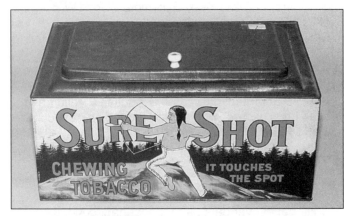

Bin, litho tin, hinged lid, "Sure Shot Chewing Tobacco, It Hits The Spot," 8" h, 15-1/4" w, 10-1/4" d, $522.50.

Tin, litho tin, "Light Sweet Cuba, Continental Tobacco Co., successor to Daniel Scotten & Co. of Detroit," 1 lb, 8-1/4" d, $35.

Pry lid, "Swansdown Brand Fresh Keeping High Grade Blend Coffee, Swansdown Coffee Company Inc., Importers, Roasters and Blenders, Pittsburgh, Pa.," oval image of swan, yellow ground, cond. 7+, 1 lb, 6-1/4" h, 4-1/4" dia......................................... 572.00

"Swansdown Brand Fresh Keeping High Grade Blend Coffee, Swansdown Coffee Company Inc., Importers, Roasters and Blenders, Pittsburgh, Pa.," oval image of swan, Good Housekeeping seal ©1964, red/black text, yellow ground, cond. 8, 3 lb, 7-1/4" h, 6" dia .......................................................... 333.00

## Sweet Burley Tobacco

Bin, countertop store bin, litho tin, "Light Sweet Burley Tobacco," red text, yellow ground, cond. 8.5+, 11" h, 8-1/2" dia......................................................... 268.00

## Sweet Caporal Cigarettes

Tin, litho tin, flat 50, Kinney Bros., cond. 8 .............. 33.00

## Sweet Cuba

Bin, cardboard, tin top/bottom, "Sweet Cuba Fine Cut, the Kind That Suits, Spaulding & Merrick, Chicago, Illinois" on front with oval image of lighthouse flanked by banners, "48 Five Cent Packages Sweet Cuba Chewing Tobacco" on side with star banner, cond. 9-, 11-1/4" h, 8" w, 6-1/2" d .......................................................555.50

Package, silver wrapper with red label, "Sweet Cuba Fine Cut Chewing Tobacco," cond. 8-8.5, 8 oz ..................................................................... 28.00

Sign, litho tin, slant-lid, "Sweet Cuba Fine Cut, 5¢," shows package, red text, yellow ground, cond. 8.5, 8" h, 8" w, 10" d................................................. 440.00

## Sweet Heart Products

Door push, porcelain, die-cut, heart shape, "Sweet Heart Products, Hard Wheat Flour, White Corn Flour, White Corn Meal," white on red ground, 1940s, cond. 9.25+, 5" h, 5" w......................................................... 275.00

## Sweet-heart Sugar Cones

Can, tin, "Sweet-heart Sugar Cones, the Perfect Sugar cone with the finished edge, There is joy in Sweetheart

Box, paper, "Sweetheart Drinking straws, drink the sanitary way," unused, 8-5/8" h, $8.

Sugar Cones," girl holding oversized ice cream cone, red/blue text, blue ground, S&S Cone Corp., New York, fading/dents/scratches/chips, 15-1/2" h, 12-1/2" dia.................................................. 269.50

## Sweetheart Peanut Butter

Pail, litho tin, "Sweetheart" in white over medallion with "Pure Peanut Butter, Made Exclusively From The Sweetheart of the Nut" in red/black, dark ground, Canadian, cond. 7.5, 1 lb, 3-1/2" x 3-3/4" ........... 99.00

## Sweetheart Straws

## Sweet Home Rolled Oats

Box, cardboard, round, "Sweet Home Quick Cooking Rolled Oats," house, "Sweet Home" in script at top, cond. 9-, 1 lb 4 oz ........................................... 110.00

## Sweet Mist Tobacco

Can, litho tin, "Sweet Mist Chewing Tobacco, Scotten, Dillon Company," pictures 3 children playing in water fountain, red text, yellow ground, scratches/dents, 11-1/2" h, 8-1/2" dia.................................................. 148.50

## Sweet-Orr

Sign, porcelain
   "Sweet-Orr Overalls," 6 men in contest of tug-of-war

Sign, porcelain, "Sweet-Orr Pants, Shirts, Overalls," red design, cobalt text, 1930s-1940s, cond. 7.5, 28" h, 72" w, $220. (Photo courtesy of Gary Metz, Muddy River Trading Co.)

with pants, graphic is fired-on ink, circa 1910s-1920s, cond. 8-8.25+, 14" h, 20" w.............. 770.00
   "Sweet-Orr Overalls," 6 men in contest of tug-of-war with pants, graphic stamped on yellow ground, rest on blue ground, cond. 8.5+, 14" h, 20" w .................1,760.00
Sign, tin, embossed, "Wear Sweet, Orr & Co.'s Union-Made Overalls and Pants," black text, yellow ground, flaking, cond. 7, 7" h, 10" w................................. 77.00

## Sweet Rose Cigars

Cigar cutter/lighter, cast iron, attached lamp and shade, keywind cutter, embossed "Sweet Rose High Grade Cigar," cond. EXC, 10-1/4" x 12" x 7" ........... 3,190.00

## Sweet Tips

Tin, vertical pocket, litho tin
   Flat, tall version "Bagley's Sweet Tips Smoking," fan of 7 tobacco leaves, dark ground, cond. 8,......... 57.00
   Short oval, "Bagley's Sweet Tips Smoking," fan of 7 tobacco leaves, dark/gold ground, cond. 8+......................................................... 83.00
   "Bagley's Sweet Tips Smoking," fan of 7 tobacco leaves, dark ground, 1910 tax stamp, cond. 8+, 4-3/4" h ......................................................... 57.00
Tin, vertical pocket, paper label, oval, "Bagley's Sweet Tips Smoking," white text, dark ground, fan of 7 tobacco leaves, broken hinge, cond. 7.5 ............ 27.50

## Swift's Ice Cream

Clock, light-up, square, plastic light-up face with metal case, 1960s, cond. 8.5, 16" sq............................ 77.00
Sign, sidewalk, porcelain, 2-sided, "Authorized Dealer" over white medallion with "Swift's Ice Cream," blue ground, cond. 6-8, 18" h, 24" w........................... 44.00

## Swift's Peanut Butter

Can, tin, "Swift's Peanut Butter," white text in blue oval, "Swift's Premium Quality" in lower oval flanked by 2 peanuts, "Swift's" repeats on white ground, Swift & Co., Chicago, chips/scratches, 25 lb, 10-1/8" h, 10-1/2" dia....................................................... 33.00

## Sycamore Wagon Works

Pocket mirror, celluloid, oval, "Sycamore Wagon Works Mfrs of Low Down Short Turn Wagons, Sycamore, Ill.," shows Clover Leaf Dairy wagon, cond. EXC .................... 577.50

## Sykes Comfort Powder

Tin, litho tin, "Sykes Comfort Powder, A Sking Healing Powder For Infants, Children & Adults," 2 children in oval, back pictures nurse, blue ground, 1920s, cond. 8, 4-1/2" h, 2-1/4" w, 1-3/4" d ........................... 215.50

## Symon's Coffee

Can, keywind, litho tin, "Symon's Best Coffee," cup with white electric bolts on red ground, dark/red text in white panel over dark band, unopened, cond. 8.5, 1 lb ................................................................. 110.00

# T

## Table King Coffee

Can, litho tin
2 couples dining, crowns in corners, no lid, cond. 8-, 1 lb, 5-1/2" h, 4-1/4" dia ........................................... 962.50
Dining scene, crowns on top, back/sides worn, cond. 7.5, 3 lb ...........................................................110.00

## Tac-Cut Coffee

Tin, keywind, litho tin, round image of chicken saying "Tac-Cut Tac-Cut Tac-Cut," red ground, cond. 7.5-8, 1 lb, 4" h, 5" dia ...................................... 242.00

## Tagolene Motor Oil

Sign, porcelain, 2-sided, "Tagolene Motor Oil, Tailor Made," white text, black "Skelly" diamond, red band, black ground, cond. 8+, 30" dia ........................ 467.50

## Taka-Kola

Tip tray, litho tin, "Taka-Kola Every Hour, Take No Other," woman in red dress with raised bottle, clock face around inner edge, cond. 8.5+, 4-1/4" dia ......... 550.00

## Talco DeRoss

Tin, paper label, "Talco DeRoss, Flores Del Paraiso, boratado-Antisetico-Confortante," man kissing woman's hand, Syndey Ross Co., Newark, N.J., 5-3/4" h, 2-5/8" dia ............................................................. 166.00

## Tampax

Sign, celluloid over cardboard, "Go where you want... do what you want... You feel so cool, so clean, so fresh with Tampax Menstrual Tampons," woman standing in sports car in field, 4 product boxes, 2-tone blue text, white ground, minor stains/scratches, 14-1/8" h, 10-1/8" w ............................................................. 82.50

## Taylor Cigars

Sign, reverse-foil on glass, "Taylor Co. Cigars, Tobacco & Sporting Goods," silver text/border, brown ground, framed, restored ground, cond. 9.5+ ................. 632.50

## Taylor Thermometers

Thermometer, wood, pointed top/bottom, beveled, "Taylor Thermometers Sold Here," black text at bottom, NOS, cond. VG, 29" h, 7-5/8" w .......................... 66.00

## Teddie Peanuts

Can, litho tin, "Jumbo Whole Teddie Salted Peanuts," peanut in black ring, white text, red ground, cond. 8.25, 1 lb, 5-1/2" h, 3-1/2" dia ............................. 82.50

## Teddy Bear Peas

Tin, paper label, shows early jointed teddy bear, cond. 8+, 4-1/2" h, 3-1/4" dia ..................................... 198.00

## Ted's Root Beer

Sign, countertop, cardboard, easel-back, "Ted's Creamy Root Beer," shows Ted Williams in Boston Red Sox uniform at left, bottle at right, cond. 8.5+, 10" h, 14-7/8" w ......................................................... 2,035.00

## Telfer Coffee

Pail, tin, "Telfer Coffee Milk Maid, Java and Mocha Coffee, Detroit, Mich.," shows woman/cow, gold stencil on yellow ground, bail with wooden handle, cond. 8+, 5 lb, 12" h, 7-1/4" dia........................................ 3,080.00

## Telling's Ice Cream

Sign, porcelain, 2-sided, red Sealtest seal, blue text, white ground, 1940s, cond. 9.5+, 2' h, 3' w .....................385.00

Can, litho tin, "Terrace Club Coffee Tops Them All, Clare E. Halladay Coffee Co., Battle Creek, Mich.," 1920s country club image, cond. 8, 1 lb, 6" h, 4" dia, $2,090. (Photo courtesy of Wm. Morford)

# Tennyson Cigars

Tin, vertical box, litho tin, held 25 cigars, "Tennyson" over large image of man on red ground, "5¢" below, cond. 7.5 .................................................................. 85.00

# Terrace Club Coffee (See Photo)

# Texaco

**History:** Partners Joseph Cullinan, a former employee of Standard Oil, and Arnold Schlaet formed the Texas Fuel Company in 1902. Initially, their oil saw duty as an industrial and household fuel, but once cars became popular, Texaco opened a chain of service stations.

**References:** Robert W. D. Ball, *Texaco Collectibles*, Schiffer Publishing, 1994; Rick Pease, *A Tour with Texaco: Antique Advertising and Memorabilia*, Schiffer Publishing, 1997

Alarm clock, Westclock, metal case, glass lens, cardboard face, star logo, NOS, cond. 9, 5-1/4" dia ............... 330.00
Banner, cloth
"Drain- Fill- then Listen," 2 Scottie dogs at right, black/red text, white ground, cond. 8, 36" h, 80" w .......... 209.00
"New Texaco Motor Oil! Lasts Longer-Crack Proof!," black/red text on white ground, yellow text on black strip at bottom, cond. 8, 36" h, 80" w .............. 93.50
Blotter, "Good Bye, Hard Carbon" in white on red band, man in hat with green can with star logo, New Jersey merchant info printed on blank at bottom, cond. NM, 6" h, 3-1/2" w ....................................................... 82.50
Calendar, cardboard/paper, die-cut, 1952, "Texaco Asphalt Roofing Products," round star logo at top, full pad, cond. 8, 26-1/2" h, 15" w .......................... 357.50
Can, litho tin
"Texaco 574 Oil," black text on white panel over red star logo with name on ringed border, green ground, cond. 8, 6-1/4" h, 3-3/4" dia ........................... 82.50
"Texaco Plastic Asbestos Roof Cement," star logo, white over green ground, farm buildings at bottom, cond. 8, 5" h, 6" dia......................................... 60.50
Clock, lightup, metal body, tin face, replaced Texaco star decal in center, reverse-painted glass cover for "Jungman Oil Co.," fluorescent tube, cond. 7, 20" dia ............. 330.00
Gas globe
Glass, Gill body, 2 glass lenses, copper base, star logo, "T" with white outline, cond. 7, 13-1/2" dia ................................................. 302.50
Glass, narrow body, 2 glass lenses, star logo, "T" with black outline, lens cond. 8.5/8, body cond. 8, 13-1/2" dia ..................................................... 396.00
Glass, wide body, 2 lenses, "Texaco" star logo, white ground, both lenses dated "Hull 4-37," lens cond. 8/7.5, body cond. 8.5, 13-1/2" dia .................... 500.50
Metal, high-profile body, 2 lenses, "Texaco Ethyl" in white on red border, star logo in center on white ground, 1 lens cracked, lens cond. 9/6, body cond. 8.5................................................................. 313.50
Milk glass, embossed, 1-pc, "Texaco Ethyl," black text, star logo, orig paint, brass collar, cond. NM, 18" h, 16" dia........................................................ 3,080.00

Can, litho tin, "Texaco Lighter Fluid," light wear, scratches, plastic neck and cap, 4 oz, $15.

Milk glass, embossed, 1-pc, "Texaco" star logo, copper base, repainted, all cond. 9, 18" h, 16" dia ..................................................... 1,237.50
Plastic Capcolite body, 1 lens, with "Texaco" star logo, white ground, both cond. 8, 13-1/2" dia ..........242.00
Grease gun, metal/brass, embossed, "Texaco" on handle, red body, cond. 8.5, 27" l ........................... 390.50
Pinback button, "Win a Texaco Scottie, Listen," shows 2 Scottie dogs, cond. EXC, 1-3/4" dia.................. 467.50
Rack, wire, litho tin sign at top, "Texaco Outboard Lubricants" in red/black, star logo at left, boat motor at right, both on black panel with white pinstripes, white ground, NOS, cond. 9, 44" h, 20" w, 11" d..........................632.00
Salt/pepper shakers, plastic, gas pump shape
Decals for "Fire-Chief" on red shaker, "Sky Chief" on gray shaker, advertise Washington station, cond. 8, 2-3/4" h, pr...................................................... 55.00
Red and blue pumps with decals, advertise Washington station, orig box with "Texaco" star logo, NOS, cond. 8+, 2-3/4" h, pr.................................... 319.00
Sign, porcelain, pump, star logo
8" dia, restored, cond. 9.................................... 165.00
10" dia, circa 1930s, cond. 8........................... 357.50
12" dia, cond. 8.5............................................ 242.00
15" dia, cond. 8............................................... 203.50
Sign, porcelain
2-sided, "Nafta Texaco" on red ground with star logo in white circle, "Gargoyle Mobiloil" in black on white ground with red gargoyle logo, diagonal divider, cond. 7, 36" dia........................................ 3,025.00
Die-cut, keyhole style, "M.N. Saunders, Tank Truck Dealer" at bottom, star logo at top, black text/border, white ground, dated 10-9-58 at edge, restored, cond. 9, 13-1/2" h, 10-1/2" w ....................... 209.00
"No Smoking, The Texas Company," black text/border, white ground, cond. 7.5, 4-3/4" h, 15" w............121.00

Sign, tin, embossed, 6-sided, "Diesel Chief," black on white ground, green border, star logo at bottom, NOS, cond. 9, 9-3/4" h, 15-1/4" w............................. 385.00

Thermometer, tin, die-cut, keyhole style, star-logo sign shape, "Compliments..." info at bottom, red/green trim, orig box, cond. 8, 6-1/4" h, 2-1/2" w.................. 121.00

Toy

Helmet, plastic, "Texaco Fire Chief," star logo, gold eagle head holding white shield on red helmet, attached microphone/speaker, orig box, NOS, box torn/faded, 8" h, 14" l ...............................110.00

Pull toy, litho tin, oil cart with air meter, red pump with round "Texaco" star globe, green wheels, J. Chein & Co., cond. G, 8" h, 3" w, 4" d ........................ 825.00

Ship, plastic, battery-op, "Texaco" on side of ship, star logo on smokestack, box mkd "Exclusive Texaco Dealer Offer, It's Motorized! Batteries Included!," fire damage to box, NOS, 28" l ..................... 357.50

## Texaco Aircraft Engine Oil

Can, litho tin, winged star logo

Red over white ground, The Texas Co., cond. 8, 5 qt, 7-3/4" h, 6-5/8" dia .......................................... 55.00

White over red ground, The Texas Co., full, cond. 8.5, qt, 5-1/2" h, 4" dia ......................................... 121.00

## Texaco Fire-Chief

Bank, metal, paper decal, pump shaped, star/hat logo, red ground, cond. 8, 5-3/4" h ........................... 302.50

Banner, cloth, "A Greater Fire-Chief, The 100% Anti-Knock 'Regular'," red helmet on black circle, white ground, red lower border, cond. 7, 30" h, 17" w ....................... 126.50

Sign, porcelain, pump sign

1954, "Fire-Chief Gasoline," red fireman's hat/Texaco star, white ground, cond. 9.25, 12" h, 8" w................................................................. 198.00

1958, "Fire-Chief Gasoline," red fireman's hat/Texaco star, white ground, cond. 8.75, 12" h, 8" w................................................................. 154.00

Sign, porcelain

Rounded (to fit on visible pump), "Fire-Chief Gasoline" red/black text, red helmet by star logo, white ground, black border, cond. 7, 18" h, 10" w.................... 176.00

"Fire-Chief Gasoline" red/black text, red helmet by star logo, white ground, black border, cond. 8.5, 18" h, 12" w................................................................. 60.50

## Texaco Motor Oil

Blotter, "All the comfort that a snappy, smooth-running motor gives. Get it by using Texaco Motor Oil. The clear, clean oil with the right body," back of car with male passenger, Texaco logo, adv for NJ dealer, cond. 8, 3-1/4" h, 6" w.................................................. 152.00

Can, tin

"Easy Pour Can, Texaco Motor Oil Extra Heavy" in black on white panel over red star logo with name on ringed border, "The Texas Company" in red at bottom, green ground, cond. 7, 15" h, 3-3/4" dia ........................................................ 803.00

"Texaco 574 Oil," black text in white panel, star logo with red text border, green ground, cond. 8, qt, 6-1/2" h, 3-3/4" dia............................................ 66.00

"Texaco Aircraft Engine Oil" in green under star logo with green wings, red over white ground, cond. 8, qt, 5-1/2" h, 4" dia........................................... 49.50

"Texaco Marine Motor Oil" over star logo, white ground, green band at top/bottom with birds/boats, cond. 8+/7+, qt, 5-1/2" h, 4" dia .................... 165.00

"Texaco Motor Oil," white medallion with small image of oil pouring beside Texaco star and "Clean, Clear, Golden," green ground, Handy Grip top, logo embossed on lid, 1/2 gal, 6-1/2" h, 8" w, 3-1/4" d ......................................................... 412.50

"Texaco Motor Oil Heavy" black in white panel over red star logo with name on ringed border, green ground, The Texaco Company, Port Arthur, TX, cond. 7, gal, 11" h, 8" w, 3" d............................................... 82.50

Sign, metal, flange, "Easy Pour Can, Two Quarts" in black on white ground with hand pouring green 2-qt can, "Texaco Motor Oil, Manufactured Only By The Texas Company" in white on red ground, cond. 7, 27-1/2" h, 17-1/2" w ........................................................990.00

Sign, porcelain

2-sided, lubester, "Texaco Motor Oil" on red border, star logo in center, cond. 9, 5" dia ............... 522.50

2-sided, "Drain And Refill With Texaco Motor Oil," oil pouring/"Clean, Clear, Golden" and star logo in octagonal panel, white ground, cond. 8/7, 27" h, 18-1/2" w ........................................................ 330.00

"Clean Clear Texaco Motor Oil," star logo on black band at top, white text, red ground, "Property Of the Texas Co. (A/Asia) Ltd." at bottom, cond. 7, 14" h, 21" w......................................................... 555.50

## Thalhimers Fountain Coffee

Can, keywind, litho tin, "Thalhimers Special Blend Fountain Coffee," white text on black panel, black/white checkered ground, cond. 8.5+, 1 lb ................... 51.70

## Thermo Royal Anti-Freeze

Sign/thermometer, tin sign, shows can of "Thermo Royal Anti-Rust, No Poison Fumes, Anti-Freeze," red/black/white text on white over red over black can, red ground, round porcelain-face thermometer with glass cover on can, cond. G, 17-5/8" h, 11-5/8" w.........................275.00

## Thins

Tin, litho tin, "No. 55 Thins Service Packet" in blue on white ground, rest in white on blue ground, "Three Rubber Prophylactics, Manufactured by Youngs Rubber Corporation, Inc., General Offices, New York, N.Y., Factory, Trenton, N.J.," cond. 8.5+, 1/4" h, 1-5/8" w, 2-1/8" d ......................................................... 907.50

## I.P. Thomas & Sons

Calendar, paper, framed, Indian illustration identified as "Hiawatha's Wedding Journey," lettered "I.P. Thomas & Son Co., High-Grade Fertilizers, Office: 1000 Drexel Building Philadelphia, Works: Nantua Point, N.J. On Delaware River," December pad only, creases, 25-1/2" h, 16" w...............................................................176.00

## Thompson's Ice Cream

Pocket mirror, round, "Thompson's Unexcelled Ice Cream, Andy Gump For President," shows Gump, cond. 8 ............................................................ 231.00

## Three Cadets Condoms

Tin, litho tin
"Three Cadets, Carefully Tested, 100% Perfect," yellow/red/blue swirls, ©1931, 2-pc, cond. 8.5+, 5/8" h, 1-5/8" dia ................................................ 275.00
"Three Cadets, Guaranteed Indefinitely, Carefully Tested, 100% Perfect," white/gray/blue swirls, ©1931, cond. 8.5+, 5/8" h, 1-5/8" dia............ 440.00

## Three Crows Jamaica Ginger

Bottle, paper label, shows crows, Atlantic Spice Co., Rockland, Maine, cond. 8, 4-1/2" h, 1-3/4" w, 1" d.................................................................... 27.50

## Three Feathers

Tin, vertical pocket, litho tin, "Three Feathers, Will Not Bite The Tongue, Choice Granulated Plug Cut," 3 feathers in crown on red medallion, blue/white ground with red/yellow trim, cond. 9.............................. 547.00

## Three Squires Pipe Mixture

Tin, vertical pocket, cardboard, sample, "Complimentary Sample," oval image of 3 men at table, red ground, cond. 9.5, 2-3/4" h, 2" w...................................... 75.00

## Three States

Tin, flat pocket, oval, "Three States Mixture, Kentucky, Virginia, Louisiana, Harry Weigginger Tob. Co.," 4-1/2" x 2-3/4" ................................................ 303.00

## 3-20-8 Cigars

Pocket mirror, round, "Now Is The Time To Smoke 3-20-8, New England's Best 10¢ Cigar," clock motif, white text on red stripe, black ground, white border with Roman numerals, cond. 8.25.............................. 33.00

## Three Twins

Tin, litho tin
Horizontal box, litho tin, "3 Twins Cut Plug," portraits of 3 women over red/white text on yellow ground, cond. 7.5, 1-3/4" h, 3-7/8" w, 2-1/2" d ............. 33.00
"3 Twins Fine Cut Smoking Tobacco," portraits of 3 women over red/white text on yellow ground, cond. 7.5, 4" x 6" .................................................... 193.00

## 3 V Cola

Sign, litho tin, "Stop for 3 V Cola, 3 Full Glasses In Every Bottle," yellow stop sign/6-pack carrier, red/black text, white ground, cond. 9.25+, 28" h, 20" w ........... 187.00

## Thurber & Co. Tea

Tin, litho tin, oval images of headquarters/screaming eagle, green ground, circa 1880s, cond. 8,1 lb, 8-1/2" h, 4-1/4" dia ............................................ 605.00

**Package, cardboard, paper label, "Bright Tiger Chewing Tobacco 5¢ Package," 11-1/2" h, $175.**

## Tidex

Gas globe, 2 lenses, wide glass body, "Tidex" in black, white/purple ground, all cond. 9, 13-1/2" dia ................... 550.00

## Tiger Chewing Tobacco

Tin, litho tin
Hinged, "Tiger Bright Chewing Tobacco," round image of tiger's head, red/gold checkered ground, cond. 8+, 2-1/8" h, 6" w, 4" d ................................ 220.00
Vertical pocket, "Tiger Bright Sweet Chewing Tobacco, P. Lorillard Co., Jersey City, N.J., 10¢" shows tiger over box with lettering, yellow ground, cond. 8-8.5 ........................................................ 431.00

## Times Square

Tin, vertical pocket, litho tin
"Times Square Smoking Mixture, Sold Only at United Cigar Stores and Whelan Drug Stores," nighttime skyline, cond. 7.5.......................................... 136.00
"Times Square Smoking Mixture," nighttime skyline, cond. 8........................................................ 331.00
"Times Square Smoking Mixture, Mellowed in Wood," nighttime skyline, cond. 8+, 4-1/4" h, 3" w........412.50

## Tintex

Display, countertop, litho tin, "Tints and Dyes Anything Any Color, Tintex, Tints As You Rinse," shows woman dying blouse pink, color chips behind her and packages of product, 35 compartments in back, cond. 8+, 23-3/8" h, 21-3/4" w, 7-1/2" d .......................... 550.00

## Tiolene

Matchbox, tin, divided image on lid, "Purol Gasoline" in

white with arrow on red ground; "Tiolene Motor Oil" with bull's eye in black on yellow ground, cond. 7, 1-1/2" h, 2-1/4" w .................................................. 88.00

Pen, "Tiolene Motor Oil, Made from Cabin Creek Crude By The Pure Oil Co." contains oil sample, North Dakota dealer, cond. 9, 5-7/8" l ........................ 104.50

Sign, porcelain, round, "The Pure Oil, Tiolene, Company, U.S.A.," "100% Pure Pennsylvania Oil' logo, zigzag border, white ground, 1930s-1940s, cond. 8, 15" dia ............................................................. 330.00

## Tiopet Motor Oil

Can, tin, "Tiopet 100% Pure Pennsylvania Motor Oil," pointing Indian in headdress, white text, red over black ground, Tiona Petroleum Co., Philadelphia, cond. 8.5+, qt, 5-1/2" h, 4" dia ................................... 660.00

## Tippecanoe

Sign, paper label, "Tippecanoe, The Best For Malaria, Tired Feeling," shows canoe with 5 seats, black text, white ground, framed, cond. 8, 8-1/2" h, 20-1/4" w ........................................................... 221.00

## Tip Top Bread

Kick plate, metal, heavy gauge, "Enriched Tip-Top Is Better Bread," shows loaf of bread in wrapper, cond. 9-9.25, 12" h, 30" w .............................................. 143.00

## Tip Top Tobacco (See Photo)

## Titusville Iron Works Co.

Sign, porcelain, oval, "Titusville, The Titusville Iron Works Co., Titusville, Pa., Since 1860," black/white text, yellow ground, cond. 7, 8" h, 18" w ........................ 77.00

## TNT Pop Corn

Tin, litho tin, round, "Barteldo's Tender Nutritious Tasty Pop Corn," enlarged "TNT" in red/"Pop Corn" in cobalt

Tin, paper label, "Sweet Tip Top, Beats All! Smoke and Chew," pictures horse-drawn fire engine, 6-1/4" h, $45.

Sign, lightup, "Ask For Toby Ale, Genuine Top Fermented," reverse-painted glass front, metal back, standup base, 17-1/2" h, 13-1/2" w, $225.

over radiating red/yellow lines in circle of popped corn, unopened, cond. 9+, 10 oz ............................... 132.00

## Tobacco Girl

Tin, litho tin, "Tobacco Girl, Comes Through With The Goods," woman peeking through tobacco leaf, red text, white ground, minor paint chips/scuffs, 5-1/2" h, 6-1/4" w, 4-1/2" d .......................................... 1,650.00

## Toby Ale (See Photo)

## Tolu Chewing Gum

Tin, litho tin, "Hoadley's Everlasting Tolu Chewing Gum, E.J. Hoadley, Hartford, Conn., Six for 5 Cents," black on yellow ground, cond. 8.5+, 3/4" h, 2-1/4" w, 1" d ............................................................... 770.00

## Toledo Scales

Sign, porcelain, "Our Weighing Service is rendered by Toledo Scales, No Springs - Honest Weight," dark text/border, white ground, cond. EXC, 11" h, 17-1/2" w .......................................................... 104.50

## Tom's Snacks (See Photo)

## Tonka Smoking Mixture

Tin, vertical box, litho tin, lid shows 2 soldiers sharing pipe outside tent on Plains, front has ornate vase with flowers on Oriental rug with "Smoking" in wisp of smoke, McAlpin Consumers Tobacco Co. Ltd., Toronto, 3-1/4" h, 5" w, 3-3/4" d ............................. 405.00

Sign, tin, "Time Out for Tom's," shows 3 snacks, 1950s, cond. 8.25+, 28" h, 20" w, $275. (Photo courtesy of Gary Metz, Muddy River Trading Co.)

Match holder, litho tin, "Topsy Hosiery, Fuess-Fischer Co.," 4-7/8" h, 3-3/8" w, $340.

## Tono-Sama Tobacco

Tin, litho tin, "Tono-Sama Long Cut Mild Smoking Tobacco," sailboat with island/mountain in background, Imperial Tobacco Co., Montreal, cond. 8, 4" x 6".................................................. 72.50

## Tootsie Rolls

**History:** After immigrating to New York City in 1896, Leo Hirshfield returned to the business of making candy. Using a formula he brought from Vienna, Hirshfield began producing rolls of chewy chocolatey candy that he sold for a penny apiece. Needing a name for his popular treat, Hirshfield chose Tootsie to honor his childhood sweetheart.

Display case, metal/glass, incised glass panel, "Tootsie Rolls, Pure, Delicious Chocolate Candy," back door missing, 1920s-1930s, cond. 7.5-8, 8-1/2" h, 7" w, 5" d.................................................. 687.50

## Topaz Coffee

Can, paper label over tin, sample, "Free Sample, Topaz High Grade Roasted Coffee, Sherman Bros. & Co., Importers of Coffee, Teas and Spices, Chicago, Ill.," oval image of person on horseback, red ground, cond. 7.5+, 2-5/8" h, 1-7/8" dia .................................. 198.00

## Topps

Greeting card, "Hope Your Christmas Is" with arrow pointing to attached piece of "Topps" gum, seal with party hat, ball on tail, wreath around neck, orig envelope, mint, 1940s, 6" h, 5" w ...................................... 33.00

## Topsy Hosiery (See Photo)

## Tops All Coffee

Can, litho tin, "Ehlers Tops All Coffee, Superior Quality, Delicious Flavors, Albert Elhers, Brooklyn, New York," shows woman holding up coffee cup while standing on globe, green ground, cond. 8-, 3 lb ................... 632.50

## Torpedo

Tin, vertical pocket, litho tin
　Destroyer version, "Torpedo Special Short Cut Smoking Tobacco," green ground, Canadian, front cond. 8, back cond. 5 ........................................ 1,452.00
　Submarine version, concave, "Torpedo Special Short Cut Smoking Tobacco," green ground, Canadian, cond. 8...................................................... 7,720.00

## Torrington Bearings

Clock, lightup, metal body, glass face/cover, "Torrington Bearings" on black panel in center with parts on red square, "Authorized Distributor" in white on red border, cond. 9, 18" dia ............................................... 143.00

## Totem Cigars

Cigar box, "Totem, Union Made, Watt & Bond, Boston," round images of Indian portrait/running/on horseback, white text on red border, label under lid and on right side, circa 1901, 100-count, cond. 8.25 .............. 93.50

## Totem Tobacco

Pack, cigarette rolling papers, "Totem Tobacco" in brown,

side view of Indian smoking pipe in front of totem pole, orange ground, cond. EXC, 3" h, 1-3/4" w ........ 280.00

## Town & Country Coffee

Can, keywind, litho tin, "Town & Country Coffee," cond. 8.25+, 1 lb ......................................................... 126.50

## Town Talk Bread

Sign

Porcelain, "Ask For Town Talk Bread, Rich In Pure Milk," blue/yellow text, cobalt oval shows bread/baker, white ground, circa 1930s, cond. 6, 14" h, 22" w .......................................................... 154.00

Tin, embossed, "Better Buy... Braun's Town Talk Bread," black/red text, black border, cond. G, 23-1/2" h, 35-1/2" w ......................................... 77.00

## Toyland Peanut Butter

Pail, litho tin, "Toyland Peanut Butter," marching band in red, white text, E.K. Pond Co., Chicago, cond. 8.5+, 1 lb ................................................................. 374.00

## Trackside Gasoline

Gas globe, 2 glass lenses, wide glass body, "Trackside Gasoline" in blue at top/bottom border, "Regular" in red script at center, all cond. 9, 13-1/2" dia .................. 582.00

## Tracto Motor Oil

Sign, tin, embossed, "Tracto Motor Oil, Reduces Friction, Saves Wear," silhouette of farm/oil wells at bottom, black/yellow text, yellow ground, cond. 8, 11-1/2" h, 35-1/2" w ........................................................... 66.00

## Trade Signs

Barbershop, "Modern Service," sign, porcelain, rounded pole design, scratches/edge chips, 48" h, 9" w .............. 242.00

"Jewelry, Watch Repairing," sign, porcelain, 2-sided, cast-iron hanger, pocket watch motif, Roman numerals, orange design, black ground, chips, 16-1/2" h, 11-1/4" w ...................................................... 1,001.00

Gun, longarm, carved wood, chips/wear, 144" l ..................................................................... 522.50

Ice cream cone, papier-mache, 3-D, hanging, dripping vanilla over 10-rib cone, 1930s-1940s, 44" h, cond. 8.5-9 ................................................................ 231.00

Ice cream sundae, tin, embossed, die-cut, 24" h, 13" w ................................................................. 264.00

Padlock/protruding key, wood/metal, circa 1970s, cond. 9.5, 22" h, 14" w ................................................ 77.00

## Trico Wiper Blades and Solvent

Thermometer, Pam style, aluminum/glass, "Trico Wiper Blades and Solvent Stop Smear," shows bottle, white over brown ground, white border, cond. 7, 12" dia ................................................................. 181.50

## Triple AAA Root Beer

Sign, tin, "Just Say Triple 'AAA' Root Beer," red octagonal

Sign, tin, "Triple Cola, 16 ounces, It's Bigger, It's Better," edge wear, 31-1/2" h, 11-1/2" w, $165.

logo, tilted bottle at right, yellow panel on white ground, minor scratches/dents, 19-1/2" h, 28" w .................. 93.50

## Triple Cola (See Photo)

## Triangle Club Baking Powder

Can, paper label on tin, "Triangle Club Brand Pure Cream of Tartar Baking Powder," red triangle design, striped ground, Montgomery Ward Co., 1 lb, cond. 8- ................................................................. 44.00

## Trillium Rolled Oats

Box, paper on cardboard, round, "Trillium Brand Quick Cooking Rolled Oats," 3 flowers/leaves, red/black text, white ground, Friedrich & Kemp Co., Red Wing MN, cond. 8-, 3 lb ................................................... 104.50

## Triplex Safety Glass

Sign, porcelain, 2-sided, "Triplex Safety Glass Authorized Dealer, no flying splinters, no jagged edges," shows shattered car windshield, cond. 8+, 17-1/4" h, 24" w ............................................................ 2,310.00

## Trojans

Sign

Celluloid, embossed, 2-sided, front with 7 images of tins/packages, back shows testing machine, cond. 8, 9" h, 8" w ................................................... 467.50

Litho tin, "The Ultra-Modern Prophylactic Package," shows cardboard box of product with foldout packets, lists products/prices, cond. 8, 10-1/2" h, 8-1/8" w ...................................................... 132.00

**Can, litho tin, pry lid, "Trophy Coffee, the Blodgett-Beckley Co., Toledo," 3 lb., $75.**

Tin, litho tin
  "Improved Trojans," Trojan logo on red over black/white bands, red/black text, cond. 8, 1/4" h, 2-1/8" w, 1-5/8" d ............................................. 49.50
  "Reservoir End Trojans," Trojan logo, white ground, red trim at each side, cond. EXC, 1/4" h, 2-1/4" w, 1-7/8" d ......................................... 165.00
  "The Gold, Trojans," gold/black Trojan logo in center on white, vertical gold bands at sides, NM, 1/4" h, 2-1/8" w, 1-5/8" d ................................ 66.50

## Trop-Artic Auto Oil

Can, litho tin, early autos in winter/summer conditions, Manhattan Oil Co., cond. 8, 1/2 gal, 6" h, 8" w, 3" d .......................................................... 1,210.00
Cup, litho tin, "Trop-Artic Auto Oil" in red, early autos in winter/summer conditions, Manhattan Oil Co., cond. 8+, 2-3/4" h, 3-3/4" dia ...................................... 440.00

## Trophy Coffee (See Photo)

## Trophy Motor Oil

Can, litho tin, "Trophy Balanced Blend Motor Oil, 40° below," H.K. Stahl Co., St. Paul MN, scene of truck in snow, yellow trophy under name, full, cond. 8.5, qt, 5-1/2" h, 4" dia ............................................... 770.00

## Tropical Coffee

Can, litho tin, diamond medallion shows scantily clad native holding up fruit, flanked by palm trees, red ground, dent/rust, slip lid possibly replaced, 1 lb, 3-1/2" h, 5" dia ............................................... 253.00

## Trout-Line

Tin, vertical pocket
  Cardboard, tin top/bottom, oval "Trout-Line Burley Cut Smoking Tobacco," round medallion with red border shows man netting fish, yellow text except Burley Cut (in red border), green ground, unsealed, cond. 8.5.............................................................. 565.00
  Litho tin, "Trout-Line Smoking Tobacco, Burley Cut," round medallion with red border shows man netting fish, green ground, cond. 8.5........................ 799.00

## Tru Ade

Thermometer, tin, rounded corners, "Cold Juicy Delicious!, Tru Ade, not carbonated," slanted bottle at bottom right, white ground, 1960s, cond. 7-7.5, 16" h................................................................. 33.00

## True Mark

Tin, typewriter ribbon, litho tin, round, classical scene of hunter with bow chasing deer, white on black ground, cond. 8 ............................................................... 27.50

## Try Me Peanut Butter

Pail, litho tin, "Try Me Brand Peanut Butter," blue/red text on white ground, "Peanut Butter" in white on red panel, schoolhouse scene with teacher/students at bottom, cond. 7.5-8, 1 lb, 3-1/4" h, 3-1/2" dia ................ 276.00

## Tryphosa Coffee

Can, litho tin, small top, "A Delicious Blend of Choice Coffees," ground in shades of yellow/blue/green, Merchants Coffee Co., Baltimore, cond. 8-, 6" h, 4-1/4" d ............................................................. 66.00

## T&T Coffee

Can, slip lid, litho tin, "T&T Vacuum Steel Cut Coffee," large "T&T," dark letters, red ground, cond. 8-, 1 lb ...................................................................... 33.00

## Tubular Cream Separator

Match holder, hanging, litho tin, "Tubular Cream Separa-

**Can, tin, "It satisfies from Pole to Pole, Trop-Artic Auto Oil, Used Everywhere," cond. 9/8, 1 gal, 10-1/2" h, 8" w, 3" d, $3,520. (Photo courtesy of Collectors Auction Services)**

tors, the Sharples Separator Co., West Chester, Pa., Toronto, Can., Chicago, Ill.," shows cattle in pasture, also mother/daughter working cream separator, wear/chips, 6-7/8" h, 2-1/8" w ...................................... 495.00

Pot scraper, "Sharples Tubular Cream Separator, The 1909 tubulars are better than ever, Foremost in dairy work, The only bottom-feed suspended bowl separa-tor," woman with milk can/red separator, cond. 9+/8.25+ ............................................................ 308.00

## Tucketts Abbey Pipe Tobacco

Can, litho tin, round, screw top, "Tucketts Abbey Pipe Tobacco, 70¢," black/white image of abbey, blue ground, cond. 8, 4" h, 4-1/4" dia ........................ 31.00

Tin, vertical pocket, litho tin
"Tucketts Abbey Pipe Tobacco, 10¢," black/white image of abbey, cobalt ground, full, cond. 9.................. 366.00
Short version, "Tucketts Abbey Pipe Tobacco, Rough Cut," black/white image of abbey, blue ground, cond. 8, 4" h................................................. 247.50
Tall version, "Tucketts Abbey Pipe Tobacco, Rough Cut," black/white image of abbey, blue ground, cond. 8, 4-1/2" h ........................................... 360.00

## Tuckett's Orinco

Tin, litho tin, round, litho slip lid, "Tuckett's Orinoco Cut Fine," seated fisherman with dog between his legs, Tuckett Tobacco Co., Hamilton, Canada, fading/rust/scratches/stains, 3-3/4" h, 4-1/4" dia ................ 121.00

## Tums

Clock, lightup, reverse-painted glass face, wood frame, metal body, "Tums for the Tummy, For Acid Indiges-tion," yellow/red text, white numbers, black ground, small crack, 16-1/4" sq........................................ 88.00

## Tung-Sol Electron Tubes

Clock, lightup, glass face/cover, cardboard body
"Radio Television Service, Tung-Sol Electronic Tubes,"

Thermometer, tin, "Tums for the Tummy, Tums Quick Relief for Acid Indigestion, Heart-burn," 9-1/8" h, 4-1/8" w, $154.

Jar, glass with clamp lid, 4 panels with paper labels, "Patter-son's Tuxedo Tobacco, R.A. Patterson Tobacco Co., The American Tob. Co.," $60.

white/orange text on blue circle, orange "ts" logo, blue Roman numerals on yellow border, 15" dia .......................................................... 154.00
"Radio Service, Tung-Sol Radio Tubes," white/orange text on blue circle, blue Roman numerals on white border, 15" dia ............................................. 220.00

## Turf Special Fine Cut

Tin, flat pocket, litho tin, shows Pegasus in central ring, Aus-tralian, cond. 8, 5/8" h, 3-1/4" w, 2-1/4" d ................. 53.00

## Tuxedo

Tin, vertical pocket, litho tin
Curved, sample, "Patterson's Tuxedo Tobacco, Spe-cially Prepared For Pipe & Cigarette," round image of man in tuxedo, green ground, cond. 8-, 2-3/4" h, 1-7/8" w ...................................................... 385.00
Cut-down sample, "Fresh Tuxedo Tobacco," yellow text, green ground, cond. 8+, 1-1/2" h, 3" w.................................................................. 55.00
"Fresh Tuxedo Tobacco, specially Prepared For Pipe or Cigarette," shows man in tuxedo in yellow circle,

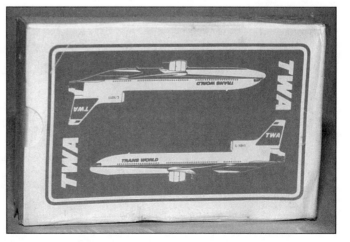

Playing cards, "TWA," pictures L-1011, full deck, $5.

**Tin, vertical pocket, embossed, flip top, "Twin Oaks Mixture," $93.50.**

yellow text, green ground, yellow stripes top/bottom, cond. 8.5 .................................................. 38.50
Sample, round image of man in tuxedo, green ground, cond. 8.5, 2-3/4" h, 2-1/8" w ......................... 248.00

## TWA (See Photo)

## Twang Root Beer

Sign, tin, embossed, "Save Caps for Premiums, Twang, Vitamin Root Beer," bottle cap above white diagonal, black ground, red border, cond. EXC, 14-1/4" dia ....................................................... 132.00

## Twin Oaks Mixture

Tin, casket-shape, litho tin, embossed, red highlights, silver ground, embossed trees/acorns, cond. 7.5, 4-1/4" h, 8" w 4-1/4" d ........................................ 45.00

Tin, vertical pocket, litho tin
Sample, embossed trees/acorns with central red ground on silver tin, cond. 9 .......................... 636.00
Tall version with flat top, embossed trees/acorns with central red ground on silver tin, silver untarnished, cond. 8.5 ...................................................... 306.00

## Two Nickels Smoking Tobacco

Pack, paper, foil-lined, "Two Nickels Cut Plug Smoking Tobacco," shows 2 Liberty-head nickels over "Good And Plenty," black/white text, orange ground, P. Lorillard Co., cond. 8.5, 4-1/2" h, 3" w ...................... 44.00

## 2 Way

Door push, embossed, "Drink 2 Way," shows bottle on yellow ground, cond. 9.25+, 10" h, 4" w ............. 66.00

## Tydol

Sign
Porcelain, "Tydol Flying" in black over flying A logo with red "A" and white wings on green stripe, white ground, red border, cond. 7, 9-1/2" dia ........... 165.00
Tin, die-cut, white winged "A" on red circle, wingtips extend past edges, cond. 8.5, 15-1/2" h, 18-1/2" w ..................................................... 335.50

## Tyee Bait

Tin, litho tin, pry lid, "Tyee Brand Prepared Salmon Eggs, Every Egg A Perfect Bait," shows 2 trout in water, J.E. Hubbart, ©1910, cond. 8.5, 2-1/2" h, 2-1/8" dia........................................................ 577.50

# U

Tin, condom, "Ultrex Platinum," full, $25.

## Ultrex Platinum (See Photo)

## U.M.C. Nitro Club

Box, shell box, 2-pc, paper label on cardboard, "U.M.C. Nitro Club Loaded Paper Shells, Smokeless Powder," name above/below flying duck, side shows shell, 12 gauge, fading/wear/soiling, 2-1/2" h, 4-1/8" sq............................................................... 27.50

## U Mix Tobacco

Box, litho tin, "Fine Tobacco, U Mix," black text/scrolled embellishments, red-green-red ground, Cameron & Cameron Co., Richmond, VA, cond. VG, 2" h, 4-1/2" w, 3-1/4" d................................................................... 82.50

## Uncle Daniel Tobacco

Pack, paper, "Uncle Daniel Fine Cut," bearded man in hat, unopened, mint, 3-1/4" h, 2-3/8" w............... 31.00

## Uncle Sam Cigars (See Photo)

## Uncle Sam Shoe Polish

Tin, "Uncle Sam Shoe Polish" in white on blue border, full-figure Uncle Sam on brown ground, boy shining Uncle Sam's boots on back, cond. 8.25, 3-1/2" dia........... 44.00

## Uncle Sam Tobacco

Tin, vertical pocket, litho tin, "Uncle Sam Smoking

Tin, litho tin, "Uncle Daniel Fine Cut Tobacco, The Scotten-Dillon Co., Detroit," 1 lb, 8-1/4" d, $55.

Tobacco," half-length portrait of Uncle Sam on red/white/blue shield, dark-blue ground, Canadian, cond. 8 ........................................................ 2,572.00

## Uncle Sam's Kisses

Box, display, cardboard, shows Uncle Sam, "Uncle Sam's Kisses" in red/white/blue shield, "2 for 1 Cent," cond. 8+, 10" h, 7-3/4" w, 6-3/4" d ................... 302.50

## Uncle Tom Peanuts

Tin, litho tin, "Phelp's Uncle Tom Salted Peanuts," round image of black family outside cabin, yellow text, black ground, cond. 8, 1/2 lb, 4-7/8" h, 3-1/8" w, 1-3/4" d ......................................................... 330.00

Sign, glass, reverse-painted, chain-hung, "Uncle Sam, American Cigar Co., Agents," uses original cigar label, 18" l, $900.

## Uneeda Biscuit

Sign

Cardboard, "We Close at (blank) P.M., Don't forget Uneeda Biscuit, Plain or Salted," child in yellow rain slicker/hat with product at left, white ground, 1920s, cond. NM, 10" h, 9" w........................................148.50

Paper, "On Land or Sea, Uneeda Biscuit, National Biscuit Company," 3-D "Uneeda Biscuit" extending into background, black/brown/red text, landscape ground with house/sea, mkd "Display During November Only," newer frame, fading/soiling, 12-1/2" h, 21-1/2" w ...........................................82.50

Paperboard, trolley, "Uneeda Biscuit" box strapped atop school books, "National Biscuit Company, Uneeda Bakers" lower-right, white ground, cond. 8+, 11" h, 21" w..............................................66.00

## Uniflo Motor Oil

Sign, litho tin, "Time for a change? Ask For Uniflo Motor Oil, Keeps Engines Extra Clean," oil-drop character at right, black/red text on gold/white/red bands, 1960s, cond. 8.25, 10" h, 17" w ....................................187.00

## Uniform Cut Plug

Tin

Paper label, "Uniform Cut Plug, Larus & Bro. Co., Richmond, Va.," shows portrait of sailor in oval wreath, 1910 tax stamp, cond. 8-, 7" h, 4-1/2" dia.........165.00

Litho tin, small top, "Uniform Cut Plug, Larus & Bro. Co.," shows portrait of sailor in oval wreath, cond. 8+, 6-1/4" h, 4-7/8" d....................................962.50

## Union Gasoline

Gas globe, 1 lens, newer high-profile metal body, "Union Gasoline" in white in shield with blue top, red/white-striped body, "Property of Union Oil" at bottom center, white ground, cond. 8.5, 15" dia.....................1,870.00

## Union Leader

Canister, litho tin, round, dome-top, "Union Leader Smoking Tobacco," eagle on branch in oval, white text, red ground, flange bottom, cond. 8.5, 5-3/4" h, 4" dia.....................................................................53.00

Lunch box, litho tin, "Union Leader Cut Plug," spread-wing eagle, gold text, basketweave ground, cond. 8.5 ........................................................42.00

Sign, litho tin, "Union Leader for Pipe or Cigarette," left side rusted, 10" h, 22-1/4" w, $60.

Milk pail, litho tin, "Union Leader Cut Plug," gold text, red ground, spread-wing eagle, cond. 7 .................156.00

Tin, litho tin, round, "Union Leader Smoking Tobacco," white text, Uncle Sam portrait in oval, red ground with blue/white stripes, cond. 8, 6" h, 5" dia...............79.00

Tin, vertical pocket, litho tin

"Union Leader (in scroll) Redi Cut Tobacco," Uncle Sam portrait in white oval, red ground with blue/white stripes, yellow wreath and "Tobacco," 5-color, cond. 8-8.5.................................................83.50

"Union Leader Redi Cut Tobacco," green wreath and "Tobacco," Uncle Sam portrait in yellow oval, red ground with blue/white stripes, cond. 8 ........147.50

"Union Leader Redi Cut Tobacco," Uncle Sam portrait in oval, red ground with blue/white stripes, green wreath, yellow "Tobacco," cond. 8, 4-1/2" h, 3-3/8" w, 1" d.........................................................91.00

"Union Leader Smoking Tobacco," Uncle Sam portrait in oval, white text, red ground with blue/white stripes, cond. 8, 4-3/8" h, 3" w........................................166.00

## Union Made

Sign, porcelain, curved, "Union Made Pants and Overalls," white on black ground, white diamond logo with trolley or RR car/heart and "The Brand," restored, 14" h, 16" w ...............................................................396.00

## Union Oil Company

Badge, cap, inlaid cloisonné porcelain lettering, red/white/blue shield, hinged pin/clip on back, small chips, 1-3/4" sq........................................................1,320.00

## Union 76

Sign, porcelain, "Union 76 plus Gasoline," white/cobalt text, orange ground, cond. 8, 11-1/2" dia..........302.50

## United Gasoline

Gas globe, 1 lens, high-profile metal body, "United Gasoline" around red "United Oil" oval, white ground, NOS, all cond. 9, 15" dia .........................................1,100.00

Sign, porcelain, "United Gasoline" in white on red panel at bottom, 3-tone blue frame in cobalt diamond on white field at top, cond. 8+, 24" sq...................242.00

## United Motor Courts

Sign, porcelain, 2-sided, rounded corners, "Member, United Motor Courts," white text, diagonal over shield with red top, black ground, cond. 8/7, 28" h, 36" w .............................................................132.00

## United Service Motors

Sign, neon

Porcelain, "United Service Motors" with "Service" in white on car silhouette, black text, orange ground, orig neon with repairs, lights blue/orange, cond. 8.5, 14" h, 24" w, 6-1/2" d............................................................2,970.00

Tin, "'United' For Service, Your Guide, United Service Motors, Wherever You Drive," white arrow points to oval logo in outline of U.S., white/blue text, blue ground, neon on oval logo lights orange/blinks, cond. 7, 36-1/2" h, 60-1/4" w ...................... 1,595.00

Sign, porcelain, 2-sided, oval, iron hanger, "United Service Motors" with "Service" in white on car silhouette, black text, orange ground, cond. 7.5, 44" h, 52" w ................................................................. 825.00

## United States Express

Sign, pressed copper, embossed and painted, "United States Express, Exclusive Special Fast Trains, Best Service-Lowest Rates, Money Orders for Sale," gold finish, light bends ........................................... 3,520.00

## United States Steel Corporation

Sign, porcelain, "Danger" in red oval, "High Voltage, Keep Away, United States Steel Corporation," skull/cross bones in black circle flanked by red electric bolts, white/black letters, black over white ground, faded, 14" h, 10" w ........................................... 121.00

## United States Tires

Fan, cardboard litho, "United States Tires are Good Tires," round logo on blue-white ribbon at top, tires at left/right/bottom, rotating die-cut car in center, cond. 8, 9-1/2" h, 8" w ........................................................ 55.00

## Universal Blend Coffee

Can, knob top, litho tin, "Universal Blend Coffee," Uncle Sam straddling sunrise, litho loss at bottom, cond. 7, 1 lb ................................................................. 110.00

## Universal Home-Wares

Clock, lightup, glass face/cover, cardboard body, "Electrical Appliances, Universal Home-Wares," white text in blue inner circle, "Universal" in red panel, red numbers on white border, new wiring, one metal cover missing on back, 15" dia ................................................. 99.00

## Universal Stoves and Ranges

Bank, litho tin, rotating globe on die-cut frame, red lettering on globe, "Save Your Money And Buy Universal Stoves And Ranges, Cribben & Sexton Company, Chicago" in yellow on stand, wreath on support at globe, cond. 8+ ........................................................... 214.00

## Upson Board

Sign, porcelain, "Upson Processed Board for walls, ceilings, partitions, insulation," red/white text, cobalt

ground, white border, chips/scratches/fade marks, 20" h, 40" w......................................................... 55.00

## U.S. Cartridge Co.

Calendar, paper, 1922, grizzly bear on hind legs, holding case of cartridges, hunter hiding in tree in background, metal strip trimmed off, December pad only, cond. 8, 34-5/8" h, 15" w............................................... 797.50

## U.S. Marine Tobacco

Tin, vertical pocket, litho tin, "U.S. Marine Flake Cut," "US" in white text in black circle, otherwise yellow text on red ground, full, cond. 8+, 4-1/2" h.............. 397.00

## U.S. Motor Gasoline

Gas globe, 2 flat lenses, high-profile metal body, "U.S. Motor Gasoline," clear text on white border, clear circular center, body repainted, all cond. 7, 14-1/2" dia........................................................ 143.00

## U.S. Navy Gas

Gas globe, 2 lenses, high-profile metal body, black text, blue zigzag border, white ground, lens cond. 9, 15" dia................................................................ 990.00

## U.S. Post Office

Sign, wood, raised wood text, "US" arched over "Post Office," white text, 12-1/2" h, 51-1/2" w............. 176.00

## U.S. Royal

Rack, litho metal, "U.S. Royal," yellow text on cobalt panel, red ground, cond. 8/7, 11" h, 15" w, 11" d................................................................ 104.50

## Utica Drop Forge & Tool Co.

Cabinet, tin, wood base, "Grip! Cut! Bend Metal! Utica Drop Forge & Tool Co., Utica, N.Y.," various pliers/wire cutters, woodgrain ground, scratches/scuffs/dents, 13-11/16" h, 18" w, 9-3/4" d.................................... 115.50

## Uzar Peanut Butter

Can, litho tin, pry lid, "Uzar Peanut Butter," yellow/white arched text, woman on purple over yellow ground, type without bail handle, cond. 8.25+, 2 lb........ 357.50

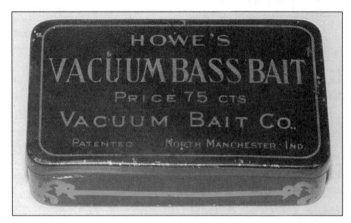

**Tin, litho tin, "Howe's Vacuum Bass Bait, Price 75 Cts, Vacuum Bait Co., Patented, North Manchester, Ind.," gold text, black ground, $450.**

## Vacuum Bass Bait (See Photo)

## Vacuum Oil Co.

**History:** Vacuum Oil Company, founded in 1866, was already manufacturing an extensive line of specialty lubricants when Standard Oil bought the company in 1879. After that time, their lubricants were sold under the Gargoyle and Gargoyle Mobiloil brands. They expanded into the world of gasoline marketing with the introduction of MOBILGAS in the late 1920s.

Lighter, chrome, inlaid cloisonné porcelain top in blue/white with red gargoyle, lighter in shape of 2 tubes, 2" h ................................................................. 440.00
Pocket knife, Remington, "Vacuum Oil Co., Gargoyle, New York, U.S.A." logo with gargoyle in inlaid cloisonné porcelain, both blades mkd "Remington UMC," cond. 7.5+ .................................................. 203.50
Straight razor, celluloid handle, "Gargoyle Marine Oils" and gargoyle symbol engraved on front of blade, "Vacuum Oil Co., New York, USA" on back, orig holder stamped "Oils That Lubricate Most," 6" l .......... 330.00

## Valdor Tobac A Pipe

Can, litho tin, round, screw top, 3 repeated images of gentleman smoking, red ground, back has paper label showing nuts, "O.B., Sweet as a Nut," cond. 8+, 4" x 4-3/8" ................................................................. 58.50

## Valley Gasoline

Gas globe, milk glass, 2 orig insert lenses, red/blue text/

border, orig shipping box, chip to base, rest cond. EXC, 16" h, 15-1/2" dia .................................... 315.00

## Valspar

Sign
Cardboard hanger or easel-back, "New Cars for Old - in any color - with Valentine's Valspar enamel, Waterproof, Weeatherproof, Accident-proof," man at sedan, cond. 7-7.5, 16" h, 12" w ................ 88.00
Celluloid over tin, easel-back, "Valentine's Valspar Varnish Stain, Some Boys will be Boys ... let the floor be Valsparred," shows boys washing a dog on indoor hardwood floor, 7 stain colors, circa 1930s-1940s, cond. 8+, 14" h, 11" w ...................... 104.50

## Valvoline

**History:** Originally founded as the Continuous Oil Refining Company in Binghamton, New York in 1866, this firm introduced its line of Valvoline lubricants in 1873. The trademark is the oldest in the petroleum industry. The line became so well known that the company's name was changed to Valvoline Oil Company in 1902.

Can, litho tin
"Valvoline Oil Company, Chicago," black text, green ground, Valvoline/Magnet Oils logos, cond. 7, 1 gal, 11-1/2" h, 6" w, 3-1/2" d .............................. 335.50
"Valvoline Oil Company, Valvoline Light Motor Oil" on front, "Best by Every Test" on sides, black on green ground, cond. 8+/7+, qt, 2-3/4" h, 6-1/8" w, 4-1/8" d ........................................................ 445.50

**Can, metal, "Valvoline Motor Oil," black text, green ground, text on all 4 sides, cond. 8, gal, 11" h, 7-1/2" w, 3" d, $203.50. (Photo courtesy of Collectors Auction Services)**

"Valvoline Oil, Valvoline Oil Company, New York, U.S.A.," white text, "Valvoline" over dotted white semi-circle, green ground red/white border, cond. 8+/7+, gal, 10-1/2" h, 8" w, 3" d .................... 209.00

Gas globe, 1 lens, glass body, "Valvoline Ethyl," black red text under triangular "Ethyl" logo, dotted semi-circle in center, white ground, metal base, lens cond. 9, body cond. 8, 13-1/2" dia............................................... 660.00

Pocket mirror, celluloid, oval, "Valvoline Oil Company, Lubricating Oils, Los Angeles, Cal.," barrel motif, 1-3/4" h, 2-3/4" w .............................................. 467.50

Sign, metal, 2-sided, "Ask for Valvoline Motor Oil," red/blue "V" logo, red/blue text, white ground, blue border, cond. 8, 30" dia .................................................110.00

Sign, tin
  Pillow sign, "Ask for Valvoline Motor Oil," yellow on black ground, cond. 8, 17-1/2" dia ................ 203.50
  "Valvoline Motor Oil" vertical over horizontal text, white text, red/white border, wood frame, Valvoline Oil Co., Portland ME, cond. 8, 60" h, 12" w ....... 423.50

Thermometer, Pam style, tin/glass, round, "Ask For The World's First Motor Oil, Valvoline, Costs More To Make... Costs Less To Use," oil can on yellow ground, cond. 8.5, 12" dia ............................................. 330.00

## Van Dam Cigars

Sign, litho tin, "Van Dam Cigars," bearded man in hat, black text, white ground, cond. 9- ..................... 308.00

## Van Dyks Peanut Butter

Pail, litho tin, Mother Hubbard nursery rhyme with images/verses, cond. 7.5, 3-7/8" h, 3-1/2" dia.................... 495.00

## Vanity Coffee

Can, keywind, litho tin
  "Vanity Kickbusch Vacuum Packed Coffee," peacock on red circle, yellow ground, wrong lid, cond. 8.25+, 1 lb ............................................................... 143.00

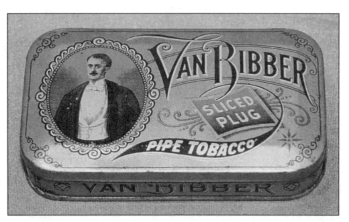

Tin, litho tin, "Van Bibber Sliced Plug Pipe Tobacco," 4-5/8" x 2-3/4", $95.

  Earlier taller version of above tin, same design, wrong lid, cond. 7.5, 1 lb ........................................... 55.00

## Vanner & Prest's Molliscorium

Clock, Baird, wood/tin/glass, "Vanner & Prest's Molliscorium, Comp Embrocation," Roman numerals repainted, cond. VG, 31" h, 18" w..................... 715.00

## Gardiner B. Van Ness (See Photo)

## Van Ogden's

Tin, paper label on cardboard, "Van Ogden's Brand Special Allspice," black chef over "VO" logo, Van Ogden Inc., Chicago, 4 oz, cond. 9- .............................110.00

## Van Ribber Tobacco (See Photo)

## Vargas

Sign, Pyraglass (celluloid-like finish over wood), standup, "Your Health, Bacillus Acidophilus Milk, Lederle," woman with glass, by Albert Vargas, circa 1930s, cond. EXC, 12-3/4" h, 9-3/4" w ................................................687.50

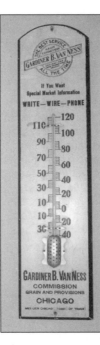

Thermometer, painted wood, "Gardiner B. Van Ness, Commission Grain and Provisions, Chicago," wear, 24" h, 6" w, $60.

Can, litho tin, "Veedol Motor Oil," unopened, 1 qt, $25.

**Box, cardboard, "Vel" detergent, cobalt on yellow ground, Colgate-Palmolive-Peet Co., unopened, 12 oz, $20.**

# Vaseline

Cabinet, tin, "Vaseline Preparations" over 6 different tubes/Camphor Ice container, woodgrain ground, rear-opening doors, 8 storage slots, cond. G, 11-1/2" h, 9-1/2" w, 5" d ...................................................... 143.00

# Veedol Motor Oil

Can, litho tin, with orig wooden box, can with "Veedol, The Motor Oil that Gives the Film of Protection," orange on black ground, box with "1-5 Gal. Can, Veedol Motor Oil, Tide Water Oil Co., New York, U.S.A.," can cond. 8.5, box cond. 8, 5 gal, can 15" h, 11-1/2" sq................................................. 313.50

Sign, porcelain, tombstone, 2-sided, "Ask for Veedol Motor Oils" in white/red text, "100% Pennsylvania, Supreme Quality" in white panel, black ground, red border, touchups/patched holes, cond. 8, 28" h, 22" w .................................................................. 258.50

Sign, litho tin, die-cut
  "Veedol" between feet of blonde ice skater in short white dress, foreign, cond. 8+, 17-1/2" h, 6-1/2" w........................................................... 550.00
  "Veedol" in blue panel under ice skates of blonde in white skating outfit with red trim, cond. 7, 14" h, 5" w.............................................................. 264.00
  "Veedol" in red on white panel under ice skates of blonde in white skating outfit with red trim, cond. 7, 14-1/4" h, 5-1/2" w ........................................ 357.50
  "Veedol" in red on white drape on skater in yellow outfit, cond. VG, 17-1/4" h, 9-1/2" w .................. 231.00

# Vel (See Photo)

# Velvet Coffee

Pail, litho tin, "Velvet Brand Coffee" in gold on orange ground, shows The W.H. Malkin Co. on one side, steaming cup of coffee on other, Canadian, cond. 8-, 5 lb, 8-1/2" h, 8-1/4" dia ................................... 220.00

# Velvet Tobacco

Sign

Porcelain, "Velvet, Aged in Wood, Sold Here, Pipe Tobacco," white text on cobalt ground, "Velvet" in smoke motif, shows open vertical pocket tin at left, chips at holes/edges, 12" h, 39" w ............... 385.00

Tin, shows dog with paw up on seated man holding child, older man seated nearby, Velvet Joe quote at top, product lower-left, newer frame, chips/dents/paint loss/rust, 31" h, 24-3/4" w ................... 253.00

Tin, vertical pocket, litho tin, sample
  Pipe on red ground with smoke spelling out "Velvet," "Tobacco" below in yellow, cond. 8+, 2-7/8" h, 2-1/8" w ............................................................ 220.00
  Pipe on red ground with smoke spelling out "Velvet," "Tobacco" below in yellow, "Free Sample" in white box at right, cond. 8+ ................................... 191.00

# Venoco

Gas globe, metal body/bands, high profile (newer), 2 glass lenses
  "-Hi- Venoco Power," blue/red text, white ground, all cond. 8.5, 15-1/2" dia .................................. 231.00
  "-Hi- Venoco Power," blue/red text, stylized blue hourglass border with 2 horizontal stripes, white ground, 1 lens cracked, lens cond. 9/6, body cond. 8.5, 15" dia ............................................................ 231.00

# Vermont Mutual Fire Insurance

Sign, litho tin, indented oval medallion showing brick structure/horse and buggy/early auto, "Montpelier, Vermont," 24-1/2" h, 20-1/4" w .............................................1,045.00

# Vernor's Ginger Ale

Sign, metal, "Vernor's Ginger Ale," leprechaun in circle at

**Sign, litho tin, "Drink Vernor's Ginger Ale, Flavor Mellowed in Wood 4 Years, deliciously different!," leprechaun holding bottle on barrel, green/white/yellow/red text, yellow ground, black border, 1940s-1950s, cond. 8.25+, 18" h, 54" w, $605. (Photo courtesy of Gary Metz, Muddy River Trading Co.)**

left, green text/border, yellow ground, stains/soiling/rust at edges, 10" h, 30" w............................................. 170.50

## Vess Cola

Display, countertop, neon, "Drink Vess Cola, First for Thirst!," yellow marquee with "Vess Cola" in red, other text in white, green ground, pointed top, neon at border, cond. 8-8.25, 10" h, 14" w ...................................... 357.50

## Veteran Peanut Butter

Pail, litho tin, "Veteran Brand Peanut Butter" in oval, round image of general in center, light-blue/white design, dark ground, Brewster Gordon Co., Rochester, NY, 1 lb, 3-3/4" h, 3-1/4" dia ............................. 198.00

## Veteran Tobacco

Pack, paper, "Veteran Tobacco For Smoking & Chewing," shows crossed guns/saber, white text, dark ground, full, cond. 8+.......................................................... 38.50

## Viceroy

Sign, tin, embossed, "Filtered Smoke with the Finest Flavor," shows pack of "Viceroy Filter Tip Cigarettes, King-Size," 1950s-1960s, rounded corners, cond. 8.5, 14" h, 27" w.......................................................... 99.00

## Vicks

Door push, porcelain, "Come In, Vicks Va-Tro-Nol for Nose & Throat, Helps Prevent Colds," white text on red bands, blue bottle/dropper, cond. 8.25, 6-1/2" h, 4" w ...................................................................... 385.00

Thermometer, tin, "Now over 159 Million Vicks Packages Used Yearly, World's Best Known," shows 5 products, yellow ground, rounded corners, cond. 8+, 13-1/2" h, 4-1/2" w ............................................................. 266.00

## Vic's Special Beer

Sign, tin over cardboard, easel back or hung, "Pic-Me

**Pocket mirror, celluloid, "Glenn W. Bodley, Victrolas and Records, Three Rivers, Michigan, Victrola," 2" dia, $50.**

Vic's Special Beer," bottle in slanted white oval at left, red/black text, red ground, black border, Northern Brewing Co., Superior WI, cond. EXC, 5-3/8" h, 11-3/8" w ............................................................ 66.00

## Victor

Tin, litho tin, tennis strings, "Victor Strings that Win," tennis player on large red "V" on all sides, white/blue ground, blue lid, cond. 8+, 7" h, 6-3/4" w, 4" d....................... 66.00

## Victrola (See Photo)

## Violet Ray Lens

Paperweight, glass, cornflower color, embossed "Use Violet Ray Lens, Safety First," figure of infant, cond. G, 4-1/4" h, base 3-1/4" dia ................................... 110.00

## Virginia Cigarettes

Tin, flat pocket, paper label on cardboard, "Virginia Cigarettes, 12, Perfectos Finos," currency-type design showing buildings on hill John Player & Sons, Nottingham, unopened, cond. 9, 1/2" h, 4-1/2" w, 3" d....................................................................... 44.00

## Virginia Dare Cut Plug

Tin, litho tin, square corner, "Virginia Dare Extra Fine Cut Plug," shows topless Leda and swan, pre-May 1901, cond. 9, rectangular .......................................... 345.00

## Virginity Smoking Tobacco

Tin, litho tin, square corner, oval medallion of woman with bare shoulders, floral design/embellishments, cond. 8+, 2-1/4" h, 4-1/2" w, 3-1/4" d..................................... 374.00

## Vitality Dog Food

Sign, tin, embossed, "Staley's Vitality Dog Foods, A.E. Staley Mfg. Co., Decatur, Ill.," black/white hunting dog over canted black/white panel with red "Vitality," small bull's-eye design at right, black/red text, yellow ground, cond. VG, 27-1/8" h, 19-1/8" w ........................... 132.00

## Vita-Var Paints

Sign, flange, metal, "Vita-Var Paints Since 1888," castle-type logo, rust/scratches, 20" h, 24" w ................... 110.00

## Vulcan Plow Co.

Match striker, litho tin, die-cut, "Vulcan Plow Company, Evansville, Ind., Vulcan Best Chilled Plows, Rose Clipper Best Steel Plows," bearded man with sledge/"Vulcan" apron beside anvil, striker at bottom, minor dents/chips/bubbling, 7-3/4" h, 2-3/4" w ..................... 616.00

# W

## Wabash Fibre Box Co.

Fan, cardboard, "The Wabash Boxes" in white panel on scene of woman driving early roadster in the country, cond. EXC, 11-1/4" h, 8" w.................................. 33.00

## Wadhams Motor Oil

Can, metal, "Wadhams Tempered Motor Oil, Heavy," oil cans over red circle, white text, "Heavy" in hang tag design, black ground, Wadhams Oil Co., Milwaukee, cond. 7, gal, 11" h, 8" w 3" d ............................ 412.50

## Wagon Wheel

Tin, vertical pocket, litho tin
Sample, "Wagon Wheel Pipe and Cigarette Tobacco, Free Trial Package Compliments of Taylor Brothers, Inc., Carries You On To That Happy Land," Conestoga wagon in front of wagon wheel rising on horizon, yellow/brown striped ground, cond. 8+, 4-1/2" h, 3" w .............................................. 1,072.50
"Wagon Wheel Pipe and Cigarette Tobacco, Manufactured by Taylor Brothers, Inc., Winston Salem, N.C., Carries You On To That Happy Land," Conestoga wagon in front of wagon wheel rising on horizon, yellow/brown striped ground, cond. 8+ ...... 1,021.00

## Waitch's Black & White

Tin, litho tin
"Waitch's Black & White Prophylactics, 1/4 doz.," small portrait of man, vertical bars at left, white on black ground, scratches/wear to bottom, 1/4" h, 2-1/4" w, 1-5/8" d ....................................................... 402.50
Same design as above with "To Open Press Corners" at top, cond. EXC, 1/4" h, 2-1/4" w, 1-5/8" d .......... 467.50

## Wales Jellies

Sign, cardboard, hanging card, girl with oversized jar of product, lists flavors, cond. 9.5+, 11" h, 7" w ........... 71.50

## Walker's Grape Juice

Bowl, enameled, "Walker's Grape Juice" in black flanked by grape clusters/leaves, inside stained/patched hole/chips, 7" h, 19" dia ........................................... 330.00

## Walk-Over Shoes

Figure, composition, male/female, late 1920s-early 1930s, soiling/chips/wear, woman repaired at base, 12" h, pr............................................................. 137.50

Sign, tin, "Walk-Over Shoes," white text flanked by white oval with man in suit standing over dress shoe, merchant info on white ground at bottom, fading/stains/edge rust/bent corners, 11-3/4" h, 23-1/2" w ........................... 60.50

## Wan-Eta Cocoa

Tin, paper label over tin, round image of Indian woman with hand shading eyes, yellow on brown ground, cond. 7, 1/5 lb, 4-1/8" h, 2-1/2" w, 1-1/2" d ................................ 143.00

## Ward's

See Lemon-Crush, Lime-Crush, Orange-Crush

## Ward's

Tin, litho tin, "Ward's Nutmeg," sailing ships near tropical shoreline, white/black bands, green ground, Ward's Medical Co., Winona MN, cond. 9, 4 oz ............. 55.00

## Warren Featherbone

Pocket mirror, celluloid, "Warren Featherbone, We should like to see your face at our office in New York, Boston, Philadelphia or Chicago, Factor, Three Oaks, Michigan," shows turkey standing on whale, worn lettering ............................................................. 440.00

## Warren's Paints and Varnishes

Sign, porcelain, 2-sided, die-cut, "Warren's Paints and

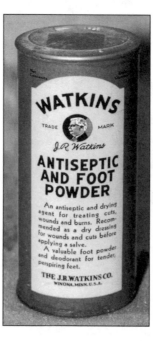

Can, paper, "Watkins Antiseptic and Foot Powder, The J.R. Watkins Co., Winona, Minn., U.S.A.," light rust and stains, 8 oz, $22.50.

Varnishes, Nashville, Tennessee, Southern Made for Southern Clime," 3 rectangular panels over round panel with slogan/cartoon portrait of painter, chips/rust/stain, 26" h, 24" w ....................................... 258.50

## Waterman's

Display case, glass top and sides with tin sign in back, "Waterman's Ideal Fountain Pen," top cracked, minor chips, 9-1/2" h, 18" w, 17" d .............................. 770.00

Sign, porcelain, "Waterman's Ideal Fountain Pen," white on blue ground, cond. 8+, 2" h, 18-1/2" w .................. 467.50

## Watkins (See Photo)

## Watta Pop

Display, plaster, Indian bust, embossed "Chief Watta Pop," 17 holes to hold lollipops in headdress, cond. 8 .............................................................. 521.50

## Waverley

Tin, flat 50, litho tin, "Straight Cut, Waverly Virginia Cigarettes, Lambert & Butler, England, Supplied to crew for personal use only," gold on blue ground, cond. 8 ................................................................27.50

## Wayne Dairy

Sign, porcelain, 2-sided, "Ask For Wayne Dairy Quality Ice Cream," black text on cream ground, 1940s-1950s, minor chips, cond. 9.25-9.75, 15" h, 20" w ............ 154.00

## Wayne Feeds

Thermometer, litho tin, die-cut chick
"Wayne Feeds, Decatur, Ind., Egg Hatchery," lists temperature for hatching eggs, 6-1/2"h, 3-1/2" w............................................................ 66.00

"Wayne Feeds" on chick, "Compliments of Your Wayne Feed Dealer, A Better Feed For Every Need" in courtesy panel, 1st/2nd/3rd Week temperatures mkd at tube, chick against striped feed bag, 6-1/4" h, 3-1/2" w ........................................... 346.50

## Wear-u-well Shoes

Sign, flange, porcelain, die-cut, oval, "Wear-u-well Shoes, Extra Value," yellow/black design with horizontal panel in center, cond. VG, 17" h, 25" w ............................... 264.00

## Web-Foot

Cigar box, "Web-Foot" repeated twice over image of Indian maiden with red-tipped white feathers in her hair, circa 1920, 10-count, cond. 9...................... 88.00

## Webster Cigars

Tin, horizontal box, litho tin, "Webster" in red above round portrait, quill pen/paper flank image, cond. 8, 1-1/4" h, 4-3/4" w, 3-1/4" d............................................... 33.00

## Wedding Bouquet Cigar

Sign, litho tin, embossed, "Wedding Bouquet Cigar, Cli-

Container, cardboard, litho paper, "Wedding Ring Rolled Oats, J.F. Humphreys and Co., Bloomington, Ill.," $100.

max of Perfection, L. Kahner & Co., Makers, New York," outdoor Puritan wedding scene, gold text/elaborate border, restoration, mounted on board, restored to cond. 8, 19-1/2" h, 27-1/2" w............................ 522.50

## Wedding Ring Rolled Oats (See Photo)

## Weeks' Remedies

Display, countertop, litho tin, wooden base, "We personally recommend that you use Weeks' Remedies," D. Weeks & Co., advertising on all 4 sides, product images on front, cond. 8, 14-1/4" h, 15" w, 5-1/2" d ........................................................... 660.00

## Weidmann's Peanut Butter

Crock, brown glaze, incised "Weidmann's Peanut Butter,

Sign, litho tin, "Drink A Bunch Of Grapes from Welch Juniors 10¢," bottle/grapes at left, white/yellow/black text, black over purple ground, yellow border, 1931, cond. 8.25, 14" h, 20" w, $275. (Photo courtesy of Gary Metz, Muddy River Trading Co.)

since 1870, Meridan, Mississippi," 4" h,
3-1/2" dia......................................................115.50

## Weikel's Justrite Coffee

Can, litho tin, pry lid, white radiating-type design on red,
Weikel and Smith Spice Co., Philadelphia, cond. 8, 5-
3/4" h, 4-1/4" dia ........................................ 132.00

## Weisert's 54

Tin, vertical pocket, litho tin, "John Weisert's 54 Smoking
Tobacco for Pipe and Cigarette, John Weisert Tobacco
Company," "54" on brown tobacco leaf, yellow ground,
cond. 8-9 ...................................................... 330.00

## Welch's Grape Juice

Sign, litho tin, "Drink A Bunch Of Grapes from Welch Juniors 10¢, Ice Cold," bottle/grapes at left, white/yellow/
black text, black over purple ground, yellow border,
circa 1931, cond. 8.5+, 18" h, 40" w ................ 660.00

## Welcome Borax Soap

Sign, porcelain, "Ask For Welcome Borax Soap," blue
text, yellow ground, red trim, cond. NM, 6" h,
36" w ............................................................ 550.00

## Welcome Guest Coffee

Tin, litho tin, oval medallion with butler carrying tray, red
ground, no lid, cond. 8, 1 lb, 5-3/4" h,
4" dia........................................................... 1,705.00

## Weldon Smoking Tobacco

Tin, vertical pocket, litho tin, short version, "Weldon Cube
Cut Smoking Tobacco, S.S. Pierce Co., Boston," crest
with rampant lion on yellow ground, cond. 8,
3-5/8" h......................................................... 545.00

Tip tray, litho tin, Welsbach Co. Mantles, cond. 9-, 4-1/4" dia,
$55.

Beater jar, stone-
ware, white
glaze, blue ink-
stamp mark,
"Wesson Oil, For
Making Good
Things to Eat,"
5-1/4" h,
4-3/4" dia, $60.

## Wellington

Tin, vertical pocket, litho tin
Black crown on red ground, "Wellington London Mixture, Christian Peper Tob. Co., St. Louis, Mo.," full,
cond. 9+...................................................... 1,055.00
Orange version, "Wellington London Mixture, Christian
Peper Tob. Co., St. Louis, Mo.," red crown in double
circle, orange ground, cond. 8 ..................... 224.00

## Welsbach (See Photo)

## Wesson Oil (See Photo)

## Western Cartridge Co.

Box, shell box, 2-pc, paper label on cardboard
"Western Field, Loaded Waterproof Paper Shot Shells,
Smokeless Powder," red/blue text, blue arched
"Field" under red diamond logo, grouse in grass at
right, white ground, red border, 12 gauge, cond. G,
2-1/2" h, 4-1/8" sq........................................ 77.00
Same design as above, script name at top, grouse at
right, white ground, red border, 12 gauge, cond. G,
2-1/2" h, 4-1/8" sq........................................ 253.00
Sign
Cardboard, cutout, easel-back, "Western Super-X
Long Range .22 Cartridges, Champions in their
class," boy with rifle in front of target, 1930s-1940s,
cond. 8.5+, 26" h, 19" w.............................. 632.50
Paper, "Patented Steel-Locked Shotgun Shells, Perfect From Primer to Crimp," blacks hunting scene
with boy in tree, father/dog on ground, cond. 8.5+,
28-1/2" h, 17" w .......................................... 1,072.50

## Western Farms

Sign, litho tin over cardboard, hanging, beveled edge,
"Western Farms, Milk That Is Milk," shows child asleep in
high chair by oversized milk bottle, green ground with
gold border, cond. 8-, 4-3/8" h, 13-3/8" w ..............550.00

# Western Union

Sign

Celluloid over metal, "Telephone Your Telegrams from here, Ask Operator for Western Union" with graphic of stick telephone, "W.V.Tel.Co. 61706 Inspected" on reverse, 9-1/2" h, 9" w ............................. 198.00

Porcelain, flange, "Western Union Telegraph And Cable Office," white text/border, cobalt ground, cond. G, 12-1/4" h, 24" w............................... 181.50

# Western Winchester

Sign, cardboard, standup, easel-back, shows hunters at breakfast in cabin with guns/decoys/shell boxes, framed, tears/paper loss/mildew, 25-7/8" h, 31-1/2" w ....................................................... 132.00

# Westfield Steam Laundry

Pinback button, celluloid over metal, "Compliments of Westfield Steam Laundry, Westfield, Mass., Carrington & Grout, Proprietors," shows horse/buggy, minor soiling, 1-3/4" dia........................................11.00

# Westinghouse Radio

Clock, lightup, glass face/cover, pressed-cardboard body, "Listen... And You'll Buy A Westinghouse Radio," black/white text on red circle, white border, black numbers, 15" dia ...................................................... 104.50

# Whale Smoking Tobacco (See Photo)

# Wheat Straw Cigarette Papers

Box, counter display, cardboard, "Roll Your Own... Wheat Straw Cigarette Papers," white text, cobalt ground, full with 24 thick packs, cond. 8.5-9, 1-3/4" h, 5-3/4" w, 3" d.................................................................... 28.50

Cloth bag, "Whale Smoking Tobacco," full, 8" h, $12.50.

Display, cardboard, die-cut, "Thirsty? Just Whistle, Golden Orange Refreshment," with unopened bottle, 1948, cond. 8.25-9.25, 11" h, 13" w, $192.50. (Photo courtesy of Gary Metz, Muddy River Trading Co.)

# Whip

Tin, vertical pocket, litho tin

"Whip Ready Rolled For Pipe or Cigarette," round image of man in red racing jacket with horse, green ground, cond. 7, tall variation ....................... 297.00

Same design as above, short variation, cond. 8.5, 3-1/2" h, 2-1/2" w .......................................... 990.00

# Whistle

Bottle holder, wall-mount, cast-iron figural hand, arm embossed "Whistle," with unopened bottle, 10" l................................................................. 1,210.00

Clock, electric

Die-cut pressed board, "Golden Orange Refreshment Time, Thirsty? Just Whistle," shows bottle of Whistle with brownie, wear/paint specks, works, 23" h, 24" w.......................................................... 1,160.50

Round, "Thirsty? Just Whistle," rectangular orange/blue logo over brownie hauling oversized bottle on handcart, yellow center, blue numbers on white border, 14-1/2" dia ............................................. 715.00

Display, countertop, cardboard, die-cut, "Golden Orange Refreshment, Thirsty? Just Whistle," shows brownies in a roadside stand, unused, 15" h, 17" w .................275.00

Fan pull, cardboard, die-cut, Brownie figure sitting on bottle, diamond logo, 1940s-1950s, cond. 9.75, 11-1/2" h........................................................... 264.00

Headband, paper, die-cut, headdress shape, NM, 5-1/2" h, 23-1/2" l ................................................11.00

Kickplate, litho tin, embossed, "Thirsty? Just Whistle, Morning-Noon-Night," black text, white ground, central horizontal band, black corners, circa 1930, NOS, cond. 9.25-9.5, 12" h, 27" w.............................. 242.00

Menu board, litho tin, embossed, "Thirsty? Just Whistle," red/blue logo, blue ground, 4 Brownies at corner of

Sign, litho tin, "Thirsty? just (image of hand holding titled "Whistle" bottle at left), The Choice Of Orange Drinks, 5¢, Whistle," rectangular logo lower-right, Good Housekeeping seal, white/orange text, cobalt ground, 1930s-1940s, cond. 9.25+, 29" w, $962.50. (Photo courtesy of Gary Metz, Muddy River Trading Co.)

    menu area in red/white border, 1948, cond. 9-9.25, 28" h, 20" w ........................................................ 797.50
Sign, cardboard
    "Thirsty? Just Whistle, Guaranteed Refreshing," Brownie sitting atop a bottle, crease, 11-1/2" h, 2-3/4" w.......................................................... 82.50
    "Whistle" in blue vertical text, Brownie at top using rope to pull "E" in place, Brownie at bottom on bottle, Brownie at bottom juggling 3 red balls on his feet, new frame, 24" h, 4-1/4" w.................... 187.00
Sign, litho tin over cardboard, easel/string back, "Thirst? Just - (shows hand with tilted "Whistle" bottle), On Ice, Get the Handy Bottle," white text, black ground, 1930s-1940s, cond. 9.25, 6" h, 9" w .............. 1,155.00
Sign, litho tin, embossed
    "Thirsty? Just Whistle, Morning-Noon-Night," blue/

orange on white ground, cracking to paint/touch-ups, 12-1/2" h, 27-1/2" w ............................ 154.00
    "Thirsty? Just... Whistle, Sparkling Orange Goodness," text in yellow/white ovals, yellow musical notes, top of bottle lower-right, diagonal orange-over-cobalt ground, yellow border, cond. G, 32" h, 56" w............................................................. 258.50
Sign, litho tin
    Arrow shape, points right, "Whistle" in black on orange rectangle, arrow with black ground, unused, 7" h, 27" w........................................................... 357.50
    Arrow shape, points left, "Whistle" in black on orange rectangle, arrow with black ground, unused, 7" h, 27" w........................................................... 357.50
    "Thirsty? Just Whistle," round scene of brownie hauling bottle of Whistle on a handcart/farm in background, orange logo, blue ground, cond. 8.75+, 30" h, 26" w...........................................................935.00
Thermometer, painted wood, "Thirsty? Just Whistle, Refreshing in any Weather, Morning-Noon-Night," white ground, 1920s, rounded top, 15" h, 4" w...............550.00

# Whitaker Automotive Cables

Display rack, tin, embossed, wire hooks, "Whitaker Automotive Cables" in red/text on green panel, yellow arched top shows red car outline/cables, cardboard slide shows different sizes, cond. 7, 9-3/4" h, 17" w ................................................................. 38.50

# White Cap Coffee (See Photo)

# White Crown Gasoline

Gas globe, milk glass, 1-pc, cond. 8, 16-1/2" h, 17" dia.......................................................... 214.50

Sign, litho tin, embossed, "Thirsty? Just Whistle, Golden Orange Goodness," blue ground, 1940s, cond. 9.5, 30" h, 26" w, $1,100. (Photo courtesy of Gary Metz, Muddy River Trading Co.)

Can, keywind, litho tin, "White Cap Coffee, The Heekin Co. Cincinnati," 1 lb, $20.

Can, keywind, litho tin, "White House Coffee, swinell-Wright Co., Boston, Chicago, Portsmouth," 1 lb, $45.

## White Eagle

Sign, porcelain, 2-sided, octagonal, "White Eagle" in white on black horizontal panel, "Gasoline and Oil" in white at border, circular red ground, white octagonal trim, restored, cond. 8.5, 28" h, 28" w ............... 440.00

## White Flash

Gas globe
   Glass Gill body, 2 glass lenses, "Atlantic White Flash" in white, 4 red/blue panels in checkered design, body with metal rings, 1 lens cracked, lens cond. 9/6, 13-1/2" dia ................................................. 367.50
   Metal body, low-profile, 2 lenses, "Atlantic White Flash" in white, 4 red/blue panels in checkered

Thermometer, painted wood, "Drink White House Coffee, 'The flavor is roasted in!' Dwinell-Wright Company, Boston, Chicago, Porstmouth Va.," light wear, 15" h, 4" w, $150.

design, body repainted, lens cond. 8/7, body cond. 8.5, 16" dia ............................................. 561.00

## White Goose

Tin, litho tin, "White Goose Brand Pure Spices, Turmeric, Shuster-Gormly Co.," round image of goose, red ground, cond. 8+, 3-1/8" h, 2-3/8" w, 1-1/4" d.................. 1,045.00

## White House Coffee (See Photo)

Can, litho tin
   Keywind, tall version, "White House Vacuum Packed Thermo-fresh Coffee, Steel Cut," medallion shows white house, white/gold/blue text, dark ground, gold band top/bottom, 1 lb, cond. 8 ....................... 51.50
   Sample size, 10¢ special souvenir made for the Jamestown Exposition, cond. 7, 3-3/8" h, 2-5/8" dia ..................................................... 154.00

## White House Ginger Ale

Tip tray, litho tin, round, "White House Ginger Ale, Purity Guaranteed, Standard Bottle & Extract Co., Boston," shows bottle, cond. 9.75 ..................................... 88.00

## White King Soap

Sign, litho tin, "Granulated White King Washing Machine Soap, It Takes So Little And It Goes So Far," shows black/white box of product with king image, white/red text, red ground, cond. 8.5+, 14" h, 10" w ........................... 220.00

## White Manor

Tin, vertical pocket, litho tin, "White Manor Pipe Mixture," shows mansion behind trees, cond. 9 .............. 430.00

Clock, neon on die-cut sign, "White King Quick Dissolving Soap, 'It Takes So Little,' Cool Water Washing," shows box of product, orig red/blue neon, clock not wired, replaced transformer/cord, cond. 7.75-8.25, 38" h, 26" w, $1,980. (Photo courtesy of Gary Metz, Muddy River Trading Co.)

## White Mountain Kisses

Sign, paper, embossed, "White Mountain Kisses, 20¢ Per Pound, Assorted Flavors," outdoor scene of boy in red kissing girl in pink dress/hat, framed, soiling, 11-1/8" h, 9" w .................................................................. 193.50

## White Rock

**History:** A spring surrounded by white limestone in Waukesha, Wis., was the inspiration for the White Rock name H.W. Culver gave to the bottled spring water he sold. After seeing a painting of Psyche kneeling on a rock and gazing at her reflection in a pool of water, the owners of the White Rock Mineral Springs Company determined that an adaptation of the work would be a wonderful trademark for the company. Over the years, the nymph's appearance has been updated several times, and she has been featured in cartoons and even walked off her rock in some advertising.

Sign, cardboard, "White Rock Sparkling Water, Don't say club soda...say White Rock," fairy kneeling on rock, silver platter with 2 bottles, green border, 1940s-1950s, framed, cond. 8.5-8.75, 30" h, 22" w ..................... 412.50

Sign, litho tin, embossed, "White Rock, Sparkling Beverages," fairy kneeling on rock looking into stream, red/black text, white ground, circa 1950s, cond. 9.25-9.5, 33" h, 57" w ..................................................... 550.00

Tip tray, litho tin

Rectangular, "White Rock, The World's Best Table Water," shows fairy kneeling on rock looking into stream, black panels, red border, cond. 8.25 ................................................................ 77.00

Round, "White Rock, The World's Best Table Water," shows fairy kneeling on rock looking into stream, wear/scratches, 4-1/4" dia ........................... 198.00

## White Rock Beer

Sign, litho tin, "White Rock Bottled Beer," woman with braided hair holding wheat, bottle at right in frame of

**Sign, flange, tin, embossed, "White Rock, Sparkling Beverages," red/black text, white ground, minor paint chips, 13" h, 18" w, $550.**

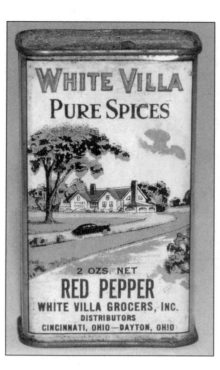

Tin, litho tin, "White Villa, Pure Spices, Red Pepper, White Villa Grocers Inc., Cincinnati/Dayton," 2 oz, $35.

wheat, Akron Brewing Co., Akron, OH, wood frame, scratches/paint chips, 24-3/4" h, 33" w ............. 616.00

## White Rose

Sign, tin, "White Rose Motor Gasoline And National Carbonless Motor Oil," roses upper-right, white/black text, black over green ground, newer frame, NOS, cond. 8+, 10-1/4" h, 14-1/4" w ..................................... 891.00

## White Rose Rye Whiskey

Stoneware jug, salt-glazed, embossed text/floral design with cobalt highlights, circa 1900, cond. 9, 8" h ................ 77.00

## White Squadron Coffee

Tin, paper label, "White Squadron Coffee, Mocha and Java, Ross W. Weir & Co., New York," image of battleships, age-toning/some label missing, 5-3/8" h, 4-1/4" dia ........................................................... 275.00

## White Swan Coffee

Tin, keywind, litho tin, drip grind, round image of swan, white text, red ground, cond. 8.5, 1 lb ................ 48.00

## White Villa

Tin, litho tin, tall version, "White Villa, America's Finest Coffee," earlier version with diamond medallion showing touring car/villa, red/dark ground, cond. 8.5, 1 lb .................................................................. 75.00

## Whitehead & Hoag Co.

Calendar, paper, 1911, "Badges, Emblems for every society, Banners for every purpose," waist-up view of woman in red coat/white scarf at wheel of open-top auto, pad begins with February, The Whitehead & Hoag Co., Newark NJ, cond. 8 .......................... 44.00

# Whiting

Sign, porcelain, 2-sided, die-cut, rounded top, "Whiting" in white on red ground, white border, white circle above name, cond. 7, 33" h, 60" w ................... 187.00

# Whiting-Adams Brushes

Pocket mirror, celluloid, "Whiting-Adams Brushes. Boston, U.S.A.," owl poem, own with brush on branch in front of crescent moon, white ground, 2-3/16" dia ............. 187.00

# Whitman's

**History:** In 1842 Stephen F. Whitman opened a fruit and candy shop in Philadelphia, incorporating rare fruits and nuts in some of the many varieties he made. With a mind for customer service, he would keep records of his buyers' preferences and even accept special orders for boxed assortments of his confections. The company became Stephen F. Whitman & Son in 1869 after Whitman's son, Horace, joined the firm. The company was awarded a bronze medal at the Philadelphia Centennial in 1876, and by 1907 their candy was being sold nationally.

The popular Whitman's Sampler was introduced in 1912, and both the cover design and the inside index were the brainchild of Walter Sharp, the company president. The illustration of a delivery boy carrying a box of chocolates under his arm became a registered trademark in 1915. The company issued special gift boxes from 1924 to 1926, with designs as varied as an Art Nouveau woman, pirates, and even heraldry. The slo-

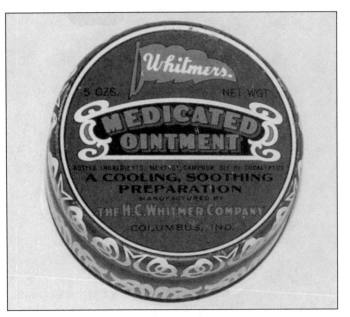

Tin, litho tin, "Whitmers Medicated Ointment," 5 oz, $15.

gan "A Woman Never Forgets a man Who Remembers" debuted in 1939.

Sign, porcelain
    Flange, "Agency, Whitman's Chocolates & Confections," white text, cobalt ground, circa 1930s, cond. 9.5+, 10" h, 20" w ......................................... 467.50
    Strip, "Agency, Whitman's Chocolates," white text, 1920s-1930s, cond. 8.25-8.5, 4" h, 24" w ..................... 330.00
    "Agency, Whitman's Chocolates and Confections Since 1842," cond. 8.75-9, 13" h, 40" w ...................... 357.50

# Whitmers (See Photo)

# Whiz

Display, litho tin, 4 shelves, "Whiz Service Center" sign on red roof, body with image of Whiz kids in crowns/ diapers working on car below "For Better Car Care," 53" h, 24" w, 21" d .............................................. 412.50

# Whiz Cigar Holders

Display, cardboard, die-cut, red "Whiz" in white oval, "Bakelite Cigar Holders" in white on red ground, "Tu Tone" on white oval center display with 12 holders, Whiz Mfg. Co. Division of Eastern Briar Pipe Co., Brooklyn, NOS, 10-1/4" h, 9" w ........................... 71.50

# Whiz Stop Leak

Can, metal, "Whiz Stop Leak Radiator Compound," 2 characters at radiator, red text, yellow ground, R.M. Hollingshead Co., Camden, NJ, unopened, cond. 7, 5-3/8" h, 2-3/8" dia ............................................... 38.50
Display, box, litho cardboard, 6 litho tin cans, "Whiz Radiator Stop Leak" in red on display back showing 2 characters with oversized can running toward man outside car, "We Guarantee Satisfaction Or Money Back," full cans cond. 7, display cond. 8, 6-1/2" x 14" x 5" ........................ 990.00

**Clock, lightup, "Whitman's Chocolate," Whitman's figure on front lightup panel, case repainted, 1930s, $2,860. (Photo courtesy of Gary Metz, Muddy River Trading Co.)**

**Can, keywind, litho tin, "Wigwam Coffee, Carpenter Cook Co. Menominee, Mich.," 1 lb., $55.**

## Wieland's Beer

Chalkware, paper label, man top half/bottle bottom half, bottle cap hat, "John Wieland's Extra Pale Lager Beer," red "W"/crown logo, Pacific Brewing and Malting Co., San Jose, CA, chips/worn label/stains, 9" h, 3" dia .................................................. 44.00

Tray, tin, "Wieland's Beer" over woman sitting at table with letter/flowers, "Brewery's Own Bottling" at bottom, red "W"/crown logo, ©1909, edge chips/scratches, crazing/soiling/touchups, 13-1/4" h, 10-1/2" w ................... 170.50

## Wigwam Coffee

Can, pry lid, litho tin, "Wigwam Brand Coffee," silhouette of Indian in white box over "Patent Cut," silhouette of Indian on horseback/teepees at bottom, orange ground, cond. 9.25+, 1 lb ................................. 187.00

## Wilbur's Cocoa

Can, paper label on tin, small top, "Wilbur's Cocoa, 10 Cents," cherub stirring cup marked "Wilbur," cond. 8, 1/5 lb, 3-1/8" h, 2-1/2" dia ................................ 495.00

**Display, litho tin, hanging, "Willard Battery Cables," 15 pegs on fold-up arm, 11-3/4" h, 22" w, $88.**

Glove hook, celluloid/metal, "Wilbur's Cocoa," cherub stirring cup marked "Wilbur," 1896, cond. 9.25+, 2-1/2" l, 7/8" dia ................................................................ 55.00

## Wildroot

Sign, tin, embossed, rounded corners, "Barber Shop, Ask For Wildroot," shows barber pole at right, black/red text, white ground, mkd "9-56," cond. G, 13-1/2" h, 39-1/2" w ............................................. 154.00

## Wild Rose Talcum Powder

Tin, cardboard, slip lid, round image of woman holding flowers, cond. 8+, 6-3/4" h, 3-1/8" dia ............... 107.00

## Willard (See Photo)

Clock, lightup, glass face/cover, metal case, "Willard Batteries," white text on red circle, black numbers in white border, new hands, cond. 8, 15" dia ................. 258.50
Sign
   Tin, embossed, "Willard Batteries," white text, red ground, black border, cond. 8+, 12" h, 39-1/2" w ....................................................... 154.00
   Glass, reverse-painted, metal frame,"Willard Super Master With Metalex Grids, 100% More Protection Against Overcharging... the No. 1 Battery Killer," car battery at left, red/black text, white ground, cond. 8.5, 12" h, 20" w ......................................... 187.00

## Williams Baby Talc (See Photo)

## Williams Root Beer Extract (See Photo on Cover)

## Willoughby Taylor

Tin, vertical pocket, litho tin, full, "Willoughby Taylor Pipe Mixture," white text, cobalt ground, lower shield with WT in white/gold on red/white stripes, cond. 8.5 ............... 115.50

**Tin, litho tin, "Williams Baby Talc," cond. 8+, 4 oz, 5" h, $385.**

## Wilson's Peanut Butter

Pail, litho tin, Old Woman in a Shoe nursery rhyme scene, wire bail, Wilson & Co., Chicago, cond. 8.5, 12 oz ............................................... 385.00

## Winchester

**History:** A Baltimore carpenter named Oliver Winchester invested in a store in 1940 and then decided to open a shirt factory to supply that store. The advent of the Civil War turned his thoughts toward firearms, and in 1867 he opened the Winchester Repeating Arms Company.

Located near his shirt factory in New Haven, Conn., the company was subsequently bought by Western Cartridge Company but continued operating under the old name until 1938. At that point the name was changed to Winchester Repeating Arms Company, Division of Western Cartridge Company.

**Collectors' Club:** The Winchester Club of America, 3070 S. Wyandot, Englewood, CO 80110

Bait box, orig paint, hand-soldered, "Winchester Trademark, Made in U.S.A.," stenciled in gold, black ground, loops for wearing on belt, cond. 7+, 2-1/8" h, 6" w, 2-1/2" d .......................................... 440.00

Box, cartridge box, paper label on cardboard, "50 Cartridges .44 Cal., Winchester Rifle Model 1873, Center Fire, Solid Head," shows "Winchester Model 1873" cartridge, shows rifle on side, soiling/wear/stains, 1-5/8" h, 4-3/4" w, 2-3/8" d .......................... 27.50

Box, shell box, cardboard, paper label, 2-pc
"Winchester New Rival Water Proofed Paper Shot Shells, Primed With The Winchester No. 2 Primer," shows single shell, green text, dirty/scuffed/corners separating, 2-3/4" h, 8-1/8" sq ......................... 55.00

"Winchester Repeater Paper Shot Shells Loaded With Smokeless Powder," shows crossed shells on side, red/blue text, white panel on yellow ground, 12 gauge, cond. G, 2-1/2" h, 4-1/4" sq ................ 27.50

Christmas card, "With Warmest Greetings and Best Wishes for the Christmas Season...Winchester," hunter on snowshoes, art by Philip Goodwin, 6" h, 4-3/4" w ............................................ 187.00

Flashlight, metal with blue/red label, unused, orig box with "The Winchester Flashlight" in medallion with gun, blue ground, cond. NM, 6-1/2" l .......................... 253.00

Sign, cardboard, 2-sided, "Winchester Super Speed Center-fire Cartridges With The New Silvertip Bullet, Effective For All Hunting Ranges," text over tree, angry bear at right, cartridges on black band, deer/elk at bottom, "Fire Cartridge Specifications and Ballistics" on back, cond. VG, 12-3/4" h, 21" w ................................. 93.50

Souvenir china, cup with gold pig, German, "Birds-Eye View of Winchester Repeating Arms, New Haven, Conn.," handcolored factory scene, cond. EXC, 3" h ............................................. 357.50

## Winchester Simmons Co.

Display case, standup tilting case, wood with sliding

cover, "Be Your Own Barber," striped poles each side, 16" h, 18-1/8" w, 2-5/8" d ................................. 412.50

## Winchester Talc

Can, litho tin, "Winchester After Shave Talc," outdoor scene of seated hunter with dog, red top/bottom, cond. 9.25 ......................................................... 247.50

## Wingold

Premium, cardboard, "Bay State - Wingold Flour, Shipped to All Parts of the World, The Quality is always Right - Sold by the grocer who gave this to you," delivery truck/2 toy cars/train engine, made to be cut out, cond. 9.5, 10-1/4" h, 12-1/2" w .................................. 71.50

## Wing's Baby Powder

Can, litho tin, "Wing's Salicylated Talcum Baby Powder with Borax, Perfumed, A Healthful and Sanitary Powder for the Nursery and Toilet," round image of infant flanked by wings, TOC, 4" h, 1-3/4" dia ........... 522.50

## Wings Cigarettes

Sign, paper, "Wings, Fifteen Cent Quality, 10¢ for 20," pack of "Wings Cigarettes" lower left, "B&W" octagonal logo, lit cigarette lower-right, yellow ground, cond. VG, 20" h, 14" w ......................................... 5.50

## Winner Cut Plug (See Photo)

## Winston

Thermometer, tin, rounded corners, "Winston tastes good... Like a cigarette should," red/black text over pack of Winston Filter Cigarettes, yellow ground, tube to right, cond. 8.5, 13" h .................................... 55.00

**Lunch box, litho tin, "Winner Cut Plug Smoke and Chew," early auto race, product on side, lid 7+, body 8.5+, 4-1/2" h, 7-1/2" w, 5" d, $401.50.**

## Wise Potato Chips

Standup, litho cardboard, die-cut, shape of an owl perched on log beside bag of Wise Potato Chips, tape repairs/cardboard added to support easel on back, 29-1/2" h, 20" w............ 715.00

Thermometer, painted wood, "Potato Storage Thermometer, Compliments of Wise Potato Chip Co., Beswick, Pa.," owl logo, cond. 8+, 8-3/8" h, 2-7/8" w .......... 357.50

## Wish Bone Coffee

Can, keywind, litho tin, blue version, shows wishbone around cup of coffee, yellow text, blue ground, 1 lb, cond. 8.5 ........... 103.00

## Wishing Well Orange

Door push, porcelain, "We Sell Wishing Well Orange," black on yellow ground, chips, 4" h, 32-1/2" w.............. 148.50

## Wm Penn Motor Oils

Sign, flange, porcelain, die-cut, round, "Wm Penn Motor Oils, Pure Pennsylvania, The Canfield Oil Co.," white/green text, red/green ground, cond. 7, 18" dia............. 522.50

## Wolf Co.

Sign, litho paper, "The Wolf Co., Flouring Mill Machinery, Chambersburg, Pa., U.S.A.," shows child in bonnet, 2 types of machines, blue/red text, white ground, framed, 25-1/4" h, 17-3/4" w ........... 440.00

## Wolf's Head Motor Oil

Sign, tin, embossed, "Wolf's Head" in black vertical text, "Motor Oil, Finest Of the Fine Since 1879" in red, red wolf's head on black stripe at top, white ground, NOS, 82" h, 12" w................. 143.00

Thermometer, tin, embossed, "How good it is, Winston," 13-1/2" h, 6" w, $55.

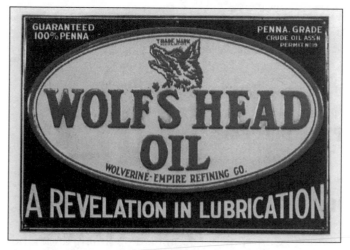

Sign, tin, embossed, "Wolf's Head Oil," red text in white oval, "A Revelation in Lubrication" in white on green ground, cond. 7+, 13-1/2" h, 19-1/2" w, $440. (Photo courtesy of Collectors Auction Services)

## Wonder Bread

Door push, painted metal, embossed, "We Suggest Wonder Bread, it's Fresh," white on red ground, minor scratches, 2-3/4" h, 27-1/2" w........... 165.00

Puppet, heavy paper, flat, die-cut jointed Howdy Doody holding loaf of "Wonder Enriched Bread," 13" h, 6" w ........... 302.50

Sign, porcelain, orange text, black ground, 1940s, cond. 8.5, 8-1/2" h, 20" w............. 121.00

Sign, tin, embossed, "Builds Strong Bodies 8 Ways," white text on black strip at bottom, loaf of "Wonder Enriched Bread, Helps Build Strong Bodies 8 Ways!" on red ground, white border, cond. VG, 18" h, 30" w ............. 132.00

## Woodbury's Talcum Powder

Tin, white text, green ground, cond. 8.5, 5" h, 2-3/8" w............. 27.50

## Woodlawn Mills

Display, cabinet, metal with wood base, litho of service station customer in shoe-shaped car getting laced up, sides with gas pump advertising quantities of colors, "Woodlawn Mills Shoe Lace Service Station, Buy Another Pair And Carry A Spare," shelves in back for storage ........... 3,520.00

## Workman's Friend

Pocket mirror, celluloid, round, "The Workman's Friend, For Removing Obstructions from Eyes And Other Uses Where Close Examination Is Required, 65¢" back view of man holding mirror, stain/lifting of silver, 2-1/2" dia............. 49.50

## Wright

Sign, porcelain, "Wright" under winged "W" logo, black design on white ground, cond. 8+, 18" h, 36" w ............. 77.00

Sign, cardboard, die-cut, standup, "Wrigley's," outdoor scene with woman in white dress/red bow with open box handing gum to girl in dress/bonnet, framed, circa 1910, cond. 7-7.5, 36" h, 26" w, $1,265. (Photo courtesy of Gary Metz, Muddy River Trading Co.)

# Wrigley's

**History:** William Wrigley, Jr., moved to Chicago in 1891 to open a new office for his father's soap company that was based in Philadelphia. Realizing that a 5¢ bar of soap wasn't profitable for dealers, he increased the price to 10¢, but, as an incentive, included an umbrella with every store box sold.

His penchant for using promotional giveaways was next exhibited when he included a cookbook with each 50-cent can of baking powder sold. Sales were so good he stopped peddling soap and focused on finding desirable premiums.

When he hit on the idea of giving away two packages of chewing gum with each can of baking powder, the promotion was such a success that he gave up baking powder in favor of gum. Ladders, desks, and even trucks were offered to storekeepers as incentives. Wrigley's inventiveness, combined with heavy advertising, paid off, and the company became a success.

Wrigley's Juicy Fruit gum and Spearmint gum debuted in 1893, while Doublemint was added to the line-up in 1914.

Box, unopened 20-pack, Wrigley's Spearmint, orig wax seal, 1940s-1950s, cond. 9-9.5............................ 88.00
Display
    Cardboard, 2 tiers, "Use Daily-Insure Attractive Smile, Sweet Inoffensive Breath-Millions Do, Healthful Refreshing Delicious Wrigley's," green arrow points to woman at right, 6-3/4" h, 12-1/2" w, 9" d........... 154.00
    Metal arrow-shaped man, celluloid face, 2 2-tier racks, circa 1930s, cond. 6-7 ................................. 550.00
Display rack, metal and celluloid, die-cut, celluloid face with moderate soiling and fading, with 4 1930s gum boxes, cond. 8+, 14" sq .................................... 632.50
Sign, cardboard, trolley
    "In Bond! Wrigley's, Next time you buy a package, notice the way it's wrapped. The Flavor Lasts," shows Wrigley's character with oversized pack over

"Sealed Tight-Kept Right," new frame, scuffs/scratches, 12-1/4" h, 22-1/4" w........................ 49.50
"Inexpensive - Satisfying, Taste the Juice of Real Mint Leaves," pack of Spearmint at left, 2 arrow characters at right, blue ground, yellow strip at bottom, 1920s, cond. 8+, 11" h, 21" w .........................110.00
"Inexpensive – Satisfying" in upper-left, "Taste the Juice of Real Mint Leaves" on lower yellow panel, pack of "Wrigley's Spearmint, The Perfect Gum" at left, boy/girl arrow-head characters carrying ice skates at right, light-blue ground, soiling/edge wear/rounded corners, 11" h, 21" w ..................... 143.00
"Wrigley's" beside pack of Juicy Fruit at bottom, top shows cartoon image of general store scene with men playing checkers, boy at counter, cond. 8+, 11" h, 21" w................................................. 385.00
Sign, tin over cardboard
    Beveled, "Wrigley's After Every Meal," shows packs of Juicy Fruit/Spearmint/Double Mint/P.K. gum, red ground, cond. 8+, 6" h, 13-3/8" w ................. 742.50
    "Finest Quality Peppermint Gum, 5¢ Per Pack," shows pack of Wrigley's Double Mint and elf-like figure, 1930s, cond. 7.75-8.25, 6" h, 13" w............. 308.00
Vending cover, porcelain, "Wrigley's P.K. Chewing Gum," yellow vertical text, green ground, 1930s, cond. 8.25-8.5, 21" h, 4" w, 3" d........................................... 330.00

# Wynola

Door push, embossed, "You'll Enjoy Wynola, Good Any Time," shows bottle, black/red text, white ground, Canadian, cond. 8.5+, 14" h ................................ 55.00

# Wyomissing Coffee

Pocket mirror, celluloid, round, hands holding crown over image of can of "William Hill & Sons Wyomissing Java and Mocha Dry Roasted Coffee," "Crowned King of Coffees" in blue at bottom, white ground, small cut/foxing, 1-3/4" dia...................................................... 98.00

Match holder, litho tin, "Juicy Fruit," tear through hole at top, 4-7/8" h, 3-3/8" w, $300.

# X Y Z

## X-tane

Gas globe
  Plastic body (newer), 2 lenses, "New Super X-tane Premium," white/blue text, white horizontal strip on red ground, all cond. 9, 13-1/2" dia............... 203.50
  Plastic body (newer), 2 lenses, "X-tane" in black on white panel, red ground above/below, all cond. 9, 13-1/2" dia ................................................. 187.00

## Yacht Club Smoking Tobacco

Tin, vertical pocket, litho tin, portrait of man in white cross on red ground, cond. 7.5-8............................. 1,049.00

## Yankee Boy

Tin, vertical pocket, litho tin
  "Yankee Boy Burley Plug Cut, S.D. Co., Union Made," shield-shaped medallion with blond boy at bat in ballpark, red/white checkered ground, cond. 8 .......................................................... 715.00
  Same design as above with brunette rusted-thru, otherwise cond. 8, 4-1/4" h ................................ 468.00

## Yankee Girl Tobacco

Box, store display, cardboard, "Yankee Girl Plug Tobacco, 1 Dozen 12 Cuts Cellophane Wrapped," yellow banner flanked by shield design with woman, red/white checkered ground, full, cond. 8+, 2-1/4" h, 8-1/2" w, 3" d.................................................................... 176.00

## Yankee Safety Razor

Tin, litho tin
  "Yankee Safety Razor," shield-shape medallion with man shaving, flanked by eagles, red ground, chips, wear, orig razor, cond. 7+, 1-1/2" h, 2-1/2" w, 1-3/4" d .......................................................... 154.00
  "Yankee Safety Razor" at top/bottom, "Blade Box" in red on panel with stars/stripes shield, Reichard & Scheuber Mfg. Co., cond. 8.25+, 2-1/4" w, 1" d ............ 82.50

## Yeast Foam

Sign, paper, "Yeast Foam, Makes Delicious Buckwheat Cakes," girl in white at table with platter of pancakes, box of product at left, red/white text, framed, minor soiling, 16-1/4" h, 11-1/2" w................................ 44.00

## Yellow Bonnet Coffee

Can, keywind, litho tin, "Yellow Bonnet Coffee," portrait of woman in yellow bonnet, white text, red ground, cond. 8.5, 1 lb ............................................................. 88.00

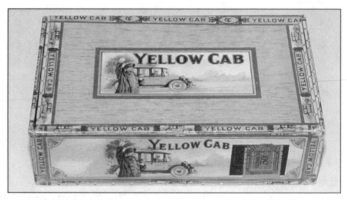

Cigar box, "Yellow Cab," $154.

## Yellow Cab Cigars

Cigar box
  Paper label, "Yellow Cab Sweets, Havana Blend 100% Tobacco, 5¢," yellow cab under awning, label on top/2 sides/under lid, cond. 7.5, 1-3/4" h, 3-7/8" w, 2-1/2" d .......................................... 207.00
  Paper label, "Yellow Cab, Takes The Right Of Way," officer with outstretched hand/early taxi, labels inside/out, outside box cond. fair-poor, inside label cond. good, 5-3/4" h, 9-1/4" w, 8-1/4" d........... 154.00

## Yucatan Gum

Display box, litho tin, hinged lid, "Chew Yucatan Gum, American Chicle Co., New York, Cleveland, Chicago, Kansas City, San Francisco," 6" h, 6-3/4" w, 4-3/4" d, $275.

Tin, litho tin, "Z.B.T. Baby Powder, The Centaur-Caldwell Division of Sterling Drugs Inc., N.Y.," 4-1/2 oz, $17.50.

## Z.B.T. Baby Powder (See Photo)

## Zenith

Thermometer, tin, embossed, square corners, "Zenith Long Distance Radio," vertical "Zenith" beside yellow thermometer over radio tower, yellow/black text, red over black ground, cond. G, 71" h, 17" w.......... 522.50

## Zeno Gum

Tin, litho tin, "Zeno Chewing Gum, Uncommonly Good in every flavor," yellow/white text on brick wall, boy reaching over for pack of gum, graphics under lid, Dutch scene around tin, cond. 8-, 2-1/2" h, 9-1/2" w, 4-1/2" d.............. 60.50

Trade card, mechanical, die-cut, "I keep my nerves steady by chewing Zeno Pepsin Gum," woman driver, cond. 8-, 6" h, 3-1/2" w....................... 357.50

## Zephyr

Gas globe

Ripple body, red, 2 glass lenses, "Zephyr" in red on diagonal over red circle, white ground, paint chips to metal rims, 13-1/2" dia........................... 1,320.00

Glass body, wide, 2 lenses, lenses glued in, cond. 7, 13-1/2" dia.................................................... 390.50

## Zerolene

Can, tin, "Zerolene, The Standard Oil For Motor Cars, No. 3," polar bear in red/blue round logo at left, white ground, Standard Oil Co., CA, orig lid, cond. 7, 1/2 gal, 6-1/2" h, 8" w, 2-3/4" d ...................................... 225.50

## Zig Zag Gum

Blotter, cardboard, "The Clark Twins, Highest Quality Great Sellers, The D.L. Clark Co., Pittsburgh, U.S.A.," text flanked by images of girl with boxes of Zig Zag and Clark Gum, unused, cond. EXC, 4" h, 9-1/4" w...............247.50

## Zig-Zag Tobacco

Can, litho tin, "Zig-Zag Mild Cigarette Tobacco," name in circle by smoking cigarette, white ground, circa 1920, cond. 8+, 4" h, 4" dia............................................ 111.00

## Zipp's Cherri-o

Sign, decal sign, framed, circa 1930s, cond. 9.5, 7" h, 16" w .................................................................121.00

Tray, round, "Drink Zipp's Cherri-o, 5¢, Delicious - Refreshing," bird on cherry branch using straw to drink from glass, 1920s, cond. 9.25........................................550.00

## Zira Cigarettes

Sign, cardboard, wood frame, "Zira, The New Cigarette, 5 Cents, A Satin Wonder In Each Package, Each One Recommends One More," product at left with woman insert card, product at right with flower insert card, red/yellow triangular ground, top corner missing, cond. VG, 13" h, 16" w..............................................................44.00

## Zobelein's

Tip tray, metal, "Serve Zobelein's Eastside Zest Cold" and "Non-Intoxicating Pure & Healthful Cereal Beverage," wood-like look with text in central oval, rust/scratches, 4-1/2" w, 6" l....................................... 49.50

## Zu Zu Ginger Snaps

Sign, cardboard, trolley, "The Best Bite You Ever Had, National Biscuit Company," box of product lower-left, face at right, cond. 7.5, 11" h, 21" w.......................385.00